Edexcel AS & A level
Politics

New for 2017

Andrew Colclough
Dr Graham Goodlad
Dr Samantha Laycock
Ian Levinson
Dr Andrew Mitchell
Kathy Schindler
Adam Tomes

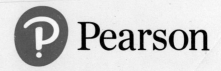
Pearson

Published by Pearson Education Limited, 80 Strand, London, WC2R 0RL.

www.pearsonschoolsandfecolleges.co.uk

Copies of all official specifications for all Edexcel qualifications may be found on the website: www.edexcel.com

Text © Pearson Education Limited 2017

Designed by Pearson Education Limited

Typeset by Phoenix Photosetting, Chatham, Kent

Original illustrations © Pearson Education Ltd

Illustrated by Tek-Art, West Sussex and Phoenix Photosetting, Chatham for Pearson Education Limited

Cover design by Pearson Education Limited

Picture research by Alison Prior

Cover photo/illustration © Arthimedes/Shutterstock.com

First published 2017

20 19 18 17

10 9 8 7 6 5 4

British Library Cataloguing in Publication Data

A catalogue record for this book is available from the British Library

ISBN (Student Book bundle) 978 1 292 187020

ISBN (ActiveBook) 978 1 292 187044

ISBN (Kindle Edition) 978 1 292 187051

Copyright notice

Printed in Slovakia by Neografia

Acknowledgements

For image acknowledgements please see page ix.

All other images © Pearson Education

The publisher would like to thank the following for their kind permission to reproduce their materials:

p.79–80 Tables 1.6, 1.7 and 1.8, data used from *How Britain Voted Since 1974* by permission of Ipsos Mori; **p.85–86** extract from *Press affiliation and the 2015 general election; who runs Britain?* by Dr Andrew Defty, used by permission of the author; **p.179** extract from *Parliamentary Scrutiny of Government* by Dr Hannah White, used by permission of the Institute for Government; **p.203** extract from *Thank goodness Theresa May has restored cabinet government – or has she? A decade of outreach* by John Rentoul, used by permission of *The Independent*; **p.318** citation, *Mahatma*, Vol. V, (1952).

We would like to thank Sarra Jenkins for her invaluable help in reviewing this book.

Websites

Pearson Education Limited is not responsible for content of any external sites. It is essential that tutors preview each website before using it in class to ensure that the URL is still accurate, relevant and appropriate. We suggest that tutors bookmark relevant websites and consider enabling students to access them through the school/college intranet.

A note from the publisher

In order to ensure that this resource offers high-quality support for the associated Pearson qualification, it has been through a review process by the awarding body. This process confirms that this resource fully covers the teaching and learning content of the specification or part of a specification at which it is aimed. It also confirms that it demonstrates an appropriate balance between the development of subject skills, knowledge and understanding, in addition to preparation for assessment.

Endorsement does not cover any guidance on assessment activities or processes (e.g. practice questions or advice on how to answer assessment questions), included in the resource nor does it prescribe any particular approach to the teaching or delivery of a related course.

While the publishers have made every attempt to ensure that advice on the qualification and its assessment is accurate, the official specification and associated assessment guidance materials are the only authoritative source of information and should always be referred to for definitive guidance.

Pearson examiners have not contributed to any sections in this resource relevant to examination papers for which they have responsibility.

Examiners will not use endorsed resources as a source of material for any assessment set by Pearson.

Endorsement of a resource does not mean that the resource is required to achieve this Pearson qualification, nor does it mean that it is the only suitable material available to support the qualification, and any resource lists produced by the awarding body shall include this and other appropriate resources.

Contents

About the authors

Andrew Colclough is Head of Politics at d'Overbroeck's, Oxford. He has taught A-level politics for more than 20 years, with a variety of material published in the area of United States politics and A-level politics skills. He is also an examiner covering UK and US politics, currently acting as team leader for Edexcel United States Politics. Andrew delivers politics CPD for A-level teachers as well as UK and US revision lectures with Philip Allan Conferences.

Dr Graham Goodlad is Head of Politics at St John's College, Southsea. He has taught A-level history and politics for 30 years. He specialises in post-war British government and politics, about which he has written widely for A-level students and undergraduates. Graham Goodlad's most recent publications are *British Prime Ministers from Balfour to Brown* (co-authored with Dr Robert Pearce) and *Thatcher* in the Routledge Historical Biographies series. He was elected a Fellow of the Royal Historical Society in 2011.

Dr Samantha Laycock is a teacher of history and politics at The Sixth Form College, Colchester. She has taught politics to A level, undergraduate and postgraduate students for more than 20 years. Her particular interests lie in elections and referendums, voting behaviour and international relations. She has been published in various academic journals, including *Electoral Studies* and *The Journal of Elections, Public Opinion and Parties*, as well as in the *Developments in British Politics* series.

Ian Levinson has been teaching politics for 17 years. He is Head of Politics at the Sixth Form College, Colchester. After his master's degree, Ian completed his training as a specialist politics teacher at the University of Leicester. His particular interests are the politics of the European Union, international relations and Holocaust education. He has led many trips to Brussels and Auschwitz. Ian Levinson has been Principal Examiner for Pre-U Comparative Government and Politics and AS-level Citizenship Studies.

Dr Andrew Mitchell is Head of Government and Politics at Peter Symonds Sixth Form College, Winchester. He has taught A-level history and politics for 25 years and before that was briefly a university lecturer. Andrew has written or co-authored several A-level textbooks covering the Russian Revolution, Mussolini's Italy and the Cold War. He has also contributed to several politics publications including *The Oxford Companion to Twentieth Century British Politics*. He is currently an A-level Chief Examiner.

Kathy Schindler has been teaching A-level politics for more than 25 years, working in a large comprehensive school in London for most of that time. Her particular interest is in political ideas, which she has always taught alongside UK politics. She has more recently extended her interests to include American politics. Kathy is also an experienced examiner and team leader for the Edexcel exam board, and was involved in drafting the new 2017 syllabus for Edexcel.

Adam Tomes is a Tutor of Politics at York College, recently rated as 'outstanding' by Ofsted. He has taught history, philosophy, politics and international relations for the last 15 years at A level and access-to-higher-education level. He has experience as an examiner in history and politics, and as a team leader in politics. Adam has a particular interest in the history, ideas and approaches of radical political movements.

How to use this book

This Student Book contains features to help you access the course content, prepare for your exams and take your knowledge and understanding further. Here are the features you will see, in the main body of the book and in the margins, along with an explanation of how you can use each one.

Key term

Egoistical individualism
the idea that individual freedom is associated with self-interest and self-reliance.

Key terms are listed in the course specification. These are terms you have to know and are encouraged to explain in your answers during the exam. Key terms are highlighted in bold in the text and are defined in handy boxes close to the main content.

Case study features look at particular examples of politics in practice, taken from recent history and the past. Each case study feature has a question or two at the end, to help you check that you have understood its relevance. It is important that you know examples of this kind, as you may be asked to use them in your answers. The case study features are examples only: you do not have to know these particular ones, and could choose your own with support from your teacher.

Case study: Tony Blair and Bernie Ecclestone

Blair faced criticism within months of becoming prime minister in 1997 following the revelation that Bernie Ecclestone, the motor-racing boss, had donated £1 million to Labour. It was alleged that there was a connection between this and a delay in implementing a ban on tobacco advertising in Formula One racing. Blair was forced to justify himself in a TV interview, in which he famously described himself as 'a pretty straight sort of guy', and the money was subsequently returned.

Question
• Following this case, were people justified in being suspicious about the relationship between parties and business interests?

Boxed features pick out a particular element of the content that needs more detailed explanation or benefits from a particular focus.

Rationalism in action

Liberals accept that competition between individuals, groups and nations regrettably will produce conflicts, but they favour the use of reasoned debate and discussion to resolve disputes. Late 19th-century liberals were at the forefront of moves to develop methods of industrial arbitration. This meant that a neutral third party would mediate between employers and trade unions in an effort to avert costly legal action or strikes. Similarly, in international relations, liberals view war as a last resort, which should be avoided if at all possible…

Pause & reflect

Research the results in your own parliamentary constituency at the last three general elections. What percentage of the vote was gained by the winning candidate in each contest?

Pause & reflect features are given at points where it may be helpful to stop and reflect on what you have been reading. You will be encouraged to check that you have understood the basics before reading on.

Extension activities give opportunities and ideas for you to explore an aspect of politics in more detail. This helps you to stretch your research and thinking, and to deepen your understanding, to help you access the higher marks available in the exam.

EXTENSION ACTIVITY

For each of the four key policy areas (economic, welfare, law and order, foreign policy), find at least one pledge from the latest Conservative election manifesto that relates to it.

Link

For more about **pressure groups**, see Section 1.3.

Link features point you to other areas of the book where you can find related content.

Assessment support features provide useful advice and guidance for students taking the A-level exams. You will find one feature at the end of each section of the book, which offers:

- information about a particular question type – which paper it appears on, how many marks are available and whether it is source-based or essay type
- general advice on how to approach answering an exam question of this type, including structure and style
- more specific ways in which you might address the particular question, including short examples of how a high-level answer might look, with explanatory notes.

Most of the sample questions provided in this book relate primarily to the chapter that they follow. In the real exams, some questions will relate to more than one chapter, as they will span more than one section of the course specification.

Assessment support: 1.1.2 Political Parties

Question 4 on AS-Level Paper 1 is worth 30 marks and must be completed in 50 minutes. It takes the form of a brief quotation, stating a point of view on a particular topic, and asking how far you agree with it. You are given a choice of two questions; you should answer one.

  'The influence of the media is the most important factor that determines the success or failure of a political party.'

How far do you agree with this view of what determines the success or failure of a political party? [30 marks]. In this answer you must refer to at least two political parties and consider this view and the alternative to this view in a balanced way.

Your answer will take the form of an essay in which you consider both sides of the argument. This question tests all three Assessment Objectives, with marks divided equally between them. Examiners are looking for comprehensive and precise knowledge and understanding of the topic, used to support a reasoned argument. You must make convincing connections between different ideas and concepts. Your arguments should be fully supported, and your essay should reach a conclusion in which you reflect both sides of the argument, in order to score highly for evaluation.

- Take a few minutes to write a brief plan – this will give you a clear sense of direction and help you make sure you do not leave out anything important.
- Aim to write about six paragraphs, including a brief introduction and a fully supported conclusion.

Your online ActiveBook

This book comes with three years' access to ActiveBook* – an online version of your textbook. Follow the instructions on the inside front cover to get started.

Your ActiveBook is the perfect way to personalise your learning. You can:

- access your content online – anytime, anywhere
- use the highlighting tool to help you study, remember and personalise your revision
- use the annotation tool to make notes – perhaps about wider reading, connections or work you need to do.

* This is for new purchases only. If the access code has already been revealed – for example, you bought the book second-hand – it may no longer be valid.

Content and assessment overview

This section shows you what is covered in each of the AS and A-level qualifications, and how each is assessed. It also explains the assessment objectives, and how these are addressed in the exam.

Advanced Subsidiary (AS) Level

The Pearson Edexcel Level 3 Advanced Subsidiary GCE in Politics consists of **two** externally-examined papers. You must complete all assessment in May/June in any single year.

Component 1: UK Politics		
How you will be assessed	Content covered	Assessment overview
Written examination: 1 hour and 45 minutes 50% of the qualification 60 marks	You will study: • democracy and participation • political parties • electoral systems • voting behaviour and the media.	**Section A** One 10-mark question from a choice of two, which assesses AO1. **Section B** Two 10-mark questions – one question focuses on a single source and assesses AO1 and AO2. The other question focuses on two comparative sources and assesses AO2 and AO3. **Section C** One 30-mark question from a choice of two, which assesses AO1, AO2 and AO3.

Component 2: UK Government		
How you will be assessed	Content covered	Assessment overview
Written examination: 1 hour and 45 minutes 50% of the qualification 60 marks	You will study: • the constitution • parliament • prime minister and executive • relationships between the branches.	**Section A** One 10-mark question from a choice of two, which assesses AO1. **Section B** Two 10-mark questions – one question focuses on a single source and assesses AO1 and AO2. The other question focuses on two comparative sources and assesses AO2 and AO3. **Section C** One 30-mark question from a choice of two, which assesses AO1, AO2 and AO3.

Explanation of Assessment Objectives (AO) for AS level

You must be able to:		% GCE AS Level
AO1	Demonstrate **knowledge** and **understanding** of political institutions, processes, concepts, theories and issues.	**42**
AO2	**Analyse** aspects of politics and political information, including in relation to parallels, connections, similarities and differences.	**33**
AO3	**Evaluate** aspects of politics and political information, including to construct arguments, make substantiated judgements and draw conclusions.	**25**
	Total:	**100%**

Advanced (A) Level

The Pearson Edexcel Level 3 Advanced GCE in Politics consists of **three** externally examined papers. You must complete all assessment in May/June in any single year.

Component 1: UK Politics

How you will be assessed	Content covered	Assessment overview
Written examination: 2 hours 33⅓% of the qualification 84 marks	You will study: 1. Political Participation • democracy and participation • political parties • electoral systems • voting behaviour and the media. 2. Core Political Ideas • conservatism • liberalism • socialism.	**Section A: Political Participation** One 30-mark question from a choice of two (each question uses a source) – you must complete one of these. Plus one 30-mark question from a choice of two – you must complete one of these. All questions assess AO1, AO2 and AO3. **Section B: Core Political Ideas** One 24-mark question from a choice of two, which assesses AO1, AO2 and AO3.

Component 2: UK Government

How you will be assessed	Content covered	Assessment overview
Written examination: 2 hours 33⅓% of the qualification 84 marks	You will study: 1. UK Government • the constitution • parliament • prime minister and executive • relationships between the branches 2. Non-Core Political Ideas – one idea from the following: • anarchism • ecologism • feminism • multiculturalism • nationalism.	**Section A: UK Government** One 30-mark question from a choice of two (each question uses a source) – you must complete one of these. Plus one 30-mark question from a choice of two – you must complete one of these. All questions assess AO1, AO2 and AO3. **Section B: Non-Core Political Ideas** One 24-mark question from a choice of two, which assesses AO1, AO2 and AO3.

Component 3: Comparative Politics

| You will study either USA or Global Politics

Written examination: 2 hours

33⅓% of the qualification

84 marks | For **USA**, you will study:
• the US Constitution and federalism
• US Congress
• US presidency
• US Supreme Court and civil rights
• democracy and participation
• comparative theories.
OR
For **Global** you will study:
• sovereignty and globalisation
• global governance: political and economic
• global governance: human rights and environmental
• power and developments
• regionalism and the European Union
• comparative theories. | **Section A**
One 12-mark question from a choice of two, which assesses AO1 and AO2.
Section B
One compulsory 12-mark question focused on comparative theories, which assesses AO1 and AO2.
Section C
Two 30-mark questions from a choice of three, which assess AO1, AO2 and AO3. |

Explanation of Assessment Objectives (AO) for A level

You must be able to:		% GCE A Level
AO1	Demonstrate **knowledge** and **understanding** of political institutions, processes, concepts, theories and issues.	35
AO2	**Analyse** aspects of politics and political information, including in relation to parallels, connections, similarities and differences.	35
AO3	**Evaluate** aspects of politics and political information, including to construct arguments, make substantiated judgements and draw conclusions.	30
	Total:	100%

Synoptic assessment

Synoptic assessment requires you to work across different parts of a qualification and to show your accumulated knowledge and understanding of a topic or subject area. Synoptic assessment enables you to show your ability to combine your skills, knowledge and understanding with breadth and depth of the subject.

The publisher would like to thank the following for their kind permission to reproduce their photographs:

(Key: b-bottom; c-centre; l-left; r-right; t-top)

123RF.com: David Fowler 35; **Alamy Stock Photo:** 615, Collection 202, Brian Harris 70, Chris Batson 17, Chris Dorney 29, Chronicle 238, 311, Classic Images 146, Clynt Graham Food and Drink 482, dpa Picture Alliance 121, 300b, 302b, 310, 418l, Everett Collection Historical 103, 261, 280, FinPics 229, foto-call 5, Granger Historical Picture Archive 281, 282, 287, History Collection 2016 102, Ian Dagnall Computing 106, Ian Francis stock 434, imageBROKER 139, INTERFOTO 137, Jeff Morgan 309, Jim West 253, KC Photography 156t, Lebrecht Music & Arts Photo Library 244, LOC 131b, Malcolm Park Wine and Vineyards 574, Michael Kemp 275, Mike Goldwater 283, New York City 592, New Zulu 25, PACIFIC PRESS 436, Paris Pierce 275l, Patrizia Wyss 521, Pictorial Press Ltd 11, 137, 318, REUTERS 206, 231, 520, Robert Hunt Library 131c, Russell Hart 188, The Print Collector 241, View Pictures Ltd 156b, World History Archive 275r, 277, 289, 586b, YAY Media AS 339, Zuma Press Inc 263, 406, 438, 587; **Fotolia.com:** Argus 225, Jose Alfonso 305r, Richard Carey 255, Unclepodger 300; **Getty Images:** 582, AFP 22, Ben Pruchnie 172, Bettmann 272r, Dan Kitwood 73, Derek Hudson 291, Fred Ramage 561, Frederic Reglain 120, Hulton Archive 138t, Joseph EID 475, KAZUHIRO NOGI 506, Keystone 30, Leon Neal 7, Martha Holmes 104, MCT 393, Michael Nicholson 114t, 131t, Sam Panthakey 301, Terry Disney 34, The Washington Post 284, Topical Press Agency 586t, W. Breeze 270, Wathiq Khuzaie 584, WPA Pool 14; **GNU Free Documentation License: Wikipedia:** 114b, 240, 242; **John Frost Historical Newspapers:** 84, 197; **Press Association Images:** PA / PA Archive 32, 164b, 179; **Red Squirrel Publishing:** 316; **Reuters:** Crispin Rodwell 201, Damir Sagol 539, Kirsty Wigglesworth 164t; **Shutterstock.com:** !000Words 41, 598246 246, Andy Rain / EPA / REX 151, Archive / UIG / REX 322t, 323, Archives / REX 121, Artist1704 493, Atlaspix 295, CCI 322b, chanrsitr 544l, Chris Capstick REX 140, Cineberg 216, David Cairns / REX 196t, David Fowler 196b, Everett Historical 119, 320, 321b, Frederic Legrand 56, Funny Solution Photo 548, George Kollidas 100, 101, 117, Georgi 321t, Giovanni Vale 60, Ian Hinchcliffe 249, ITV / REX 74, JetKat 505, Joe Gough 537, Joe Partridge / REX 305l, Justin Lane / EPA / REX 237, kwest 526, lazyllama 458, Makus Gann 449b, Maury / EPA / REX 377r, MH Anderson Photography 347, Misha Abesadze 544, Nils Jorgensen 83, Paul Rookes 248, Peter Hermes Furian 320t, petrmalinak 532, Press Eye Ltd / REX 64, Ray Tang 514, REX 140, 272r, 293, 332, 454, Ricardo Seigem Uema 257, S Meddle / REX 51, Shawn Thew / EPA 12r, 378, Steve Cukrov 327, Stuart Forster / REX 109, Sutton-Hibbert / REX 302t, The Art Archive / REX 118, 243, Vlad G 449t, Wasan Ratthawon 319, WEF / SIPA / REX 500, Xinhua / REX 377l, 507, Zuma / REX 453; **© Steve Bell / All Rights Reserved:** 186, 199

Cover images: *Front:* **Shutterstock.com:** Arthimedes

All other images © Pearson Education

Studying politics at A level

Welcome to the study of politics.

You have chosen a subject that, more than any other, explains the society in which we live. Politics is not an abstract academic discipline, remote from everyday life. It is relevant to almost every aspect of the world around us. Politicians are responsible for the public services we use and how they are organised and funded. The decisions that affect our schools and colleges, our health service, transport network and armed forces are all political decisions. Our rights and responsibilities as citizens – the power of the state over us, and our ability to choose and influence those in authority – are all related to politics. How fair and representative is our voting system? How do people organise themselves to put pressure on government? How powerful is parliament? If you are interested in these and similar questions, then this is the subject for you.

To begin with, you will be learning about the processes and institutions at the heart of politics and government in the UK. The A-level specification also gives you an opportunity to examine the key ideas that have influenced modern politics, and then to look beyond the UK – either at the working of the US political system, or at major issues in global politics.

What will be asked of you as a politics student?

As with any A-level subject, your teacher and your textbook will be vital resources, providing a firm foundation of knowledge and understanding. You should make sure that you can recall and explain the key concepts that you will encounter throughout the course. Get hold of the specification, the sample questions and the mark schemes produced by the examination board. These are essential tools for learning the subject and for understanding what will be expected of you as a student.

However, politics is about much more than that. One of the most important things to note is that politics is not a static subject. Of course, certain key ideas and concepts will remain broadly the same, but the way in which they are applied in the real world is constantly changing. For example, the policies of political parties develop in response to new circumstances, such as an election defeat or a change of leadership. It is important, therefore, to keep up to date. Use websites such as those of the BBC, parliament and Number 10. Read a quality newspaper, either in print or online, and watch news and current affairs programmes on television. Articles in journals such as *Politics Review*, *Think Tank* and *Total Politics* are other useful resources.

Your teacher will advise you on how to organise your studies, but it is a good idea to have a ring binder for your notes, subdivided into different topic areas. You can add new examples as they occur, in the appropriate section, to create your own bank of up-to-date, relevant material to support your answers. Some sections of the specification explicitly require knowledge of older examples, such as a study of one prime minister from the period 1945–97 and one since 1997. However, you should also be able to discuss more recent developments and make connections between them and earlier material.

A secure basis of knowledge and understanding will enable you to develop the study skills you need. Politics is about discussion and debate, and being able to develop and defend a point of view. From the beginning you will get used to reading about, analysing and evaluating different arguments. In politics there is no right and wrong, but rather different types of opinion. Sometimes these will be sharply opposing positions, held by politicians who profoundly disagree with each other. You will be looking at the ideas and facts on which these competing viewpoints are based.

You will also learn how to put forward your own opinion, and to back up the points you make with evidence.

Become familiar with the types of questions asked in the examination as soon as you can. Get used to the command words used by the examiners – such as 'describe', 'explain', 'assess' – and what they are asking of you. Read the question carefully so that you can ensure your answer is relevant, and you do not waste time writing out material that is not helping you to gain marks. Use the mark allocations to decide how much time to spend on a particular part of a question. Make timed question practice a regular part of your preparation for the examination. Be systematic in your learning – make sure that your notes on each topic are complete and well organised, learn the topic, then test yourself by attempting an examination question.

What might a qualification in politics lead to?

After the A-level course is over, a number of possibilities are open to you. It may be that you decide to extend your knowledge of politics by taking a university degree in the subject, or in a related area such as international relations. This might lead you to become involved in politics in a practical way – by working for a political research organisation or as an assistant to an MP, or possibly even by seeking election to local government or parliament. Who knows where A-level politics may lead you?

Whether or not you decide to take politics further, you will have learned valuable skills that can be applied to a wide range of situations and disciplines. At A level you will have learned how to select and analyse information, how to discriminate between different viewpoints and how to make a case. All of these are essential skills in a great variety of career paths, including law, journalism, the media and the civil service. And of course you will never look at the news in the same way. You will have a deeper understanding of the stories behind the headlines, and be much better equipped to play your part as an active citizen in the world you are about to enter.

Online support

An extended case study on the 2017 general election, with analysis and commentary, is available online. Teachers and students can also access free presentations to download, covering all the key terms in this book. The case study and presentations are available at:

www.pearsonschools.co.uk/edalevelpoliticssupport or www.edexcel.com/alevelpoliticssupport

Democracy and Participation

Democracy means literally 'rule by the people'. However, it is a broad and imprecise term. Democracy refers to political systems in which the people are involved in decision-making in some way, either directly or indirectly.

In this chapter you will look at:

- the different forms democracy can take, and how democratic the UK political system is
- the right to vote and other ways in which people can participate in politics
- development of the concept of rights and the debates surrounding them.

1.1 Current systems of representative and direct democracy

Features, similarities and differences

There are two main democratic systems.

Key terms

Direct democracy
all individuals express their opinions themselves and not through representatives acting on their behalf. An example of direct democracy is a referendum.

Representative democracy
a form of democracy in which an individual selects a person (or political party) to act on their behalf to exercise political choice.

- **Direct democracy:** in which individuals express their opinions themselves. This system originated in ancient Athens, where adult male citizens had the right to take part in decision-making at public meetings. Clearly such a system would not be practical as a regular means of decision-making in a large modern state.

- **Representative democracy:** in which people elect representatives who take decisions on their behalf. This is the usual form of democracy in the modern world. Representatives do not act as delegates, merely taking instructions from the voters. They are expected to exercise their judgement. If they do not satisfy the voters, they can be held to account and removed at the next election.

Both systems are based on the concept of majority rule, although a representative system may include more safeguards for minorities.

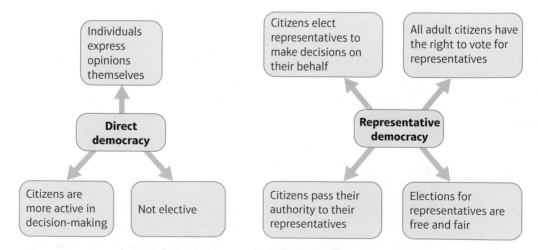

Figure 1.1: Direct and representative democracy – features and differences

Advantages and disadvantages of direct democracy and representative democracy

Advantages of direct democracy	Disadvantages of direct democracy
Gives equal weight to all votes, unlike a representative system where the varying sizes of constituencies mean that votes do not all have equal value.	Impractical in a large, heavily populated modern state where decision-making is complicated.
Encourages popular participation in politics by expecting people to take their duties as citizens seriously.	Many people will not want to – or feel qualified to – take part in decision-making, so political activists decide what happens.
Removes the need for trusted representatives, as people can take responsibility for their own decisions.	Open to manipulation by the cleverest and most articulate speakers, who will persuade people to support their viewpoint.
Develops a sense of community and encourages genuine debate.	Will of the majority is not mediated by parliamentary institutions, so minority viewpoints are disregarded.

Table 1.1: Direct democracy – advantages and disadvantages

Advantages of representative democracy	Disadvantages of representative democracy
The only practical system in a large modern state, where issues are complex and often need rapid response (for example, the deployment of troops).	May lead to reduced participation as people choose to hand responsibility to politicians.
Politicians form parties, bringing coherence and giving people a real choice of representative. Pressure groups form to represent different interests, promoting debate and encouraging **pluralist democracy**.	Parties and pressure groups are often run by elites pursuing their own agendas, not truly representing the people.
Reduces chances of minority rights being overridden by 'tyranny of the majority'.	Minorities may still find themselves under-represented as politicians are more likely to follow the views of the majority to secure election.
Elections allow people to hold representatives to account.	Politicians are skilful in avoiding accountability, especially as general elections are usually 5 years apart in the UK.
Politicians are (in theory) better informed than the average citizen about the many issues on which they must take a view.	Politicians may be corrupt and incompetent, may betray election promises or put loyalty to their party before responsibility to the electorate.

Table 1.2: Representative democracy – advantages and disadvantages

Key term

Pluralist democracy
a type of democracy in which a government makes decisions as a result of the interplay of various ideas and contrasting arguments from competing groups and organisations.

Although both systems are different, there are instances where direct democracy can be used within a representative system.

- **National referendums:** A referendum is a direct vote on a single issue, usually requiring a response to a straight yes/no question. The UK has had only three nationwide referendums: on Britain's membership of the European Economic Community (or European Union) in 1975 and 2016; and on whether to change the system of voting for the Westminster parliament in 2011.

Link

For more on **referendums**, see Section 3.2 of Electoral Systems.

- **The 2015 Recall of MPs Act:** This allows a petition to be triggered if an MP is sentenced to be imprisoned or is suspended from the House of Commons for more than 21 days. If 10 per cent of eligible voters in the constituency sign the petition, a by-election is called. Direct democracy is thus used to hold representatives to account.

The case for reform of the UK democratic system

There is an ongoing debate about how well the democratic system in the UK functions. This is important because it is generally accepted that, in the modern world, government derives its **legitimacy** from the consent of the people. Democracy validates the policies of those who exercise power.

The UK political system has a number of positive democratic features.

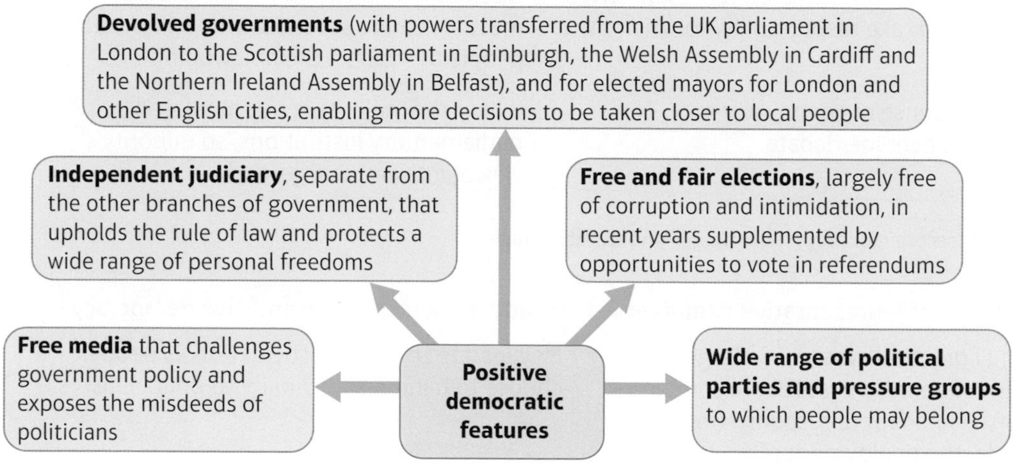

Figure 1.2: Positive democratic features of the UK political system

> **Key terms**
>
> **Legitimacy**
> the legal right to exercise power, for example, a government's right to rule following an election.
>
> **Democratic deficit**
> a perceived deficiency in the way a particular democratic body works, especially in terms of accountability and control over policy-making.

> **Link**
>
> For more on the **first-past-the-post voting system**, see Section 3.1.

However, some commentators hold that the UK is suffering from a **'democratic deficit'**, as decisions are taken by people whose appointment lacks adequate democratic input, or who are not subject to proper accountability.

They argue that the UK political system is undemocratic in important respects.

- **Under-representation of minority viewpoints due to the voting system:** The House of Commons is elected by the **first-past-the-post system**, which produces a mismatch between the votes cast for UK political parties and the seats that each party wins in parliament.
- **House of Lords lacks democratic legitimacy:** The UK is unusual in having one of the two chambers of its parliament, the House of Lords, wholly unelected. Periodic attempts at reform have failed, leaving the UK with a mainly appointed second chamber. The greater part of its membership has been appointed by successive prime ministers, with smaller numbers chosen by other party leaders, and non-party 'crossbench' peers nominated since 2000 by an independent House of Lords Appointments Commission. This ensures that a number of different professions and fields of experience are present in the upper house, but it continues to lack democratic legitimacy.
- **Lack of protection for citizens' rights:** The European Convention on Human Rights, incorporated into UK law in 1998 (the Human Rights Act), arguably provides inadequate guarantees for the rights of citizens in their relationship with the state. Governments can 'derogate from' articles of the Human Rights Act, officially stating that parts of the act no longer have legal authority in certain situations.
- **Control of sections of the media by wealthy, unaccountable business interests:** For example, the powerful Murdoch group has owned a number of British newspapers simultaneously, including *The Times*, *The Sunday Times* and *The Sun*.

There is a widely held belief that the UK's democratic system suffers from a '**participation crisis**' due to a lack of engagement with the political system among a significant section of the population.

Voter turnout

Voter turnout is one of the most obvious measures of participation. Falling turnout is important because it means that governments are elected on a reduced share of the popular vote, thus calling the strength of their mandate into question.

The average turnout at general elections from 1945 to 1997 was 76 per cent. Since then, as Figure 1.3 shows, it has been lower. The percentage for 2001 was the lowest since the end of the First World War in 1918. There has been a modest recovery at the last three general elections, although it is still some way from the levels seen at most post-war contests.

Turnout is even lower, as a rule, in so-called 'second order' elections, such as those for the devolved bodies in Scotland, Wales and Northern Ireland, and in local council elections. Average turnout in the May 2016 local elections in England was 33.8 per cent. This may be because voters see these less powerful bodies as unlikely to make a major difference to their lives. Turnout in parliamentary by-elections is often low because people are not helping to choose a government. In the February 2017 Stoke-on-Trent by-election, for example, only 38.2 per cent of the electorate voted. This was significantly less than the already low 49.9 per cent turnout in the seat at the 2015 general election. On the same day, the Copeland (Cumbria) by-election saw a turnout of 51.3 per cent, down from 63.8 per cent at the general election.

> **Key term**
>
> **Participation crisis**
> a lack of engagement with the political system, for example where a large number of people choose not to vote, join a political party or stand for office.

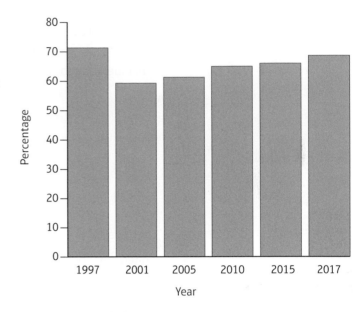

Figure 1.3: General election turnout since 1997

In spite of publicity encouraging people to vote, the Police and Crime Commissioner elections in 2012 had the lowest average turnout at any UK contest, at 15 per cent. Voters did not fully understand the purpose of these elected individuals. There was a slight improvement to 27 per cent in the 2016 elections.

Party membership

Party membership is another indicator of a participation crisis. Only 1.6 per cent of the electorate now belongs to one of the three main UK-wide political parties, whereas in 1983 the figure was 3.8 per cent. However, this differs significantly from party to party.

- The Conservative Party had just under 150,000 members by 2016, a significant drop from an estimated 400,000 in the mid-1990s.
- The Labour Party's membership increased in the run-up to the 1997 election but fell while the party was in government to around 190,000 members. The election of Jeremy Corbyn as leader has been associated with a remarkable increase in membership, with a total of 515,000 by July 2016.
- The Liberal Democrats had about 70,000 members in the early 2000s, falling to 49,000 during the 2010–15 coalition with the Conservatives. In 2016, they had recovered to about 76,000 members, and by 2017 claimed a membership exceeding 82,000.

Another recent trend has been an increase in the membership of some smaller parties. At the 2015 general election a record 24.8 per cent of the vote went to parties other than the Conservatives, Labour and Liberal Democrats.

Political party	Membership (Dec 2013)	Membership (July 2016)
Scottish Nationalist Party (SNP)	25,000	120,000
Green Party	13,800	55,000
United Kingdom Independence Party (UKIP)	32,400	39,000

Table 1.3: Membership of selected smaller parties

Link

For more on **pressure groups**, see Section 1.3.

Is there a crisis of participation?

There are other, less formal ways in which people can get involved in politics. Membership of **pressure groups**, particularly those concerned with single issues such as the environment, has been increasing. The last two decades have seen numerous well-attended demonstrations on issues as diverse as fuel prices, the Iraq War, fox hunting and student tuition fees. Direct action has become a recognised feature of modern politics, indicating that people may be turning to new methods of expression because they feel that conventional politics has let them down. Society has become more consumerist – people make up their minds more on an individual basis and are used to making choices between different options.

In the last decade the emergence of social media has enabled people, especially the young, to exchange political views and participate in online campaigns on particular issues, without engaging in the real world. An example of e-democracy is support for e-petitions, which allow people to register a viewpoint online. An e-petition on the Downing Street website in 2007, against proposals for road-charging, was signed by 1.8 million people.

The rise of new forms of political engagement may be seen as a positive development, but it is still a cause for concern that so many people are uninvolved in traditional politics. One explanation is political apathy – a lack of interest or awareness of contemporary events and political issues that affect society. An alternative version of this is known as 'hapathy' – a blend of the words 'happiness' and 'apathy', meaning that people are generally contented and see no need to push for political change. This may possibly help to account for the unusually low levels of voter turnout in 2001 and

2005 (the economy was booming and presumably levels of contentment were higher) but not for the 2010 election (which took place against a much less optimistic economic background).

To some extent levels of participation depend on the type of issue at stake. Turnout for the Scottish independence referendum in September 2014 was 84.6 per cent, while 72.2 per cent of voters took part in the June 2016 EU referendum across the UK. These figures suggest that on critical issues affecting the way that the country is governed, people will still express a view.

A factor that helps explain both declining voter turnout and increasing interest in alternative types of political activity is the generally negative public perception of politicians in recent decades. Examples of dishonest behaviour by MPs and broken electoral promises, together with a general sense that voting does not change anything, have reduced levels of trust in democratic politics.

Case study: The 2009 parliamentary expenses scandal

The parliamentary expenses scandal featured stories that some MPs had made false claims for mortgage repayments, home insurance and other costs – including in one case, the purchase of a duck house.

In 2009 *The Daily Telegraph* published evidence of widespread abuse of the system that allowed MPs to claim expenses for living costs. The affair dragged in MPs from across the political spectrum, leading to a number of apologies, forced repayments and decisions not to contest seats at the next general election. Five former MPs and two members of the House of Lords were sentenced to prison terms. Although steps have been taken to regulate the expenses system, this does not seem to have fundamentally altered popular perceptions. A 2015 survey by market research company Ipsos MORI found that politicians were the profession least trusted by the public, below estate agents, journalists and bankers.

Question

- Apart from the expenses scandal, can you think of other reasons why levels of trust in politicians are so low?

Pause & reflect

Review the discussion so far. How plausible do you think it is to talk of a 'crisis of political participation'? Alternatively, is it more appropriate to talk about a change in the way that people participate in politics?

What should be done to reform the system?

Some recent reform proposals have focused on increasing turnout at elections by making it easier for people to vote, such as:

- changing the day for elections from Thursday to the weekend, as in mainland Europe
- allowing people to vote anywhere in their constituency, rather than insisting on attendance at a particular polling station
- allowing voting to take place over several days.

Two other suggestions are to encourage wider use of postal voting, and to allow electronic voting (e-voting). These methods are open to questions about security. When all-postal ballots were trialled in four regions at the 2004 European parliament elections, there were complaints of an increase in electoral fraud, including multiple voting and intimidation. Voters also disliked being deprived of other means of voting. E-voting is open to problems arising from cyberattack and the possibility of online impersonation of voters. The need to access technology may also discriminate against older people, who are less familiar with it, and poorer voters who cannot afford computers.

There has also been a suggestion that the **voting age be reduced** from 18 to 16, which was allowed in the 2014 Scottish referendum, but is still not the practice in UK elections.

Another radical proposal is to make voting compulsory. This is the practice in certain countries, including Belgium and Australia, where failure to turn up at the polling station attracts a small fine. Table 1.4 shows the arguments for and against this idea.

> **Link**
>
> For more on **reducing the voting age**, see Section 1.2.

Voting should be made compulsory	It should remain voluntary
Voting is a social duty as well as a right; people should be engaged in the processes that affect their lives.	In a preferential voting system, where voters number candidates in order, compulsory voting might lead to participants simply placing candidates in rank order (1,2,3 or 3,2,1).
It would produce a parliament that is more representative of the population as a whole.	It is undemocratic to force people to take part in something that should be a matter of choice.
Politicians would have to run better quality campaigns, and governments would have to frame their policies with the whole electorate in mind.	It would not stop politicians focusing their campaigning on marginal seats, and neglecting safe seats where the outcome is predictable.
Voters are not obliged to vote for one of the candidates if they conscientiously cannot do so; it would still be legal to spoil one's ballot paper, or a 'none of the above' box could be provided on the paper.	Compulsory voting does not address the deeper reasons why people decide not to vote.

Table 1.4: Compulsory voting – for and against

However, these proposals will have a limited impact if the reasons for non-participation lie deeper than apathy or the inconvenience of actually taking part in the electoral process.

Here are some broader reforms of the UK democratic system that could be considered.

- Changing the electoral system for Westminster to one based on proportional representation, so that it more accurately reflects voters' preferences. People who wish to vote for a minority party might then feel that there is more chance of their viewpoint being represented.
- Further reform of parliament, to make its processes more democratic and transparent, and enabling it to bring governments more effectively to account for their actions.
- The transfer of more government powers and functions to local bodies – for example, devolving power to the English regions or to an English parliament.

However, there is little willingness to undertake reform on this scale. A comprehensive overhaul of the kind that radical reformers want to see seems unlikely.

1.2   A wider franchise and debates over suffrage

The **suffrage** (also known as the **franchise**) is the ability or right to vote in public elections. In the present day all adults over the age of 18 possess this right, provided they have registered to vote. British and Irish citizens have reciprocal rights to vote in each other's countries. Commonwealth citizens are allowed to vote, as are UK nationals who have lived abroad for less than 15 years. The only categories of people who are excluded from taking part in parliamentary elections are:

> **Key term**
>
> **Franchise/suffrage**
> the ability, or right, to vote in public elections.

- people under the age of 18
- EU citizens (apart from those from the Irish Republic), although they can vote in local elections
- Members of the House of Lords (on the grounds that they have a permanent voice as members of one of the two Houses of Parliament)
- prisoners (this exclusion is subject to a challenge from the European Court of Human Rights, but to date the government has ignored it)
- those convicted of a corrupt or illegal electoral practice, who are barred for 5 years
- people who are compulsorily detained in a psychiatric hospital.

Key milestones in the widening of the franchise

From the late Middle Ages to the early 19th century, no major reform of the electoral system occurred. There were numerous anomalies.

- There were two types of constituency: the counties and the boroughs (or towns), which varied considerably in size. In the counties, the right to vote was restricted to those who owned freehold property worth at least 40 shillings, or £2 in value. Voting qualifications in boroughs varied according to a range of local rules and traditions. In some boroughs all freemen were entitled to vote, whereas in others it depended on property ownership or the payment of some kind of local tax.
- The distribution of parliamentary seats had not kept pace with economic growth and population movement, so some tiny boroughs retained an historic right to return MPs. In many cases a wealthy patron effectively nominated the MP. Meanwhile, emerging industrial towns were yet to acquire representation of their own.
- Plural voting allowed wealthy men, who owned property in more than one constituency, to vote more than once.
- By custom, women were excluded from voting, although there had been occasional examples of women who owned property in their own right exercising the franchise.

This meant that the electorate totalled approximately 400,000 men by the early 19th century.

The Great Reform Act of 1832

The Great Reform Act of 1832 brought about the first major change, by:

- abolishing the separate representation of the most underpopulated 'rotten boroughs' and creating seats for urban areas, such as Manchester
- granting the vote to some new categories of people in the counties, including tenant farmers and smaller property holders

- creating a standard qualification for the franchise in the boroughs, so it now applied to all male householders living in properties who paid a yearly rental of £10 or more – i.e. the middle classes, who were growing in importance as a result of the industrial revolution.

The electorate increased to an estimated 650,000, equivalent to 5 per cent of the adult population.

The vote was extended further in a series of stages, as it became clear to the governing classes that gradual reform would not provoke violent revolution. They were persuaded that the cautious admission of more people to the franchise was the best way to avert such an upheaval.

However, property (owned or rented) remained the test for admission to the franchise throughout the Victorian era. It was not until 1918 that possession of the vote was treated as a citizen's right, and even then it was not granted to women on the same basis as men. Although class, gender and age remained obstacles to voting for centuries, ethnicity was never specified as grounds for exclusion from the franchise.

1867
Borough householders (e.g. tradesmen, shopkeepers) enfranchised
Electorate rises from 1–2 million = 13 per cent of adult population

1884
Rural householders (e.g. farm workers, miners) put on same footing as borough ones
Electorate over five million = 25 per cent of adult population

1918
All men over 21 and women over 30 enfranchised
75 per cent of adult population can vote

1928
Terms for men and women equalised; both sexes can vote at 21
Full adult suffrage

1948
End of plural voting
One person, one vote

1969
Voting age reduced to 18
Reflecting changing attitudes in society about adulthood

Figure 2.1: The development of the electoral system after the Great Reform Act of 1832

> **Pause & reflect**
>
> Which of the developments in Figure 2.1 would you describe as the most important turning point in the growth of democracy in the UK? Give reasons for your answer.

The work of the suffragists and suffragettes to extend the franchise

The exclusion of women from the franchise was largely unchallenged until the late 19th century. It was assumed that married women were represented by the votes cast by their husbands. Illogically, women were allowed to vote in local council elections but not in parliamentary elections, on the grounds that only men should have a say in issues of national and imperial importance.

The situation began to change with the establishment of the National Union of Women's Suffrage Societies (NUWSS) in 1897, under the leadership of Millicent Fawcett. Members, known as 'suffragists', were mainly middle-class women who believed in non-violent methods of persuasion, such as peaceful demonstrations, petitions and lobbying MPs. There was evidence that the climate of opinion was changing by the turn of the century, but for more radical campaigners progress was too slow. Emmeline Pankhurst, a former suffragist who was supported by her daughter Christabel, formed the Women's Social and Political Union in 1903. Dubbed 'suffragettes' by the popular press, the WSPU attracted both working- and middle-class support and used more militant tactics than the NUWSS. Its aim was to attract publicity and put pressure on parliament through attacks on well-known institutions and the disruption of political meetings and other prominent male-dominated public activities. For example, in 1913, suffragette Emily Davison threw herself under the king's horse at the Epsom Derby.

The suffragettes attracted hostility but also a degree of sympathy for their strength and endurance. Suffragettes who were imprisoned for their activities went on hunger strike, leading the authorities to resort to force-feeding. This gave the movement valuable publicity and depicted the liberal government of the day as unreasonably harsh. Nonetheless, the suffragettes showed moderation in suspending their campaigning on the outbreak of the First World War in 1914.

Suffragette leader Emmeline Pankhurst in prison during the suffragette campaign for equal voting rights.

Female enfranchisement, admittedly on a limited basis, eventually came through the 1918 Representation of the People Act. The act was passed mainly due to growing pressure to give the vote to all working-class men, in recognition of the fact that many who had served in the armed forces were not householders – so they had no stake in the political system for which they were expected to lay down their lives. Women over the age of 30, who were householders or wives of householders, were granted the vote at the same time.

The effectiveness of the two female suffrage movements remains controversial. Some historians have argued that the quiet, undramatic work of the suffragists has not been recognised, and that the violent methods of the suffragettes alienated potential supporters. Another line of argument is that the willingness of women to serve in vital industries during the war, filling the gaps left by men on military service, persuaded the government of their fitness for the vote. However, the vast majority of female war workers were younger, unmarried women, who did not benefit directly from the 1918 legislation.

It seems likely that the suffragette movement was important because it kept the issue of voting rights on the agenda in the decade before the First World War. Politicians of all parties may have concluded in 1918 that, if they did not grant the vote to some women, the campaign would restart, in a political environment much more favourable to the idea of equality.

A case study of a current movement to extend the franchise: Votes at 16

The most prominent group still excluded from the franchise are 16 and 17 year olds. The Votes at 16 Coalition, formed in 2003, won an early success by securing a study of the issue by the Electoral Commission. Although the report came down on the side of no change, a number of individual Liberal Democrat, Labour and SNP MPs kept the issue alive in the House of Commons. Labour MP Julie Morgan sponsored a private member's bill in 2008, which ran out of parliamentary time.

An important boost for the campaign came when 16 and 17 year olds were allowed to vote in the Scottish independence referendum in 2014, and the Scottish parliament voted the following year to allow them to take part in its own elections. At UK level, by the time of the 2015 general election, all major parties except the Conservatives were in favour of extending the precedent. The Electoral Reform Society also supports votes at 16.

Figure 2.2: What are the arguments for and against votes at 16?

EXTENSION ACTIVITY

Which recent developments have strengthened the case for lowering the voting age? How convincing do you find the arguments? Look at the website of the Votes at 16 campaign for more information.

1.3 Pressure groups and other influences

Pressure groups differ from political parties in that they do not usually enter their own candidates at elections and do not seek to exercise power themselves. Rather they seek to influence the government (or another authority) to adopt their ideas, or not to pursue a policy of which they disapprove.

Pressure groups: how they exert influence

The term 'pressure group' is very broad. There is a huge variety of types of group, from purely local ones, often created for a specific purpose such as campaigning against a new road, to well-established national and even transnational organisations. The methods that they use also vary considerably.

There are three main types of pressure groups.

- **Sectional groups (or interest groups)** seek to promote the interests of an occupation or another group in society. For example, trade unions represent their members in negotiations with employers over wages and working conditions. Membership of a sectional group is usually restricted to people who meet specific requirements, such as professional qualifications in a particular field. For example, the Law Society is open to solicitors in England and Wales.

- **Cause groups (or promotional groups)** are focused on achieving a particular goal or drawing attention to an issue or group of related issues. Membership is usually open to anyone who sympathises with their aims. For example, Greenpeace promotes awareness of environmental concerns and tries to influence the government to adopt 'green' causes. A special category of cause group is one that promotes the interests of a group in society – usually one that cannot stand up for itself. Members do not belong to the social group for which they campaign. For example, most members of the housing charity Shelter are not themselves homeless.

- **Social movements** are similar to cause groups but are more loosely structured. Some participants may also belong to more traditional pressure groups, while others are simply moved to take part in a specific protest. Social movements are usually politically radical and seek to achieve a single objective. For example, the Camps for Climate Action were created for short periods in 2006–10 to protest against the expansion of Heathrow airport, coal-fired power stations in Yorkshire and other environmental targets.

Pause & reflect

Find the websites of the following pressure groups and decide what type of group they are. Look at the list of campaigns they run (usually prominent on their home page or in the 'What we do' section). Are any hard to categorise?

- The National Union of Teachers.
- Campaign for Nuclear Disarmament.
- Friends of the Earth.

- The Road Haulage Association.
- The Countryside Alliance.

Another way to categorise pressure groups is to look at the nature of their relationship with the government.

There are broadly two different kinds of group.

- **Insider groups** rely on contacts with ministers and civil servants to achieve their aims. Some, like the National Union of Farmers, have close links with the relevant government department (in this case, Defra). Insider groups tend to have objectives that are broadly in line with the views of the government, increasing their leverage. Insider groups are also sub-divided into low- and high-profile groups. Low-profile groups, such as the Howard League for Penal Reform, rely on discreet behind the scenes contacts rather than seeking publicity. High-profile groups, such as the Confederation of British Industry (CBI), supplement their lobbying with use of the media to make their case.

- **Outsider groups** are not consulted by the government. Their objectives may be so far outside the political mainstream (for example, animal rights protestors who try to intimidate animal testing laboratories into ceasing their work) that the government is unlikely to enter into dialogue with them. Alternatively, an outsider group may wish to preserve its independence and reputation for ideological purity by keeping government at a distance. For example, the 'Occupy' movement, which organised sit-ins in late 2011, sees government as closely aligned to the global capitalist movement against which they are protesting.

Some groups move from insider to outsider status (and vice versa) according to changing political circumstances. In the post-war era, trade unions enjoyed privileged access to influence, especially when Labour governments were in power, but with the election of the Thatcher government in 1979, union leaders were deliberately excluded from the corridors of power.

How pressure groups' methods vary

A pressure group's choice of methods will be determined largely by the resources available and by its status as an insider or outsider group. Insider groups tend to negotiate quietly behind the scenes, using their private contacts in Whitehall. They may even be given the opportunity to offer their views on draft legislation. Organisations such as the National Farmers Union are able to offer the government the benefit of their specialised knowledge in return for influence over policy. Pressure groups may also lobby MPs, briefing them on issues of concern or giving evidence to committees. Lawyers acting for the human rights group, Liberty, have done this in order to put their views across on counterterrorism policies that affect people's civil liberties.

Outsider groups typically resort to less discreet methods to draw attention to their concerns. Lacking contacts within government, they may try to exercise influence through email campaigns and petitions, or staging demonstrations and publicity stunts. Members of the pressure group Black Lives Matter UK, for example, obstructed flights at London City Airport in September 2016 to draw attention to their claim that ethnic minorities are disproportionately affected by pollution.

Direct action is not always peaceful. Some of those who took part in the 2010 student demonstrations against increased university tuition fees were prosecuted for disorderly conduct. Other pressure groups, usually those that are well funded, may initiate legal challenges against policies to which they are opposed. The Countryside Alliance took its case against the banning of fox hunting (in vain) to the High Court in 2004.

Some groups may use a combination of 'insider' and 'outsider' methods. Much depends on the nature of the issue and the degree to which the government is willing to respond. The British Medical Association (BMA) usually enjoys insider status but, faced with the Conservative government's determination to impose a new contract on junior doctors, it indicated its support for strike action in the autumn of 2016 – a classic outsider group tactic. It later called off support for more extended strikes in response to concerns about patient safety.

Why do some pressure groups have more influence than others?

What constitutes success for a pressure group? Success for some groups may consist of winning publicity for an issue rather than actually changing government policy. It is particularly hard to gauge the success of insider groups, as they do not usually publicise their achievements to avoid offending their government contacts.

The success of different pressure groups can vary considerably as a consequence of the wider context. Much depends on the climate of public opinion and the willingness of the government to make concessions. Access to effective methods of communication is another factor that may promote success. An example is the dramatic sequence of events that followed a period of rising petrol prices in September 2000. Online groups that mobilise opposition through petitions are also becoming increasingly effective. For example, in 2016, the 38 Degrees group collected 321,437 online signatures, helping to persuade the government not to privatise the Land Registry.

The UK economy almost ground to a halt when road hauliers and farmers spearheaded a movement to blockade oil refineries, in a bid to get the government to reduce the tax on fuel. These activists had considerable leverage and made use of mobile phones to assemble their supporters rapidly with little warning. They also enjoyed widespread public approval. They secured a limited success by catching the Blair government unprepared – they gained a freeze rather than a cut in the duty – but two later attempts to replicate this mass protest, when the cost of fuel began to rise again, failed to attract significant support.

Several factors are usually relevant in deciding the effectiveness of pressure group activity.

- **Resources:** A large membership who pay subscriptions means that a group is likely to have the financial resources to run offices, pay permanent staff and organise publicity. For example, the RSPCA employs about 1600 people, supported by thousands of volunteers, and can afford to take out full-page advertisements in national newspapers. The size of a pressure group's membership can also be important in persuading government that it reflects a significant section of public opinion. However, this is not always the case. The Campaign for Nuclear Disarmament had an estimated 110,000 members in the mid-1980s but the Thatcher government could afford to ignore its large and well-orchestrated demonstrations, because it could rely on the passive support of the majority of the population.

- **Tactics and leadership:** Experienced, capable leadership is vital to success. For example, the RSPCA played a key role in securing the ban on hunting with dogs in 2004 by collaborating with two similar groups, the League Against Cruel Sports and the International Fund for Animal Welfare, so that they were not competing with each other. Another key to success is knowing which 'access points' in the UK political system to target – the points at which a group can apply pressure. The European Union can also have an important role, such as developing and policing environmental standards. Friends of the Earth ran a long and ultimately successful campaign to compel the UK government to clean up beaches, as required by the EU.

- **Public support:** Pressure groups whose agenda is in step with public opinion are usually more successful than those whose objectives fail to engage it, or whose methods alienate potential sympathisers. The Snowdrop campaign to ban the use of handguns was successful largely because of public reaction to the 1996 Dunblane Primary School massacre, when a gunman killed 16 children and their teacher. Favourable media coverage can play an important role in winning support, as can the involvement of a well-known personality. TV celebrity Joanna Lumley's support for retired Gurkha soldiers was important in overturning a government ban on their right to live in the UK.

- **Government attitudes:** Insider contacts with government ministers and civil servants are often a key to success. The National Farmers Union's links to Defra were instrumental in bringing about the 2013 badger cull, intended to protect cattle against tuberculosis, despite the wishes of animal welfare groups, who advocated vaccination of herds as a more humane approach. Government will usually listen to the groups on which it relies for specialist knowledge of a policy area, and with whose agenda it can see some common ground.

Case study: The BMA and the ban on smoking in cars carrying children

The BMA is a sectional group whose main purpose is to protect the interests of doctors. It can also function as a cause group on issues that affect public health. Its professional status and ability to provide scientific evidence give it credibility with government. The BMA had already contributed to the introduction of a ban on smoking in enclosed public spaces from 2007. It saw the prohibition of smoking in private vehicles as the next stage in its campaign for a smoke-free UK.

When the BMA first made its case in November 2011, on the grounds that passive smoking is particularly harmful in a confined space, the government had no plans for legislation. Instead it preferred to discourage drivers from smoking by publicising the health risks. The BMA did not secure all of its objectives. Originally it argued for an outright ban on smoking in cars, regardless of whether passengers were being carried. There was insufficient support for this, so the BMA concentrated on campaigning for prohibition when children were being carried. This attracted the support of other pressure groups such as Asthma UK. The BMA used online technology to lobby for support, providing its members with a web-based form to personalise and send to their MPs. It also made its case to members of the House of Lords. A Labour peer introduced an amendment to the 2014 Children and Families Bill, which was passed by the Lords and later accepted by the Commons. The ban came into force in October 2015.

This is a good illustration of successful pressure-group politics. The BMA showed a willingness to focus on an attainable goal. It proved patient and resourceful in mobilising support and using the parliamentary process. It was also fortunate in that public opinion and the government were willing to protect children as a vulnerable group, while they would have seen a total ban on smoking in cars as an unnecessary intrusion into people's private lives.

Case study: The Occupy London movement

In October 2011 a group of protestors occupied the square in front of St Paul's Cathedral in London, where they erected tents until they were evicted by order of the High Court 4 months later. They were protesting about corporate greed in the City of London, which they held responsible for social inequality. Their actions were echoed by demonstrations in other cities, including in Wall Street, New York. Superficially they had some success in drawing attention to their cause, at a time when the coalition government's spending cuts were widely condemned on the left of British politics for making life harder for the poor, while wealthy people in the financial sector seemed unscathed. A senior clergyman at St Paul's resigned his post in solidarity with the protestors and there was some sympathy for them when the police were sent in to clear the camp. However, Occupy London failed to achieve long-lasting results. In part this was due to the strong stand taken by the authorities. Although initially they tolerated the camp, when they decided to take action they were determined not to allow the protestors to settle elsewhere in London. Fundamentally, the movement's objectives were too broad and incoherent to give them any chance of success. They represented a generalised hostility to global capitalism and did not have practical, achievable goals. Even if the government had been prepared to negotiate with the campaigners, it is hard to see what it could have done to satisfy them.

Another problem for the Occupy movement was that, although social media helped to bring people together quickly, it was of little use in building a long-term organisation. Ultimately it lacked the capacity to channel its unfocused idealism into practical political activity.

The Occupy London camp outside St Paul's Cathedral in London.

Questions

- After reading both case studies do you agree that the most important factor in the success of the BMA and the failure of Occupy London was the extent to which their respective goals were acceptable to the public?

- What lessons can pressure group organisers draw from these two examples?

Other collective organisations and groups

There are a number of other organisations and groups that seek to exercise influence in various ways within the UK political system. Here are three key types.

Think tanks

Think tanks are groups of experts from different backgrounds who are brought together to investigate particular topics and to offer solutions to complicated economic, social or political issues. For example, the shift of Conservative Party thinking towards a more overtly free-market-oriented approach in the 1970s owed a great deal to Margaret Thatcher's patronage of right-wing think tanks, such as the Centre for Policy Studies and the Adam Smith Institute.

> **Key term**
>
> **Think tank**
> a body of experts brought together to investigate and offer solutions to economic, social or political issues.

Think tanks are an alternative source of ideas to the civil service, with more time and expertise than political parties to carry out research. Some have a definite influence on government policy. For example, the Centre for Social Justice was set up by former Conservative Party leader Iain Duncan Smith in 2004 to look for new solutions to the problems of people living in disadvantaged communities. Duncan Smith's appointment as Work and Pensions Secretary in the coalition government 6 years later enabled him to implement some of its ideas, notably the 'universal credit' plan that seeks to reduce the dependence of poor people on welfare benefits.

However, in government it is necessary to make compromises, so the less politically practical ideas dreamed up by think tanks are often ignored. The work of think tanks is often said to lack the academic rigour expected in university circles. Typically, think tanks are staffed by young, ambitious individuals who see their time there as a springboard to a political career. For example, David Miliband went from working at the centre-left Institute for Public Policy Research to become an adviser to Tony Blair, then an MP and eventually a senior minister in the **New Labour** governments.

> **Link**
>
> For more on **New Labour**, see Section 2.2 of Political Parties.

> **Key term**
>
> **Lobbyist**
> someone who is paid by clients to seek to influence government or parliament on their behalf, particularly when legislation is being considered.

Lobbyists

Lobbyists are members of professional organisations who are paid by clients seeking access to government, or to MPs and members of the House of Lords. Their purpose is to gain influence on behalf of their clients, particularly when legislation that affects their clients' interests is under consideration. This is an extension of a long-established principle that members of the public may lobby their MPs in person or by letter. The word 'lobby' is derived from the hallways of the Houses of Parliament where, in the past, people would meet their MP to ask for help. However, there is unease about the legitimacy of some professional lobbying activities. Many people dislike the idea that influence can be bought by wealthy individuals and organisations, who can afford the lobbyists' fees. Attention has been focused on the system recently by undercover journalists posing as lobbyists to entrap MPs with offers of financial rewards. The parliamentary code of conduct strictly bars MPs from accepting money for agreeing to represent a viewpoint.

Another concern has been that the lobbying system for many years was expected to regulate itself, with lobbyists being allowed to decide whether or not their names appeared on a public register. In 2014 the government made it a legal requirement for anyone lobbying on behalf of a third party to register if their activities include discussing policy, legislation or government contracts with a minister or senior civil servant. This did not allay the anxieties of critics who wanted greater transparency.

Lobbying remains big business in the UK, employing an estimated 4000 people, and a total of £2 billion is spent on it each year. How much influence lobbying really has over government is uncertain. Under David Cameron, Number 10 denied that lobbying firms changed government policy, but stated that companies frequently discuss their concerns with the Business Department or the Treasury. Governments carry out regular consultation exercises to discover what the impact of proposed legislation on relevant groups may be, and they may modify their plans in response to pressure.

Corporations

The role of corporations, or large business organisations, in UK government circles is a related area of concern for some pro-democracy campaigners. There has also been discussion of the so-called 'revolving door' process, where senior politicians and officials take well-paid jobs in the private sector after they leave government service. This brings with it the suspicion that they use their knowledge and contacts to benefit the interests of these corporations. In addition a number of business leaders have become ministers by being appointed to the House of Lords.

Powerful corporations may lobby the government in an attempt to modify policies that affect their business interests. For example, in October 2016, during a social event at the Conservative Party Conference attended by the Business Secretary, Greg Clark, it was reported that the British Soft Drinks Association had expressed its opposition to a planned tax on sugary drinks. However, in this case, the government persisted with its policy. It was commended by health group campaigners for not being deflected from a policy it viewed as important in combating obesity.

Another issue is how far multinational corporations that operate in the UK can be compelled to pay what is accepted as a fair level of tax. In 2016, after a prolonged negotiation with HM Revenue and Customs, the internet-search organisation Google agreed to pay £130 million in taxes dating back to 2005. However, opposition MPs argued that this was a lenient figure given the level of profits made by the firm in the UK.

1.4 Rights in context

Citizens of a democracy enter into a contract with the state. It guarantees them certain rights, and in return they have obligations. Some are legal obligations, such as obeying the law, paying taxes and performing jury service. Others are moral responsibilities, include voting in elections and playing a part in protecting the environment, such as recycling. The notion of 'active citizenship' goes further to include offering voluntary service to help the community.

'Rights' are legally protected freedoms, also known as civil liberties. In the UK these rights are now guaranteed by the 1998 Human Rights Act, but there was an understanding of people's entitlement to them long before this. It was also broadly accepted that they might have to be limited in time of war or other major national emergency.

They include the right to:

- fair and equal treatment under the law, including the right to a fair trial and to peaceful possession of one's property, and to freedom from arbitrary detention
- freedom of expression in speech and writing
- freedom of conscience, including worshipping as one wishes (and not being compelled to take part in religious observance)
- vote, to stand for election and to join a party or pressure group
- belong to an association such as a trade union
- freedom of movement.

More contentious are 'social rights', including the right to education, employment, health care and welfare provision.

Major milestones in the development of rights in the UK

The notion of civil rights developed gradually over an extended period. Until 1998 there was no single document that positively set out citizens' rights. Instead there were 'negative rights' – things people were entitled to do unless the law explicitly prohibited them. For example, people had a right to freedom of expression, subject to laws of defamation and blasphemy. Some rights were protected by acts of parliament, while others were derived from custom or common law.

- **Magna Carta ('Great Charter')**, a document drawn up in 1215, is usually regarded as the oldest statement of rights in the UK. It was presented to King John by nobles who disapproved of his tyrannical rule, and its original purpose was to limit royal power. Many of its clauses are now outdated, but the following excerpt has been widely hailed as the foundation of the rights of the citizen:

No free man shall be seized or imprisoned, or stripped of his rights or possessions, or outlawed or exiled; nor will we proceed with force against him except by the lawful judgement of his equals or by the law of the land. To no one will we sell, to no one deny or delay right or justice.

This clause is regarded as establishing the right to trial by jury and to *habeas corpus*, which means literally 'you may have the body' in Latin – this refers to a court order to produce a person before a court so that it can be determined whether he or she has been lawfully detained.

- **The European Convention on Human Rights** was drawn up in 1950, with the UK as one of its signatories, by the Council of Europe (not part of the European Union). It was very similar to the United Nations Declaration of Human Rights, drawn up in the aftermath of terrible violations of rights in the Second World War. The European Court of Human Rights was set up in Strasbourg to hear cases where people felt that their rights had been infringed in their own countries. UK citizens were allowed to appeal to the Court, but it was time-consuming and expensive.

- **The Human Rights Act (1998)** was passed by the New Labour government, which incorporated the Convention into UK law with effect from 2000. These rights – including the right to life, the prohibition of torture or degrading treatment, freedom from arbitrary arrest, the right to a fair trial and rights to privacy and family life – could now be defended in UK courts without having to go to Strasbourg.

- **The Equality Act (2010)** brought together earlier pieces of legislation that had sought to outlaw discrimination and unfair treatment, such as the 1970 Equal Pay Act, the 1975 Sex Discrimination Act and the 1976 Race Relations Act. It identified nine 'protected characteristics': age, disability, gender reassignment, marriage or civil partnership, pregnancy and maternity, race, religion or belief, sex, and sexual orientation. It made it illegal for public bodies, employers, service providers and other organisations and individuals to discriminate against people on any of these grounds, in the workplace or in wider society.

EXTENSION ACTIVITY

Research the Human Rights Act. A useful summary of its provisions can be found on the website of the human rights pressure group, Liberty. How far do you think that its provisions have been upheld in the UK?

Debates over the extent, limits and tensions within the UK's rights-based culture

Since the passing of the Human Rights Act it has often been claimed that the UK has developed a 'rights-based culture'. All new legislation must be compliant with the act. Judges can declare earlier acts of parliament incompatible with it, although they cannot legally compel parliament to make changes. This is because of the all-important concept of **parliamentary sovereignty**.

One indicator of the growing prominence of rights has been an increased use of judicial review. The number of reviews rose from around 4240 in 2000 to around 15,600 by 2013. Examples of successful challenges to government policies include High Court rulings that retired Gurkha soldiers should be allowed to settle in the UK (2008), and that the government had not consulted fairly on compensation for people affected by the planned high-speed rail link (2013).

Its defenders say that judicial review is a vital means of defending citizens' rights, enabling the legality of government actions to be properly scrutinised; its critics argue that it places too much power in the hands of unelected and unaccountable judges.

A prominent example of judicial review – sometimes called 'judge-made law' – is the issue of privacy. Judges have been accused of effectively creating a privacy law through the way they have interpreted the Human Rights Act. In a series of high-profile court cases, they appeared to give priority to Article 8 of the European Convention on Human Rights (the right to privacy) over Article 10 (the right to freedom of expression), as claimed by the press. This occurred even though specific legislation on the subject had not been passed by parliament and it was not explicitly covered by

Link

For more on **parliamentary sovereignty**, see Section 4.4 of Relations Between Institutions.

common law. It seemed that wealthy individuals, who could afford to take legal action, had an unfair advantage. For example, in 2008 the High Court awarded Max Mosley, the head of the Formula 1 motor racing organisation, substantial damages when the *News of the World* published a story about his sex life, which he argued had breached his privacy. On the other hand it is worth noting that Mosley failed in a subsequent action in the European Court of Human Rights, which refused to rule that newspapers should notify people before printing stories about their personal lives.

For many on the right of British politics, a more serious fault of the Human Rights Act is the way that it seems to show favour to undeserving individuals, rather than protecting the legitimate freedoms of UK citizens. The Conservatives have argued for many years for the replacement of the act with a new 'British Bill of Rights', which would establish the supremacy of British courts over the European Court of Human Rights. The case of Abu Qatada illustrates the frustration caused by the way in which the Human Rights Act was implemented.

Case study: The Abu Qatada deportation case and the Human Rights Act

Abu Qatada, a radical Muslim cleric living in London since the 1990s, had made speeches justifying the use of violence to promote the Islamist cause and had served time in British jails. The security services regarded him as a threat and ministers wanted to deport him to his country of origin, Jordan, where he was wanted for trial. However, his legal advisers were able to fight deportation for 8 years on the grounds that he might be tried using evidence obtained under torture, a breach of the Human Rights Act. Only in 2013, after the UK had signed a treaty with Jordan pledging that such evidence would not be used, was Abu Qatada flown back to face trial. He was cleared of involvement in terrorist bomb plots in Jordan. Nevertheless the British authorities continued to view him as a dangerous influence.

Question

- Another high-profile extradition case was that of the Islamic fundamentalist preacher, Abu Hamza. Research this case to find out the part played by the European Convention on Human Rights.

The lack of clarity over the definition of rights can lead to conflicts between pressure groups and individuals. One example concerns the pressure group, the Campaign for Freedom of Information, that worked to help bring about the Freedom of Information Act (2000), which gives the public the right to access data held by public authorities. In 2006–07 this group opposed an attempt by a group of MPs to exclude parliament from the scope of the act. The MPs had argued that they should be exempt on the grounds that they were entitled to confidentiality in their correspondence with constituents. The bill passed the Commons but failed to find a sponsor in the Lords and was dropped.

Another example of this kind of conflict concerns walkers' 'right to roam' in the countryside, for which the Ramblers' Association campaigned for many years. This right was finally given legal force in the Countryside and Rights of Way Act (2000). Pop star Madonna and her film director husband, Guy Ritchie, were two celebrity landowners who contested the right of the public to walk across their land. The planning inspectorate ruled in 2004 that ramblers would have access to part of their Wiltshire estate that was out of sight of their home, meaning that their right to privacy would not be infringed.

Perhaps the most emotive area where the rights of the individual have come into conflict with the priorities of government is that of counterterrorism. The 9/11 terror attacks in the USA in 2001, and the 7/7 London Underground and bus bombings in 2005, led to government measures that limited civil liberties in the interests of protecting the wider community. Ministers argued that they were entitled to detain terror suspects without trial on the grounds that a national emergency existed. In December 2004 the law lords (the highest court in the land before the creation of the Supreme Court) ruled that indefinite detention of foreign nationals, on suspicion of involvement in terrorism, was discriminatory. Faced with this legal challenge, the government passed a new law to introduce a system of control orders that enabled suspects to be closely monitored, such as through electronic tagging, a requirement to report to the police and removal of mobile phones and internet access. Control orders were kept in place, despite adverse rulings by judges, until 2011 when the coalition government replaced them with a modified version known as Terrorism Prevention and Investigation Measures (TPIMs).

EXTENSION ACTIVITY

Choose one of the campaigns highlighted on Liberty's website, and another one from the website of the Howard League for Penal Reform. Find out how successful these two pressure groups have been in promoting their chosen causes.

It would not be true to say that there has been an unremitting erosion of human rights in response to fears of terrorism. Some restrictive measures have been abandoned in face of parliamentary and public opposition. For example, in November 2005, the Blair government's proposal to extend the period that a suspect could be held before being charged, from 14 to 90 days, was defeated in the Commons. The government then compromised on 28 days and abandoned a subsequent attempt to increase it to 42 days, following a defeat in the Lords in 2008. Under the coalition the 28-day period was halved, and the Labour government's plan for compulsory identity cards was scrapped.

However, the public has been remarkably willing to sacrifice some liberties at a time of heightened concern over security. Governments have tended to place the safety of society above the protection of individual rights. This explains why pro-human rights pressure groups such as Liberty have had limited success in deflecting government policy. For example, in 2013 the organisation failed to stop the introduction of so-called 'secret courts', which permit terrorist suspects and major criminals to be tried without the evidence against them being disclosed in full. Nor did they arrest the passage of the Investigatory Powers Bill – the so-called 'Snoopers' Charter' – which increases the power of the intelligence agencies by obliging internet companies to store information about customers' browsing history.

Similarly the Howard League for Penal Reform, which campaigns for the rights of prisoners, has struggled to persuade the government to implement its agenda. The rights of convicted criminals do not constitute a popular cause. However, the Howard League tends to win victories on relatively minor issues, such as securing a 2014 High Court ruling that obliged the government to drop its ban on prisoners' families sending books to them. On the wider issue of securing a reduction in the size of the prison population the League has been less successful, noting in a review in May 2016 that 'there is no public service in such disarray as the prisons'. As a rule, governments are unlikely to side with pressure groups that campaign for the rights of minority groups whom the wider public regards as undeserving of sympathy.

The terrorist bombings on the London transport network on 7 July 2005 highlighted the tension between human rights and national security.

Assessment support: 1.1 Democracy and Participation

Question 3 on AS-Level Paper 1 is worth 10 marks and must be completed in 20 minutes. It is based on two short source extracts, which may be written text, data or a combination of the two.

Using the sources, assess whether UK democracy is facing a 'participation crisis'. [10 marks]

In your response you must compare both sources by analysing and evaluating them. You will not gain credit for use of knowledge and understanding alone. Any knowledge and understanding used in your response must support your analysis and evaluation of both sources in order to gain credit.

Table 3.1: Source 1: A table showing turnout in selected elections in the UK

Election	Date	% turnout
European parliament	2014	35.6
UK general election	2015	66.1
Scottish parliament	2016	55.6
Welsh Assembly	2016	45.3
Northern Ireland Assembly	2016	54.9
London Mayor	2016	45.3
Police and crime commissioners (England/Wales average)	2016	26.6

Source 2: Adapted from a Houses of Parliament report entitled 'Trends in Political Participation', published June 2015.

> *Traditionally, the role of the citizen in Western democracies has been perceived as a series of civic duties, including the duty to vote, but this conception appears to be declining. For example, a 2015 British Social Attitudes report noted that in 2013 57 per cent of respondents considered that they had a duty to vote compared with 76 per cent in 1987. However… many academics and political commentators have argued that the way that people understand politics and how they choose to express themselves politically is changing. Factors affecting this include increasing internet access, levels of university education, the rise of consumerism, and a preference for individual, rather than collective, decision-making and action. This may be leading people to participate in politics in new ways.*

The sources will present contrasting messages and are intended to encourage you to write a comparative answer. The mark scheme emphasises that answers that do not attempt comparison cannot attain higher than Level 1 (3 marks at most). This question tests AO2 (analysis) and AO3 (evaluation), with available marks split evenly between the two.

- Spend a few minutes – no more than five – reading the sources and noting the key things that you will include in your answer, before starting to write.

- Aim to write about three paragraphs, including a conclusion, in which you make an overall judgement, which must be convincingly supported.

- Remember to pick out similarities as well as differences, and where relevant to make connections between the points you make.

Here is the last part of a student's answer to this question.

The two sources differ in that Source 1, a table of statistics, presents figures on just one aspect of political participation: electoral turnout. This is an important but still quite narrow measure of involvement in politics. Source 2 interprets political participation more broadly than that. Also we do not know how typical the data selected in Source 1 may be. It is drawn from a narrow time period of just 2 years and so is of limited value on its own. Source 2 is part of a balanced report commissioned by the UK parliament. Unlike Source 1 it offers explanations for trends in political participation, and it uses data taken from a longer time period.

- The student highlights the ways the two sources are alike, as well as their differences.

- By questioning the value of the data used in Source 1, the student demonstrates that they can evaluate as well as analyse.

CHAPTER

2 Political Parties

Political parties are a vital part of the UK's representative democracy. In this chapter you will learn about:

- the role of parties within the political system and the arguments surrounding party funding
- the development and ideas of the main UK parties: the Conservatives, Labour and Liberal Democrats
- the part played by smaller parties that have emerged in recent years, including the Scottish National Party, Greens and UKIP
- the various models of party system associated with UK politics, and the factors that shape the fortunes of individual parties.

2.1 Political parties

The functions and features of political parties in the UK's representative democracy

A political party is a group of people drawn together by a similar set of beliefs, known as an ideology, even if they do not have identical views – on some issues they may be deeply divided. Most parties aspire to form a government and adopt an agreed programme of policy commitments, linked to their core ideas. Some parties are defined by a single issue (for example, UKIP's overriding cause has been withdrawal from the EU), but they will usually develop policies on other issues to broaden their support base.

Parties are different from **pressure groups**. Pressure groups may represent a single sectional interest or be concerned with a narrow range of ideas, such as the environment. Pressure groups may try to influence parties to adopt their ideas, but do not usually enter their own candidates at elections.

Political parties perform a number of functions within a democratic system.

- **Representation:** Perhaps the main function of parties is to represent the views of people with a certain set of beliefs. Those who have a broadly **right-wing** outlook have historically been drawn to the Conservative Party; those with a **left-wing** frame of mind have tended to gravitate towards Labour. This representative function could be performed by lots of individuals or pressure groups, but the value of parties is that they bring order to the political system.

Link

For more about **pressure groups**, see Section 1.3.

Key terms

Right wing
supporting the *status quo* – for little or no change. Supporters of right-wing parties (often known as conservatives) stress the importance of order, stability, hierarchy and private property.

Left wing
desiring change, reform and alteration to the way that society operates, including socialists, who are critical of the capitalist or free-market economy.

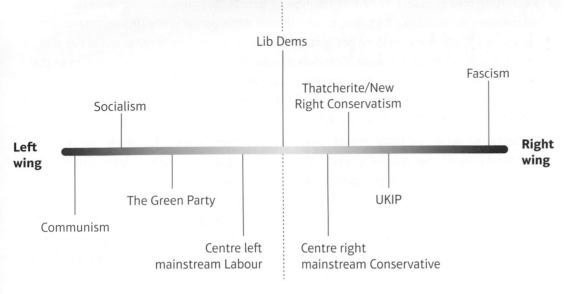

Lib Dems

Fascism

Thatcherite/New
Right Conservatism

Socialism

**Left
wing**

**Right
wing**

The Green Party

UKIP

Communism

Centre left
mainstream Labour

Centre right
mainstream Conservative

Figure 1.1: The political party spectrum in the UK

- **Participation:** In order to win power or influence, parties encourage people to participate in politics – to vote, join a party and to support it through funding to get its message across. Parties vary in how far they allow their members to shape party policy, but all the main UK parties have procedures that involve members in selecting candidates to stand for local and national elections, and in choosing the party leader. For example, the Labour Party increased its membership by allowing supporters to join for an annual subscription of £3 (later raised to £25), a development that played a part in the election of Jeremy Corbyn as leader in September 2015.

Jeremy Corbyn's election as Labour leader was associated with a rise in grassroots party membership.

- **Recruiting office holders:** For a small number of people, party membership leads to recruitment as candidates for public office and thus participation in the UK's representative democracy. Candidates can learn political skills as campaigners and organisers. Parties also have the right to reject or 'deselect' candidates who fail to live up to their expectation so that they cannot stand for that party in any upcoming election. Before the 2015 general election, Conservative activists in Thirsk and Malton (in North Yorkshire) and South Suffolk did not allow the sitting MPs to stand again as candidates.

- **Formulating policy:** Parties generate policies that embody the ideas for which they stand. At a general election they put these proposals before the electorate in a manifesto, a document setting out their programme for government. For example, at the 2015 general election the NHS was a key battleground. The Conservatives promised to give people access to their GP 7 days a week, while Labour pledged that patients would be given an appointment within 48 hours. Parties can also be said to have an educative function, by communicating and explaining their ideas to the public (although they do this to win popular support, so are likely to distort opponents' policies in their own interests).

- **Providing government:** The winning party at a general election has the opportunity to form a government. That party then controls the business of parliament, with a view to passing its manifesto into law. The prime minister is not directly elected by the people, but is usually the leader of the largest party. A prime minister who loses the confidence of their party is vulnerable. For example, in November 1990 Margaret Thatcher lost the support of a large number of Conservative MPs, and failed to win a leadership contest outright. She resigned and was replaced by John Major, who was regarded as better placed to unite the party and lead it to renewed electoral success.

EXTENSION ACTIVITY

How would you judge the success or failure of political parties? Should this be measured solely by their success in winning parliamentary seats, or are other features just as important, such as the size of their membership or their influence on government policies? Find examples of UK parties that have been successful in different ways in recent years.

The funding of UK political parties

MPs are paid from general taxation (their basic annual salary in April 2017 was £76,000). They are also allowed to claim expenses to cover the cost of running an office, living in Westminster and their constituency, and travelling between the two. However, in the UK there has been resistance to state funding of parties (a practice that happens in some other countries). Instead parties must meet most of their election costs from the voluntary subscriptions of their membership and from fundraising events in MPs' constituencies. However, there is special state provision to support the activities of the opposition in parliament, known as Short money.

Party funding has been a controversial area because of the suspicion that powerful interests offer financial support in return for political influence (see the Case study). While the Conservative Party has historically been seen as the party of big business, Labour has traditionally been funded by the trade unions, which played a major role in founding the party and shaping its policies. During the 'New Labour' years (1994–2010) this was to some extent replaced by donations from successful individuals as Labour became friendlier towards the business community. The Liberal Democrats (the least well-funded of the main UK parties) often criticise their opponents for being bankrolled by the wealthy. The large parties have been accused of offering political honours, such as places in the House of Lords, to their most generous benefactors, a practice that seems to run counter to principles of democracy and openness.

Case study: Tony Blair and Bernie Ecclestone

Blair faced criticism within months of becoming prime minister in 1997 following the revelation that Bernie Ecclestone, the motor-racing boss, had donated £1 million to Labour. It was alleged that there was a connection between this and a delay in implementing a ban on tobacco advertising in Formula One racing. Blair was forced to justify himself in a TV interview, in which he famously described himself as 'a pretty straight sort of guy', and the money was subsequently returned.

Question

- Following this case, were people justified in being suspicious about the relationship between parties and business interests?

In an attempt to overcome the perception that party funding had become an undemocratic feature of the UK political system, the Blair government passed the 2000 Political Parties, Elections and Referendums Act.

As a result of the 2000 act:

- an independent electoral commission was set up to supervise party spending on election campaigns
- the amount that a party could spend was capped at £30,000 in a constituency
- donations of more than £5,000 (nationally) or £1,000 (to a constituency party) had to be declared, and parties had to publish details of donations at regular intervals
- donations from individuals not on the UK electoral roll were banned.

This did not, however, put the issue of funding to rest. In the 'cash for peerages' scandal in 2006, it transpired that several wealthy individuals who had loaned money to the Labour Party had been nominated for honours. It seemed as if the party was exploiting a loophole in the law, which only regulated outright gifts. Blair was interviewed by the police and two of his aides also faced questioning. Although no charges were brought, the affair cast a shadow over Blair's last months in office. It was later decided that loans would be subject to the same rules as donations, and spending limits for parties were revised in the run-up to the 2010 election.

Potential reforms

In 2007 a report by a former civil servant, Sir Hayden Phillips, proposed to address the problem of private donations by moving towards a system where parties are funded from taxpayers' money. However, no subsequent government has acted on this recommendation. Pressure to make public spending cuts under the coalition government meant that this was not the time to place an additional burden on the taxpayer.

A suggestion supported by Labour and the Liberal Democrats at the 2015 election was to impose limits on individual donations to parties. This debate was complicated by issues of party-political advantage because the Conservatives, who stood to lose most from such a move, wanted to place corresponding restrictions on Labour's trade union backers. The Conservative government's 2016 Trade Union Act obliged new trade union members to choose whether to 'opt in' to making payments towards the political levy. This was expected to lead to a significant drop in the funding received by the Labour Party from the unions.

Pause & reflect

Why do you think it has been so difficult to find agreement on the subject of party funding?

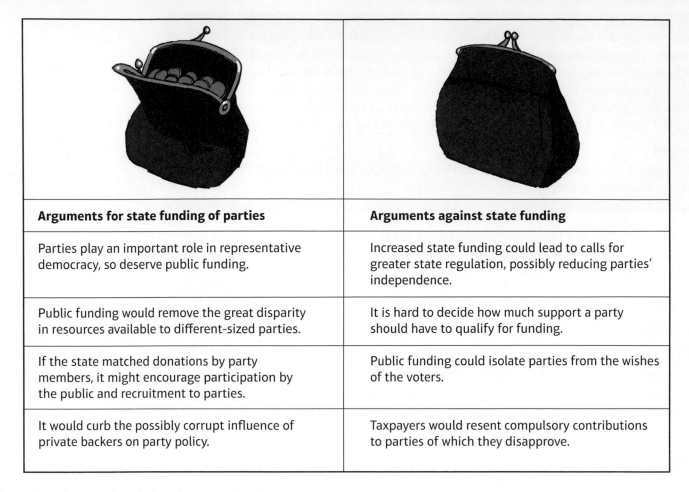

Arguments for state funding of parties	Arguments against state funding
Parties play an important role in representative democracy, so deserve public funding.	Increased state funding could lead to calls for greater state regulation, possibly reducing parties' independence.
Public funding would remove the great disparity in resources available to different-sized parties.	It is hard to decide how much support a party should have to qualify for funding.
If the state matched donations by party members, it might encourage participation by the public and recruitment to parties.	Public funding could isolate parties from the wishes of the voters.
It would curb the possibly corrupt influence of private backers on party policy.	Taxpayers would resent compulsory contributions to parties of which they disapprove.

Table 1.1: State funding of political parties – for and against

2.2   Established political parties

In this section you will learn about the origins and historical development of the three main UK political parties and how this has shaped their ideas and current policies.

The Conservative Party

Traditional conservatism

The Conservative Party can trace its origins back to the Tory Party of the late 17th century, an aristocratic grouping that first came together in defence of the historic privileges of the Crown and the Church of England as powerful landowning institutions. By the 1830s, under the leadership of Sir Robert Peel (prime minister 1834–35 and 1841–46), it was evolving into a party dedicated to the defence of property and traditional authority against the threat of revolution. Peel stressed the importance of gradual reform in order to protect, or conserve, established institutions – hence the name 'Conservative'. The party was remarkably successful in the late-19th and 20th centuries, broadening its support by appealing to the middle classes as well as the land-owning aristocracy.

One-nation conservatism

A development from traditional conservatism was **one-nation** conservatism, originally associated with one of the party's most colourful leaders, Benjamin Disraeli (prime minister 1868 and 1874–80). The name came from a passage in one of Disraeli's books, *Sybil*, in which he contemplates the growing division between rich and poor in the mid-19th century, produced by the development of industrial capitalism. The 'one-nation' philosophy sought to bridge the gulf between the classes through a paternalistic social policy. The 'natural leaders' of society would accept an obligation to act benevolently towards the disadvantaged, in return for acceptance of their right to rule. Disraeli, and later Conservative leaders who shared his approach, sought to win popular support by means of social reform and a 'patriotic' foreign policy, designed to strengthen national unity.

One-nation conservatism peaked in the generation after the Second World War, when the party broadly accepted the changes introduced by the Labour administration of 1945–51: the mixed economy, a welfare state and government action to maintain a high level of employment. They prided themselves on a pragmatic, non-ideological approach, maintaining the party contest between themselves and the Labour Party, while undoing few of their opponents' policies when they held office. Post-war Conservatives balanced an attachment to free enterprise with state intervention in economic and social policy.

A statue of Benjamin Disraeli (1804–81), author of one-nation conservatism.

EXTENSION ACTIVITY

Review the points made in Table 1.1. Develop an explanation of why each argument might be good for the UK's political system or not. In thinking about the arguments in favour of state funding, ask yourself the following questions.

• If parties are to be state funded, how should the amount allocated to each party be decided?

• Should all parties be eligible for funding?

• Should parties be allowed to continue raising some of their funds privately, or should it all come from taxation?

Thatcherism and the New Right

Margaret Thatcher (Conservative Party leader 1975–90) gave her name to a more sharply ideological form of conservatism. 'Thatcherism' was linked intellectually with the rise of a school of thought known as the **New Right**. It sought to reduce state intervention in the economy, while restoring order to society in the face of rising challenges from militant trade unions and other groups on the left. Its radical policy agenda rejected the instinct of one-nation conservatives to seek compromise.

Thatcherism comprised the following key themes.

- Control of public spending, combined with tax cuts to provide incentives for business leaders and to stimulate economic growth.
- Privatisation of industries and services taken into state ownership to promote improvement and wider consumer choice through competition.
- Legal limits on the power of trade unions to deter industrial action.
- A tough approach to law and order, with increased police and judicial powers.
- Assertion of British interests abroad, in relation to the challenges posed by the Soviet Union and other external threats.
- A desire to protect national sovereignty against the growth of the European Community (European Union).

Key term

New Right
an approach that combined:

- the thinking of neo-conservatives who wanted the state to take a more authoritarian approach to morality and law and order

- the thinking of neo-liberals who endorsed the free market and the rolling back of the state in people's lives and businesses.

Thatcherites aimed to 'roll back the state' and encourage individuals to take more responsibility for themselves. However, in practice the popularity of the National Health Service and the need to maintain a framework of state welfare provision limited the scope for radical reform.

Margaret Thatcher's sale of council houses to their tenants was part of her attempt to make citizens more independent of the state.

A post-Thatcherite party?

Margaret Thatcher was a dominant but divisive figure who aroused both admiration and hostility within and beyond her party. Following her departure in November 1990, the party struggled for a decade and a half to develop an identity independent of her. Thatcher's immediate successor, John Major (prime minister 1990–97) to some extent represented the continuation of Thatcherism, with the privatisation of coal and railways, but he projected a less confrontational image. After a narrow general election victory in April 1992, his premiership was troubled by growing divisions over Europe. A moderate pro-European, Major sought without success to reconcile two competing party factions – hard-line Eurosceptics wanted stronger resistance to what they saw as the encroaching power of the European Union, while a smaller pro-European group sought to keep British influence over a now rapidly integrating continent. These divisions, together with a series of scandals and a growing sense of exhaustion on the part of the government, contributed to a devastating general election defeat in May 1997.

The next three leaders of the party failed to unseat a triumphant Tony Blair, who successfully held the centre ground of British politics to win two more electoral victories for Labour in 2001 and 2005. William Hague, Iain Duncan Smith and Michael Howard failed to distance themselves sufficiently from Thatcherism, which the public identified with a now discredited past. All three seemed unable to move the party beyond an association with traditional issues such as Europe, immigration and law and order. With an ageing membership and outdated policies, the party failed to appeal to an increasingly diverse society.

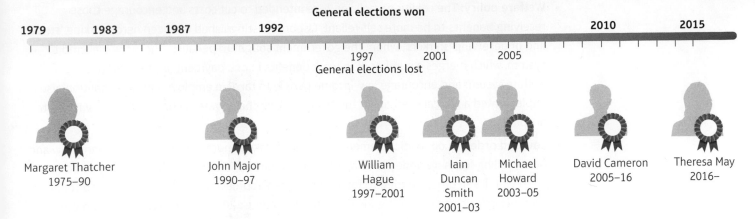

Figure 2.1: Leaders of the Conservative Party since 1975

Only with the election of David Cameron as leader in December 2005 did a serious attempt to 'detoxify' the Conservative brand begin. Cameron brought the fresh thinking of a new generation – respectful of Thatcher but aware that Britain had changed considerably since she had left office. He learned from the way in which Blair had reinvented the Labour Party to win support beyond its traditional core vote. Cameron identified himself as a 'liberal conservative', tolerant of minority groups and different lifestyles. He showed an interest in the environment, which was assuming greater importance as a political issue, even if his critics accused him of staging superficial photo opportunities, such as posing with husky dogs on a visit to a melting glacier in Norway. He also demonstrated that he valued public services such as the NHS, on which the majority of the population relied.

Both Cameron and his successor, Theresa May, maintained that they stood on the side of ordinary people, rather than just the interests of a well-off elite. Where Thatcher had presented the Conservatives as the party of thrusting individualism, Cameron emphasised the bonds between people, arguing the case for co-operation between the state and the voluntary sector in building the 'Big Society'. The morally authoritarian tone of Thatcherism was replaced by, for example, support for the legalisation of gay marriage. In many ways the new approach seemed like an updated version of one-nation conservatism.

Cameron's moderate tone helped him to form a coalition government with the Liberal Democrats when he failed to win an outright majority in the May 2010 general election. Although there were tensions – for example, over reform of the voting system and the upgrading of Britain's nuclear weapons system – he managed to work with his coalition partners for a full 5 years, before winning a slim victory and forming a purely Conservative government in May 2015.

Nonetheless there were important respects in which Cameron (and still more his party) remained close to the ideas of Thatcherism.

- **Economic policy:** Cameron's priority was to reduce the budget deficit inherited from the previous Labour government. In traditional conservative fashion Cameron and his chancellor, George Osborne, accused their predecessors of irresponsible overspending, which they blamed for the financial crisis of 2008. Their response in office was to insist on a programme of public spending cuts, dubbed 'austerity', to maintain the confidence of the financial markets and prevent Britain's borrowing costs from rising. The budgets of Whitehall departments (with some exceptions, such as health, schools and international aid) were cut by up to 25 per cent. The concept of the 'Big Society' had never been properly defined, and some now came to regard it as a smokescreen for cutting costs, by withdrawing the state from the provision of public services.

- **Welfare policy:** The coalition's policies were intended to cut costs and encourage those receiving benefits to be more self-reliant. Osborne distinguished between hard-working 'strivers' and undeserving 'shirkers', whom the government sought to penalise. The 'universal credit' system, which merges a number of in-work benefits in one payment, is intended to simplify the welfare system and encourage low-income people to take up employment. The coalition also implemented a radical overhaul of the NHS, allowing the private sector to compete with state hospitals.

- **Law and order:** In opposition Cameron seemed to take a more liberal attitude towards law and order, calling for more understanding of young offenders in a speech dubbed 'hug a hoodie' by the media. In office he tried to follow a balanced approach to crime. He supported tough sentencing for certain crimes, especially after the August 2011 London riots, but promoted a 'rehabilitation revolution' to reduce the problem of reoffending by people leaving prison unprepared for life on the outside. The coalition government rewarded private firms and charities that helped criminals in their rehabilitation, using a 'payment by results' scheme. Cameron's policies on law and order resembled Tony Blair's insistence that government must be 'tough on crime, tough on the causes of crime'.

- **Foreign policy:** Cameron's approach was consistent with Thatcherism in most important respects, featuring strong links with the USA, support for air strikes against Islamic terror groups in Syria and Iraq, and a pragmatic Euroscepticism. Cameron tried, as Thatcher did in the 1980s, to fight his corner in the EU. He renegotiated the terms of British membership before holding a referendum, in which he championed the 'Remain' side. He resigned in July 2016 after the referendum resulted in a majority vote to leave the EU. Theresa May adopted a similarly tough approach to getting the best available deal from the remaining members of the EU in the 'Brexit' negotiations.

Architects of Conservative modernisation: David Cameron with his successor as party leader, Theresa May, flanked by their respective chancellors, George Osborne (left) and Philip Hammond (right).

Pause & reflect ✔

Use the information here, and other resources, to create a table with two columns and complete it with the following information:

- evidence that David Cameron and Theresa May have broken with Thatcherism
- evidence that their governments have continued its key principles.

The Labour Party

'Old Labour' and social democracy

The Labour Party was founded in 1900 by a group of socialist societies and trade unions. It was known until 1906 as the Labour Representation Committee, revealing its original purpose – to get more working class MPs into parliament, where they could push for improved working and living conditions for the working class. Politically active working people had tended to support the Liberal Party, but by the dawn of the 20th century it was felt that they needed a party specifically concerned with their interests. Within the party's 1918 constitution, Clause 4 committed it to campaign for the 'common ownership of the means of production, distribution and exchange' – the state was to take over or 'nationalise' key industries and services to run them in the interests of the community rather than for profit alone.

The first Labour government took office in 1924 under Prime Minister Ramsay MacDonald but it was a short-lived administration that did not command a parliamentary majority. The same was true of the second Labour government (1929–31), which was frustrated and divided by the onset of economic depression following the disaster of the Wall Street Crash. Not until 1945 was a majority Labour government, headed by Clement Attlee, able to make important changes. These included the nationalisation of coal, railways, power, steel and civil aviation, a comprehensive system of social security inspired by the wartime Beveridge Report and a National Health Service, free at the point of need.

Post-war Labour governments between 1945 and 1979 described themselves as socialist but in practice they were social democratic; they did not try to abolish capitalism, but aimed to manage it so that it did not exploit the workforce. Social democrats emphasised the importance of welfare policy in redistributing wealth and creating a fairer society. A good example of the social democratic approach was the creation of comprehensive schools, intended to promote greater equality of opportunity.

The defeat of the last '**Old Labour**' prime minister, James Callaghan, at the 1979 general election, heralded a division between moderate social democrats and more left-wing elements, who captured the party under the leadership of Michael Foot. Labour lost the 1983 election on a hard-line socialist programme calling for further nationalisation, increased taxation and spending, the abolition of Britain's nuclear defences and withdrawal from the European Economic Community, which the left viewed as a capitalist organisation. Following this catastrophic defeat and the election of a new leader, Neil Kinnock, drawn from the party's centre-left, the slow work of rebuilding began.

From 'Old' to 'New Labour'

To broaden its support, the Labour Party began to move away from the its hard left position of the early 1980s. This involved a gradual recognition that, as the old industrial base of the country disappeared and people became more affluent, policies that appealed solely to the traditional working class would not be enough to win a general election. It took two more defeats, in 1987

Key term

Old Labour (social democracy)
key Labour principles embodying nationalisation, redistribution of wealth from rich to poor and the provision of continually improving welfare and state services – an approach which largely rejected the more free market approach associated with Thatcherism or New Labour.

Two 'Old Labour' prime ministers: Clement Attlee (left, prime minister 1945–51) and Harold Wilson (prime minister 1964–70 and 1974–76).

Link

For more on the **Social Chapter**, see Section 4.3 of Relations Between Institutions.

Key term

New Labour (Third Way) a revision of traditional 'Old Labour' values and ideas, involving a shift in emphasis from a heavy focus on the working class to a wider class base, and a less robust alliance with the trade unions.

and 1992, and the election of a forceful new leader, Tony Blair, to complete this process. The party dropped unpopular policy proposals, crucially revising Clause 4 of its constitution in 1995 so that it was no longer committed to nationalisation. The role played by the trade unions in the party was downgraded, and the party leadership developed links with the business community. At the same time Labour became more pro-European as the EU adopted policies that protected workers' rights, such as the **Social Chapter**.

The party was rebranded as '**New Labour**' and, under the influence of progressive thinker Anthony Giddens, aimed to find a 'third way' between old-style socialism and free-market capitalism. A strong emphasis was placed on managing the media to project a more modern image, and great efforts were made to ensure that Labour demonstrated unity and discipline. Aided by the disintegration of John Major's Conservative government, Blair won a landslide victory in May 1997. He was re-elected twice more before making way for the succession of his long-serving chancellor and fellow architect of New Labour, Gordon Brown, in June 2007.

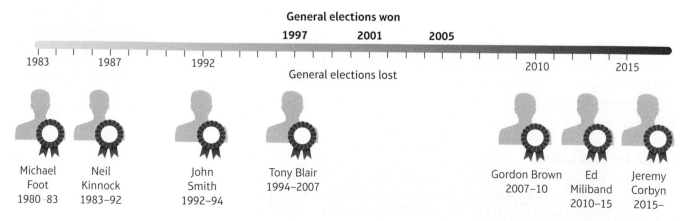

General elections won

1997   2001   2005

1983   1987   1992   2010   2015

General elections lost

Michael Foot 1980–83

Neil Kinnock 1983–92

John Smith 1992–94

Tony Blair 1994–2007

Gordon Brown 2007–10

Ed Miliband 2010–15

Jeremy Corbyn 2015–

Figure 2.2: Labour Party leaders since 1980

New Labour: a departure from socialism?

The creation of New Labour aroused intense controversy. Many traditional socialists rejected these modernising efforts as a betrayal of their heritage. They felt that Blair was too much at home with business leaders and too enthusiastic for the values of the market. His building of close links with the US government, culminating in the 2003 Iraq War, further damaged his credentials as a progressive figure. On the other hand, Blair's supporters argued that New Labour was a necessary adaptation to a changing society and that, in the words of Deputy Prime Minister John Prescott, it embodied 'traditional values in a modern setting'.

Here are the key features of New Labour in power.

- **Emphasis on wealth creation rather than redistribution:** The New Labour governments sought to reduce poverty but did not make the elimination of inequality a priority. For example, they introduced a national minimum wage, a long-standing ambition of the Labour Party, but at a less generous level (£3.60 an hour for adults) than the trade unions wanted. Blair in particular regarded individual aspiration to a better standard of life, achieved through a person's efforts, as entirely natural.

- **People need to be aware of their responsibilities to the community as well as their rights:** Blair sought to impose conditions on the receipt of welfare benefits, and brought in legal measures to deal with anti-social behaviour, known as ASBOs (Anti-Social Behaviour Orders). These could be imposed by a magistrate, banning an individual from particular activities or entering a specific area. In a famous soundbite, Blair declared that a Labour government must be 'tough on crime and tough on the causes of crime' – willing to punish criminal behaviour, while continuing to tackle poor social conditions.

- **Responsibility in handling the national finances:** The New Labour governments aimed to differentiate themselves from earlier social democratic administrations, by conserving resources before investing more in key public services. A major turning point was the increase in National Insurance contributions in 2002, which led to the largest ever rise in spending on the NHS.

- **Enlisting the public sector to deliver public services:** For example, Private Finance Initiative (PFI) contracts were awarded to private firms to build new schools and hospitals.

- **Influence of liberal ideology on Labour thinking:** This showed in devolution – the transfer of central government functions to new representative bodies in Scotland, Wales and Northern Ireland – and the passage of the Human Rights Act. However, New Labour governments proved willing to curb civil liberties in their campaign against crime and terrorism, extending the time that suspects could be detained before being charged, widening police powers and proposing the introduction of identity cards.

New Labour's Tony Blair and Gordon Brown.

Labour under Gordon Brown and Ed Miliband: politics after the crash

The financial crisis and recession of 2008–09 led to a shift in policy by the Brown government.

- The Treasury pumped money into the banking system in an attempt to boost economic activity.

- The government nationalised, or part-nationalised the most vulnerable banks in order to restore confidence.

- Brown broke an earlier promise not to raise income tax levels by creating a new 50 per cent band, to be paid by those who earned more than £150,000 a year – a sign that Labour wanted the better-off to assume some responsibility for dealing with the perilous economic situation.

- Brown proposed to maintain public spending, arguing that drastic cuts, recommended by Conservatives, would starve the economy of resources and prolong the downturn.

This led to claims that New Labour ideology had been abandoned. However, these were emergency measures at a time of heightened concern for the future of the financial system and were quite unlike the ideologically driven commitment to public ownership of the 'Old Labour' period.

The period of opposition from 2010 to 2015 saw the party take up a not always coherent position. Under Ed Miliband's leadership it maintained some elements of New Labour policies, while shifting slightly to the left. The new leader called for the restoration of the 50 per cent top rate of income tax, which the coalition had reduced to 45 per cent, and for a temporary energy price freeze. However, it is important not to exaggerate the extent to which Miliband broke with the party's recent past. The need to re-establish Labour's reputation as a competent manager of the economy was an important concern for Miliband and his shadow chancellor, Ed Balls. In practice they concentrated their attack on the most controversial aspects of the 'austerity' programme, such as the unpopular 'bedroom tax' (the end of the spare room subsidy that led to the reduction of housing benefit for tenants living in council properties too large for their needs), rather than rejecting the coalition's whole economic strategy.

Miliband tried to combine New Labour's support for business with the defence of the party's core working-class constituency by drawing a distinction between what he called 'predatory' and 'responsible' capitalism. In calling for a crackdown on tax avoidance and more spending on the NHS, he was only echoing the coalition parties. His call for a 10 per cent starting income tax band for the lowest paid was a return to a policy originally introduced (but later scrapped) by Brown as chancellor. At the 2015 election Miliband pledged to reduce the deficit every year of the next parliament. He insisted that Labour's spending plans would be paid for without additional borrowing.

Notwithstanding the actual moderation of many of Miliband's policy proposals, he was dubbed 'Red Ed' and many media commentators ascribed his defeat in the May 2015 election to his perceived hostility to the private sector and willingness to return to 'tax and spend' policies. However, by 2015 there was pressure from the left of the party for Labour to adopt a much more radical approach. Some party members attributed the landslide victory of the SNP in Scotland, where Labour was left with just one Westminster seat, to the party being insufficiently left wing.

This was the background to the overwhelming victory of a staunchly socialist backbencher, Jeremy Corbyn, in the September 2015 leadership election after Miliband's resignation. It was remarkable that he was preferred by the party membership – and by a large margin – to either of the most experienced candidates, Andy Burnham and Yvette Cooper, who had served in the New Labour government. The most Blairite contender, Liz Kendall, won less than 5 per cent of the vote. Corbyn's left-wing agenda meant that he struggled to create a united shadow cabinet, and opponents in the parliamentary party forced a second leadership contest in the autumn of 2016, which he won triumphantly. Never before had there been such a divide between the party's MPs, who favoured a more cautious, centrist approach, and its rank-and-file membership, who warmed to Corbyn's unconventional, anti-establishment style.

Pause & reflect ✔

Why did Jeremy Corbyn arouse such enthusiasm in the Labour Party?

Here are Labour's policies in the Corbyn era.

- **Economic policy:** Jeremy Corbyn took the Miliband-Balls idea of increased investment in the economy further, calling for large-scale funding of industry and infrastructure organised by a National Investment Bank. An important aim of this was to reduce regional inequalities. Corbyn called for the renationalisation of the railways, a policy the New Labour governments refused to adopt. Instinctively supporting intervention of an Old Labour kind, he demanded, for example, that companies publish pay audits with the aim of countering discrimination in the workplace. Like Miliband he favoured restoration of the 50 per cent top rate of income tax. However, Corbyn was much more clear-cut in his opposition to austerity, characterising it as a 'political choice' that harmed the most vulnerable members of society, rather than an 'economic necessity'.

- **Welfare policy:** Corbyn strongly opposed benefit cuts. As a socialist he regarded the poor as the victims of capitalism, who are entitled to public support. He opposed the use of the private sector to deliver public services – a central aspect of New Labour. Thus he argued for a wholly state-run NHS. In order to promote lifelong education and training, he called for a 'national education service', and opposed student tuition fees. By contrast Ed Miliband confined himself to advocating their reduction from £9,000 to £6,000 a year.

- **Law and order policy:** Corbyn was opposed to the more hard-line policies of the New Labour era, such as increased powers to combat terrorism and the introduction of identity cards. This became a less controversial policy area within the Labour Party – both Blairites and Corbynites found common ground in opposing government cuts to police numbers, which they described as jeopardising public safety.

- **Foreign policy:** Corbyn consistently voted against the use of force, and favoured the withdrawal of the UK from NATO's military structure and the abolition of the Trident nuclear weapons system, again placing him at odds with New Labour. He and his then shadow foreign secretary, Hilary Benn, took opposing positions in the December 2015 Commons vote on military intervention against 'Islamic State' terrorism. The party was so divided on the issue that Corbyn had to allow his MPs a free vote. Corbyn followed the mainstream of his party in supporting continued British membership of the EU, emphasising its positive role in protecting workers' rights, but more enthusiastic Labour pro-Europeans felt that he campaigned in a lukewarm manner in the 2016 referendum.

Pause & reflect

Review the information here on the policies of Jeremy Corbyn's Labour Party, and supplement it with your own research on the internet. Which policies most clearly mark a break with the New Labour era? On which policies is there agreement within the party?

The Liberal Democrat Party

From Liberals to Liberal Democrats

The Liberal Democrat Party was founded in 1988 but is descended from a much older political grouping. Its distant ancestors were the Whigs, an aristocratic faction who originated in the 17th century as opponents of the Tories. In the mid-19th century they joined with a variety of middle- and working-class supporters of political and social change to form the Liberal Party.

Key terms

Classical liberals
early liberals who believed that individual freedom would best be achieved with the state playing a minimal role.

Modern liberals
liberals who believe that, under free-market capitalism, many individuals are not truly free, and that the state must help them in a more active way.

Classical liberals were committed above all to the freedom of the individual and wanted the state to play a minimal role in society. In the 19th century this expressed itself in support for free trade, the widening of the franchise, the extension of civil liberties to people who did not belong to the established Anglican Church, and the widening of educational opportunity. Their most notable leader, W.E. Gladstone (prime minister 1868–74, 1880–85, 1886 and 1892–94), also attempted without success to extend self-government to Ireland as part of the UK.

The 'New Liberal' governments of the Edwardian era (1901–10) adopted a range of social reforms, including old age pensions and National Insurance, in a bid to discourage working people from supporting the newly founded Labour Party. This was the beginning of **modern liberalism** – a recognition that many individuals could not be truly free on account of the inequalities produced by free-market capitalism. Freedom could no longer be defined merely as being 'left alone' but required an active state to support people and enable them to reach their potential.

In the decades after the First World War the Liberal Party declined rapidly, a victim of rivalry between its two most significant figures, H.H. Asquith (prime minister 1908–16) and David Lloyd George (prime minister 1916–22). The Liberals attempted to appeal to both middle- and working-class voters, but suffered from an inability to define their identity clearly in an age of growing polarisation on class lines between the Conservatives and Labour. In the post-1945 consensus era, Liberal Party representation fell to single figures.

The party experienced short-lived revivals in the early 1960s and again in the early 1970s. It was unable to make a breakthrough under the 'first past the post' electoral system, which favoured its larger rivals, whose support was concentrated in certain areas. However, in 1981 the Liberals received a boost from a division in the Labour Party that led a group of moderate MPs to create the Social Democratic Party (SDP). The SDP formed an electoral pact with the Liberals, fighting the 1983 and 1987 general elections as the Alliance. In 1988 the two parties merged to form the Liberal Democrat Party.

The Liberal Democrat share of the vote grew modestly and in the 1997 election – aided by popular disillusionment with the Conservatives and careful targeting of seats – this translated into a parliamentary total of 46. Tactical voting was also a factor – this is the practice of not voting for your preferred candidate, but using your vote to prevent another candidate from winning. In this instance, the Liberal Democrats had a boost from Labour supporters in some constituencies when they voted for their Liberal Democrat candidate, knowing they had a better chance of beating the Conservatives than Labour. By 2005 this had risen to 62 seats – an impressive achievement although not enough to make the Liberal Democrats a credible independent challenger for power. The one political reform that might have helped them become a major player – a change to a voting system based on proportional representation – was denied them.

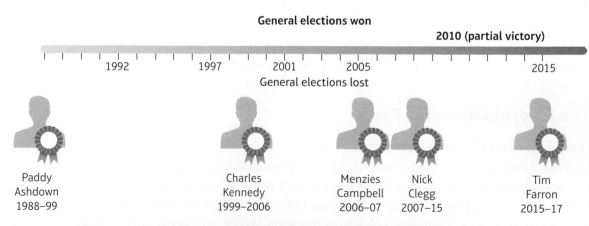

Figure 2.3: Leaders of the Liberal Democrat Party since 1988

The experience of coalition government

The Liberal Democrats have consistently emphasised a number of themes including constitutional reform, civil liberties and internationalism, expressed for example in a positive attitude towards the European Union. However, in other ways they have not been in complete agreement on how to project themselves. In the period of New Labour government, especially under the leadership of Charles Kennedy, they were essentially a centre-left party rather than aiming to be equidistant between the two larger parties. They were opposed to the Iraq War, identity cards and student tuition fees, and in favour of a 50 per cent income tax rate on those earning more than £100,000. Kennedy exemplified the priorities of the social liberals – modern liberals who were influenced by the tradition of generous welfare provision, which could be traced back to the wartime Beveridge Report. They differed from another group within the party, the 'economic' or 'Orange Book' liberals, who took their name from a 2004 publication of the same title. They supported free market solutions to problems and emphasised the party's traditional commitment to the freedom of the individual, whereas social liberals took a more collectivist approach.

Nick Clegg, one of the authors of *The Orange Book*, became party leader in 2007. His approach was to position the party so that it could conceivably work with one of the two larger parties in coalition. Following the May 2010 general election this became a reality for the first time since 1945. The political arithmetic dictated a coalition with the Conservatives, with the Liberal Democrats now in possession of 57 seats.

Clegg had envisioned the Liberal Democrats as moderating the policies of their coalition partner – a less confrontational style of politics that proved difficult to achieve. The party was persuaded that because of the gravity of the financial crisis, it needed to demonstrate its credentials as a responsible party of government by going along with the programme of cuts advocated by the Conservatives. In truth, the smaller party was in a bind. If it refused to enter the coalition, it would have been accused of running away at a time of national emergency, but by taking part in government, it incurred the unpopularity of association with a number of policies contrary to its centre-left heritage. Although Clegg secured a referendum on electoral reform in May 2011, the rejection of the option for Alternative Vote (a voting system that allows voters to rank candidates in order of preference), for which the Liberal Democrats campaigned, effectively buried the cause for a generation. The party's preferred system was the Single Transferable Vote, but the leadership felt that the Alternative Vote was the maximum they could hope to achieve in the circumstances – a sign of their limited bargaining power within the coalition partnership. The ensuing disillusionment of party activists contributed to the Liberal Democrats' heavy losses in the 2015 general election, which saw them reduced to eight seats.

What do the Liberal Democrats stand for?

The party membership elected Tim Farron as their leader after the 2015 defeat and the resignation of Nick Clegg. The choice of a left-leaning MP who had not served in the coalition seemed to indicate that the Liberal Democrats wanted to dissociate themselves from their record in office. It is not easy to decide where exactly to place them on the political spectrum. A policy statement on their website says that they aim to keep Britain 'open, tolerant and united' – but this does not distinguish them much from other mainstream UK parties.

- **Economic policy:** At the 2015 general election the Liberal Democrats emphasised their continued commitment to eliminating the budget deficit, the most important policy underpinning their coalition with the Conservatives. However, it must be done in a way that was fair to the poor. In government they introduced a policy, to which the Conservatives signed up, of progressively raising the basic income-tax threshold so that more low-income people were relieved of paying tax. They promised to 'borrow less than Labour, cut less than the Tories'. They stressed their environmental credentials more than their rivals, with a commitment to renewable energy and the expansion of the Green Investment Bank they had helped to establish, to attract funding for projects such as offshore wind farms.

- **Welfare policy:** In coalition the Liberal Democrats shared the Conservative objective of controlling spending on benefits, while uprating pensions and extending free childcare to enable parents to return to work. They differentiated themselves by pledging to curb benefits paid to better-off pensioners, in order to afford more support for the low-paid. On the NHS, just like the Conservatives and Labour, they pledged increased funding from 2015.

- **Law and order:** The Liberal Democrats aim to see that personal freedom is not eroded as a consequence of giving the authorities more powers to fight crime. They regard the defence of civil liberties as one of their key characteristics, distinguishing them from other parties. In coalition they opposed the Conservatives' plans for the so-called 'Snoopers' Charter', the Communications Data Bill, the purpose of which was to allow the monitoring of internet use. In their emphasis on the rehabilitation of prisoners, and the use of community service as an alternative to short-term prison sentences, they are close to the position taken by moderate Conservatives and Labour.

- **Foreign policy:** The Liberal Democrats have consistently been the most enthusiastic of all the UK parties for British membership of the EU. Perhaps the party's most distinctive policy position in opposition was its reluctance to accept the result of the Brexit referendum. This contrasted with the views of both Theresa May and Jeremy Corbyn who, although they had backed the 'Remain' cause, stated that they would respect the popular verdict.

Pause & reflect

Look back at the section on the functions of parties in the UK's system of representative democracy. How effectively do you think the Conservative, Labour and Liberal Democrat parties have fulfilled these functions in recent years?

EXTENSION ACTIVITY

Copy out the table below. Use the information on the current policies of the three main parties to complete each section. For each one, make sure that you provide a specific example of a policy.

Where do the main groups within the three parties stand on each of the key policy areas?

Groups within the main parties	Economic policy	Welfare policy	Law and order policy	Foreign policy
Thatcherite/ New Right Conservative				
Present day/ One-Nation Conservative				
Moderate Labour				
Corbynite Labour				
Liberal Democrat				

2.3   Emerging and minor UK political parties

The importance of other parties in the UK

One of the most remarkable developments of recent decades has been the emergence of smaller parties that have challenged the dominance of the three older, traditional parties. It was a sign of this change when, in one of the televised debates held in the course of the 2015 general election campaign, no fewer than seven parties took part.

The party leaders who took part in the televised general election debate in 2015. From left to right: Natalie Bennett (Green), Nick Clegg (Liberal Democrat), Nigel Farage (UKIP), Ed Miliband (Labour), Leanne Wood (Plaid Cymru), Nicola Sturgeon (SNP), David Cameron (Conservative).

Two of these small parties, the United Kingdom Independence Party (UKIP) and the Green Party, have derived their importance from campaigning to promote a particular issue or group of related issues. They have no expectation of winning enough seats to form a government. Instead their aim is to force the larger parties to accept their agenda, either in whole or in part. In this sense they have behaved more like pressure groups than traditional political parties.

The other small parties are regionally based. The Welsh Nationalist Party (Plaid Cymru), established in 1925, is officially committed to independence for Wales within the EU, but in practice has been more concerned with the preservation of a distinctive Welsh language and culture. The party has never had more than four MPs at Westminster at any one time (at the 2015 general election it had a total of three) but it has been more successful in the National Assembly for Wales. In 2007 Plaid Cymru became the second largest party in the Assembly and was in coalition government with Labour until it dropped to third place after the 2011 election.

The Scottish National Party

The Scottish National Party, founded in 1934, is a centre-left party whose main purpose is to secure independence for Scotland from the UK. The growing strength of the SNP helped persuade the Labour Party to take up the cause of devolution ahead of the 1997 general election.

The Blair government believed that granting devolution would ensure that Labour would remain the dominant political force in Scotland. Its strategy was to give the Scottish people just enough self-governing power to ensure that they did not vote for the SNP. The strategy worked until 2007 when a talented nationalist leader, Alex Salmond, formed a minority SNP government, transforming this into a small majority in the 2011 election. This was undoubtedly a major reason why the Westminster government was prepared to support the extension of more powers to the

Link

For more on **devolution**, see Section 1.3 of The Constitution.

Edinburgh administration (for example, taxation and borrowing). The fruits of this were the 2012 Scotland Act and the holding of a referendum on Scottish independence in September 2014. Towards the end of the referendum campaign, all three major party leaders agreed to abandon Prime Minister's Questions at Westminster, in order to go to Scotland to present a united front for staying in the Union. Although the independence option was defeated, it was clear that the issue would not go away. A new SNP first minister, Nicola Sturgeon, argued that as Scotland faced being taken out of the EU against its will, following the June 2016 'Brexit' referendum vote, the SNP was entitled to hold another vote on independence in the near future.

Another area of concern has been the SNP's capacity to influence legislation at Westminster, especially after the 2015 general election, when it won 56 of Scotland's 59 seats. The SNP's official position (unlike, for example, that of Scottish Labour MPs in the past) has been one of refraining from voting on purely English issues, in order to underscore the nationalist argument that the two countries should not interfere in each other's internal affairs.

Since October 2015, the passing of the English votes for English laws (EVEL) measure has placed limits on all Scottish MPs at Westminster, but with important exceptions. In March 2016, SNP MPs helped to defeat the Cameron government's proposal for an extension of Sunday trading laws in England and Wales. The party's argument was that the measure would affect Scottish workers because UK-wide employers would use it to set new, less advantageous rates of pay on both sides of the border. The 2017 general election, however, saw the SNP lose 24 of its seats, and, with it, some of its influence at Westminster.

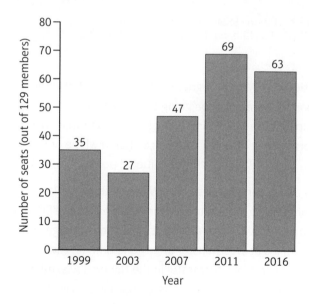

Figure 3.1: Number of seats won by the SNP in Scottish parliament elections

The ideas and policies of two minor parties: UKIP and the Green Party

The United Kingdom Independence Party (UKIP)

UKIP began as a fringe nationalist party in 1991, and by the 21st century was associated with one man – Nigel Farage – and one issue – opposition to Britain's membership of the EU. It owed its slowly growing national profile to a sense of dissatisfaction with the way in which the three main parties seemed constantly to accommodate themselves to the quickening pace of European integration. In the 2014 European elections UKIP gained a total of 24 MEPs, making it the largest

UK party in the European parliament. It won 3.9 million votes in the 2015 general election, although under the first-past-the-post voting system this total returned only one MP.

UKIP is a radical right-wing populist party, whose supporters tend to be older, more traditional people who feel left behind in a rapidly changing world. They are often people with lower levels of education and job security, anxious about what they see as challenges to their way of life. For many, immigration has been a major concern. UKIP supporters saw the arrival of large numbers of Eastern Europeans, following the expansion of the EU in 2004, as a threat to 'British jobs' and to the native British way of life. Unlike the older British National Party (BNP), which was associated with overt racial prejudice, UKIP seemed a more 'respectable' option. Its most prominent figure, Nigel Farage (party leader 2006–09 and 2010–16), was a charismatic individual whose chummy, outspoken persona was one to which many ordinary people could relate. By not conforming to the image of mainstream 'liberal establishment' figures such as Cameron, Clegg and Miliband, he appealed to voters who felt disillusioned with the three main parties.

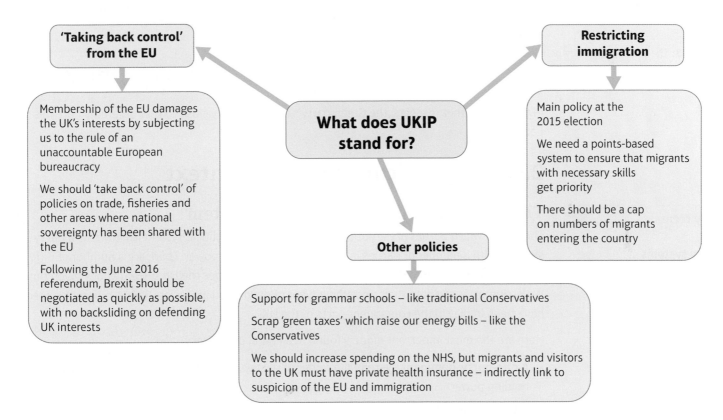

Figure 3.2: UKIP's key policies

The Green Party

The Green Party evolved from a party founded in 1973 as 'PEOPLE', later changing its name to the Ecology Party before assuming its present identity in 1985. The Green Party won its first seat at Westminster in 2010, when Caroline Lucas became MP for Brighton Pavilion. The party won more than one million votes across the UK in 2015, but failed to win any more seats.

The Green Party is a centre-left party that is not only concerned with environmental issues, but also with reducing social inequality. It is also strongly pro-European, seeing the EU as a safeguard for environmental protection.

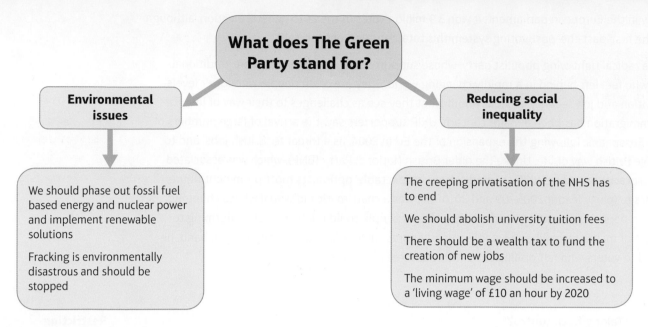

Figure 3.3: The Green Party's key policies

In these and other respects, the Green party's agenda is very close to that of Jeremy Corbyn's Labour Party.

2.4   UK political parties in context

The development of a multi-party system

The way in which parties are grouped and structured in a political system is known as a **party system**, with a number of parties in contention for political power. There are a number of different models, and it is open to debate which of these best describes the UK system at any given time. It is also important to note that, since the advent of devolution in the late 1990s, different systems have been in play in the component parts of the UK.

Here are the most important models found in a liberal democracy.

- **A one-party-dominant system:** A number of parties, but only one has a realistic prospect of holding power.

- **A two-party system:** Two parties compete for power at elections; other parties have no real chance of breaking their monopoly.

- **A two-and-a-half-party system:** Two large parties are the main players, but are challenged by the growth of a smaller third party.

- **A multi-party system:** A number of parties contend to form a government; coalitions become the norm.

Which of these models most closely fits UK politics at present? The Westminster elections are a good starting point.

Westminster: survival of the two-party system

The classic era of the two-party system was the period 1945–74, when Labour and the Conservatives won, on average, a combined 91 per cent of the votes and almost 98 per cent of the seats at Westminster. This was clearly coming under strain from the mid-1970s, with a period

> **Key term**
>
> **Party systems**
> the way in which the political parties in a political system are grouped and structured.

of minority Labour government followed by two long periods of single party dominance – the Conservatives from 1979 to 1997 and Labour from 1997 to 2010. The Liberals made modest gains, especially after forming an alliance with the Social Democrats in 1981, then merging with them to form the Liberal Democrats in 1988. Between 1979 and 2010, the two main parties' combined average share of the vote fell to 73 per cent.

Nonetheless the two-party system survived, largely as a result of the distorting effect of the **first-past-the-post voting system**, which limits smaller parties' ability to win seats. The two largest parties shared an average of 91 per cent of the seats, and they continued to monopolise government without the participation of the UK's third party.

The period of coalition government (2010–15) could be described as a two-and-a-half-party system. The Liberal Democrats secured 23 per cent of the vote in 2010 and enough seats to play a part in government, though only as the partner of a larger party in a coalition. Almost 35 per cent of voters supported parties other than the Conservatives and Labour in this election.

However, this proved a short-lived development. The 2015 general election heralded a return to 'business as usual' at Westminster. The Liberal Democrats were devastated at the polls, losing all but eight of their seats. The most startling aspect of the 2015 contest was the landslide victory of the SNP in Scotland, where they took all but three of the 59 seats. However, the SNP is a regional party, which is not a contender for power at Westminster, even if it is able to influence the outcome of some votes in the House of Commons. Essentially Westminster remains dominated by the two largest parties. As long as the first-past-the-post system remains in place, this is unlikely to change.

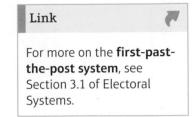

Link

For more on the **first-past-the-post system**, see Section 3.1 of Electoral Systems.

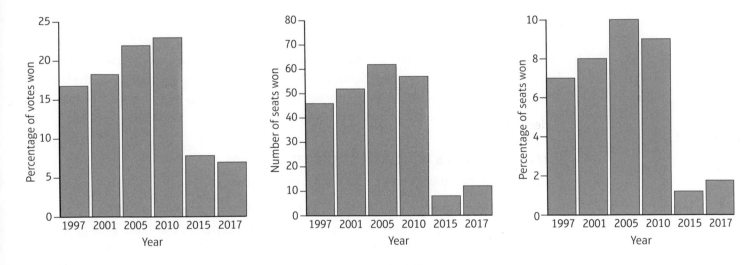

Figure 4.1: The fortunes of the third party – Liberal Democrat share of votes and seats since 1997

The devolved bodies: a variety of multi-party systems

The use of the Additional Member System (AMS) for elections to the Scottish parliament and Welsh Assembly has produced very different outcomes from the trends observed at Westminster. A partly proportional system, it tends to increase the representation of smaller parties. Although the SNP has been in power in Scotland for almost a decade now, it formed a minority government from 2007 to 2011 and once again after the May 2016 election. Before 2007 Scotland was governed for 8 years by a Labour-Liberal Democrat coalition. Similarly in Wales there have been periods of minority Labour government, a Labour-Liberal Democrat coalition and a Labour-Plaid Cymru coalition.

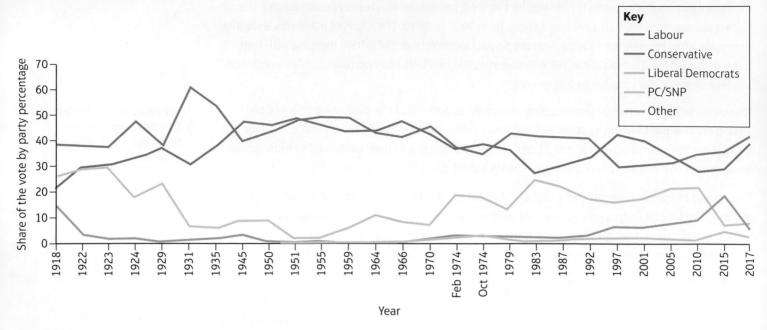

Figure 4.2: Share of the vote by party at UK general elections, 1918–2015

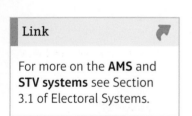

Link

For more on the **AMS** and **STV systems** see Section 3.1 of Electoral Systems.

In Northern Ireland a fully proportional system, Single Transferable Vote (STV), is used to elect the assembly. Until January 2017, when the power-sharing executive collapsed owing to internal disagreement, the first minister and four other members were drawn from the largest party, the Democratic Unionist Party; the deputy first minister and three others were from the second largest party, Sinn Fein; and one post was held by an independent. In the March 2017 election the Democratic Unionists remained the largest party with 28 seats, but were only one seat ahead of Sinn Fein. The moderate nationalist Social and Democratic Labour Party won 12 seats, the Ulster Unionists ten and the neutral Alliance Party eight seats. It would thus be fair to describe the regions of the UK as having multi-party systems.

Various factors that affect party success

A number of factors influence the success or failure of parties.

- **The strength of a party's leadership:** Voters tend to respond positively to party leaders who demonstrate a clear sense of direction. They also reject parties that fail to get a grip on events in times of crisis. For example, the Labour government of James Callaghan seemed weak because it was unable to control trade union demands for pay increases in the so-called 'winter of discontent' (1978–79), when a wave of strikes brought many public services to a halt. Margaret Thatcher, the Conservative leader, won the May 1979 election not because she was personally popular but because she offered a tough response to the strikers whom she dubbed the 'wreckers in our midst'. This built on the success of a Conservative advertising campaign, featuring an image of a dole queue under the slogan 'Labour isn't working', which reminded voters of rising unemployment under Labour. In more recent times, opinion polls consistently placed Theresa May ahead of Labour leader Jeremy Corbyn because she was seen as a stronger leader, even though a majority of respondents also viewed her as having a cold personality and being out of touch.

- **The extent to which parties are united or divided between different party factions:** Divided parties do not perform well at general elections. John Major's Conservatives suffered a heavy loss in the 1997 general election, largely because they were seen as incompetent and divided on the subject of Britain's relationship with the European Union. At the election, both pro- and anti-EU Conservatives lost their seats, showing that it was not the issue of Europe in itself that mattered, but the voters' perception of a weak and divided party. By contrast Tony Blair had reshaped the Labour Party since becoming its leader in 1994, imposing strong discipline so that it appeared united.

- **The role of the media in projecting a particular image of a party:** The growing importance of the media in recent decades has tended to reinforce the general public's impression of parties and their leaders. Newspaper comment and TV images play an important role in modern politics. The use of televised debates between the party leaders in the 2010 general election enhanced the appeal of Nick Clegg, the Liberal Democrat leader, whose party gained enough support to deny the Conservatives an overall majority, enabling them to take office in a coalition government. However, the importance of the debates should not be exaggerated, since the Liberal Democrats actually emerged with five fewer seats than in the 2005 contest.

Assessment support: 1.1.2 Political Parties

Question 4 on AS-Level Paper 1 is worth 30 marks and must be completed in 50 minutes. It takes the form of a brief quotation, stating a point of view on a particular topic, and asking how far you agree with it. You are given a choice of two questions; you should answer one.

> *'The influence of the media is the most important factor that determines the success or failure of a political party.'*
>
> *How far do you agree with this view of what determines the success or failure of a political party? [30 marks].*
> *In this answer you must refer to at least two political parties and consider this view and the alternative to this view in a balanced way.*

Your answer will take the form of an essay in which you consider both sides of the argument. This question tests all three Assessment Objectives, with marks divided equally between them. Examiners are looking for comprehensive and precise knowledge and understanding of the topic, used to support a reasoned argument. You must make convincing connections between different ideas and concepts. Your arguments should be fully supported and your essay should reach a conclusion in which you reflect both sides of the argument in order to score highly for evaluation.

- Take a few minutes to write a brief plan – this will give you a clear sense of direction and help you make sure you do not leave out anything important.

- Aim to write about six paragraphs, including a brief introduction and a fully supported conclusion.

- Focus first on the factor in the question – the role of the media. In what ways is it important to the fortunes of political parties? Then compare it with other factors, such as the quality of party leadership and the extent to which parties are united or divided.

- In your conclusion you should assess the overall contribution of the media to party success or failure. If you feel that another factor is more important, say so – with your reasons.

Here is an extract from the middle part of a student's answer. The student has already explained the ways in which the presentation of party leaders in the media is important to their success.

On the other hand, you should not assume that public image is always crucial in winning or losing elections. Liberal Democrat leader Nick Clegg briefly became very popular and well known because he performed well in the first television debate in the 2010 general election, but this did not have a major impact on the result. His party did well enough to enter a coalition with the Conservatives, but they actually ended up with five fewer seats than in 2005. A charismatic leader is not always the key to success. Voters can be influenced by issues as much as personalities. Margaret Thatcher trailed James Callaghan by twenty percentage points in opinion polls in the 1979 campaign, but her party won the election because the voters thought Labour had a poor record in government, particularly because of its failure to control the trade unions, whose strike action had crippled the country in the so-called 'winter of discontent'.

- By saying 'On the other hand' at the start, the student indicates clearly to the examiner they are now going to look at the other side of the argument.

- The argument is supported with specific examples drawn from different elections and parties. This is important because the mark scheme states that you cannot reach Level 2 (7 to 12 marks out of 30) if you do not refer to at least two political parties.

Electoral Systems

In this section you will learn about:

- the different voting systems used in the UK and their advantages and disadvantages, including **'first past the post' (FPTP)** and alternatives wholly or partly based on proportional representation
- referendums and how they are used
- how different electoral systems are used in the UK and their impact on governments, the representation of parties and the choice open to voters.

Key term

First past the post (FPTP) an electoral system, sometimes known as a plurality system, where the candidate with the largest number of votes is elected. Victory is achieved by having at least one more vote than other contenders.

3.1 Different electoral systems

An electoral system performs a vital function in a democracy by turning the votes cast at an election into seats – each of which is held by a single representative, known in the UK as a Member of Parliament (MP) – whose number reflects the strength of each party in a representative body.

Elections have a number of functions.

- **Representation:** The most fundamental purpose of elections at all levels – local, regional and national – is to choose a representative to speak on behalf of a community and to provide a link between them and those who take decisions on their behalf. MPs are said to be 'trustees' – individuals in whom voters place their trust – who have autonomy to speak and vote as they see fit in the interests of their constituency. They are entitled to think independently in response to changing circumstances. Following the Burkean theory of representation, MPs are not mere 'delegates' – people sent to speak and act with a predetermined agenda to replicate the views and wishes of others.

  The representative function is complicated in the Westminster system by pressure from the party leadership to support an agreed line. The promise of government posts, which are at the disposal of the prime minister, may influence ambitious MPs. But MPs who displease their constituents can be removed by the voters at the next general election.

- **Choosing the government:** At a general election voters are choosing a government and granting it legitimacy. The leader of the party that wins the largest number of seats has the right to form a government. With 'first past the post' this is usually a straightforward matter – the winning party normally commands a working majority of MPs, outnumbering all the other parties in the House of Commons put together. However, recent elections have seen a couple of exceptions to this. The 2010 general election left the Conservatives 20 seats short of a majority, which saw them enter into a coalition with the Liberal Democrats. Again in 2017 the Conservatives were eight seats short of a majority and so agreed a more informal arrangement with the Democratic Unionist Party (see page 168).

- **Holding a government to account:** Usually, every 5 years a government has to face the electorate at a general election in order to renew its mandate to govern. The voters have the right to reject an unpopular government that is perceived to have failed. Individual MPs can also be held to account for their performance. Following the revelations of abuse of parliamentary expenses in 2009, a number of MPs stood down rather than face the voters at the general election the following year.

Since 2015 the Recall of MPs Act has strengthened the power of voters to remove MPs who have behaved poorly. If an MP is sentenced to a prison sentence, or is suspended from the Commons for more than 21 days, a by-election is triggered if at least 10 per cent of constituents sign a recall petition.

- **Participation:** Voting in elections is the most obvious way ordinary people can take part in politics. Party manifestos provide information on which voters can make a judgement, although many people do not read them, or they mistrust the promises politicians make. The information provided may be misleading. For example, the 2001 Labour manifesto stated 'we will not introduce "top-up" fees (for university tuition) and have legislated to prevent them'. There was outrage from students, and many Labour MPs, after the election when the government decided to increase fees from their previous level of £1,000 per annum.

- **Influence over policy:** Voters have limited influence over the policies that political parties put before them. However, election defeats do send a message to parties not to persist with unpopular policies. Labour's catastrophic defeat in the 1983 general election, followed by a slightly less disastrous performance in 1987, led the party leadership gradually to drop unpopular policies and move towards the centre ground.

  Elections also allow small parties, which cannot hope to form a government, to put their views across. This enables them to draw attention to the issues they stand for, and sometimes to influence the larger parties to adopt some of their policies. For example, the increased public profile of the Greens in the 1990s was one reason why other parties began to emphasise the importance of countering climate change.

How should different voting systems be judged?

In deciding which voting system is the best, it is important to be clear on what you expect it to deliver. The most important criteria would probably be:

- a fair result that gives, as far as possible, equal value to people's votes across the country
- a choice of candidates
- an effective link between the elected representative and the constituency
- a strong government that can pass laws but can be held to account by the electorate.

No electoral system will deliver all of these to the same degree. It is a question of deciding which of these features you consider to be the most important.

First past the post

The voting system used for UK general elections and by-elections, and local council elections in England and Wales, is known as first past the post (FPTP). Voters cast a single vote by placing a cross next to the name of their preferred candidate. FPTP is a simple plurality system – the person with the largest number of votes in a constituency (or seat) is elected. The winner does not have to gain a majority of the votes cast. The party with the largest number of seats (not necessarily a majority of the votes cast across the country) has the right to form a government. Indeed, in 1951 and February 1974, the party forming the government secured fewer votes than the main opposition party, suggesting that FPTP can distort voters' wishes.

General elections are supposed to take place every 5 years, on the first Thursday in May (as stipulated by the 2011 Fixed Term Parliaments Act). Before that, the prime minister could choose the date at any time within the five-year period. However, as Theresa May demonstrated when she called an election for June 2017, the act does allow a prime minister to dissolve parliament with the support of two-thirds of MPs.

The continued use of FPTP for Westminster elections has aroused controversy for decades.

In modern times the UK's parliamentary system has been based on single-member representation – each constituency elects one MP. Until 1948 some constituencies returned more than one member (for example, several Lancashire towns, including Blackburn and Bolton, were dual-member constituencies).

The average number of voters in a constituency is roughly 70,000, but there is considerable variation. The size of constituencies is regulated by an independent Boundary Commission, which recommends periodic changes based on movements of population. In 2005 the number of Scottish constituencies was reduced from 72 to 59 to bring its representation more closely into line with that of the rest of the UK. Before the 2015 general election it had been agreed to reduce the number of constituencies in the UK from 650 to 600. This reform was delayed owing to disagreements within the **coalition government**, but the election of a Conservative government put it back on the agenda again. It is expected to involve an extensive redrawing of constituency boundaries. Among the planned changes is the splitting of the Isle of Wight, which currently has 110,000 voters, into two separate seats.

>
> ### Key term
>
> **Coalition government** a government formed of more than one political party, normally accompanied by an agreement over policy options and offices of state (for example, the Conservative–Liberal Democrat coalition of 2010–15).

Advantages of FPTP

- **Speed and simplicity:** FPTP is easy to use, with voters making a single cross and choosing one candidate. The result is usually known early in the morning after polling day and a new government is rapidly formed, allowing a swift and orderly transfer of power. The May 2010 general election was an exception, when negotiations between the prospective parties of government did not produce a result for 5 days. This would be the norm under a proportional system. The outcome of a general election would be determined by bargaining between the party leaders, which can take time. After the 2010 general election in Belgium, which uses a proportional system, it took almost 18 months to form a government. Admittedly this is an extreme example, but the fact remains that proportional systems are far less decisive than FPTP. The ease and familiarity of FPTP help to explain continuing public support for its retention. When voters were given the opportunity to replace it with the Alternative Vote (AV) in a referendum held in May 2011, almost 68 per cent of those who voted chose to retain FPTP.

- **Strong and stable government:** FPTP tends to promote a two-party system, which gives voters a clear choice. At general elections it usually gives a clear majority to one party, which then has a mandate to carry out its programme. The government can be removed at the next general election if the voters disapprove of its record. For example, it enabled Margaret Thatcher to carry out her plans for the reduction of trade union power and privatisation in the 1980s, and allowed Tony Blair to undertake extensive constitutional reforms after his 1997 victory. Supporters of FPTP argue that, by boosting the significance of smaller parties, proportional systems give them undue influence. In Germany between 1969 and 1998, the Free Democrats never gained more than 10 per cent of the popular vote but were able to hold the balance of power between the two largest parties. They sustained the Social Democrats in office until 1982, when they switched their support to the Christian Democrats or German Conservatives. Proportional representation is far more likely than FPTP to produce a coalition government. This means that the government's programme will be worked out behind closed doors in negotiations between the party leaders, without the voters having the opportunity to give their verdict on it. In addition coalitions are sometimes unstable and can break up if one of the coalition parties has a fundamental disagreement with its partner.

- **Exclusion of extremists:** Although critics of FPTP point to the way it under-represents smaller parties, the advantage of this is that extreme parties – which may feed on racism, xenophobia and other extremist views – are much less likely to gain a foothold.

- **A strong link between MPs and their constituencies:** The relatively small size of most FPTP constituencies, and the fact that a single MP is responsible for representing those who live within the constituency, are often seen as strengths. MPs handle correspondence from their constituents and hold surgeries at which they make themselves available to those seeking help and advice.

Case study: Stephen Timms MP

Labour MP Stephen Timms, who represents East Ham in London, held the record for the greatest number of surgeries in 2011. He did so in spite of being stabbed by an Islamic extremist at a surgery the previous year, insisting that it was important for him to continue to be accessible.

Question

- Can you think of ways in which MPs can help their constituents? A starting point for your research is 'What your MP can do for you' on the parliament website.

Disadvantages of FPTP

- **MPs and governments can be elected on less than 50 per cent of the vote:** More than half of MPs typically do not command majority support within their constituency. This is because they do not need an overall majority of the votes cast, but can win by gaining just one more vote than the second placed candidate. It is quite possible for more votes to be cast against rather than for the winning candidate, as Table 1.1 shows. Support for parties is even lower when turnout figures are taken into account. The turnout in Belfast South was 60 per cent, so Alasdair McDonnell only polled 14.7 per cent of the electorate.

Candidate	Political party	% of the vote
Alasdair McDonnell	Social Democratic and Labour Party (SDLP)	24.5
Jonathan Bell	Democratic Unionist Party (DUP)	22.2
Paula Bradshaw	Alliance Party	17.2
Máirtín Ó Muilleoir	Sinn Fein	13.9
Rodney McCune	Ulster Unionist Party	9.1
Clare Bailey	Green Party	5.7
Bob Stoker	UKIP	4.9
Ben Manton	Conservative	1.5
Lily Kerr	Workers Party	0.9

Table 1.1: FPTP in action – Belfast South in the 2015 general election

- **At national level:** FPTP regularly produces governments elected on a minority of the popular vote. The lowest percentage was recorded in 2005, when Tony Blair was re-elected on 35.2 per cent of the vote. This weakens the mandate enjoyed by the winning party, especially as general elections since 2001 have been characterised by low voter turnout. This feature means that significant numbers of voters feel that the system lacks legitimacy.

- **Lack of proportionality:** FPTP does not translate the number of votes into seats for each party with any real accuracy. The system favours parties whose vote is concentrated, rather than those whose support is spread across a large geographical area. A party may come second in a large number of seats, but FPTP does not reward this because only one candidate can win in each constituency. For example, UKIP won almost 3.9 million votes in 2015, but only one seat.

Pause & reflect

Research the results in your own parliamentary constituency at the last three general elections. What percentage of the vote was gained by the winning candidate in each contest?

Key terms

Marginal seats
seats held by a small majority, where a small swing to an opposition candidate can cause the seat to change hands.

Safe seats
constituencies in which the sitting MP has a secure majority over the nearest rival, and is largely immune from swings in voting choice.

By contrast the Scottish National Party replaced Labour as the largest party in Scotland, taking 56 out of 59 seats with 50 per cent of the vote, because it campaigned only in one part of the UK. FPTP does not reflect the fact that the number of people voting for the two largest parties has been in decline for some time. Between 1945 and 1970, on average ten MPs from smaller parties were elected in each parliament. By 2015 that figure had risen to 87 MPs.

- **The winner's bonus:** The winning party under FPTP enjoys a share of the seats in excess of the share of the vote it receives. This occurs if a large number of seats are **marginal** between the two main parties. For example, in the elections of 1983 and 1987 Margaret Thatcher won majorities of 144 and 102 respectively, on 42 per cent of the vote. In the 2015 election the winner's bonus was much less marked, with David Cameron winning only a 12 seat majority, but there was still a mismatch between votes and seats. The Conservatives won 50.9 per cent of the seats with 36.9 per cent of the vote. There is no precise percentage or winning margin to which this aligns, but a 10 per cent margin would need only a 5 per cent swing to the rival party to take it. Although marginal seats comprise only a minority of seats at Westminster, they are where general elections are commonly determined. Parties focus their resources heavily on these seats, spending large amounts of money on campaigning and enlisting the support of high-profile figures to lend support to their candidates.

- **Limited voter choice:** FPTP limits the choice for voters in several ways. Each party puts forward a single candidate, so there is no choice between individuals representing different shades of opinion within the party. The prevalence of **safe seats** means that many voters have little hope of seeing their favoured candidate win. This can depress voter turnout, as people feel that there is no point in voting for a candidate who cannot hope to be elected, because the same political party holds the seat in every election. In the run-up to the 2015 general election the Electoral Reform Society estimated that 364 seats – 56 per cent of the total – were safe seats. An example is Theresa May's Maidenhead constituency in Berkshire, which she held with a majority of 29,059 in 2015, and which has been Conservative since 1885. Alternatively, people may resort to tactical voting – voting not for their favourite but for the candidate most likely to prevent the party they dislike from winning. In 2015 a number of vote-swapping websites were set up. These enabled people living in constituencies where their vote would be wasted to swap with someone in an area where it would make a difference. This is not illegal (unless inducement or pressure is applied) but it does shed a light on the way that the UK's system of representative democracy works.

- **Votes are of unequal value:** In a small constituency a vote usually counts for more than it does in a larger one. For example, it took only 9407 votes to elect the MP for Orkney and Shetland, compared to 28,591 for the Isle of Wight MP. Votes are said to be 'wasted' if they are cast for a losing candidate, or if they are cast for a winning candidate, in excess of the plurality needed for him or her to win. The Electoral Reform Society calculated that 74.4 per cent of votes cast in the 2015 election were wasted, compared to 71.1 per cent in 2010.

Case study: A marginal seat – Thanet South, Kent

This seat has been won by the winning party at every general election since its creation: Conservative in 1983, 1987 and 1992; Labour in 1997, 2001 and 2005; Conservative again in 2010. In 2015 it was held by the Conservative candidate, Craig Mackinlay, against a challenge from UKIP Leader, Nigel Farage, with a majority of 2812 and was retained by Mackinlay in 2017.

Questions
- How do marginal seats demonstrate the limitations of FPTP as a democratic system?
- Thanet South has sometimes been described as a 'barometer' of national opinion in general elections. What does this mean?

Pause & reflect

Look back at the functions of elections. Does FPTP adequately fulfil these?

FPTP produces another kind of distortion known as 'electoral deserts' – areas of the country where one party cannot win seats. South-east England is an electoral desert for Labour. An area that is an electoral desert for one party may be described as a 'heartland' for its opponent. For example, north-east England, Merseyside and South Wales are Labour heartlands.

The additional member system, single transferable vote and supplementary vote: their advantages and disadvantages

In the late 1990s the Blair government introduced new voting systems for different elections, while leaving first past the post unchanged for Westminster.

- The **additional member system** is a hybrid or mixed system, combining elements of FPTP and proportional representation.
- The **single transferable vote** is a form of proportional representation.
- The **supplementary vote** is majoritarian, not proportional.

In this section you will learn how each of these systems works, as well as its advantages and disadvantages.

Additional member system (AMS)

Where is it used?
The Scottish parliament, Welsh Assembly, Greater London Assembly (GLA)

How does it work?
- Voters have two votes: the first is for a constituency representative, who is elected using FPTP; the second is for a party list and uses multi-member regional constituencies, introducing an element of proportional representation.
- There are fewer list members than constituency representatives, and so they are known as 'additional' or 'top-up' members. In the Scottish parliament, 73 of the 129 members are elected in single-member constituencies, with the remaining 56 seats being filled by list members. In the Welsh Assembly 40 of the 60 members represent single-member constituencies, with 20 list members. In the GLA 14 of the 25 members are elected in single-member constituencies and 11 are top-up members.
- These bodies have 4-year fixed terms.

Advantages
- The top-up component introduces a proportional element, acting as a corrective to the FPTP part of the system. A calculation is made using the d'Hondt formula to determine how many members a party should be allocated from the lists. For example, in Scotland the Conservative Party won no seats in the 1997 Westminster election under FPTP, but the list enabled it to win a total of 18 seats in the first Scottish parliament elections in 1999.
- The FPTP element maintains a strong link between the member and the constituency.
- Electors have wider choice than under FPTP; they can vote for a 'split ticket' if they wish, using their constituency vote to choose a representative from one party, and their top-up vote to support another party.

Pause & reflect

Using your knowledge of the advantages and disadvantages of FPTP, do you think AMS represents a better option for the UK?

Disadvantages

- It creates two different types of member – some with constituency responsibilities and some without. However, there is little evidence that the second category is seen as having less legitimacy.
- A closed list system is used, which means that the party leadership ranks candidates in order on the list. It can use this power to limit the chances of dissident members of the party being elected.
- Smaller parties achieve less representation than under a fully proportional system. This is especially true in Wales where the small number of top-up seats has advantaged Labour (see Table 1.2). The SNP has been the dominant party in Scotland since 2007, running a majority government in 2011–16.

Party	Constituency seats	Top-up seats	Total seats
Labour	27	2	29
Plaid Cymru	6	6	12
Conservative	6	5	11
UKIP	0	7	7
Lib Dem	1	0	1
Green	0	0	0

Table 1.2: AMS in action – the Welsh Assembly elections, May 2016

Single transferable vote (STV)

Where is it used?
The Northern Ireland Assembly, European parliament elections in Northern Ireland, Scottish council elections

How does it work?
- It uses multi-member constituencies; in the case of the Northern Ireland Assembly, there are 18, each returning five members.
- Voters number their choices preferentially: 1, 2, 3 etc.
- In order to be elected, a candidate needs to achieve a quota, arrived at using the Droop formula, which divides the number of votes cast by the number of seats contested plus one.

The results are calculated using a complex counting process that takes into account voters' second preferences. If a candidate reaches the quota on the first round of counting, they are elected and their second preferences are redistributed. If no one attains the quota, the least popular candidate is eliminated and the second preferences of those who voted for this candidate are transferred. This process is continued until all the seats are filled.

Advantages
- There is a close correlation between votes and seats.
- Voter choice is high; it is possible to choose between candidates standing for the same party as well as between candidates from different parties.
- In Northern Ireland it has created a power-sharing government that enables representatives of the two rival communities, the unionists and nationalists, to work together, ending 30 years of violent disturbance in Northern Ireland.

Disadvantages

- It is not fully proportional, particularly where smaller multi-member constituencies are used.

- In large multi-member constituencies, the link between the member and the voters may be weak.

- Power-sharing governments may bring rival groups together but they are still prone to conflict. The Northern Ireland executive was suspended several times in its early years, including for almost five years in 2002–07 as a result of a breakdown of trust. Co-operation between the parties broke down again early in 2017, triggering further elections. STV did not help the more centrist parties in the long term. The dominant parties are now the Democratic Unionist Party and republican Sinn Fein. Since 2007 they have replaced the more moderate Ulster Unionist Party and Social and Democratic Labour Party. Voting across community lines is still rare.

Party	% of seats	% of the vote
Democratic Unionist Party	35.2	29.2
Sinn Fein	23.1	24.0
Ulster Unionist Party	14.8	12.6
SDLP	11.1	12.0
Alliance Party	7.4	7.0
Green Party	1.9	2.7
People before Profit	1.9	2.0
Traditional Unionist Voice	0.9	3.4
Independent	0.9	3.3
UKIP	0	1.5
Progressive Unionist Party	0	0.9
Conservative	0	0.4
NI Labour Representation Committee	0	0.2
Others	0	1.0

Table 1.3: STV in action – Northern Ireland Assembly elections, May 2016

Supplementary vote (SV)

Where is it used?
- Elections for the London Mayor and other elected mayors, Police and Crime Commissioners in England and Wales

How does it work?
- Each voter is allowed a first and a second preference vote.

- Any candidate who gains more than 50 per cent of first preference votes is elected automatically.

- If this does not occur, all candidates except the top two are eliminated. Second preference votes for these two candidates are now added to produce one overall winner.

Advantages
- It ensures broad support for the winner. Sadiq Khan, elected Mayor of London in May 2016, has the largest personal mandate of any elected politician in British history (see Table 1.4).

- It is simple and straightforward to use.

- It has allowed some independent candidates to win; for example 12 out of 40 police and crime commissioners were independents in the 2012 contest, although the number fell in the second elections in 2016.

Disadvantages

- SV is not proportional as one individual is being elected to a single office.
- The winner does not need to get an absolute majority of the votes cast.
- Voters need to be able to identify the likely top two candidates in order to have influence over the outcome, and this is not always clear (with the exception of London).

MAYOR OF LONDON

Labour's Sadiq Khan became the first Muslim Mayor of London in May 2016, as well as the individual with the largest personal mandate in British political history.

Candidate	Party	1st round: % of 1st preference votes	1st round: % of 2nd preference votes	2nd round: Final total % of votes
Sadiq Khan	Labour	44.2	65.5	56.8
Zac Goldsmith	Conservative	35.0	34.5	43.2
Sian Berry	Green	5.8	–	–
Caroline Pidgeon	Liberal Democrat	4.6	–	–
Peter Whittle	UKIP	3.6	–	–
Sophie Walker	Women's Equality Party	2.0	–	–
George Galloway	Respect	1.4	–	–
Paul Golding	Britain First	1.2	–	–
Lee Harris	Cannabis is Safer than Alcohol	0.8	–	–
David Furness	British National Party	0.5	–	–
Prince Zylinski	Independent	0.5	–	–
Ankit Love	One Love Party	0.2	–	–

Table 1.4: SV in action – London Mayoral Elections, May 2016

EXTENSION ACTIVITY

Is it now time to reform the UK electoral system? In support of your answer, consider the election results in the examples presented in this section. Which is the fairest of the available systems?

Case study: a comparison between FPTP and STV

STV is the preferred system of the Electoral Reform Society. It is worth comparing it with the FPTP system to determine which best delivers the four qualities identified earlier as desirable features of an electoral system.

- **A fair result that gives, as far as possible, equal value to people's votes across the country:** STV translates votes into seats more fairly, helping smaller parties that are under-represented under FPTP. It does away with tactical voting as voters do not have to vote for the candidate who is most likely to block the one they dislike.

- **A choice of candidates:** STV gives voters a wider choice, even allowing a choice between candidates from different wings of the same party in a multi-member constituency. On the other hand, it may encourage 'donkey voting' – voters may list candidates in rank order as stated on the ballot paper.

- **An effective link between the elected representative and the constituency:** This is weaker under STV, especially in underpopulated multi-member constituencies which are too large for their representatives to know well. On the other hand, the absence of safe seats under STV makes candidates work harder for votes, so that they have to address concerns across the whole of the constituency. FPTP encourages parties to focus on key marginal seats at the expense of others.

- **A strong government that can pass laws but can be held to account by the electorate:** Votes take longer to count under STV, possibly delaying the formation of a government. It is likely to produce a coalition – this may encourage a more consensual style of government, or it may lead to instability. Coalitions pursue a programme agreed by politicians after the election, on which voters have not given a verdict. Or it may result in a weak **minority government**. Both can occur under FPTP, but they are much less common.

Party	Actual results under FPTP	Projected results under STV
Conservative	331	276
Labour	232	236
Liberal Democrat	8	26
UKIP	1	54
Green	1	3
SNP	56	34
Plaid Cymru	3	3

Table 1.5: The 2015 general election – number of seats under FPTP and STV (England, Scotland and Wales only).

Questions

- Is the creation of a possibly weaker government under STV a price worth paying for the advantages offered by this system?

- Does the evidence here suggest that STV necessarily weakens the link between MPs and their constituencies?

EXTENSION ACTIVITY

Research the role of the Electoral Reform Society. Do you agree with their case for electoral reform in the UK? Explain your answer.

Key term

Minority government a government that takes office but does not have a majority of seats in parliament, which makes passing legislation very difficult. After an indecisive general election, Labour leader Harold Wilson took office in March 1974 as leader of a minority government, although he was able to win a small majority in a further election in October.

EXTENSION ACTIVITY

Use the data in Table 1.5 to work out what kind of government Britain might have had if STV had been used rather than FPTP in the 2015 general election. Would the most likely outcome have been a minority Conservative government?

3.2   Referendums and how they are used

How referendums have been used and their impact on UK political life since 1997

What is a referendum?

A referendum is a vote on a particular issue, usually requiring a yes/no response. It is an example of direct democracy within a representative system. There is no constitutional mechanism requiring a prime minister to hold a referendum; they are called at the discretion of the government. Technically the result does not have legal force and it has to be approved by parliament, which has legal sovereignty. However, in practice it is highly unlikely that the country's elected representatives would ignore the will of the people.

Referendums were unknown in the UK until 1973 when voters in Northern Ireland were asked whether they wanted to stay in the UK. The first national referendum was held in June 1975, when Labour Prime Minister Harold Wilson gave the electorate a vote on whether they wanted to stay in the European Economic Community. Since the election of the New Labour government in 1997 they have become more common. Indeed, there is now an expectation that a referendum will be called when an important, possibly irreversible, constitutional change is contemplated. Major developments, such as devolution for Scotland, Wales and Northern Ireland, have been given public approval in this way. Possibly the most far-reaching change to the UK constitution in a generation, the decision to leave the European Union, would not have occurred had it been left up to parliament. The vote for 'Brexit' in the June 2016 referendum led directly to a change of prime minister and confronted Theresa May's government with a hugely complex challenge, to negotiate the terms of Britain's departure. Table 2.1 shows the growing use of referendums since 1997. Before that time, they were a rarity in the UK.

Since 2000 the conduct of referendums has been regulated by the Electoral Commission. This independent body is responsible for checking the wording of the referendum question, as proposed by the government, to ensure that it is as objective as possible. In the 2016 EU referendum, the government had originally proposed to ask: 'Should the United Kingdom remain a member of the European Union?' The Commission considered this to be insufficiently neutral, and insisted that the ballot paper should present two options: 'Should the United Kingdom remain a member of the European Union or leave the European Union?' The Commission also monitors expenditure by the rival campaigning groups, and designates one approved 'lead campaign organisation' on each side. In the EU referendum, the official groups representing the two sides were 'Vote Leave' and 'Britain Stronger in Europe'. This designation entitled them to receive a pre-determined amount of public funding.

In what circumstances is a referendum held?

- **Legitimising a major government initiative:** Since the advent of the Blair government, it has become the accepted practice to secure a demonstration of public support before embarking on important, possibly irreversible constitutional changes. The 1997 referendums on devolution for Scotland and Wales, and in Northern Ireland on the 1998 Good Friday Agreement, are examples.
- **Getting a government out of a difficult situation:** Referendums have sometimes been used when a government faces serious internal disagreement. By handing the decision to the people, and insisting that colleagues then rally behind the popular verdict, the government can maintain its unity. Harold Wilson held a referendum in 1975 because his party was split between pro- and anti-European factions. If he had tried to insist on the government taking a particular position, he would have faced damaging resignations from ministers on the other side.

Date	UK-wide? Regional?	Topic	% Yes vote	% No vote	% Turnout
Sept 1997	Scotland	Establishment of a Scottish parliament	74.3	25.7	60.4
Sept 1997	Scotland	Tax varying powers for Scottish parliament	63.5	36.5	60.4
Sept 1997	Wales	Establishment of a Welsh Assembly	50.3	49.7	50.1
May 1998	London	London Mayor and Assembly	72.0	28.0	34.0
May 1998	Northern Ireland	Approval of the Good Friday Agreement	71.1	28.9	81.0
Nov 2004	North-East England	Creation of an elected regional assembly	22.0	78.0	48.0
Mar 2011	Wales	Extension of powers for Welsh Assembly	63.5	36.5	35.6
May 2011	UK	Change to AV for the Westminster electoral system	32.1	67.9	42.2
Sept 2014	Scotland	Scottish independence	44.7	55.3	84.6
June 2016	UK	Remain or leave the EU	48.1 Remain	51.9 Leave	72.2

Table 2.1: National and regional referendums held in the UK since 1997

- **A result of a deal between political parties:** David Cameron agreed to hold a vote on changing the electoral system for Westminster because this was a demand of the Liberal Democrats, as part of the coalition agreement establishing the government in May 2010.

- **In response to pressure to hold a referendum:** Cameron initially did not want to hold an in/out EU referendum. He joined forces with the Liberal Democrats and Labour in October 2011 to defeat Conservative backbenchers who were pressing for a referendum. He changed his mind in January 2013 as the demand refused to go away, and he began to fear the possible loss of Conservative voters to UKIP if he did not concede. By announcing that he would hold a referendum if re-elected in 2015, he took the issue off the agenda at the ensuing general election. After the election he had to make good his promise, resulting in defeat for the 'Remain' side that he had championed and bringing about his resignation as prime minister.

> **EXTENSION ACTIVITY**
>
> Compare the differing levels of turnout in the referendums in Table 2.1. Why do you think there is so much variation in participation? Does low turnout undermine the legitimacy of the result?

Election	Referendum
Elections must be held at regular intervals by law. The 2011 Fixed Term Parliaments Act has set the date for general elections at intervals every 5 years. In an election, voters are pronouncing on a range of different policy issues, not a single question.	In the UK there is no legal or constitutional requirement to have a referendum – it is a political choice. Referendums are on major issues, when government needs to secure public backing or feels obliged to consult the electorate directly. The government proposes the question, although the wording is now approved by the neutral Electoral Commission.

Table 2.2: How a referendum differs from an election

A 'Yes' supporter in the 2014 Scottish independence referendum inviting debate.

The case for and against referendums in a representative democracy

For referendums

- Referendums involve the people directly in decision-making on important issues. In a democracy the electorate has the right to be consulted. Trust in politicians is low, and many questions are too important to leave to them. In a general election the people are expressing a view on a great many policy matters. The virtue of a referendum is that it enables a single issue to be isolated, so that an unambiguous popular verdict can be given. Some issues, such as the UK's membership of the EU, cut across party lines with pro- and anti-EU politicians in both major political parties, so a real choice cannot be given in a general election.

- Referendums are a check on what the Conservative politician, Lord Hailsham, famously called the UK's 'elective dictatorship' – the idea that executive dominance of the House of Commons gives it undue power, over which usually the electorate has control only once every 5 years. The holding of referendums between general elections gives the people an opportunity to have their say more frequently, and prevents the government from becoming remote and unaccountable. They prevent a government, possibly one with a small parliamentary majority, from rushing through a change without consulting the people.

- By demonstrating clear public support for a change, referendums settle arguments and entrench reforms. This is not to say that such a change could never be reversed by a future parliament, but to do so would entail another major public debate. The demonstration of support for the Scottish parliament and for the Northern Ireland peace process has helped bring stability to the new institutions created in these parts of the UK.

- Referendums raise voters' political awareness. The Scottish referendum in September 2014, for example, has been praised for giving an opportunity to air a wide range of issues related to independence. These included the likely impact of independence on the economy, the future of the nuclear deterrent based on the River Clyde and Scotland's relationship with the EU. All of these topics were thoroughly debated during the campaign.

- The conduct of referendums has been subject to independent supervision by the Electoral Commission since 2000. This reduces the chances that the result will be skewed as a result of unfair influence, because the expenditure of the competing sides is limited and the wording of the referendum question is subject to review by an independent body.

Against referendums

- Referendums are a challenge to parliamentary sovereignty. Voters elect representatives to take decisions on their behalf and this was the accepted way of doing so until the 1970s. Ordinary people lack the expertise to make decisions on complex questions such as, for example, whether Britain should join the euro – a subject that the New Labour government declared that it would put to the popular vote if it ever recommended joining.

- If the arguments are not explained clearly to the public, popular participation may be low. This was a factor in the low turnout in the 2011 referendum on electoral reform. After the 2016 EU vote, the Electoral Commission reported that the arguments used by the leaders of both campaigns included a degree of distortion, and that there should be greater regulation of referendum campaigns to ensure that people receive a fair presentation of the arguments.

- Governments choose whether or not to call a referendum. Blair and Brown denied the electorate a say on the Lisbon Treaty of 2007, which extended the process of European integration, on the grounds that previous governments had not held popular votes on treaties. This caused outrage among the opposition, who maintained that voters had been denied a chance to vote on an agreement that transferred significant authority to the EU. In addition, governments sometimes hold referendums for their own political purposes, for example, to defuse opposition and (as with the 2011 referendum) to overcome their own differences. There is an argument for greater regulation of the circumstances in which a referendum can be triggered.

- Low turnout has been the norm, with outstanding exceptions such as the Scottish independence referendum in 2014. This limits the legitimacy of the decision. Turnout in the 1997 Welsh devolution vote, for example, was barely above 50 per cent, which cast a shadow over the new Assembly for some time.

- The outcomes of referendums can be influenced by factors that have nothing to do with the subject being put before the electorate. They can be a way of registering a protest against the government of the day. For example, the defeat of the Alternative Vote proposal in the 2011 referendum was affected by the unpopularity of the Liberal Democrats.

3.3 Electoral system analysis

Debates on why different electoral systems are used in the UK

Why has FPTP survived for Westminster elections?

First past the post has survived largely because the outcomes it produces usually suit the interests of the two largest parties, who have largely monopolised government since 1945. The Labour Party offered a referendum on FPTP before the 1997 general election, but had no incentive to deliver this after winning a large independent majority under the existing system. The coalition offered a referendum on AV after taking office in 2010 because this was a key demand of the Liberal Democrats when they agreed to participate in the government.

Voters accept FPTP because it is familiar and easy to use, and there is little desire to change it for an untried system that may bring problems of its own. The outcome of the May 2011 referendum demonstrated the lack of popular support for change.

The other systems discussed in this chapter were chosen by the Blair government when it established new institutions in the different parts of the UK. In each case different reasons applied.

Why was AMS adopted for Scottish and Welsh devolved elections and for the Greater London Assembly?

AMS was the price that Labour paid for winning acceptance of its devolution plans from the other political parties. The Liberal Democrats and SNP would have preferred STV for the Scottish parliament as they expected that Labour would sweep the board under a less proportional system. AMS was chosen as a compromise that would result in a broadly representative parliament, but without involving such a radical change as STV. It pacified the other parties by providing an element of proportionality but was also acceptable to Labour because it retained local representation (a feature of FPTP). Labour expected that AMS would enable it to play a part in government in Scotland and, at least until the SNP victory in 2007, this proved to be correct. After AMS had been agreed on for Scotland it was decided to use the same system for Wales, where support for devolution was much weaker.

AMS was adopted for the Greater London Assembly because it had already been selected for Scotland and Wales. It would broadly reflect the views of the population of the capital while retaining an element of geographical representation.

Why was STV adopted for the Northern Ireland Assembly?

STV was chosen for Northern Ireland after the 1998 Good Friday Agreement because it is a highly proportional system, likely to ensure the broadest possible representation of different parties. In view of the background of conflict between unionist and nationalist communities in Northern Ireland, it was important to avoid single-party domination, which could have derailed the fragile peace process. The use of STV ensures that governments are power-sharing bodies drawn from both sides of the divide. Another reason is that STV was already used in the Republic of Ireland. It had also been used for short periods when a previous Northern Ireland parliament had been in existence, between the 1920s and 1970s, and so had roots in the province.

Why was SV used to choose elected mayors?

Both SV and AV were considered as possibilities when the Labour government was deciding which method to use for choosing the London Mayor – and thus the mayor for other cities. SV was chosen partly because it was simpler to use. It was also preferred because only the top two candidates, after first preferences had been counted, would make it through to the final round. This meant that candidates with little positive support would be less likely to win merely because they were a 'lowest common denominator' second or third choice. In this way the winner would have a clear mandate.

The impact of the electoral system on the government or type of government appointed

Coalition governments and new voting systems

An important consequence of the adoption of proportional (or partly proportional) electoral systems is that coalition or minority governments have become much more common in Scotland, Wales and Northern Ireland. This is in contrast with Westminster, which continues to experience single party rule as the norm (with the exceptions in modern times of the 2010–15 coalition and the 2017 agreement between the Conservatives and the Democratic Unionist Party). However, the worst predictions made by critics of proportional representation have not been fulfilled. Coalition governments in different parts of the UK have proved to be stable and, unlike in some other countries that use PR, there have not been frequent changes of government. The devolved administrations have mostly served for sustained periods.

The politics of compromise

There has also been a change to the way in which governments are formed and policy is made. Negotiations between political parties, which remain rare at Westminster, are the normal way in which business is conducted in Edinburgh, Cardiff and Belfast.

As Table 3.1 shows, majority government has been the exception to the rule in Scotland. When it was in a minority, the SNP government had to win the support of other parties in order to pass legislation. In February 2011, in order to win support for its budget, the administration had to make concessions to the Conservatives and Liberal Democrats. In response to claims that its budget did not do enough to promote economic recovery, the SNP agreed to measures to increase youth employment and training. Claims that new voting systems would produce a more consensual style of politics have not entirely been fulfilled. There has been conflict on the central issue of Scottish independence, since the SNP is outnumbered by parties that support the Union.

In Wales, Labour has consistently been the strongest party but, as Table 3.2 shows, the proportional element of AMS has frequently denied it the opportunity to govern alone. Like the SNP in Scotland, Welsh Labour has so far formed only one majority administration.

In Northern Ireland, the Good Friday Agreement requires that representatives of the main unionist and nationalist parties are included in the executive. The choice of STV for Assembly elections guarantees that members of the two rival communities are elected, rather than Northern Ireland submitting to single-party domination as this could risk a return to sectarian violence. The first minister and deputy first minister – nominated by the two largest parties – are equal in status and share governmental responsibilities. The system of government is designed to ensure joint participation by unionists and nationalists or republicans.

Term of office	Type of government
1999–2007	Labour–Liberal Democrat
2007–2011	SNP (minority government)
2011–2016	SNP (majority government)
2016–	SNP (minority government)

Table 3.1: Scottish governments since devolution

Term of office	Type of government
1999–2000	Labour (minority government)
2000–2003	Labour–Liberal Democrat
2003–2007	Labour (majority government)
2007 (May–June)	Labour (minority government)
2007–2011	Labour–Plaid Cymru
2011–16	Labour (minority government)
2016–	Labour–Liberal Democrat

Table 3.2: Welsh governments since the introduction of devolution

First Minister Arlene Foster (Democratic Unionist Party) and Deputy First Minister, the late Martin McGuinness (Sinn Fein), who held office jointly until the breakdown of the Northern Ireland power-sharing executive in January 2017.

Term of office	Party of first minister	Party of deputy first minister	Ministers from different parties
1999–2002 (Devolved institutions suspended 2002–07)	Ulster Unionist Party (UUP)	Social and Democratic Labour Party (SDLP)	UUP 4 SDLP 4 DUP 2 Sinn Fein 2
2007–11	Democratic Unionist Party (DUP)	Sinn Fein (SF)	UUP 2 SDLP 1 DUP 5 Sinn Fein 4 Alliance Party 1
2011–16	Democratic Unionist Party (DUP)	Sinn Fein (SF)	UUP 1 (until 2015) 0 (2015–16) SDLP 1 DUP 5 (until 2015) 6 (2015–16) Sinn Fein 4 Alliance Party 4
2016–17	Democratic Unionist Party (DUP)	Sinn Fein (SF)	DUP 5 Sinn Fein 4 Independent 1

Table 3.3: Composition of the Northern Ireland executive since devolution

EXTENSION ACTIVITY

What does the composition of the Northern Ireland executive, shown in Table 3.3, tell you about the effects of the STV electoral system?

By contrast, at Westminster the main parties remain in an adversarial relationship, with one major opposition party clearly playing the role of an alternative government and smaller parties having much less influence. From the 1990s to the 2010 general election, the electoral system for Westminster tended to favour the Labour Party – a trend now beginning to reverse. This was because with FPTP the distribution of votes is important. In the Blair–Brown era, safe Labour seats tended to have lower populations, as the revision of constituency boundaries had not kept pace with the movement of people away from inner cities to more affluent suburban and rural areas. In short, it took fewer votes to return a Labour MP than a Conservative. This, together with a slightly lower average turnout in the seats it held, gave Labour an advantage. The Conservatives' vote was less efficiently distributed across the constituencies. This unevenness does not occur under proportional systems.

Policy-making in devolved governments

Sub-national governments have used their devolved powers to differentiate themselves in terms of policy from what happens at Westminster. Under the Scottish Labour–Liberal Democrat coalition it was decided that university students in Scotland would not pay tuition fees and elderly people would receive free nursing care. In both Scotland and Wales, prescription charges were abolished. None of these benefits were extended to people living in England. This means that there is no longer a uniform welfare state across the UK. This can be directly attributed to the selection of AMS as the electoral system for the Scottish parliament. It ensured that, by obliging it to enter coalition with the centre-left Liberal Democrats, Scottish Labour did not follow the rightward drift of the party at Westminster in the New Labour era.

The impact of different electoral systems on party representation and on voter choice

Effects on party representation

As you have seen, the adoption of fully or partly proportional systems has assisted smaller parties to varying extents. The systems used in 'second order' elections are not affected to the same degree as FPTP by the geographical distribution of votes. So in the 2015 general election, the only third parties that did well were those, like the SNP or DUP, that campaigned in particular regions of the UK where their support is concentrated.

Smaller parties have a vested interest in reforming the electoral system but little realistic chance of achieving it. The experience of coalition government at Westminster has not encouraged a public demand for reform. This is despite the fact that in 2015 almost a quarter of the electorate voted for a party other than the Conservatives, Labour and the Liberal Democrats.

Effects on voter choice

AMS allows people two votes, for a constituency and a list candidate. Even more choice is offered by STV, where a preferential voting system allows voters to differentiate not only between political parties but also between candidates from the same party. STV involves fewer 'wasted' votes than FPTP, and offers greater potential to choose the winning candidate because of its proportional character. SV allows voters a first and a second preference vote.

All of these systems provide more choice than FPTP, under which voters can choose only one candidate. However, if they live in a safe seat, even this has little chance of affecting the expected outcome.

EXTENSION ACTIVITY

Look back at the information on AMS, STV and SV. Which one of these systems, on balance, provides the fairest representation for different parties and offers the widest choice for voters? How does this compare with the effects of FPTP? Support your answer with examples.

Assessment support: 1.1.3 Electoral Systems

Question 2 on A-Level Paper 1 gives you a choice of two 30-mark questions, to be completed in 45 minutes.

Evaluate the extent to which the increased use of referendums would improve democracy in the UK. You must consider this view and the alternative to this view in a balanced way. [30 marks].

These questions require an essay-style answer. They test all three Assessment Objectives, with 10 marks available for each. The highest level (25 to 30 marks) requires in-depth knowledge and understanding, supporting strong skills of analysis and evaluation. The mark scheme stresses that you must consider both sides of the question – in this case, the arguments for and against the increased use of referendums.

- Begin with a brief introduction in which you outline your argument. You need to set out a minimum of two key points on each side of the question, which you will develop in the course of the essay.

- Typically, you will be following your introduction with four paragraphs – one for each major point you intend to make – and finally a conclusion.

- The instruction to **evaluate** means that you must present arguments for and against the use of referendums. Each argument should be supported with accurate and relevant examples.

- In your conclusion, reach an overall judgement, after reviewing the balance between the two sides of the argument. Don't bring new factual material in at this point. Your conclusion should emerge naturally from the way you have constructed your argument.

Here is an example of an introduction written by a student.

Supporters of referendums make several points in favour of their use. They mainly base their arguments on the shortcomings of the UK's representative system. Referendums provide an opportunity to gauge public opinion between general elections. They encourage political participation and help to educate the public by focusing attention on important issues. On the other hand, a simple yes/no response is not necessarily the best way of making a decision on a complex political issue. Moreover, referendums can produce a distorted result because the media and pressure groups can present issues to the public in a subjective and often unfair way.

- This introduction is effective because it outlines the main arguments for and against the use of referendums.

- Notice the use of 'on the other hand' to show that the student is looking at the other side of the argument.

- The student does not go into factual detail at this stage. The right place for this is in the body of the essay, as the student takes each argument in turn and explains it fully. The purpose of the introduction is to indicate the 'direction of travel' we can expect to see as the essay develops.

Voting Behaviour and the Media

In this section you will learn about:

- case studies of three key general elections, the various factors that explain their outcomes and other aspects of voting behaviour
- the changing role of the media, from newspapers and television to the internet and social media, both during and between elections.

4.1 Case studies of three key general elections

The elections, their results and the impact on parties and government

This section looks at voting behaviour in three key general elections: those held in 1979, 1997 and 2010. The results of these three contests were very different. However, all three are widely regarded as critical turning points in post-war politics. It should be noted that in 1979 there were typically three or four candidates per constituency (2576 candidates in 635 constituencies), but by 1997 the number rose to 3724 candidates in 659 constituencies and in 2010 to 4150 candidates in 650 constituencies. This shows a development that gave greater choice to voters, reducing the dominance of the two large parties.

1979

3 May 1979 *Thatcher's first victory*

- The election initiated 18 years of Conservative rule, under Margaret Thatcher up to 1990 and then under John Major to 1997. Seen as bringing to an end years of post-war consensus.
- Called after James Callaghan's minority Labour government lost a vote of no confidence in the House of Commons – the most recent time this has happened.
- Thatcher's initial majority was modest, but it increased in 1983 and 1987; John Major clung to power in the 1992 election.
- Labour descended into a prolonged period of left/right infighting over policy until the reinvention of the party under Tony Blair enabled it to return to power in 1997.

Turnout: 76% Size of majority: 43

Party	Number of seats	Increase/loss of seats	% of popular vote
Conservative	339	+62	43.9
Labour	269	-50	36.9
Liberal	11	-2	13.8

Table 1.1: Results of the 1979 general election

1997

1 May 1997 *Blair's New Labour victory*

- The landslide victory of New Labour, which removed John Major's Conservatives from office and opened the way to 13 years of Labour government.
- Tony Blair was prime minister until 2007 when he was succeeded by Gordon Brown.
- The Liberal Democrats emerged as a significant third force at Westminster.
- The Conservatives were troubled by ongoing divisions, poor leadership and an inability to appear relevant to contemporary society. They were unable to dislodge Labour from power in the next two elections (2001 and 2005).

Turnout: 71.4 %   Size of majority: 179

Party	Number of seats	Increase/loss of seats	% of popular vote
Labour	418	+145	43.2
Conservative	165	-178	30.7
Liberal Democrat	46	+28	16.8

Table 1.2: Results of the 1997 general election

2010

6 May 2010 *The first post-war coalition*

- The election that saw Blair's successor, Gordon Brown, removed from office, ending the New Labour era.
- David Cameron's Conservatives increased their share of the seats, benefiting from 4 years of efforts at modernisation under their new leader.
- The Conservatives did not gain an independent majority, so had to form a coalition – the first since 1945 – with the Liberal Democrats. Against predictions, the coalition survived a full term, partly due to the Fixed Term Parliament Act on which the Liberal Democrats had insisted.
- Cameron won a slender Conservative majority in the 2015 election.

Turnout: 65.1%   Size of majority: None following the election; the Conservative–Liberal Democrat coalition that was formed afterwards had a majority of 77.

Party	Number of seats	Increase/loss of seats	% of popular vote
Conservative	306	+96	36.1
Labour	258	-90	29.0
Liberal Democrat	57	-5	23.0

Table 1.3: Results of the 2010 general election

The factors that explain the outcome of these elections

A number of factors explain the outcome of different electoral contests. These include the impact of party policies and the **manifesto** – the document that enables a winning party to claim a **mandate** – and the techniques that parties use in their election campaigns. It is also important to examine the wider context of particular elections. The state of the economy, the public image of party leaders, and the assessment that voters make of a government's record may all play an important part in determining the result.

1979

Party policies and manifestos

Both the Labour and Conservative manifestos were notable for their moderation. Both gave high priority to bringing inflation down. Callaghan came from Labour's traditional centre-right and he resisted pressure for more extreme proposals from his party's left wing. Thatcher's policy statement contained very little indication that she intended to move her party to the right. There was a mention of returning recently nationalised industries to private hands and removing some trade union powers, but no suggestion of a radical crusade to scale down the state sector. This meant that when Callaghan warned the electorate of a lurch to the right if the Conservatives won, it had little credibility.

The election campaign

The Conservatives adopted many of the techniques of modern advertising under the guidance of two professional publicity specialists, Gordon Reece and Tim Bell. The Labour campaign lacked awareness of the finer points of presentation, whereas Thatcher proved amenable to her advisers' invention of photo opportunities, and was pictured doing everything from tasting tea to holding a newborn calf. The real impact of the campaign is hard to measure. Although the Conservatives outpaced Labour in the opinion polls, when voters were asked who would make the better prime minister, 'Sunny Jim' Callaghan was 20 points ahead of Thatcher on average. In spite of his mistakes, voters still respected his air of experience. Thatcher was wise to turn down the offer of a televised debate, which would have highlighted this difference between them. It was perfectly acceptable to do so as a debate had not been held at any previous election.

The wider political context

The real reason for Thatcher's victory was the weakness of the Labour government, which precipitated the dissolution of parliament. In spite of Callaghan's personal popularity, and tentative signs of economic improvement, there was never much doubt that the Conservatives would win. Callaghan's government was a minority administration that survived by constructing deals with smaller parties. This left it vulnerable to defeat in the Commons. Moreover, Callaghan mistimed the election. There was widespread expectation that he would call an election in the autumn of 1978, but he backed away from doing so. During the 'winter of discontent', which followed in the early months of 1979, the government's attempt to impose a 5 per cent limit on pay increases collapsed as a series of strikes – by lorry drivers, health workers, refuse collectors and even, in one local authority, gravediggers – created a sense of national paralysis.

Callaghan's failure to control militant trade unions handed the Conservatives a winning card. The media showed images of a miserable, strike-bound Britain. When Callaghan returned from a Caribbean island summit meeting of world leaders, and dismissed questions by a journalist about the situation at home, *The Sun* accused him of being out of touch. A politically lethal headline summarised his off-the-cuff remarks in three words: 'Crisis? What crisis?' This provided the Conservatives with an irresistible theme: that the country needed a new direction and a government that could grapple with economic and social breakdown.

Key terms

Manifesto
the document in which a political party details what actions and programmes it intends to introduce if it is successful in the next election – a set of promises for future action.

Mandate
the authority to govern, which a government derives from an election victory. This means that it has the right to introduce its policies as stated in its manifesto. It also allows it to take decisions on other issues as they arise during its term of office, which could not have been foreseen when the manifesto was produced.

The election was triggered by a withdrawal of support for the government by nationalist parties, after the result of referendums on Scottish and Welsh devolution went against the government. This forced Callaghan to go to the country at the worst possible time for his party.

Images of uncollected rubbish in the 'winter of discontent' aided the Conservatives' return to office in 1979.

1997

Party policies and manifestos

As Labour leader, Tony Blair drove forward the policy of modernisation that had tentatively begun under his predecessors, Neil Kinnock (1983–92) and John Smith (1992–94). The 'New Labour' project abandoned old-fashioned party policies such as nationalisation, tax increases and the strengthening of trade union powers, which might put off non-committed middle-class voters. Blair also gave off reassuringly tough signals on law and order, an issue that mattered to voters following rising crime rates in the early 1990s, and emphasised his links to the business community. Crucially, Labour won the endorsement of the greater part of the press, including *The Sun* and *The Times*. The message was that New Labour was a moderate party with the interests of 'middle England' at heart. As a sign of the party's desire to show how responsible it was, its 1997 platform stressed specific policy details where it promised to make a difference, such as reducing the size of primary school classes and cutting hospital waiting lists. There was no stark difference between Labour and the Conservatives.

Another of Labour's policies that helped the party win was Blair's emphasis on constitutional reform, which gave the party common ground with the Liberal Democrats. This made it easier for Liberal Democrats to vote tactically for Labour in marginal seats, which their own candidates could not hope to win. This may have added up to 30 seats to the Labour majority.

The election campaign

New Labour placed a huge emphasis on developing a professional vote-winning machine. It employed public-relations experts to handle the media, used focus groups to assess public opinion and systematically targeted marginal seats rather than safe seats. However, the importance of this strategy should not be exaggerated. Labour's share of the vote increased on average by 12.5 per cent in its target seats, but by 13.4 per cent in constituencies that it neglected. In fact, despite the

A 'pledge card', carried by Labour candidates in 1997, showed the modesty of the party's policy objectives at this stage, which included no cuts to NHS waiting times and no rise in income tax rates.

central control over the campaign exerted by Labour headquarters, the party's lead in the opinion polls actually declined in the course of the campaign.

The wider political context

Labour could not have won on such a large scale without the damage the Conservatives inflicted on themselves after their narrow victory in the 1992 election. Turnout in 1997 was relatively low, at 71.4 per cent, which meant that under 31 per cent of the registered electorate actually voted Labour. This does not suggest a mass popular movement in support of Labour. The Conservatives had their worst election result since 1832, winning only 30.7 per cent of the vote. The 1997 result can only be fully explained by looking at the failures of John Major's government.

Economic policy played an important role. By 1997 the economy was recovering from the recession of the early part of the decade, but voters did not give the Conservatives credit for this. They remembered the catastrophe of 'Black Wednesday' in September 1992 rather than the modest economic improvement that followed. There was no tangible 'feel good factor' in 1997, as the fruits of recovery failed to feed through into either tax cuts or increased investment in public services. Monthly opinion polls show that Labour was consistently ahead of the Conservatives from the autumn of 1992 onwards. The Conservatives had lost their reputation as efficient managers of the economy and failed to retrieve it.

The image of Tory incompetence was confirmed by a series of financial and sexual scandals (which the media called 'sleaze') and continuing divisions over Britain's relationship with the European Union. The impression of weak leadership was fatal for the Conservatives.

> **Link**
>
> For more about **Black Wednesday**, see Section 3.3 of Prime Minister and Executive.

2010

Party policies and manifestos

There was little difference between the three main parties on the main issue of the election – the need to reduce the budget deficit – which had increased to £163 billion since the financial crisis of 2007–08. All three parties pledged to make savings without sacrificing essential public services. The differences were on the timing and extent of public-spending cuts. The Conservatives were alone in calling for immediate cuts; their rivals argued that this would jeopardise the fragile recovery of the economy from recession, and the cuts should be phased in gradually. From 2008 Cameron and his team focused their attacks on Labour's alleged mismanagement of the economy, accusing the party of reckless overspending and a failure to regulate the banking system effectively. This gained considerable traction with the electorate; in one opinion poll 59 per cent of voters agreed that most of the extra money spent by the Labour government had been wasted.

The election campaign

The 2010 election provides further evidence of the limited importance of campaigns in determining the final result. The Conservatives had begun intense targeting of marginal seats early in the 2005–10 parliament, striving to get their candidates established at local level, market-testing policies with voters and emphasising their support for public services on which people depended. Yet in spite of these efforts, the Conservatives were still 20 seats short of an overall majority.

On the Labour side much was made of Gordon Brown's unscripted meeting with a voter in Rochdale, Lancashire. After she embarrassed him with a hostile question about immigration, a radio microphone picked him up describing her as a 'bigoted woman' while he was being driven away. The incident was seized on by the media but its actual significance was limited. Brown was already behind in the polls and in fact Labour held Rochdale, where the incident took place.

The most remarkable innovation of the 2010 campaign was the decision to hold televised debates featuring the three main party leaders. Brown was generally felt to have come across as rather wooden, and his tendency to reply 'I agree with Nick' was derided at the time. Nick Clegg experienced a boost in the opinion polls after an unexpectedly good performance in the first of the three debates, but this fell back before polling day. Although the Liberal Democrats were able to enter government in coalition with the Conservatives, they lost a total of five seats.

The wider political context

A similarity with James Callaghan's 1979 defeat was Gordon Brown's choice of election date. When he succeeded Tony Blair as prime minister in June 2007, Brown briefly encouraged speculation that he would call an autumn election in order to secure a personal mandate. When he decided not to do so, he was widely ridiculed for alleged cowardice ('Bottler Brown') and his reputation never fully recovered. He then had to grapple with the financial crisis and ensuing recession, which gave the Conservatives ammunition to use against him. Although many independent commentators commended him for the emergency action he took, in bailing out the banks and partly nationalising those on the brink of failure, he received little political credit for this.

Brown was harshly treated in the media, being depicted as an insecure, cantankerous workaholic who could not articulate a convincing vision for the country. An Ipsos MORI poll shortly before the election showed that 33 per cent of people regarded Cameron as the most capable potential prime minister, compared to 29 per cent for Brown. But when asked about particular leadership characteristics, Brown was consistently ahead on such criteria as 'who best understands the problems facing Britain' or 'who would be best in a crisis'. Clearly the electorate was not fully convinced that Cameron was ready to take over. Opinion polls showed the Conservatives ahead of Labour on some issues, but in spite of Cameron's efforts at modernisation of the party, these still tended to come from traditional Conservative territory, such as immigration and law and order. On the main question facing the country, management of the economy, 29 per cent of voters felt that the Conservatives had the best policy, compared to 26 per cent for Labour. A further 36 per cent did not choose any of the parties. This helps to explain why the Conservatives were unable to secure an independent majority.

The Conservative campaign in 2010 focused on Gordon Brown's alleged incompetence in leading the economy from 'boom to bust'.

EXTENSION ACTIVITY

Can you find common factors that help to explain the outcome of the three general elections you have been studying?

Class-based voting and other influences on voting patterns

Up to about 1970, voters in Britain were strongly influenced by their social class background. Generally speaking, working class people – who earned a living from manual labour – voted for the Labour Party. It was closely linked to the trade union movement and looked after the interests of those who worked in the traditional heavy industries of coal, steel, textiles and shipbuilding. The middle classes (non-manual or 'white collar' workers, property owners and business people) voted Conservative. This is known as class voting – voting in line with the political party that supposedly best protects and serves the interests of a particular class. In the final third of the 20th century, class began to lose its importance as a determinant of voting behaviour – a process known as **class dealignment**.

Of course there was never a completely clear-cut social divide between the two parties. Labour also commanded the support of a section of the middle class, especially those who worked in the state sector, such as teachers and social workers, and it had a following among university intellectuals. The Conservatives appealed to deferential and patriotic working class voters who valued established institutions such as the monarchy. Without an appeal beyond the ranks of the middle classes, they would not have held office for the greater part of the period.

> **Key term**
>
> **Class dealignment**
> the process where individuals no longer identify themselves as belonging to a certain class and do not vote for the party they may be expected to, given their background.

A BBC comedy sketch from the 1960s depicting upper, middle and working-class stereotypes. The clear-cut distinction between classes, parodied here, was to be eroded in subsequent decades.

The link between class and voting is no longer as pronounced as it was in the years after the Second World War. As society has become more affluent and working-class people have aspired to a middle-class way of life, the differences between people in terms of class have not been as visible. This was already apparent by the time of the 1979 election, but it gathered pace in the 1980s, promoted by the sale of council houses to their tenants under the Thatcher government. The decline of the old heavy industries reduced trade union power, while the service sector, which was less unionised, expanded. The privatisation of many industries and services reduced the size of the public sector, which was traditionally a source of support for the Labour Party. The creation of **New Labour** in the 1990s was a recognition of this trend.

Tony Blair's victory in 1997 owed a great deal to his ability to broaden the appeal of the party, appealing to middle-class voters, as well as Labour's traditional working-class base. This was symbolised by the dropping of its historic commitment to the public ownership of key industries – such as the railways and energy companies – in 1995.

However, it is still the case that voters in the highest classes are more likely to vote Conservative than Labour. The reverse is true in the lowest occupational groups. There is also a link between class and patterns of turnout at general elections. Members of the electorate who have more at stake financially – through the ownership of property, savings and investments – are more inclined to vote than the poor, who may believe that the political system delivers little for them. In 2010, 76 per cent of the two highest social classes voted, compared with 57 per cent of the two lowest classes. Another indicator was the gap between those who owned their own homes (74 per cent) and those living in social housing or in the private rented sector (55 per cent).

Partisanship and voting attachment

Another feature of the last third of the 20th century, and the early years of the 21st, has been **partisan dealignment**. This is a decline in the attachment felt by many voters to one of the two major parties. In the past this loyalty had been instilled by family tradition and the influence of the workplace and local community. These bonds were weakened as people became less likely to work in the same industry for their whole lives; improving education reinforced this process.

Link

For more on **New Labour**, see Section 2.2 of Political Parties.

Key term

Partisan dealignment the process where individuals no longer identify themselves on a long-term basis as being associated with a certain political party.

More people have become floating, or swing, voters who do not identify with a particular party and are open to persuasion at each election. In part this is the result of a growing sense of **disillusion** and **apathy**: a loss of confidence in the capacity of politics and politicians to solve problems and make a difference. The size of the core vote for the Conservatives and Labour – the section of the electorate who can be relied upon to support one of these two large parties – has diminished. In 1979, 81 per cent of the electorate cast their votes for Labour and the Conservatives. By 1997 this had fallen to 74 per cent, and to 65 per cent by 2010.

> ### Pause & reflect
>
> What do you think are the most important reasons for the decline of the core vote for the two largest parties since 1945?

Governing competency and voter choice

Another way of explaining voting behaviour is known as rational choice theory: the idea that voters behave like consumers, deciding how to vote by evaluating what is the most beneficial option for them as individuals. Voters look at the policies on offer and choose the party most closely aligned to their preferences. This is linked to the growth of a more educated electorate, with more access to political information, particularly since the rise of the internet. This approach is problematic because it assumes that voters make rational choices based upon a knowledge of party policies. It does not explain elections where voters feel differently about different issues, or where there is no single overriding issue.

A refinement of rational choice theory is that voters are influenced not by detailed party policies but by questions such as:

- Who is the best potential prime minister among the available party leaders?
- Who is expected to manage the economy most successfully?
- Who will provide the best-quality public services?

Many skilled workers voted Conservative for the first time in 1979, in response to Margaret Thatcher's populist style, and because they had become disenchanted with the perceived incompetence of Labour governments in the 1970s. They stayed with the Conservatives for the next three general elections (1983, 1987 and 1992). However, they transferred their support to New Labour in 1997 as evidence of poor management by John Major's government began to accumulate. They also voted Labour in 2001 and 2005, but abandoned the party in 2010 after their faith in it was weakened by the financial crisis and the ensuing recession.

At each of these elections, voters were passing judgment on the **governing competency** of the main parties. For a party in office, this means assessing how successfully it has managed the business of government. Policy success – notably in the management of the economy, together with evidence of a clear agenda and united, strong leadership – are key indicators. In the case of an opposition party, voters are deciding on its potential governing competence if it were to achieve office.

A variant of the rational choice theory is the economic voting model. This holds that voters are more likely to support a governing party if it has managed the economy successfully. Alternatively, they may give their support to a party that is thought likely to deliver economic prosperity, either to voters themselves and their families, or to the population as a whole. Voters may be influenced by factors such as inflation, unemployment, interest rates and taxation, or more generally by a

Key terms

Disillusion
disappointment from discovering something is not as good as one believed it to be; for example, having no confidence in politics and politicians as being able to solve issues and make a difference.

Apathy
lack of interest, enthusiasm, or concern; for example, not caring about political activity, which manifests itself in low turnout at elections and poor awareness of contemporary events.

Key term

Governing competency
the perceived ability of the governing party in office to manage the affairs of state effectively. It also applies to the way that voters regard the potential competency of an opposition party, if it were to win office.

broader sense of well-being, sometimes known as the 'feel good factor'. Public anger over the 'winter of discontent' played a major part in the Conservatives' election victory in 1979. The absence of the 'feel good factor' also worked to the Conservatives' advantage in the 2010 election, as they were able to portray Labour as having responded inadequately to the financial crisis.

The public image of party leaders has become more important in recent decades as politics has become increasingly personalised. Commentators have talked about the 'presidentialisation' of British politics since the 1979 election. The suggestion is that UK election campaigns are increasingly shaped by voters' perceptions of the leading figures, as they are in United States' presidential contests. Blair modelled himself to a great extent on Thatcher's strong leadership qualities. Brown notoriously failed to come across as a dynamic, assured leader in 2010, although the election result suggests that voters were not fully persuaded by Cameron as a replacement for him.

Parties appreciate the importance of presenting their leaders in a good light. Attention is given to 'photo opportunities' that will show the leader's human touch. In the run-up to the 2010 elections, the parties agonised over arrangements for the first televised debates between the leaders. Leaders' appearances have become increasingly stage-managed, to avoid possibly awkward encounters with members of the public who may react in a negative manner. Most meetings featuring cheering, placard-waving crowds do not really involve the general public. Instead trusted supporters are drafted in to give the impression of spontaneous enthusiasm for the leader.

> ### Pause & reflect
>
> Reviewing the evidence discussed so far in this chapter, what do you feel is the most important single influence on voter choice: the image of the party leaders, the economic record of the government, or a more general perception of a party's competence to govern? Justify your answer.

Gender, age, ethnicity and region as factors in influencing voting behaviour, turnout and trends

Historically women had a slightly stronger preference for the Conservatives than male voters did. This may have been because women favoured a stable society and, as the main carers in most households, they responded to the traditional Tory emphasis on the family.

In the Blair era the difference between male and female voting habits lessened, with younger women being slightly more likely than men to vote Labour. This may be because, by the 1990s, women were as likely as men to have a job outside the home, so their worlds became more similar. Alternatively they may have been responding to New Labour's more family-friendly policies, such as the provision of free nursery places.

Older women are more likely to vote Conservative than younger women. In this sense they are similar to men. In the 2010 election 30 per cent of women aged 18–24 voted Conservative, while for women over 55 this rose to 42 per cent. The party leaders recognised the importance of younger women as a constituency, targeting them through platforms such as the parenting advice website Mumsnet.

Turnout does not differ significantly between men and women. In the 2010 election, 66 per cent of men and 64 per cent of women voted. Turnout among men and women of the same social class was also strikingly similar.

Age

Older people exhibit a greater tendency than the young to vote Conservative. As they are more likely to own property, they will vote for the party that can be expected to protect their material interests. Age means that they are also less likely to vote idealistically, or with the aspiration of fundamentally changing society.

In addition, political outlooks are shaped by voters' experiences. Older voters today will remember the difficulties faced by Labour governments in the 1970s, when trade unions enjoyed greater power, and this may influence them to support the Conservatives – not a factor for voters in their 20s. In 2010, 44 per cent of over-65-year-olds favoured the Conservatives, compared to just 30 per cent of 18–24 year olds. In recognition of this trend David Cameron refused to cut pensioner benefits, while Labour and the Liberal Democrats argued for the removal of the winter fuel allowance from better-off retired people.

Age is an important factor in patterns of turnout. Older people are more likely than the young to vote – 76 per cent of those over 65 did so in 2010, compared to 44 per cent of the 18–24 age group. The elderly have acquired habits of voting earlier in their lives, and tend to see the outcome of elections as having more impact on their lives. Younger people are more likely to feel alienated from a political system that has not, as they see it, made a significant difference to their lives.

Ethnicity

Ethnic minorities are traditionally more inclined to vote Labour, which has focused more strongly than its opponents on promoting a multi-cultural and anti-discrimination agenda. There is a link to class here, as members of minorities are disproportionately employed in low-wage jobs. One exception is that Asians are more likely to support the Conservatives than voters of African descent, because the former respond in particular to the party's emphasis on small business values. However, overall, ethnic minority voters have remained loyal to Labour. In 2010 they preferred Labour to the Conservatives by 60 to 16 per cent. Ethnicity is also a significant discriminator when it comes to turnout, with 67 per cent of white people voting in 2010, compared to only 51 per cent of ethnic minority groups.

While gender, age and ethnicity seem to be the current variables, the relative importance of different factors varies. For example, in the 2016 EU referendum, education was possibly the most important factor. Those without qualifications went 75 per cent for Brexit, while those with university degrees went 75 per cent against.

Region

There is a strong regional bias to voting patterns, linked in part to class differences. Most voters in the south (with the important exception of London) and in rural areas and suburbs – the most prosperous areas with the highest levels of employment and home ownership – are typically Conservative supporters. Conversely, in industrial and urban areas, in the north of England, Wales and (to a lesser extent) the Midlands – the poorer areas of the country – there is much stronger loyalty to Labour.

As Table 1.4 shows, it is not easy to see patterns in turnout across the countries that make up the UK. Participation in Northern Ireland has fallen. This may be because the political situation had stabilised by the early 21st century. When conflict was more marked, turnout tended to be higher, possibly because voters were more concerned about the outcome of elections.

Election	UK	England	Wales	Scotland	Northern Ireland
1997	71.4	71.4	73.5	71.3	67.1
2001	59.4	59.2	61.6	58.2	68.0
2005	61.4	61.3	62.6	60.8	62.9
2010	65.1	65.5	64.7	63.8	57.6
2015	66.1	65.8	65.7	71.1	58.1
2017	68.7	69.1	68.6	66.4	65.4

Table 1.4: Percentage turnout in different parts of the UK at general elections since 1997

However, there is a class dimension in relation to turnout in different English regions. In the 2010 contest, turnout in the south-east and south-west was 68.0 per cent and 69.1 per cent respectively, while in the less affluent north-west it was 62.6 per cent.

Class retains some importance as a determinant of voting behaviour. There is a link between voting and the degree to which people feel included in society. The elderly, the better-off, white people and those who live in more prosperous parts of the country are more likely to believe that they can affect the outcome of elections and so protect their interests.

EXTENSION ACTIVITY

Look at the policies of the main political parties during the most recent general election. Can you find evidence in their manifestos that their policies were designed to win the support of particular groups such as the elderly and the more prosperous?

Analysis of the national voting behaviour patterns for the 1979, 1997 and 2010 elections

Class and voting behaviour

Class remains a factor in determining voting habits. The UK Office for National Statistics uses the following descriptors of social class, based on occupation.

Social class	Description
AB	Higher and intermediate managerial, administrative and professional occupations
C1	Supervisory, clerical and junior managerial, administrative and professional occupations
C2	Skilled manual occupations
DE	Semi-skilled and unskilled manual occupations, unemployed and lowest grade occupations

Table 1.5: Social class and voting behaviour

Voters in the highest classes are more likely to vote Conservative than Labour. The reverse is true in the lowest occupational groups, as is shown in Table 1.6.

General election	1979	1997	2010
Middle class (ABC1)			
Conservative	59	39	39
Labour	24	34	27
Liberal/Lib Dem	15	20	26
Skilled working class (C2)			
Conservative	41	27	37
Labour	41	50	29
Liberal/Lib Dem	15	16	22
Semi/unskilled working class (DE)			
Conservative	34	21	31
Labour	49	59	40
Liberal/Lib Dem	13	13	17

Table 1.6: The relationship between class and voting behaviour in the 1979, 1997 and 2010 general elections showing percentage support for the main parties

---

Pause & reflect

Review the evidence presented in Table 1.6. Do these figures support the view that there has been a process of class and partisan dealignment since the 1970s?

Gender and voting behaviour

General election	1979	1997	2010
Men			
Conservative	43	31	38
Labour	40	45	28
Liberal/Lib Dem	13	17	22
Women			
Conservative	47	32	36
Labour	35	44	31
Liberal/Lib Dem	15	18	26

Table 1.7: The relationship between gender and voting behaviour in the 1979, 1997 and 2010 elections showing percentage support for the main parties

---

Pause & reflect

What does Table 1.7 show about the relationship between gender and voting behaviour in these three elections? How might you explain this?

Age and voting behaviour

General election	1979	1997	2010
18–24 year olds			
Conservative	42	27	30
Labour	41	49	31
Liberal/Lib Dem	12	16	30
25–34 year olds			
Conservative	43	28	35
Labour	38	49	30
Liberal/Lib Dem	15	16	29
Over 65 year olds			
Conservative	No data	36	44
Labour	No data	41	31
Liberal/Lib Dem	No data	17	16

Table 1.8: The relationship between age and voting behaviour in the 1979, 1997 and 2010 general elections showing percentage support for the main parties

> **Pause & reflect**
>
> What does Table 1.8 show about the relationship between age and voting behaviour? Suggest possible explanations for any trends that you find.

4.2 The influence of the media

The role of the media in politics and its impact

It is not easy to give a categorical answer to the question, how far does the media influence politics? By the 21st century a variety of forms of media were available in the UK, which impacts on politics in different ways both at elections and in the intervals between them.

The oldest form of media is the newspaper press. Circulation of most newspapers has declined in recent years as voters have increasingly turned to new media, notably the internet from the 1990s and social media from the 2000s. However, the press continues to be important. Many people now read newspapers online. Television and radio news programmes take up stories that the press has publicised, and newspaper journalists are often quoted and interviewed on other media.

Television still dominates media coverage of elections, and is probably the most important means by which voters obtain political information. An estimated 9.6 million people watched the first of the leaders' debates in the 2010 election campaign. Seven million viewers watched the leaders' debate on ITV in the 2015 election and 4 million watched a further BBC debate in which only the opposition party leaders took part. In 2017, ahead of the June general election, just 3.5 million viewers watched a leaders' debate on the BBC, which saw Prime Minister Theresa May deputised for by Home Secretary Amber Rudd.

Newspaper title	Party endorsed at 2015 election	1997	2010	2016
The Sun	Conservative	3,877,097	3,006, 565	1,787,096
Daily Mail	Conservative	2,344,183	2,120,347	1,589,471
Daily Mirror	Labour	2,442,078	1,218, 425	809,147
Daily Express	UKIP	1,241,336	674,640	408,700
Daily Telegraph	Conservative	1,129,777	691,128	472,033
The Guardian	Labour	428,010	302,285	164,163
The Times	Conservative	821,000	508,250	404,155
The Independent	Continuation of coalition/Liberal Democrat	288,182	185,815	55,193

Table 2.1: Average daily circulation figures for selected national newspapers since 1997, and broad political affiliation

> **Pause & reflect**
>
> How do you think the leadership debates may have influenced voters? How important were they in shaping people's voting behaviour?

Opinion polls

Polls, run by firms including Ipsos MORI, Populus and YouGov, aim to gauge the popularity of political parties by asking a sample of people how they intend to vote. They also ask the public more detailed questions about their opinion of the party leaders and their policies. Opinion polls have become an integral part of election campaigns. The parties take note of their findings and conduct their own polls. Another variation is the exit poll, which asks voters how they have voted as they leave the polling station. This does not, of course, take account of people who have voted in advance by post.

Opinion polls are not always accurate. In 1992 most failed to predict John Major's 21-seat majority. Instead the majority of polls predicted either a narrow Labour victory or a hung parliament. There were different explanations for the inaccuracy. Some commentators suggested that there was a 'boomerang effect' – the polls had shown Labour in the lead early in the campaign, causing voters who did not want a Labour victory to turn out and cause a late swing to the Conservatives. It was also suggested that the results had been skewed by the phenomenon of so-called 'shy Tories': people who intended to vote Conservative but did not want to declare themselves in public because they felt self-conscious about supporting a party that was viewed as 'uncaring'. In response to this, the polling firms adjusted the way in which they selected their samples, and made more use of telephone polling, which was considered more accurate than face-to-face interviews.

The polling agencies were wrong again in 2015. They correctly predicted that the Scottish National Party would overwhelm Labour, which had previously been a powerful force in Scotland but, at UK level, on average they predicted that Labour and the Conservatives would each win about 34 per cent of the vote. This proved to be some way off the mark: in the event the Conservatives won a small majority with 36.9 per cent of the vote, leaving Labour with 30.4 per cent. An inquiry found that the polling firms had not surveyed a representative selection of the nation's voters.

In particular, they did not question enough retired people, who were more likely to be Conservative supporters, and they interviewed too many politically engaged young people, who were untypical of their age group and were more likely to vote Labour.

What has the impact been of changing types of media?

The internet played little if any part in politics during the first decade of its existence, the 1990s. As late as 2000 only 26 per cent of households had internet access. This figure had risen to 82 per cent by the time of the 2010 election, leading the political parties to make extensive use of the internet to reach the electorate. Most MPs had their own websites, which became the most important way for the public to learn about their activities and to communicate with them. Established media outlets such as the BBC set up their own websites, and major newspapers had started to appear online as well as in print.

Another new feature by 2010 was the rise of social media, such as Facebook and Twitter. By 2015 these platforms had been joined by Snapchat and Instagram, and this was widely expected to be the first general election in which social media would play a major role. The parties were certainly aware of the potential of the new media. They learned from the success of Barack Obama in making extensive use of social media to target different groups of voters in the 2012 US presidential election. For example, in the 2015 election campaign, the Conservatives reportedly spent £100,000 a month on Facebook advertising.

These developments have helped parties to reach the young in particular. A survey on the eve of the 2015 election indicated that 79 per cent of 18–24 year olds relied almost totally on online sources to inform themselves, while 59 per cent depended on social media to discover others' opinions on politics. This generation has not acquired habits of buying and reading newspapers, which they see as too expensive, less convenient and not fully up to date in an era of 24-hour news coverage.

However, these considerations do not apply with the same force to older people, who are much more likely to turn out to vote. They continue to derive their news from the press and television, and to read the contributions of columnists and commentators for interpretations of political events. There is little evidence that social media played a major role in shaping the overall outcome of the 2015 election.

The political parties clearly believe in the continued importance of the press and television. In the 2015 election, Conservative-supporting newspapers repeated David Cameron's claim that if voters did not choose his party, they risked putting a weak Labour government in office, propped up by the SNP. *The Daily Telegraph* printed an appeal from 5000 small business owners not to place the economic recovery in jeopardy, and to give Cameron a mandate to finish what he had started under the coalition. Similarly, Cameron was anxious in 2015 to make sure that, if he could not evade participation in televised debates, the timing and format of these events should work in his favour.

More generally, over the last three decades political leaders have become more conscious of the importance of projecting a favourable image in the media, and of seeking to control the news agenda as far as possible. This reached a peak under the New Labour governments, which took the business of news management very seriously. This was the era when the term 'spin doctor' was coined. To cope with the arrival of 24-hour news in the 1990s Tony Blair recruited a press secretary, Alastair Campbell, who was the political editor of *Today* newspaper at the time. Blair's Number 10 developed a so-called 'grid' of forthcoming events so that news announcements could be made around them, presenting the government in the best light.

Later governments have been no less controlling. In his memoirs Kenneth Clarke, an independent-minded member of David Cameron's coalition Cabinet, tells a story that illustrates this. Early in 2014 he was informed by Downing Street that he was not needed for the BBC's *Question Time* because the programme makers had inadvertently booked another minister to appear. When Clarke telephoned to verify the story, the programme makers expressed surprise; they had been told by the Number 10 Press Office that he could not be on the panel because he was unwell. The only possible conclusion was that Number 10 preferred to have a spokesman who could be relied on to toe the agreed government line.

Alastair Campbell (left), pictured with Tony Blair during his time as Downing Street Press Secretary and Director of Communications and Strategy, 1997–2003.

Another sign of the importance of the media is that governments have been increasingly making important policy announcements in television studios rather than in the traditional arena of the House of Commons. Ministerial speeches are often summarised in the press before they have been delivered. As long as politicians continue to believe that the media is important, it will retain its influence.

Debates around bias and persuasion in the media

The media in a democratic society

A free media is a vital feature of a healthy democracy and can play an essential role in holding governments to account, especially when parliamentary opposition is weak, as it was for much of the New Labour era. However, there are concerns about the role of the media in politics. Popular newspapers, in particular, tend to present an unduly simplified interpretation of political issues, focusing excessively on personalities. Newspaper owners are primarily interested in boosting their circulation figures and cannot be held to account in the same way that politicians can.

Case study: The 2011 phone hacking scandal

The 2011 phone hacking scandal, which revealed that employees of Rupert Murdoch's News International had been involved in illegal information gathering, further reduced public trust in the press. The scandal led to the closure of the newspaper involved, the *News of the World*, and to an inquiry into the culture, practices and ethics of the press, headed by a senior judicial figure, Lord Justice Leveson. The inquiry resulted in the creation of a new body to regulate the press more effectively, the Independent Press Standards Organisation, headed by a retired judge. The powers of this body remain a matter of controversy. Supporters see it as a reasonable response to concerns about press behaviour, since the previous practice of self-regulation had been shown to have serious shortcomings. Critics, on the other hand, have voiced anxieties regarding the future of freedom of speech.

Question

- What happened in the phone hacking scandal? Use the internet to research more details of this episode.

Media bias and the political parties

Newspapers are notoriously partisan and will alter their allegiance in response to changing circumstances as much as to any ideological loyalties. For example, *The Sun* began as a Labour-supporting paper but switched to the Conservatives in the mid-1970s. Its owner, Rupert Murdoch, responded to Margaret Thatcher's hard-line approach to the trade unions, which was in line with his business interests. In the run-up to the 1997 election *The Sun* abandoned the Conservatives as John Major's government disintegrated and Tony Blair showed that business had nothing to fear from New Labour. It returned to the Conservatives after repudiating Gordon Brown prior to the 2010 election.

Television is less biased in its coverage than newspapers. Terrestrial television must be balanced; by contrast the press, in spite of Leveson, is practically free from regulation. The BBC Charter insists on political neutrality, and this is by and large followed by the other terrestrial channels. Parties are allocated agreed amounts of air time for their election broadcasts, based on their voting strength in the last contest and the number of constituencies they are contesting.

Websites and social media platforms are not subject to control of their content, and so are likely to be more biased than traditional broadcasters.

How much influence do the media have on the public?

It seems unlikely that the influence of the press causes people to change their voting behaviour. It is best to be sceptical of claims that newspapers have decided the outcome of elections, the best known example of which was *The Sun* editorial on the day of the 1992 election, picturing Labour leader Neil Kinnock's head in a lightbulb and urging its readers: 'If Kinnock wins today will the last person to leave Britain please turn out the lights.' After Labour lost, the paper celebrated with a headline that was to become notorious: 'It's *The Sun* wot won it.'

In fact most people read newspapers that broadly reflect their outlook, so papers usually confirm their readers' existing political views. However, the importance of the press as a reflection of public opinion should not be discounted – the winning party at each recent election was supported by the majority of the press. In 2010 and 2015 the *Daily Mirror* was the only major popular national daily that still backed Labour. The press may also shape the political agenda through the way it covers political issues. This may be more important in an age of class and party dealignment, when voters' loyalties to political parties are more changeable.

The self-congratulatory headline on the front of *The Sun* after Labour's defeat in the 1992 general election.

The influence of television is also hard to judge with certainty. A survey found that 62 per cent of respondents cited television as the strongest influence in helping them form an opinion in the run-up to the 2015 election, while only 25 per cent put newspapers first. Figures for other forms of media were much smaller. However, it is important not to exaggerate the role of television in changing people's opinions. In the 2010 election, Nick Clegg enjoyed a boost in the polls following an impressive performance in the first televised debate. This proved to be a temporary triumph as voters swung back to the two larger, more familiar parties in the final stages of the campaign. Nonetheless, the raising of the Liberal Democrat leader's profile may have helped to deny the Conservatives an independent majority and so had an indirect influence on the outcome.

The importance of television lies in the way that it projects visual images, helping voters to form an impression of the party leaders. The relentlessly negative coverage of Jeremy Corbyn since his election as Labour leader in September 2015 centred as much on his personality and appearance as on his policies. This did not damage his reputation among the party faithful, who chose him as leader in preference to his more conventional parliamentary rivals, but it may have prevented him from becoming established with the wider public.

It seems reasonable to conclude that electronic media, like the press, reinforces rather than changes political attitudes. So many differing views are available on websites, blogs and other online forums that it is unlikely that many users will deliberately seek out those that conflict with their own views. Social media more often provides a vehicle for trivial political stories, rather than a serious forum for debate. It is hard to make a case that it has so far done much more than register the increasingly fragmented, personalised nature of modern politics.

Assessment support: 1.1.4 Voting Behaviour and the Media

Question 1 on A-Level Paper 1 gives you a choice of two 30-mark questions, to be completed in 45 minutes. Each question is based on one or possibly two sources. You may be given a piece of written text or a combination of text and data, such as a table, pie chart or graph.

This source is adapted from a blog by Dr Andrew Defty of the University of Lincoln, entitled 'Press affiliation and the 2015 General Election', posted 19 November 2015.

'*At the 2015 general election five out of 11 national daily newspapers supported the Conservative Party. Only two supported Labour,* The Mirror *and* The Guardian. *Conservative press share in 2015 was 71% compared to 15% for Labour and 5% for the Liberal Democrats. The overwhelming Conservative domination of the press would seem to reinforce the argument that press support is central to electoral fortunes.*

However, it is hard to know exactly what influence, if any, the press has on voting behaviour. The newspaper one reads does not necessarily define one's political affiliation. There is clearly some link; polling data from 2015 clearly indicates that the majority of Guardian *and* Mirror *readers vote Labour while the overwhelming majority of* Telegraph *and* Daily Mail *readers vote Conservative. However, a small proportion of* Guardian *readers vote Conservative (6%), and research shows that a large proportion of Labour MPs are avid readers of* The Daily Mail, *and not always to find out what the Conservative opposition thinks.*

The circulation of daily newspapers in the UK is in seemingly terminal decline. Out of a total electorate in May 2015 of around 45 million, the total daily circulation of national newspapers in the UK was around 7 million, one in six voters. It is hard to attribute significant political influence to newspapers which are read by such a small proportion of the voting public. However, while print sales are in decline this has been at least partly offset by the online presence of Britain's daily newspapers, which has grown significantly in recent years.

Britain has a highly partisan press and in recent years political parties have spent a great deal of energy and money chasing the endorsement of various sections of the print media. However, there are significant questions about whether this has a significant or indeed any impact on electoral fortunes.'

Source: whorunsbritain.blogs.lincoln.ac.uk/2015/11/19/press-affiliation-and-the-2015-general-election

Using the source, evaluate the view that the newspaper press does NOT have a major influence on voting behaviour. [30 marks]

In your response you must:

* *compare the different opinions in the source*

* *consider this view and the alternative to this view in a balanced way*

* *use knowledge and understanding to help you to analyse and evaluate.*

Sources used in this type of question will contain different viewpoints. In this case, the source puts forward some evidence that newspapers played an important role in the 2015 general election, although overall it argues that the influence of the press on voting behaviour should not be exaggerated.

You are expected to write a comparative answer, in which you offer analysis and evaluation related to information drawn from the source. The question assesses all three Assessment Objectives, with the marks divided equally between them. If you do not provide any comparative analysis of the source, or you do not consider both views in a balanced way, you cannot get higher than the top of Level 2 – a maximum of 12 marks out of 30.

* Don't start writing straight away. Take a few minutes to read through the source carefully, annotating it with comments that may form part of your answer.

* At the highest level, examiners are looking for thorough and in-depth knowledge and understanding.

* Make sure that you consider both views presented in the extract.

* Finally, provide a conclusion in which you reach an overall judgement on the two different views.

Here is an example taken from the middle part of a student's answer to this question.

The author shows that there is a strong correlation between the voting habits of many people and their choice of newspaper. He does show that there are some exceptions to this. However, the examples he gives are not necessarily very significant; the six per cent of *Guardian* readers who vote Conservative, mentioned here, are not a very large proportion. It is more striking that many Labour MPs read the *Daily Mail*, a traditional Conservative-supporting newspaper, but they may of course also read other media with a different political slant. It certainly seems unlikely, whatever their motives may be for reading the *Daily Mail*, that it affects their political views. These examples do not necessarily invalidate the basic point, that most people tend to choose papers which fit with their political preferences.

* This is an effective paragraph because it links together relevant pieces of information taken from within the source.

* The student does not just extract information, but offers possible explanations of the points made in the source. The paragraph is clearly part of a reasoned, analytical answer.

* The student offers a judgement on the evidence presented in the source. This would score highly for evaluation.

Conservatism

Conservatism aims to conserve society in its existing form and conservatives are wary of change. They prefer pragmatism to ideological thinking and they attempt to adapt conservatism's core ideas and principles gradually over time, in line with changes in society. During the 1970s and 1980s, however, New Right conservative thinking challenged many of the key elements of traditional conservatism.

In this section you will learn about:

- the core ideas and principles of conservatism
- the differing views and tensions within conservatism
- key conservative thinkers and their ideas.

1.1 Core ideas and principles

Pragmatism

Arguably, the key core value of conservatism is pragmatism, an idea usually associated with conservative thinkers such as **Edmund Burke** (1729–97) and **Michael Oakeshott** (1901–90). In political terms, pragmatism rejects theory and ideology in favour of practical experience – the approach to society should be flexible, with decisions made on the basis of what works. Oakeshott summarised that 'to be a Conservative is to prefer the tried to the untried'. Pragmatism also implies a flexible approach to politics that considers what is in the best interests of the people, what is acceptable to the public and what will maintain social stability and cohesion.

Link

For more on **Edmund Burke**, see Section 1.3.

For more on **Michael Oakeshott**, see Section 1.3.

Conservatives' preference for pragmatism is strongly linked to their view of human rationality. They contend that humans lack the intellectual ability and powers of reasoning to fully comprehend the complex realities of the world. As a result, conservatives tend to dismiss abstract ideas, theories and ideologies that claim to 'explain' or 'improve' human life and development. Principles and ideas such as human rights, a classless society and equality are dangerous because they can promote a radical reordering of society (often through revolution) that leads to worse rather than better conditions. Conservatives try to avoid a rigid ideological approach to issues, preferring to act in a pragmatic way that emphasises caution, moderation and a sense of historical continuity.

Critics argue that pragmatism reveals a lack of political principle and encourages politicians to follow rather than lead public opinion. In practice, political behaviour or action cannot be wholly separated from ideological or theoretical considerations.

Link

For more on **traditional conservatism**, see Section 1.2.

For more on **one-nation conservatism**, see Section 1.2.

Traditional and **one-nation conservatism** are the two strands of conservative thinking usually linked to pragmatism. For traditional conservatives, such as Edmund Burke, pragmatism was an essential element in facilitating 'natural' or inevitable change within a state or society. This type of change, he argued, should not be opposed because a state 'without the means of some change is without the means of its conservation' – for the state to keep going, it would have to adapt to some extent. Burke's conservatism maintained that cautious pragmatism would bring about necessary change peacefully, through evolution, whereas the unbending pursuit of revolution or reaction would lead to conflict and chaos. The key features of society – such as order, property,

Key term

Change to conserve
the idea that society should adapt to changing circumstances by introducing moderate reforms, rather than reject change outright and risk rebellion or revolution.

tradition and established institutions – can only be preserved through a pragmatic policy that takes into account shifting circumstances and recognises occasions when it is necessary to **change to conserve**.

One-nation conservatives hold similar attitudes to social reform. However, more recently they have also adopted a pragmatic 'middle way' approach to the economy that combines market competition with government regulation. These conservatives argue that this moderate economic course promotes growth and social harmony by encouraging wealth creation through private enterprise and generating the funding for state welfare programmes.

Case study: Conservative administrations 1951–64

Perhaps the clearest example of one-nation conservative pragmatism occurred in the years 1951–64 when a series of moderate Conservative administrations governed the UK. In opposition, the Conservative Party had opposed many aspects of the Labour government's domestic reform programme between 1945 and 1951. However, once back in power the Conservatives made no concerted attempt to reverse Labour's nationalisation of British industry or to dismantle the newly created welfare state. Aware that these initiatives were popular and, apparently, working well, successive Conservative governments took a pragmatic decision to retain Labour's reforms.

Question
- Were the Conservative governments of 1951–64 motivated purely by pragmatism?

Tradition

Another important core value of conservatism is its attachment to tradition – the institutions, customs and practices of a society that have developed over time. Originally, the conservative justification for tradition had religious roots. Conservatives who believed that the world was created by a divine being saw society's institutions and practices of society as 'God-given'. Humans who attempt to alter these longstanding social arrangements are challenging the will of God and consequently are likely to undermine society, rather than improve it.

Although religious fundamentalists still put forward this argument for tradition, this divine justification has been severely weakened by the impact of Enlightenment thinking (with its emphasis on rationalism and anti-clericalism) from the 18th century and the incorporation of obviously man-made innovations over time, such as representative democracy.

Nowadays, most conservatives offer two secular (or non-religious) arguments for the value of tradition.

First, drawing on the ideas of Edmund Burke and the writer G.K. Chesterton (1874–1936), conservatives maintain that tradition constitutes the accumulated wisdom of the past. According to this view, the institutions, customs and practices of the past (such as the monarchy, the constitution, the nuclear family and heterosexual marriage) have demonstrated their value to earlier societies as they have proved 'fit for purpose' over time and survived. For this reason, they should be preserved so that current and future generations can also benefit from them. For example, the monarchy has promoted a sense of national unity and pride over the centuries, seen most recently at the 2011 royal wedding. Thus, tradition establishes continuity and social stability.

This was Burke's point when he famously stated that society was a 'partnership not only between those who are living, but between those who are living, those who are dead and those who are to be born'. Each generation has a solemn duty to safeguard and pass on the accumulated wisdom of tradition to the next generation.

This view of tradition clearly influences the conservative attitude to change. According to conservatives, reform or change can only be justified if it evolves naturally in a peaceful, gradual way in order to strengthen existing institutions, customs and practices. Conservatives argue that, by seeking to destroy all traditional political and social institutions, the French in 1789 and the Bolsheviks in Russia in 1917 were cutting themselves off from their past and paving the way for regimes that were more tyrannical (such as the Terror of 1793–94, the Napoleonic Empire and the Stalinist dictatorship) than the ones they had toppled.

Secondly, conservatives champion tradition because, in their view, it provides society and the individual with a strong sense of identity. Long-established institutions, customs and practices are familiar and provide individuals with a historically based sense of belonging to a particular society.

Tradition fosters social cohesion and security because it offers humans a reassuring collective sense of who they are, and establishes powerful ties between people and specific societies. Conservatives claim that any attempt to implement radical, wide-ranging changes will cut people off from the 'traditional' basis of society and inevitably lead to instability, anxiety and insecurity.

Such arguments were used by Conservative opponents of the New Labour government's constitutional changes in the late 1990s. They asserted that innovations such as devolved assemblies and House of Lords reform would undermine the constitutional stability of the UK and create a mood of public uncertainty.

Human imperfection

Conservatives have a pessimistic view of human nature, arguing that people are flawed and incapable of reaching a state of perfection. Conservatism also asserts that human nature is immutable (remains constant). **Human imperfection** has to be kept in check due to the human capacity for evil.

Following from this, conservatives stress that:

- a tough stance on law and order is required, to deter criminal behaviour
- as human nature cannot be transformed, foreign policy has to be based on national security rather than 'liberal' notions of international co-operation and harmony
- human behaviour is competitive, so any successful political system will recognise that self-interest is a more powerful motivator than altruism.

For conservatives, humans are flawed in three ways: psychologically, morally and intellectually.

Organic society or state

Given that conservatives regard humans as dependent and security-seeking, it follows that people cannot exist separately from society as a whole or from social groups, such as the family or the local community. Society and social groups provide individuals with a sense of security and purpose, and prevent the development of anomie – a condition of instability affecting individuals and societies, produced by a breakdown in social standards and values or by a lack of purpose or ideals.

In turn, humans accept the duties, responsibilities and bonds that go with belonging to society or social groups, such as being a caring parent, a considerate neighbour, or a respectful son or daughter. For conservatives, this represents true freedom – the willing acceptance of the value of social obligations and ties. If people did not acknowledge and act on these responsibilities and bonds, human society would lack social cohesion and descend into **atomism**.

Key terms

Human imperfection
the traditional conservative belief that humans are flawed in a number of ways, which makes them incapable of making good decisions for themselves.

Atomism
the idea that society is made up of self-interested and self-sufficient individuals (also known as egoistical individualism). It can also describe increasing social breakdown and isolation.

Conservative view of human imperfection		
Psychological	**Moral**	**Intellectual**
Humans are limited and dependent. People crave safety, familiarity and the security of knowing their designated place in society.	Humans are morally imperfect because they are naturally selfish and greedy. Anti-social or criminal behaviour is due to basic human nature and cannot be attributed to economic or social disadvantage.	The intellect and reasoning of humans are limited. Humans do not possess the mental faculties to make sense of a complex modern world.
Such a view places a premium on social order rather than liberty because order provides humans with much-needed security, predictability and stability.	A robust law and order system that imposes severe sanctions on such conduct is the only effective deterrent to combat the moral imperfections of humans.	Consequently, conservatives reject overarching theories or ideologies that claim to explain or predict the development of human society.
In contrast, liberty raises the unsettling prospect of choice, change and uncertainty. For this reason, conservatives have frequently endorsed Thomas Hobbes' argument that social order has to come before liberty.		Instead humans need to draw on tradition, history and practical experience to understand their place in the world.

Figure 1.1: The three aspects of human imperfection

These assumptions lead conservatives to endorse organicism – the idea of an organic society or state. This perspective views society as a living organism, with all its parts working together in harmony to ensure that the 'body' remains healthy.

Here, two considerations are important.

- The internal elements of an organic society or state cannot be randomly reconfigured. Like a living creature, an organic society is maintained by a delicate set of relationships between these elements. If this careful balance is disturbed, the society will be undermined and possibly destroyed. For this reason, an organic society represents more than a collection of individual elements.

- An organic society is based on natural needs and instincts such as affection, security and concern, rather than an ideological blueprint devised by political theorists. Such a view of society – where its component parts have been moulded by natural forces beyond human control – suggests that its members should sustain this careful balance of interacting elements. In particular, long-standing institutions have played a key role in preserving the 'health' of society and should not be changed or removed.

Key terms

Hierarchy
the conservative belief that society is naturally organised in fixed and unequal tiers, where one's social position or status is not based on individual ability.

Authority
for conservatives, the idea that people in higher positions in society are best able to make decisions on behalf of other people or society as a whole; authority comes naturally from above and rests on an accepted obligation from below to obey.

Underpinning the idea of an organic society is the conservative belief in **hierarchy** and **authority**. Traditionally, conservatism has argued that society is naturally hierarchical – it is based on fixed social ranks and inequalities. This is partly to do with the fact that individuals vary in terms of their talents, intellect, skills and work rate. However, conservatism maintains that an organic society must rest on inequality, not just because of individual differences but also because different classes and groups (like different limbs and organs) have to perform specific roles. For example, some have to provide political leadership or manage commercial enterprises, while others have to perform routine manual or non-manual work, or raise children at home. Consequently, an organic society produces natural inequalities in terms of financial rewards and social status.

Such an arrangement, according to conservatives, can be justified because the most advantaged also bear the heaviest social responsibilities. Managers and employers enjoy higher living standards than their workers, but they carry the burden of protecting the jobs and economic well-being of their workforces. In this sense, a hierarchical organic society encourages **paternalism** as a means to ensure social cohesion.

For conservatives, the hierarchical structure of organic society is reinforced by authority. Conservatism contends that authority develops naturally or organically in much the same way as society. This form of authority operates in a top-down manner, shapes relations between the different social groups and permeates all social institutions. Authority therefore resides with political leaders, employers, managers, teachers, parents and so on.

Conservatives argue that authority performs a vital and positive function by providing humans with security, direction and support. Authority also promotes social cohesion by giving people a clear sense of how they 'fit in' and what they are expected to do. The leadership exercised by those in authority not only offers discipline, but also an example to be admired, respected and accepted.

Most conservatives assert that the actions of people holding such authority are limited by the natural responsibilities that accompany their privileged position. Employers, for example, have authority over their workers but this does not give them the right to abuse employees.

Paternalism

In conservative thought, paternalism is the idea of government by people who are best equipped to lead by virtue of their birth, inheritance and upbringing. Conservatives' belief in paternalism is inextricably linked to their views on hierarchy, order and the organic society. Traditional conservatives, such as Burke, argued that the 'natural aristocracy' presided over society much like a father did over his family; the social elite provides leadership because of its innate or hereditary abilities, just as a father exercises authority, ensures protection and provides guidance. Its skills and talents cannot be obtained by hard work or self-improvement. Those at the top of society have a duty to care for the lower social ranks. In the 18th and early 19th centuries, some conservative aristocrats acted in a paternalistic fashion by improving material conditions for their tenants and employees, and by involving themselves in charitable and philanthropic works.

The wisdom and experience of paternalistic leaders confer natural authority, because they 'know what is best' for the rest of society. Traditionally, these leaders were drawn from the aristocratic elite that had been educated in the values of social obligation and public service, and had provided the senior political decision-makers for generations. The Cecil family (Marquesses of Salisbury) and the Stanley family (Earls of Derby) are good examples of high-born paternalistic conservative political leaders. More recently, one-nation paternalistic conservatism has relied on government regulation of the economy and social welfare measures to improve conditions for the poorest in society. UK Conservative Prime Minister David Cameron (2010–16) also drew on paternalism when he called for 'compassionate conservatism'.

Paternalism can take two forms:

- soft – when those who are the recipients give their consent
- hard – when paternalism is imposed, regardless of consent or opposition, in a more authoritarian manner.

The origins of one-nation paternalistic conservatism are usually traced back to the works of Benjamin Disraeli (1804–81), who served as Conservative prime minister from 1874 to 1880. In his novels *Coningsby* (1844) and *Sybil* (1845), Disraeli warned that Britain was dividing into two nations – the rich and the poor – and that this increased the likelihood of social revolution. For Disraeli, such a situation could be averted only by the privileged in society recognising their social obligation and duty to look after the less fortunate. The well-off would preserve their advantages, but they would also alleviate the hardships faced by the lower orders and strengthen the social cohesion and stability of the nation. In this way, Disraeli's one-nation paternalism blended self-interest with principle. As prime minister, Disraeli translated this idea of paternalism into practice to a certain extent by passing a series of limited social reforms.

By the mid-20th century, one-nation conservatism had added a 'middle way' economic approach to social reform in its pursuit of paternalistic policies. The moderate UK Conservative governments of the 1950s and 1960s steered a central course between free-market economics and state planning, on the grounds that the former led to social fragmentation and failed to protect the poorest, while the latter stifled individual initiative and entrepreneurial flair. Economic policy combined government regulation and market completion to produce, in the words of Harold Macmillan, Conservative prime minister in the UK between 1957 and 1963, 'private enterprise without selfishness'. This effectively meant that one-nation conservatives fully accepted that the state had an obligation to intervene in the economy and maintain the welfare state to combat poverty and deprivation. Nevertheless, there were limits to paternalism, in the sense that improving conditions for poorer groups was principally motivated by a desire to strengthen the hierarchical nature of society by removing threats to the social order.

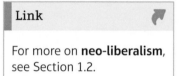

Link

For more on **neo-liberalism**, see Section 1.2.

In contrast, **neo-liberalism** completely rejects the idea of paternalism. Based partly on free-market economics, neo-liberalism aims to reduce the size of the state so that the unregulated market can generate a more dynamic and efficient economy leading to increased growth and prosperity. From this perspective, government intervention in the economy (a key element of the one-nation conservative paternalistic approach) or state control undermines human initiative and enterprise, resulting in economic stagnation. Similarly, the neo-liberal faith in individualism also challenges conservative notions of paternalism. By stressing the importance of self-help, individual responsibility and personal initiative, neo-liberals view welfare programmes and social reforms negatively. In their view, they promote a dependency culture among poorer people and undermine the free market.

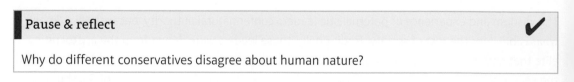

Pause & reflect ✔

Why do different conservatives disagree about human nature?

Libertarianism

Libertarianism is a political philosophy that emphasises the rights of individuals to liberty, advocating only minimal state intervention in the lives of citizens. The primary role of the state is to protect individual rights. Libertarianism, with its emphasis on maximum economic freedom and minimal government regulation in social affairs, provides a rival conservative core value to paternalism.

This libertarian idea has been evident in conservative thinking since the late 18th century, influenced by Adam Smith's arguments for economic liberalism. For example, Burke advocated free trade and a market economy on the grounds that such arrangements were efficient, just and 'natural' (due to the human desire for wealth). For conservatives, the operation of the capitalist free market represented a natural law that could not be altered without damaging prosperity and working conditions.

In its modern form, libertarian conservatism is more commonly known as the liberal **New Right** or neo-liberalism. Associated with the policies of UK Conservative Prime Minister Margaret Thatcher (1979–90) and US Republican President Ronald Reagan (1981–89), neo-liberalism rejects state intervention and champions the free-market economy. It fundamentally opposes **Keynesian**-style demand management and welfare programmes.

According to neo-liberal economists, the free market is the only mechanism that can efficiently supply goods and services on the basis of consumer demand. Only the market, not government intervention, can ultimately determine the 'natural' level of unemployment.

Neo-liberals consider inflation to be the biggest threat to the market economy. By undermining financial confidence, inflation inhibits all forms of economic and business activity. To combat inflation, neo-liberal thinkers call for government spending cuts to control the money supply. Both Thatcher and Reagan adopted this approach during the 1980s.

Neo-liberals also dismiss the mixed economy and public ownership on the grounds of expense and inefficiency, while endorsing 'supply side' economics as the path to growth and general prosperity. Government should focus on the 'supply side' to create the conditions to facilitate the highest possible levels of production. In practice, this means that producers' access to key economic resources (including capital, labour and land) has to be unrestricted – so obstacles such as government regulation, high taxation and trade union influence over the labour market must be removed. Underlying this is the assumption that the innovative and dynamic qualities of entrepreneurs and wealth creators can only flourish when freed from these restraints.

Neo-liberalism also justifies its opposition to state intervention by calling for individual liberty. Personal freedom can only be guaranteed by 'rolling back' the state, particularly social welfare programmes. The neo-liberal objection to state welfare is partly economic (public services are inefficient and increasingly expensive, placing greater burdens on taxpayers) and partly moral, as can be seen in Figure 1.2.

> **Link** ↗
>
> For more on the **New Right**, see Section 1.2.

> **Link** ↗
>
> For more on **Keynesianism**, see Section 2.2.

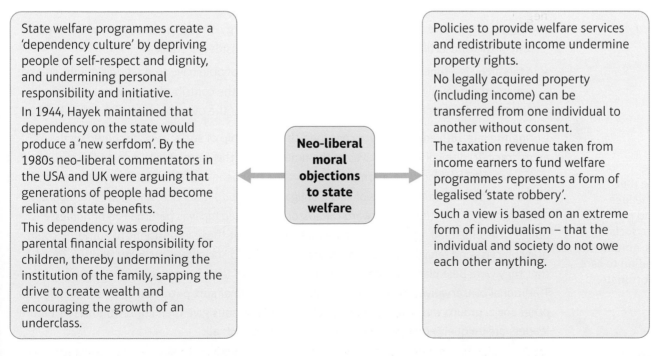

Figure 1.2: Neo-liberal moral objections to state welfare

1.2 Differing views and tensions within conservatism

Traditional conservatism

Traditional conservatism originated in the late 18th century as a reaction to the Enlightenment and the French Revolution. This strand of conservative thought is most clearly set out in Edmund Burke's *Reflections on the Revolution in France*, published in 1790. Broadly speaking, traditional conservatism defends the established order in society based on a commitment to organicism, hierarchy and paternalism. Traditional conservatives regard society as a sort of living or organic entity with complex interconnections and relationships. Any changes to one part will affect all the other parts, possibly in unforeseen and negative ways. Radical or abrupt changes are to be avoided. When change is desirable to adapt to a new situation, an organic society must evolve naturally at its own speed through small, pragmatic reforms to minimise any harmful consequences.

For traditional conservatives, an organic society is founded on tried and tested institutions (such as the family, the church and the monarchy) that in various ways confer privileges, authority, responsibilities and obligations. These social arrangements are held in place by custom and tradition – the accumulated wisdom and experience of the past – to maintain a society bound together by powerful bonds of loyalty, affection and duty. Any changes that are introduced must preserve the best features of society and reconcile them to new circumstances. Reform has to be pragmatic, drawing on the lessons of history and tradition to establish practical, effective solutions.

Traditional conservatives also argue that the implementation of ideological blueprints and abstract theory to bring about an ideal society can only lead to disaster, as the example of the Jacobins in the French Revolution demonstrates. Such an approach is not based on previous human experience and introduces drastic and swift changes that lead to social breakdown and destruction.

In order to sustain itself, say traditional conservatives, the organic society has to be organised as a hierarchy for two main reasons.

- People do not have the same abilities, talents and energy, so it is 'natural' that society should reflect this and 'artificial' that all humans should be considered equal.
- A hierarchy is a functional necessity because different people have to do different jobs and are rewarded differently (in pay and status) depending on the contribution they make. Hierarchy ensures that everyone works together harmoniously for the overall health of the social body.

During the late 18th and early 19th centuries, the leadership of society was assumed by the aristocracy. Traditional conservatives at the time justified this form of elite rule on the grounds that it was natural since, for generations, the upper class had been raised to govern at all levels and had also been educated in the values of social obligation and public service. Another contemporary conservative justification put forward for aristocratic leadership was paternalism or **noblesse oblige**. The longstanding practice of elite rule ensured that those in positions of authority could draw on class and family traditions of leadership, duty and social responsibility, and this meant that they were best placed to make decisions on behalf of (and for the good of) society as a whole. Traditional conservatives would consider this to be a form of **soft paternalism** since, in their view, other social groups within an organic society accept (and thus give their consent) that the 'natural' leaders are uniquely equipped to act in the best interests of all.

Key term

Noblesse oblige
a French phrase that encapsulates the idea that nobility and privilege bring with them social responsibilities, notably the duty and obligation to care for those less fortunate.

Link

For more on **soft paternalism**, see Section 1.1.

One-nation conservatism

One-nation conservatism, an updated version of traditional conservatism, emerged in response to the development of **laissez-faire** capitalism and industrialisation in the 19th century. Its central figure, Benjamin Disraeli, felt that capitalism encouraged a self-interested individualism that undermined the idea of social responsibility, and threatened to split Britain into two nations – the rich and the poor. If left unaddressed, he argued, this division would lead to class conflict, a declining sense of community and national identity, and possibly revolution.

To remedy this situation, Disraeli called for conservatism to renew its commitment to the concepts of reform and social obligation. His motives were both pragmatic and principled. Reforms to improve conditions for the poorest in society would reduce the likelihood of large-scale social discontent, preserving the position of the upper classes. Such measures would probably increase working class support for the Conservative Party too. Disraeli also maintained that the wealthiest and most privileged social groups had a moral duty to help the poor. Organic society depended not only on 'top down' authority, but also on the governing elite's acceptance of social responsibility for less fortunate people. In an industrialised capitalist society, Disraeli concluded, conservative paternalism should now embrace social reform or 'welfarism' to strengthen national unity and thus preserve 'one nation'. Table 2.1 shows the main features of Disraeli's one-nation conservatism.

Maintenance of traditional institutions	Imperialism	Reforms to improve conditions for the working class
In speeches at Manchester and Crystal Palace in 1872, Disraeli signalled his determination to uphold traditional British institutions, such as the monarchy and the Church of England. This was based on the 'one nation' view that such institutions had proved themselves over time, provided stability and offered a focus for national loyalty and identity across the classes. Disraeli's defence of these institutions included creating the title 'Empress of India' in 1876 for Queen Victoria, to link the monarch with Britain's sense of imperial pride.	At Manchester and Crystal Palace (1872), Disraeli also praised imperialism, arguing that the British Empire was not only a source of great national pride but also allowed Britain to play an influential role on the world stage. Disraeli's support for imperialism was an important element in 'one nation' thinking because the theme of empire appealed to all classes and linked conservative values to the 'mass politics' that was beginning to emerge in Britain from the late 1860s.	Social and other reforms were introduced to forge an alliance between the traditional ruling class and the workers, and to offset the negative effects of laissez-faire capitalism and remove the possibility of revolution. Examples: • Artisans' Dwellings Act (1875) • Sale of Food and Drugs Act (1875) • Conspiracy and Protection of Property Act (1875) • Second Reform Act (1867)

Table 2.1: Main features of Disraeli's one-nation conservatism

Disraeli's conception and pursuit of one-nation conservatism had a powerful influence on the development of conservative thinking. One-nation conservatism was most dominant in the years just after the Second World War. Between 1951 and 1964, successive Conservative governments in the UK based their policies on the one-nation perspective. They adopted **Keynesian** economic management techniques to maintain high employment, accepted the mixed economy and supported an expanded welfare state.

> **Key term**
>
> **Laissez-faire**
> minimal intervention in business and the state by the government.

> **Link**
>
> For more on **Keynesianism**, see Section 2.2.

This 'middle way' approach tried to navigate a path between unbridled liberalism (free-market economics and individualism) and socialist collectivism (extensive state planning and control). Harold Macmillan, the UK Conservative prime minister from 1957 to 1963, first coined the term 'the middle way' in 1938, in his book advocating a form of planned capitalism. For Macmillan, this was to be 'a mixed system' that combined 'state ownership, regulation or control of certain aspects of economic activity with the drive and initiative of private enterprise'. There was a clear link between the one-nation conservatism of mid-20th century Britain and Disraeli's original thinking. Another 'one-nation' Conservative minister during the 1950s and 1960s, R.A. Butler, argued that government policy at that time was focused on 'bringing together what Disraeli called the Two Nations into a single social entity'.

In recent years, the one-nation approach has continued to influence aspects of Conservative Party thinking and policy. David Cameron, the former Conservative prime minister (2010–16), drew on this legacy when he argued that a new 'compassionate conservatism' would underpin his government. His successor Theresa May did much the same thing in early 2017 when she called for the creation of a 'shared society' that would focus 'rather more on the responsibilities we have to one another' and respect 'the bonds of family, community, citizenship and strong institutions that we share as a union of people and nations'.

Pause & reflect ✔

Why was one-nation conservatism dominant in the early post-war decades?

The New Right

The New Right strand of conservatism gathered momentum from the mid-1970s as a rival to one-nation conservatism. New Right conservatism is founded on two distinct but, in certain respects, seemingly opposed ideological traditions:

- neo-liberalism or the liberal New Right – a modernised version of classical liberalism, based on a commitment to the free-market economy, the minimal state, and individual freedom and responsibility
- neo-conservatism or the conservative New Right – an updated form of traditional conservative social thinking, based on a commitment to order, traditional values and public morality.

By amalgamating these neo-liberal and neo-conservative ideas, the New Right contains **radical**, traditional and reactionary elements. Its determination to abandon government interventionism in economic and social affairs, and attack 'permissive' social attitudes (the belief that people should make their own moral choices) is clear evidence of the New Right's radicalism. At the same time, neo-conservatives stress the benefits of traditional values. New Right conservatism also exhibits reactionary tendencies. Both neo-liberals and neo-conservatives often appear to want to turn the clock back to the 1800s, which they regard as a mythical age of economic liberty and moral responsibility.

During the mid-1970s, Western governments using orthodox interventionist policies (based on **Keynesianism** and welfarism) were unable to combat 'stagflation' in their economies – a mixture of persistent inflation combined with high unemployment and stagnating demand. New Right thinking exerted a powerful influence in the USA and the UK where it became popularly associated with President Ronald Reagan and Prime Minister Margaret Thatcher. The terms 'Reaganism' and 'Thatcherism' became political labels for this New Right perspective, which also proved influential in Australia and other parts of Europe.

Key term 💬

Radical
a term used to describe beliefs, ideas or attitudes that favour drastic political, economic and social change.

Link ↗

For more on **Keynesianism**, see Section 2.2.

Neo-liberal features of Thatcherism	Neo-conservative features of Thatcherism
• Tight control of money supply through monetarist policies to control inflation and so encourage economic activity and investment • Privatisation of state-controlled industries (gas, electricity, water) on grounds of freedom, competition and efficiency • Promotion of free market through policies of deregulation affecting London's financial sector – the 'Big Bang' (1986) • Belief that trade union power was endangering UK's economic competitiveness led to anti-union legislation	• Defence of traditional values including support for heterosexual marriage and the nuclear family • Strong law-and-order policies based on support for police and punitive criminal justice • Opposition to permissive attitudes and 'alternative' lifestyles led to Section 28 (1988), a law prohibiting promotion of homosexuality • Determination to protect public morality led to government regulation of the UK video market, following concerns about 'video nasty' horror films

Table 2.2 Core principles and ideas of Thatcherism in action

Neo-liberalism

The economic problems affecting the West in the 1970s appeared to discredit Keynesianism and helped create a more receptive environment for neo-liberal thinking. Liberal New Right ideas call for:

- a minimal state
- self-reliant individuals capable of making rational decisions in their own interests
- the rejection of collectivism and
- the elimination of government intervention.

Neo-liberalism, promoted by the work of economists such as Milton Friedman and Friedrich Hayek, principally champions the free-market economy. It sees the free market as the only mechanism that can meet consumer demand for goods and services efficiently and widely, maximise the use of resources, and achieve the greatest overall prosperity. Neo-liberals argue that government intervention cannot solve economic problems (such as rising unemployment and inflation in the 1970s) or properly allocate resources within a developed economy. Government involvement merely causes these economic problems or makes them worse.

The liberal New Right maintains that the operation of the free market has to be protected against three main threats: monopolies, inflation and government intervention. Industrial or business monopolies, in their view, reduce economic competition, leading to distorted prices and consumer choice. Neo-liberals also contend that inflation is the 'great evil' in the market economy because any fall in the value of money discourages economic activity and investment, and breaks the relationship between price level and demand. Overcoming inflation, they argue, is the one vital role government can play in the economy.

Friedman asserted that **Keynesian** policies to stimulate demand create inflation by encouraging governments to print too much money or provide too much credit. His solution, known as monetarism, is for the government to reduce inflation by controlling the money supply through cuts in public spending. Both Thatcher and Reagan pursued monetarist policies to tackle inflation in the 1980s, convinced that the market would address the problem of mounting unemployment. The overall neo-liberal approach to economic policy is known as 'supply-side' economics, to distinguish it from the Keynesian focus on demand.

The liberal New Right regards government intervention in the economy as the most potent threat to the free market. State planning, nationalisation and high taxation are all rejected on the grounds that they distort the market and contribute to, rather than alleviate, economic problems. Margaret Thatcher embarked on an extensive privatisation policy in the 1980s that transferred state-owned industries to the private sector. Thatcher's justification was that nationalised industries were

Link

For more on **Keynesianism**, see Section 2.2.

inefficient and lacked the dynamism associated with the private sector's need to generate profits. Similar neo-liberal reservations apply to state welfare provision. In this view, welfare and social programmes expand, irrespective of demand, due to the vested interests of the professionals concerned (such as doctors, teachers and administrators) and politicians (who promise increased government spending on these services in order to secure votes at election time). The end result is higher taxation, rising inflation, and increasingly inefficient and bloated state services artificially protected from free-market competition. Consequently, many neo-liberals maintain that to improve efficiency, public services and other government agencies should be exposed to the competitive forces of the market economy.

Finally, neo-liberalism advocates atomistic individualism (the idea that individuals are rational, self-interested and self-sufficient), which is clearly linked to the liberal New Right belief in free-market economics. According to the liberal New Right, the freedom of the market is the guarantee of individual freedom. Neo-liberals view freedom in negative terms, stressing the need to remove external constraints or limitations on the individual. Individual freedom can only be preserved by opposing collectivism and rolling back the state. In this context, neo-liberals criticise state welfare policies for creating a dependency culture and infringing property rights by imposing high taxes on individuals to fund benefit payments. Such a system, in their view, actually institutionalises poverty and unemployment, and undermines atomistic individualism. If people no longer face government intervention and interference, they will be free to deal with each other without restrictions. These unhindered human interactions will create a 'natural' order vastly superior to any imposed model because it is based on everyone's consent.

The liberal New Right concludes that although humans may be selfish, they are rational and entitled to pursue their own interests in their own way as long as they accept others can do the same. This approach to individualism, claim neo-liberals, releases human potential and creates natural harmony through free relations between people.

Neo-conservatism

The other element of the New Right, known as neo-conservatism, can be seen as a mild type of authoritarianism. The development of neo-conservatism (or the conservative New Right) in the USA during the 1970s was a reaction against the reforms, ideas and permissive attitudes of the so-called 'liberal' 1960s. For neo-conservatives, these unwelcome changes threatened society with social fragmentation, which could only be stopped by strong political leadership and authority. Unlike the neo-liberals, the conservative New Right were driven primarily by political considerations.

Nevertheless, both components of the New Right agree on the necessity of reducing the state's role in the economy. The neo-conservative stress on authority and the need to preserve society shows that the conservative New Right is influenced to some extent by traditional conservative notions of organicism. However, neo-conservatism is much more authoritarian than one-nation conservatism, because it seeks to strengthen society by reasserting authority and social discipline, rather than through social reform and welfare measures.

Neo-conservatives focus mainly on the need to uphold social order and protect public morality. The conservative New Right maintains that since the 1960s authority and respect have declined in Western nations, leading to higher crime figures and increased rates of anti-social behaviour. Neo-conservatives have argued for the re-imposition of authority and discipline at every level of society, to restore the authority of traditional social structures such as the family with its 'natural' internal relationships based on hierarchy and patriarchy. In addition, the conservative New Right promotes the 'strong state' or state authoritarianism, with increased police powers and harsher punishments, to tackle crime and public disorder. Both Thatcher and Reagan adopted a tough stance on law and order in the 1980s, believing that prison sentences had to provide 'hard lessons' for those convicted of offences.

The neo-conservatives reject permissiveness suggesting there is no objective right and wrong. This **anti-permissiveness** and concern with public morality also stem from the emergence of a 'free-for-all' or 'anything goes' culture in some Western countries during the 1960s. The 'permissive society' of that era was roundly condemned by politicians such as Margaret Thatcher who advocated 'Victorian values', and organisations such as the Moral Majority in the USA that campaigned for traditional values. From the conservative New Right standpoint, there are two problems if a person is free to adopt their own moral code or lifestyle.

- The individual concerned may opt for an 'immoral' lifestyle – particularly unacceptable to religious elements within the neo-conservative ranks in the USA.

- People should not be free to choose different moral positions because this prevents the development of common moral standards, undermining social cohesion. For similar reasons, the conservative New Right is critical of multiculturalism, which, in their view, threatens social and national unity by dividing society along ethnic, racial and religious lines.

> **Key term**
>
> **Anti-permissiveness**
> a rejection of permissiveness, which is the belief that people should make their own moral choices.

> **EXTENSION ACTIVITY**
>
> How similar are the ideas of neo-liberals and neo-conservatives? Make a table that shows areas of overlap and difference.

Human nature	Most conservatives are pessimistic about human nature and regard people as imperfect, insecure and limited. Furthermore, from a conservative perspective, human nature is immutable, so it cannot be altered by changing economic, social or political conditions. This negative view of human beings shapes much of the conservative ideological outlook. Without firm government and a tough criminal justice system, argue conservatives, human behaviour would inevitably deteriorate. They also contend that idealistic or utopian political schemes (for example, based on fraternity or equality) will never curb humans' aggressive instincts. According to conservatives, capitalism is the only viable economic system because human nature is essentially competitive and self-interested. Neo-liberal conservatives, however, adopt atomistic individualism, maintaining that human beings can be self-reliant and rational in their decision-making.
The state	For one-nation conservatives, the state is a neutral agency and its primary role is to preserve social order through welfare programmes, economic interventionism and the defence of traditional institutions and values (such as the family and respect for authority). In contrast, the New Right exhibits both liberal and authoritarian attitudes towards the state. Neo-liberals call for the rolling back of the state on the grounds that state intervention stifles economic initiative and growth and creates a debilitating dependency culture. Neo-conservatives agree that the state's role in the economy needs to be reduced. Nevertheless, neo-conservatives also call for a 'strong state' (based on increased police powers, tougher punishments and anti-permissive policies) to combat crime, anti-social behaviour and 'permissive' attitudes.
Society	Traditional and one-nation conservatives have an organic view of society. All parts of this society, they argue, work together harmoniously to ensure a healthy 'social body'. Any change to internal elements of the organic society may jeopardise social stability by undermining tried and tested institutions. Such a society rests on the conservative belief in hierarchy and authority to give people the security of knowing their place and role in the social order, and the leaders' 'natural' top-down control over the other social groups. For conservatives, the privileges of the elite are balanced by a strong sense of social responsibility or paternalism towards the less fortunate. Neo-liberal conservatives, in contrast, reject the assumptions underpinning the organic society such as a 'natural' hierarchy and paternalism. Instead, neo-liberals view society as composed of independent and rational individuals operating within a free market. From this perspective, society is based on an individualism that releases human potential and establishes harmonious free relations between people.
The economy	All conservatives favour private enterprise but their views on the economy vary. One-nation conservatives endorse limited interventionist economic management techniques to maintain high employment levels, a mixed economy of private and public concerns, and state welfare programmes. They adopt this approach to avoid the perceived drawbacks of an unbridled free market and socialist collectivism, and prevent social instability. Both neo-conservatives and neo-liberals, in contrast, argue that the state's role in the economy has to be reduced. Neo-liberals, in particular, call for a free-market economy on the grounds that it is the best mechanism to meet consumer demand, maximise the use of resources and generate prosperity.

Table 2.3: Core principles and ideas of conservatism in action

1.3 Conservative thinkers and ideas

Thomas Hobbes (1588–1679)

Key ideas

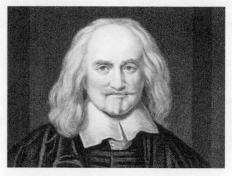

- An ordered society should balance the human need to lead a free life.

- Humans are needy, vulnerable and easily led astray in attempts to understand the world around them.

Thomas Hobbes, arguably the most celebrated English political philosopher, made important contributions to conservative thought. In his most famous work *Leviathan* (1651), he argued for almost total obedience to absolute government, as the only alternative was chaos.

Thomas Hobbes: 'How could a state be governed, or protected in its foreign relations if every individual remained free to obey or not to obey the law according to his private opinion?'

According to Hobbes, freedom without order and authority would have disastrous consequences for human society. He created a hypothetical situation known as the 'state of nature' where people were equal and free, and did not have to answer to any form of higher authority. Hobbes argued that under such circumstances, humans would exhibit a 'restless desire' for power, leading to conflict and turning the state of nature into a 'war of every man against every man'. In his view, the state of nature would become a state of war and life would become 'solitary, poor, nasty, brutish and short'. Fearful, self-interested and rational people would choose to sacrifice many of their rights and freedoms in return for order and security. They would enter into a social contract to establish political authority, surrendering all but one of their natural rights (the right to self-defence) to the individual or group to whom they grant authority. In this way, Hobbes argued, government is established by the consent of the people, who authorise those in power to do everything necessary to preserve order and peace. Thus, the people jointly submit to the absolute authority of the state (what Hobbes terms 'Leviathan') which represents 'a common power to keep them all in awe'.

Hobbes' arguments about the state of nature and the need for political authority are clearly shaped by his views on human nature.

- **Humans are needy and vulnerable.** People will compete violently to get the basic necessities of life and other material gains, will challenge others and fight out of fear to ensure their personal safety, and will seek reputation, both for its own sake and so that others will be too afraid to challenge them.

- **Humans are easily led astray in their attempts to understand the world around them.** The human capacity to reason is fragile, and people's attempts to interpret the world around them tend to be distorted by self-interest and the concerns of the moment.

Unsurprisingly, Hobbes concludes that the best people hope for is a peaceful life under strong government authority to guarantee order and security. The alternative is to accept the 'natural condition of mankind' with its violence, insecurity and constant threats.

Edmund Burke (1729–97)

Key ideas

- Change has to be undertaken with great caution, mindful of the delicate balance inherent in an organic society.

- Tradition and **empiricism** should be respected because they represent practices passed down from one generation to the next.

The Irish-born politician and writer, Edmund Burke, is commonly regarded as a founder of modern conservatism. His reputation rests largely on his book *Reflections on the Revolution in France* (1790) in which he criticised the French Revolution and developed a number of key conservative arguments.

For Burke, the fundamental problem with the French Revolution was that it represented an attempt to create a new society and system

Edmund Burke: 'It is with infinite caution that any man ought to venture upon pulling down an edifice which has answered in any tolerable degree for ages the common purposes of society, or on building it up again without having the model and patterns of approved utility before his eyes.'

Key term

Empiricism
the idea that knowledge comes from real experience and not from abstract theories.

of government based on abstract principles (such as liberty and equality) rather than the lessons of the past. Since these principles were not well established in France, he argued, such drastic changes could only end in chaos or tyranny. In Burke's view, the state resembled a living organism like a plant that may be changed when necessary through gentle 'pruning' or 'grafting' to preserve the political stability and social harmony. Reform should be limited and cautious, take account of the past, and be based on empiricism and tradition. Revolutionary change threatened to cut off society's 'roots' (such as its institutions and customs), leading to complete social and political breakdown.

Burke's endorsement of the value of tradition and empiricism is clearly linked to his attitude towards **organic, gradual change**. In his view, tradition and empiricism represent the accumulated and 'tested' wisdom of the past residing in society's long-standing institutions, customs and practices, and so they should be respected. As he explained: 'we procure reverence to our civil institutions on the principle which Nature teaches us to revere individual men: on account of their age, and on account of those from whom they are descended'.

According to Burke, continuing respect for tradition and empiricism promotes social continuity and stability. It also establishes an obligation or duty for each generation to protect and pass on the accumulated wisdom of tradition and empiricism to their successors. Furthermore, Burke advocated respect for tradition and empiricism on the grounds that they provide society and the individual with a strong sense of historical identity, offering people a sense of being 'rooted' in, and tied to, their particular society.

Link

For more on **organicism**, see Section 1.1.

Michael Oakeshott (1901–90)

Key ideas

- People's actions should be guided by pragmatism, rather than by ideology.
- Theories and ideologies oversimplify complex situations.

Michael Oakeshott, a British political philosopher, made a significant contribution to conservative thinking on human imperfection and pragmatism in works such as *Rationalism in Politics* (1962) and *On Human Conduct* (1975).

Michael Oakeshott: 'The office of government is not to impose other beliefs and activities upon its subjects, not to tutor or educate them, not to make them better or happier in another way, not to direct them, to galvanize them into action, to lead them or co-ordinate their activities… the office of government is merely to rule.'

According to Oakeshott, modern society is both unpredictable and complex. Consequently, it cannot be understood in terms of abstract principles or theories. 'Rational' attempts to make sense of society's behaviour inevitably distort and simplify the facts – a problem compounded by human imperfection, as people do not have the mental faculties to make sense of a complex modern world. Also, the 'rationalist' political leader's impulse is to act solely on the 'authority of his own reason' rather than practical experience. This encourages the dangerous idea that the leader fully understands society and knows how it should be changed. Oakeshott considered that the brutal fascist and communist regimes established in the 20th century were clear examples of this misguided human rationalism in politics. He also concluded that parliamentary government in Britain had developed pragmatically over time, and had not followed a rationalist or ideological path, as shown in Figure 3.1.

Oakeshott maintained that politics can only be successfully conducted if it accommodates existing traditions, practices and prejudices. This pragmatic approach:

- can deliver what is in the best interests of the people without overstepping the limits of public acceptance
- maintains social stability and cohesion by emphasising moderation, cautious change where necessary, and a sense of historical continuity
- is flexible, reflecting complex and shifting social realities, unlike rigid theories and ideologies which encourage dogmatic decision-making.

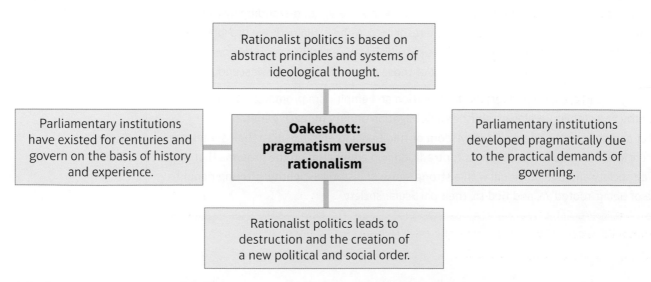

Figure 3.1: Oakeshott: pragmatism versus rationalism

Ayn Rand (1905–82)

Key ideas

- People should pursue their own happiness as their highest moral aim.
- People should work hard to achieve a life of purpose and productiveness.

Ayn Rand: 'The question isn't who is going to let me; it's who is going to stop me.'

The rise of fascism and communism in the 20th century led many thinkers in the West to reconsider the role of the state in the lives of individuals. The Russian-born American philosopher, novelist and conservative Ayn Rand was one of them. Rand's response was objectivism, a libertarian philosophical system that advocates the virtues of rational self-interest and maintains that individual freedom supports a pure, laissez-faire capitalist economy. These ideas were publicised chiefly through Rand's novels *The Fountainhead* (1943) and *Atlas Shrugged* (1957).

Objectivism was Rand's most important contribution to political thought. She claimed that it offered a set of principles covering all aspects of human life, including politics, economics, culture and human relationships. In her view, reason provided the fundamental basis of human life and this led her to endorse a form of ethical individualism that claimed that the rational pursuit of self-interest was morally right.

Any attempt, said Rand, to control or regulate an individual's actions corrupted the capacity of that person to work freely as a productive member of society, mainly by undermining his or her practical use of reason. For example, she rejected government welfare and wealth redistribution programmes because the state, in her view, relies on the implicit threat of force to ensure that people contribute to such schemes through taxation. Rand referred to this opposition to external coercion of the individual as the 'non-aggression principle'. Rand also condemned all forms of personal altruism (the idea that an individual should put the well-being of others first) because such acts created an 'artificial' sense of obligation and expectation, and did not accord with an individual's rational self-interest.

A self-proclaimed 'radical for capitalism', Rand argued that the unrestricted expression of human rationality was entirely compatible with the free market. She called for 'a full, pure, uncontrolled, unregulated laissez-faire' economy, maintaining that this was morally superior to the rest because it fully respects the individual's pursuit of rational self-interest and is fully consistent with the non-aggression principle. Under such economic arrangements, free individuals can use their time, money, and other resources as they see fit, and can interact and trade voluntarily with others to their mutual advantage. For these reasons, she concluded, libertarian conservatives 'must fight for capitalism, not as a practical issue, not as an economic issue, but, with the most righteous pride, as a moral issue'.

Robert Nozick (1938–2002)

Key ideas

- Individuals in society cannot be treated as a thing, or used against their will as a resource.

- Individuals own their bodies, talents, abilities and labour.

Robert Nozick, the US philosopher and right-wing libertarian, was one of the most important intellectual figures in the development of the New Right. In his major work *Anarchy, State, and Utopia* (1974), Nozick argued for a rights-based libertarian system and a minimal state.

Robert Nozick: 'Individuals have rights and there are things no person or group may do to them (without violating their rights).'

Nozick's libertarianism was partly based on Kant's moral principle that humans should be treated 'always as an end and never as a means only'. By this, Kant meant that since humans are rational, self-aware beings with free will, they should not be treated as mere things, or used against their will as resources. The assumption that individuals are inviolable end in themselves, Nozick argued, gives them rights to their lives, liberty and the rewards resulting from their labour. According to Nozick, these rights act as 'side-constraints' on the actions of others by setting limits on how a person may be treated. For example, an individual cannot be forced against his or her will to work for another person's purposes (even if those purposes are good).

From this, Nozick reached the radical conclusion that the taxes levied to fund state welfare programmes are immoral because:

- they amount to a type of forced labour imposed on the individual by the state

- they treat individuals as a means or resource to further the goals of equality and social justice and, in so doing, violate the principle that humans should be seen as better ends in themselves.

The only type of state that can be morally justified is a **minimal or 'night watchman' state** with powers limited to those necessary to protect people against violence, theft and fraud.

Nozick also used the concept of self-ownership to support this right-wing libertarian position. Dating back at least to the liberal political philosopher **John Locke** (1632–1704), self-ownership is based on the idea that individuals own themselves – their bodies, talents, abilities and labour, and the rewards or products created by their talents, abilities and labour. Nozick maintained that self-ownership gives the individual the right to determine what can be done with the 'possession'. Self-ownership gives a person rights to the various elements that make up one's self.

For these reasons, Nozick asserted, self-ownership also opposes taxation to fund welfare programmes and supports the minimal state. Viewed from this perspective, such taxation is a form of slavery – in effect, the state gives others an entitlement (in the form of welfare benefits) to part of the rewards of an individual's labour. Citizens entitled to benefits become partial owners of the individual since they have partial property rights over his or her labour. In this way, Nozick argued, the principle of self-ownership is undermined. Similarly, anything more extensive than the minimal state also compromises self-ownership. For example, a state that regulates what people eat, drink, or smoke interferes with their right to use their self-owned bodies as they want.

Key term

Minimal or 'night watchman' state
the idea that the role of the state must be restricted in order to preserve individual liberty.

Link

For more on **John Locke**, see Section 2.3.

Assessment support: 1.2.1 Conservatism

Question 3 on A-Level Paper 1 gives you a choice of two 24-mark questions. Pick the question you feel most confident about and complete your answer in approximately 30 minutes.

To what extent do different conservatives agree on the importance of paternalism? [24 marks]

You must use appropriate thinkers you have studied to support your answer.

These questions require an essay-style answer. They test all three Assessment Objectives, with 8 marks available for each. The highest level (20 to 24 marks) requires in-depth knowledge and understanding, supporting strong skills of analysis and evaluation. The mark scheme stresses that you must also offer a focused and justified conclusion – in this case, on the extent to which different conservatives agree on the importance of paternalism.

- Begin with a brief introduction in which you outline your argument. You need to set out a minimum of two key points on each side (in agreement and disagreement) of the question to develop later.

- Typically, you will write four main paragraphs (one for each major point) and round off with a conclusion.

- You are asked to review and make a substantiated judgement about the extent of conservative agreement on the importance of paternalism. Begin with the 'agree' arguments, then provide balance by dealing with the 'disagree' arguments. Each argument should be supported with accurate and relevant evidence, such as key thinkers and policies.

- In your conclusion, review the balance between the two sides, then reach a substantiated judgement. Your conclusion should not contain new factual material. Your judgement should emerge naturally from the way in which you have constructed your argument.

Here is an example of a main 'disagree' paragraph from a student's answer.

Although traditional and one-nation conservatives agree on the importance of paternalism, the neo-liberal wing of the New Right completely rejects the concept, viewing it as counterproductive. For instance, neo-liberals raise two moral objections to state welfare programmes, a key feature of one-nation conservative paternalism. First, in their view, such welfare provision creates a 'dependency culture' rather than a safety net by stripping individuals of their self-respect, dignity, drive and sense of personal responsibility. In 1944, Friedrich Hayek maintained that such dependency on the state would create a 'new serfdom'. By the 1980s, US and British neo-liberals were claiming that extensive reliance on state benefits was eroding parental financial responsibility for children (undermining the institution of the family in the process), draining the motivation to create wealth and promoting the growth of an underclass. Second, neo-liberals such as Robert Nozick oppose the paternalistic assumptions underpinning state welfare by defending individual rights. Nozick claims that welfare and redistribution programmes undermine property rights because legally acquired property (including income) cannot be transferred from one person to another without consent. So from a neo-liberal perspective, tax revenues taken from income earners to finance welfare measures represent a form of legalised 'state robbery'. Neo-liberals therefore sharply disagree with traditional and one-nation conservatives about the importance of paternalism.

This 'disagree' paragraph is effective for the following reasons.

- It is precisely focused on answering the question.

- It clearly explains why neo-liberals reject one-nation conservative paternalism in the form of state welfare.

- The student includes relevant own knowledge to add depth to the analysis – for example, references to Hayek's 'new serfdom' and neo-liberal concerns in the 1980s about the growth of a dependent underclass.

- It incorporates relevant information about a thinker (Robert Nozick) to develop and support the argument that neo-liberals disagree with other conservatives over the importance of paternalism.

CHAPTER 2

Liberalism

Liberalism has been one of the most widespread political ideologies of the last two centuries. It has influenced most mainstream political parties in the UK and other Western countries. Ideas such as the protection of civil liberties, freedom of choice and equal opportunities are broadly supported across the political spectrum in democratic societies.

This chapter covers:

- the key concepts and values of liberalism
- the various ways in which different types of liberal – 'classical' liberals and their modern successors – have interpreted these ideas
- the contributions of a number of leading liberal thinkers.

You will learn how the core ideas and principles of liberalism relate to human nature, the state, society and the economy.

2.1 Core ideas and principles

Liberalism emerged in reaction to the rule of monarchies and aristocratic privilege in the early modern world. It reflected the views of the educated middle classes, who sought wider civil liberties and opportunities to better themselves. Liberalism was part of the Enlightenment, an 18th-century intellectual movement that rejected traditional social, political and religious ideas, and stressed the power of reason and the importance of tolerance and freedom from tyranny. Thinkers who were influenced by this movement believed in abolishing traditional restrictions on the freedom of the individual, whether these were imposed by government or the church. They held that people are born with different potential, but all are equal in rights (though at the time most definitions of this excluded women and ethnic minorities). People should be free to take their own decisions and to make the most of their talents and opportunities.

The classic statement of this outlook was the United States Declaration of Independence (1776), primarily written by the future President, Thomas Jefferson. The Declaration states that 'we hold these truths to be self-evident, that all men are created equal, that they are endowed by their Creator with certain unalienable rights (natural rights), that among these are life, liberty and the pursuit of happiness.'

The signing of the Declaration of Independence, 4 July 1776. Representatives of the former royal colonies in North America stated their intention to govern themselves, rather than continue under British rule.

Individualism

Liberals stress the importance of the individual over the claims of any social group or collective body. Immanuel Kant (1724–1804), the German Enlightenment thinker, argued that all individuals are unique and have equal worth; they should always be used as 'ends' and never merely as 'means'. In other words, people should not be treated as instruments to achieve a particular goal, but should be regarded as possessing their own intrinsic value. He described this as a 'categorical imperative' – an absolute moral requirement to perform an action for its own sake, rather than for any gain.

Individualism can be interpreted in two different ways. Classical liberals believe in 'egoistical individualism' – the view that people are essentially self-seeking and self-reliant. This view minimises the importance of society, seeing it as little more than a collection of independent individuals. More widely held in the modern world is a version known as **developmental individualism**. This concept plays down the pursuit of self-interest, and has been used to justify support for some state intervention in society to help the disadvantaged.

Another idea linked to the importance of the individual is **tolerance**. This is one of the natural rights that liberals believe everyone should have, which should not be taken away against the will of the individual. Originally this referred primarily to tolerance of different religious beliefs, but today it has been extended to a wide range of views and practices. For example, liberals tend to take a relaxed view of sexual matters, supporting measures to put same-sex relationships on the same legal footing as heterosexual relationships because these are private lifestyle choices.

> **Link**
>
> For more on **individualism**, see Section 2.2.

> **Key terms**
>
> **Developmental individualism**
> the view that individual freedom is linked to the desire to create a society in which each person can grow and flourish.
>
> **Tolerance**
> a willingness to accept values, customs and beliefs with which one disagrees.

Pause & reflect

'A liberal is a person who prioritises the rights of the individual, and would only restrict these rights if someone holds beliefs or acts in a way that endangers others.'

Is this a good working definition of a liberal?

Freedom or liberty

Freedom is the most important of all liberal values. Early liberals objected to the way in which authoritarian governments claimed a right to take decisions on behalf of people and attempted to regulate their behaviour. However, they and their successors did recognise that freedom can never be absolute but must be exercised under the law, in order to protect people from interfering with each other's rights. This is why the early liberal thinker **John Locke** (1632–1704) argued that 'the end of law is not to abolish or restrain, but to preserve and enlarge freedom… where there is no law, there is no freedom.'

The concept of liberty was central to the work of the early 19th-century school of thought known as utilitarianism. Its leading thinker, Jeremy Bentham (1748–1832), maintained that each individual can decide what is in his or her own interests. He argued that human actions are motivated mainly by a desire to pursue pleasure and to avoid pain. Government should not prevent people from doing what they choose unless their actions threaten others' ability to do the same for themselves. This was a mechanistic view of human behaviour that saw people as driven by rational self-interest. When applied to society at large it produced the idea of 'the greatest happiness for the greatest number'. This could mean that the interests of minorities are overridden by those of the majority.

> **Link**
>
> For more on **John Locke**, see Section 2.3.

Link

For more on **John Stuart Mill**, see Section 2.3.

Key terms

Negative freedom
freedom from interference by other people.

Positive freedom
having the capacity to act on one's free will and to realise personal potential.

Limited government
where the role of government is limited by checks and balances, and a separation of powers, because of the corrupting nature of power.

Laissez-faire capitalism
an economic system organised by the market, where goods are produced for exchange and profit, and wealth is privately owned.

Link

For more on the **Bill of Rights**, see Section 4.4 of The Supreme Court and Civil Rights.

John Stuart Mill (1806–73) was perhaps the most important classical liberal thinker of the 19th century. He began as a follower of Bentham, but came to see the pursuit of pleasure and avoidance of pain as too simplistic. He put forward what became known as the idea of **negative freedom**. Individuals should only be subject to external restraint when their actions potentially affect others, not when their actions affect only themselves.

From the late 19th century onwards, many liberals found Mill's concept of liberty too limited because it viewed society as little more than a collection of independent atoms. The Oxford thinker T.H. Green (1836–82) argued that society was an organic whole, in which people pursue the common good as well as their own interests. They are both individual and social in nature. From this came the concept of **positive freedom**. Individuals should be able to control their own destiny, to develop personal talents and achieve self-fulfilment. Some limited state intervention was necessary to make this possible.

The state: a 'necessary evil'

There is a complex relationship between liberalism and the state. Liberals accept that the state is needed to avert disorder and to protect the vulnerable from exploitation. However, they mistrust power because they believe that human beings are essentially self-seeking, so may use any position of power to pursue their own interests, probably at the expense of others. Liberals oppose the concentration of political power, fearing that it gives people a greater incentive to benefit themselves and to use other people for their own ends. The classic statement of this was by the Victorian liberal historian Lord Acton (1834–1902): 'Power tends to corrupt, and absolute power corrupts absolutely.'

Liberals therefore argue for **limited government**, with checks and balances on the exercise of power. They support the idea of constitutionalism (government in which power is distributed and limited by a system of laws) in order to prevent a concentration of power. Typical features of a liberal constitution include the separation of powers, which means that authority is shared between the three branches of government: the legislature, executive and judiciary. Linked to this is the concept of checks and balances. The branches are given some influence over each other and they act to check abuses of power, as in the United States Constitution. Liberals also favour a bill of rights, which provides a clear statement of citizens' rights and defines the relationship between citizens and the state. In the United States, the first ten amendments to the Constitution are known as the **Bill of Rights**.

Liberals' suspicion of the concentration of political power often leads them to support its devolution from central government to regional bodies. This occurred in the UK in the late 1990s, with the creation of the Scottish parliament and assemblies for Wales and Northern Ireland. An alternative is federalism – a system of government like that in the USA or Germany, where a number of states form a union under a central government, while each state retains responsibility for its own internal affairs.

The liberal emphasis on a limited role for the state also has an economic dimension. Liberals of the 18th and 19th centuries believed in **laissez-faire capitalism**. The fullest statement of this idea was by the Scottish economist Adam Smith, one of the most prominent Enlightenment era thinkers, in *The Wealth of Nations* (1776). Smith emphasised the part played by self-interest in driving economic growth, famously writing 'it is not from the benevolence [unselfish goodwill] of the butcher, the brewer or the baker that we expect our dinner, but from their regard for their own interest'.

Rationalism

At the heart of Enlightenment thinking is a belief in human reason. It holds that individuals should be free to exercise their judgement about their own interests without needing to be guided by external authorities, such as the state or church leaders. People will not always make correct decisions, but it is better for them to take responsibility for themselves than to take instruction from above. Liberals were encouraged by the development of scientific learning in the 18th and 19th centuries, which pushed back the boundaries of human understanding and liberated people from a blind faith in established authority, tradition and superstition.

Faith in reason is linked to the idea of a progressive society, in which the personal development of the individual promotes wider social advancement.

Rationalism in action

Liberals accept that competition between individuals, groups and nations regrettably will produce conflicts, but they favour the use of reasoned debate and discussion to resolve disputes. Late 19th-century liberals were in the forefront of moves to develop methods of industrial arbitration. This meant that a neutral third party would mediate between employers and trade unions, in an effort to avert costly legal action or strikes. Similarly, in international relations, liberals view war as a last resort, which should be avoided if at all possible. In the early 20th century liberals were in the forefront of campaigns in support of the League of Nations, the forerunner of today's United Nations, which sought to bring countries together to discuss their disputes. Many liberals today support the European Union on the grounds that, by surrendering some of their national sovereignty, member states derive benefits through association with each other, such as access to a large trading area.

Equality and social justice

Liberals place emphasis on **equality of opportunity**. Liberals accept differing outcomes because people have different abilities and potential. They should be free to reach that potential.

Traditionally liberalism is based on a belief in **foundational equality**. This implies a belief in formal equality, in that individuals should enjoy the same legal and political rights in society, ensured by equality before the law and equal voting rights in free and fair elections.

Socialists criticise liberalism on the grounds that it does not tackle inequality because it is closely linked to the capitalist idea of competition. Instead, socialists aim to achieve equality of outcome by using the power of the state to redistribute wealth. However, classical liberals believe that individuals with different talents should be rewarded differently. The resulting social inequality is beneficial for society because it gives people an incentive to work hard and make the most of their abilities. The good society is a **meritocracy**. For example William Gladstone, the British Liberal prime minister, introduced competitive examinations for entry to the civil service in the 1870s, bringing to an end the practice of making appointments on the basis of aristocratic connections.

Statue in Edinburgh of the Enlightenment economist Adam Smith (1723–90) whose *The Wealth of Nations* argues for a self-regulating economic system, free of the distortions caused by the granting of monopolies and other privileges to different interest groups.

Key terms

Equality of opportunity
the idea that all individuals should have equal chances in life to rise and fall.

Foundational equality
rights that all humans have by virtue of being born, which cannot be taken away.

Meritocracy
a society organised on the basis that success is based on ability and hard work.

Link

For more about **Mary Wollstonecraft**, see Section 3.2 of Feminism.

Link

For more about **John Rawls**, see Section 2.3.

Until the 20th century liberals did not all extend the same rights to women as to men. The early feminist writer **Mary Wollstonecraft** (1759–97) argued that women were no less rational beings than men, and were entitled to the same rights to pursue a career and to own their own property when married – something the law prohibited at the time. Modern liberals support full civil rights for women and minority groups. For example, US President Barack Obama supported the right of transgender pupils to use bathrooms of their choice at school.

There are different views within liberalism on equality. Most modern liberals favour some degree of state intervention to narrow social inequalities. They believe that true equality is not possible without social justice. However, they do not believe that total equality of outcome is either possible or desirable. **John Rawls** (1921–2002), author of *A Theory of Justice* (1971), is known for attempting to reconcile the concepts of liberal individualism with the prevention of excessive inequality.

Liberal democracy

Since the 19th century most liberals have supported the concept of liberal democracy. This involves:

- free elections to give expression to the will of the people
- limitations on the power of the state, which should act as a neutral arbiter between different interests in society
- respect for civil liberties and toleration of different viewpoints.

The idea that government should be based on the consent of the people is central to liberalism and long pre-dates modern notions of democracy. Liberals argue that, without this foundation, government lacks legitimacy. Thomas Hobbes (1588–1679) in his book *Leviathan* (1651) argued that the people should come together to erect a great power over them to guarantee peace and security.

Key term

Social contract
an unofficial agreement shared by everyone in a society in which they give up some freedom in return for security.

The idea of a **social contract** between the people and their rulers was explained by John Locke in his book *Two Treatises of Government* (1690)**.** He argued that the people must freely give, and renew, their consent to be governed. They have a right of rebellion if the government breaks the contract.

Liberals support democracy on the grounds that it enables citizens to hold government to account. It also extends popular participation and performs an educational function in society, promoting the personal development of individuals. Democracy also gives a political voice to different groups and interests. In this way it promotes consensus and underpins political stability giving equilibrium or balance to the political system.

On the other hand, liberals have feared excessive democracy on the grounds that it may lead to the 'tyranny of the majority', suppressing minority rights or individual freedom, or it may create a culture of dull conformism. Mill proposed to allocate more votes to the educated (plural voting) as a way of curbing the influence of the uneducated masses. Modern liberals would not support this idea because it gives undue weight to the views of an elite. They have been generally supportive of democracy, as long as it is limited by a constitutional framework, and individual and group rights are protected. The **electoral college** system used in the USA was devised partly as a buffer against the manipulation of the masses by an unscrupulous campaigner for the post. The people do not directly choose the president; instead this is done by electors corresponding to the number of representatives each state has in Congress.

Link

For more on the **US electoral college,** see Section 5.1 of US Democracy and Participation.

Pause & reflect

How far is liberal concern about democracy motivated by fear that the masses cannot be trusted to make the 'right' decisions, as viewed by the educated elite? Some commentators of a liberal persuasion gave the impression that they regarded those who voted to leave the EU in Britain's 2016 referendum in this light. They reacted in a similar way a few months later to the election of the abrasive populist, Donald Trump, as US President.

Human nature	The starting point for liberals is the importance of the individual. Liberals see people as rational individuals, capable of perceiving their own interests and taking their own decisions. They stress the positive potential of human nature. People should be free to make the most of their talents, enjoying equality of opportunity. A good society is also one in which there is tolerance of different values, customs and beliefs. Classical liberals believe that people should be restricted only where there is risk of their threatening the freedom of others. Modern liberals have been more conscious of social injustice, and favour some external intervention by the state to counter this.
The state	Central to liberal political thought is the concept of the social contract – the idea that the state is based on the agreement of the people, who choose to give up some freedom in return for security. According to mechanistic theory, people created the state to serve them and act in their interests. Liberals therefore believe in limited government, with checks and balances to prevent abuses of power. They are keen that the state does not deprive people of their civil liberties. Liberals often support the decentralisation of power, so that authority is dispersed between different levels of government and not concentrated at the centre.
Society	Classical liberals downplayed the importance of society, seeing it primarily as a collection of individuals, pursuing their own interests. They advocated the concept of a meritocracy, whereby individuals succeed through their own ability and hard work. This entails a belief in the importance of foundational equality – people are born equal. Linked to this is the notion of formal equality, whereby individuals are entitled to the same legal and political rights. Modern liberals believe that this, on its own, is not enough to guarantee true social equality. People should still be free to make their own choices, but society is more than the sum of the individuals it contains. For example, some assistance by the state in combating poverty is necessary to enable people to flourish and for a fair society to develop, in which inequality is minimised.
The economy	Classical liberalism's emphasis on the individual led to a belief in free-market capitalism – the idea that the economy is best served by limited state intervention. By contrast in the 20th century, modern liberals were more conscious of the failings of the market, and argued that state intervention is necessary to promote sustainable growth and to limit the injustice associated with large-scale unemployment and poverty.

Table 1.1: Core principles and ideas of liberalism in action

2.2 Differing views and tensions within liberalism

The two main varieties of liberalism are known as classical and modern liberalism.

Classical liberalism is the earliest form of the ideology. It is associated with the rise of industrial capitalism in the 18th and 19th centuries. Followers of classical liberalism prized freedom above other values, and believed that freedom could best be achieved by restricting the power of government. In the late 20th century, classical liberalism was reinvented in Britain and the USA as **neo-liberalism**. It was associated with the New Right, an important influence on the British Conservative Party under the leadership of Margaret Thatcher (1975–90) and her successors.

Modern liberalism emerged in the early 20th century in reaction to the growth of free-market capitalism. It did not wish to abolish capitalism and replace private ownership with state control of the economy, but its adherents did believe in regulating the market in order to counter excessive deprivation and inequality. Modern liberals do not believe that people can be truly free if simply 'left alone' by the state.

Classical and modern liberals take different approaches to two key areas: freedom and the state.

Different views of freedom

Both classical and modern liberals value freedom, but they disagree over its nature. Classical liberals believe in negative freedom, a principle often linked to the idea of freedom of choice or privacy. Freedom can be expanded most clearly by restraining state power. Classical liberals also believe in **egoistical individualism**.

The logic of negative freedom leads to the rolling back of the state, to encourage individuals to take more responsibility for themselves. Self-reliance is a key virtue for classical liberals. Dependence on the state is damaging because it undermines the self-respect of the individual and saps the spirit of enterprise on which economic growth depends.

Current debates over the growth of a 'dependency culture' are linked to the ideas of classical liberalism. The idea of the dependency culture has come from the expansion of the UK welfare state since 1945, which has been associated with a loss of personal responsibility, the breakdown of the traditional family and the persistence of unemployment across generations. Neo-liberals argue that social welfare should be targeted at those who really need it, and that others should be encouraged to lift themselves out of poverty through their own efforts.

Modern liberals believe that negative freedom is necessary but not sufficient for a good society. It can amount to little more than 'freedom to starve' for those facing disadvantages over which they have no control – for example, working in an occupation prone to periods of unemployment, or suffering an industrial accident. These people need assistance to live truly free and fulfilling lives.

This is why modern liberals support the idea of positive freedom. This defines freedom as self-mastery or self-realisation. Freedom can be expanded by qualified state intervention in the economy and society, to widen individual opportunity and liberate citizens from social evils such as poverty. Modern liberals favour developmental individualism – enabling individuals to enjoy personal growth and empowerment.

Link

For more on **neo-liberalism**, see Section 1.2 and Section 1.3 of Conservatism.

Key term

Egoistical individualism the idea that individual freedom is associated with self-interest and self-reliance.

Different views of the state

Classical and modern liberals have some common ground on the nature of the state. Both believe in the decentralisation of government and protection of civil liberties. In the 19th century, Gladstone tried to grant Home Rule or **self-government** to Ireland. In the 20th century, this equated to the concept of devolution – the transfer of certain central government functions to elected bodies in the different parts of the UK. This influenced the New Labour governments of 1997–2010, which set up elected bodies for Scotland, Wales and Northern Ireland. Liberal reforms of the constitutional framework in the same period included the Human Rights Act and Freedom of Information Act, which guaranteed certain rights for citizens.

Liberals do not revere the state. They differ from conservatives, who attach importance to the accumulated wisdom of the past and view the state as an organic entity whose component parts cannot be rearranged at will. Liberals subscribe to a **mechanistic theory** of the state – they see it as a machine created to serve the individual. Its parts are equal in worth and interchangeable.

However, there are different liberal views of the role that the state should play. Classical liberals believe that the state should merely lay down the conditions for orderly existence and leave other issues in the hands of private individuals and businesses. They support the idea of a minimal or 'night watchman' state, whose role is to maintain social order, enforce contracts and provide defence against external attack. The state should not interfere in economic and social life more than is strictly necessary, since this would risk undermining individual liberty. Its role is to maintain a stable framework for trade, uphold the value of the currency and generally create an environment within which laissez-faire capitalism can thrive.

In the 19th century, some classical liberals went further and developed what later became known as Social Darwinism. They borrowed from the naturalist Charles Darwin the concept of natural selection, which they applied to human society. They argued that, because individuals differ in their abilities, it is unavoidable that some will succeed and others will fail. Their most important figure was Herbert Spencer (1820–1903), author of the classic text *The Man Versus the State* (1884), who coined the phrase 'survival of the fittest'. He maintained that those who do well are those who adapt most successfully to their economic environment. The logic of this position is that government should not intervene to support people through the provision of social welfare.

By contrast, modern liberals believe in an **enabling state**. They arrived at this position through a growing awareness of the inequality of late 19th-century society, which they linked to low pay, unemployment, slum housing and poor working conditions. Known in the late-Victorian and Edwardian periods as 'New Liberals', they supported policies of welfare as the way to bring about equality of opportunity. They argued that if individuals and groups are held back by their social circumstances, the state has a social responsibility to reduce or remove these disadvantages. This responsibility is known as welfare or social liberalism. It was expressed in the reforms of the Liberal governments of H.H. Asquith before the First World War, including the first old-age pensions, National Insurance and labour exchanges, the forerunner of today's job centres.

Link

For more on **self-government**, see Section 1.3 of The Constitution.

Key terms

Mechanistic theory
the theory that people created the state to serve them and act in their interests.

Enabling state
a larger state that helps individuals to achieve their potential and be free.

A poster advertising the social reforms introduced by David Lloyd George, chancellor of the exchequer in the New Liberal government.

The Beveridge Report

These ideas were taken further in the mid-20th century by Sir William Beveridge, a leading civil servant and academic. He was the author of the influential *Beveridge Report* (1942), the foundation of the post-war British welfare state. He argued that liberty should be available equally to all, and this was impossible if part of the population was held back by the 'five giants': poverty, lack of education, ill health, poor living conditions and unemployment. Beveridge's report had a major influence on the post-war Labour government. Comprehensive National Insurance, the National Health Service and improved housing and education were all responses to the challenges he outlined.

A Second World War cartoon depicting Beveridge fighting the 'five giants' threatening people's well-being: Want (poverty), Ignorance (lack of education), Disease, Squalor (poor living conditions) and Idleness (unemployment).

Beveridge declared that 'a starving man is not free because, until he is fed, he cannot have a thought for anything but how to meet his urgent physical needs'. This is a good summary of the approach of modern liberals: to enable individuals to flourish, they argue that some state intervention is necessary.

The Beveridge Report captured the wartime desire for a more equal and just society. People who were fighting for their freedom against Nazism felt entitled to a better standard of living after the war. The report's promise to protect people from the 'cradle to the grave' against social injustice became famous.

The publication of the report was the culmination of a distinguished career for Beveridge. He had become an expert on unemployment and social security as an adviser to the Liberal government before the First World War. He was director of the London School of Economics from 1919 to 1937, before becoming Master of University College, Oxford. Between 1944 and 1945 he was briefly a Liberal MP. After losing his seat, Beveridge was appointed to the House of Lords.

Modern liberalism also includes economic management on the lines proposed by the economist John Maynard Keynes (1883–1946). Keynes was a talented Cambridge University academic who first came to attention with his book *The Economic Consequences of the Peace* (1919), a critique of the allied powers' treatment of Germany at the Versailles peace conference, written while he was an adviser to the Treasury. Keynes' most important contribution to economic thought came in reaction to the Great Depression of the 1930s. He argued that the image of a self-regulating free market is a myth, and that government intervention is necessary to ensure that market economies deliver sustainable growth and keep unemployment low. In particular, governments should prevent a slump by managing the level of demand in the economy so that full employment is maintained. In his best-known book, *The General* (1936), Keynes argued for a programme of public expenditure to create jobs and stimulate the economy. In the final stages of the Second World War, Keynes represented the British government in talks in the USA, which led to the creation of two important financial institutions, the World Bank and the International Monetary Fund. **Keynesianism** was most influential in the decades immediately after the war, when governments became more willing to act in order to correct the failings of the market.

> **Key term**
>
> **Keynesianism**
> an economic system that requires government involvement to stimulate the economy to achieve full employment and price stability.

Is modern liberalism a contradiction or a continuation of classical liberalism?

There is a clear difference between the classical liberal fear of the state and modern liberals' willingness to use its power to promote social justice. In the 19th century, liberals were sceptical of the benefits of state intervention. Gladstone described it as 'construction', a term that to him had negative connotations. He believed that it would take responsibility out of the hands of the individual.

Nevertheless, both classical and modern liberals are concerned in their different ways with expanding the freedom of the individual. Modern liberals see the state as helping individuals to help themselves and they regard state provision of welfare and education as a means to ensure equality of opportunity.

Both types of liberal are anxious to resist the idea of an over-powerful government. They share a commitment to holding government to account, to decentralising power and to protecting the rights of the citizen. Where they differ is in the extent to which they are prepared to use the state to achieve liberal objectives.

Classical and modern liberalism similarities	Classical and modern liberalism differences
• Both types of liberal seek to enhance individual freedom – but in different ways. Individuals have inherent value, and are capable of rational thought and decision-making. • Both believe in equality of opportunity and in equal civil rights. • Both wish to place limits on the power of the state. They believe in the decentralisation of power and in the importance of citizens holding government to account. The purpose of the state is to serve the individual and its institutions should be reformed as necessary to promote this. • Both support the fundamental concepts of private ownership and capitalism, as opposed to a state-controlled economy.	• Classical liberals believe in negative freedom – individuals thrive when left alone by the state. Modern liberals argue that under free-market capitalism, not all people can be truly free because they are held back by disadvantaged circumstances. • Classical liberals see society as essentially a collection of individuals. Modern liberals have a more holistic view of society, in which the promotion of the common good must go hand in hand with individual freedom. • Classical liberals fear that state intervention may take decision-making out of the hands of individuals and reduce their self-reliance. By contrast, modern liberals believe that some state intervention is necessary to promote a fair society, in which people can make the most of their talents and opportunities. They believe in an 'enabling state' which helps people to help themselves. This means government provision of welfare services to relieve poverty, rather than expecting individuals to rely on themselves. • Classical liberals believe in a largely self-regulating free market economy. Modern liberals see the flaws in capitalism. They argue that government management is necessary to minimise the effect of economic downturns, which lead to mass unemployment and poverty if not corrected.

Table 2.1: Similarities and differences between classical and modern liberals

EXTENSION ACTIVITY

Review the information presented here on classical and modern liberalism. Do you feel that the similarities between them are more significant than the differences?

2.3 Liberal thinkers and ideas

John Locke (1632–1704)

Key ideas

- Society, state and government are based on a voluntary agreement or contract.
- Government should be limited and based on consent from below.

John Locke: 'It is evident that absolute monarchy… is indeed inconsistent with civil society, and so can be no form of civil government at all.'

Locke was the leading philosopher of the Whig movement, the forerunner of the Liberal Party. Locke was a supporter of the 'Glorious Revolution' of 1688, which entailed the replacement of the Catholic King James II with his Protestant son-in-law and daughter, William III and Mary II. This was an event of huge importance because it was the foundation of Britain's constitutional monarchy.

Locke's most important work was *Two Treatises of Government* (1690). He was strongly opposed to the exercise of power unrestrained by law. He argued that both the rulers and the people must be subject to law. Without this, the people would be like animals in a farmyard – kept by the farmer from harming each other, but with no guarantee that the farmer will not abuse them. This was the concept of limited government – the power of government should be limited and based on consent from below.

Locke based his philosophy on the doctrine of natural rights and natural laws. People are equal in rights and must respect each other's rights. Government derives its legitimacy from the people and should govern in accordance with natural rights. It does not have an inherent, God-given right to rule over others.

From this came the concept of the social contract – the idea that society, state and government are based on a theoretical voluntary agreement. People should accept the authority of the government as long as it fulfils its part of the contract. This means that government should protect property rights. Indeed Locke wrote that 'the great and chief end of men uniting into commonwealths, and putting themselves under government, is the preservation of their property'. Government should also exercise tolerance in religious matters and not interfere in the area of private conscience. If government breaks its contract with the people by abusing their natural rights, they are entitled to resist the government and, if necessary, overthrow it.

Locke's philosophy is based on reason. He argued that no rational person would submit to arbitrary rule – a form of government in which the ruler has unlimited power and is not restrained by law – because this would not be in anyone's best interests. This is the classical liberal view that the state should serve the individual. However, Locke did not believe in democracy or political equality in the modern sense. His writings are unclear on whether he believed in the equality of men and women, and he would not extend toleration to atheism. However, he emphasised the importance of civil society, and of basing authority on consent – ideas that have been central to liberalism in later centuries. These ideas make Locke perhaps the most important classical-liberal theorist of government and society.

Mary Wollstonecraft (1759–97)

Key ideas

- Women are rational, independent beings capable of reason.

- In order to be free, women should enjoy full civil liberties and the opportunity to pursue a career.

Mary Wollstonecraft: 'The divine right of husbands, like the divine right of kings, may, it is hoped, in this enlightened age, be contested without danger.'

Mary Wollstonecraft was an early feminist writer, best known for her book *A Vindication of the Rights of Woman* (1792). Her work represents an extension of liberalism into an area that is now taken for granted, but which in the 18th century made her ahead of her time. She believed that women were no less rational than men, and therefore entitled to the same rights.

Wollstonecraft lived at a time when women lacked legal independence. When they married, their husbands took control of almost every aspect of their lives, including their property, and it was extremely difficult for them to pursue a career outside the home. Wollstonecraft described women as 'slaves… in a political and civil sense'. She wanted women to have **formal equality**, to enjoy full civil liberties and be allowed to have a career, rather than being economically dependent on men. The key to achieving this, she argued, was education, which would enable a woman to gain self-respect and to realise her potential.

At the same time Wollstonecraft valued marriage as an institution. She herself was married to a radical intellectual, William Godwin, and died soon after giving birth to their daughter, Mary Shelley, best known as the author of *Frankenstein*. Where Wollstonecraft differed from most of her contemporaries was in her insistence that marriage must be a partnership of equals. The tyranny of the male over the female in a marital relationship must be resisted because it prevents people from being good citizens.

However, there were limits to her ambitions for women, which can be explained by the period in which she lived. She recognised that, as a result of biology, women were more likely to opt for marriage and bringing up children. She argued that this was no less virtuous than a career. Essentially she wanted women to be able to choose between these two routes. She therefore exemplifies the liberal concept of equality of opportunity, an idea that she wanted to see extended to both men and women without distinction.

Key term

Formal equality
the idea that all individuals have the same legal and political rights in society.

John Stuart Mill (1806–73)

Key ideas

- Individuals should be free to do anything except harm other individuals.

- It is important to tolerate behaviour or ideas that are different from one's own.

John Stuart Mill: 'The only purpose for which power can be rightfully exercised over any member of a civilised community, against his will, is to prevent harm to others.'

John Stuart Mill was the son of a utilitarian philosopher, James Mill. He was initially influenced by his father and by the founder of the movement, Jeremy Bentham. From the utilitarian movement he derived the idea that individuals are best qualified to judge their own interests. However, he disagreed with their view that the pursuit of pleasure and avoidance of pain was the sole motivation of human beings. He argued that the betterment of human civilisation was no less important as a goal.

Mill's most important contribution to liberal thought, explained in his book *On Liberty* (1859), was the **harm principle**, from which flowed a strictly limited view of the role of government. He made a distinction between actions that were 'self-regarding' (those that affected only the individual responsible for the action) and those that were 'other-regarding' (behaviour that did affect others). The first category would include, for example, the expression of personal beliefs. Mill believed that government had no business interfering in this kind of area. However, it was entitled to restrict behaviour that adversely affected the freedom of others, such as violent or disorderly conduct.

Later in life Mill modified his limited view of the role of government. He accepted that some degree of state intervention was justified to prevent the poor from enduring injustice. He believed that income should be taxed at a single rate (the so-called 'flat tax'), but he was in favour of inheritance tax because the transmission of wealth across the generations gave some individuals an advantage over others. In this sense he represents a bridge between classical and modern liberalism.

Mill also upheld the idea of tolerance and the right of people to express a minority view. He believed that just because an opinion was widely held across society, that did not necessarily make it correct. For example, he spent a night in jail for trying to advise the poor on contraception, which in Victorian England was seen as a taboo subject. His private life was unconventional, especially by the standards of his time; he lived for 21 years with the love of his life, Harriet Taylor, and her first husband, marrying her after the latter died. Mill believed in the complete equality of men and women, which was unusual even among radical liberals in his time, and during his brief period as a Liberal MP (1865–68) he unsuccessfully championed votes for women.

Key term

Harm principle
the idea that individuals should be free to do anything except harm other individuals.

John Rawls (1921–2002)

Key ideas

- Society must be just and guarantee each citizen a life worth living.
- A fair society is one in which the difference in outcomes for the richest and the poorest is kept to a minimum.

John Rawls: 'It may be expedient but it is not just that some should have less in order that others should prosper.'

Rawls was an American academic whose best-known work *A Theory of Justice* (1971) attempts to reconcile individual freedom with the avoidance of excessive inequality in society. He rejected utilitarianism because it did not take account of the range of desires and goals pursued by individual people, and some would find their interests ignored. Rawls' starting point was that everyone has an equal entitlement to certain basic rights and liberties. However, it is also important to create a society in which there is economic justice. His ideas are intellectually linked to the social contract, as developed by Locke and other liberal thinkers.

Rawls accepted that there would always be a degree of inequality, but said that a just society should aim to minimise the difference between the outcomes for the best off and the poorest. He envisaged what he called the 'original position' – a hypothetical state of affairs before human society had been formed. People would have to decide on a basis for society that was fair to all, devising it behind a 'veil of ignorance' so it would not be skewed by knowledge of their own class, gender, race, talents or other characteristics. They would not be certain about how successful they would be, so they would need to adopt a low-risk strategy so that if they found themselves at the bottom of society, they would not suffer unduly.

In these circumstances, Rawls argued, people would agree on the importance of equal rights including freedom of speech and the right of assembly. They would also want an accepted minimum standard of living. This 'difference principle' would allow people to enjoy as much freedom as possible, provided that it was not exercised at the expense of others. There would be inequality in such a society, but it would be tolerated only if it did not make those at the bottom worse off.

Rawls rejected the two extremes of communism and unregulated capitalism, instead favouring a 'property-owning democracy', in which ownership is widely distributed and the poorest members of society can be economically independent.

In *Political Liberalism* (1993), Rawls modified his original theory because he realised that, in a pluralist society, not everyone would agree with his model. He therefore envisaged a range of liberal principles, with his two principles of equal rights and economic justice forming just one of a number of options. It would be enough for there to be what he termed an 'overlapping consensus', as opposed to unanimous agreement on the principles of a just society.

Betty Friedan (1921–2006)

Key ideas

- Women are as capable as men and oppressive laws and social views must be rejected.

- Women are held back from fulfilling their potential by unfair ideas about the kind of employment they can take up.

Betty Friedan: 'A girl should not expect special privileges because of her sex but neither should she adjust to prejudice and discrimination.'

Betty Friedan was an American liberal feminist whose most important work was *The Feminine Mystique*, published in 1963. She also helped to found the National Organization for Women (NOW), which became the largest women's rights organisation in the world. Its aim was to bring women fully into the mainstream of society alongside men and to secure the enforcement of anti-discrimination laws by the federal government.

Friedan's starting point was a belief that conditioning rather than biology led women to become wives and homemakers, rather than seeking to pursue a career. This path was set early, with the family and school, and was reinforced by social, cultural and religious influences. Friedan argued for wider opportunities for women and for a change of attitudes in favour of greater equality between the sexes. She maintained that, for many women, being confined to a domestic role led to a lack of fulfilment and to deep unhappiness.

Friedan was a liberal because she wanted to make reforms within the existing structure of society, rather than fundamentally transforming it. She accepted that many women do have a deep desire to be wives and mothers, and this was no less valid than following a career. All she wanted was for women to be able to choose between the two.

In many ways her work represents a continuation of that of Mary Wollstonecraft; the fact that she was making her case almost two centuries later shows the limited progress made by the feminist movement in the intervening period. Like Wollstonecraft, Friedan's philosophy was grounded in a liberal belief that individuals are of equal worth and therefore are entitled to equal rights. Her main concern was with the creation of a level playing field to enable women to compete equally with men, and not be restricted to a narrow range of what were considered 'acceptable' occupations.

Pause & reflect

Can you trace common themes in the work of the five thinkers you have studied? List any areas of agreement, and try to find ways in which the later thinkers have developed ideas in which their predecessors were interested. In particular, look out for common ground on key areas such as:

- freedom of the individual
- equality and rights
- the role of the state.

Assessment support: 1.2.2 Liberalism

Question 3 on A-Level Paper 1 gives you a choice of two 24-mark questions, to be completed in essay form in 30 minutes. This means that one of the core political ideas (Conservatism, Liberalism and Socialism) will not appear on the paper – indeed it is possible that both alternatives could be focused on one political idea. You must ensure that you learn all three ideas!

To what extent is there agreement between classical and modern liberals?

You must use appropriate thinkers you have studied to support your answer. [24 marks]

This kind of question tests all three Assessment Objectives, with marks divided equally between them. Each question will ask about one core political idea. You will not be asked to make comparisons between different ideas – for example, you will not be comparing the liberal and socialist views of the state. Instead, you will be asked to discuss key concepts associated with just one political idea, or tensions within a single idea.

- Questions begin with 'To what extent', so you must consider both sides of the argument – in this case you are looking for areas where different types of liberals agree and disagree. If you cover only one side you cannot achieve higher than Level 2 (5 to 9 marks).

- It is worth writing a brief plan to help you organise your ideas and make sure that you do not omit an important feature of your argument. You do not need to write a long introduction; outline the main areas that you will be covering and get started. Aim to write a minimum of three paragraphs, followed by a conclusion in which you draw the threads of the argument together, reflecting both sides presented in the question.

- You should use the ideas of some of the key thinkers from the specification to illustrate your answer, integrating this material into the answer rather than presenting it in a free-standing way. The mark scheme makes it clear that you cannot be awarded a mark higher than Level 2 unless you do so. But you do not need to refer to all five specified thinkers in your answer.

Here is part of a student's answer to this question.

Classical and modern liberals' differing views of individual freedom affect their attitudes towards the role of the state. Classical liberals believe that the state is at best a necessary evil and should therefore fulfil only a minimal role. As far as possible matters should be left in the hands of individuals and businesses, in order to avoid the risk of undermining people's independence. The classic statement of this viewpoint was made by John Stuart Mill in his book '*On Liberty*'. His 'harm principle' was based on the idea that the state should intervene only to protect individuals against the abuse of their own freedom by others.

By contrast, modern liberals believe in an enabling state. They argue that without some state intervention, some individuals and groups will remain disadvantaged by their social circumstances and thus not truly free. Freedom to starve is not true freedom. John Rawls, for example, argued that if people were invited to design a society that is just for all citizens, from behind a 'veil of ignorance', they would aim for one in which inequality is not too great. This is because if they do not know what the outcome will be for themselves, they will want to make sure that those at the bottom do not fall below a certain minimum standard. This will give individuals the best chance of realising their potential and enjoying freedom to make decisions about their own lives.

This is a good piece of analysis for the following reasons.

- The answer clearly contrasts the views of classical and modern liberals. The coverage of modern liberals is particularly good – the answer could have been improved by briefly explaining what classical liberals mean by a 'minimal state', but this is a small omission.

- The answer refers to one thinker for each of the two schools of liberal thought, giving just enough information to make their contribution to the debate clear.

CHAPTER
3

Socialism

The most distinctive feature of socialism is its opposition to capitalism, an economic system based on individualism, competition and inequality. Socialism seeks to provide a more humane alternative by creating a society founded on collectivism, co-operation and social equality. Within socialism, there are various traditions that aim either to remove or reduce class divisions.

In this section you will learn about:

- the core ideas and principles of socialism
- the differing views and tensions within socialism
- key socialist thinkers and their ideas.

You will be learning how the core ideas and principles of socialism relate to human nature, the state, society and the economy.

3.1 Socialism: core ideas and principles

Collectivism

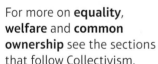

Link

For more on **equality**, **welfare** and **common ownership** see the sections that follow Collectivism.

Collectivism is one of the most important ideas underpinning socialist ideology, informing other socialist values and principles including **equality**, **welfare** and **common ownership**.

It maintains that humans can achieve their political, social and economic objectives more effectively through collective action than through individual effort. Collectivism also implies that society can only be transformed by collective endeavour – for socialists, it offers a way of achieving an ideal society.

Socialists endorse collectivism for two fundamental reasons.

- From a moral perspective, the interests of the group – such as a society or a community – should take priority over individual self-interest. Collective effort encourages social unity and a sense of social responsibility towards others.

- In practical economic terms, collectivism utilises the capabilities of the whole of society efficiently, avoiding the wastefulness and limited impact of competitive individual effort inherent in the capitalist economy.

Collectivism, therefore, reflects the socialist view that it is more important to pursue the interests of a society or a community rather than individual self-interest.

Key term

Fraternity
literally a 'brotherhood' – humans bound together by comradeship and a common outlook because they share the same basic nature and interests, while differences due to class, religion, nationality and ethnic background are far less significant.

This emphasis on collectivism is rooted in the socialist view of human nature, which argues that humans are social animals; as such, they prefer to live in social groups rather than alone. It follows that humans have the capacity for collective action and can work together in order to achieve their goals. In this sense, they are tied together by the bonds of **fraternity**.

Socialists also argue that human nature is moulded by social conditions – the experiences and circumstances of a person's life. According to the socialist view, people can only be defined or understood in terms of the social groups they belong to. This line of argument leads socialists to conclude that membership of a community or society offers humans true freedom and fulfilment.

Most socialists call for some form of state intervention and state planning to promote collectivist goals and ensure that the distribution of goods and services is not left to free-market forces. The pursuit of collectivism is commonly seen to involve the growth of the state, the expansion of state services and responsibilities, and an increase in state spending.

However, in practice, different strands of socialism vary in their commitment to collectivism.

Marxists and state socialists advocate collective action through a centralised state that organises all (or nearly all) production and distribution. For example, in the USSR after 1929, most industries were nationalised and all agricultural land was collectivised in order to transform a backward state into a modern industrial society, using complete state control of the economy to bring about change. After the Second World War, **communist** regimes in China and eastern Europe pursued similar policies of state-controlled collectivism.

Moderate socialists who accept some degree of free-market **capitalism** in the economy have pursued collectivism in a more limited way. For instance, the 1945–51 Labour government in the UK nationalised key industries – such as coal, electricity, and iron and steel – but left much of the economy in private hands.

Key terms

Marxism
an ideological system, within socialism, that drew on the writings of Marx and Engels and has at its core a philosophy of history that explains why it is inevitable that capitalism will be replaced by communism.

Communism
an economic and political system advocated by Karl Marx in which private ownership of the means of production is abolished in favour of common ownership. A classless society is established, production is based on human need, and the state withers away. Marxists argue that it is only under such a system that humans can realise their full potential.

Capitalism
wealth is privately owned and goods and services are produced for profit, as determined by market forces. The capitalist system has developed over the last five centuries to become the economic driving force of the modern global economy.

Figure 1.1: The most common forms of socialist collectivism

In many ways collectivism is a difficult concept to pin down precisely. This is partly because it is often used to describe very different things. The term has been applied to small self-governing communities (such as those based on the ideas of the 19th-century socialists Robert Owen and Charles Fourier), general opposition to individualism, and a system of centralised state control that directs the economy and society.

There are two basic criticisms of collectivism.

- Because collectivism emphasises group action and common interests, it suppresses human individuality and diversity.

- As collectivist objectives can only really be advanced through the agency of the state, it leads to the growth of arbitrary state power and the erosion of individual freedoms.

Since the 1970s, socialists generally have attached less importance to collectivism. This is due to a growing perception that collectivism in developed countries such as the UK (mainly in the form of state welfare, trade union power and government intervention in the economy) was producing a **dependency culture** and a sluggish, uncompetitive economic sector. The end of the Cold War in 1989 and the collapse of the USSR in 1991 reinforced this view as collectivism suffered a significant ideological defeat.

Common humanity

The socialist belief in a common humanity is also based on assumptions about human nature. Socialists see humans as social creatures with a tendency towards **co-operation**, sociability and rationality; humans naturally prefer to co-operate with, rather than compete against, each other. In fact, the individual cannot be understood without reference to society, because human behaviour is socially determined.

Socialists advocate co-operation based on their positive view of human nature. They argue that humans are naturally inclined to work together for the common good and that co-operative effort produces the best results for society. Co-operation also reinforces and reflects the socialist idea of a common humanity, in both moral and economic terms. People who co-operate rather than compete with each other form connections based on understanding, respect and mutual support. They also channel the capabilities of the whole group or community, rather than just the potential of a single individual.

By contrast, according to the socialist view, competition (particularly within a capitalist economy) is wasteful, promotes social divisions and generates conflict, hostility and resentment. Socialists maintain that capitalist economic competition sets one person against another, a process that encourages people to reject or disregard their common humanity (and social nature) rather than accept it. It encourages humans to be self-centred and belligerent.

This emphasis on a common humanity has led socialists to conclude that human motivation can be driven not just by material considerations but also by a moral view of people's role in society. People should work hard in order to improve their society or community because they have a sense of responsibility for other humans, particularly the least fortunate. The moral incentive to improve society rests on the acceptance of a common humanity.

For the economy to function properly, most contemporary socialists accept the need for at least some material rewards to motivate people, but they also stress that these should be linked to moral incentives. For example, co-operative effort to boost economic growth not only increases living standards for the working population but also provides the funds (through taxation) to finance welfare measures to help the vulnerable and the poor.

Finally, the belief in a common humanity has led socialists to support an interventionist role for the state. Marxists and state socialists argue that the agency of the state can be used to control economic production and distribution for the benefit of everyone. Social democrats also advocate state intervention, in the more limited form of welfare and redistribution programmes, to help those in the greatest need.

> **Link**
>
> For more on **dependency culture**, see Section 1.1 of Conservatism.

> **Key term**
>
> **Co-operation**
> working collectively to achieve mutual benefits.

EXTENSION ACTIVITY

Research one co-operative movement and produce a short report on what your chosen example reveals about socialist attitudes to human nature, the state, the economy and society.

Equality

The pursuit of social equality or equality of outcome is, arguably, the fundamental value of socialism. Socialists argue that this form of equality can be justified in several ways.

Social equality ensures fairness

Economic inequality (differences in wealth), according to the socialist view, is due to the structural inequalities in a capitalist society, rather than innate differences of ability among people. For this reason, some socialists tend to reject equality of opportunity because, in their view, such a concept justifies the unequal treatment of people on the grounds of innate ability. This argument reflects a view of human nature that emphasises people are born with the potential to be equal.

Other socialists maintain that, since it is part of human nature to have different abilities and attributes, inequality in the form of differential rewards is inevitable to some extent. These socialists tend to endorse an egalitarian approach to ensure that people are treated less unequally, in terms of material rewards and living conditions. Without this commitment to socialist egalitarianism, formal political and legal equality is compromised because, on its own, the latter does nothing to tackle the structural inequalities (such as social class) inherent in capitalism.

Social equality reinforces collectivism

A second argument is that social equality reinforces collectivism, co-operation and solidarity within society and the economy. Put simply, human beings are more likely to co-exist harmoniously in society and work together for the common economic good if they share the same social and economic conditions. For example, modern Sweden has high levels of social equality based on extensive wealth redistribution and social welfare. Socialists argue that such measures have made a major contribution to the stability, cohesion and economic output of Swedish society.

Social inequality, on the other hand, encourages conflict and instability. Societies with great economic and social inequalities are unstable because they are sharply divided into the 'haves' and 'have-nots'. Eventually, if the situation is not addressed, the disadvantaged sections of society will revolt in protest against their conditions, as happened in Russia in 1917 and Mexico in 1910–20. In a similar way, socialists also condemn equality of opportunity for fostering a competitive 'dog-eat-dog' outlook.

Social equality is a means of satisfying basic human needs

A third view is that social equality is a means of satisfying basic human needs that are part of human nature and essential to a sense of human fulfilment. Given that all people's basic needs are the same (such as food, friendship and shelter), socialists call for the equal, or more equal, distribution of wealth and resources to promote human fulfilment and realise human potential. In terms of the economy, most socialists agree that the free market, driven by the profit motive, cannot allocate wealth and resources fairly to all members of society. In their view, only the redistributive mechanism of the state can provide for everyone, irrespective of social position, and combat the divisive effects of the free market.

Debates about equality

A key debate within socialism focuses on the extent to which social and economic equality can or should be achieved. In many ways, this is a debate about the role of the state. Revolutionary socialists, such as **Marxists**, demand absolute equality for everyone in terms of material rewards and life opportunities. Such equality can be guaranteed only by the controlled distribution of goods and services, the abolition of private property and the introduction of **common ownership** of all means of production. Under this system, the state exercises common ownership and supervises the distribution of resources to prevent the return of social and economic inequalities.

> ## Link
>
> For more on **Marxists**, see Section 3.2.

> ## Key term
>
> **Common ownership**
> the means of production is owned by the workers so that all are able to participate in its running and to benefit from the wealth of society.

By contrast, **social democrats** call for more limited state intervention to achieve relative equality within society via welfare measures, government spending and progressive taxation. Their primary aim is to remove absolute poverty and, if this can be achieved, then a certain level of inequality can be tolerated. For social democrats, the state does not own or control all the means of production – its role is to adjust distribution to narrow differences in wealth and life chances. In essence, social democrats seek to reform rather than abolish capitalism and for this reason maintain that material incentives continue to play an important role in human motivation. As a result, the social-democrat position on social equality is flexible enough to embrace equality of opportunity.

> **Link** ↗
>
> For more on **social democrats**, see Section 3.2.

Common ownership

Socialists endorse common ownership because, in their view, private property (productive wealth or capital, rather than personal belongings) has several important drawbacks.

- As wealth is created by the communal endeavour of humans, it should be owned collectively, not by individuals.
- Private property encourages materialism and fosters the false belief that the achievement of personal wealth will bring fulfilment.
- Private property generates social conflict between 'have' and 'have-not' groups, such as owners and workers.

Broadly speaking, socialists have argued either that private property should be abolished entirely and replaced with common ownership or that the latter should be applied in a more limited way. In the USSR from the 1930s, the Stalinist regime implemented an all-encompassing form of common ownership by bringing the entire economy under state control. More moderate socialists, including the Attlee Labour government in the UK (1945–51), have opted for limited common ownership by nationalising only key strategic industries, including the coal mines, the railways and steel-making, leaving much of the economy in private hands. However, in recent decades, western socialist parties have placed less emphasis on common ownership in favour of other objectives.

> **Link** ↗
>
> For more on **the Third Way**, see Section 3.2.

Equality of outcome
Equality of outcome maintains that rewards should be based on an individual's contribution. Since this will vary from person to person some inequality will persist but differences in rewards will not be as marked as in the free-market system. Equality of outcome tends to be supported by fundamentalist socialists (who reject capitalism) as a way of removing the free market's influence but opposed by social democrats and **the Third Way** as a form of artificial social and economic 'levelling'.

Absolute equality
Absolute equality is based on the notion that everyone will receive the same rewards, providing they make a contribution to society. Over time, each person will make a broadly equal contribution. This approach is supported by Marxists as the basis of a communist society but rejected by social democrats and the Third Way as impractical and potentially destabilising.

Disagreements among socialists about the nature of equality

Equality of opportunity
Equality of opportunity is based on the principle that everyone should have an equal chance to make the best of their abilities. There should be a 'level playing field' with no artificial barriers to progress for those with ability, talent and a positive attitude to hard work. This approach is supported by social democrats and the Third Way on meritocratic grounds but rejected by Marxists because it does not seek to remove capitalism and its structural inequalities.

Equality of welfare
Equality of welfare accepts that human society is inevitably unequal but also maintains that every individual is entitled to have an equal minimum standard of living guaranteed by state welfare provision. Equality of welfare is endorsed by social democrats and the Third Way because it provides a vital safety net for the most vulnerable in society. Marxists reject it because this welfare provision does not seek to remove capitalism and its structural inequalities.

Figure 1.2: The main disagreements among socialists about the nature of equality

Pause & reflect ✔

Why do different socialists disagree about the nature of equality?

Political opponents of socialist ideology have rejected social equality because:

- **it is unjust** – in treating everybody the same irrespective of their attributes, it does not reward people according to their skills and abilities
- **it lowers human ambition, motivation and initiative** by removing or downgrading material incentives, leading to economic underperformance
- **it restricts the liberties of the individual** because it can only be implemented through extensive state intervention and control
- **it stifles diversity and individuality**, encouraging a 'colourless' social uniformity.

Social class

For socialists, the existence of social classes explains the most important divides in society, rather than the actions of individuals or the essence of human nature itself. At one level, socialists have used the concept of social class to enhance their understanding of social and political development. This approach has led them to conclude that people with a similar socio-economic position in society share a similar outlook and have common aims. It follows that social classes, rather than individuals or human nature, have been the principal agents of change throughout history. For example, Marxists assert that conflict between ruling and revolutionary classes is the driving force behind such change in society.

At another level, socialism's focus on social class is based on an ideological commitment to represent the interests of, and improve conditions for, the working class. Indeed, for socialists, the working class provides the means for bringing about a socialist transformation of society and the economy. Having said this, social class is not viewed as either an essential or everlasting feature of society because communist societies aim to eradicate all class distinctions, and other socialist societies seek to diminish class inequalities significantly.

Categorising social classes

Social class provides a way of categorising and analysing society by dividing it into different economic and social groups. In basic terms, a social class consists of a group of people with similar social and economic characteristics. Marxism, in particular, has offered a highly influential class analysis of society and politics. From a communist perspective, a person's class is determined by their position within the economy (such as a landowner, a capitalist or a wage earner) and these economically based class distinctions powerfully shape the nature of society. The crucial Marxist class division is between capital and labour – between the bourgeoisie (who own productive wealth) and the proletariat (who have to sell their labour power in order to survive).

Other definitions of class commonly focus on how occupational groups – such as middle class/white collar/non-manual workers and working class/blue collar/manual workers – differ in terms of income and status.

Marketing organisations have developed a more sophisticated classification scheme that distinguishes between six categories:

A	Higher managerial, administrative or professional
B	Intermediate managerial, administrative or professional
C1	Supervisory, clerical
C2	Skilled manual worker
D	Semi-skilled and unskilled manual worker
E	State pensioner, casual worker and unemployed

The British Election Study, which analyses voting behaviour, uses another class scheme. This distinguishes between owners and managers, and between the petite bourgeoisie (small proprietors) and the working class. Most contemporary political commentators maintain that social class now exerts a declining influence on society due to deindustrialisation and dealignment (a trend that sees a social group abandoning its previous partisan loyalty to a particular party, resulting in less predictable voting patterns).

Although clearly central to the ideology, socialists disagree over the importance of social class. Marxists traditionally emphasise the fundamental role of class politics based on the economic division between capital and labour. In this analysis, a person's class position is economically determined by their relationship to the means of production. Marxism maintains that conflict is inevitable between the owners of productive wealth (the capitalists or the bourgeoisie) and those who have to sell their labour to survive (the proletariat or working class). Under the capitalist system, argue Marxists, the state becomes an instrument of class rule, with the bourgeoisie using institutions and agencies (such as the political and legal systems, the bureaucracy and the police) to maintain their dominance. Nevertheless, this class conflict, according to Marxist theory, grows in intensity and inevitably divides society sharply into two antagonistic groups – the 'haves' and 'have-nots'. Eventually, this process leads to a proletarian revolution that overthrows the capitalist state and the bourgeoisie. For Marxists, the state will only wither away once the workers' gains have been consolidated and social class differences are replaced by a classless, equal society.

By contrast, social democrats define social class in more fluid terms, emphasising income and status differences between non-manual and manual occupational groups. Social democrats also tend to argue that socialist objectives can be achieved through targeted state intervention to narrow (not remove) class distinctions. The state, according to social democrats, does not represent an instrument of oppressive class rule but rather provides the welfare and redistribution schemes by which class inequalities can be reduced. Unlike Marxists, who stress class conflict and revolutionary action, social democrats advocate class consensus in society and peaceful social improvement.

Over the last 50 years or so, the connection between socialist ideology and class politics has weakened considerably. The decline in class politics, reflected in the social democrats' more moderate stance, has been an important consequence of significant changes in the economy, notably deindustrialisation and the rise of the service sector. Deindustrialisation has led to the decline of traditional staple industries (such as coal mining and steel making), which had previously supported a culture of working-class solidarity, pro-socialist-worker politics and powerful trade union organisations. The contraction of the staple industries has undermined working-class solidarity and working-class communities, and has reduced the size of the manual workforce. Deindustrialisation has created post-industrial societies with service- and information-based economies and expanding middle classes.

As a result, in recent decades, moderate socialist parties have adapted their programmes to appeal to non-manual workers. They have also attempted to redefine their brand of progressive politics in terms of 'classless' concerns, such as green and feminist issues, and have placed less emphasis on the redress of working-class grievances.

Workers' control

Link

For more on **syndicalism**, see Anarchism chapter.

The term 'workers' control' refers to the complete or partial ownership of an economic enterprise (such as a business or factory) by those employed there. It can also be used in a wider and more political sense to mean workers' control of the state. The concept has influenced different strands of socialist thought, including Marxism and **syndicalism**. Workers' control covers a range of schemes that aim to provide workers with full democratic control over their places of employment. These schemes go beyond the right to be consulted and participate by seeking to establish real decision-making powers for workers in their particular industries or occupations.

Such a system is often justified in terms of core socialist ideas and principles. First, workers' control is clearly based on socialist views about human nature, as it promotes collective effort and the pursuit of group (rather than individual) interests. Furthermore, some socialists have argued that workers' control, with its emphasis on fully involving employees in all aspects of the production process, can maximise human potential by combating alienation at the workplace and undermining the capitalist view of labour as a mere commodity.

Second, workers' control has significant implications for the economy. Some socialists maintain that, as the workers are the key factor in the production process, they should have the right to control the means of production. Workers' control aims either to dilute or replace capitalist control of the economy. For example, French syndicalists in the late 19th and early 20th centuries called for the overthrow of capitalism and the introduction of workers' control of the economy based on the trade unions and proletarian political institutions.

Third, those endorsing workers' control hold contrasting views regarding the role played by the state in the socialist transformation. Syndicalists are hostile towards the state, regarding it as an instrument of capitalist oppression and an inefficient bureaucratic structure incapable of initiating meaningful reform. Consequently, they call for the state to be forcibly replaced with a form of workers' control based on a federation of trade union bodies. British guild socialism, a pro-workers' control movement that emerged in the early 20th century, was internally divided over the role of the state. Although all guild socialists argued for state ownership of industry in the pursuit of workers' control, some called for the state to remain essentially in its existing form, whereas others called for the state to be turned into a federal body composed of workers' guilds, consumers' organisations and local government bodies.

Finally, workers' control can be seen as an important step towards a socialist society. At one end of the spectrum, 'moderate' workers' control in a capitalist society (such as increased trade union and shopfloor influence over manager's decisions) provides a method of introducing limited reforms to the social and economic structure. At the other end, industrial self-management by workers living under state socialism (such as the workers' councils operating in Yugoslavia in the 1950s and 1960s) reinforces the idea that a socialist society should raise the condition and status of the working class.

Critics reject such schemes on the grounds that they are utopian and fail to acknowledge that business needs risk-takers and investors as well as workers. According to this view, workers often lack the entrepreneurial attributes necessary for success. In taking over the management functions of appointments, promotions and dismissals, manual employees may adversely affect the economic viability of their workplace.

Case study: Russian Revolution

- In mid-1917, the Russian economy collapsed under strain of the First World War. Workers' factory committees were established to supervise or replace managers, to try to maintain production. By October 1917, this involved about 40 per cent of the Russian industrial working-class.

- Bolsheviks issued the Decree on Workers' Control (November 1917), giving additional powers to factory committees.

- Lenin was worried that factory committees would not follow Bolshevik directives. By 1918, he was taking steps to curb their powers. Factory committees later merged with trade unions under firm Bolshevik control.

Case study: Guild socialism in Britain

- Emerged in the early 20th century and gained momentum during the First World War, due to rise of left-wing shop stewards' movement, which called for workers' control in war industries.

- Guild socialists advocated state ownership of industry and workers' control by delegating authority to democratically run national guilds.

- The movement collapsed in 1920s, but stimulated debate in the Labour Party and trade-union movement about workers' control.

Case study: Syndicalism in France

- Militant trade-union movement began in France in the 1890s, heavily influenced by Georges Sorel's thinking on direct action and use of general strike to secure working-class objectives.

- Once a general strike had destroyed capitalist order, syndicalists envisaged a system where each industry would be run by trade unions and political institutions; the state would be replaced by workers' control based on a federation of trade-union bodies.

- Syndicalist ideas influenced the development of labour organisations in Italy, Spain and USA in the early 20th century.

Questions

- Which labour movement detailed in the three case studies above do you think has had most influence on labour relations in modern-day Europe?

- Which do you think would have done most to have improved working conditions at the time?

3.2 Differing views and tensions within socialism

Revolutionary socialism

Revolutionary socialism rejects the use of democratic methods in the pursuit of a socialist society. In the 19th century, this 'revolutionary road' to socialism was popular with many on the left for two reasons.

- The early development of industrialisation and capitalism brought poverty, exploitation and unemployment, which was expected to radicalise the working classes who were at the sharp end of these changes.

- As the workers were not part of the 'political nation', they had little ability to influence policies in government systems usually dominated by the landed aristocracy or bourgeoisie.

Socialism through revolution is also based on the conviction that the state is a 'bourgeois' instrument of class oppression, defending capitalist interests against those of the working classes. The primacy of the ruling class is reinforced by key institutions and agencies of the state, such as the parliamentary system, the mass media and high finance. Piecemeal or gradual change will not lead to a genuinely socialist society because the ruling class and bourgeois values are too firmly entrenched. For example, capitalists are adept at infiltrating political parties, representative assemblies and labour organisations in order to blunt their radicalism.

Furthermore, revolutionary socialism calls for a total transformation of society, so the existing state has to be completely uprooted and replaced with new revolutionary institutions. Such a fundamental change often leads to violence; the ruling class is unlikely to give up its power without a fight. Thus revolutionary socialists in Russia (1918–21), China (1946–49) and Mexico (1910–20) had to fight bloody civil wars to establish their regimes.

Finally, revolutionary socialists maintain that any attempt to 'humanise' capitalism, a system based on inequality and exploitation, would completely undermine the principles and objectives of socialism.

After the Second World War, revolutionary socialism was adopted by many national liberation movements in Africa, Asia and South America, including the Chinese communists led by Mao, the Viet Cong directed by Hoàng Văn Thái and the Cuban insurgents under Castro. These movements concluded that such a strategy was the only way to remove the colonial powers and their domestic allies and dismantle outdated social and economic systems. The intention was to bring about rapid modernisation to enable these societies to catch up with the more prosperous and technologically advanced industrial countries.

The pursuit of the 'revolutionary road' has usually resulted in fundamentalist socialist regimes, such as those established in the Soviet Union, the People's Republic of China and Cambodia under the Khmer Rouge. In all three cases, successful insurrection destroyed the old order, which permitted the creation of a new socialist society based on state control of the economy. Revolutionary strategy also encouraged the establishment of rigid hierarchical parties with dominant leaders and the use of ruthless dictatorial political methods to remove all opposition and introduce totalitarianism.

The end of the Cold War in the late 1980s and early 1990s delivered a hugely damaging blow to revolutionary socialism as communism collapsed in the Soviet Union and the satellite states of the Eastern bloc.

Social democracy

Social democracy emerged after 1945 as western socialist parties embraced electoral politics and switched to the more limited aim of reforming, rather than abolishing, capitalism.

Ideologically, social democracy attempts to reconcile free-market capitalism with state intervention, based on three assumptions.

- Although the capitalist system is a dependable creator of wealth, the way it distributes wealth produces inequality and poverty.
- State intervention in economic and social affairs can protect the public and remedy the weaknesses of capitalism.
- Peaceful and constitutional methods should be used to bring about social change.

Social democracy is chiefly concerned with the just or fair distribution of wealth in society; its defining core value is **social justice**. This form of socialism rests on a moral, rather than a Marxist, critique of capitalism: socialism is morally superior to capitalism. Christian principles have also

> **Pause & reflect**
>
> Why has revolutionary socialism held relatively little appeal in developed countries in the West?

> **Key term**
>
> **Social justice**
> a commitment to greater equality and a just distribution of wealth in order to achieve a more equitable distribution of life chances within society.

informed the social-democratic position, notably the Christian socialist tradition in the UK and 'liberation theology' in Latin America. Social democracy can encompass a variety of perspectives, including the acceptance of private-sector productivity and personal responsibility.

By the late 19th century, some socialist thinkers concluded that the Marxist analysis of capitalism was flawed. Eduard Bernstein published a **revisionist** study, *Evolutionary Socialism* (1899), which argued that capitalism was not developing along Marxist lines. Instead of succumbing to economic crises and promoting ever-deepening class conflict, the capitalist system was proving resilient and adaptable.

Bernstein argued, for example, that joint stock companies had widened the ownership of wealth through shareholders, rather than concentrating it in the hands of fewer and fewer capitalists. Bernstein concluded that capitalism was not a brutally exploitative system and it could be reformed peacefully through electoral politics. He advocated state ownership of key industries, and legal safeguards and welfare measures to protect the workers.

During the 20th century, western socialist parties increasingly recognised the dynamism and productivity of the market economy, abandoned their commitment to economic planning and pursued a revisionist policy of reforming capitalism. The Swedish Social Democratic Labour Party and the West German Social Democratic Party made this shift officially in the 1930s and 1950s respectively. The British Labour Party remained formally committed to common ownership until 1995, but post-war Labour governments never subjected the British economy to extensive state control.

Social democracy adopted a more limited programme, with three key elements.

- Support for a mixed economy of both state and privately owned enterprises, with only key strategic industries nationalised, as under the Attlee Labour government of 1945–51.
- **Keynesianism** as a means of regulating the capitalist economy and maintaining full employment.
- Reform of capitalism chiefly through the welfare state, which would redistribute wealth to tackle social inequality and the problem of poverty.

In 1956, the British socialist **Anthony Crosland** put forward the intellectual case for social democracy in his book *The Future of Socialism*. Crosland maintained that a new skilled governing class of salaried managers, technocrats and officials had now taken over the control of industry from the old capitalist class. The pursuit of profit was only one of its objectives because this new technical and administrative elite also had wider concerns, such as the maintenance of good employer-worker relations and the protection of the business's reputation. Consequently, Crosland asserted, capitalism was no longer a system of harsh class oppression, and extensive state direction and control was now irrelevant.

Instead, Crosland emphasised the need for social justice (rather than common ownership) by stressing the redistributive role of the welfare state funded by progressive taxation. Under such a system, Crosland argued, economic growth would sustain social democracy. An expanding economy would provide the taxation revenue to pay for welfare spending and improve the living standards of the more affluent, who were expected to finance this social expenditure.

The early post-1945 decades were the heyday of social democracy, but this depended on two potentially conflicting features. By viewing market economics as the only secure way to create wealth, social democrats effectively conceded that capitalism could be reformed but not removed. At the same time, social democracy retained its socialist credentials by calling for social justice and distributive equality – the reduction of poverty and some redistribution of wealth to assist poorer social groups.

Key terms

Revisionism
a revised political theory that modifies the established or traditional view. Here, revisionism refers to the critical reinterpretation of Marxism.

Evolutionary socialism
a form of socialism advocating a parliamentary route to deliver a long-term, radical transformation in a gradual, piecemeal way through legal and peaceful means.

Keynesian economics
the economic theory developed by British economist John Maynard Keynes, which argued that governments should:

- spend or invest money to stimulate the economy and boost demand in times of recession
- use taxation and interest rates to manage demand within the economy, sustaining growth and deterring recession.

Link

For more on **Anthony Crosland**, see Section 3.3.

In short, social democracy was a balancing act that attempted to deliver both economic efficiency and egalitarianism. This central tension within social democracy was concealed during the early post-war boom-decades when economic growth, high employment and low inflation delivered rising living standards for most people and the tax revenues to expand welfare programmes.

By the 1970s and 1980s, however, a sharp economic downturn exposed this central tension within social democracy. With unemployment mounting, the demand for welfare services increased as the tax-based funding for such social support declined (due to fewer people having a job and company profits falling). Now, social democrats faced a fundamental dilemma: should they reduce inflation and taxes to stimulate the economy or prioritise the funding of welfare to protect the lower paid and unemployed? Other factors also exacerbated the difficulties of social democracy in the 1980s and 1990s. The impact of the shift to a post-industrial service-based economy, and the contraction of the working class due to deindustrialisation, reduced social democracy's traditional electoral base. The collapse of the Soviet communist bloc (1989–91) inflicted further damage on social democracy. Popular rejection of the Soviet system also discredited other forms of socialism, including social democracy, which looked to the state to deliver economic and social reform.

Third way

Partly in response to this crisis of social democracy, from the 1980s reformist socialist parties in Europe and elsewhere revised their ideological stance and moved away from traditional social-democratic principles. Their new position, known as the 'third way' or 'neo-revisionism', attempted to formulate an ideological alternative to traditional social democracy and free-market neo-liberalism in the context of a modern globalised economy. New Labour first introduced neo-revisionism in the UK during the 1990s. There is considerable disagreement over the third way's relationship to socialism due to the ideologically nebulous nature of neo-revisionism.

Nevertheless, five key features characterise third-way thinking.

The primacy of the market over the state

The third way accepts the primacy of the market over the state and rejects 'top down' state intervention. Neo-revisionists accept globalisation and the 'knowledge economy' where information and communication technologies ensure competitiveness and productivity. By endorsing a dynamic market economy and an enterprise culture to maximise wealth creation, the third way has ideological links with neo-liberalism. Under New Labour, for example, the private sector became involved in the provision of public services through Private Finance Initiative (PFI) schemes and Public-Private Partnerships (PPP). This pro-market-economy stance also led neo-revisionists to downplay the socialist policy of redistributing wealth through progressive taxation.

The value of community and moral responsibility

Neo-revisionists also endorse the value of community and moral responsibility. Here, third-way thinking distances itself from the perceived moral and social downside of neo-liberal economics – a market-driven free-for-all. New Labour attempted to resolve this tension in the late 1990s and early 2000s by linking communitarian and liberal ideas. The resulting communitarian liberalism emphasised that personal autonomy operates within a communal context based on mutual dependence and benefit, balancing rights with responsibilities. Neo-revisionist initiatives in the UK regarding welfare and parental involvement in schools reflected these assumptions.

A social model based on consensus and harmony

Third-way thinking puts forward a social model based on consensus and harmony that clearly differs from the traditional socialist focus on class differences and inequality. Consequently, third-way advocates see no contradiction in endorsing what might be seen as opposing values or concepts. Neo-revisionists, for example, champion self-reliance and mutual dependence, and the market economy and fairness.

Social inclusion

Third-way supporters have also shifted away from the socialist commitment to equality in order to endorse the concept of social inclusion (individuals can only participate fully in society by acquiring the appropriate skills, rights and opportunities). Neo-revisionists, therefore, emphasise equality of opportunity and the benefits of a meritocratic social system. The third way does not oppose great individual wealth providing it helps to improve the overall prosperity of society. Furthermore, welfare should target socially marginalised groups and provide people with the assistance they need to enable them to improve their own situation. Tony Blair, the UK Labour prime minister, summed up this approach as 'a hand up, not a handout'. The neo-revisionist assumption here is that welfare support should target those who are actively seeking employment and want to be self-reliant.

A competition or market state

The third way also takes a different view of the state's function, with neo-revisionists promoting the concept of a competition (or market) state to develop the national workforce's skills and knowledge base. With its focus on social investment, the competition state emphasises the importance of education for improving a person's job prospects and boosting economic growth. This explains why an early New Labour government slogan was 'Education, education, education'.

Although New Labour was electorally successful in 1997, 2001 and 2005, many socialists criticise third-way thinking for its lack of real socialist content (for example, watered down commitments to equality and redistribution of wealth). In their view, neo-revisionism was essentially a Labour rebranding exercise to make the party more attractive to middle-class voters and business interests following four consecutive general-election defeats. Growing disillusion with the third-way approach certainly helps to explain the election of an avowedly left-wing Labour leader, Jeremy Corbyn, in 2015.

Nevertheless, third-way ideas have influenced various left-of-centre parties, including the German SDP and the South African ANC. Furthermore, under New Labour, neo-revisionism introduced important measures that promoted social justice and improved the position of the most disadvantaged in society (such as educational maintenance grants, the minimum wage and family tax credits).

Pause & reflect

How similar are the ideas of social democracy and the third way? Make a table that shows areas of overlap and difference.

Human nature	Socialists have a positive view of human nature and regard people as social creatures who are co-operative, sociable and rational. From this perspective, human behaviour is socially determined and people naturally prefer to work together rather than compete against each other. This co-operative outlook enables humans to form connections (based on understanding, mutual support and respect), harness the capabilities of the whole community or society, and experience personal growth. Marxist socialists maintain that the true co-operative and communal instincts of humans can be liberated only by the removal of the exploitative and oppressive capitalist system and the creation of a communist society.
The state	In theory, Marxism regards the state as an instrument of class rule. Marxist socialists argue that, under capitalism, the ruling bourgeoisie use the state apparatus (such as the political and legal system) to maintain their dominance over the proletariat. In their view, the state will wither away once communism has established a classless equal society. However, in practice, Marxist and state socialist regimes have used a centralised state to organise most or all production and distribution, and control their populations. Social democrats, by contrast, argue that limited state intervention in social and economic affairs can safeguard the public and remedy the shortcomings of capitalism. Third-way supporters, or neo-revisionists, adopt a more sceptical attitude towards the state, asserting that 'top down' state intervention in economic and social matters is both inefficient and ineffective. For neo-revisionists, the state should focus on social investment in infrastructure and education to improve job opportunities and encourage self-reliance.
Society	Traditionally, socialists have seen society as being characterised mainly by class inequalities, economic divisions and significant disparities in property ownership. For example, Marxists argue that capitalist society is dominated by class conflict between the ruling bourgeoisie and the proletariat. In their view, only communism, with its commitment to classlessness and absolute equality, can deliver a stable and unified society. Social democrats tend to view society in more fluid terms. They accept that class inequalities exist, but also maintain that these social differences can be reduced through peaceful improvements, such as welfare and redistribution schemes. Social democrats also recognise that deindustrialisation and the rise of the service economy has made society increasingly 'middle class'. Neo-revisionist thinking on society rejects the traditional socialist emphasis on class distinctions and inequality. Instead, the third-way model of society stresses harmony, consensus and social inclusion.
The economy	Most socialists call for some form of intervention or planning in economic affairs because they maintain that the profit-driven free market cannot allocate wealth and resources fairly. Marxists and state socialists advocate replacing capitalism with a centrally planned economy based on common ownership of the means of production. Under communism, Marxists argue, economic production will be determined solely by human need. In contrast, social democrats accept a degree of free-market capitalism, and favour a mixed economy of nationalised key industries and privately-owned enterprises. Social democrats also endorse Keynesian interventionist techniques to regulate capitalism and maintain employment. In addition, they support welfare policies to redistribute wealth. Neo-revisionists readily accept the primacy of the free market in the economy since, in their view, it is the most efficient system of production – the resulting economic growth benefits everyone and encourages desirable personal qualities such as responsibility. Third-way thinking also rejects state intervention in the economy on the grounds that it discourages investment and stifles entrepreneurial initiative.

Table 2.1: Core principles and ideas of socialism in action

3.3 Socialist thinkers and their ideas

Karl Marx (1818–83) and Friedrich Engels (1820–95)

Key ideas

- Social class is central to socialism.
- Human nature is socially determined and can only be expressed under communism.

Karl Marx and Friedrich Engels are the most famous revolutionary socialists. Their works include *The Communist Manifesto* (1848) and *Capital* (1867, 1885, 1894). For Marx and Engels, social class is central to socialism and underpins three key elements of Marxism: **historical materialism**, **dialectical change** and revolutionary **class consciousness**.

Karl Marx and Friedrich Engels: 'The proletarians have nothing to lose but their chains. Working Men of All Countries, Unite!'

- Historical materialism maintains that historical and social development can be explained in terms of economic and class factors. The economic system powerfully influences or 'conditions' all other aspects of society.
- Dialectical change is a process of development that occurs through the conflict or struggle between two opposing forces. Marx and Engels thought that at each stage of human history, dialectical change is propelled by the struggle between exploiters and the exploited (for example, capitalists and workers). This process only ends with the establishment of a communist society.
- Class consciousness is needed for the oppressed to overthrow their oppressors. For example, under capitalism, before a socialist revolution can take place, the proletariat has to become a 'class for itself', aware of its own interests and determined to pursue them.

Like most socialists, Marx and Engels view humans as essentially social beings, whose behaviour and potential are influenced more by nurture than by nature. Humans are sociable, rational and co-operative, capable of leading satisfying lives based on fulfilling work, where the conditions for free creative production exist.

Under capitalism, these conditions do not exist, so the individual cannot realise his or her true human potential. The solution, Marx contends, is the creation of a communist society that abolishes private property, class differences, the state apparatus and divisions between mental and physical labour. Freed from such constraints, the individual can become a fully developed person, engaging in many activities and achieving their potential through creative work in co-operation with others. This ideal stands in sharp contrast to the brutal and oppressive Marxist regimes of the 20th and 21st centuries.

Key terms

Historic materialism
Marxist theory that the economic base (the economic system) forms the superstructure (culture, politics, law, ideology, religion, art and social consciousness).

Dialectic
a process of development that occurs through the conflict between two opposing forces. In Marxism, class conflict creates internal contradictions within society, which drives historical change.

Class consciousness
the self-understanding of social class that is a historical phenomenon, created out of collective struggle.

Pause & reflect

Can you trace common themes in the work of the five thinkers on pages 137–141? List areas of agreement and disagreement and try to find ways in which later thinkers have developed the ideas of earlier socialist theorists. In particular consider key areas such as:

- the state
- equality
- capitalism
- social class
- route to socialism.

Beatrice Webb (1858–1943)

Key ideas

- The 'inevitability of gradualness'– establishing socialism peacefully by passing democratic reforms through existing parliamentary institutions.

- The expansion of the state will deliver socialism.

Beatrice Webb: 'Nature still obstinately refuses to co-operate by making the rich people innately superior to the poor people.'

The daughter of an industrialist, Beatrice Webb was an early member of the Fabian Society. With her husband, Sidney Webb, she wrote a number of pro-socialist works, including *A Constitution for the Socialist Commonwealth of Great Britain* (1920), *The Decay of Capitalist Civilisation* (1923) and *Soviet Communism: A New Civilisation?* (1935).

Webb rejected the Marxist theory of class struggle, endorsing the 'inevitability of gradualness'. She thought that the new mass age of democratic politics would lead inevitably to policies to secure the interests of the working class. The move towards socialism could be speeded up by presenting reasoned arguments and painstaking research to show the efficiency of socialism compared to capitalism.

At first, Webb opposed the idea of a working-class party, focusing instead on spreading evolutionary socialist ideas among leading liberals and conservatives. Her attitude to suffrage was just as elitist. She thought the average voter was limited, selfish and uninformed, so she rejected direct democracy and the 'self-interested' nature of workers' control. Representative democracy was preferable because it would lead to a skilled governing class subject to democratic constraints.

Webb and her husband Sidney believed that the expansion of the state was critical in order to deliver socialism – the 'economic side of democracy'. They saw the gradual growth of state power as evidence that collectivism would bring in a new socialist age. For example, local authorities were increasingly providing utilities and amenities such as gas, public transport and parks. The expanding state had 'silently changed its character… from police power to housekeeping on a national scale', and would ensure the peaceful emergence of socialism.

Webb emphasised that the state's ability to deliver socialism would depend heavily on highly trained specialists and administrators to organise society and the economy. Over time, municipal and state intervention would increase as more areas of life would need to be regulated and planned. The role of the disciplined elite would be to run the state 'to guide the mass of citizens to a Socialist State'.

Webb and her husband increasingly recognised that central state action would further the development of socialism. Webb's participation in the Royal Commission on the Poor Laws (1905–09) made her aware that problems such as unemployment had national rather than local characteristics. This belief in centralised state action, 'rational' planning and bureaucratic direction led them, rather naively, to endorse Stalinist Russia in the 1930s. They claimed that their interest had been stimulated by 'the deliberate planning of all the nation's production, distribution and exchange, not for swelling the profit of the few but for increasing the consumption of the whole community.'

Rosa Luxemburg (1871–1919)

Key ideas

- Evolutionary socialism is not possible as capitalism is based on economic exploitation.
- Struggle by the proletariat creates the class-consciousness needed to overthrow the capitalist state.

Rosa Luxemburg was a Polish Marxist and revolutionary, and was regarded as the most prominent left-wing member of the German Social Democratic Party (SPD). In a series of influential books, Luxemburg developed important critiques of evolutionary socialism and **revisionism**, and disagreed with Lenin over key features of Marxism.

Rosa Luxemburg: 'The mass strike is the first natural, impulsive form of every great revolutionary struggle of the proletariat and the more highly developed the antagonism is between capital and labour, the more effective and decisive must mass strikes become.'

Link

For more on **revisionism**, see Section 3.2.

In *Social Reform or Revolution* (1899) she argued that socialism could not be created gradually from within capitalism through a series of reforms. Instead it was essential for the proletariat to achieve a revolutionary conquest of political power for two key reasons.

- Any evolutionary or revisionist socialist strategy would leave the capitalist system of economic exploitation intact. Worker organisations would never be able to determine their wages or resolve the contradiction between social production and the private appropriation of wealth. Socialist parties would lose their sense of political purpose and the revolutionary instincts of the working class would be dampened.
- An evolutionary or reformist socialist strategy could never smooth away the exploitation inherent in the capitalist economy, because the contradictions and crises of capitalism made its collapse inevitable.

In *The Accumulation of Capital* (1913), Luxemburg said that the capitalist market could not absorb all the surplus value generated. By accessing less economically developed territories and markets, capitalist states effectively exported the capitalist system. Eventually, capitalism would run out of new territories and markets to exploit and the system would collapse.

Luxemburg also maintained that struggle by the proletariat for reform and democracy was essential for the creation of the worker class-consciousness that would overthrow capitalist society. In *The Mass Strike, the Political Party and the Trade Unions* (1906) she argued that this consciousness would develop naturally from within the workers themselves. Proletarian discontent against state control would erupt in numerous unsuccessful and successful strikes, culminating in a spontaneous mass strike, which would radicalise the workers and bring about a socialist revolution.

Luxemburg's views brought her into direct conflict with the Bolshevik leader, Lenin. In *Organizational Questions of Social Democracy* (1904), Luxemburg rejected Lenin's argument that the workers had to be led by a small, rigidly centralised vanguard party in order to overthrow capitalism. In her view, a revolutionary party that demanded blind obedience would create an 'absolute dividing wall' between the leaders and the mass membership, preventing workers from becoming 'free and independent directors' of society under socialism.

Anthony Crosland (1918–77)

Key ideas

- The inherent contradictions in capitalism.

- State-managed capitalism.

Crosland was the leading post-war revisionist theorist in British socialism and had a major influence on the Labour Party. In his 1956 book *The Future of Socialism*, Crosland claimed that capitalism had radically changed and no longer resembled an economic system based on inherent contradictions, as described by Marx. Modern capitalism lacked the internal tensions to drive social change or bring about revolution.

Anthony Crosland: 'Marx has little or nothing to offer the contemporary socialist.'

For Crosland, this was in part due to the extension of democracy, the growth of industrial bargaining and the dispersal of business ownership. Decision-making in business was now in the hands of professional managers, key industries had been nationalised and a comprehensive welfare state had been established. Now governments pursuing Keynesian economics could maintain high employment, ensure low inflation and promote continuous growth. Rather than collapsing, capitalism had produced rising living standards.

Crosland argued that the main aim of socialism now was to manage capitalism to deliver greater social equality and social justice, with more egalitarian distribution of rewards, status and privileges, and no class barriers. Crosland put forward four justifications for equality.

- Economic efficiency – there was no clear relationship between an individual's status and rewards and the importance of their economic function.

- Creation of a more communitarian society – existing inequalities created resentments, which had an adverse effect on economic progress.

- The injustice of rewarding talents and abilities – these were largely due to nature and nurture, not individual responsibility.

- The need for social justice – Crosland called this 'democratic equality' and argued that socialism had to move beyond equality of opportunity.

Crosland's more egalitarian society depended on high levels of government spending on welfare services and the redistribution of income and wealth. He was convinced that Keynesian demand-management of a mixed economy, with some nationalised industries in a system based on private ownership, was the best way to generate sustained economic growth. Economic expansion would provide the government with funds for welfare and social spending to improve life for those at the bottom of society, while enabling the more affluent to preserve their standard of living.

Another important part of Crosland's revisionist socialism centred on his call for the development of comprehensive secondary education and the expansion of higher education, where children of all abilities and backgrounds would share similar educational experiences. As Education Secretary (1965–67), Crosland issued the famous Department of Education and Science circular 10/65, inviting all education authorities in England and Wales to submit plans for the reform of secondary education on comprehensive lines. He reportedly said to his wife: 'If it's the last thing I do I'm going to destroy every grammar school in England and Wales.'

Anthony Giddens (1938–)

Key ideas

- The 'third way' – a new political approach to social democracy.
- The rejection of state intervention.

Anthony Giddens, the British sociologist and social theorist, was arguably the most important intellectual figure in the development of the 'third way'. Widely seen as Tony Blair's 'favourite academic', Giddens influenced the political direction taken by the US Clinton administration and the New Labour government in the UK.

Anthony Giddens: 'The new mixed economy looks… for a synergy between public and private sectors.'

In his book, *The Third Way: The Renewal of Social Democracy* (1998), Giddens argued for a new political approach that drew on the strengths of the social democratic and neo-liberal free-market traditions while avoiding their weaknesses. Two key themes were:

- the rejection of state intervention and acceptance of the free market in the economy, with the emphasis on equality of opportunity over equality, and responsibility and community over class conflict
- the role of the state in social investment in infrastructure and education, not economic and social engineering.

According to Giddens, by the late 20th century social democracy had to be modernised due to the impact of globalisation, the rise of the new knowledge economy and the growth of more individualistic aspirations. He argued that 'top down' state intervention was now both inefficient and ineffective. The left should 'get comfortable with the markets' because the free-market economy was not only the most efficient system of production (and economic growth would benefit everyone) but also encouraged personal qualities such as responsibility.

Giddens tempered this view by stressing that, for this market-driven system to be fair, everyone needed an equal opportunity to better themselves through their ability and effort. Nevertheless, he called for government action to control the widening inequalities of outcome that he saw as an inevitable consequence. In particular, he rejected the idea that the success or failure of one generation should increase or restrict the opportunities of the next. Giddens also stressed the importance of community and responsibility, partly to offset the negative effects of the free market (such as excessive materialism and competitive individualism), but also to reflect the declining importance of hierarchy and class conflict in modern Britain. Community was 'fundamental to the new politics' of the third way because it promoted social cohesion, shared values, and individual and social responsibility.

Giddens rejected the economic and social engineering that underpinned the extensive state-welfare and wealth-redistribution programmes of previous social-democratic governments. This form of state intervention, he argued, encouraged a culture of dependency, and the tax revenues required discouraged the investment and entrepreneurial effort needed to sustain a competitive economy. Instead, Giddens called for a 'social investment' state – essentially a 'contract' between the government and the citizen. The state, benefiting from the economic growth generated by the free market, had a responsibility to invest in the infrastructure of society (such as education, training, subsidised employment and expert advice) to provide better job opportunities. In return, people had a duty to take advantage of what was on offer, a responsibility to help themselves and an obligation not to settle for a life on benefits.

> **Assessment support: 1.2.3 Socialism**
>
> Question 3 on A-Level Paper 1 gives you a choice of two 24-mark questions. Pick the question you feel most confident about and complete your answer in 30 minutes.
>
> *To what extent do different socialists agree over the role of the state? [24 marks]*
>
> *You must use appropriate thinkers you have studied to support your answer.*
>
> These questions require an essay-style answer. They test all three Assessment Objectives, with 8 marks available for each. The highest level requires in-depth knowledge and understanding, supporting strong skills of analysis and evaluation. The mark scheme stresses that you must also offer a focused and justified conclusion: in this case, on the extent to which different socialists are committed to collectivism.
>
> • Begin with a brief introduction in which you outline your argument. You need to set out a minimum of two key points on each side (agree and disagree) of the question, to develop.
>
> • Typically, you will write four main paragraphs – one for each major point – and round off with a conclusion.
>
> • You are asked to review and make a substantiated judgement about the extent to which different socialists agree over the role of the state. Begin with the 'agree' arguments, but you must then provide balance by dealing with the 'disagree' arguments. Each argument should be supported with accurate and relevant evidence, such as key thinkers and policies.
>
> • In your conclusion, review the balance between the two sides then reach a substantiated judgement. Your conclusion should not contain new factual material. Your judgement should emerge naturally from the way in which you have constructed your argument.
>
> Here is part of a student's answer – the conclusion.
>
> In conclusion, most socialists call for some form of state intervention and state planning to promote collectivist goals and ensure that the distribution of goods and services is not left to the free market. Having said this, it is evident that different socialists do disagree over the role of the state. Marxists (in practice) and state socialists are committed to a centralised state that organises all or most production and distribution. Left-wing regimes organised on this basis include the former Soviet Union and present-day North Korea. Moderate socialists, in contrast, adopt more limited forms of state control (such as the nationalisation of selected industries) within the framework of a mixed economy. However, in recent decades, social democrats and third way adherents have downgraded the importance of the role of the state even more. For example, neo-revisionists have rejected 'top down' state intervention and accepted the primacy of the free market. This shift is partly due to a growing perception that the role of the state in the UK and other developed countries (state welfare, nationalisation and government economic intervention) has fostered a dependency culture and a sluggish, uncompetitive economy. The end of the Cold War and the collapse of the Soviet Union and Eastern bloc in 1989–91 reinforced this trend as the socialist concept of state control sustained a major ideological defeat. Overall, in the late 20th and early 21st centuries, different socialists have shown less agreement over the role of the state than in post-war decades.
>
> This conclusion is effective for the following reasons.
>
> • It offers a substantiated and reasoned judgement that is precisely focused on the question set. In doing so, it clearly reviews the balance between the two sides of the argument.
>
> • Using contextual factors – the perceived negative consequences of the role of the state in countries such as the UK, and the impact of the collapse of the Soviet Union and Eastern bloc – adds weight to the student's overall judgement.
>
> • The final sentence makes the student's judgement explicit and uses the key terms in the question.

The Constitution

In the modern world the political system of a state is organised according to rules and practices laid down in a **constitution**. The purpose of a constitution is to set out the powers and responsibilities of the different institutions of government, and to describe the relationships between these institutions and between the government and the citizens. The USA, Germany and France are examples of countries where a single document performs this role. The UK constitution, on the other hand, consists of a collection of written and unwritten elements. It has many sources rather than just one.

> **Key term**
>
> **Constitution**
> a set of laws and guidelines setting out how a political system works, and where power is located within the system. It defines the powers and functions of government and the rights of ordinary citizens in relation to the government.

In this section you will learn about:

- how the UK political system operates
- how the UK political system has evolved over time
- how the UK political system has changed as a result of reforms introduced since the election of the New Labour government in 1997, and the process of devolution, which includes the dispersal of power from the central government in London to new bodies in different parts of the UK
- the arguments for making further changes in the future.

1.1 The development, nature and sources of the UK constitution

The development of the constitution

The UK constitution is different from those of most of its neighbours because, for a long period, the country has not undergone a fundamental, transforming change, such as a revolution or a military defeat followed by occupation by a foreign power. Instead the political system of the UK has evolved gradually and, at least since the civil wars of the 17th century, without dramatic breaks in continuity. This contrasts, for example, with the United States, whose constitution dates from 1787 after the American people had established their independence from Britain and their leaders had decided how they wanted to govern themselves.

Elements of the UK constitution can be traced back more than a thousand years. In the Middle Ages, power was concentrated in the hands of the monarch. However, in order to govern the country, the Crown required the co-operation of a class of landowning nobility, who gradually gained more rights over time. From the 13th century the nobles and other interest groups gained representation in an assembly – parliament – that met to advise the monarch, pass laws and give consent to taxation. Parliament consisted of an upper house, made up of the hereditary aristocracy and senior members of the church (the House of Lords), and an elected House of Commons, which initially consisted of representatives of the landed gentry and prosperous merchants. The Commons increasingly took on a representative function, and expected to be heard when it presented grievances to the monarch.

The balance of power between the Crown and parliament was adjusted in favour of the latter as a result of the civil wars of the mid-17th century. By the 19th century, Britain was governed by a constitutional monarch who acted on the advice of ministers. The ministers were accountable to parliament as the country's supreme law-making body. Voting rights were progressively extended to the middle- and working-classes, creating a more democratic society by the early 20th century and ending the monopoly of power traditionally enjoyed by the aristocratic elite. Within parliament this was reflected in the emergence of the elected House of Commons as the more powerful of the two chambers.

In parallel with these developments, it was recognised from the 17th century that the judiciary should be independent of political influence and control. Judges became increasingly important through their role in upholding the rule of law – the idea that no body, including the government, should be above the law.

Even if it lacks a single founding document, the UK constitution does have important written components. Table 1.1 shows the most important historical 'landmark' documents that have influenced the growth of the UK's political system, some of which date back several centuries. The overall effect of these developments has been to:

- reduce the powers of the monarchy, and to extend those of parliament
- increase the rights and freedoms of the ordinary citizen
- draw together the component parts of the United Kingdom
- increase the power of the elected House of Commons at the expense of the unelected House of Lords
- define the UK's relationship with the institutions that later evolved into the European Union.

Document	Date	Overview	Development of constitution
The Magna Carta also known as the Great Charter	1215	Agreement between King John and the barons, who had rebelled against the abuse of royal power. Largely a concession to specific demands of the nobility. Many clauses have been repealed or superseded by later legislation. Remains a powerful symbol of English liberties.	The Magna Carta stated the principle that no one should be deprived of liberty or property without due process of law.
The Bill of Rights	1689	Passed by parliament in reaction to the arbitrary rule of King James II, who was driven from the throne in the 'Glorious Revolution'. His successors – William III and his wife, Mary II – affirmed the rights of parliament when they accepted the throne.	The Bill of Rights included provisions for: • regular parliaments • free elections • freedom of speech within parliament.
The Act of Settlement	1701	Motivated by a desire to exclude James II and his heirs from the throne. At the time their adherence to the Catholic religion was widely associated with tyrannical rule.	The act established the right of parliament to determine the line of succession to the throne.
The Acts of Union	1707	United England and Scotland, which had had a shared monarch since 1603 but had retained two separate parliaments. Both countries were now placed under one parliament based in Westminster.	This was the basis of the United Kingdom until Tony Blair's New Labour government passed legislation to set up a Scottish parliament once again in 1997.

Table 1.1: Key historical documents

Document	Date	Overview	Development of constitution
The Parliament Acts	1911, 1949	Reduced the power of the House of Lords to interfere with the agenda of the House of Commons. The 1911 act was provoked by the action of the Lords in rejecting the radical tax-raising 'People's Budget', introduced by the Liberal chancellor of the exchequer, David Lloyd George.	1911 act affirmed that the Lords could not delay money bills. For non-financial bills, the power of veto was replaced with a two-year delaying power. 1949 act reduced this delaying period to one year.
The European Communities Act	1972	Passed by Edward Heath's Conservative government, the act took Britain into the European Economic Community, the forerunner of the European Union (EU).	Established the principle that EU law would take precedence over UK law where a conflict occurred. This act is expected to be repealed after a majority of people in the UK voted to leave the EU in a referendum in 2016.

Table 1.1: Key historical documents (continued)

William III and Mary II accepting the throne in 1689 on the basis of the Bill of Rights. This established the principle that the Crown's authority rests on the consent of parliament.

Key terms

Codified
a constitution in which laws and practices are set out in a single document.

Entrenched
a constitution protected by a higher court and requiring special procedures to amend it.

Unitary
a political system where all legal sovereignty is contained in a single place.

Link

For more on **devolution**, see Sections 1.2 and 1.3.

The nature of the UK constitution

The UK constitution is distinctive in several important respects.

- It is uncodified – there is no single legal code or document in which its key principles are gathered together. Instead, it is derived from a number of sources, some written down, while others are unwritten.

- It is unentrenched – it can be altered relatively easily, by a simple majority vote in parliament. It therefore has a higher degree of flexibility than a **codified** constitution. There is no special legal procedure for amending the UK constitution. In the UK all laws have equal status. By contrast, a codified constitution has a higher status than ordinary laws and some or all of its provisions are said to be **entrenched**. For example, an amendment to the United States constitution requires the support of two-thirds of Congress and three-quarters of the states to become law.

- It is **unitary** – sovereignty (or ultimate authority) has traditionally been located at the centre, with the component parts of the country – England, Scotland, Wales and Northern Ireland – all essentially run from London and treated in a similar way. This has been modified since the introduction of **devolution** in the late 1990s.

Some would now use the term 'union state' to describe the UK since, although the centre remains strong, the individual sub-national units are governed in different ways. The distribution of power between the central and regional governments of the UK can still be altered by act of parliament. This is an important difference with a federal constitution like that of Germany or the USA.

The twin pillars of the UK constitution: parliamentary sovereignty and the rule of law

Writing in 1885, the Victorian constitutional theorist A.V. Dicey identified two key principles of the UK constitution. The first of these was **parliamentary sovereignty**.

Figure 1.1 shows the three main ways in which parliament can be said to be sovereign.

> **Link**
>
> For more on **sovereignty**, see Section 4.4.

> **Key terms**
>
> **Parliamentary sovereignty** the principle that parliament can make, amend or unmake any law, and cannot bind its successors or be bound by its predecessors.
>
> **The rule of law** the principle that all people and bodies, including government, must follow the law and can be held to account if they do not.

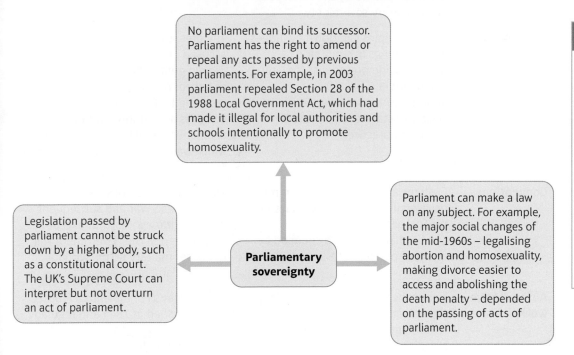

Figure 1.1: Three main ways parliament can be said to be sovereign

The other major principle identified by Dicey was **the rule of law**. Dicey argued that this was the main way in which the rights and liberties of citizens are protected. Respect for the rule of law is important because it acts as a check on parliamentary sovereignty, which in theory might take away people's liberties. Under the rule of law:

- everyone is entitled to a fair trial and no one should be imprisoned without due legal process
- all citizens must obey the law and are equal under it
- public officials are not above the law and they can be held to account by the courts
- the judiciary must be independent of political interference.

The five main sources of the UK constitution

In the absence of a single document, the origins of the UK's constitutional practice can be found in five main areas, as Table 1.2 shows.

Source	What is it?	Examples
Statute law	The body of law passed by parliament. Not all laws are constitutional, only those that affect the nature of the political system and citizens' rights. It is the most important source as it is underpinned by the concept of parliamentary sovereignty.	The 1998 Scotland Act, Government of Wales Act and Northern Ireland Act created devolved legislative bodies, which were given some powers previously held by Westminster.
Common law	Legal principles laid down by judges in their rulings in court cases, which provide precedents for later judgments. Important in cases where it is not clear how statute law should be applied in practice.	The presumption that a person accused of a crime is innocent until proven guilty. The medieval concept of *habeas corpus* (a Latin phrase meaning literally 'you may have the body') is a common-law protection against unlawful imprisonment, which was converted into a statute in 1679.
Conventions	Customs and practices that do not have legal force, but which have been broadly accepted over time. Can be challenged and changed by an act of parliament.	The principle, established since the 2003 Iraq War and subsequent parliamentary votes, that except in an emergency, the government will not order military action without prior parliamentary approval
Authoritative works	Textbooks that explain the working of the political system. A useful guide, but lacking legal standing.	Erskine May's *Parliamentary Practice*, first published in 1844 and regularly updated, explains the rules of parliamentary life.
Treaties (including European Union law)	Agreements with other EU member states, which UK governments have signed since joining what is now the EU in 1973. Following the 2016 referendum, preparations are being made for the UK to leave the EU.	Arguably the most important treaty was Maastricht (1992), which transformed the European Community into the European Union.

Table 1.2: Origins of the UK constitution

Pause & reflect

Review the information contained in this section and make a list of the ways in which the power and importance of the UK parliament developed up to the late 20th century.

1.2 How the constitution has changed since 1997

The election of a Labour government in 1997, after 18 years in opposition, led to a range of constitutional reforms that were more far-reaching than anything attempted by governments for generations. Since the end of the Labour government some of these reforms have been developed further.

Why did this period see such extensive reform?

Pressure for reform in the 1990s

- **Demands for modernisation:** Tony Blair's New Labour Party was sympathetic to the idea of constitutional reform as part of its plan to modernise British institutions. Old Labour had adopted some political reforms, such as extending the vote to 18 year olds in 1969 and attempting to pass devolution for Scotland and Wales in 1979. However, it had been primarily concerned with economic and social issues. New Labour was more open to demands from pressure groups such as Charter 88 (later renamed Unlock Democracy), who wanted more open democracy and stronger guarantees of citizens' rights. Before winning a large independent majority in the 1997 election, Blair expected that he might need support from the Liberal Democrats, who were also committed to constitutional change – particularly reform of the first-past-the-post electoral system.

- **The experience of Conservative rule, 1978–97:** The Conservative governments had refused to undertake constitutional reforms. This had helped to build up pressure for change, especially in Scotland, where the population felt ignored by a distant government in London. Scottish opinion rejected a number of Conservative policies. For example, the unpopular poll tax (a controversial way of financing local government) had been trialled there in 1989 before its introduction in England and Wales. Accusations of corruption or 'sleaze' against many parliamentarians in the 1990s also helped to create a climate of opinion where the health and integrity of traditional institutions were questioned.

Changes under Labour, 1997–2010

The Labour governments focused on five major areas of reform.

- **House of Lords reform:** When the Labour government took office in 1997, the House of Lords was dominated by hereditary peers who owed their titles to inheritance. In what was intended as a transitional reform two years later, the government ended the right of all but 92 of these peers to sit in the Lords. House of Lords reform would reduce the influence of Labour's opponents within the political system, as the majority of hereditary peers supported Conservative governments. The removal of most hereditary peers also gave the Lords a more 'modern' appearance. The majority of its members were now life peers, who were supposed to have been appointed on grounds of merit, reflecting a wide variety of fields of activity, including politics, business, the trade union movement, the arts and the military. No political party now enjoyed a dominant position in the Lords. From 2000 a House of Lords Appointments Commission nominated a proportion of peers who were not linked with a party. However, the prime minister and other party leaders continued to make nominations on party political grounds, and no agreement was reached on making the Lords either wholly or partly elected, so it continued to lack democratic legitimacy.

- **Electoral reform:** Various forms of proportional representation were introduced for elections to the Scottish parliament, Welsh Assembly, Northern Ireland Assembly and European parliament. However, although the government commissioned a report into the system used

EXTENSION ACTIVITY

Use the internet to investigate Unlock Democracy and find out what the purpose of this pressure group is. Identify three issues on which it campaigns. Why does it consider these issues to be important?

Link

For more on **voting systems** see Section 3.1 of Electoral Systems.

Key term

Devolution
the dispersal of power, but not sovereignty, within a political system.

Link

For more on these **devolved bodies** see Section 1.3.

for Westminster, chaired by Roy Jenkins (former Labour Cabinet minister, subsequently a Liberal Democrat peer), no action was taken. Supporters of proportional representation concluded that, having won a crushing victory under the old system, Labour had no interest in changing arrangements for Westminster.

- **Devolution:** Devolved bodies were created for Scotland, Wales and Northern Ireland following referendums in 1997–98 in these parts of the UK. Labour's devolution reforms were a pragmatic package, designed to damp down support for the pro-independence Scottish National Party (SNP) and to bring together the conflicting unionist and nationalist factions in Northern Ireland. Demand for devolution in Wales was always weaker and the Welsh Assembly did not gain comparable powers to those of the Scottish parliament.

  The government had no answer to the so-called 'West Lothian question' – the anomaly that Scottish MPs at Westminster were able to vote on purely English matters, yet English MPs had no influence over issues devolved to the Scottish parliament. Another source of grievance for England was the persistence of the Barnett formula, devised by Labour minister Joel Barnett in 1978, long before devolution. This determines relative levels of public spending for the component parts of the UK on the basis of population. It means that Scotland, Wales and Northern Ireland receive more spending per head of population than England.

  An attempt to set up elected regional assemblies in England was abandoned after the only area in which a referendum was held to test public opinion, the North-East, decisively rejected the idea in 2004.

- **The Human Rights Act:** This act incorporated the European Convention on Human Rights (ECHR) into UK statute law, enshrining rights such as those to a fair trial, freedom from slavery and degrading treatment, and respect for privacy and family life. All future legislation had to be compatible with the ECHR. Judges could not strike down laws that were incompatible with it but could highlight such legislation for amendment by parliament. The limitations of the Human Rights Act were demonstrated by the government's decision to 'derogate from' (declare an exemption from) Article 5, which gave individuals the right to liberty and security, in cases of suspected terrorism. The introduction of control orders in 2005, which allowed the authorities to limit the freedom of movement of such individuals, highlighted the unentrenched nature of the act.

- **The creation of the Supreme Court:** The 2005 Constitutional Reform Act led to the establishment, four years later, of a Supreme Court as the highest court of appeal in the UK for civil cases, and (except in Scotland) for criminal cases. Previously senior judges known as the law lords, sitting in the House of Lords, had performed this function. This development is an example of the separation of powers – the idea that the different branches of government (in this case law-making and judicial) should be independent of each other.

Pause & reflect

Did the Labour governments deliver a major overhaul of the constitution, or was their record disappointing? Draw up a table showing their achievements on one side and areas where they left reforms unfinished on the other.

Reforms under the coalition (2010–15) and the Conservative government since 2015

Conservative Prime Minister David Cameron (left) with Liberal Democrat Deputy Prime Minister Nick Clegg outside 10 Downing Street.

The Conservatives and Liberal Democrats had a certain amount of common ground on constitutional reform. This was reflected in the coalition agreement between the two parties, which launched the new government in May 2010. Areas of agreement included openness to further devolution to Scotland and Wales and to parliamentary reform, including a wholly or mainly elected House of Lords. However, the coalition government was noteworthy for conflict and disappointment, as well as achievement.

Areas of disagreement under the coalition included the following.

- **House of Lords reform and House of Commons boundary reform:** Plans for a mainly elected House of Lords were dropped after a rebellion by 91 backbench Conservative MPs. The Liberal Democrats, who were the more committed of the two parties to a democratically chosen upper house, retaliated by blocking the implementation of legislation designed to reduce the number of MPs from 650 to 600. The effect would have been to produce a smaller number of constituencies, of more equal size, so that that all votes would have had more equal value across the country. The Liberal Democrats halted the change because it would have mainly favoured the Conservatives. However, after the end of the coalition, the new Conservative government confirmed that the reform would be introduced in time for the 2020 general election. This was before Theresa May called an early general election in June 2017.

- **Electoral reform:** A referendum was held in May 2011, with the two parties taking up entrenched positions: the Conservatives campaigned strongly to retain first past the post, while the Liberal Democrats argued for the adoption of the Alternative Vote (AV), a preferential, though not proportional, voting system, only to see their proposals rejected by 68 per cent of those who voted. This was a major disappointment for the Liberal Democrats, for whom progress towards a change in the voting system had been a priority in negotiating the coalition agreement. They had in fact preferred the proportional Single Transferable Vote system, but had opted for AV as the maximum that they expected to gain at the time. The result seemed to be more a vote against the Liberal Democrats themselves than against the electoral system they were promoting.

- **Rights:** The Conservatives wanted to replace the Human Rights Act with a British Bill of Rights, whereas the Liberal Democrats were determined to retain the act. A commission tasked with investigating the issue failed to find a way forward. The Conservative manifesto at the 2015 general election pledged to revisit the issue.

The most significant changes were as follows.

- **Devolution**
  - **Wales:** A referendum was held in Wales in March 2011 on proposals to grant further powers to the Welsh Assembly. This resulted in the assembly receiving direct law-making power in all of the 20 policy areas that had been devolved to it, without the need to consult Westminster.
  - **Scotland:** The Scottish parliament received more powers under the 2012 Scotland Act, including borrowing powers, the right to set its own rate of income tax and control over landfill tax and stamp duty. In September 2014 a referendum was held in Scotland on proposals for independence, resulting in a 55 per cent vote to stay in the UK. In the course of the campaign, Prime Minister David Cameron and the leaders of the other main UK parties pledged to grant more powers to the Scottish parliament.
  - **England – English votes for English laws (EVEL):** As a concession to English opinion, the Conservative government that took office in May 2015 offered a solution to the West Lothian question. Under 'English votes for English laws' (EVEL), if a measure that concerns only England (or England and Wales) comes before the House of Commons, it can pass only with the approval of a 'grand committee', consisting solely of English (or English and Welsh) MPs. The measure was used for the first time in January 2016, to pass a housing bill without the involvement of Scottish MPs.
- **The Fixed Term Parliaments Act (2011):** This ended the prime minister's historic power to choose the date of a general election by establishing that a new parliament must be elected on a fixed date, at five-year intervals. An earlier contest can be held only if two-thirds of MPs vote for one, or if a prime minister loses a vote of no confidence and fails to form a new government within a 14-day period. This reform suited the interests of both partners in the coalition by giving the government a guaranteed period in which to implement their programme, free from speculation about the date of the next election. However, by calling an early general election in June 2017, only two years after the previous contest, Theresa May showed that it is possible for a prime minister to get around the act. Opposition MPs do not want to appear afraid of facing the electorate, and it is unlikely that a determined prime minister would fail to get the necessary support in parliament for an early election.
- **Reform of the House of Commons:** The coalition implemented reforms recommended by a committee chaired by Labour MP Tony Wright, which reported before the 2010 general election. Chairs of House of Commons select committees, which scrutinise the activities of government departments, were to be chosen by MPs, rather than have their selection influenced by the party leaders. A backbench business committee was created, which chooses topics for debate, including some proposed by the public in e-petitions. The first such debate was triggered by people seeking justice for the 96 Liverpool football supporters who died in the 1989 Hillsborough disaster.
- **The Recall of MPs Act (2015):** This was a response to the fact that voters had no legal means of removing scandalous MPs who refused to resign their seats. It means that if an MP is sentenced to a custodial sentence, or is suspended from the Commons for more than 21 days, a by-election is triggered if at least 10 per cent of constituents sign a recall petition.

1.3 The role and powers of devolved bodies in the UK

Devolution in England

Local government in England has undergone several reorganisations since the late Victorian period when a two-tier system was created, based on county and borough councils and, at a lower level, district councils. In the 1990s some areas moved to a single tier of local government known as 'unitary authorities'. London had a single authority – the Greater London Council – from 1965, and six other metropolitan councils followed for England's main urban areas (the West Midlands, South Yorkshire, West Yorkshire, Tyne and Wear, Greater Manchester and Merseyside). These authorities gained a reputation for high spending and were abolished by the Thatcher government in 1986.

One of the objectives of the Blair government was to recreate a democratically elected strategic authority for the capital. This led to the establishment of two new institutions from 2000 – an elected mayor with executive powers (an idea inspired by large US cities), supported by the Greater London Assembly. They share oversight of policy areas such as policing, transport and economic development. The first mayor, Ken Livingstone, introduced a congestion charge for drivers entering central London in response to increased traffic and air pollution. By 2015 a further 16 urban areas, including Bristol, Liverpool and Greater Manchester, had decided to adopt the elected mayor model.

The Blair government tried to extend regional decision-making by setting up unelected Regional Development Agencies. Their purpose was to promote economic development on behalf of central government. An attempt to go further by creating elected regional assemblies failed to win support. The government slimmed down its plans for referendums on regional assemblies to proposals for just three in the North-East, North-West and Yorkshire and the Humber. These were considered to be the areas where the sense of regional identity was strongest, but in the end only one referendum was held, in the North-East. Even here the idea was heavily defeated when put to the test, with a 78 per cent 'no' vote in 2004. People were not persuaded that they needed a possibly expensive layer of additional bureaucracy, with few powers to make a real difference to regional regeneration.

The coalition abolished Labour's Regional Development Agencies but tried to breathe life into the concept of regionalism by combining local authorities in so-called 'city regions'. Each would be led by a directly elected 'metro mayor'. Some of these new bodies are located in the north of England and are intended to develop what former Chancellor George Osborne called the 'northern powerhouse'. This was a plan to drive regional growth through improved transport links and investment in science and innovation.

The new city regions are:

- Cambridgeshire and Peterborough
- Greater Manchester
- Liverpool
- Sheffield
- Tees Valley
- West Midlands
- west of England.

The powers of the new metro mayors vary but they include developing an economic growth strategy and making policy on housing, skills and transport.

There has also been discussion of the idea of an English parliament, but there is little public support for this and it is not espoused by any major political party. There is evidence that the cultural sense of 'Englishness' is strengthening, partly in reaction to the perceived advantages enjoyed by Scotland under devolution. However, this has yet to translate into a serious political demand for England to have the same constitutional arrangements as Scotland. The 'English votes for English laws' measure was intended to stem demands for a more fundamental overhaul of devolution arrangements.

Devolution in Scotland, Wales and Northern Ireland

More extensive changes have taken place in Scotland, Wales and Northern Ireland. Devolution in these parts of the UK involved the transfer of powers over certain policy areas to new, sub-national bodies. In each case Westminster retained control of what are known as 'reserved powers', which include defence, foreign policy, constitutional matters, welfare benefits and important areas of economic policy including trade, the currency and interest rates. These are the main powers that indicate a fully fledged independent state. They were not granted to the devolved bodies because the purpose of devolution was to keep the four nations within the United Kingdom.

There were important differences between the three bodies when it came to deciding which areas would be 'devolved powers', as Figure 3.1 shows.

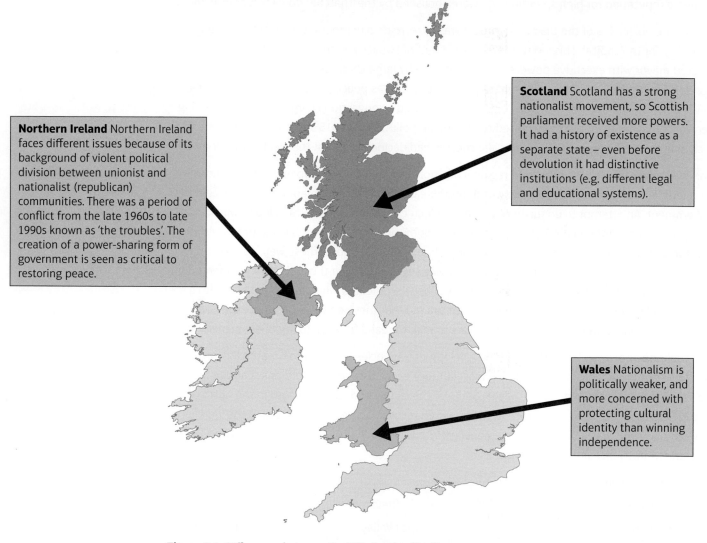

Northern Ireland Northern Ireland faces different issues because of its background of violent political division between unionist and nationalist (republican) communities. There was a period of conflict from the late 1960s to late 1990s known as 'the troubles'. The creation of a power-sharing form of government is seen as critical to restoring peace.

Scotland Scotland has a strong nationalist movement, so Scottish parliament received more powers. It had a history of existence as a separate state – even before devolution it had distinctive institutions (e.g. different legal and educational systems).

Wales Nationalism is politically weaker, and more concerned with protecting cultural identity than winning independence.

Figure 3.1: Differences between the UK's devolved bodies

Scottish parliament and government

The Scottish parliament and government were set up in Edinburgh in 1999. The parliament consists of 129 MSPs (Members of the Scottish parliament), elected every 4 years using the **Additional Member System**. It scrutinises the work of the Scottish government. It is sometimes referred to as 'Holyrood' after the part of Edinburgh where it is located, close to the royal palace of the same name.

Link

For more on the **Additional Member System**, see Section 3.1 of Electoral Systems.

The Scottish government devises and implements policy on matters devolved to Scotland, and proposes an annual budget to the parliament. The head of the Scottish government is known as the first minister. Since 2014 this has been Nicola Sturgeon, leader of the largest party in the parliament, the SNP.

The areas that the main devolved powers cover are shown in Figure 3.2.

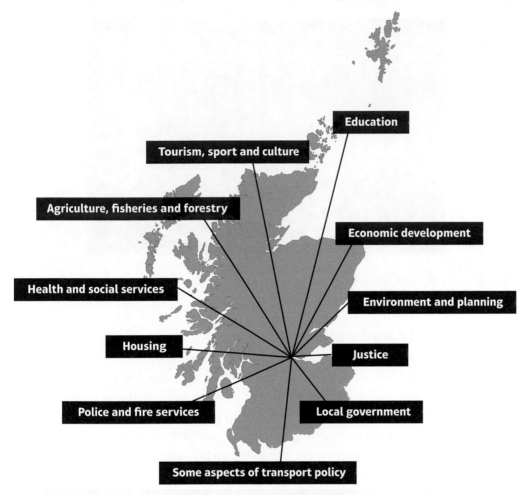

Figure 3.2: The main devolved powers exercised by the Scottish parliament

The Scottish government was also allowed to vary income tax by 3p above or below the UK rate, although this power was never used. However, it did make use of other devolved powers to develop a distinctive position for Scotland on social policy. For example, Scottish students do not pay university tuition fees and there is free nursing care for the elderly. In 2016 there was another break with the general direction of UK policy, when the Scottish government ended the right of council tenants to buy their own homes – something that had been started across the UK by Margaret Thatcher's government in 1980.

The Calman Commission, set up under Gordon Brown's government, led in 2012 to the granting of additional powers including:

- taxation powers, including the right to set a Scottish income tax rate and control of stamp duty and landfill tax
- borrowing powers
- regulation of air weapons
- drink driving alcohol limits.

The Scottish independence referendum, held in September 2014, followed by the establishment of the Smith Commission, led to further powers being transferred in 2015–16. The main areas relate to taxation and welfare. New powers include control over air passenger duty, licensing of onshore oil and gas prospecting and some welfare benefits. The changes mean that the parliament now has control over taxation representing 36 per cent of devolved expenditure, compared with less than 10 per cent when it was established.

The horseshoe-shaped layout of the Scottish parliament was designed to avoid the adversarial appearance of the Westminster parliament.

Welsh Assembly and government

Like the Scottish parliament, the National Assembly for Wales based in Cardiff, dates to 1999. Assembly Members (AMs) are elected by the Additional Member System. Their role is to represent the Welsh people, to make laws on the areas devolved to Wales and hold the Welsh government to account. However, with only 60 members the Assembly is much smaller than its Scottish counterpart. The Welsh government was originally located within the Assembly but the two were formally separated in 2006. The government is headed by a first minister, a post held by Carwyn Jones, leader of a minority Labour administration, from 2009.

The Welsh Assembly encourages the public to see the Senedd ('senate' or 'parliament') as a public building not just for Members, as part of 'Welsh democracy in action'.

There are 20 specified devolved powers, including those shown in Figure 3.3.

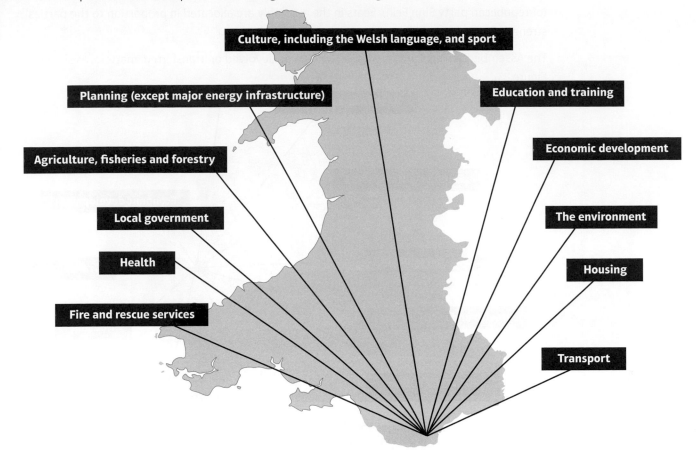

Culture, including the Welsh language, and sport

Planning (except major energy infrastructure)

Education and training

Agriculture, fisheries and forestry

Economic development

Local government

The environment

Health

Housing

Fire and rescue services

Transport

Figure 3.3: Some of the specified devolved powers of the Welsh Assembly

Unlike in Scotland, police and justice are not devolved areas and the Welsh Assembly has not gained powers over income tax and borrowing. Since the 2011 referendum the Assembly has been able to pass laws in all 20 devolved areas, without regard to the views of the UK government.

Northern Ireland Assembly and executive

Devolution in Northern Ireland was established following the 1998 Good Friday Agreement, which sought to bring the two main communities in the province together. These are the unionists, who want to keep Northern Ireland within the UK, and the nationalists and republicans, who wish to see a united, independent Ireland. These political divisions broadly correlate to the differing religious identities of the two communities – unionists are historically linked to Protestantism, and nationalists to Catholicism. The creation of a power-sharing executive, in which both sides were to be represented, was the most important feature of devolution in Northern Ireland. The process of devolution has been more uneven than in Scotland and Wales, with the Northern Ireland Assembly being suspended by the UK government in London on more than one occasion following a breakdown of trust between the Unionist and republican groups. This included a period of suspension that lasted for almost 5 years, from 2002–07.

The Northern Ireland Assembly, located in Belfast, consists of 90 (originally 108) Members of the Legislative Assembly (MLAs), elected by Single Transferable Vote. The use of STV, a highly proportional voting system, ensures the representation of both sides rather than the dominance of the larger grouping, and thus leads to the adoption of a power-sharing system of government. The executive is headed by a first minister and a deputy first minister, who until January 2017

EXTENSION ACTIVITY

Ron Davies, Welsh secretary in the Blair government, described devolution as 'a process, not an event'. How has the experience of devolution in Scotland and Wales since the late 1990s shown this to be a correct observation?

were Arlene Foster (leader of the Democratic Unionist Party) and the late Martin McGuinness (of republican party Sinn Fein). Seats in the assembly are allocated in proportion to the parties' strength in the Assembly.

The Assembly can legislate on what are known as devolved or 'transferred' matters, as shown in Figure 3.4.

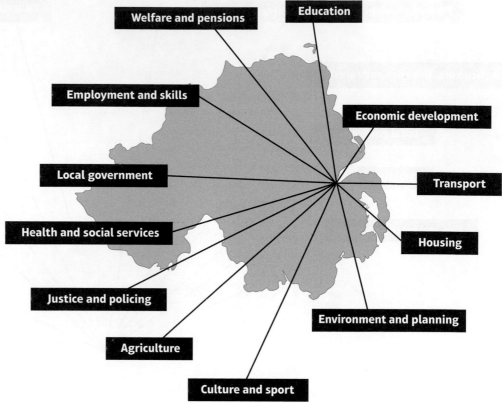

Figure 3.4: Transferred matters for the Northern Ireland Assembly

In addition there are a number of 'reserved matters' that are normally the domain of Westminster, but on which the Assembly can legislate with the consent of the Northern Ireland secretary (a member of the UK Cabinet). These include financial services, broadcasting, consumer safety and firearms.

Pause & reflect	

Devolution in the UK is sometimes described as 'asymmetric' – each of the devolved bodies has different powers and features. Make a table showing the ways in which the three bodies differ from each other.

1.4 Debates on further reform

It is now time to assess the main constitutional reforms introduced since 1997. How adequate are they and to what extent should they be taken further?

Devolution

Devolution has modified the UK's heavily centralised constitution by enabling policies that meet the needs and wishes of people at local level. In Northern Ireland devolution has helped to end violence between the unionist and nationalist communities by creating a power-sharing system of government.

On the other hand Scottish independence, which was rejected in the 2014 referendum, has been revived since the UK voted to leave the European Union in 2016. The Scottish National Party administration has called for a new referendum on independence. It argues that the wishes of the majority in Scotland, who wanted to remain in the EU, have been ignored.

The devolution settlement is uneven in the way it applies to the component parts of the UK. A federal solution would create greater uniformity.

Electoral reform

Electoral reform has produced more proportional results in elections to the Scottish parliament, Welsh Assembly and Northern Ireland Assembly. The rejection of AV in the 2011 referendum indicates that there is no public appetite for the extension of reform to Westminster. First past the post usually delivers strong governments with a clear mandate, and it preserves the valuable link between MPs and their constituencies.

The under-representation of smaller parties, and the way in which the current system produces governments with a majority of seats but a minority of votes, are arguments for further reform.

House of Lords reform

We now have an upper house based much more firmly on merit and experience. Its greater assertiveness in holding the government to account is an argument for leaving the Lords as it is. An elected chamber would mirror the Commons, producing a house dominated by professional politicians and reducing the range of expertise currently available.

On the other hand the Lords lacks democratic legitimacy because none of its members are elected. This is highly unusual in the modern age.

The Human Rights Act

The 1998 act brought the UK into line with other European states by incorporating the European Convention on Human Rights into national law. It provides protection of citizens' rights without threatening parliamentary sovereignty. As the act is not entrenched, the government can modify the way it operates when required, such as the creation of control orders in 2005.

However, there is a case for strengthening the act on the grounds that governments can currently take away important liberties by a simple majority vote in parliament.

Conservative critics would like to see the act replaced with a British Bill of Rights, which would make the UK Supreme Court the final judge of citizens' rights.

Overview

There is a case that no more reform is needed.

- The current settlement protects the rights of citizens and recognises the desire for autonomy in the component parts of the UK. At the same time it enables the election of strong governments, which are able to act in the national interest.
- There is a lack of clear agreement on the form that any further change should take.

On the other hand, the opposite can be argued.

- In many respects, the current settlement is incomplete and illogical. The UK is out of step with most other Western democracies in having an unelected upper house and a voting system that imperfectly reflects the preferences of the electorate.

- A federal solution could remove the anomalies created by the current 'asymmetric' devolution arrangements.
- Citizens need greater clarity on the nature of their rights, and stronger protection against arbitrary government actions.

To what extent should the constitutional reforms introduced since 1997 be taken further?

To conclude this section, here are two further questions about specific aspects of constitutional reform, which could be the subject of examination questions. In both cases there are two sides to be considered.

- Should devolution be extended within England? (See Table 4.1)
- Should the UK constitution be entrenched and codified, including a Bill of Rights? (See Table 4.2)

Arguments for extending devolution in England	Arguments against devolution within England
England is the most prosperous and heavily populated part of the UK, but it's the only one without a devolved body. Under the 1978 Barnett formula for deciding on levels of public spending, England receives less per person than the other parts of the UK. A federal solution would promote greater equality between the different parts of the UK.	England's size and wealth mean that it would dominate a federal structure. Also how would an English parliament relate to Westminster? For example, a separate English executive could clash with the UK government over the handling of domestic English issues.
'EVEL' makes Scottish MPs second-class representatives at Westminster, weakening the unity of the UK. It doesn't really resolve the West Lothian question.	'EVEL' may have resolved the West Lothian question. It has been used at Westminster to pass a housing bill in 2016. Scottish MPs dislike it but its introduction has not thus far caused the UK to break up.
Devolution has led to policies to meet the differing needs of the Scottish, Welsh and Northern Irish peoples, so why would it not work for England?	Most English people don't make a logical distinction between England and Britain as a whole, and see Westminster as 'their' parliament.
There is a strong regional identity in some parts of the UK, for example in Devon and Cornwall. This could be a basis for regional assemblies which might co-ordinate local policies and attract inward investment.	The defeat of Blair's proposals in 2004 suggests that there isn't a strong enough sense of identity across the UK to make regional assemblies viable.

Table 4.1: Arguments for and against devolution within England

EXTENSION ACTIVITY

Use the internet to research the West Lothian question and the Barnett formula in greater depth. How convincing do you find the arguments for greater devolution to England?

Arguments for the UK constitution to be entrenched and codified, including a Bill of Rights	Arguments against the UK constitution being entrenched and codified, including a Bill of Rights
Codification would educate the public about constitutional issues and promote greater respect for political institutions.	There is almost no public demand for change of this kind. It would be extremely difficult to find consensus on what to include in a codified constitution and such a project would probably entail years of debate and consultation.
Entrenchment would not make it impossible to amend the constitution, but doing so would entail an orderly and careful process. This would reduce the chances of a government pushing through ill-considered changes.	An uncodified constitution allows for greater flexibility. The UK constitution is an organic entity that is able to adapt to political and social change. Constitutional reforms since 1997 can be seen as evidence of the ability of the UK constitution to absorb change.
An entrenched Bill of Rights would provide stronger protection of individual liberties than the current Human Rights Act, as for example the introduction of control orders in 2005 demonstrated. With an uncodified constitution there is a tendency for governments to push the boundaries of what is politically possible, increasing their own power.	A strong executive, provided that it is answerable to parliament (and thus to the electorate) is able to take decisions rapidly in changing situations, for example in countering the threat of terrorism. Government would be unduly constrained by a codified constitution.
Codification would mean greater clarity about the rights of citizens and the powers of government – for example clearing up the uncertainty arising from conventions governing the power of the PM, the circumstances in which ministers should resign and what happens in the event of a 'hung parliament' with no clear election winner.	Much of the historic constitution is written, with acts of parliament and works of authority providing clear guidance. Few codified constitutions are self-explanatory and (as in the USA) they require extensive interpretation.
A constitutional court – as in Germany and the USA – staffed by senior judges with expert knowledge, would be able to assess the constitutionality of actions by parliament and the executive, judging their behaviour by a clear set of rules. This would increase the legitimacy of the political process.	This would put an unjustified degree of power in the hands of unelected, unaccountable judges who may be out of touch with public opinion. A codified constitution would be a direct challenge to parliamentary sovereignty, on which the UK system of government has been founded, because it would bind future parliaments.

Table 4.2: Arguments for and against the UK constitution to be entrenched and codified, including a Bill of Rights

EXTENSION ACTIVITY

Do you feel that the weaknesses of the UK constitution are sufficiently serious to make it worthwhile to overturn centuries of historical practice? Or is a new start needed, to bring the UK into line with most other Western political systems?

Assessment support: 2.1.1 The Constitution

Question 1 on AS-Level Paper 2 gives you a choice of two 10-mark questions, to be completed in 15 minutes.

Describe the key features of the UK constitution. [10 marks]

These questions require a short essay-style response. They are targeted at Assessment Objective 1 (knowledge and understanding). To reach the highest level (8–10 marks), accurate and comprehensive knowledge and understanding are required.

- Given the time constraints, your introduction should do no more than list the points you will be making. Here you are being asked in effect to write a concise 'pen portrait' of the UK constitution. Make sure that you include its key features:

  ○ its uncodified and unentrenched character

  ○ its unitary nature

  ○ the concept of parliamentary sovereignty

  ○ the rule of law.

- Each of these points will require a paragraph consisting of a few lines of explanation. Do not let yourself focus so heavily on one area that you neglect the others.

- You are describing, rather than developing an argument, so there is no need for a conclusion.

Here is an example taken from a student's answer. In this paragraph the student describes the unitary nature of the constitution.

The UK is said to have a unitary constitution. This means that sovereignty, or ultimate authority, is located at the centre, in London. Until the late 1990s the different parts of the UK were all governed in roughly the same way. This changed with the introduction of devolution – the creation of a Scottish parliament and assemblies with lesser powers in Wales and Northern Ireland, which are responsible for policies in their own area, such as health care and education. The UK parliament can still alter the powers of the different bodies and so it still has ultimate sovereignty. The UK is sometimes described as a 'union' rather than a 'unitary' state because the various 'sub-national' parts have different powers and functions. It is not a federal state like the USA, where the powers of the different levels of government are guaranteed by a codified constitution.

- This paragraph gives the right amount of detail for this kind of question. Notice, for example, that the student defines devolution but does not go into great detail about it. More than this would not be expected. Although important, devolution is still only one aspect of the UK constitution.

- The answer shows a comprehensive understanding of the concept of a unitary constitution, and the points made by the student are related to the wider context of how the UK is governed.

- The student uses relevant terminology, such as 'union state' and 'federal', which shows a confident level of knowledge and understanding.

CHAPTER
2 Parliament

Parliament, sometimes referred to as 'Westminster' after the district of London where it meets, is at the centre of the UK political system. It dates back to the 13th century, when the king permitted the election of an assembly to assist him in governing the country. The UK has a 'bicameral' parliamentary system – a parliament with two chambers, an elected **House of Commons** and an unelected **House of Lords**.

In this section you will learn about:

- how the two Houses are structured, and their respective functions
- their comparative powers
- the stages through which a bill passes to become law
- the interaction between parliament and the executive.

2.1 The structure and role of the House of Commons and House of Lords

The selection of members

Members of the House of Commons

Members of the House of Commons are all chosen through election to represent single-member constituencies, using the first-past-the-post electoral system. At the 2015 general election there were 650 constituencies; this is expected to be reduced eventually to 600. The number of candidates seeking election had risen to 3971 by 2015 – an average of six per constituency, mainly chosen and supported by political parties.

Under the Fixed Term Parliaments Act (2011) general elections are supposed to be held at regular intervals, at the end of a fixed five-year parliamentary term. An early general election can be held in one of two possible situations: if a government loses a vote of no confidence and the prime minister cannot form another administration within 14 days; or if two-thirds of MPs support a motion calling for an early election. Theresa May called an early election for June 2017 with the support of the necessary proportion of MPs.

If an MP dies or retires during a parliamentary term, the vacancy is filled by holding a by-election in that constituency.

Most MPs are elected as members of a political party. Only one independent, Lady Hermon – MP for North Down in Northern Ireland – was elected at the 2010 and 2015 general elections. Sometimes an MP may resign or be expelled from a party, and serve out the rest of the parliamentary term as an independent. For example, UKIP's only MP, Douglas Carswell (member for Clacton, Essex), left the party to become an independent in March 2017.

The majority of MPs – roughly three-quarters of the total membership of the Commons – are known as **backbenchers**. The rest are the frontbenchers, who are sub-divided into members of the government, and 'shadow' ministers, who are members of the **opposition**, occupying the front bench that faces the government. The Shadow Cabinet is headed by the leader of the opposition. Since September 2015 this has been Jeremy Corbyn, the leader of the Labour Party.

Key terms

Parliament
the British legislature (law-making body), made up of the House of Commons, House of Lords and monarch.

House of Commons
the primary chamber of the UK legislature, directly elected by voters.

House of Lords
the second chamber of the UK legislature, not directly elected by voters.

Backbenchers
MPs who do not have a ministerial or shadow-ministerial position. They occupy the benches in the debating chamber behind their leaders. Their main role is to represent their constituencies. They are also expected to support the leaders of their respective parties.

Opposition
the official opposition is usually the party with the second-largest number of seats in the Commons. Its role is to criticise the government and to oppose many of its legislative proposals. It also seeks to present itself as an alternative government.

Members of the House of Lords

The House of Lords does not have an upper limit on the size of its membership. In late 2016 it consisted of a total of 809 peers; the parliament website (www.parliament.uk/mps-lords-and-offices/lords/composition-of-the-lords/) is regularly updated with details of membership. There are three main categories of peer: hereditary peers, life peers and 26 'Lords Spiritual' (Anglican archbishops and bishops) who sit in the Lords for historic reasons, as the Church of England is the official church of the British state.

Pause & reflect

The composition of the House of Lords is one of the undemocratic features of the UK constitution, which makes it different from the political systems of most other Western countries. Do you think that parliament would benefit from reform of the House of Lords, and if so, what form should such reform take?

The House of Lords debating chamber.

The House of Commons debating chamber.

The main functions of parliament

Both the Commons and the Lords perform three main functions:

- passing legislation
- scrutiny of the executive (including debating)
- providing ministers.

In addition the Commons has the function of representing the electorate. This section outlines each of these roles in turn, with some assessment of how well they are fulfilled.

Passing legislation (Commons and Lords)

This is the most important function of parliament. Parliament is the supreme legislative body in the UK, with authority to pass or amend laws on any subject. The House of Commons has exclusive power to give consent to taxation – as the elected chamber it represents the public, and the Lords is not allowed to interfere with the passage of what are known as 'money' bills. The Lords has the right to amend non-financial legislation.

Most legislation is initiated by the government and there is limited opportunity for backbench and opposition MPs to propose measures of their own. Parliament mostly reacts to measures put before it by the executive, rather than developing its own legislative proposals, and it is rarely able to defeat or significantly amend legislation. To succeed, this requires solid opposition from the opposition parties combined with rebels on the government side. An example is David Cameron's defeat in March 2016 on plans to extend Sunday trading, when Labour and the SNP joined with Conservative dissidents.

The adversarial nature of the party system, in which the opposition constantly confronts and challenges the government, is reinforced by the work of the party whips. They are responsible for ensuring that MPs attend parliamentary votes (known as 'divisions') and for granting leave of absence if their vote is not essential. They issue MPs with a written instruction to attend – also known as a 'whip' – which indicates how important it is for an MP to be present. The most important votes are underlined three times and these occasions are therefore known as a 'three-line whip'. Less important requests for attendance may be underlined just once or twice. Government whips may offer the prospect of ministerial posts in order to encourage and reward loyalty. Whips can also impose sanctions on those who do not accept the party line. Persistent rebels may have the whip withdrawn, meaning that they are effectively suspended from the party and have to sit as an independent. This can also happen in cases of misconduct where it is felt that an MP has damaged the party's reputation. Smaller teams of whips operate in the Lords.

Governments can use the argument of overriding necessity to push through legislation. The 2005 Prevention of Terrorism Act, which introduced control orders for individuals suspected of terrorist offences, completed all its stages in just 18 days. On the other hand, only a small number of bills are so poorly drafted that they are virtually unworkable. The usual example given is the 1991 Dangerous Dogs Act, which was passed in response to a series of tabloid stories about dog attacks. Critics argued that, instead of prohibiting certain breeds of dog, it should have targeted irresponsible owners. A review by the RSPCA, 25 years later, showed that of 30 deaths caused in that period by dogs, 21 involved breeds that were not specified in the act.

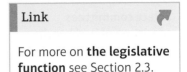

Link

For more on **the legislative function** see Section 2.3.

Link

For more on **the scrutiny function** see Section 2.4

Key term

Select committees consisting of backbench MPs, the composition of Commons select committees reflects the make-up of the Commons. Select committees in the Commons investigate and report on the activities of government departments. Their counterparts in the Lords (such as the Constitution Committee and the Science and Technology Committee) carry out topic-based inquiries.

Parliamentary scrutiny (Commons and Lords)

Parliament has a responsibility to exercise oversight of the executive's actions. The opposition seeks to hold the government to account and to expose its errors. Ministers have a duty to explain and defend their policies in parliament. Most senior ministers sit in the Commons, where the main action of politics takes place. Theresa May's first Cabinet, appointed in July 2016, contained only one member of the Lords (the Leader of the Lords, Baroness Evans), which is typical of recent practice. However, most government departments are represented in the Lords by a junior minister, whose role is to oversee the passage of business through the upper house.

There are a number of ways in which the function of scrutiny is performed. The most important are:

- **questions to ministers**, which may call for oral or written answers. Prime Minister's Questions, a weekly question-and-answer session in the chamber of the Commons, has been criticised for being unduly theatrical and largely a point-scoring exercise dominated by the prime minister and the leader of the opposition.

- **select committees**, which shadow individual government departments in the Commons.

- **debates**, which can be impressive set-piece events, such as the August 2013 House of Commons debate in which the Cameron government was defeated on its proposal to undertake military action in Syria. Since 2010 the creation of the Backbench Business Committee has given MPs more power to shape the agenda by allowing them to choose the topic for debate on one day per week. Debates in the Lords are often given credit for their high quality, with participants commonly including recently retired individuals with expertise in a particular field, but they rarely influence the course of events.

Providing ministers (Commons and Lords)

In a parliamentary system of government, the convention is that ministers must sit in one of the two houses. Parliament acts as a recruiting ground for future ministers, with the whips making recommendations to the prime minister on suitable candidates for promotion. The prime minister possesses wide powers of patronage.

The award of a peerage can on occasion be used to secure the services of a particular individual as a minister, if that person is not an MP. For example, following the 2008 financial crisis, Gordon Brown recalled Peter Mandelson from the European Commission, appointing him to the Lords so that he could serve as business secretary.

Representing the electorate (the Commons only)

The Commons has a representative function since it is the elected house. The Lords is representative only in the sense that it contains people with a wide range of professional backgrounds, although this aspect is not organised systematically. The Lords is not dominated by a single party in the way that the Commons often is, as a consequence of the distorting effects of the first-past-the-post voting system. However, the Lords does not reflect the composition of wider UK society. More than half of its members are over the age of 70, three quarters are male and only around five per cent come from ethnic minorities.

The Commons has a representative function as the elected house. By long-standing tradition, MPs are not delegates of their constituencies – they use their judgement on how to vote, rather than taking instructions from those who elect them. The first-past-the-post system means that there is a strong link between an MP and their constituency. MPs are expected to respond to issues raised by individual constituents and to stand up for local interests at Westminster. For example, a number of the 44 MPs who voted against plans for the London to Birmingham High Speed Rail link (HS2) in March 2016 represented constituencies that would be affected by the planned route. If an MP does not fulfil the expectations of the local electorate, the voters have a right to choose a different representative at the next general election.

Nicky Morgan MP

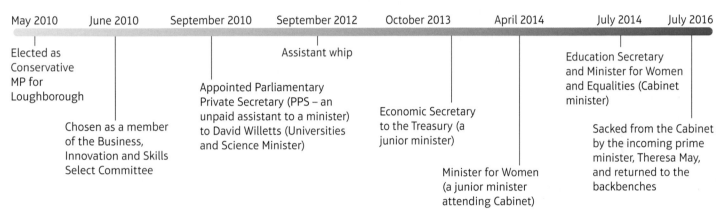

Figure 1.1: Typical steps in a parliamentary career: Nicky Morgan MP

How effectively does parliament perform its representative function?

- One concern is that an MP's loyalty to their party, reinforced by the desire to win promotion to the government, may come into conflict with the need to represent a constituency. However, skilful MPs are good at reconciling the two roles. The ministerial code, which regulates the conduct of ministers, advises them to take care to avoid conflicts of interest. But they are allowed to make representations to colleagues in government, as long as they make it clear that they are acting as their constituents' representative and not as a minister. For example in 2006 Hazel Blears, a member of Tony Blair's Cabinet, supported protests against a planned closure of part of a hospital in her Salford constituency.

- Another issue is that, although there has been considerable improvement since the 1980s, the Commons is still not truly representative of society as a whole. 29 per cent of MPs elected in May 2015 were female – an increase on the 2010 figure, which was 22 per cent – compared to 51 per cent of the UK population. Similarly ethnic minority MPs make up 6 per cent of the Commons, compared to 13 per cent of the population. A pattern has also been developing in recent decades in terms of the class and occupational background of MPs, as Table 1.1 on the next page demonstrates.

> ### Pause & reflect
>
> What does the table below reveal about the background of MPs elected in 2015? (The equivalent percentage for the 2010 election is given in brackets.) Note that there is some double counting as some MPs have more than one kind of job.
>
> | Occupation | Percentage of MPs elected in 2015 (2010) |
> |---|---|
> | Business | 22 (19) |
> | Finance | 15 (15) |
> | Law | 14 (14) |
> | Media | 10 (10) |
> | Teachers | 5 (6) |
> | Lecturers | 4 (6) |
> | PR/Marketing | 8 (11) |
> | Health | 4 (2.5) |
> | Manual work | 3 (4) |
> | Politics | 25 (24) |
> | Agriculture | 1 (2) |
> | Voluntary work | 8 (9) |
> | Armed services | 4 (4) |
> | Unions | 6 (7) |
>
> **Table 1.1:** Background of MPs

2.2 The comparative powers of the House of Commons and House of Lords

The exclusive powers of the House of Commons

Most of the powers and functions of parliament are shared by the two houses. There is one important area, however, where the Commons has exclusive authority – to give consent to taxation and public expenditure. Since the Commons represents the taxpayer, there is a tradition that although the Lords debates money bills, it cannot interfere with them. For this reason the chancellor of the exchequer is obliged to sit in the Commons, where the annual budget is always presented.

Another area where the Commons can exercise power is the situation known as **confidence and supply**. This can occur in the event of a minority government, where the governing party does not join a formal coalition, but relies on a limited agreement with another party (or parties) to keep itself in office. The Conservative Party's arrangement with the Democratic Unionist Party following the general election in June 2017, when the Conservatives were eight seats short of a majority, was a confidence and supply agreement. This means that the supporting party will provide backing on a vote of no confidence, and will vote through the government's budget (the 'supply' part of the arrangement). In return the smaller party will receive certain concessions. It is an agreement that is more flexible (and thus less stable) than a full coalition.

Key term

Confidence and supply
A type of informal coalition agreement sometimes used in the event of a hung parliament where the minority partner agrees to vote with the government on key issues, usually in exchange for policy concessions.

Another relatively recent occurrence in the UK was in 1977–78, when James Callaghan's minority Labour government concluded the 'Lib–Lab Pact' with the smaller Liberal Party. There was talk of the SNP supporting a minority Labour government on these terms, had the 2015 election resulted in a hung parliament.

The main powers of the House of Lords

The Lords is definitely less powerful than the Commons, as suggested by one of its informal alternative names, the 'second chamber'. Since the early 20th century, when the UK started to become more democratic, its powers have been limited by both law and convention. It is widely accepted that this is appropriate, since it lacks the democratic legitimacy of an elected chamber.

The most important legal restraints on the power of the Lords are provided by the Parliament Acts of 1911 and 1949. The first of these came about when the Lords broke with the convention, established since the late 17th century, that they should not interfere with matters of taxation. Aristocratic outrage at new taxes on land and wealth, proposed in the Liberal government's 'People's budget' of 1909, led the Lords to break with this tradition. By rejecting the budget they brought about a prolonged constitutional crisis, which was resolved by the passing of the Parliament Act two years later. This set out in law that:

- the Lords had no right to delay money bills
- its power to veto non-financial bills was to be replaced by a power of delay lasting two parliamentary sessions (equivalent to two years).

Clement Attlee's Labour government, faced with opposition from the Lords to its iron and steel nationalisation bill, used the 1911 act to push through a modification, halving the length of time that the upper house could use its delaying power. This was embodied in the 1949 Parliament Act.

The power of the Lords is also constrained by the 1945 **Salisbury convention**, a convention agreed shortly after the election of the Attlee government. Named after the Conservative opposition leader in the upper house, Lord Salisbury, the convention stated that the Lords would not oppose a bill that gave effect to a commitment contained in the manifesto of the winning party at a general election. The convention was a response to the election of Britain's first majority Labour government, which was committed to a radical reforming programme.

The Lords, then, has the following distinctive powers:

- It acts mainly as a revising chamber, proposing amendments to government legislation, which it is up to the government to decide whether to accept or reject.
- It can delay non-financial legislation for one year.
- The only scenario in which the Lords retains its veto is an extremely unlikely one: if a government were to attempt to prolong the life of parliament beyond its legal maximum term of five years, the Lords is legally empowered to force it to hold a general election.

Debates about the relative powers of the two houses

Although the formal powers of the Lords are quite restricted, as with so much else in British politics, what the upper house can actually do depends to a large extent on the particular circumstances of the time. In recent years some commentators have argued that the Lords is becoming more assertive in its relationship with the elected chamber.

> **Key term**
>
> **Salisbury convention**
> the convention whereby the House of Lords does not delay or block legislation that was included in a government's manifesto.

> **EXTENSION ACTIVITY**
>
> Is a House of Lords still necessary? Make a list of the competing arguments for retaining and abolishing the upper house.

In what ways is the Lords becoming more important?

The removal of most hereditary peers from the Lords in 1999 meant that the upper house was now dominated by life peers, who had mostly been appointed for service in different walks of life. This increased the Lords' sense of legitimacy. Life peers were also more likely to play a regular part in the work of the House, whereas many hereditary peers rarely appeared at Westminster. As a result the reformed House was more inclined to challenge the government, as Table 2.1 demonstrates.

Government	Dates	Number of defeats
Conservative	1979–97	241
Labour	1997–2010	528
Conservative–Liberal Democrat Coalition	2010–15	99
Conservative	2015–16	60

Table 2.1: Government defeats in the House of Lords since 1979

Source: adapted from www.parliament.uk/about/faqs/house-of-lords-faqs/lords-govtdefeats

---

Pause & reflect

Using Table 2.1, work out how many times per session (i.e. each year) the Lords defeated the government, in each of the four time periods. Does this suggest that the 1999 reform of the Lords has made a difference to the way that it behaves?

Another consequence of the departure of most hereditary peers was that the traditional dominance of the House by the Conservative Party came to an end. No party now has overall control of the Lords and so careful management of the House has become more important for governments. Liberal Democrat peers demonstrated growing independence during the period of the New Labour government. For example, after the 2005 general election, they opposed Tony Blair's proposals for identity cards, even though this policy had been announced by the Labour Party in advance. They argued that the Salisbury convention no longer applied because the government had been re-elected on a very low share of the popular vote (only 35.2 per cent). The formation of the coalition government in 2010 cast further doubt on whether the Salisbury convention still applied. This was because the government programme was based on a coalition agreement – between the Conservative and Liberal Democrat leaders – that had never been put to the voters.

Cross-bench peers also began to play a more important role in holding the government to account. As neutral figures, they are more likely to assess a bill on its merits and to decide accordingly whether to support or oppose the government. For example, the cross-bench peer Lord Owen, a former doctor, played a leading role in opposing the coalition government's controversial Health and Social Care Bill. The measure was passed in March 2012 after the government accepted all the amendments proposed in the Lords.

EXTENSION ACTIVITY

What potential problems for the current Conservative government are indicated by the party-affiliation figures in Table 2.2?

Party/group	Number (at 18 April 2017)
Bishops	25
Conservative	254
Cross-bench	178
Labour	202
Liberal Democrat	102
Non-affiliated	30
Others	14
Total	805

Table 2.2: Membership of the House of Lords by party affiliation

How does the Commons maintain its supremacy?

Although the Lords is clearly more assertive, the Commons remains the dominant house. The two houses are not always in conflict with each other – in fact, many amendments in the Lords are sponsored by the government itself, on occasions when it belatedly notices flaws in its own legislation. But when clashes occur, the government can usually make use of its majority in the Commons to overturn critical Lords amendments if it chooses to do so. In February 2012, for example, the coalition government rejected seven amendments to its Welfare Reform and Work Bill, arguing that only the Commons was entitled to take decisions with large financial implications.

A bill can go back and forth between the two houses in a process known as 'parliamentary ping pong'. An extreme example of this was the debate between the two houses on the 2005 Prevention of Terrorism Bill, which introduced control orders. This entailed a marathon sitting of 30 hours. The Lords wanted the bill to include a 'sunset clause' – in other words it would automatically expire after a year unless further legislation was passed to renew it. In the end it is up to the government to decide whether to accept or reject any changes proposed by the Lords. In the case of the Prevention of Terrorism Bill, the Lords backed down following a compromise – the government promised a review a year later.

If the upper house maintains its opposition to the Commons, as a last resort the government can use the Parliament Act to force a bill through. This is rare, but it was used three times by the Blair government for the following.

- Changing the voting system for European parliament elections (1999).
- Equalising the age of consent for gay and heterosexual people (2000).
- Banning hunting with dogs (2004).

In practice, the Lords will usually drop its opposition after making its point, recognising that it lacks the democratic legitimacy needed to push its case further. The following case study illustrates the willingness of the Lords to take a stand on an issue, but also the self-restraint that usually prevails in clashes between the two houses.

EXTENSION ACTIVITY

Choose one of the examples given above in which the Blair government made use of the Parliament Act. Research your chosen example online to find out what led up to the act being invoked, and the issues that it raised at the time.

Case study: the Lords' defeat of the Cameron government's plans for cuts to tax credits, October 2015

The controversy over tax credit cuts found members of the Lords on the same side of the argument as the progressive campaign group, 38 Degrees.

The House of Lords attracted publicity in the autumn of 2015 by voting to delay planned cuts to tax credits and to compensate those who were affected. This was an emotionally charged issue because the purpose of tax credits was to support low-income working people. The vote raised a constitutional issue, with supporters of the government arguing that because this was a financial measure, the Lords should not have become involved. However, strictly speaking, the peers were within their rights because the tax credit changes were incorporated in a 'statutory instrument' (or secondary legislation) rather than in primary legislation. The government was acting on the basis of power delegated to it under a previous act of parliament, which enabled it to make changes to the law, rather than bringing forward a new bill. The Lords was allowed to reject a statutory instrument.

At the same time the episode highlighted the limits of the Lords' power. Peers showed restraint in choosing not to support a more controversial Liberal Democrat motion to block the changes completely. This is typical of the Lords' approach; the upper house normally tries to avoid all-out conflict with an elected government. The government ordered a review of the Lords' power to take this kind of action in the future, but eventually backed away from further confrontation on the issue.

Questions

- What does the House of Lords' stance on tax credits tell you about how it sees its constitutional role?

- Why do you think the Conservative government decided not to bring forward legislation to curb the Lords' power to block statutory instruments?

2.3   The legislative process

The different stages a bill goes through to become law

Before looking at the process itself you need to be aware of the difference between a **legislative bill** and an act of parliament, and to understand the various types of bill that can pass through parliament.

- A legislative bill is a proposal for a new law, or a change to an existing law, which is brought before parliament. A bill can be introduced in either the Commons or the Lords.
- An act of parliament is a bill that has completed all its stages in parliament and has become law.

Types of bill

Government bill or public bill

The most important type of proposal that can be debated in parliament. These are brought forward by government ministers to change public policy, for example the reorganisation of the NHS which was brought about by the 2012 Health and Social Care Act.

Private bill

Much less common. It is sponsored by an organisation such as a company or a local authority, with the intention of changing the law as it affects that organisation. A group affected by such a bill has the right to petition parliament against it. An example is the 2013 Local Local Authorities and Transport for London Act, which introduced new powers for dealing with obstructions caused by builders and road users in the capital.

Hybrid bill

Has characteristics of both a public and a private bill. It proposes changes to the law which would affect the general public, but certain groups or areas in particular. The bill to build the HS2 rail link from London to Birmingham (and then to Manchester and Leeds) is an example.

Private member's bill

Affects the whole population, introduced by an individual backbench MP or a member of the Lords. These are much less likely than a government bill to become law, as they depend on time being found for them to complete all their stages in parliament. In the Commons, at the start of each session the names of MPs applying to introduce a private member's bill are drawn in a ballot. An alternative is for a member to make a proposal using the 'ten minute rule', but this allows for little more than the airing of an issue in a speech which must last no more than ten minutes.

Some landmark bills have, however, originated as private member's bills. An example of such a measure is the imposition of a duty on councils and NHS services to look after people with autism, passed in 2009, which was initiated by Cheryl Gillan MP.

Figure 3.1: Different types of bill that can pass through parliament

How a bill becomes law

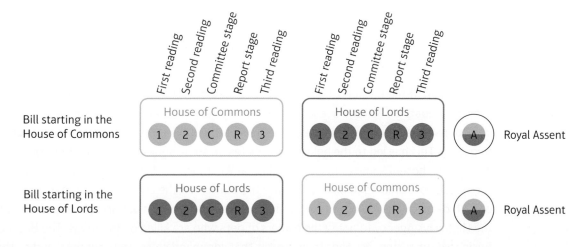

Figure 3.2: The stages a bill goes through to become law

Origin: A bill may originate as a Green Paper (a document setting out options for legislation and inviting consultation) and/or a White Paper (a more detailed statement of the government's intentions) – but this whole stage is not compulsory.

First reading (in the Commons in this example): First compulsory stage. The bill is made available to MPs but is not debated or voted on at this stage.

Second reading: Principle of the bill is debated and a vote may be taken if it is contested.

Committee stage: Bill is scrutinised in detail by a **public bill committee**, formerly known as a standing committee, whose membership reflects the strength of the parties in the Commons. Amendments may be made at this stage if the government is prepared to accept them.

Report stage: Whole House considers amendments made at the committee stage and may accept or reject them.

Third reading: Amended bill is debated and voted on by the whole House.

House of Lords stages: Bill goes through the same stages in the Lords, with the exception of the committee stage, which is carried out by the whole House. The Lords can propose amendments. The Commons has to decide whether to accept, reject or further amend these. The bill can go back and forth between the two Houses for up to a year before it becomes law, in a process popularly known as 'parliamentary ping pong'.

Royal assent: Monarch signs the bill, making it law. This stage is a formality as the sovereign is a constitutional monarch, who would not get involved in politics by refusing to sign a bill.

2.4   The ways in which parliament interacts with the executive

The role and significance of backbenchers

Crucial to the ability of MPs and peers to carry out their functions is the concept of **parliamentary privilege**. This means that, within the confines of parliament, they may say what they like, without being subject to outside influence. This includes immunity from being sued for libel. It does not mean that they cannot be prosecuted for criminal activity; several MPs and peers were jailed, for example, following revelations in 2009 that they had made false claims for parliamentary expenses. The role of parliamentary privilege is to ensure that MPs and peers enjoy their historic right to freedom of speech.

Some commentators have suggested that backbench MPs are playing an increasingly significant role within parliament, especially in scrutinising government activity and holding the executive to account. There is some evidence in support of this claim.

- The creation of the Backbench Business Committee in 2010, which is allowed to choose the topic for debate on 35 days in each parliamentary session. Some of these subjects are chosen in response to e-petitions signed by members of the public; 100,000 signatures are required to qualify. This has led to the holding of debates on some subjects that might not otherwise have been chosen. Some of these take place in Westminster Hall, the oldest surviving part of the Houses of Parliament, in order to ease the burden on the Commons chamber. Examples of such debates include one in 2015 that led to the introduction of Harvey's law, which obliges the Highways Agency to notify the owners of pets who are killed on the roads. The Backbench Business Committee responds to proposals that command cross-party support, and so there is an incentive for MPs to work together in requesting a debate.

> **Key term**
>
> **Public bill committees** committees responsible for looking at bills in detail.

> **EXTENSION ACTIVITY**
>
> Use the internet to research the various stages through which a particular bill became law. Prominent examples from the coalition government include the Welfare Reform Act (2012) and the Marriage (Same Sex Couples) Act (2013).

> **Key term**
>
> **Parliamentary privilege** the right of MPs or Lords to make certain statements within parliament without being subject to outside influence, including law.

- A rise in the number of backbench rebellions against government measures, even if the average number of MPs involved in particular rebellions has declined. Political scientists Philip Cowley and Mark Stuart have calculated that coalition MPs rebelled in 35 per cent of divisions during the 2010–15 parliament; the equivalent figures for government rebellions under Labour in the 2005–10 parliament was 28 per cent. Note also that if a government is not certain of getting its business through, it may choose not to proceed rather than risk an actual defeat in the Commons. The coalition government's dropping of its House of Lords reform bill after the second reading in 2013 is an example of this.

- An increase in the use of 'urgent questions' – a device that, subject to the approval of the Speaker of the House, allows an MP to raise an important matter requiring an immediate answer from a government minister. A study conducted during the coalition government found that Speaker John Bercow allowed a total of 3547 urgent questions in 2009–13, while his predecessor, Michael Martin (2000–09) presided over only 1234 in a much longer period. An example is the summoning of Work and Pensions Secretary Damian Green in February 2017. He was summoned to answer an urgent question put by Labour MP Stephen Timms regarding changes to Personal Independence Payment, a benefit paid to disabled people.

There are important limits on the influence of backbenchers.

- MPs can use various methods to draw attention to issues in which they are interested, but this does not mean that they will succeed in getting any action taken. One example of this is an adjournment debate. After the official business of the House is over, there is an opportunity to raise an issue and a minister will reply. Another option for backbenchers is the 10-minute rule. This allows MPs to speak for 10 minutes on their chosen subject before the beginning of official business on certain days. However, in both cases, the only result is likely to be an airing of the MP's concern in debate.

- Public bill committees give MPs an opportunity to propose amendments to legislation, and each clause of a bill is scrutinised. However, the government has a majority on these committees and often it will use its position of strength to introduce its own amendments, rather than listening to proposals from opposition MPs.

- The power of patronage and ties of party loyalty, reinforced by the party whips, remain important factors in the Commons.

Backbench members of the House of Lords are usually established figures in their own fields, and many are retired politicians. The promise of a government post cannot therefore influence them as much as it might a backbench MP, and so they are likely to act independently. The growing prominence of cross-benchers who have no party affiliation has already been noted. For almost any conceivable area of public life or interest, there will be peers with experience and expertise who can contribute to debates in particular areas. Current examples include Professor Lord Hennessy, one of Britain's leading experts on constitutional matters, and Baroness Greenfield in the field of science and technology. A full list of cross-benchers can be found on the following website: www.crossbenchpeers.org.uk/role.html

The work of select committees

House of Commons select committees in their current form were introduced by Norman St John Stevas, Leader of the House at the beginning of the Thatcher government in 1979. There is a select committee to scrutinise the policy, administration and spending of each government department.

In addition there are several non-departmental select committees with specific functions.

- The Public Accounts Committee examines government expenditure, seeking to ensure that value for money is being obtained.
- The Liaison Committee, which consists of the chairs of all the select committees, questions the prime minister twice a year across the whole field of government policy.
- The Committee on Standards oversees the work of the parliamentary commissioner on standards, an official who is in charge of regulating MPs' conduct, including their financial affairs.

Each departmental select committee consists of a *minimum* of 11 backbench MPs. Their composition reflects the balance of party strength in the House of Commons. For example, the Education Select Committee was chaired by Conservative MP Neil Carmichael following the 2015 general election. Of the ten other members, a further five were Conservatives, four were Labour and one was a member of the SNP.

Following a reform introduced in 2010, chairs are now elected by their fellow MPs rather than chosen by the party whips, a move which has increased their independence. Members are chosen by secret ballot within party groups.

The members of a select committee decide on the areas that they will investigate. They have the power to gather written and oral evidence and to summon witnesses, including ministers, civil servants, experts and members of the public with a relevant interest. Select committees may appoint specialist advisers – possibly an academic in the field they are investigating – to assist them in their work. They produce a report, to which the government is expected to respond within two months.

Select committees are important for a number of reasons.

- Their work is respected because it is evidence-based. Their hearings are televised and reported in the media, which increases their influence. They air issues of public interest. The Transport Select Committee, for example, held Transport Secretary Patrick McLoughlin to account for the controversy over the West Coast Main Line rail franchise in 2012.
- The scope of the committees' work has widened in recent years to include the scrutiny of legislation. They also hold pre-appointment hearings, in which they interview candidates for some public roles. The Treasury Select Committee, for example, has the right to veto the chancellor of the exchequer's choice for the head of the Office for Budget Responsibility.
- Long-serving members can accumulate more knowledge of a particular policy area than a minister, who may stay in a government department for only two or three years. Some experienced chairs of select committees have become considerable public figures, and this role is now recognised as an alternative career path to the ministerial ladder. An example is Margaret Hodge, chair of the Public Accounts Select Committee from 2010 to 2015, who has said that she had more influence in this role than as a government minister earlier in her career.
- Select committees can have a direct influence on government policy. For example, in 2014 the Home Office took the Passport Office back under ministerial control, following a critical report by the Home Affairs Select Committee. The chief executive of the Passport Office, organised as an executive agency at the time, had been criticised for a large backlog in applications that had caused considerable public anger during the summer.

On the other hand, the influence of select committees should not be exaggerated.

- A majority of select-committee members will be drawn from the governing party (or parties in the case of a coalition) and there is a tradition that MPs from the government side chair the influential Treasury, foreign affairs and defence committees.

- Although the resources available have increased, the committees can cover only a limited range of topics in depth and there is a tendency to avoid investigations into more long-term, strategic issues.
- There is still a high turnover rate for membership of committees, and some MPs do not attend regularly.
- The government accepts an estimated 40 per cent of select-committee recommendations, but these rarely involve major changes of policy.
- Committees' power to summon witnesses is considerable but not unlimited. For example, in 2013, as home secretary, Theresa May blocked the Home Affairs Select Committee from interviewing the head of MI5, Andrew Parker.

House of Lords select committees operate on a different basis to those in the Commons. They do not shadow government departments, but instead scrutinise legislation and investigate particular issues. An example is the Constitution Committee, which examines public bills for their constitutional implications and investigates broad constitutional issues. Lords committees deliberately seek to avoid duplicating the work of their counterparts in the Commons. Thus a Treasury Select Committee is to be found in the Commons, which examines the work of the Treasury and HMRC. The Lords has an Economic Affairs Committee, which looks at wider issues, such as the economic case for the HS2 rail link. Lords committees can draw on the services of a range of well-qualified experts in different fields. For example, former Chancellor Lord (Nigel) Lawson was a member of the Economic Affairs Committee. Yet, however learned and thoroughly researched the reports of these Lords committees may be, their wider impact is usually limited.

> ### Pause & reflect
>
> How effective do you feel select committees are in holding the government to account, compared with other methods that are available to MPs?

The role and significance of the opposition

Opposition parties are not in a strong position to hold the government to account in parliament unless its majority is small. Even a leader of the opposition who is judged to be an effective performer in the Commons, such as William Hague in the period of Tony Blair's first government, may make little real impression on the general public, as his defeat in the 2001 general election showed. Opposition leaders may choose instead to concentrate on attacking the government through the media, where they reach a larger audience. They have a constant dilemma in that they need to criticise ministers, while also projecting themselves in a statesmanlike light as a government in waiting. The leader of the opposition does, however, have certain opportunities to hold the government to account. They take the leading role in responding to the government programme, as set out in the annual Queen's speech, and replies to the chancellor of the exchequer's budget speech.

The opposition parties are allocated 20 days a year to propose subjects for debate. Of these, 17 days are at the disposal of the leader of the official opposition – the largest opposition party – leaving the other three days to the second-largest opposition party. The SNP, for example, used its allocation in November 2015 to instigate debates on the Trident nuclear defence system, to which they are strongly opposed, and on the closure of HMRC offices. These occasions are of only symbolic importance, allowing opposition parties to register their views on aspects of government policy. The government will usually table an amendment to the opposition motion, cancelling it out by commending its own policy. With an in-built majority it will usually have no difficulty in carrying the amendment.

Assistance is available to help opposition parties carry out their parliamentary business, in the form of 'Short money'. The fund also provides help with the running costs of the leader of the opposition's office. The purpose of Short money is to compensate for the fact that, unlike the government, opposition parties do not have access to support from the civil service. It is supposed to be spent on policy research and the salaries of staff who work for the opposition in parliament, rather than in their party headquarters. The Conservative government cut the amount available after the 2015 general election, on the grounds that opposition parties should make sacrifices at a time when Whitehall departments' funding was being reduced.

> **Pause & reflect**
>
> How justified was the Labour spokeswoman who described the government's cuts to Short money as 'anti-democratic' and designed to give it an 'unfair advantage' over the opposition? Do you believe that political parties should receive more state funding for their activities?

Ministerial questions and Prime Minister's Questions

Prime Minister's Questions is one of the regular set-piece events of the parliamentary calendar. It is held once a week, at 12 p.m. for half an hour each Wednesday when the Commons is sitting. It attracts considerable attention in press and television reporting. Its defenders argue that it obliges the prime minister to engage with the opposition on a range of topics, and the intensive preparation that goes on inside Number 10 suggests that it is a significant event. Tony Blair later described it as 'the most nerve-racking, discombobulating, nail-biting, bowel-moving, terror-inspiring, courage-draining experience' in his political life.

Critics, however, point to the 'gladiatorial' nature of the encounter between the prime minister and the leader of the opposition, which tends to reveal more about their respective personalities than it does about the detail of government policy. Clashes between David Cameron and Jeremy Corbyn, for example, were notorious for their displays of prime ministerial scorn, with Cameron on one occasion attacking his opposite number's choice of suit. There is considerable stage management, with MPs on the government side deliberately asking 'planted' questions to present the prime minister in a good light. In 2012, for example, it was revealed that Cameron's parliamentary private secretary, Desmond Swayne, had orchestrated heckling of the Labour leader, Ed Miliband, and had asked Conservative MPs to create a 'protective wall of sound' around the prime minister when he faced opposition criticism.

Better scrutiny of government activity is arguably provided by the rota on which ministers answer questions about their own departments. This usually entails more detailed questioning and ministers are given notice of oral questions so that they can prepare with the assistance of civil servants. MPs can also submit written questions that are answered by civil servants. This allows opposition MPs to inform themselves about government policy, and individual members can raise issues of interest to their constituents. This is, of course, much less well-known than the highly theatrical verbal duels between the prime minister and the leader of the opposition.

The trivial nature of much of Prime Minister's Questions was highlighted by David Cameron's comment about the leader of the opposition Jeremy Corbyn's choice of outfit in February 2016.

Assessment support: 2.1.2 Parliament

Question 1 on A-Level Paper 2 gives you a choice of two 30-mark questions – 1a and 1b – with one to be completed in 45 minutes. This kind of question is based on a source presenting more than one opinion on a topic.

This source contains extracts from a briefing document entitled 'Parliamentary Scrutiny of Government', published in 2015 by the Institute for Government. This is an independent research body concerned with the way in which government works.

> *Parliament has long played a central role in our system of government as the forum in which government must explain itself and be held to account. The two Houses of Parliament fulfil their scrutiny role through three key mechanisms: debate, questions and committees… politicians have real opportunities to influence the government's agenda. However, the fact that parliamentary scrutiny is undertaken by politicians means that it is shaped by many motivations besides the ambition to improve the effectiveness of government. These may compromise the effectiveness of scrutiny. For example, a backbench government-party MP might treat a minister gently in a select committee hearing or ask a helpful question at Prime Minister's Questions in order to enhance their own career prospects. More seriously, they might ask a question to serve outside interests for personal gain…*

> *The MPs who undertake scrutiny do so in their capacity as the democratically elected representatives of the taxpayer and citizen. An awareness of this contributes legitimacy and importance to the process. Parliamentary scrutiny is bolstered by certain powers (including the power to send for 'persons, papers and records', which facilitates the gathering of evidence) available by virtue of parliament's role within the constitution (as a check on the executive)…*

> *Parliamentary scrutiny involves an accountability relationship: parliament can 'require' an explanation from ministers of their performance, decisions and actions in relation to the expenditure, administration or policy of the government… however, the enforceability of the 'right to ask questions', which is generally understood as a key power of parliamentary committees, is uncertain in practice.*

(Source: www.instituteforgovernment.org.uk/sites/default/files/publications/Parliamentary%20 scrutiny%20briefing%20note%20final.pdf [pp. 15–16])

Using the source, evaluate the view that parliament is effective in carrying out its work of scrutinising the UK government. [30 marks]

In your response you must:

- *compare the different opinions in the source*

- *consider this view and the alternative to this view in a balanced way*

- *use knowledge and understanding to help you analyse and evaluate.*

This kind of question tests all three Assessment Objectives, with the marks equally divided between them. You are expected to compare the different opinions given in the source and to analyse and evaluate them, using your knowledge and understanding of the topic to support your answer. If you do not provide any comparative analysis of the source, or you do not consider the different views in a balanced way, you cannot score higher than the top of Level 2 – a maximum of 12 marks out of 30. Your analysis and evaluation must relate to the information in the source.

- Read the source carefully before you start writing, noting the arguments that it puts forward on how effective parliament is in carrying out its scrutiny function.

- The source gives three main ways in which parliamentary scrutiny is carried out: debates, questions (to ministers and the prime minister) and committees.

- After identifying these methods in a brief introduction, examine each one in turn in separate paragraphs. For each method, you need to offer analysis and evaluation of its effectiveness, firmly underpinned by your knowledge and understanding of the topic.

- It is important to consider both sides presented in the source, and to reflect the balance between the two in your conclusion.

Here is part of a student's answer to this question, focusing on the role of select committees.

House of Commons select committees shadow government departments and carry out evidence-based inquiries, which may be reported by the media, increasing their influence. Since 2010 they have become more independent of government as MPs have been allowed to elect their chairs, rather than having them appointed by the party whips. The source points out that the committees have a right to summon witnesses, including ministers, and documents as part of their investigations. This potentially gives them considerable importance but the source does go on to say that this right is not completely enforceable. For example, as Home Secretary Theresa May blocked the appearance of Andrew Parker, the director of MI5, before a meeting of the Home Affairs Select Committee. The source also notes that MPs on the government side may treat a minister gently in order to demonstrate their loyalty and improve their chances of promotion. This is linked to the rise of the professional politician in recent decades, who is keen to win government posts.

- The student correctly uses a combination of material drawn from the source and from outside knowledge. For example, the point about the summoning of witnesses is backed up by a specific example concerning the director of MI5.

- The paragraph shows the skill of comparative analysis, picking up and expanding on points from the source to demonstrate both effective and less-effective features of select committees.

- This approach would score highly for analysis and evaluation.

CHAPTER
3

Prime Minister and Executive

The **executive** is sometimes referred to as the government. It is the decision-making body at the heart of the political system, the collective group consisting of the prime minister, **Cabinet** and junior ministers.

In this section you will look at:

- how the executive functions and the powers that it exercises
- what it means for ministers to be responsible, both as individuals and collectively as members of the government
- the relationship between the prime minister and Cabinet, and their ability to control events and policy.

3.1 The structure, role and powers of the executive

The structure of the executive

The prime minister
- Head of the **executive** who chairs the **Cabinet** and manages its agenda
- Appoints all members of the Cabinet and junior **ministers**, and decides who sits on Cabinet committees
- Organises the structure of government – can create, abolish or merge departments

The Cabinet
- Consists of 20 to 23 senior ministers, including those who hold the title secretary of state
- Several senior figures are not members of the Cabinet but attend its meetings
- Administrative support and help in delivering policy is provided by the Cabinet Office, headed by the Cabinet secretary, the UK's most senior civil servant
- Many decisions taken in Cabinet committees, which deal with particular areas of policy such as economic affairs and national security

Government departments
- Each one responsible for an area of policy, e.g. the Ministry of Defence, Department for Transport
- Each headed by a Cabinet minister, supported by several junior ministers responsible for specific aspects of the work of the department

Executive agencies
- Semi-independent bodies that carry out some of the functions of **government departments**, for example, the DVLA (Driver and Vehicle Licensing Agency) is overseen by the Department for Transport

Figure 1.1: Power structure of the executive

An example of a government department: the Department for Education

> **Justine Greening MP**
> Secretary of State for Education
> (also Minister for Women and Equalities) – leads the department

> **Junior ministers**
> - **Nick Gibb MP** – Minister of State for School Standards
> - **Jo Johnson MP** – Minister of State for Universities, Science, Research and Innovation
> - **Robert Halfon MP** – Minister of State for Apprenticeships and Skills
> - **Edward Timpson MP** – Minister of State for Vulnerable Children and Families

> - **Caroline Dinenage MP** – Parliamentary Under Secretary of State for Women, Equalities and Early Years
> - **Lord Nash** – Parliamentary Under Secretary of State for the School System

Figure 1.2: Hierarchy of a typical government department

Ministers of state are senior to parliamentary under secretaries of state. Notice that the department has a junior minister (Lord Nash) to represent it in the House of Lords.

The main roles of the executive

Link

For more details on **devolved bodies**, see Section 1.3

The executive decides how the country is run. It represents the UK abroad and manages the defence of the country. It is responsible for public services including the National Health Service, welfare benefits and the criminal justice system. Since devolution, some of these functions have been transferred from the core executive in London to devolved bodies in Scotland, Wales and Northern Ireland.

Proposing legislation, proposing the budget and making policy are all important roles of the UK executive.

Proposing legislation

The executive introduces proposals for new laws or amendments to existing laws. It announces a new programme at the start of each parliamentary session in the Queen's speech, which is read out to both Houses of Parliament by the monarch, but is written by the government. For example, the May 2015 Queen's speech reflected the priorities of the Conservative government that had just been elected under the leadership of David Cameron, including proposals for:

- an in/out referendum on the UK's membership of the European Union
- measures to ensure that decisions affecting England, or England and Wales, would be taken only with the consent of MPs from those parts of the UK
- legislation to protect essential public services against strikes.

The executive does not, of course, confine itself to measures proposed in a party manifesto at a general election. It also has the power to introduce legislation to contend with emergencies, such as the threat of terrorism, and to amend existing statutes in order to bring the UK into line with international law. This is known as a 'doctor's mandate'.

Ministers will often consult with interested parties, such as pressure groups and professional bodies, before introducing legislation. For example, in 2015 the Cameron government undertook a consultation exercise with employers on its proposal to introduce an apprenticeship levy, a requirement for large companies to contribute towards the cost of training new workers. This was introduced in 2017.

Proposing the budget

The government needs to raise revenue in order to fund public services and to meet its spending priorities. The budget is created by the chancellor of the exchequer in consultation with the prime minister, and is revealed to the rest of the Cabinet shortly before it is delivered. The budget is an annual statement of the government's plans for changes to taxation and public spending. In recent years, the budget has been presented to the House of Commons for approval in March, but this moved to November from 2017. If a new government comes to power after a general election, it introduces a budget of its own, even if the previous government has already presented one. For example, in June 2010 George Osborne, chancellor in the new coalition government, delivered an 'emergency budget' only 90 days after the previous Labour government's budget.

Making policy decisions

The executive has to decide how to give effect to its aims for the future direction of the country. Examples of important policy decisions taken by the 2010–15 coalition government include:

- streamlining the welfare system by introducing a single benefit for working-age people, known as Universal Credit
- allowing parents and voluntary groups to set up 'free schools', independent of local councils
- introducing more competition into the National Health Service (at least in England) and putting GPs in control of the commissioning of care for patients.

Pause & reflect

Check that you are clear on how the role of the UK government differs from that of parliament. You can find a useful summary on the parliament website at: www.parliament.uk/about/how/role/parliament-government/. Use the information to produce a table setting out the roles of the two in bullet-point form.

The main powers of the executive

The executive has at its disposal a number of powers, some of which it exercises collectively, while others are in the hands of the prime minister, who may make use of them in consultation with a handful of senior ministerial colleagues and officials. The way in which these powers are deployed has given rise to the debate on whether the UK can be said to have a system of Cabinet government, or of '**prime ministerial government**'.

Royal prerogative powers

Royal prerogative powers are powers that historically belonged to the Crown, but which over time have been transferred to the prime minister or other ministers. Many of these are not properly defined. They are not set out in statutes but are based largely on the practice of previous governments. The main prerogative powers that still exist today are shown in Figure 1.3:

Link

For more on **prime ministerial government**, see Section 3.3

Key term

Royal prerogative
a set of powers and privileges belonging to the monarch but normally exercised by the prime minister or Cabinet, such as the granting of honours or of legal pardons.

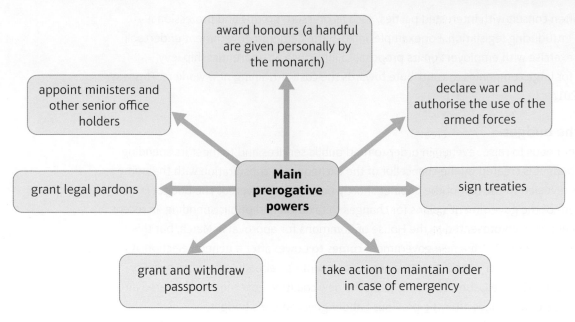

Figure 1.3: Main prerogative powers

Both Gordon Brown's Labour government (2007–10) and the coalition government (2010–15) were open to the idea of placing some prerogative powers under parliamentary authority.

Two powers have been abolished or reformed.

- The 2011 Fixed Term Parliaments Act removed the right of the prime minister to determine the date of the general election. However, as in the case of Theresa May, who called an early general election for June 2017, it is possible for the prime minister to override the act with the support of enough MPs.

- Since the parliamentary debate on the Iraq War in 2003, and the 2013 debate on air strikes in Syria, governments have accepted that military action requires prior parliamentary approval. In case of an emergency, the government retains the right to deploy troops and then to secure approval afterwards.

Initiation of legislation

The executive controls most of the parliamentary time available for legislation. The exceptions to this are 20 opposition days, 13 days set aside for private member's bills, and a variable amount of time allocated for debates chosen by the Backbench Business Committee. Legislation can be introduced in either the Commons or the Lords but it is usual for the most important bills to go to the Commons first.

Link

For more on **MP rebellions**, see Section 2.2 of Parliament.

If the government has a majority in the Commons, it can usually rely on the party whipping system and the power of patronage to push through its programme. **Rebellions** can occur, although it is rare for a government to be defeated on the second or third reading of a bill.

The executive has several tools to strengthen its hold over the passage of legislation. The guillotine – formally known as an 'allocation of time' motion – which dates back to 1887, is a procedure that allows the government to curtail debate on the individual clauses of a bill. It applies only in the Commons. An attempt by the Cameron government to use the guillotine in a Lords debate on the redrawing of constituency boundaries was abandoned after opposition in 2011. The programming motion, introduced by the Blair government, enables the executive to set out in advance the time limits for each stage in the passage of a bill. In addition, since 2002 it has been possible for the government to carry over uncompleted legislation from one session to another, without having to start again from the beginning of the legislative process in the new session.

Secondary legislation

Secondary (or delegated) legislation is law made without passing a new act of parliament. Instead the government uses powers created by an earlier act. The most common form of secondary legislation is statutory instruments. These enable a government to modify or repeal existing legislation without introducing a new bill. Clearly it would be pointlessly time-consuming to enact new legislation every time the government needs to amend or update the detail of existing regulations. However, critics have raised concerns about the growing use of statutory instruments to make more controversial changes. For example, in 2016 statutory instruments were used to abolish maintenance grants for university students and to allow fracking in national parks. Opposition politicians and press commentators argued that the government was sneaking these changes through the back door. Statutory instruments are sometimes called 'Henry VIII clauses' because they enable the government to evade parliamentary scrutiny. Although parliament can debate and, in theory, reject a statutory instrument, about two-thirds of them simply become law on a specified date in the future, without being put before MPs.

> **Link**
>
> For an example related to **secondary legislation**, see the case study in Section 2.2 of Parliament.

3.2 The concept of ministerial responsibility

What does it mean to say that ministers are 'responsible' or 'accountable' for what they do? The concept of responsibility is a convention, not a fixed law which can be enforced. This means that political circumstances are important in determining how the concept of responsibility is applied in practice. In particular, there are no hard and fast rules governing the circumstances in which ministers may be obliged to take responsibility for their actions by resigning from the government.

The concept of individual ministerial responsibility

Individual ministerial responsibility is the idea that ministers are responsible for the running of their department and its policies. They also have responsibility for the standard of their own personal conduct. The official definition of **individual responsibility** is set out in a document known as the *Ministerial Code*, issued at the start of a new government by the prime minister. The latest version states that 'Ministers have a duty to parliament to account, and be held to account, for the policies, decisions and actions of their departments and agencies'. They are obliged to give accurate information to parliament, and if they knowingly mislead parliament, they are expected to resign. Ministers are responsible for deciding how to conduct themselves but, importantly, they 'only remain in office for so long as they retain the confidence of the prime minister'. The latter is described as 'the ultimate judge of the standards of behaviour expected of a minister and the appropriate consequences of a breach of those standards'.

It is now widely accepted that the business of government is so large and complex that a minister cannot be expected to know about everything that goes on within their department, and so would not be expected to resign over a minor mistake. It is hard to be certain how the concept of individual responsibility will work out in a given situation.

> **Key terms**
>
> **Secondary legislation** powers given to the executive by parliament to make changes to the law, within certain specific rules.
>
> **Individual responsibility** the principle by which ministers are responsible for their personal conduct and for their departments.

Case study: Charles Clarke and the foreign prisoners issue, April 2006

The case of Charles Clarke, home secretary in Tony Blair's government, illustrates how flexible the concept of individual ministerial responsibility can be. Clarke was challenged by opposition MPs in April 2006 over the inability of the Home Office to account for the movements of more than 1000 foreign prisoners after they had served their sentences in the UK. It appeared that they had been freed without being considered for deportation. Clarke admitted that his department had taken its 'eye off the ball' but also told the BBC that 'I certainly don't think I have a duty to the public to go – I have a duty to sort this out.' It was reported that he did in fact privately offer to resign but initially the prime minister backed him to continue in office. However, 10 days later, with the affair showing no signs of abating, Blair sacked Clarke as part of a wider Cabinet reshuffle, following poor results for the Labour Party in the local elections. This example demonstrates the extent to which the interpretation of ministerial responsibility depends on the circumstances at the time.

Question

- Does the case of Charles Clarke suggest that the concept of ministerial responsibility has become so elastic that it is actually outdated?

The fate of an individual minister depends on:

- how serious the issue is perceived to be
- the level of criticism in parliament and the media when a mistake is made
- the attitude of the prime minister of the day.

Alastair Campbell, who served as Tony Blair's press secretary, was believed to have had a 'golden rule' that a minister would have to go if he or she was at the centre of a media storm for a given length of time. However, when later asked to clarify what he had actually said, Campbell was unable to recall having laid down any such rule.

One factor that has eroded the concept of individual responsibility is the way in which, since the late 1980s, many government functions have been delegated to executive agencies under a director general, rather than a minister. This has led to some doubt about who is accountable, with the minister assuming responsibility for making overall policy, while the head of the agency exercises 'operational responsibility'. For example, in 1995 the Home Secretary Michael Howard controversially sacked Derek Lewis, the director general of the Prisons Service, following criticism of the escape of prisoners from Parkhurst Jail.

The blurring of lines of accountability has meant that in some cases, civil servants rather than ministers have been held responsible for departmental errors. Traditionally civil servants were anonymous, taking neither credit nor blame for the actions of governments, but this has been eroded in recent decades. For example, in 2012 Transport Secretary Patrick McLoughlin admitted that mistakes had been made in the awarding of a franchise to companies to run trains on the West Coast Main Line. Three civil servants were suspended as a result, one of whom launched a successful legal action, leading to the officials' reinstatement. Constitutional expert Professor Vernon Bogdanor made the case for the traditional relationship between ministers and civil servants. He argued that ministers were responsible for ensuring that officials had the necessary skills to carry out the work of the department, and that ministers should be in a position to assure parliament that all was in order.

Personal misconduct is a more common cause of resignations than failures of policy or administration. In some cases the *impression* that a minister's behaviour has fallen short of expected standards of integrity has been enough to bring about a departure from office. For example, Peter Mandelson was obliged to resign twice from Tony Blair's first government because of a perception of wrongdoing. In 1998 he left his post as trade and industry secretary after it was revealed that he was buying a house with the help of a loan supplied by a Cabinet colleague, whose business affairs were being investigated by Mandelson's department. Brought back as Northern Ireland secretary, he was forced out in 2001 by accusations that he had used his influence to fast track a passport application by an Indian businessman. Mandelson was exonerated by an independent enquiry but by then he had already gone. In both cases he had to resign simply to clear the air, regardless of the facts.

The concept of collective ministerial responsibility

Collective ministerial responsibility is the convention that ministers must support all decisions of the government in public. It means that they are responsible as a group to parliament and thus to the people, and that discussions in Cabinet should be confidential. If defeated in a vote of no confidence in the Commons, the government as a whole resigns. The practice is designed to maintain the unity of the government in face of attacks by the opposition. While ministers are free to argue their case with each other in private, once a decision has been reached it is binding on them all. If a minister cannot accept such a decision, in theory they should resign. One of the best-known examples of such a resignation in recent times was in 2003 of Robin Cook, leader of the House of Commons, in opposition to the Blair government's decision to go to war with Iraq. He stated that he could not 'accept collective responsibility for the decision to commit Britain now to military action in Iraq without international agreement or domestic support'.

Clear-cut resignations on grounds of disagreement with government policy are quite rare in practice. To take such a step may well end a political career. It is more common for ministers who are unhappy with government policy to grumble from within, or 'leak' their dissatisfaction to the media, rather than take a public stand. Not all resignations are purely concerned with matters of principle but may be complicated by personality clashes and ambitions.

EXTENSION ACTIVITY

How significant has the creation of executive agencies been for the concept of ministerial responsibility? An example you could look at is the dispute over the relaxation of border control checks, which led to the suspension of Brodie Clark, head of the UK Border Agency in 2011.

Key term

Collective responsibility principle by which ministers must support Cabinet decisions or leave the executive.

Case study: Iain Duncan Smith and disability benefit cuts, March 2016

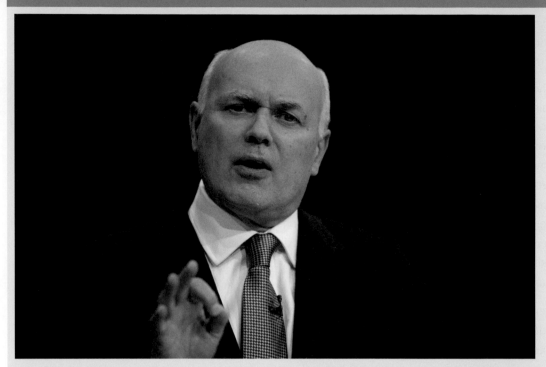

Iain Duncan Smith resigned in 2016 as work and pensions secretary in David Cameron's government, stating that he could not accept cuts to disability benefits, on which the Treasury was insisting. He objected to the fact that, at the same time, Chancellor George Osborne had made other changes in his budget to benefit higher earners. However Duncan Smith's decision was not based on his reaction to a single budget, but was the culmination of growing resentment. In his opinion Osborne was too inclined to make cuts for narrow political reasons rather than in the national economic interest. Duncan Smith also disliked the Treasury's demand that the Department of Work and Pensions should take responsibility publicly for what he regarded as unfair measures. Personality differences played a part. It was widely believed that Osborne considered Duncan Smith to be too intellectually limited to take responsibility for complex government policies. Duncan Smith's desire to see Britain leave the European Union, which had recently brought him into conflict with Cameron and Osborne, may also have played a part in causing the clash.

Question

- Which of the reasons discussed here do you feel was the most important cause of Duncan Smith's resignation?

Exceptions to collective responsibility

There have been occasions when collective responsibility has been modified for political reasons. A notable example was the need to find a compromise between the Conservatives and Liberal Democrats in order to form a coalition government in 2010. There were four issues on which, it was agreed at the outset, Liberal Democrat ministers would not be bound by collective responsibility. These were areas where they were most likely to come into conflict with the views of their Conservative partners. Liberal Democrats were allowed to abstain in votes on the construction of new nuclear power stations, tax allowances for married couples and higher education funding; and to propose an alternative to the renewal of the Trident nuclear deterrent. There were other instances, during the lifetime of the government, where members of the two parties took opposing standpoints. One example was the 2011 referendum on the Westminster electoral system, in which David Cameron defended first past the post, while Nick Clegg campaigned for the alternative vote.

Since 1945 it has proved necessary to suspend collective responsibility on two occasions, during both referendum campaigns on the troubled issue of Britain's membership of the European Union. In 1975 Labour Prime Minister Harold Wilson recognised that, in order to prevent resignations by anti-Europeans, he had to allow ministers to campaign on both sides of the argument. The understanding was that, having been allowed to argue their cases in public, they would then unite behind the people's verdict. Labour ministers were allowed to share platforms at public meetings with members of other parties who shared their views. The only condition was that, as the official government position was to remain in Europe, opponents could not speak against membership from the despatch box in the House of Commons. Industry Minister Eric Heffer was sacked for breaking this rule.

In the spring of 2016 David Cameron, faced with an equally divided Conservative Party, reluctantly agreed to suspend collective responsibility on the European issue. The ensuing referendum was more bitterly fought than the 1975 campaign, with five anti-EU Cabinet ministers joined by the charismatic former London Mayor, Boris Johnson, in attacking the terms on which Cameron proposed to continue British membership. Unlike Wilson four decades earlier, Cameron took personal charge of the 'Remain' campaign and, when his side lost the vote in June 2016, had no real alternative but to resign as prime minister.

Pause & reflect

Date of resignation	Minister	Post	Reason for resignation
2010	David Laws	Chief Secretary to the Treasury	Claimed parliamentary expenses to pay rent to his partner
2011	Liam Fox	Defence Secretary	Allowed a personal friend to accompany him as an adviser to official meetings
2012	Chris Huhne	Energy and Climate Change Secretary	Charged with perverting the course of justice over an earlier speeding prosecution
2012	Andrew Mitchell	Chief Whip	Accused of insulting policemen on duty in Downing Street
2014	Maria Miller	Culture Secretary	Parliamentary expenses claims related to family home
2014	Baroness Warsi	Minister of State at Foreign Office and Minister for Faith and Communities	Disagreed with government policy on the Israel–Gaza conflict

Table 2.1: Resignations during the Coalition government, 2010–15

Check that you understand the difference between individual and collective responsibility. Can you see the differences in practice? Using the information in the table and other resources available to you, decide which resignations are examples of **(a)** individual responsibility and **(b)** collective responsibility. Are the resignations in the former category examples of ministers taking responsibility for departmental errors, or cases of personal misconduct?

3.3 The prime minister and Cabinet

The power of the prime minister and Cabinet

Prime minister	Term of office	Political party
Clement Attlee	1945–51	Labour
Winston Churchill	1951–55	Conservative
Anthony Eden	1955–57	Conservative
Harold Macmillan	1957–63	Conservative
Alec Douglas-Home	1963–64	Conservative
Harold Wilson	1964–70 and 1974–76	Labour
Edward Heath	1970–74	Conservative
James Callaghan	1976–79	Labour
Margaret Thatcher	1979–90	Conservative
John Major	1990–97	Conservative
Tony Blair	1997–2007	Labour
Gordon Brown	2007–10	Labour
David Cameron	2010–16	Coalition 2010–15; Conservative 2015–16
Theresa May	2016–	Conservative

Table 3.1: Prime ministers since 1945

The factors governing the prime minister's selection of ministers

The power to appoint, reshuffle and dismiss ministers belongs exclusively to the prime minister. There has only been one exception to this in recent times. As part of the negotiations to form the coalition in May 2010, David Cameron had to allow the Liberal Democrats five of the 22 Cabinet posts. Nominations to these (and to an agreed number of junior posts) were the preserve of the Liberal Democrat leader and Deputy Prime Minister, Nick Clegg. When a Liberal Democrat minister resigned, Clegg found a replacement from his own party. This meant that there was a formal constraint on the prime minister's power of appointment.

However, even in a single-party government a prime minister does not in practice have total freedom to appoint whom they want. In practice the composition of a Cabinet will depend on a range of considerations.

- **The importance of including individuals with ability and experience:** Prime ministers do not have the luxury of an unlimited pool of talent in the parliamentary party. There will always be a large number of MPs who are 'natural backbenchers' – who do not have the aptitude for high office, or whose views place them too far outside the mainstream to make them acceptable as ministers. General ability as an administrator and communicator is more important than detailed knowledge of a particular policy area, as each department is staffed by civil servants who supply an incoming minister with the necessary specialist support. There are some exceptions: both Gordon Brown and George Osborne served substantial apprenticeships as shadow chancellor before taking over at the Treasury. In any party there will be senior figures who will need to be included. A prime minister who has come to office by winning a leadership contest will usually include their defeated rivals in recognition of their standing within the party. For example, John Major retained Douglas Hurd at the Foreign Office in 1990 and offered the other leadership candidate, Michael Heseltine, a choice of senior posts.

- **Establishing a prime minister's authority:** An incoming prime minister, even one who replaces a premier of the same party midway through a parliament, will want to stamp their own authority on the government. Not all prime ministers make radical changes to the team they inherit. For example, John Major did not remove key people associated with Margaret Thatcher when he took over in 1990, but waited until he had won his own general election 18 months later. By contrast Theresa May was determined to distance herself from David Cameron's administration when she became prime minister in 2016. The former chancellor, George Osborne, was the most prominent figure from the previous government to be sacked. A further nine senior ministers lost their jobs over the next 24 hours.

- **Rewarding loyalty and including key allies – but also conciliating potential rivals:** Blair began his second term in 2001 by appointing several committed supporters of the New Labour project to key positions, including David Blunkett as home secretary and Alan Milburn as health secretary. They were also personally loyal to him. It is politically wise to occupy potentially troublesome MPs with senior posts, even if this means handling tensions within the team. Blair's appointment of Brown as chancellor, and his acceptance that he could not move him to another post against his wishes, is a good example of this limitation on a prime minister's freedom of action.

- **Maintaining a balance between different factions within the governing party:** In order to maintain party unity it is often necessary to find posts for MPs with different ideological views from those of the prime minister. Taking over after the 2016 EU referendum, Theresa May had to include prominent supporters of 'Brexit', such as Boris Johnson (Foreign Secretary) and Liam Fox (International Trade Secretary), as well as individuals who – like her – had supported the 'Remain' side, such as Philip Hammond (Chancellor) and Amber Rudd (Home Secretary).

- **Meeting expectations of diversity:** When he formed his first Cabinet in 1990, John Major faced adverse comment for including no women – something that he later corrected. Since then it has become the norm for prime ministers to appoint a number of female ministers, and not only to middle- and lower-ranking Cabinet posts. Margaret Beckett, made foreign secretary by Tony Blair in 2006, was the first woman to hold one of the three most senior posts under the prime minister. There has also been greater representation of ethnic-minority groups in recent years. Sajid Javid, a leading MP of Asian background, has served in both the Cameron and May governments.

The relationship between Cabinet and prime minister

The Cabinet is formally responsible for policy-making. However, in recent times it has been more usual for decisions to be taken elsewhere, and it is often claimed that the executive is now dominated by the prime minister to an undue degree. Some commentators have argued that the result has been the rise of **presidential government** – the idea that leadership is becoming much more personalised, and that prime ministers are distant from, and much less dependent on, traditional institutions such as the Cabinet.

> **Key term**
>
> **Presidential government** an executive dominated by one individual. This may be a president but can also describe a strong, dominant prime minister.

Factors that affect the relationship and how they have changed

In practice the relationship between the prime minister and Cabinet is shaped by a range of factors, whose relative importance depends heavily on the particular circumstances of the time. Key factors include the following.

- **The management skills of the prime minister:** A determined and astute prime minister will exploit the elastic nature of the office to assert control over the Cabinet. The right to appoint and dismiss ministers can be used to reshape the top team, to remove poor performers and bring in new blood, and to marginalise opponents. This power should, however, be deployed with care. For example, after establishing herself as prime minister in the early 1980s, Margaret Thatcher promoted supporters such as Nigel Lawson and Norman Tebbit in order to build a Cabinet in her own image. However, by the end of the decade her dominance of the Cabinet and alienation of senior colleagues was starting to undermine her position. The resignation of Deputy Prime Minister Sir Geoffrey Howe triggered a leadership challenge in November 1990. When Thatcher needed the support of her Cabinet she found that goodwill had evaporated at the top, leading directly to her resignation.

- **The prime minister's ability to set the agenda:** Decisions are rarely, if ever, taken in Cabinet by holding a vote. The views of the most senior figures will usually command more weight. Most ministers will, in any case, be too concerned with their individual departmental responsibilities to challenge the consensus view on a matter of which they may have limited knowledge. The prime minister's traditional right to chair the meeting and to sum up at the end is an important source of influence. They can also keep certain items off the agenda of Cabinet meetings. Harold Wilson, for example, refused to allow discussion of devaluation of the pound in the period 1964–67, even though several ministers wanted to open up the argument.

- **The use of Cabinet committees and informal groups to take decisions:** Since 1945 prime ministers have made increasing use of Cabinet committees to take decisions, which are later ratified by the full Cabinet. By choosing the membership of these committees and taking the chair of the most important ones – or placing this responsibility in the hands of a reliable ally – the prime minister can exercise a significant degree of control. On entering Number 10, Theresa May decided to chair three important committees, including the one dealing with the crucial issue of Britain's exit from the EU. Many decisions are taken in smaller, informal groups, or in bilateral meetings involving the prime minister and one colleague. For example, the market-sensitive decision to place management of interest rates in the hands of the Bank of England was taken by Tony Blair and Gordon Brown within days of the 1997 election victory, and the rest of the Cabinet were informed later. Under the coalition, the presence of two parties in government meant that it was necessary to have more discussion of policy in Cabinet. Yet, even then, an informal body known as 'the Quad' – David Cameron, Nick Clegg and their two most senior colleagues, Chancellor George Osborne and Chief Treasury Secretary Danny Alexander – met regularly to resolve differences between the coalition partners.

- **The development of the Prime Minister's Office and the Cabinet Office:** Although there is no official 'Prime Minister's Department', the prime minister has access to more resources than other ministers, with a Prime Minister's Office in Number 10 Downing Street staffed by a combination of civil servants and special advisers drawn from the governing party. Harold Wilson created the Policy Unit in 1974 to enable the prime minister to gain an overview and to drive policy across departments. Under Blair there was close co-operation between the Prime Minister's Office and the Cabinet Office to support the co-ordination and implementation of policy. Cameron initially adopted a more 'hands off' approach to government departments, allowing individual ministers more autonomy than under Blair and Brown but, after some policy embarrassments, he strengthened the centre once again with the creation of a Policy and Implementation Unit in 2011. The Press Office, which handles the government's presentation in the media, also works closely with the prime minister. Under Blair it gained enhanced importance as part of a newly created Communications and Strategy Directorate in Downing Street. Although media management has been less obtrusive under later prime ministers, the capacity to get the government's message across remains an important function of the Downing Street machine.

- **The impact of the wider political and economic situation:** It is important to note that the degree to which the prime minister can dominate the Cabinet is affected by a variety of external pressures. A prime minister with a large parliamentary majority and a united party, such as Blair in the wake of the 1997 Labour landslide, will find it much easier to gain ascendancy than one like Major, whose control over the Commons was precarious from 1992 onwards. Popularity with the public, a booming economy and an ability to master events rather than appear as their victim all strengthen the hand of the prime minister in dealing with the Cabinet. Margaret Thatcher's standing improved enormously after victory in the 1982 Falklands War. Gordon Brown was harmed by his decision not to hold a general election on becoming prime minister, after allowing expectations of a contest to build, and his authority was further undermined by the financial crash of 2007–08. The weakness of his position was underlined in 2009 when it became known that Alistair Darling, the chancellor, had refused to take another post so that Brown could replace him with his favoured candidate, Ed Balls. Brown could not afford the additional damage that the high-profile resignation of his chancellor would cause at a time of economic crisis.

Pause & reflect

Reviewing what you have read so far, what do you regard as the three or four most important qualities of a successful prime minister? In your opinion, which of these does the current prime minister possess?

The balance of power between prime minister and Cabinet

What conclusions can be drawn about the relationship between the prime minister and Cabinet? It is a good idea to be sceptical of generalisations. As should be clear by now, the balance between the two depends heavily on changing circumstances. The table below summarises the main arguments.

The Cabinet remains an important body.	The prime minister is the dominant force in government.
The Cabinet approves government decisions, so confers legitimacy on them in the eyes of parliament and the public. A minister who cannot accept the agreed line, such as Robin Cook over the Iraq War, should resign from the Cabinet.	Decisions are commonly taken by Cabinet committees, hand-picked by the PM, or in small groups and bilateral meetings, such as the 1997 Blair/Brown decision to hand control of interest rates to the Bank of England. Cabinet 'rubber stamps' decisions taken elsewhere.
On important issues the PM recognises the need for Cabinet support. After completing his renegotiation of the UK's membership of the EU in 2016, Cameron presented the deal to a full Cabinet meeting. The Cabinet is also important in times of national crisis, such as a military conflict, although (as in the Falklands War in 1982) day-to-day decisions may be taken by a smaller 'War Cabinet' of key ministers and armed service leaders, whose decisions are then reported to the full Cabinet.	The PM controls the agenda and length of Cabinet meetings (less than an hour under some PMs). It only meets once a week, and then only while parliament is sitting, unless an emergency occurs. Most ministers do not feel qualified, and are too immersed in their own departments, to be able to offer an informed view on the detail of matters outside their remit. Most are reluctant to challenge the PM, who has the power to dismiss or demote ministers.
The Cabinet is where the programme of government business in parliament is discussed. In theory it is also where disagreements between government departments are resolved.	In practice disputes are usually resolved outside the Cabinet, in committees or by the intervention of the PM (for example, Cameron's settlement of the 2011 clash between Energy Secretary Chris Huhne and Business Secretary Vince Cable on the level of carbon emission targets to which the UK should sign up).
The UK does not have a 'presidential' system in reality, even if it has some characteristics of one. The fall of Thatcher demonstrates the continuing importance of keeping the support of the Cabinet.	The media focus heavily on the PM (for example, in the televised leadership debates in the 2010 and 2015 elections). Modern PMs tend to project themselves as national leaders, separate from the institutions of government, and with a personal mandate from the people for action.

Figure 3.1: Main arguments about the balance of power between the prime minister and the Cabinet

The powers of the prime minister and the Cabinet to dictate events and policy

The nature and extent of the prime minister's powers have been a matter for debate for generations. The reason for this is that, under Britain's uncodified constitution, there is no precise and comprehensive definition of the role. The Cabinet Office prepared a list of the prime minister's functions in 1947, during the premiership of Clement Attlee, which was updated by the historian Lord Hennessy in 1995 and again in 2011. However, this does not have the force of a legally binding document.

EXTENSION ACTIVITY

Read Peter Hennessy's article on 'The role and powers of the prime minister', available at: www.publications.parliament.uk/pa/cm201012/cmselect/cmpolcon/writev/842/pm04.htm. A fuller discussion is to be found in Chapter 7 of Hennessy's book *Distilling the Frenzy: Writing the History of One's Own Time* (Biteback Publishing, 2013).

Compare the list of powers and functions prepared by the Cabinet Office in 1947 with Hennessy's 2011 analysis. In what ways has the job of prime minister changed in this period?

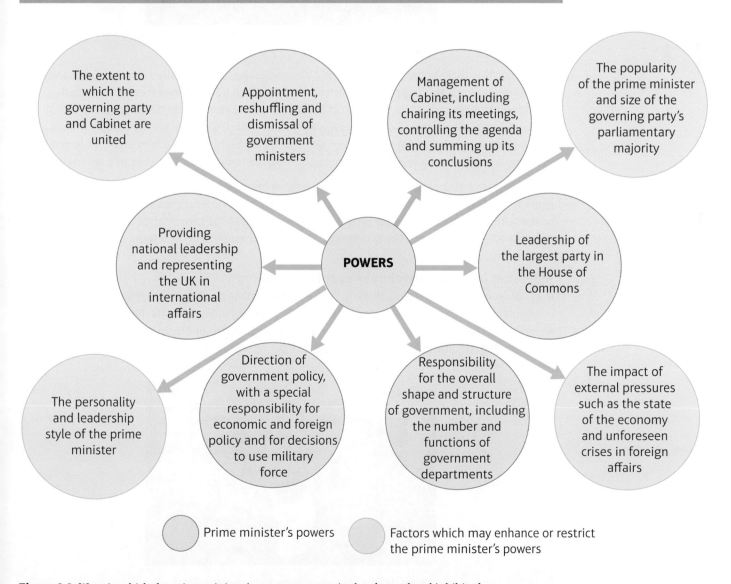

Figure 3.2: Ways in which the prime minister's powers are exercised, enhanced and inhibited

Influence of prime ministers

In order to understand more fully how these factors come into play, here are two case studies, which offer some similarities as well as differences. You need to know in depth about one prime minister from the period 1945–97, and one from the post-1997 period.

Case study: Prime Minister John Major (November 1990 to May 1997)

John Major (right) with Tony Blair.

John Major was little-known to the general public when he unexpectedly took over from a very dominant and long-serving prime minister, Margaret Thatcher, in November 1990. He had served less than four years in the Cabinet before becoming prime minister, more than half of this time as chief secretary to the Treasury, a position that does not normally give its occupant a high profile outside Westminster. Major was chosen partly because he was expected to provide calm and stability, and a less divisive approach to government than Thatcher had adopted.

Major surprised many observers by winning (with a small majority of 21 seats) a further general election victory for the Conservatives in April 1992. However his second term as prime minister was fraught with problems and in May 1997 his Labour rival, Tony Blair, won a crushing 179-seat majority. For this reason Major is commonly seen as a weak and unsuccessful prime minister.

Assessing Major's control over events and policy

✔ Major won credit in his first 18 months in office by acting decisively to replace the unpopular poll tax with the less-controversial council tax, which remains the system of local government finance today. This helped to distance his government from the confrontational and 'uncaring' reputation of his predecessor. The speed with which the new system was put in place helped Major to win re-election in 1992.

Protesters demonstrate against the Thatcher government's unpopular poll tax.

✔ Major was regarded as having handled the first Gulf War in early 1991 effectively. The war was fought to expel Iraq's dictator, Saddam Hussein, from Kuwait, which he had invaded shortly before Major took office. Major worked effectively with Britain's US allies, led by President George H.W. Bush, and struck the right note both in dealing with British forces and in uniting British public opinion. This enhanced Major's standing as a national leader.

✘ On the other hand Major's economic policy record is more mixed. As chancellor of the exchequer in October 1990, he had persuaded a reluctant Thatcher to join the European Exchange Rate Mechanism (ERM). On 'Black Wednesday' in September 1992, market pressure forced the pound out of the ERM, even though the government frantically raised interest rates in a bid to uphold its place within the specified exchange-rate limits imposed by the system. This event fatally damaged Major's reputation for economic competence and, although the economy recovered, with both inflation and unemployment falling by the mid-1990s, he gained no credit with the general public. Major was also unfortunate that Labour, steered by Tony Blair and Gordon Brown, was distancing itself from the damaging 'tax and spend' image of the party in previous years, and so appeared more responsible as a potential manager of the economy.

A newspaper headline highlights the dramatic events of 'Black Wednesday'.

✔ ✘ Major adopted a more collegial style of Cabinet management than Thatcher, allowing more discussion and deliberately acting in a more inclusive way. His lack of ideological commitments also seemed attractive. However, when things started to go wrong, these strengths became weaknesses. Colleagues did not respect and fear him as they had done his predecessor, and some doubted if he had firm beliefs on issues that mattered.

✘ Major's control of his party and Cabinet was seriously undermined during his second term. Conflict over the European Union was one of the root causes of his difficulties. His party contained a hard core of 'Eurosceptic' backbenchers, who saw the EU as a threat to the UK's national sovereignty, and were particularly hostile to the Maastricht Treaty. Certainly, Major secured opt-outs for Britain from joining the planned single European currency, and from the 'Social Chapter' that increased European intervention in social policy. However, many Conservative MPs were not pacified by these concessions. Backbench revolts meant that Major secured the Treaty's passage through the Commons by only one vote in July 1993. He presided over an increasingly divided Cabinet. A sympathetic view of Major would argue that he successfully balanced pro- and anti-European ministers by taking a moderate line, whereas a leader with more pronounced views, such as Michael Heseltine (who served as environment secretary, trade and industry secretary and finally deputy prime minister), might have provoked a worse split. More negatively, however, the spectacle of disunity created an impression of weak leadership, which led to open ridicule of Major in parliament and the media. His attempt to restore his authority in June 1995, by resigning the party leadership and inviting any of his critics to run against him, failed to achieve its purpose. Although he comfortably saw off the challenger, former Welsh Secretary John Redwood, the infighting continued and contributed to the government's catastrophic defeat at the polls two years later.

✘ The fact that Major and his team had to devote so much time to day-to-day parliamentary management, with a disappearing majority and a divided party, hampered his chances of leaving a distinct legacy in terms of policy. He seemed to spend an inordinate amount of time on crisis management, trying to paper over the cracks on Europe and also coping with a series of financial and sexual scandals involving junior ministers and backbenchers, dubbed 'sleaze' by the press. One of Major's aims was to make public services more accountable to their users – an approach that was sometimes called 'Thatcherism with a human face' – but little came of this. The 'Citizen's Charter' was an attempt to lay down expectations for the performance of schools, hospitals and other bodies, but it failed to capture the public imagination. Rail privatisation was consistent with Thatcher's policy of reducing the size of the state sector and bringing in competition. However, the way that it was accomplished led to widespread criticism, in particular of the decision to separate responsibility for track from the running of train services. Overall Major appeared to be reacting to events rather than driving forward a clear and popular agenda.

✔ Progress towards a peace deal in Northern Ireland, which had been riven for over two decades by sectarian conflict between unionists and republicans, was one of the more positive aspects of Major's premiership. He managed to establish trust with both sides through the December 1993 Downing Street Declaration, which ruled out the imposition of a united Ireland against the wishes of the unionists, while showing respect for the aspirations of the nationalist community. There was a return to violence in Major's final year as prime minister, but he had laid the foundations on which Tony Blair was able to build.

✔ After a promising start, a combination of adverse circumstances and Major's own personality combined to cause him to lose control. Within months of his knife-edge 1992 election victory, Britain's departure from the Exchange Rate Mechanism blasted his government's reputation for economic competence. Grappling with internal party divisions over Europe, and with a series of damaging scandals, Major seemed always to be reacting to events rather than driving forward an agenda of his own. He never gained credit for the positive achievements of his premiership, such as the beginnings of economic recovery and peace in Northern Ireland.

Date	Event
1990	Major succeeds Thatcher as prime minister
1991	Gulf War: Saddam Hussein driven out of Kuwait
1992	General election victory (21 seat majority) 'Black Wednesday': Britain leaves the European Exchange Rate Mechanism
1993	Downing Street Declaration on Northern Ireland
1995	Major faces Conservative Party leadership challenge
1997	General election defeat; Major resigns

Table 3.2: Major's premiership: key dates

Question

- Review what you have read about John Major's time as prime minister. Was there a steady decline from the 1992 election onwards, or can you identify a 'point of no return', after which it was impossible to rescue his premiership from disaster?

Case study: Prime Minister Tony Blair (May 1997 to June 2007)

An intelligence report was supposedly edited to over-emphasise the risk that Iraq posed to the West. The cartoon also makes reference to President Bill Clinton's difficulties explaining away accusations that he had 'relations' with an intern while in office.

Tony Blair was a strong contrast with John Major in terms of governing style. While still leader of the opposition he taunted Major mercilessly over his divided following. 'There is one very big difference,' he told the Commons in April 1995, 'I lead my party, he follows his.' Blair combined a ruthless insistence on unity and discipline with an acute awareness of how to project a winning image through the media. The remodelling of Labour as an attractive, modernising centre party, together with the evident weaknesses of Major's government, gave Blair a decisive victory in May 1997. He went on to win again, almost as overwhelmingly, in June 2001. Even after the loss of 100 seats in his final general election in May 2005, Blair still had a majority of 66. This meant that he did not suffer a defeat in the Commons until the autumn of 2005, on a proposal to extend the time that the police could hold terror suspects before charging them. Blair was, for a time, extraordinarily popular, with a mandate to make significant policy changes. The fact that he inherited a recovering economy, and left office before the financial crisis of 2007–08, meant that he always operated within a favourable economic context. After he took Britain into the controversial Iraq War in 2003, however, he began to lose credibility, and by the end of his time in Downing Street there was a serious question mark over the nature of Blair's achievement.

Assessing Blair's control over events and policy

✔ ✘ Blair placed a strong emphasis on strengthening the centre of UK government in order to tackle problems in a more 'joined up' manner, cutting across individual departments. Jonathan Powell, the prime minister's chief of staff – itself a role borrowed from the US White House and denoting a more 'presidential' style – announced 'a change from a feudal system of barons to a more Napoleonic system'. By this he meant that individual Cabinet ministers would have less autonomy than in the past and they would work to a much more centrally managed agenda. The Cabinet Office and Downing Street Policy Unit worked more closely together, and from 2001 a newly created Prime Minister's Delivery Unit sought to drive reform of the public sector.

The methods of media management pioneered in opposition by Blair's press secretary, Alastair Campbell, were transferred to government, with the creation of a Strategic Communications Unit to respond to the 24-hour news media of the new century.

All recent prime ministers had to some extent used informal meetings with selected colleagues and advisers, rather than collective decision-making in the full Cabinet. However, under Blair this became the normal practice, with bilateral meetings with Cabinet ministers being used to review progress on the attainment of policy goals. Blair's preference for informal meetings, bypassing established committee structures, and at which proper records were not kept, was dubbed 'sofa government'. At one level this increased the prime minister's power to direct events. The most spectacular example was the way in which decisions were taken prior to the launching of the Iraq War in March 2003. Although Iraq featured on the Cabinet agenda, there was little genuine discussion around the table, and ministers were denied access to many key documents. The practice was criticised in a 2004 review chaired by former Cabinet Secretary Lord Butler, which warned that the exclusion of the Cabinet from the process 'risks reducing the scope for informed collective political judgement'.

✘ There was one important individual whose presence placed a significant limitation on Blair's power within the government. This was the chancellor throughout the Blair years, Gordon Brown. The two men had struck an informal deal in May 1994, after the sudden death of Labour leader John Smith. Brown had given Blair a clear run at the party leadership in return for the post of chancellor when they came to power. In addition, Brown believed that Blair would eventually step down, allowing him to become prime minister. When this did not happen before the end of Labour's second term, relations between the two deteriorated. The need to keep a powerful colleague on side influenced Blair's decision to announce that his third general election victory would be his last. The ensuing public speculation about when exactly the handover would occur reduced Blair's authority. The difficult relationship between prime minister and chancellor also meant that Blair had to concede a significant amount of control over a number of policy areas. For example, Brown effectively denied Blair his wish to take Britain into the European single currency. He devised five economic tests that would first have to be passed, and insisted that the Treasury would determine whether they had been met. These tensions at the top meant that, although Blair had the advantage of a broadly united party – most Labour MPs were grateful to him for delivering three successive election victories – there were destabilising conflicts between 'Blairite' and 'Brownite' factions.

✔ The Blair government had a number of important policy achievements to its credit. In his first term Blair put through a range of constitutional reforms that modernised the political system without jeopardising the authority of central government. Most hereditary peers were removed from the House of Lords, ending the Conservative Party's control of the upper house, but the more radical step of replacing an appointed chamber with an elected one was not taken. Devolution was granted to Scotland and Wales, with new representative bodies elected using proportional systems, but Blair avoided holding a referendum on electoral reform for Westminster, preferring to retain a model that delivered Labour victories.

✔ Blair's most outstanding personal success was his revival of the peace process in Northern Ireland, culminating in the creation of power-sharing institutions following the April 1998 Good Friday agreement. He showed his skills as a negotiator in finding just enough common ground to bring unionists, moderate nationalists and hard-line republicans together. Although trust between the rival communities broke down more than once, leading to the re-imposition of direct rule from London for five years, Blair succeeded in restoring devolved government shortly before he left office. This was due to a combination of firmness and a talent for building constructive personal relationships with key individuals on both sides of the sectarian divide.

A nationalist-leaning newspaper heralds the peace agreement in Northern Ireland.

✔ Public service reform was an area close to Blair's heart. He had some success in introducing the ideas and methods of the business sector to improve the delivery of education and health. Self-governing city academies, which took their funding directly from central government rather than from local authorities, began to replace failing state schools, providing a model that was developed by later governments. Foundation hospitals, whose managers were given additional powers and funding, were another break with the traditional Labour idea that the state should guarantee a uniform model of welfare provision. The principle that university students should contribute to the cost of their education was established, and the level of tuition fees was hiked in 2004 in the teeth of bitter Labour backbench opposition. At the same time some distinctively 'Labour' measures were introduced, including a national minimum wage, free nursery places and Sure Start centres to help families in the most deprived areas. Their overall effect was to halt the widening of the gap between rich and poor, if not to reverse it. Blair's insistence on a socially liberal agenda, which was at least as important to him as the battle against poverty, was reflected in the introduction of civil partnerships for same sex couples.

✗ There were areas where change was frustrated. Blair himself blamed the opposition of vested interests within the public sector, talking of 'scars on his back', for his unsuccessful attempts to reform the way in which services were delivered. Perhaps more important was the fact that in his second term issues of national security and foreign policy diverted his attention. Blair's premiership reminds us that even the most driven of leaders is subject to the problem of overload. After the terrorist attacks of 11 September 2001 in New York and Washington, Blair showed the ability of a powerful prime minister to shape overseas policy. He committed the UK to support US President George W. Bush's 'war on terror', which saw British troops engaged in lengthy campaigns in Afghanistan and Iraq. Unlike the first Gulf War under Major, neither operation concluded with a clear-cut result. The Iraq War in particular inflicted lasting damage on Blair's reputation as, although the tyrant Saddam Hussein was rapidly removed, order inside the country disintegrated and allied troops faced prolonged guerrilla resistance. Critics focused on Blair's willingness to take the country to war on the basis of unsubstantiated claims that Iraq's government possessed weapons of mass destruction. He was also blamed for his failure to formulate a plan with the US for the reconstruction of Iraq after the toppling of Saddam. He gave the impression of having surrendered his judgement in order to keep in line with the US administration. Blair's premiership illustrates both the immense potential of the office – to transform governmental structures and to embark on major departures in policy – and its limitations. The erosion of trust that followed the Iraq War severely limited Blair's chances of leaving a positive legacy in other areas.

US troops on patrol during the Iraq War.

Blair's legacy

Blair shaped Downing Street to place Number 10 at the centre of power, pushing forward policy initiatives and managing the government's public image in a pro-active way. He pursued a modernising agenda in both constitutional reform and the delivery of public services, achieving notable success in bringing about a peace settlement in Northern Ireland. His authority was enhanced by three consecutive general election victories but undermined by the persistent tensions with his ambitious chancellor, Gordon Brown. Blair's decision to take the UK to war in Iraq, on questionable grounds, reduced levels of trust in him. His pursuit of the 'war on terror' alienated core support and diverted him from a focus on domestic reform.

Date	Event
1997	Blair wins general election (179 seat majority) Devolution for Scotland and Wales
1998	Good Friday Agreement in Northern Ireland
2001	Second general election victory (167 seat majority) 9/11 events signal start of 'war on terror'
2003	Iraq War
2005	Third general election victory (66 seat majority)
2007	Blair resigns as prime minister

Table 3.3: Blair's premiership: key dates

Question

• There is little doubt that Blair was a more successful prime minister than Major. Do you think that this was due more to their personal characteristics or to the different circumstances they faced?

Assessment support: 2.1.3 Prime Minister and Executive

Question 2 on AS-Level Paper 2 is based on a short source extract. It is worth 10 marks and should be completed in 20 minutes. Alongside Question 3 this is a compulsory question– you must answer it.

Source 1 is adapted from an article published 29 October 2016 in The Independent *newspaper. It discusses how far prime ministers govern in a 'collegiate' way, working collaboratively with their Cabinet colleagues rather than taking their own decisions.*

Source 1: 'Thank goodness Theresa May has restored cabinet government – or has she?' by John Rentoul

> *'Relief all round that the new Prime Minister [Theresa May] has revived traditional collegiate government. "She has brought back proper cabinet government with formal committees," reported Laura Kuenssberg, the BBC's Political Editor…*
>
> *Strong personalities tend to dominate government, but even the supposedly most collegiate prime ministers are more first than equals. For example, Clement Attlee, often held up as the model of the chairman type, went behind the back of his Cabinet – because he thought most of them couldn't be trusted – to authorise the building of Britain's nuclear weapons.*
>
> *Most new prime ministers claim to be restoring cabinet government. John Major did after Thatcher. Gordon Brown did after Blair. David Cameron did after Brown. But in all cases the extent to which a prime minister works collaboratively with colleagues depends on their ideological unity and the nature of the challenges facing them.*
>
> *Cameron, for example, was forced to work closely with Nick Clegg in a coalition government, but the way he did it was not traditional cabinet government, it was the 'Quad' of two leading Tories and two Lib Dems, a device improvised as they went along.'*

(Source: from www.independent.co.uk/voices/thank-goodness-theresa-may-has-restored-cabinet-government-or-has-she-a7386411.html)

Using the source, explain how prime ministers relate to their Cabinet colleagues in government. [10 marks]

In your response you must use knowledge and understanding to analyse only points that are in the source. You will not be rewarded for introducing any additional points that are not in the source.

This type of question tests AO1 (knowledge and understanding) and AO2 (analysis), with the marks split equally between the two. You are asked to extract relevant information from the source and explain it. Anything you write should develop and analyse points made in the source. You should not introduce factual material from outside the source. For this question you would explain how the appearance of 'Cabinet government' has often proved deceptive in modern times. The source mentions, for example, the 'Quad' or inner group of four ministers responsible for many key decisions in David Cameron's coalition government. Some explanation of how this and similar 'inner Cabinets' have worked would receive credit.

- Spend a few minutes reading the source and noting the key points that you will need to include in your answer.

- Aim to write about three paragraphs, with analysis of the source supported throughout by precise knowledge and understanding.

- Close with a short conclusion in which you draw together and emphasise the main points you have made.

Here is the final part of a student's answer to this question.

Theresa May is the latest in a long line of prime ministers who have given the impression that they are restoring true Cabinet government after it has been abused by their predecessor. However, as we have seen, in practice much depends on the personality of the prime minister and the circumstances they face, which are always changing. Where there are significant differences within a Cabinet, a prime minister may go behind the backs of the Cabinet as a whole, to work with a smaller number of colleagues whom he or she can manage more easily. This enables the prime minister to make sure that the most important aspects of his or her agenda are implemented.

- The conclusion underlines the key points made in the answer, with no additional material drawn from outside the source.

- The student reaches a supported judgement: in practice, it is not the case that prime ministers uphold an ideal model of Cabinet government.

Relations Between Institutions

The UK system of government has traditionally featured what is known as a fusion of powers. This means that there has been an overlap between three branches of government. For example, members of the government sit in one of the two Houses of Parliament, where they are held to account for their policies.

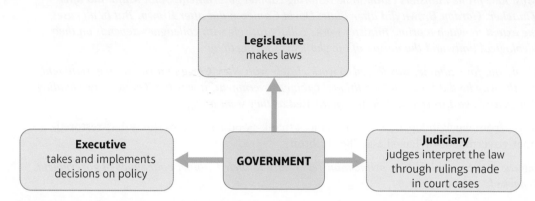

Figure 1.1: The three branches of government

Key term

Supreme Court
the highest court in the UK political system.

In one important respect the UK has moved towards a greater *separation* of powers in recent years. This is in the establishment of the **Supreme Court**, which brought to an end the situation in which the highest court in the land was located within the House of Lords. The role of the Supreme Court, and its relationship with the executive and parliament, is covered in this section.

The other areas you will learn about are:

- the relationship between the executive and parliament
- the impact of membership of the EU on UK government since 1973
- the debate over where sovereignty is located in the UK.

4.1 The Supreme Court and the legislative and policy-making processes

The role and composition of the Supreme Court

The Supreme Court was opened on 1 October 2009. It was established by the Constitutional Reform Act of 2005 but did not begin work until the premises chosen for it, Middlesex Guildhall in Parliament Square, had been prepared. The Court was designed to end the fusion of powers at the highest level of the UK judiciary. Previously the most senior judges – the 'law lords' – had sat as members of the House of Lords, and were known as the Appellate Committee of the House of Lords. The reform was to create greater transparency, and to bring the UK into line with most other Western countries, by establishing that the country's highest court was clearly independent of parliament. The Constitutional Reform Act also changed the role of the lord chancellor, whose historic office had combined three functions.

- Cabinet minister, who supervised the legal system (executive).
- Chairman of sittings of the House of Lords (legislature).
- Head of the judiciary, who appointed other judges (judiciary).

The act removed the last two of these responsibilities from the lord chancellor. The Lords is now chaired by the lord speaker, who is chosen by their fellow peers. Judges are selected by an independent Judicial Appointments Commission.

The Supreme Court's role

The UK does not have a single unified legal system. There are three different systems: one for England and Wales, one for Scotland and one for Northern Ireland. The Supreme Court is the only UK-wide court and it acts as a final court of appeal for rulings made by the lower courts. The Supreme Court is the final court of appeal for criminal cases in England, Wales and Northern Ireland, and for civil cases across the whole of the UK.

The Supreme Court also hears appeals on arguable points of law where matters of wider public and constitutional importance are involved. Until the UK leaves the European Union, the court has a responsibility to interpret law passed by the EU. The Court also makes rulings on cases where the devolved authorities in Scotland, Wales and Northern Ireland may not have acted within their powers.

Case study: The Supreme Court and the powers of the UK's devolved bodies

In July 2016 the Supreme Court overruled the Scottish government's scheme to introduce the 'named person' service, which planned to appoint state guardians, such as health visitors or head teachers, to be responsible for the well-being of children. The Supreme Court ruled that the legislation was in conflict with Article 8 of the Human Rights Act (the right to a private and family life) because it would allow public bodies to share personal information without consent. This is an example of the Supreme Court ruling that a devolved body had exceeded its powers.

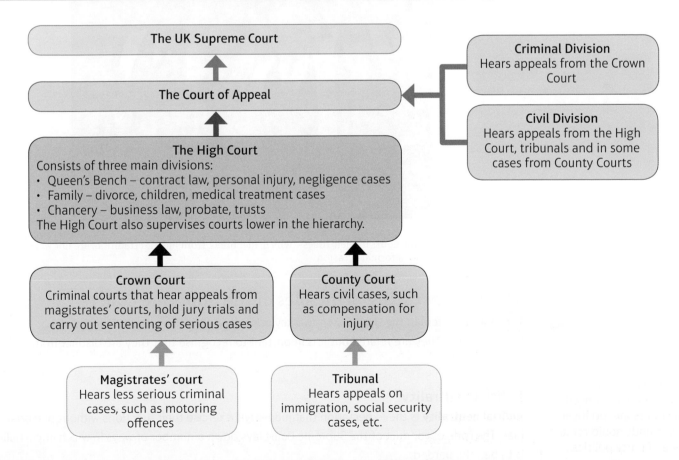

Figure 1.2: The Supreme Court's position in the structure of the judiciary for England and Wales

Appointment of members of the Supreme Court

The Supreme Court consists of 12 members, although cases are always heard by an odd number of justices so that a majority verdict can be reached. In most cases five or possibly nine justices take part; reflecting the importance of the issue, 11 took part in the 2016–17 review of the High Court ruling that parliament rather than the government should initiate the UK's exit from the European Union.

The most senior figure is designated as the president. This post was held by Lord Phillips from 2009 to 2012, and since then has been held by Lord Neuberger. There is only one female justice, Lady Hale – a fact that has attracted some attention, given the pressure on public institutions to reflect diversity in their composition. Even the leading newspaper of the establishment, *The Times*, used the phrase 'pale, male and stale' to head an article on the judiciary in 2011. Although they are known as 'Lord' or 'Lady', members of the Supreme Court do not sit in the House of Lords until their term of office has come to an end.

Supreme Court justices will usually have served as a senior judge for two years, or been a qualified lawyer for at least 15 years. The original members were the former law lords, who moved from the House of Lords to their new premises. When a vacancy occurs, nominations are made by an independent five-member Selection Commission, consisting of the president and deputy president of the Court, a member of the Judicial Appointments Commission and a member of each of the equivalent bodies for Scotland and Northern Ireland. The lord chancellor (also known as the justice secretary) either confirms or rejects the person put forward, although he or she cannot reject names repeatedly. The appointment is confirmed by the prime minister and then by the monarch.

Members of the Supreme Court in their robes – which, in a break from judicial tradition, are not worn for everyday work – during a formal occasion.

The key operating principles of the Supreme Court

The judicial system in the UK rests on two key principles: judicial neutrality and judicial independence. They are related but it is important to recognise that they are distinct from each other.

Judicial neutrality

Judicial neutrality is the expectation that judges will exercise their functions without personal bias. The code of conduct of the Supreme Court lays down a number of ways in which impartiality is to be safeguarded.

 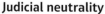

Here are the most important points.

- **Conflicts of interest:** Judges must refuse to sit in a case that involves a family member, friend or professional associate, which might give rise to doubt about the justice's detachment.
- **Public activities:** Judges may write and give lectures as part of their function of educating the public, and they may involve themselves in charitable and voluntary activities, but they must avoid political activity. A judge may serve on an official body such as a government commission provided that it does not compromise their political neutrality.

The Supreme Court is more transparent in explaining its rulings than its predecessors. Its website carries full details of its decisions, and the reasoning behind them, allowing for greater public scrutiny. The Court welcomes visitors and its proceedings are televised over the internet.

How neutral is the Supreme Court?

The narrowness of the Supreme Court's composition in terms of gender, social and educational background is a real concern. This reinforces a long-standing anxiety about the senior judiciary as a whole – that it contains a disproportionate number of white, privately educated males.

The fact that it has only one female member was significant in the case of *Radmacher v Granatino* (2010). This was a case involving a pre-nuptial agreement between marriage partners, in which a majority of the Supreme Court justices upheld the principle that claims made in the event of a divorce should be limited. Lady Hale was the only one of the nine justices to dissent from the majority verdict. She gave as her reason the likelihood that the vast majority of people who would lose out as a result of this precedent would be women. In an interview in 2015, Lady Hale called for an effort to promote greater diversity of background in appointments to the Supreme Court. She pointed out that of 13 justices sworn in since her own appointment, all were men, all were white, all but two were educated at independent schools, and all but two attended Oxford or Cambridge Universities.

Judicial independence

Judicial independence is the principle that judges must be free from political interference. This is vital because they may be called on to administer justice in cases where there is a conflict between the state and an individual citizen. People must know that they will receive impartial justice and judges need to be confident that they can make a decision without fear that their career prospects will suffer.

The UK judiciary has a number of in-built guarantees of independence.

- **Terms of employment:** Judges cannot be removed from office unless they break the law. The only limit on their service is an official retirement age, which is 70 for those who have been first appointed to a judicial post since the end of March 1995. This is known as security of tenure. Judges are also immune from legal action arising from any comments they may make on cases in court.
- **Pay:** Judges' salaries are paid automatically from an independent budget known as the Consolidated fund, without the possibility of manipulation by ministers.
- **Appointment:** The Judicial Appointments Commission and the Selection Commission for the Supreme Court are transparent in their procedure and free from political intervention.

The fact that the Supreme Court is physically separate from parliament is another, more visible sign of its independence. There was never any suggestion that the law lords were subject to government pressure, and indeed there were a number of cases where they demonstrated their independence. However, their transfer to new premises removed any possible doubt of this.

> **Key term**
>
> **Judicial independence** the principle that judges should not be influenced by other branches of government, particularly the executive.

How independent is the Supreme Court?

In most important respects the Supreme Court is independent of government. However, some concerns were raised in 2011 by its first president, Lord Phillips, on the subject of funding. This came in response to the spending cuts imposed on the court system as part of the coalition government's strategy to eliminate the budget deficit. Lord Phillips argued that the independence of the Court was at risk unless it could be allocated pre-set, ring-fenced funding. He spoke of a 'tendency on the part of the Ministry of Justice to try to gain the Supreme Court as an outlying part of its empire'. The justice secretary at the time, Kenneth Clarke, dismissed this argument. He insisted that the Supreme Court was independent of political interference and that the government accepted its judgments, even those that went against it, and that the Supreme Court could not uniquely be permitted to set its own budget.

> **Pause & reflect**
>
> Are you clear on the difference between the concepts of judicial independence and neutrality? Do you feel that on the whole, both principles are adequately upheld by the Supreme Court?

The influence of the Supreme Court on the executive and parliament

One of the most important roles of the Supreme Court is to interpret the 1998 Human Rights Act. If it believes that an existing piece of UK legislation is in conflict with the European Convention on Human Rights, it can issue a 'declaration of incompatibility'. There is an expectation that parliament will modify the law to bring it into line with the Convention. However, the doctrine of parliamentary sovereignty means that the Supreme Court does not have the power to strike down laws as its counterpart in the USA is entitled to do. In the UK there is no codified constitution against which the Supreme Court could test legislation. This is an important way in which the power of the Supreme Court is limited.

Instead the Supreme Court has the power of **judicial review**. The Court can inquire whether ministers have followed correct procedures in the way that they implemented legislation. It can examine the actions of public bodies to investigate whether they have acted **ultra vires**, a Latin term that means 'beyond one's powers' – in other words, have they gone beyond the authority granted to them in law?

Sometimes the Supreme Court's rulings work in favour of the government and on other occasions they do not, as Figure 1.2 demonstrates.

> **Pause & reflect**
>
> Review the four Supreme Court rulings in Figure 1.2. Do they support the statement that the Supreme Court takes its decisions independently of the UK executive and parliament? More detail is available on the website of the Supreme Court (www.supremecourt.uk) – click on the 'Decided cases' tab and locate the cases by date. The press summary of each case gives the key facts.

Key terms

Judicial review
the power of the judiciary to review, and sometimes reverse, actions by other branches of government that breach the law, or that are incompatible with the Human Rights Act.

Ultra vires
literally 'beyond the powers' in Latin. An action that is taken without legal authority.

The right of sex offenders to appeal against registration for life, 21 April 2010

The government's position was that individuals who had committed serious sexual offences in England and Wales must register with the police for life after being released from prison. The Supreme Court ruled that this breached their human rights and that they should have the right to appeal against registration 15 years after leaving jail. This infuriated the government and police who argued that dangerous individuals do not change their behaviour. Given public concern over the safety of children, this was a particularly sensitive issue.

The case of Private Jason Smith, 30 June 2010

Private Smith was a UK serviceman who died of heatstroke on campaign in Iraq in 2003. His family brought a case against the Ministry of Defence arguing that the authorities should have safeguarded him. The High Court ruled in their favour but when the case was appealed to the Supreme Court, this judgment was overruled by a majority of six to three. The Supreme Court held that the jurisdiction of the Human Rights Act did not extend to troops in combat situations.

The Al Rawi case and secret hearings, 13 July 2011

The case was brought by former inmates of the US prison at Guantanamo Bay on Cuba, who claimed that the UK security services had contributed to their detention and mistreatment. The security chiefs, supported by the government, argued that in the interests of national security, they must be allowed to give evidence in secret. The Supreme Court rejected this argument on the grounds that it breached one of the principles of a fair trial. Each side must be able to see the evidence put before the judge.

The HS2 rail link, 22 January 2014

Campaigners against the government's planned London to BIrmingham high speed rail link requested a judicial review to investigate whether the project complied with EU environmental directives. The Supreme Court unanimously dismissed the appeal on the grounds that parliament had not yet reached a final decision on the scheme and so its merits remained open to debate.

Figure 1.3: Four Supreme Court rulings

Case study: The Supreme Court and Brexit

The most important constitutional case to come before the Supreme Court to date has been the January 2017 ruling on Brexit – on whether the government needed the authority of parliament to trigger the process of leaving the EU, following the referendum the previous June. The case was brought by a businesswoman, Gina Miller, who argued that the prime minister could not take such a step simply by using prerogative powers. The Supreme Court upheld an earlier ruling in Ms Miller's favour by the High Court, on the grounds that EU membership had introduced statutory rights for UK citizens, which only parliament could remove. Supporters of

Key term

Elective dictatorship
a government that dominates parliament, usually due to a large majority, and therefore has few limits on its power.

Brexit were outraged, claiming that the justices had set themselves against the democratic will of the people. However, the Supreme Court was not opposing the decision to leave the EU, only reasserting the constitutional principles governing how Brexit should be carried out.

Question

• Why do you think the law was so unclear on whether the authority to trigger the process of leaving the EU required the authority of parliament?

4.2 The relationship between the executive and parliament

It is now more than 40 years since the senior Conservative politician Lord Hailsham (1907–2001) coined the phrase **'elective dictatorship'** to describe the way in which power had become concentrated in the hands of the executive. He was giving a lecture on the BBC in 1976, at a time when a Labour government was in office with a small parliamentary majority, yet was still able to get most of its legislation through the House of Commons. Hailsham argued that the only real check on executive power is the periodic holding of general elections. In the intervals, the executive can do more or less as it wishes, introducing far-reaching, even irreversible changes.

Here are some instances where this has occurred in recent times.

• In 2003 the Blair government (elected two years earlier on 40 per cent of the vote) first attempted to abolish the post of lord chancellor, without any prior consultation. On meeting constitutional difficulties with its plans, it then carried out a drastic remodelling of the office in the 2005 Constitutional Reform Act.

• In 2011 the coalition government, created the previous year through an agreement that had not been put before the electorate, passed the Fixed Term Parliaments Act.

• David Cameron, backed by the leaders of the Labour and Liberal Democrat parties, offered to devolve more powers if the Scottish people rejected independence in the 2014 referendum.

Executive dominance has tended to arise as a result of a combination of factors:

• the first-past-the-post electoral system, which tends to deliver single-party government, sometimes enjoys the benefit of a large parliamentary majority based on a small share of the popular vote

• the whip system and the prime minister's use of patronage, which reinforce party loyalty and discipline

• government domination of the legislative timetable

• the use of the Salisbury convention and the Parliament Acts to limit opposition to a government's programme from the House of Lords.

In the absence of a codified constitution, the doctrine of parliamentary sovereignty effectively means that the Commons is the main chamber, and whoever controls the Commons is the dominant force in the political system.

The concept of the 'elective dictatorship' is a starting point for posing some broader questions about the relationship between the executive and parliament.

The influence and effectiveness of parliament in holding the executive to account

The fusion of powers in the UK parliamentary system enables members of the two Houses to question and criticise the executive. At the same time, as you have seen, it also places formidable powers in the hands of a government with a majority in the Commons.

The task of holding the executive to account can be assessed under three headings.

Parliament's influence over government legislation

Parliamentary rebellions have become more common in recent years. However, defeats for government measures are rare. Blair did not lose a vote in the Commons until after the 2005 election, when his majority dropped by 100 seats, and even then it took a combination of Labour rebels and the opposition parties to defeat his plans to extend the detention of terrorist suspects to 90 days. More commonly, a government that fears defeat will withdraw a contentious measure. In July 2015 Cameron shelved plans for a vote on relaxing the ban on hunting after the SNP made it clear that they would vote against.

Sometimes opposition can compel a prime minister to allow a free vote. Cameron did so in May 2013 on the issue of same-sex marriage, knowing how strongly opposed many Conservative MPs were to the move. He won the vote thanks to the support of the Labour Party, in spite of an attempt by almost half of his own MPs to block the measure.

These are exceptions to the general rule. Normally the pressure of party discipline and loyalty will ensure that a government secures the passage of even the most controversial parts of its programme. In December 2010 the coalition won a vote to increase student tuition fees, even though this meant that the Liberal Democrats had to abandon an election promise, and the government majority fell from 83 to 21. On certain issues a government can rely on support from opposition MPs. Blair won a vote on the renewal of the Trident nuclear weapon system in March 2007 because Conservative support cancelled out a rebellion on his own side.

The Lords has become increasingly willing to oppose government measures since the removal of most hereditary peers and the ending of single-party control in the upper house. It has used its power of amendment to secure compromises from the government, as with the 'sunset clause' in the 2005 Prevention of Terrorism Act, but as the unelected chamber it will normally defer to the Commons after making its point. The Parliament Act was used three times by the Blair government to push legislation through.

Parliament's scrutiny of other government activities

Changes to select committees, notably the 2010 decision to allow MPs to elect their chairs, has enhanced their status. Long-serving chairs such as Andrew Tyrie (Treasury Select Committee) have accumulated expertise and gained public standing. Their role has expanded to include pre-appointment hearings and scrutiny of legislation. However, ministers can block the appearance of officials as witnesses, and although governments have to respond to select committee reports, they do not have to act on their recommendations. Resources available to them for research remain limited. The prime minister appears twice a year at the Liaison Committee, which consists of the chairs of the select committees. Even so, the prime minister is likely to be treated more leniently by committee chairs from their own party.

Select committee proceedings allow for more in-depth scrutiny of policy than the theatrical duels with the leader of the opposition that occur each week in Prime Minister's Questions. Of more practical value are oral and written questions to departmental ministers, although these receive less publicity.

Debates on major events, such as the one on military action in Syria in August 2013, can occasionally lead to government defeats, but this can be partly attributed to poor management of MPs by government whips. The opposition parties are allocated 20 days in each session to choose the topic for debate, but the government can ordinarily rely on its Commons majority to carry an amendment to a hostile motion. The Backbench Business Committee, created in 2010, has scheduled debates on topics that the government would not have chosen. It works on a cross-party basis. However, with some exceptions, such as the release of documents on the Hillsborough football-stadium disaster, its work has attracted limited media attention. It is also worth noting that the government determines how much time is allocated to its debates.

Parliament's ability to remove governments and ministers

In modern times parliament's power in this area has been limited. In theory the Commons can remove a government using a vote of no confidence, but this has not happened since March 1979. By making a vote a matter of confidence in the government, as John Major did on a crucial division on the Maastricht Treaty in July 1993, a prime minister can face down opposition; MPs will not normally risk triggering a general election in which they may lose their seats. The Fixed Term Parliaments Act has in any case introduced safeguards for the executive, allowing a prime minister who loses such a vote a 14-day period in which to form a new government.

Some individual ministers' careers have been ended as a result of criticism from MPs, when they scent evidence of incompetence or a scandal, but in all the best-known recent cases, parliamentary pressure has been supplemented by attacks in the media. Alastair Campbell's supposed rule about adverse publicity applied to the downfalls of Peter Mandelson, Charles Clarke, Maria Miller and others. David Cameron's premiership was ended by the defeat of the 'Remain' side, which he had championed, in the June 2016 EU referendum, and not by events in parliament.

The influence and effectiveness of the executive in attempting to exercise dominance over parliament

This section looks at the relationship between the executive and parliament from a slightly different angle. Has it become easier or harder for the executive to control parliament? Table 2.1 outlines some key arguments. From your study of this topic, can you find examples to support the points made here, to enable you to expand this skeleton into a fuller answer?

Government control over parliament has reduced	Government still retains a large degree of control over parliament
The last decade has seen an increased number of rebellions in the Commons. Although governments rarely lose legislation in votes in the Commons, they do withdraw bills on which they fear defeat, or make an issue a free vote.	The power of the whips, and the inducements of prime-ministerial patronage, remain important tools of government. Including parliamentary private secretaries, the government can call on an extensive 'payroll vote' of about 100 MPs. With a secure majority it is difficult to defeat a government in the Commons.
Government has accepted restrictions on the exercise of certain prerogatives, such as the right to authorise military action. Even if this is not legally binding an important precedent has been set. The Fixed Term Parliaments Act has removed the PM's power to choose the date of a general election, unless two-thirds of MPs support such a move.	Government retains a number of powers including the right to change laws using secondary legislation, which has been used increasingly in recent years.

The creation of the Backbench Business Committee in 2010 gives backbench MPs more control over the choice of topics for debate, airing issues that might otherwise have been neglected.	Government controls the greater part of the legislative schedule. The limited amount of time allocated to Private Member's Bills, and to debates selected by the opposition parties, supports this point.
Select committees have grown in status due to the decision to allow MPs to elect their chairs, and their powers have increased.	Ministers can still obstruct select committees from summoning officials to their hearings, and they do not have to act on their reports.
The increasing assertiveness of the House of Lords has led to several government defeats. No single party controls the Lords, making management of the House more difficult. Cross-benchers have become increasingly important.	The Lords usually defers to the will of the elected House after a period of 'parliamentary ping-pong'. The Salisbury convention protects a government's manifesto commitments. The Parliament Acts are available to help governments overcome persistent opposition from the Lords.

Table 2.1: Arguments for and against the executive's control over parliament

4.3 The aims, role and impact of the European Union on UK government

The UK joined the organisation that later became known as the **European Union (EU)** in 1973. In a referendum held on 23 June 2016, the British people voted by 52 to 48 per cent to leave the EU. This means that the government now has to negotiate the terms of Brexit – a complex process that is expected to take at least two years. In spite of Brexit, you still need to learn about the EU. Membership of the organisation has had a profound impact on the UK system of government, economy and other aspects of national life. It is also likely that the government will seek some kind of looser relationship with the EU after the country has ceased to be a member.

> **Key term**
>
> **European Union (EU)**
> an association of 28 states (including, at present, the UK), originally founded as the European Economic Community (EEC) in 1957, which has evolved into a political and economic union.

Aims of the EU and how far have they been achieved

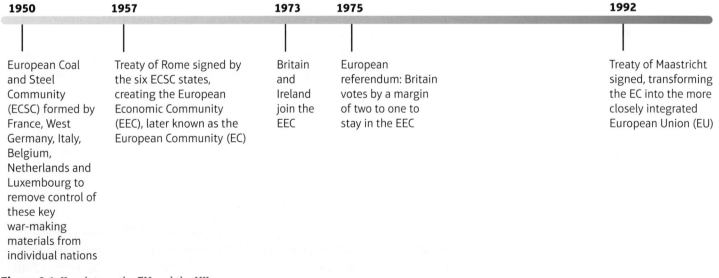

1950	1957	1973	1975	1992
European Coal and Steel Community (ECSC) formed by France, West Germany, Italy, Belgium, Netherlands and Luxembourg to remove control of these key war-making materials from individual nations	Treaty of Rome signed by the six ECSC states, creating the European Economic Community (EEC), later known as the European Community (EC)	Britain and Ireland join the EEC	European referendum: Britain votes by a margin of two to one to stay in the EEC	Treaty of Maastricht signed, transforming the EC into the more closely integrated European Union (EU)

Figure 3.1: Key dates – the EU and the UK

The process of closer European integration has been driven by a number of different factors.

Promoting peace

The continuation of peace was an important motive in the early years. The founding members were determined to avoid another conflict in Europe after the devastation of the Second World War.

Economic integration and the single market

Key term

Four freedoms
the principle of free movement of goods, services, people and capital within the EU's single market.

The member states wanted to promote economic growth by breaking down internal barriers to trade in order to create a customs union. Economic integration took a step further with the passing of the Single European Act in 1986. Its aim was to create a single European market based on the **four freedoms**: free movement of goods, services, people and capital. Much of this was accomplished by the target date of 1992, with the abolition of customs controls at borders and the recognition of common product standards. However, the single market in services, such as energy and digital products, has not yet been completed. Different national policies present obstacles to this. The free movement of EU citizens to live and work in other member states was guaranteed from 1995 by the Schengen agreement. The UK and Ireland negotiated opt-outs from the Schengen area, while a further four states (Bulgaria, Romania, Croatia and Cyprus) are expected to join in due course. Some states have introduced temporary restrictions on internal movement within the EU in response to the 2015 migrant crisis. This saw more than one million refugees arriving in EU states bordering the Mediterranean as they sought to escape conflict in parts of the Middle East and North Africa. Tensions arose between states that were willing to accept asylum seekers, and those that feared that their infrastructure could not cope with the rising numbers.

Economic and monetary union

The establishment of Economic and Monetary Union (EMU) was the eventual goal for a majority of EU member states. This meant the creation of a European Central Bank and a single currency. The Euro was introduced as a trading currency in 1999 and was issued as notes and coins from 2002. The intention was to promote cross-border trade and travel by eliminating the uncertainties caused by fluctuating exchange rates and the costs of converting currencies. In the long run the project was meant to underpin closer political union. By 2014, 19 states had become members of the Eurozone. Britain and Denmark exercised the right to opt out. They were not prepared to surrender economic sovereignty, with a single interest rate set by the European Central Bank. After the global financial crisis of 2007–08 some Eurozone members in southern Europe encountered difficulties. This was because they did not follow the rules laid down to prevent countries from running up unsustainable levels of government debt. Greece, Spain, Portugal, Ireland and Cyprus all required bailouts from EU funds. In return they were expected to implement tougher budgetary rules, embodied in the 2012 Fiscal Compact Treaty. In another sign of a desire to distance itself from EMU, the UK (and the Czech Republic) refused to sign up to this treaty.

Enlargement

With the end of the Cold War, the EU turned its attention to expanding its borders to include eastern and central European states that, until the early 1990s, had been under communist rule. This led to the admission of ten new members in 2004, followed by Romania and Bulgaria in 2007 and Croatia in 2013. The aims of enlargement were to further European unity and to create an expanded and more influential trading bloc, embracing some 500 million people. The new states could not be admitted until they had evolved into liberal democracies with functioning market economies. Applicant states also had to have administrative structures capable of implementing an array of EU laws and regulations. There was some doubt whether some of the countries were sufficiently developed to meet these criteria. Another issue was the influx of eastern European workers into established member states, provoking concern about competition for jobs and leading to the imposition of short-term restrictions on freedom of movement for Bulgarian and Romanian citizens. Anxiety over the arrival of migrants from these countries, together with the fear that the EU might expand to admit even more states, including Turkey, was an important factor in the UK's vote to leave the EU in June 2016.

Social policy

To balance the economic freedoms of the single market, from the 1980s the EU developed a social dimension to ensure that workers did not suffer disadvantage and discrimination. Another aim was to create a 'level playing field' for business, countering the danger that, if there were significant inequalities between member states, firms might move to countries where workers' rights were weaker and labour was cheaper. Advances in workers' rights have varied from one state to another.

Political union

The political system of the EU is unusual in that there is no single institution corresponding to the executive or the legislature of a typical nation state. Instead there is a perpetual state of balance between institutions that operate in an intergovernmental way and those with a supranational character. Intergovernmental operations mean that member states co-operate with each other in decision-making, protecting their respective interests and sovereignty while working towards common goals. Supranational operations mean that decision-making power is transferred to a higher body, which operates independently of nation states. Figure 3.2 shows the five main EU institutions.

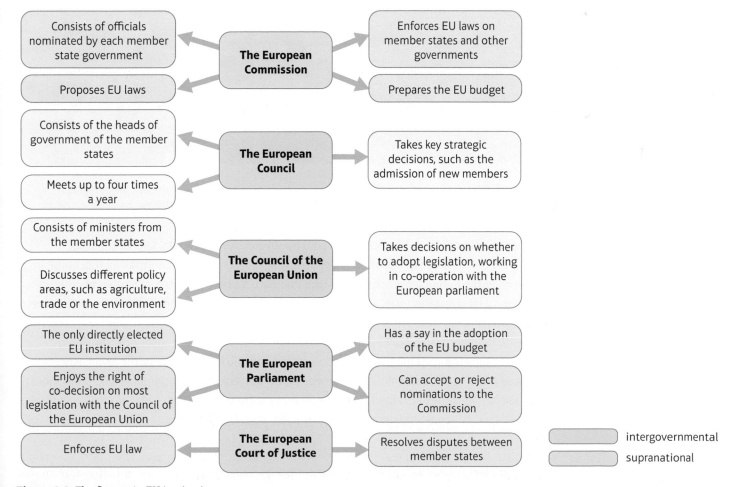

Figure 3.2: The five main EU institutions

The debating chamber of the European parliament in Brussels. Members of the European parliament are elected to represent large, regional constituencies. They sit in party groupings, alongside politicians from other parts of the EU with a similar political outlook.

The cause of political union has been furthered by several developments. One of the most important is the adoption of qualified majority voting as the main decision-making procedure in the Council of the European Union. This means that each state is allocated a number of votes in proportion to its population size. The number of policy areas in which one state can exercise a veto has been steadily reduced. There have also been moves to create a common foreign and security policy, with member states pooling their defence forces for specific purposes, such as peace-keeping and humanitarian missions. A further strand was the involvement of the EU in aspects of justice and policing. For example, the European arrest warrant allows individuals who are wanted by the authorities to be extradited from one member state to another.

The Lisbon Treaty, which was agreed in 2007 and came into force in 2009, introduced a number of institutional changes.

- The European Council was given a permanent president, serving a two-and-a-half-year term that could be renewed once.

- A High Representative of the Union for Foreign Affairs and Security Policy was appointed to co-ordinate an agreed EU foreign policy.
- A system of double majority voting was introduced, enabling legislative proposals to be passed with the support of 55 per cent of the member states, representing at least 65 per cent of the population.
- It incorporated the Charter of Fundamental Rights (which the UK refused to accept as legally binding). This included, for example, rights to education and health care, and the right to strike.

Pause & reflect

By the early 21st century the pace of European integration was causing growing opposition in the UK from 'Eurosceptics' – people who wanted to restore more control to the Westminster parliament, and who regarded the EU as an aspiring federal 'super-state'. From the information presented so far, can you see why this viewpoint gained support in the UK?

Member	Date of accession	Eurozone member?	Schengen area member?
France	1958	x	x
Germany	1958	x	x
Italy	1958	x	x
Belgium	1958	x	x
Netherlands	1958	x	x
Luxembourg	1958	x	x
UK	1973		
Ireland	1973	x	
Denmark	1973		x
Greece	1981	x	x
Spain	1986	x	x
Portugal	1986	x	x
Austria	1995	x	x
Finland	1995	x	x
Sweden	1995		x
Poland	2004		x
Czech Republic	2004		x
Slovakia	2004	x	x
Slovenia	2004	x	x
Hungary	2004		x
Estonia	2004	x	x
Latvia	2004	x	x
Lithuania	2004	x	x
Cyprus	2004	x	
Malta	2004	x	x
Bulgaria	2007		
Romania	2007		
Croatia	2013		

Table 3.1: European Union member states

The role of the EU in policy-making

The negotiation of European treaties

Treaties are the legal documents that set out the powers of the EU institutions and the rules for decision-making. The key body in negotiating a new treaty is the European Council. The heads of government who make up the Council have the authority to commit their countries to the deals they make with each other.

The European parliament then votes on the treaty. Finally, it is ratified by each member state using its own chosen procedure. The usual method is for national parliaments to take a vote. Ireland is an exception in that its constitution requires a referendum to be held. The first Irish referendum on the Lisbon Treaty rejected it. A second referendum was held after amendments had been made, leading to a 'yes' vote.

The passing and enforcement of European directives and regulations

EU laws are of two main kinds: directives and regulations.

* A directive sets out a goal that all EU member states must work towards. They are then expected to pass their own laws to achieve this. An example is the 1998 Working Time Regulations, passed in the UK to give effect to the Working Time Directive (sometimes known as the 48-hour week).

* A regulation is binding on all member states and is immediately enforceable, for example the 2015 regulation on common safeguards on goods imported from outside the EU.

Figure 3.3 below shows the main stages in the passing and enforcement of an EU law.

The European Council sets the broad guidelines for the Commission in its task of proposing laws. The EU treaties set out the basic goals and rules for law-making.

The European Commission proposes new laws. Before doing this it assesses the impact of new legislation and consults with relevant parties.

The Council of the European Union and **European parliament** jointly decide on the adoption of the new law. If they cannot agree, a 'conciliation committee' is convened to find a compromise.

Implementation of a law is the responsibility of committees of the **European Council** and of the Commission. The latter can bring a case before the **European Court of Justice** if a member state does not comply within a given timescale.

Figure 3.3: Main stages in passing and enforcement of an EU law

The impact of the EU on the UK

Long before the vote to leave the EU, the UK was commonly described as Europe's 'awkward partner'. This indicated that, on a range of issues, it was unenthusiastic about further integration.

The following case studies illustrate the UK's sometimes difficult relationship with the EU.

Case study: The UK and social policy

One example of the UK's ambivalence towards the EU is the attitude of governments towards the development of social policy. The Social Chapter, which formed part of the 1992 Maastricht Treaty, is the most significant EU measure to protect workers' rights. John Major's Conservative government initially negotiated an opt-out since it did not want businesses to be held back by 'red tape'. When the New Labour government took office in 1997, one of its first actions was to sign up to the Social Chapter. Gains for workers included equal rights for part-time and full-time workers, parental leave and entitlement to paid annual holidays. However, the Blair government was concerned to strike a balance between social protection and labour-market flexibility, and was reluctant to support further extension of the EU's role in social policy. The coalition government was also concerned to boost economic growth by giving more freedom to businesses. For example, it increased the minimum period required for workers to claim unfair dismissal from one to two years of employment. Another conflict arose after the European Court of Justice ruled that time spent by tradesmen travelling to a job must count towards the maximum 48-hour working week. Cameron's government took the side of business leaders, who argued that this would increase their costs.

Case study: The UK and the Common Fisheries Policy

From 1983 the EU regulated the amount of deep-sea fish that could be caught with a system of quotas. It also allowed fishing boats from different member states to have equal access to each other's fishing grounds. Critics argued that the policy allowed large fishing fleets from other countries to drive small UK trawler operators out of business. They also maintained that the policy was ineffective in conserving fish stocks. A particular grievance was that, as a result of the policy, fish had to be thrown back into the sea in order to meet the quota. Fishing was at the centre of a landmark ruling in the 1990 Factortame case. A Spanish fishing company, Factortame, sued the UK government for restricting its access to UK waters. The law lords, who formed the highest UK court at the time, followed the European Court of Justice in ruling that the 1988 Merchant Shipping Act, which the government was using to support its position, could not be allowed to stand because it violated EU law. This controversial case established the primacy of EU law over an act of parliament.

Question

- Do these two case studies help to explain the growth of hostility to the influence of the EU in certain sections of British society since the 1990s?

How has the EU affected the UK's political system and policy-making?

It is perhaps not surprising that the UK system of government has adjusted to membership of the EU without being fundamentally changed by it. The executive has altered the way it works in an ad hoc fashion, in order to co-ordinate British policy and to get the best available deal in negotiations with other member states and EU institutions. The process of 'Europeanisation' – the adaptation of UK government structures and domestic politics to EU policies and procedures – is an uneven one.

EU membership has heightened the profile of the prime minister, whose annual routine has included attendance at regular European Council meetings. David Cameron visited his fellow heads of government individually early in 2016, as well as attending the Council, in a bid to renegotiate the terms of UK membership. Following the vote to leave the EU, Theresa May was thrust unexpectedly into the limelight as Britain's new prime minister, conducting a series of meetings with her counterparts in pursuit of a deal that protects vital national interests.

The foreign secretary plays an important role in support of the prime minister, attending meetings of the European Council as well as the Council of the European Union. Other ministers attend meetings of the latter according to their departmental responsibilities. The chancellor of the exchequer represents the UK when the Council of Finance Ministers, known as Ecofin, is in session. Ministers responsible for other policy areas that are affected by EU policy, such as agriculture or business, travel to Brussels at other times to meet their counterparts. It should be noted that to a large extent the Council simply ratifies decisions drafted by a body of civil servants, drawn from the member states, known as Coreper. A minister who has numerous other responsibilities, and who may spend only two to three years in a particular department, is likely to rely heavily on the work of these permanent officials.

A Cabinet committee on European affairs has been set up to develop UK policy towards the EU. A European and Global Issues Secretariat, located within the Cabinet Office, seeks to co-ordinate the approach of different Whitehall departments to Britain's role in the EU.

Parliament has a responsibility to examine EU legislation, and ministers should not agree to new laws unless it has been debated or reviewed by the House of Commons European Scrutiny Committee. In practice, however, the sheer volume of EU legislation makes this a difficult task to perform effectively. The House of Lords EU Select Committee produces thoughtful reports on developments in Brussels, but its status as an organ of the second chamber means that it lacks real influence.

Table 3.2 shows how relative EU and national government responsibilities vary from one policy area to another. Some government departments are much more extensively involved in EU deliberations than others. In areas such as social security, health care and education, the EU does not try to influence the content of national policy, but it insists on equal treatment for all EU citizens. This caused problems for David Cameron in his efforts to revise the terms of Britain's EU membership, when he tried to restrict EU migrants' access to the UK's welfare benefits system.

EU has exclusive competence	EU and member states share competence	EU co-ordinates the individual policies of member states	Member states have exclusive competence
Competition policy	The single market	Common foreign and security policy	National defence
Trade with non-EU states	Social and employment policy	Some aspects of macroeconomic policy	Most taxation
Customs union	Agriculture and fisheries		Health
	Regional development		Education
	Environmental policy		Social security

Table 3.2: How relative EU and national government responsibilities vary

Another layer of complexity is supplied by devolution. A number of policy areas in which the EU shares competence with the UK have been devolved to Scotland, Wales and Northern Ireland, including agriculture, fisheries and the environment. On the subject of the UK's overall relationship with the EU, central government has to consult the administrations in Edinburgh, Cardiff and Belfast in order to produce an agreed negotiating position. This is why some writers now describe the UK as having a system of 'multi-level governance', in which policy-making is shared between the national government, the sub-national bodies in Scotland, Wales and Northern Ireland, and the institutions of the EU.

The institutional architecture described above is, of course, set to change as the UK begins the process of leaving the EU. Theresa May set up two new central government departments on taking office. The Brexit process is to be handled by the Department for Exiting the European Union, headed by David Davis. The Department for International Trade, under Liam Fox, is charged with negotiating new trade deals with non-EU countries. This is necessary for the UK, as the EU exercises this responsibility on behalf of its members. There have, however, been rumours of unseemly 'turf wars' within Whitehall, with the new International Trade Department seeking to take control of economic diplomacy from the Foreign Office.

Another minefield for the UK government is the demand from the SNP-led Edinburgh government for a second independence referendum. The case for this is that a majority of Scottish people voted to stay in the EU, and thus face being removed from it against their will as a result of the Brexit vote by the UK as a whole. Constitutionally, Scotland cannot negotiate its own relationship with the EU as part of the UK, so the independence issue has been reopened. Extricating the UK from the EU is far from a straightforward process after more than 40 years of close involvement between the two.

EXTENSION ACTIVITY

There has been considerable speculation on what kind of relationship the UK may have with the EU after Brexit takes place. In particular there is great interest in what kind of trade deal may be concluded between the UK and the other 27 EU members. Research the evolving debate on the process of the UK's disengagement from the EU. The BBC website is a good source of information on this subject.

4.4 The location of sovereignty in the UK political system

Sovereignty has been a recurrent topic in this unit. In broad terms it means the ultimate authority to make decisions in a political system. There are, however, different varieties of sovereignty.

The distinction between legal sovereignty and political sovereignty

Legal sovereignty is a concept defined in law. It belongs to the person or body in a state with unlimited legal authority. In the distant past it was exercised by the monarch, but in the present day it belongs to the UK parliament. There is no higher legal authority than parliament – it can legislate on any subject and no parliament can bind its successors.

Political sovereignty stands above legal sovereignty. In a democracy, the legal sovereign body derives its authority from the people. When the people elect a parliament, they delegate their

Key terms

Legal sovereignty
the right to ultimate legal authority in a political system; in the UK, this belongs to parliament.

Political sovereignty
the ultimate political power; in the UK's democracy, the electorate holds this power, which it delegates to parliament.

political authority to their representatives. Parliament is accountable to the electorate for the way in which it exercises its powers, and the electorate has the right to elect a new parliament at regular intervals.

In other words, parliament is entrusted with formal, legal sovereignty – the *authority* to make laws – but it can do so only because the people, who possess ultimate political *power*, allow it to do so.

How far sovereignty has moved between different branches of government

It can be argued that although parliament is theoretically sovereign, in practice real authority has long since moved to the executive. A government with a secure parliamentary majority can use the whipping system and its control of the legislative timetable to assert its dominance. It can use the Parliament Act to override opposition from the House of Lords. It has important royal prerogative powers at its disposal. Although it is now an accepted convention that the government should consult parliament in advance on the deployment of troops, this is not legally binding.

The creation of the Supreme Court could be seen as a challenge to parliamentary sovereignty, in the sense that it ended the function of the House of Lords as the UK's final court of appeal. However, the Court itself was established by act of parliament and it could in theory be abolished by a future act. The Supreme Court's own website describes its role as one of interpreting the law and developing it where necessary. It cannot strike down a law, and it is up to parliament to decide whether to amend legislation.

Other developments that have caused some commentators to question whether parliament is still sovereign include the following.

- **Devolution:** This process involves a transfer of powers and functions to new bodies, giving them the authority to make law on certain specified subjects within their own part of the UK. This does not amount to a federal settlement, which would mean a formal, legal sharing of sovereignty between different levels of government. In theory, the UK parliament could abolish the devolved assemblies. In reality, as long as these bodies command public support, this is highly unlikely. Political reality overrides constitutional theory in the real world.

- **Referendums:** The increased use of referendums since 1997 is sometimes cited as a threat to parliamentary sovereignty. At a theoretical level this is not the case since a referendum is advisory and not legally binding. However, political reality makes it extremely unlikely that parliament would dare to ignore the outcome of a popular vote. This lesson was underlined after the June 2016 EU referendum, when some constitutional lawyers argued that parliament was legally entitled to reverse the result of the vote. In practice, MPs are most unlikely to risk the public backlash that would follow an attempt to defy the clearly expressed will of the people. This highlights the difference between legal and political sovereignty.

- **The Human Rights Act:** The passing of the Human Rights Act has increased the power of judges by giving them the right to declare existing legislation incompatible with the act. They cannot, however, compel parliament to change the law. Technically parliament should implement rulings of the European Court of Human Rights but it has, for example, rejected calls to allow prisoners voting rights. The Conservative Party has proposed to pass a British Bill of Rights, which is likely to make the Supreme Court the final arbiter of human rights, and parliament would be within its rights to pass such legislation.

- **EU membership:** Supporters of the UK's membership of the EU often argued that sovereignty had not been lost but 'pooled'. This means that all member states had voluntarily shared some of their sovereignty for an agreed common purpose. The UK had gained influence that it could not have obtained on its own. Given the pace of globalisation, they argued, it was no longer possible for any state to be truly independent. Meanwhile moderate Eurosceptics believed that sovereignty could be reclaimed by negotiating opt-outs from EU policies to which they objected, or by securing the return of powers to the UK parliament. The hard-line Eurosceptics who campaigned for Brexit, on the other hand, viewed sovereignty as indivisible. They insisted that the only way to regain it was to withdraw from the EU.

The **Factortame case** is often cited as evidence that, by joining the EU, parliament had accepted that EU law would take priority if it conflicted with national legislation. It could be argued that this did not actually involve a surrender of sovereignty, since it was parliament that had agreed to limit its own power in the first place, when it passed the 1972 European Communities Act. However, the doctrine that 'no parliament can bind its successor' creates a paradox. The provisions of the 1988 Merchant Shipping Act were effectively overturned by an act passed 16 years earlier. Brexit of course means that this is soon to become a purely academic argument. Parliament has always retained the right to withdraw from the EU and in this sense its sovereignty can be said to have been in abeyance rather than permanently lost.

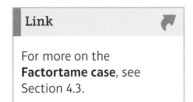

Link

For more on the **Factortame case**, see Section 4.3.

Where sovereignty can now be said to lie in the UK

- There are arguments to support the idea that parliamentary sovereignty is still a reality.

- It remains the ultimate legal authority in the UK, with power to pass laws on any subject, and it is not subordinate to any other body in law.

- Parliament retains the right to abolish devolved bodies in the component parts of the UK, to which it has transferred powers and functions – but not sovereignty. The UK is not a federal state, even if it has acquired some characteristics of one.

- Judges may recommend laws for amendment that do not conform to the Human Rights Act, but it is up to parliament to decide whether to change them.

- Parliament retained sovereignty when the UK entered the EU, because it voluntarily gave up some sovereignty when it passed the 1972 European Communities Act. This is why the principle that EU law took precedence over UK law (illustrated by the Factortame case) became established. Parliament is allowed to repeal the 1972 act to end the UK's membership of the EU.

There are also some counter arguments.

- Parliament derives its legal sovereignty from the political sovereignty that belongs to the people.

- The steadily growing power of the executive means that parliament is to a large extent controlled by the government, which uses parliament to pass its legislation.

- Legal sovereignty is a theoretical concept. The practical realities of politics mean that there are constraints on what it can do, for example, it would be inconceivable for parliament to abolish the Scottish parliament against the wishes of the Scottish people. Similarly, even though referendums are advisory rather than binding, politically it would be virtually impossible for parliament to ignore the result.

- In the modern world, globalisation makes sovereignty a less meaningful concept. It is more realistic to think of sharing sovereignty with other international actors, in order to maximise influence.

Assessment support: 2.1.4 Relations Between Institutions

Question 2 on A-Level Paper 2 gives you a choice of two essay-style questions. Each of these is worth 30 marks and should be completed in 45 minutes.

Evaluate the extent to which the balance of power has shifted from the executive to parliament in recent years. [30 marks]

In your answer you should draw on relevant knowledge and understanding of the study of Component 1: UK Politics and Core Political Ideas and consider this view and the alternative to this view in a balanced way.

This kind of question tests all three Assessment Objectives, with the marks divided equally. Your knowledge and understanding should underpin your analysis and evaluation. As with Question 2 on Paper 1, you must evaluate – in this case, develop arguments that both agree and disagree with the suggestion that parliament has increased its power at the expense of the executive. However, you must also draw on relevant information from Component 1. This is a 'synoptic' question – it requires you to draw on knowledge and understanding acquired in other parts of the specification. If you do not make any synoptic points, you cannot achieve the highest level (between 25 and 30 marks).

- Write a brief plan before you start writing, to help you produce a logically structured answer.

- The introduction needs to explain briefly what is meant by the 'balance of power' between the executive and parliament. The UK's uncodified constitution provides few clear-cut checks and balances. However, this situation is constantly changing. In the essay you are going to explain and evaluate changes that may have altered the balance between the two.

- What is meant by 'recent years'? This is obviously open to debate but as a general rule you should focus on developments since 1997 (and in particular since 2010).

- Aim to cover two to three changes that have arguably increased the power of parliament, and the same number of areas where the executive retains important powers.

- Make connections between your points – a particular development can increase the power of parliament, but can also have limitations. Finally, reach a clear and supported overall judgement.

Here is a paragraph from a student's answer.

Recent governments have accepted an increased role for parliament in the exercise of prerogative powers. For example, David Cameron consulted the Commons on his proposals to use military force in Syria in August 2013, and publicly accepted the will of parliament when he lost. This shows that government does not always have full control, and parliament now exercises greater oversight of its policies and actions. On the other hand it is still comparatively rare for a majority government to lose a vote in the Commons. Cameron suffered only six defeats in the five years of coalition government, and three more in his 14 months as head of a Conservative government with a small majority. The continuing influence of the whips over how MPs vote, and the prime minister's power of patronage, are important tools reinforcing the authority of the government. In addition the first-past-the-post voting system usually enhances the lead of the winning party over its opponents in the Commons. For example, Blair was not defeated until November 2005 (on proposals to increase the time that terror suspects could be held before being charged), which was more than eight years into his term of office.

- This is effective because it uses precise and accurate examples to support the points that it makes. It covers both sides of the argument.

- It also meets the requirement to include synoptic material. The reference to the use of the first-past-the-post voting system draws on UK Politics: Electoral Systems chapter, Sections 3.1 and 3.3.

CHAPTER 1

Anarchism

One of the most iconic graffiti symbols seen spray-painted onto walls is the 'A' in a circle – an anarchist symbol. Although the symbol is common, anarchists have struggled to communicate their views clearly. The term 'anarchy' is often used in a negative way – to describe chaos, disorganisation and disorder. However, the word itself comes from ancient Greek and simply means the absence of government or authority. These two interpretations of the word have become linked because many people cannot imagine the absence of authority or government without imagining chaos.

An anarchist symbol, which represents Proudhon's idea that 'anarchy is order, government is civil war'.

EXTENSION ACTIVITY

Read this short introductory article, *Are you an anarchist? The answer may surprise you!* by David Graeber (https://theanarchistlibrary.org/library/david-graeber-are-you-an-anarchist-the-answer-may-surprise-you). Can you imagine a world without government, laws and the police? What does it look like? What does this tell you about your view of human nature?

This chapter looks at:

- the core ideas of anarchism
- how these ideas apply to human nature, the state, society and the economy
- the different views and tensions within anarchism
- the key ideas of some key anarchist thinkers.

1.1 Core ideas and principles

Anarchism is an ideology based on freeing people from political domination and economic exploitation, ending the misuse of one person by another. Its goal is anarchy, which has been described as being without government, 'statelessness', complete freedom and equality. However it is described, anarchists agree this future society will be an ordered way of life.

Human nature	Anarchists hold an essentially positive view of human nature. At their core, humans have universal qualities, with the potential for development but also for selfishness and corruption. Human nature is seen as plastic and moulded by its environment, which explains why the existing state and existing society is responsible for the selfish, anti-social, competitive traits that we see in humanity today. The removal of the state and society will reveal true universal qualities and allow them to develop. The key disagreement is over the nature of those universal qualities, with collectivists seeing humans as altruistic, solidaristic and co-operative, while individualists see humans as self-interested, rational and competitive.
The state	Anarchism as an idea is defined by its rejection of the state. This includes rejecting all forms of government and government power, as well as authority based on hierarchy such as the church, capitalism and social relationships, such as sexism. The state in any form is unjustifiable as it is unjust, immoral, commanding, controlling and corrupting. The rejection of the state is necessary to create liberty. For individualists, this means the ability to be autonomous and explore your individuality to the full, while collectivists see that liberty must include equality to allow people to be altruistic and co-operative, and to allow solidarity to flourish.
Society	Anarchy is order, so anarchists believe that the future society is peaceful, stable and stateless. It will be based on liberty and economic freedom. This argument is often attacked as utopian, but anarchists argue that order occurs naturally and spontaneously. Collectivists see humans' universal qualities of altruism, solidarity and co-operation as the basis of natural order, while individualists argue that the self-interested, rational and competitive qualities of human nature are key. There is no clear blueprint for an anarchist society, but it is likely to include the principles of direct democracy, decentralisation and the voluntary co-operation of free and equal individuals.
The economy	Anarchists are in agreement that the economy should be a space where free individuals can manage their own affairs without state ownership or regulation, as the state supports exploitation. Anarchists are opposed to all existing economic systems and see them as a restriction on liberty. The key area of difference among anarchists is over matters of economic organisation – both between collectivists and individualists, and within the strands themselves. Collectivist anarchists support collective ownership and mutual co-operation, while anarcho-capitalists have endorsed private property and the competitive, free market. Mutualists attempt to blend elements of collectivism with individualism.

Table 1.1: Core principles and ideas of anarchism in action

Rejection of the state

Anarchism as an idea is defined by its rejection of the state. **Emma Goldman** described the state as a 'cold monster', a sovereign body that exerts total authority over all individuals and groups living within its defined geographical limits.

Anarchists oppose government, authority and political **power**. 'Government' here generally means a system of rule, from monarchism to dictatorship to liberal democracy, which anarchists see as immoral because it restricts liberty. Government is tyranny, and must be rejected.

In modern democracies, anarchists believe that the government rules by deceit, backed up by the threat of violence. There has never been a social contract into which individuals have freely entered (as liberals like to argue), so the state always restricts liberty. The people are said to be sovereign and to rule, but they give away their power at the ballot box. If the people were sovereign, there

Link

For more on **Emma Goldman**, see Section 1.3.

Key terms

State
a sovereign body that exerts total authority over all individuals and groups living within its defined geographical limits.

Power
the means or instruments – such as the law, the police and the use of ideology – by which the state and other social institutions secure their authority.

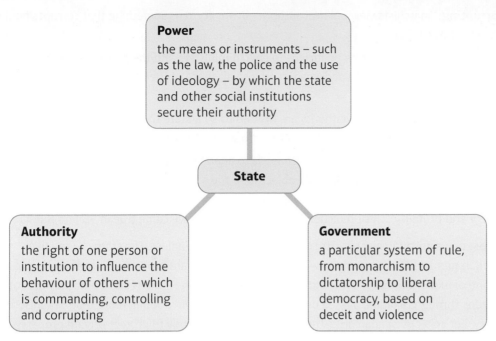

Figure 1.1: The anarchist view of aspects of the state

would be no government and no governed, so the state would not exist. The vote is nothing more than a trick that hides the massive power of the state based on the police, the banks and the army, which it uses to secure its authority. As Goldman famously stated: 'If voting changed anything, they'd make it illegal.'

Within a liberal democracy, violence will only be used when deceit fails, but evidence of such violence is clear, anarchists believe. British anarchists would point to the brutal repression of the miners' strike in 1984–85; American anarchists to the suppression of protest in Ferguson (2014) or Standing Rock (2016) by a heavily militarised police.

Anarchists reject the state and all forms of **authority** based on hierarchy: authority that divides society into the few (who give orders) and the many (who take orders). This includes social institutions such as the church, social relationships such as sexism, racism and homophobia, and capitalism, where the workers are wage slaves.

For anarchists, hierarchical authorities should be rejected as commanding, controlling and corrupting of human nature.

- **Commanding:** The state can force an individual to act in a way they would not have done voluntarily. This forces the individual to suspend their reason and lose their **autonomy** – their freedom and responsibility to decide for themselves. Autonomy is not possible under the state, so the state must be rejected to allow this core element of human nature to flourish.

- **Controlling:** Authority exerts control over people, and stifles creativity and initiative. People lose their ability to understand their own individuality and to think for themselves. This stops individuals being able to fully explore their nature and express themselves. **Max Stirner** took this thinking to the extreme by rejecting the authority of the state, the church, moral truths, family values and existing sexual morality.

Key terms

Authority
the right of one person or institution to influence the behaviour of others. Seen as commanding, controlling and corrupting.

Autonomy
a form of self-government involving a combination of freedom and responsibility, in which the individual is not subject to the will of the state or any other person.

Link

For more on **Max Stirner**, see Section 1.3.

Link

For more on **Mikhail Bakunin**, see Section 1.3.

Key terms

Government
a particular system of rule, from monarchism to dictatorship to liberal democracy, which anarchists believe is based on deceit and violence.

Solidarity
a relationship of sympathy, co-operation and harmony between people that anarchists believe means that they have no need to be regulated by the state (any regulation makes solidarity impossible).

Mutual aid
the anarchist idea that the most successful species are those that employ solidarity and co-operation rather than individualistic competition.

Direct action
a range of political actions, both non-violent and violent, that are taken outside the legal and constitutional framework.

Link

For more on **direct action**, see Section 1.1 of UK Democracy and Participation.

Link

For more on the **Zapatistas**, see the case study on pages 231–2.

Link

For more on **Peter Kropotkin**, see Section 1.3.

- **Corrupting:** Anarchists view political authority in any form as something that corrupts human nature for everyone.
  - Those with authority, from politicians to church ministers and the police, are raised above others by power, privilege and wealth and lose all sense of their true nature, which is co-operative and altruistic.
  - Those who are subject to authority are brutalised by a state that creates social conflict through inequality and resolves disputes through violence and coercion, not through reason.

The state in any form is unjustifiable, which leads to anarchism splitting from Marxism and classical liberalism. In particular, **Mikhail Bakunin** objected to the socialist state, stating that the 'red bureaucracy' would become corrupted by authority and predicted that 'socialism without freedom is slavery and brutality'. This prediction is seen by many to have come true in Stalin's Russia.

The most powerful anarchist criticism of the state is that it is unjust. The state is a relatively new creation in human history, emerging with the creation of private property. Since then its role has been one of exploitation. For some individualist anarchists, the state is like a parasite that robs its citizens through taxation, backed up by the threat of force – nothing more than organised banditry. For collectivist anarchists, the state develops as a body to protect private property and the inequalities between the wealthy and the masses. The state is controlled by the wealthy, who are willing to use mechanisms of the state to their fullest extent to protect their privilege. On the global stage, the state protects the interests of elites in advanced industrial countries through organisations such as the World Bank, the IMF and the G20.

Pause & reflect ✔

How do the anarchist views of the state suggest that the state is an unnecessary evil?

The arguments against the rejection of the state have implications for anarchist tactics and strategies. Anarchists have been critical of party politics: parties are based on hierarchical authority and seek conformism and obedience from their membership. There can be no attempt to capture **government**, either by the ballot box or by revolution, as the state is immoral and unjust, and the exercise of authority will be corrupting. This means other less orthodox strategies are required.

- **Direct action or 'propaganda by the deed':** This Bakuninist approach involves using any form of direct action – including non-payment of taxes, rents and debts, the mass strike or the refusal of conscription to acts of violence – to stir up a revolution. Modern examples of propaganda of the deed might include the **Zapatista** uprising in Mexico in 1994 or the non-payment of the poll tax in the UK under Thatcher.

- **Acts of violence:** Propaganda by the deed has become associated with acts of violence, and in particular with acts of terror, such as Alexander Berkman's attempt to murder the US businessman Henry Frick in 1892.

- **Emerging revolution:** Terrorism is widely discredited as ineffective and immoral by anarchist thinkers such as **Kropotkin** and Goldman. The revolution will emerge out of a process of direct action and DIY politics that exposes and undermines the nature of the state. This approach involves acting as if you are already free rather than trying to influence or change the decisions of the government. These actions will allow individuals to become autonomous and learn about the benefits of **solidarity**, **mutual aid** and collective action, creating a spirit of revolt. The spread of ideas will reach a boiling point, hastened by misery and oppression, and then explode into revolutionary action.

- **Creating new institutions:** Proudhon rejected any form of violence. He argued that change would be won by an evolutionary process of creating new institutions, within the cracks of the current state, to replace the existing ones. This could be done through education, instruction and peaceful action, as well as mutualist experiments, such as worker associations and a People's Bank.

- **Insurrection:** Stirner opposed revolution as a political and social act, and an authoritarian one, because revolution involves the overthrow of existing conditions to be replaced by new conditions. He favoured insurrection – a rising up of individuals who elevate themselves above the established institutions through self-liberation, leaving the establishment to decay and die rather than be overthrown.

EXTENSION ACTIVITY

Investigate the attempt by Alexander Berkman to murder Henry Frick. Why did he target Henry Frick? What was Berkman hoping to achieve and what was the result?

Key term

Insurrection
an egoistic, not a political or social act, that anarchists believe allows individuals to elevate themselves above the established institutions, leaving the establishment to decay and die.

Case study: Reclaim the Streets

The Reclaim the Streets movement began in London as an effort to take back the streets from cars and businesses and turn them into public spaces to be enjoyed by all. The tactics mixed a blend of political protest and partying with music, costumes and art. In 1996 a nine-hour party on the M41 included two stilt walkers in 18th century costumes who had RTS members hidden under their enormous skirts, using the cover to drill holes in the road to plant trees, with the party music covering the noise. This carnival approach became a key part of the anti-globalisation movement worldwide. In May 1998, carnivals were held in more than 70 cities to coincide with the G8 meetings, and in 1999 a mass street action was organised in Seattle to shut down the WTO Conference.

Posters for Reclaim the Streets adorn walls in Finland's capital Helsinki.

Questions

- Why do anarchists adopt direct action as a political tactic?

- How do group, carnival-type actions fit with anarchist thinking?

Liberty

For liberals, liberty can be defined as individuals pursuing their own good in their own way. This involves freedom from want, as well as freedom of expression, thought, assembly and movement for all. For socialists, liberty also means freedom from the economic controls of the state and from economic hardship. The liberty of anarchism includes the freedoms of both liberalism and socialism, blending their views about human nature. This informs anarchists' rejection of the state and their ideas about the best way to realise freedom.

Individualist anarchists see human nature as rational, individualist and autonomous. Because authority is commanding, the individual cannot be autonomous in making decisions based on reason and conscience; because authority is controlling, the individual cannot fully explore their individuality. Liberty is the freedom to be autonomous and to explore one's individuality to the full. It is freedom from control by the state or other social institutions, such as the church, or social relationships such as patriarchy, which are based on hierarchical authority.

Key term

Altruism
concern for the interest and welfare of others based on a belief that humans are social beings with a capacity for social solidarity.

Collectivist anarchists see humans as rational, but emphasise that human nature is **altruistic** and co-operative. The unjust nature of the state means that the individual is not free to be altruistic and co-operative. Liberty under capitalism is a cruel joke: it means nothing more than the ability for the wage slave to choose their own boss. So for collectivists the individual can only be free when all are free to realise their potential. Liberty is only possible if there is equality, where people treat each other equally, have an equal economic position and have an equal say in their workplace or community. Liberty is achieved by the overthrow of the class-based, hierarchical society based on inequalities of power, wealth and privilege.

Anarchists agree that individuality does not exist outside of society, as every individual needs others in order to develop, expand and grow. However, anarchist views of liberty are on a sliding scale between individualist and collectivist tendencies.

- Collectivists such as Bakunin emphasise the collective more, arguing that the liberty of the individual should be absolute and unlimited, but that individuality can only be achieved through work and the collective.

- Even the most radical of individualists, Max Stirner, argues that the individual needs voluntary associations with others, but never for the common good and always for their own personal interest.

- Proudhon was critical of the obsession with individuality and felt that collectivism absorbed and devalued the individual. His ideas sought a balance between the two, arguing that the first element of human nature is individuality, but that individuals coming together in a group create a force that is more than the sum of the individuals.

Anarchy is order

In an anarchist society, there would be no centralised body to impose its will on the people, no recognised hierarchical authority and no coercive machinery to impose laws. There is no clear anarchist blueprint for what this society would look like – free individuals decide how they want to live. However, it is clear that the new society would be some form of decentralised federation of autonomous districts, based on the voluntary co-operation of free and equal individuals, where decisions are made directly by the people in a form of self-government. In this society, order will occur naturally and it will be both stable and peaceful.

Opponents of anarchism see this as the weakest argument in anarchism, pointing to the selfish, antisocial and competitive aspects of human nature that make the idea of 'anarchy is order' unrealistic and unachievable. The anarchist response is to go back to human nature. Anarchists see humans at their core as social, co-operative and intellectually enlightened, but with the potential for corruption and selfishness. Human nature is socially determined, moulded by the institutions and relationships that frame everyday life. In the modern state, these institutions and relationships are based on hierarchical authority, and have created selfish, antisocial and competitive traits. Their replacement with alternatives will lead to nurturing of the core aspects of human nature.

These alternatives vary by the different strands of anarchism, as shown in Figure 1.2.

Anarchists have an optimistic view of human nature, believing in the unlimited potential for human development. The removal of the state, existing social institutions and relationships will allow conflict to be resolved by reason, not violence. It will allow for the flourishing of our social, co-operative and enlightened core nature, providing the basis for natural harmony and order.

Collectivist

Altruism is undermined by the competitive, exploitative and divisive nature of the capitalist state. Common ownership and mutualist institutions will help grow altruistic and co-operative behaviour, which will sustain natural order.

Egoistic-anarchist

The individual should act as they see fit and must not be constrained by any laws, political obligation, social norms and moral or religious principles. The removal of the state will nurture rationalism, autonomy and self-interest, which are the best guarantors of social order.

Anarcho-capitalist

The free market will allow rational, autonomous, competitive and self-interested individuals to make judgements in their own best interests, creating natural order.

Figure 1.2: Alternatives under the different strands of anarchism

Case study: The Zapatistas

Subcommandante Marcos of the Zapatistas: 'We are sorry for the inconvenience, but this is a revolution.'

In the Chiapas region of Mexico, indigenous communities live with high levels of poverty as well as a lack of education and health care. In the 1990s, the Mexican government ended its commitment to land reform based on community-owned land and signed up to NAFTA (a free-market deal with the US and Canada). This forced millions of campesinos (peasant farmers) to become cheap labour in the industrial workforce. After consultation with local communities, the Zapatistas rose up on the day NAFTA came into force to take over the major population centres and around 500 ranches. The Zapatista project is built on the idea of autonomy, which means building a world where all communities have a place and are rooted in the local cultures. Power is devolved to community level, where 'Juntas of good government' make key decisions. The members are selected by community assemblies for one-year terms and work under the idea of 'mandar obedeciendo' or 'lead by obeying'. There is collective education and health care, and the economy is based on a co-operative model – Mut Vitz is its largest coffee co-operative. Co-operative members make decisions together and distribute its income equitably.

Questions

- In what way can the Zapatista project be seen as anarchist?

- How can the Zapatista project be criticised from an anarchist perspective?

Economic freedom

Anarchism rejects the state and all forms of hierarchical authority, as well as the oppression they create. This has led anarchists to oppose capitalism and its particular form of private property. As Proudhon says in *What is Property?*: 'Property is theft'.

For anarchists, the state was founded not on a social contract between rational individuals, but on social conflict, to protect property and inequality while exploiting the masses.

Economic inequality is built into the state, which emerged when society began to produce a surplus that was taken by the few. The state became necessary to protect private property, which was often acquired unjustly. For example, in the UK the Land Enclosures Acts of the 18th century parcelled up common land and turned it over to private ownership, creating a landless working class. Historian E.P. Thompson saw this as class robbery. Anarchism aligned itself with the exploited masses and aimed to overthrow both the state and capitalism.

Analysis of existing economic systems and plans to create future economic freedom highlight some of the clearest tensions within anarchism.

Proudhon's analysis of the political economy is crucial. Proudhon calls private property 'the right to own without the need to occupy'. This means the ability to earn income without doing any productive work, by exploiting the labour of others through rent, interest and wage labour. The masses must work and be exploited or suffer starvation and misery. This is the argument taken up by collectivist anarchists, who see private property, defended by the state, as the root cause of exploitation. Private property encourages selfishness, conflict and social disharmony; inequality promotes greed, envy and resentment. Collectivists would abolish private property and replace it with collective ownership or **mutualism**, which would nurture the altruistic elements of human nature and create liberty, leading to natural order.

Anarcho-capitalists, on the other hand, support an entirely free, competitive market, including the principle of private property. The state must be removed from the market, even with the provision of public goods like roads, education or health care. The market is always more effective than the state and will allow rational, autonomous, competitive and self-interested individuals to make judgements in their own best interests, creating natural order.

Key term

Mutualism
a system of equitable exchange between self-governing producers – organised individually or in association – and small-scale private property based on use or possession.

All anarchists are opposed to all existing forms of capitalism that have existed in liberal democracies since 1945, including neo-liberalism. This is reflected in the leading role played by anarchists in the anti-globalisation movement, dating back to the Battle of Seattle in 1999. Anarchists are also opposed to forms of state socialism that have been tried in China and the USSR. However, tensions emerge again with the reasons behind each group's opposition, as Table 1.2 shows.

Link

For **neo-liberalism**, see Section 1.2 of Conservatism.

Collectivist objections	System	Anarcho-capitalist objections
State intervention has followed policies of full employment, inclusive welfare and progressive taxation. However, capitalism is still a system based on inequality and exploitation, so liberty cannot exist. Neo-liberalism is seen as widening inequality and increasing exploitation, leading to anarchists' role in the anti-globalisation and occupy movements.	Capitalism	State intervention in the economy distorts the market and creates both public and private monopolies that restrict competition and choice – and therefore restrict liberty. Intervention is still a problem, even under the neoliberal approach in the UK and USA since the 1980s.
In state socialism, the state has merely replaced the ruling elite as the exploiting power, so there is no liberty.	State socialism	State socialism based on state planning and ownership of production is an attack on property rights and liberty.

Table 1.2: Objections to state capitalism and state socialism

Anarchists agree on the need for a future economic system where free individuals can manage their own affairs. This entails no state regulation or intervention in economic life, as the rejection of the state is the core principle of anarchism. However, anarchists have endorsed various economic systems to create that freedom.

Pause & reflect

To what extent do anarchists agree in their analysis of existing economic systems, and in their proposals for future economic systems?

Utopian

Utopianism is a form of political thinking that constructs a model of an idealised future society in order to develop a critical analysis of existing society. This ideal society is based on an optimistic view of the potential of human nature for development, and will be a society of peace, harmony, unrestricted liberty and order. For collectivist anarchists, altruism will be nurtured by common ownership or mutualism; for individual anarchists, autonomy and rationalism will flourish with the absence of the state, allowing natural order to develop spontaneously.

Some anarchists, including Kropotkin, have defended this form of utopian thinking. It forces revolutionaries to question their assumptions about the existing order, such as the right to private property. Revolutionaries also need to consider what they want to achieve and what concrete, practical strategies they will need to put into place to achieve it.

Criticism of anarchism as utopian comes in two forms – and anarchists have responses to each form.

- **Criticism:** Anarchism has been a historical failure as no anarchist society has been created, so in this sense it is unachievable.

233

- **Response:** No ideal socialist or liberal society has been achieved either. Anarchist experiments have been seen during the Spanish Civil War in the 1930s and the Rojava revolution in Syria (2012 to the present). Anarchists may also point to the Zapatista rebellion, which is still in place more than 20 years after the initial uprising. Kropotkin would also argue that his philosophy is 'scientific', based on natural laws that show that the struggle for survival in nature is collective, and only the most co-operative will prosper.

- **Criticism:** Anarchism is unrealistic as its view of human nature is wrong, and natural order will not happen. If selfish, competitive and antisocial traits are natural and not caused by social institutions, society will be a free-for-all where the rich, the cunning and the powerful dominate.

- **Response:** Anarchism is based on a realistic understanding of human potential. Despite the state, humans have shown their altruism in forming organisations without authority. This is seen in how people organise in times of revolution as in Rojava, or in times of emergencies, strikes and disasters. At the fringes of the state, people organise into direct-action communities, co-operatives and community action, such as Reclaim the Streets or Occupy Wall Street. Anarchist organisation is a seed in modern society, buried under the weight of the state and capitalism, but ready to grow.

Pause & reflect

To what extent is a future society based on liberty and economic freedom where anarchy is order possible?

Case study: Anarchism and punk

Anarchism and punk are closely linked. Many think that the Sex Pistols' *Anarchy in the UK* put anarchy and punk together.

Opposition to repression by state and society summed up the punk ethic. This can be seen in the sarcasm of *Leaders of Men* by Joy Division, the anti-monarchy theme of *God Save the Queen* by the Sex Pistols and The Clash's cover of *Police and Thieves*, which attacks the police and politicians. The establishment and the mainstream press identified punk as a threat to the state and society.

Another element of punk that links into anarchism is its 'do it yourself' nature. Many punk bands refused to work with major labels, setting up their own labels to produce, market and distribute their records, while fanzines sprung up in place of the music press. Musicians could keep control over the production of their music and how it would be used in the future. For example, Crass organised their own record label, packaged their own work, distributed it and organised their own concerts. The aim was to get music out there, make enough money to live on and not to have to bow down to the capitalist instincts of the major labels.

Questions

- How can punk and anarchism be linked?
- Can punk's DIY nature be seen as a form of anarchist direct action?

1.2 Different types of anarchism

Anarchists agree on many central themes and assumptions, as shown in Figure 2.1.

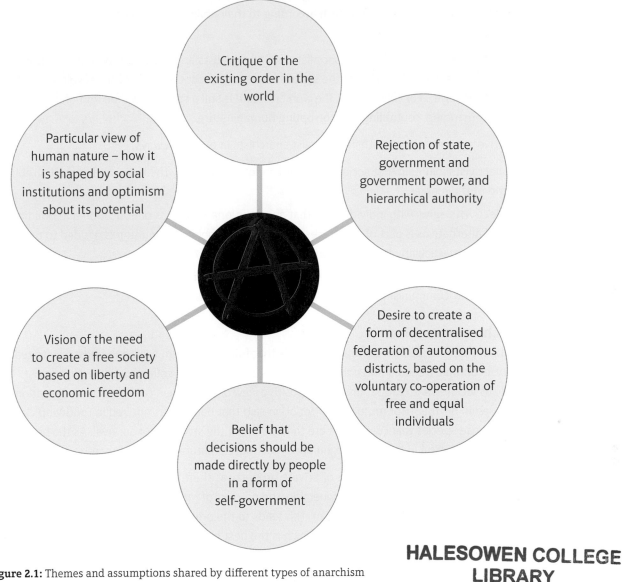

Figure 2.1: Themes and assumptions shared by different types of anarchism

However, within this broad agreement, anarchists hold very different views about human nature, leading to a range of criticisms of the existing order and different views of liberty and the ideal society.

Collectivist anarchism

Proponents of collectivist anarchism argue for the stateless society, where common ownership will nurture the rational, altruistic and co-operative elements of human nature. Collective anarchism has its roots in socialism. Closely associated with Bakunin, it pushes socialist collectivism to its furthest limits. Collectivism is essentially the view that, at its core, human nature is altruistic, co-operative and sociable. The natural relationships between people are mutual aid, social solidarity and harmony, which can be nurtured by the right social institutions. However, human nature is socially determined and the state's limiting of freedom, defence of inequality and private property creates disharmony, greed and envy.

Collectivism involves the dismantling of the state and the abolition of private property. Land and the means of production are held in common ownership, but the individual would own the product of their own labour. Society would be organised from the bottom up into voluntary collectives of producers and consumers, who would organise the production and distribution of goods. Within this society, the principle of 'from each according to their ability and to each according to their work done' would apply.

While all collectivist anarchists are socialists, not all socialists are anarchists. Anarchists disagree with the Marxist view that calls for the socialist state to protect the gains of the revolution until the state withers away. For collectivists, the workers' state is still a state, so will be immoral and unjust while commanding, controlling and corrupting human nature.

Collective anarchists clash with individualist anarchists in two main ways.

- Collectivists maintain that social problems cannot be solved by the individual or the invisible hand of the market.
- Collectivists agree with individualists that an evolutionary process of education and building social alternatives is part of the process of change, but believe revolution is needed to destroy authority (particularly the institution of private property).

Within the collectivist strand, there are three sub-strands that develop this thinking in different ways: anarcho-communism, mutualism and anarcho-syndicalism.

Anarcho-communism

The theory behind anarcho-communism holds that full communism will be the best way to realise liberty, economic freedom and natural order. This is the strand of collectivist anarchism most closely associated with Kropotkin and his positive view of the human capacity for co-operation, expressed in his theory of mutual aid. Kropotkin said that nature was not 'red in tooth and claw'; in fact, those species that co-operate are the winners in the struggle for survival. As the human species is successful in this struggle, humans must have a natural capacity for co-operation.

Anarcho-communists view all forms of private property as theft. As well as land and the means of production being held in common ownership, the product of individuals' labour should be held in common too – a break from collectivism. This leads to the principle of 'from each according to their ability, to each according to their need', which is the best basis to nurture the human capacity for mutual aid and altruism. In terms of society, Kropotkin focuses on the commune, made up of the entire local population, rather than the collective, made up of producers and consumers. These communes would be small scale, allowing for **direct democracy**, and all the wealth would be held in common. Individuals would be part of these communes based on voluntary agreement, and communes would be connected in voluntary federations that would work on all levels, from local to international.

Mutualism

The bridge between collectivist and individualist anarchism is mutualism. It emerges from Proudhon's critique of property. When Proudhon said 'Property is theft', he was targeting large property owners who could exploit the masses by charging high rents and interest, and pay them low wages that did not reflect their hard work. This criticism of property has returned to the centre of politics in the wake of the global economic crash of 2008, with the slogan 'We are the 99 per cent' and the Occupy Wall Street movement.

> ### Key term
>
> **Direct democracy**
> a form of popular self-government in which citizens make law and policy decisions in person, rather than through elected representatives.

The Occupy movement has anarchist roots with David Graeber, an anarchist activist and thinker closely involved in its early stages.

However, Proudhon is also critical of collectivism for valuing the collective over the individual – a form of oppression and servitude. He supports the right to possession – the right to use the land, tools and skills necessary to ensure that the individual is economically independent – which breaks with the idea of common ownership. Possession is his antidote to both collectivism and private property and the basis for his theory of mutualism.

The economic organisation of mutualism is based on individuals and small associations with the right to possession, who would keep the full fruits of their labour. These individuals and associations could then exchange their produce based on a system of labour notes, to make sure everyone had access to the necessities of life. Labour notes would record the working time that went into the making of each product. There would also be a People's Bank that would not make any profit, but would provide credit to the associations.

On a political level, these associations would be drawn together in a vast federation, with councils co-ordinating at local and international level. The councils would be made up of delegates from the associations, who would be subject to instant recall. The whole system would be organised from the bottom up, with no central authority, and would be based on voluntary agreements.

Anarcho-syndicalism

The ideas behind anarcho-**syndicalism** build on Bakunin's view of collectivism and his strategy of propaganda by the deed. In this strand of anarchist thinking, the trade-union movement is the revolutionary agent of change. Trade unions will continue to campaign for improved conditions and pay for workers, as well as educating them. Trades unions can then build economic institutions that are horizontal, not hierarchical, and provide self-management in the economy. These new institutions, built within the existing state, will prepare the way for the mass strike as the 'propaganda by the deed' to trigger a social revolution. After the revolution, these institutions will provide the basis for the future stable, stateless and peaceful society.

Key term

Syndicalism
revolutionary trade-unionism that uses direct action and the mass strike as an expression of working-class power to inspire popular revolt.

237

Case study: The Confederación Nacional del Trabajo (CNT)

The highpoint of anarcho-syndicalism came in the Catalonia region of Spain, from 1911 through to the late 1930s. The CNT was formed in 1911 as a non-hierarchical, horizontal federation of many syndicates or unions. During the Spanish workers' revolution of 1936, which began during the outbreak of the Spanish Civil War, the CNT put its ideas into practice. Free collectives organised and administered factories, mills, docks, transport, shops and utilities without managers or the state. Peasant collectives took control of the land owned by the church and landlords. A committee was elected to run each collective and work was parcelled out among small groups, with delegates from each collective coming together to co-ordinate. Economic equality was created on the principle 'to each according to their need, from each according to their ability'. George Orwell described his first-hand impressions of anarchist Spain in his book *Homage to Catalonia*. He describes his time in Catalonia as like emerging into 'an era of equality and freedom' where 'human beings were trying to behave as human beings and not as cogs in the capitalist machine'. The revolution was finally crushed by the Nationalists under General Franco, leading to the establishment of his dictatorship.

Questions

- How can the Spanish revolution be seen as anarchism in practice?

- How far does the Spanish revolution show that anarchism is not utopian?

'The final blow must be struck' – the worker in anarcho-syndicalist colours of red and black defeating the snake representing Franco. The swastika on the snake's tongue represents the Nazi support of Franco in the Civil War.

Individualist anarchism

Classical liberalism is pushed to its extremes by individualist anarchism. It sees society as a collection of separate individuals whose autonomy must not be restricted in any way. The state with its coercive powers of taxation, conscription and law is totally incompatible with autonomy. This goes beyond classical liberalism as it rejects the need for a 'night watchman' state to protect freedom. Provided there is no restriction on individuals, their rational nature will allow them to work together through voluntary association, resolving all disputes by reason rather than violence. This is the basis of natural order and a peaceful society.

This leads to a direct tension with collectivist anarchism in two areas.

- **Fear that individuality and autonomy will become subject to the collective:** The individualist fears being forced to join a community and losing their freedom. In particular, the abolition of private property will leave the collective with power over the individual. This leads to individualists accepting the ideas of Proudhon's possession rights added to real, free competition in their economic model.

- **Tension over strategies for overthrowing the state:** Individualists argue for education, the use of non-violent forms of social protest and the creation of alternative horizontal institutions like workers co-operatives and the People's Bank. These new organisations, built within the shell of the existing state, will finally replace the state in an evolutionary process. They oppose the revolutionary strategy of overthrowing the state, as it involves the forcible taking of property – an authoritarian act that violates autonomy and individuality.

Within individualism, there are two sub-strands that develop this approach in different ways: egoism and anarcho-capitalism.

Anarcho-capitalism

Supporters of anarcho-capitalism wish to dismantle the government, which they believe is exploitative through its use of taxation, violating the private property of the individual. The state also intervenes in the market, creating public and private monopolies that restrict freedom. In anarcho-capitalism, all contracts would be entered into freely and would only be regulated by the market, rather than the individual being forced to pay tax and having to use public services. All services currently provided by governments, such as policing, courts and roads, would be handed over to the free market. Competition will give consumers a choice, forcing the suppliers to be efficient, cost effective and more likely to reflect consumers' needs.

The critical element of anarcho-capitalism is the belief in the invisible hand of the free market and private property, so the profit motive and the wage system would remain. This has led many anarchists to argue that anarcho-capitalism is not a strain of anarchism at all, because its view of liberty does not include equality. Only the rich and powerful will be free, and they will be free to protect their own privileges through private protection bodies and resolve disputes through private courts, that would only serve those who paid the most.

Egoism

The concept of egoism can be seen as the most challenging and radical version of individualism. It argues that individuals are entirely self-interested; their only concern is the 'ego'. The individual should act in any way they choose, and there should be no restriction on autonomy or individuality. The state is a tyranny that limits, controls and subordinates the individual to the general will, so it must be abolished. Egoism also argues that the individual must reject society and in particular religion, sexual morality and the moral values imposed on all by their parents.

Egoism is most closely associated with Stirner. In economic terms, Stirner rejects capitalism, believing that anyone who works for another is exploited and alienated. Work should be purposeful and useful to the individual, and they should retain the full fruits of their labour while rejecting the right to private property.

To many, this looks like Hobbes' state of nature and a war of all against all. However, egoism disputes this, saying that, in the Union of Egoists, individuals will come together through voluntary agreements, which would not involve any giving away of individual liberty. As individuals are entirely rational and serve their own interests, they will make agreements to benefit themselves, as it will be fulfilling for their own ego. This will be the basis for a union that is peaceful and stable.

Pause & reflect

What are the key differences and similarities between individualist and collectivist anarchism?

1.3 Anarchist thinkers and their ideas

This section explores how the anarchist thinkers and their ideas have influenced anarchist thought in relation to the state, society, economy and human nature.

Max Stirner (1806–56)

Key ideas:

- The individual 'ego' must be placed above all else, and not limited or controlled.

- The Union of Egoists is based on the conscious, self-interested will of each individual.

Max Stirner is the most radical and challenging of anarchist thinkers. In his book, *The Ego and His Own*, he develops a comprehensive criticism of the state and existing society. This was based on his view of human nature as one of autonomy, rationalism and self-interest.

Max Stirner: 'There is no judge but myself who can decide if I am right or wrong.'

- **The Ego:** Stirner underlines the unique individuality of each person, which should not be limited. The 'ego' must be placed above all else and there must be an end to the control of our thoughts by existing societal institutions, such as the church and morality. In economic terms, Stirner rejected existing work as limiting the 'ego', because it is not fulfilling and the individual cannot keep the full fruits of their labour. This criticism of the state and hierarchy has power for anarchists today, who feel individuality is crushed by law, habit, custom and prejudice, while in the workplace people are increasingly carrying out tasks that are unnecessary and unrewarding.

- **Union of Egoists:** Stirner's vision of the future is of a free society living in the interests of all individuals, based on voluntary agreements made as they serve the individual's own personal interest, not for the common good. This Union of Egoists will be achieved not by revolution, which is authoritarian, but by insurrection. This insurrection involves the individual becoming an egoist and withdrawing from capitalist labour and the state, so that the state will decay and die.

Pierre-Joseph Proudhon (1809–65)

Key ideas:

- Private property is exploitative and divisive.
- Mutualism is the economic basis of liberty.
- Change should be evolutionary, not revolutionary.

In his book, *What is Property?*, Proudhon provides the bridge between individualism and collectivism in anarchism.

Pierre-Joseph Proudhon: 'Property is theft.'

- **Opposition to private property:** Proudhon attacks the view of private property – the ability to extract rent, interests and profits – as exploitative and divisive, and at the heart of capitalism. This view is further developed by collectivist anarchism and is central to the idea of the 99 per cent vs the 1 per cent, which has been developed by the Occupy movement. Proudhon endorses the right to possession, and the right for the individual to keep the full fruits of their labour, as a protection for the individual against the collective. Within this system, worker co-operatives would organise their own work and mutually exchange their goods with other individuals and co-operatives, based on labour notes that record the working time taken to create a product. An example of co-operatives working in the modern world would be the Mondragon Co-operative Federation in Spain, which has as its slogan 'Humanity at work', and has a wage differential of around 1:6 between the lowest and highest wage earners within its individual co-operatives.

- **Mutualism:** This idea fits more closely with individualist anarchism. This system of mutualism would be the economic basis of liberty; the political aspect would be based on federalism and decentralisation. The latter would be organised from the bottom up, with most power lying in the small, local bodies and the least power in the largest bodies. All federations would join together using voluntary agreements and have the liberty to leave at any time.

- **Evolutionary, not revolutionary:** Proudhon rejects the state as entirely without morality but makes the case for constructing the new society within the shell of the existing state. Anarchists should establish mutualist organisations, such as worker co-operatives and a People's Bank, which would form the basis of future society. In this evolutionary process, the state will die away rather than being overthrown in a revolutionary action.

Mikhail Bakunin (1814–76)

Key ideas:

- Human nature as social.
- Propaganda by the deed.

Bakunin is one of the most notorious radicals in history. His form of radical, revolutionary anarchism was critical of capitalism, Marxism, the state and religion, and is the foundation of collectivist anarchism.

Mikhail Bakunin: 'If there is a state, there must be the domination of one class by another and, as a result, slavery.'

- **Human nature as social:** Bakunin's view of human nature stressed rationality and individuality but argued that humans were, by their very nature, social beings who could not exist outside of society. Bakunin argued that human beings are shaped by the society they live in, so need to achieve liberty to explore the full potential of their human nature. This liberty can only be achieved by the rejection of the state and the authority of the church. In terms of the economy, Bakunin calls for **collectivisation**. This involves the abolition of private property and its replacement with the collective ownership of the means of production, because liberty without equality is just privilege and injustice.

- **Propaganda by the deed:** In his revolutionary strategy, Bakunin rejected all traditional forms of parliamentary politics and all Marxist calls for capturing the state. Bakunin argued the masses had to free themselves, and this could only be achieved by the destruction of the state. This belief in the revolutionary will of the people led Bakunin to argue for the 'propaganda by the deed', such as the non-payment of taxes, rents and debts, mass strikes and the refusal of conscription or the draft. These actions would be the catalyst for a spontaneous revolution from below and the people would be freed through the practice of direct action, empowering individuals and exposing the mechanisms of power. In many ways, this emphasis on direct action and DIY politics feeds into the spirit of political rebellion today, inspiring the Occupy Wall Street movement and the anti-globalisation movement as a whole.

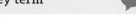

Key term

Collectivisation
the abolition of private property and its replacement by a system of common ownership.

Peter Kropotkin (1842–1921)

Key ideas:

- Mutual aid.

- Education then revolution.

- Utopian.

Kropotkin adopted a scientific approach to his study of human nature and society, and used this to underpin his philosophy of anarchism. He is a key influence on the anarcho-communist strand.

Peter Kropotkin said that anarchism is 'not only against Capitalism, but also against these pillars of Capitalism: Law, Authority, and the State.'

- **Mutual aid:** In his book *Mutual Aid*, he argues that, in nature, the survival of the fittest is a race between species, and mutual aid is the key factor for success. Where members of the same species show high levels of sociability and work together, they succeed in the evolutionary race. Kropotkin then applies this to human nature, arguing that humans have always been co-operative and altruistic – this can be seen in the types of society that pre-date the emergence of the modern state. The logical outcome of this is the emergence of anarchism. Kropotkin opposed the state and capitalism and argued that, if they were removed, humans would act in line with their true nature of altruism. This type of mutual aid, outside the existing state structures, can be seen in society in examples such as the Black Panther food and survival programmes of the 1960s and 1970s, which included free ambulance provision, breakfast for children and dental services.

- **Education then revolution:** Kropotkin endorsed a strategy for change based on education, but he realised that any revolution to end the oppression and injustice of the state and capitalism would be violent. It would be necessary for the masses to take the land, the means of production and social goods to satisfy their needs and see that the new world works for them, leading to a future society where war and violence would no longer exist.

- **Utopian:** Future society had to be utopian in order to develop criticisms of existing society and practical strategies for change. Kropotkin only gives an outline of what that future society might look like. Economically, it would be based on communism, where the means of production would be owned collectively. Each would work according to their ability and receive according to their need. The communes would be voluntary and connected in federations based on direct democracy, starting from the local unit upwards. This would nurture altruism and, together with the end of private property and poverty, would create a peaceful, harmonious society.

EXTENSION ACTIVITY

Read the principles of solidarity from the Occupy Wall Street movement at www.occupywallstreet.net/learn. To what extent are these principles based on anarchist ideas?

Emma Goldman (1869–1940)

Key ideas:

- The state and violence.
- Opposition to parliamentary politics.

Emma Goldman offers a powerful contribution to anarchism in her critique of the state, which was tied closely to her view of human nature. Goldman drew on the ideas of Stirner in that she supported the autonomy of the individual, but also those of Kropotkin, in her theory of social harmony.

Emma Goldman said that the machinery of government is made up of 'the club, the gun, the handcuff, or the prison'.

- **The state and violence:** Goldman argued that all forms of government rely on violence, particularly focusing her anger on patriotism and militarism. Internally the state uses the law, the police and the threat of violence to control; it is immoral as it restricts autonomy and individuality. Externally, the state is a body of competitive struggle, constantly looking to expand its power through the use of the military. Patriotism is used by the state to force obedience to the flag and state, stir up divisions with others and fund a growing military to control the increasing discontent of the masses, both domestically and globally. This patriotic lie undermines social harmony and universal brotherhood. Goldman's criticisms of patriotism have grown in relevance with the rise of patriotism and nationalism in the increasingly unstable 21st-century world.

- **Opposition to parliamentary politics:** Goldman contributes to anarchism by developing a critique of parliamentary politics, which she believed was reformist and corrupting. She did this using the example of the women's suffrage movement. Once women have won seats in the legislature, rather than reforming the system, Goldman argued, they will become corrupted by authority in the same way as working men have been. Even if reform could be achieved, working within the state will not tackle the real causes of oppression that lie in the state, hierarchical authority structures like the church, private property, and existing social and sexual conventions. Goldman argued that the ballot would not set women free, and that emancipation can only come from within by each woman asserting her individuality. This view is important both as a development of individualist anarchism and in relation to the modern **feminist** movement.

Link

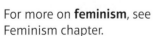

For more on **feminism**, see Feminism chapter.

EXTENSION ACTIVITY

Noam Chomsky is regarded as one of the leading voices in anarchism today. Research Chomsky to find out his views on anarchism and its prospects for being realised.

Pause & reflect

Draw a grid with the key thinkers as the rows and the state, the economy, human nature and society as the columns. Add in the key ideas of the thinkers where they apply.

Assessment support: 2.2.1 Anarchism

The non-core political ideas question is on Paper 2, Section B. It is worth 24 marks and must be completed in 30 minutes. All ideas questions start 'To what extent', a key instruction directing you to look at conflicting or competing views. You are given a choice of two questions in this format, of which you should answer one.

EITHER

3 (a) To what extent is anarchism more united than divided? [24 marks]

OR

3 (b) To what extent do anarchists agree over their view of the economy? [24 marks]

You must use appropriate thinkers you have studied to support your answer and consider both sides in a balanced way.

This question tests all three Assessment Objectives, with marks divided equally between them. You must:

- set out the nature of the debate

- draw similarities and differences between the different strands or tensions

- use at least two relevant thinkers.

Your answer should make judgements based on evidence about the significance of the differences and similarities, leading to a clear and justifiable conclusion.

- Always plan before you write. What are the key similarities and differences between the main strands (collectivist versus individualist)? Expand these into the sub-strands (mutualism or anarcho-capitalism) to develop your answer. What ideas from key thinkers are valid for this answer? Try planning answers to the two questions listed above.

- Your essay should include a brief introduction outlining the main arguments, four main points and a conclusion that should reach an overall judgement that naturally flows from the question.

Here is part of a student's answer – the first paragraph after the introduction – to question 3 (b). The introduction laid out the main ideas and the similarities between the strands over their desire for economic freedom and opposition to existing economic systems. This next paragraph explores the differences in their views about the economy.

The collectivist anarchist views private property, which Proudhon defines as the right to own without the need to occupy, as the key issue in modern capitalism as it drives inequality and exploitation. The ownership of private property means the wealthy can earn income through rent, interest and the exploitation of labour whilst doing no work themselves. The masses have no choice but to work under the threat of violence as if they don't they will lose their homes, be imprisoned for debt or left to starve. No choice means no freedom, so private property, inequality and the state that enforces it must be overthrown and this idea was a driving force behind the Occupy Wall Street's slogan, 'We are the 99%'. However, within collectivist anarchism, there is disagreement as to whether private property should be replaced by collective ownership, as Bakunin argued, or ownership based on use under mutualism, as Proudhon argued.

- This paragraph reveals a clear understanding of the key ideas that unite collectivist anarchists in their opposition to private property and inequality.

- It makes the key point that without economic equality there can be no freedom, which is a core principle of anarchism.

- Key thinkers are used to explore the core ideas within collectivist anarchism.

CHAPTER

2 Ecologism

The Earth is under severe stress. It faces a range of different threats: global warming, climate change, ozone depletion, **biodiversity** depletion, deforestation and the poisoning of the Earth through pesticides, fertilisers and waste. If humanity continues to damage the Earth at its current rate, its ability to sustain life may come to an end. This is the idea that has placed ecologism at the forefront of politics in the 21st century.

Key term 💬
Biodiversity the diversity of species within a biotic community, which brings the benefits of health and stability to the community.

This chapter looks at:

- the core ideas of ecologism
- how these apply to human nature, the state, society and the economy
- the different views and tensions within ecologism
- the key ideas of some of ecologism's key thinkers.

Pause & reflect ✔
Before reading on, think about what you know on the following questions. What are the main threats facing the Earth? How seriously do politicians take these threats? What measures have been put in place to tackle the threats?

2.1 Core ideas and principles

Ecologism is a broad movement that shares some common ideas and values. It sees humans as an integral part of nature, and so by harming nature, humanity is also harmed. It agrees that current rates of economic growth and consumption are not sustainable so action must be taken. Its goal is a future, sustainable society.

Ecology

All strands of green thinking have ecology as the central principle. Ecology is a science that studies animals and plant systems in relation to their environment. It looks at ecosystems – interacting communities of living organisms and non-living components of their environment, such as air, water and mineral soil. The key lessons of ecology are the interdependence of all different life forms and how they are sustained by the ecosystems within which they live. Humans must live in harmony with their ecosystems so they maintain the balance that supports all life.

Ecology challenges the view that humanity is nature's master. Instead, ecology sees a planetary web of interrelationships between all forms of life and the environment. These interrelationships indicate a sense of equality, as all life forms and the environment are dependent on each other.

EGO   ECO

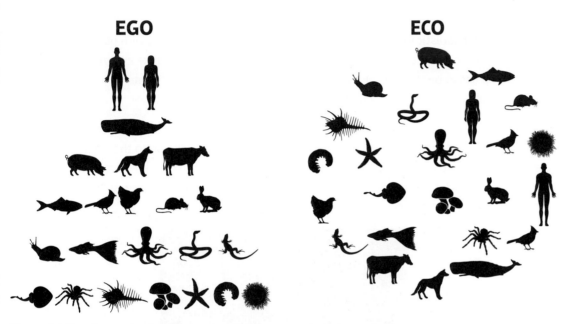

Figure 1.1: Does humanity dominate nature or is it one species among many?

The ecosystems, which support all life including humanity, are at their most stable when they have high levels of biodiversity. The natural world is made up of many ecosystems, such as lakes or forests, which make up the largest ecosystem of all, the Earth. However, humankind, through its desire for economic growth, has depleted natural resources such as oil and polluted the air and water, and forced species into extinction. Humanity is damaging the stability and balance of the Earth on which it relies for life.

This radically different understanding of nature and humanity's relationship to it has led to the rise of **ecocentrism**, which contests **anthropocentrism**.

The different strands of green thinking have developed ecology in two separate ways.

- **Shallow green** thinking argues that people should love and protect the natural world so that it continues to sustain human life (enlightened anthropocentrism). This leads to a focus on reducing pollution and using renewable sources of energy, such as solar power.
- **Deep green** thinking argues that ecology shows that humanity is not at the top of the pyramid of nature and that all species, including humans, are equal. Nature does not exist to sustain human life but rather nature has intrinsic value (ecocentrism).

Key terms

Ecocentric
a nature-centred rather than human-centred system of values that gives priority to ecological balance.

Anthropocentric
humans are separate from and superior to nature. Humans have intrinsic value while the rest of nature is just a resource that may be exploited to benefit humanity.

Link

For more on **shallow green** and **deep green ecologism**, see Section 2.2.

Link

For more on **Carolyn Merchant**, see Section 2.3.

Key term

Mechanistic world view the post-Enlightenment view in science that nature is a machine where the parts can be understood, fixed or replaced in isolation.

Holism

Holism is a core idea within ecologism. It states that the properties of a given system cannot be explained by its component parts alone. Instead, the system as a whole determines how the parts behave.

Mainstream political thinking has always seen nature as an economic resource, ready for human use. Ecologist **Carolyn Merchant** argued that this way of viewing nature was formalised during the Enlightenment, which radically changed scientific and philosophical thinking.

- Francis Bacon developed scientific methods and aims based on the idea that nature exists for humanity's use and benefit.
- René Descartes saw animals and plants as biological machines, subject to universal laws.
- Isaac Newton argued that the world could be best understood by reducing it to a collection of separate particles.

This led to a **mechanistic world view** that considered nature as a machine, with parts that can be repaired, improved or even replaced – a reductionist approach that broke everything into constituent parts to be studied in isolation. Under this view, nature is a resource to be exploited and ecological issues can be tackled through technological solutions.

Ecologism argues for a move away from this mechanistic world view towards holism. The parts of our world are interdependent and each can only be understood in relation to the whole. This leads to a drive to understand the large-scale cycles that link soil, rock, atmosphere, water and organisms together. These cycles are deeply complex and not fully understood by science, so humanity should respond to nature with respect and caution.

Ecologists argue that those who want to intervene in nature – such as fracking companies – need to prove that their actions will not harm the environment.

Green pressure groups and political parties are often criticised by deep greens as not pushing holism far enough as they tend to focus on single issue environmental concerns such as the energy crisis, animal rights and protection of the oceans. This form of shallow green thinking sees each environmental problem as a separate issue, with an individualised campaign and separate solution. It fails to take into account the need for a more radical holism that sees all the issues as interlinked and proposes a radical solution that tackles the main underlying issue of humanity's relationship to nature.

Case study: Fracking

Despite protests outside North Yorkshire County Council in May 2016, approval was granted for a fracking operation in Ryedale – the first in England since a ban was lifted in 2012.

Fracking is the process of drilling down into the Earth, then pumping a high-pressure mixture of water, sand and additives at the rock to release the oil and natural gas inside. The British Geological Survey estimates that UK shale gas resources may be 50 per cent larger than conventional gas resources. It is argued that shale gas has the potential to provide the UK with greater energy security, growth and jobs while producing electricity at half of the carbon-dioxide emissions of coal.

However, opponents of fracking, such as Friends of the Earth, raise many environmental concerns. Fracking needs huge amounts of water, which have to be transported to the fracking site. The additives include potentially carcinogenic chemicals that may escape into the groundwater (the industry says that this would only happen due to bad practice, but opponents say it is an inherent risk of fracking). Opponents say that, ultimately, electricity generated by shale gas and oil would still be emitting carbon dioxide, so instead there should be a commitment to renewable energy from wind, wave and sun.

In the UK, the issue is made more controversial by the fact that in 2015 parliament voted to allow fracking 1,200 metres below national parks, areas of outstanding natural beauty and world heritage sites. Fracking in North Yorkshire has attracted considerable opposition from local groups who argue it will create water contamination, earthquakes and noise and traffic pollution close to urban populations.

Questions

- Should fracking be banned?
- How is the debate about fracking similar to the debate about nuclear power?

Pause & reflect

What are the key principles of ecologism and holism? How can they be applied to politics?

Environmental ethics

Conventional ethics are clearly anthropocentric – they only apply to human beings. The only value placed on nature is its value to humanity. For example, a living forest has no value until it is cut down and sold as timber. There is still an environmental ethic here, but it is in human terms – people should respect the environment because pollution damages human health, loss of biodiversity threatens the ecosystems humans are part of, and climate change puts human lives at risk.

However, ecologists aim to move beyond conventional ethics to environmental ethics. This has been attempted in three main ways.

Intergenerational equity

In 1987, the World Commission on the Environment and Development issued *Our Common Future*. The report called for development that would meet the needs of the present 'without compromising the ability of future generations to meet their own needs'. This extended moral obligation to include the principle of intergenerational equity – giving rights to those yet to be born – because many environmental issues, such as resource depletion and climate change, will have a far greater impact on future generations than on current ones.

This raises two key questions.

- How can the needs of the present generation be weighed against the needs of future generations?
- What are the needs of the present and future generations?

Animal rights

Peter Singer and Tom Regan led the way in extending ethical theory to the animal world. In *Animal Liberation*, Singer argued that animals are sentient – they can experience pleasure and pain like humans – so should have rights. For Regan, animals are 'subjects of a life' – they are a somebody, with a life of their own where what happens to them matters to them, so they should have rights. Both extend rights to animals and raise the issue of speciesism – discrimination on the grounds of species alone – asking whether it can be justified.

Theories of animal rights can be seen as too individualistic, failing to take account of the need for holism in terms of wider ecosystems. The introduction of the European rabbit into Australia in 1859 created a rabbit population explosion that has led to serious soil erosion through burrowing and overgrazing. Does humankind have a responsibility to control the population through extermination? How does this fit with animal rights?

Holistic ethics

Holistic ethics takes the ideas of environmental ethics much further and is closely associated with deep green thinking. It has two key elements.

- Moral obligations must extend to a much broader community. For example, **Aldo Leopold** included 'soils, waters, plants and animals, or collectively: the land'.
- All aspects of the non-human world have intrinsic value, rather than just the value placed on them by humanity. This would make an action right, as Leopold argues, if it preserves 'the integrity, stability and beauty' of the biosphere, and wrong if it did otherwise.

This raises the question of what happens when the rights of humans clash with the rights of the non-human world, or with the rights of the Earth. If the biggest danger to the Earth is humans, what should be done with humanity?

Link

For more on **Aldo Leopold**, see Section 2.3.

EXTENSION ACTIVITY

Consider the R. Attfield thought experiment: if all humans and animals have died and you were the last person on Earth, faced by the last surviving elm tree, would it be morally wrong for you to cut it down? Consider your own view then use conventional ethics and the three environmental ethics to answer the question.

Environmental consciousness

Some deep green thinkers have challenged the idea that creating additional moral principles to protect the environment is productive. Instead they demand an entirely new world view – an 'eco-philosophy' that puts consciousness first.

The idea is that human nature needs to undergo a radical change, an inner revolution. Individuals need to move from an egoistic sense of self to a wider sense of self, based on the idea that humanity is not separate from nature, but is interconnected with it. This has to involve the widest possible identification with the non-human world. There will be no need for ethics, because the individual will have an **environmental consciousness**, which will lead them to protect nature and let it flourish, as that will allow the self to flourish.

This consciousness idea has drawn on eastern mysticism, especially Zen Buddhism, which preaches the unity of all things and pantheism – the view that God is identical with the entire universe, so all things are God.

However this view has taken considerable criticism from shallow greens as too vague to be of practical use. Social ecologists, such as **Murray Bookchin**, criticise it as spiritual 'eco-la-la' built around mysticism rather than rational thought.

Key term

Environmental consciousness
a state of being where an individual's sense of self comes from a deep identification with the non-human world.

Link

For more on **Murray Bookchin**, see Section 2.3.

> **Pause & reflect** ✔
>
> How does green thinking move beyond traditional ethics?

Post-materialism and anti-consumerism

Ecologism looks to change not just the ethical framework, but also what is meant by happiness and fulfilment. This includes criticisms of the existing understanding of the world and proposals for future society.

The first key concept of existing society that ecologism opposes is materialism, the tendency to consider material possessions and physical comfort as more important than spiritual values. Materialism links happiness to the consumption of material goods; happiness can be bought. Greens criticise materialism because ever-increasing consumption drives ecological problems. The consumption of material goods depletes the planet's finite resources and increases production, which drives increasing pollution.

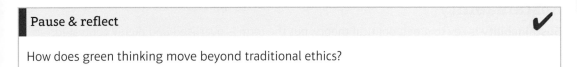

Figure 1.2: The chain of drivers of ecological problems

Consumerism worsens the problems of materialism by increasing the desire for consumption. Consumerism is the idea that the increasing consumption of goods is good for the economy and for the individual. Consumerism keeps generating new needs so consumers keep aspiring to own the latest car, gadget and fashionable home with the right address to increase their social status.

However, the consumption of material goods creates the constant desire for more, leading to unhappiness. This idea was best explained by Herbert Marcuse, who differentiated between false

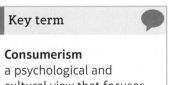

Key term

Consumerism
a psychological and cultural view that focuses on consuming goods and services as a means to feel good about oneself and drive economic growth.

needs and basic needs. Consumerism, driven by advertising, creates false needs. In their desire to meet their false needs, individuals are driven to overwork, often in jobs they do not enjoy, and miss out on activities that bring happiness, so generating toil and misery. False needs also drive us to fulfill these needs at the expense of the basic needs of others.

For shallow greens, the answer to consumerism and materialism is to do more with less.

For deep greens, this is not enough – society should do less with less, and needs a radical transformation in order to value quality over quantity. There needs to be a clean break between happiness and consumption, as greens such as **E.F. Schumacher** argue, and a move to 'right livelihood', which generates a maximum of well-being from a minimum of consumption. This will be a society built around satisfying everyone's basic needs. It will be 'poorer' in conventional economic terms, but in fact richer, as it will be a life built around justice for all peoples, more rewarding work, greater care and compassion and deeper respect for the planet.

> ### Pause & reflect
>
> How and why do ecologists challenge existing ideas of human happiness and fulfillment?

Sustainability

Sustainability is key to green political theory, but the term is overused and highly contested. Sustainability is the capacity of the ecological system (the Earth) to maintain its health over time. Ecologists see the current system of production and growth as unsustainable as it will damage the health of the Earth beyond repair, so plan for what a future sustainable society might look like.

Mainstream political thinking has the view that there are unlimited possibilities for economic growth, and supports **industrialism** – where human life is dominated by industrial mass-production and limitless growth. Green theory directly challenges this view, arguing that there are limits to growth because resources are finite and scarce. In 1972, the Club of Rome global think-tank commissioned a report called *The Limits to Growth*. The report presented the results of a computer model designed to show what would happen in a world with economic and population growth, but finite resources. When they ran the model on the basis of consumption as usual, the **limits to growth** were reached due to resource depletion. When they doubled the resources available, the model collapsed due to pollution. The modelling continued introducing a new solution to fix the previous reason for its collapse. Ultimately, the modelling showed that the limits to growth were always reached, even when all solutions were in place, showing industrialism to be unsustainable.

The problem is clear. A growth rate of 3 per cent is considered desirable in economic terms, but this implies a doubling of production and consumption every 25 years on an Earth that is finite. This is not sustainable, as it damages the ability of the planet to maintain its health and very existence over time.

Green thinking suggests some solutions.

Shallow greens support weak sustainability – the idea of getting richer but at a slower pace. Economic growth is desirable but should meet the needs of the present generation, without compromising future generations. This approach allows natural capital – the world's natural resources such as geology, soil, air, water and all living things – to be used up as long as it contributes to creating manufactured capital of equal value. So coal and oil can be used up, and carbon dioxide emitted into the atmosphere as long as enough infrastructure such as roads,

Link

For more on **E.F. Schumacher**, see Section 2.3.

EXTENSION ACTIVITY

Can the deep green view of a society that is poorer in economic terms but richer in terms of quality of life attract widespread popular support?

Key terms

Sustainability
the capacity of the ecological system to maintain its health over time – one of the most contested ideas in ecologism.

Industrialism
based on large-scale production, a faith in science and technology and limitless growth to satisfy material needs.

Limits to growth
the finite Earth, with the scarcity it implies, places limits on industrial growth.

airports and sea ports are built with it. And there is a strong belief that technological solutions can solve the environmental problems caused by increased production of goods and services.

Weak sustainability can be achieved in two ways.

- **Green capitalism** uses the market to deliver environmental solutions through technology solutions and capitalism's response to ecologically aware consumers.
- **Managerialism** uses regulations at state, regional or global level to tackle environmental problems. It takes forward the idea that the state and international bodies will take a managerial approach to capitalism using regulations and targets to deal with environmental issues.

Deep greens and social ecologists are very critical of this position. They support strong sustainability, which opposes economic growth, materialism and consumerism. This viewpoint holds that natural capital should be preserved and proposes a living economy that works within the Earth's budget of energy and resources, often based on E.F. Schumacher's 'small is beautiful' theory.

The energy debate illustrates the issues around sustainability. Economic growth and increasing levels of wealth have been driven by energy from fossil fuels such as coal, gas and oil. However, fossil fuels are natural capital and they are non-renewable so cannot be replaced. With 80 per cent of the world's consumption of energy coming from these sources, they are running out and becoming harder to extract. At the same time, they are seen as largely responsible for human-created global warming. Does sustainable policy involve drastic cuts to fossil-fuel use and a move to renewable energy? Or does it involve going further and offering an alternative view of how the economy needs to work?

Key term
Green capitalism the idea that the market will deliver environmental solutions, based on a faith in technology solutions and capitalism's response to ecologically aware consumers.

Link
For more on **green capitalism** and **managerialism**, see Section 2.2.

Mojave Desert solar power plant: an example of sustainability?

Case study: Sustainable development

Sustainable development has become the mantra of international bodies such as the UN, World Bank and IMF. Economic growth over recent decades has come at the expense of the environment and poor communities. There are 1.2 billion people who still lack access to electricity, 870 million are malnourished and 780 million are still without access to clean, safe drinking water. At the same time, natural capital has been used in ways that are wasteful, inefficient and have created high levels of pollution with real consequences for the environment. The World Bank says sustainable development is growth that 'must be both inclusive and environmentally sound to reduce poverty and build shared prosperity for today's population and to continue to meet the needs of future generations'.

Sustainable development is based on three key pillars: economic growth, social justice and stewardship (the duty to protect and conserve the environment). One complication is the idea of social justice and how sustainable development can work to tackle poverty and inequality. For example, if living standards for all humans were to be raised to the level of an American citizen, resource consumption would increase sevenfold – impossible, given the limits to growth.

Questions

- Can poverty be tackled today while meeting the needs for future generations?
- Can development be sustainable?

Pause & reflect

What are the different interpretations of sustainability?

2.2 Different types of ecologism

Deep green

Deep green thinking argues for a radical change in how the world is seen.

- It calls for the adoption of a new world view to replace the mechanistic and reductionist thinking that has dominated since the Enlightenment. This is holism taken to a radical extreme.
- It dismisses the idea that humanity is master of nature or the steward of nature.
- It dismisses the idea that the lessons of ecology can be balanced with anthropocentrism, and so argues for ecocentrism. This argument clashes with the shallow green view of enlightened anthropocentrism.
- Human beings need to undergo a radical change in consciousness to embrace ecocentrism.

The opposition to anthropocentrism emerges from two key sets of ideas.

- Deep green thinking moves beyond traditional ethics. Nature is viewed as having intrinsic value rather than just the value attached to it by humanity for the benefits it brings them. All living beings have the 'equal right to live and bloom', which is most clearly expressed in the concept of **biocentric equality**. A clear example of this type of moral thinking is found in **Aldo Leopold's** land ethic. This raises criticisms from shallow greens and social ecologists as it appears to give an equal right to humanity and the smallpox virus.
- Deep green thinking offers a philosophical challenge to the way humanity understands the world. The human spirit should be understood to be fundamentally interconnected and

Link

For more on **Aldo Leopold**, see Section 2.3.

Key term

Biocentric equality
the radical idea that all beings within the biotic community have equal intrinsic value.

interdependent with nature. This spiritual merging of the self with the universe leads to the radical shift in consciousness necessary to accept ecocentrism.

This leads deep green thinking to see environmental damage not as the result of a particular system such as capitalism or industrialism, but rather as the result of the mechanistic world view that underpins these ideas. This world view regards nature as inert and without value, just a pool of resources to be exploited to meet the desires of humanity. This view has to be challenged and overthrown in favour of an ecocentric view that gives priority to ecological balance rather than achieving human aims.

Deep ecology has some wider objectives in terms of state, society and economy to achieve its ideals.

- **Population control:** Since Paul Ehrlich's *The Population Bomb* (1968), deep green thinking has been associated with the idea that population growth threatens the biosphere. Most deep greens now oppose this idea, saying it is not about how many people, but how society is organised. The concentration of land in the hands of the few is crucial. The halving of the Central American forest between 1950 and 1990 was not due to population explosion but because the land was concentrated in the hands of rich ranchers growing crops for export. Many deep greens would also say that it is the greed of the wealthy, not population growth, that is degrading environments. About 80 per cent of natural resources are consumed by about 20 per cent of the Earth's population.

Forest being cut down to make way for an African oil plantation.

- **Living economies:** Economies must be rooted in strong sustainability, protect the Earth and people's livelihoods, and provide for their vital needs. All goods and services should be produced locally, with local resources and knowledge wherever possible. These sustainable local economies support national or international economies. The work and livelihoods of people within these local communities should be equitable, fulfilling and closely tied to local ecosystems. It is about promoting the quality of life rather than materialism and consumption. Humans will become reconnected with the land, nature and natural cycles and so their wealth will come from their ability to fully experience life.

- **Living democracy:** Democracy will be based on local communities, based on diversity and inclusion. Decisions, taken locally, will be ecologically and socially responsible as the people are so connected to the natural world. These local communities will be organised within 'bioregions'

– geographical areas based around ecosystems, whose boundaries are created by physical and environmental features – and will create a local living based on the resources available. This is a radical challenge to existing territorial divisions, which are based on national or state borders.

> **Pause & reflect**
>
> What are the key similarities and differences between shallow and deep ecologism?

Shallow green

Shallow green thinking is reformist as it believes it can reconcile the lessons of harmony and balance from ecology with anthropocentrism. In their principle of enlightened anthropocentrism, humans must live in harmony with nature and maintain its balance so the Earth can sustain human life. There are three key features of shallow green thinking.

- **There are limits to growth:** The Earth's finite and limited resources probably cannot support the existing rates of economic and population growth due to the environmental damage it will cause. Pollution, resource depletion and the impact of carbon-dioxide emissions on climate change threaten future prosperity.

- **Weak sustainability:** There is a commitment to getting richer more slowly and more smartly by developing a form of environmentally sound capitalism.

- **Intergenerational equity:** The current generation has a duty to conserve nature and the Earth for the benefit of the next generation and all generations to come. This places humanity as the steward of nature rather than its master.

There are three main policy approaches that develop from shallow green thinking.

- **Green capitalism:** This is an emphasis on market-based solutions to environmental problems, which can be achieved in four ways.
  - The ethical consumer can use their purchasing power to make sure goods are produced in a more environmentally sensitive way. Campaigns can be used to target the bottom line for companies, such as Greenpeace's campaign against Nestlé in 2010 including its KitKat spoof advert, which led to Nestlé announcing a zero-deforestation policy in its palm-oil supply chain.
  - As natural resources, such as oil and coal, become scarce, rising prices will increasingly restrict their use.
  - Rising prices will force companies to innovate and research cheaper substitutes, decreasing the use of natural resources.
  - Corporations are committed to making profit, and the only way this can be achieved in the long term is by adopting a sustainable approach.

- **Managerialism:** The state and international bodies take a managerial approach to capitalism using regulations and targets to deal with environmental degradation.
  - At an international level, the UN Framework Convention on Climate Change is an example of emerging treaties and conventions that aim to provide a framework for environmental protection at an international level.
  - These plans are enacted at state level, with developed countries taking the lead through the idea of common but differentiated responsibilities. The UK government will have to focus on UK emission cuts, as well as supporting developing countries to move to low-carbon

economies, deal with climate disasters and adapt to the adverse effects of climate change. The UK passed its own Climate Change Act in 2008, which commits the UK to reducing carbon-dioxide emissions by 80 per cent by 2050, at an estimated cost to the UK economy of about 1 per cent of GDP each year.

- Governments can use green taxes to adjust prices so that they reflect the true cost of an economic activity – including its environmental cost. This uses the strength of the market to deliver sustainability by driving companies to seek technological solutions. For example, a tax on air emissions would lead some factories to add pollution controls, some to change to cleaner manufacturing processes and others to redesign their products to make them more sustainable.

- **Technological solutions:** Research and developments in science can help tackle environmental degradation and allow for sustainable growth. For example, a key strategy to meet the target of keeping climate change by 2100 to 2 degrees or less is the development of carbon-capture technology, to capture and store carbon dioxide from the atmosphere to combat global warming. According to the International Energy Agency, this will involve removing and storing carbon dioxide power plant emissions by more than 2 billion metric tonnes per year by 2030, and 7 billion metric tonnes by 2050. Currently there is only the capacity to capture and store 40 million metric tonnes per year, and the technology is too expensive and too limited to be commercially successful.

Such was the high level of air pollution that in 2013 The World Health Organization equated a day breathing the air in Cairo to smoking one packet of cigarettes.

There is debate within shallow green thinking over whether protection over the environment is best left to the unregulated market (green capitalism) or managed capitalism (managerialism), although both viewpoints have faith in technological solutions.

Case study: IPCC

The Intergovernmental Panel on Climate Change (IPCC) is the international body for assessing the science related to climate change. In its fifth assessment report of 2014, the IPCC made the following points.

• Human interference on the climate system is clear and various scenarios are modelled up to 2100 to show how different levels of temperature increase will impact on humanity and the planet. Climate change is a collective problem that will need to be solved by nations working together to tackle it.

• The business-as-usual model shows humanity continuing to burn significant amounts of coal, and greenhouse gas emissions continuing to increase at their present rapid rate. This model will lead to a 4 to 6 degree temperature rise by 2100. The results are severe and widespread impacts on unique and threatened systems, substantial species extinction, large risks to global and regional food security, and the combination of high temperature and humidity compromising normal human activities, such as outdoor work. Climate-change impacts are expected to worsen poverty in developing countries and create increasing inequality in both developed and developing countries.

• The Paris Agreement of 2016 established the international aim of keeping global warming below 2 degrees, with the best case being 1.5 degrees or less. In order to meet the target, carbon-dioxide emissions need to be cut by 40 to 70 per cent by 2050, with the burning of fossil fuel almost entirely phased out by 2100. At the same time, low- or zero-carbon energy sources, such as wind, solar and nuclear, will need to increase from the current share of 30 per cent to more than 80 per cent by 2050. This will also involve the use of untested technologies, such as carbon capture. Even at less than 2 degrees, there is likely to be increasing water scarcity, more people affected by heat stress, more people affected by flooding, lower crop-productivity and the loss of biodiversity.

Questions

• How significant are the risks of doing nothing?

• How far do you agree that the target of keeping global warming below 2 degrees is possible?

EXTENSION ACTIVITY

Do some research to find three examples where ethical consumers or political campaigns have been used to challenge companies to become more environmentally friendly.

Pause & reflect ✔

Can markets protect the environment?

Social ecology

Social ecology refers to a wide river of ideas that link present ecological problems to deep-seated social problems. In order to solve ecological problems, it is necessary to tackle the way human beings deal with each other. Like deep green thinking, a radical change is needed. However, for social ecology, this will involve a radical social change that will overthrow societies built on hierarchy, domination and class relationships.

Social ecology breaks downs into three strands: ecosocialism, eco-anarchism and ecofemimism.

Ecosocialism

Capitalism, with its never-ending desire for greater profit, is the core cause of social exclusion, inequality and environmental degradation. So the ecological crisis is best tackled by the overthrow of capitalism.

Capitalism is seen as ecologically destructive for a variety of reasons.

- **The desire for profit in capitalism is relentless:** Profit can only continue to grow in a system with continuous and exponential growth in production.
- **Capitalism is based around commodity production:** This leads to the commodification of nature, best explained through the Marxist term 'exchange value'. Everything is valued for its monetary exchange value (the price of water) and not for its use (water's use of sustaining life).
- **Green capitalism cannot save the planet:** Capitalism is based on exponential growth, which cannot be greened. Technology cannot save capitalism as the technology available is decided by large corporations based on the profit motive, not on ecological motives. As Henry Ford explained, his company did not make mini-cars for the US, as mini-cars make mini-profits.
- **Private property:** Ownership of land is constantly encouraging the idea that humanity dominates nature. By moving to collective ownership, humanity will use the land in the best interests of all, not the few.

For John Bellamy Foster, an environmental proletariat is being created by economic and environmental hardship. Capitalism will suffer worsening economic and environmental problems in its desire for profit. These crises will drive the environmental proletariat, who cannot afford the increasing cost of scarce resources, such as food, water or energy to revolt.

Eco-anarchism

Eco-anarchism, which is closely identified with **Murray Bookchin**, argues that the idea that humanity must dominate nature comes from the concept that human beings must dominate each other. All forms of hierarchy, such as the state, capitalism or racism involve the domination of one individual or group by another. These hierarchies are linked to the hierarchy that places humanity above nature, with the Earth seen as just a pool of resources to be exploited. It is this that is driving the ecological crisis. For example, social oppressions within capitalism force peasants to cut down forests to survive, destroying their way of life in the process.

Eco-anarchism sees a clear relationship between the principles of anarchism and the lessons of ecology. In ecology, harmony and balance develop naturally on the Earth without the need for any external control or authority. In the same way, in anarchism a peaceful, stateless society develops naturally out of social solidarity between humans. It is the imposing of authority and control on human by human, and by human on nature that disrupts that natural order.

As the ecological crisis has its roots in the social problems of hierarchy and domination, then the solution must lie in radical social change. The hierarchical structures such as the state and capitalism must be overthrown and replaced with social solidarity and mutual respect. These principles are best expressed in **decentralised**, community-based and directly democratic means of organisation. The harmony between humans would extend to a harmony with nature, leading to a strong-sustainability approach.

Bookchin is critical of anthropocentrism, based on the lessons of ecology, as he dismisses the idea that humanity can be the master of nature. He is equally dismissive of ecocentrism, as it blames humanity for the ecological problems, not the impacts of the hierarchy of human relations with each other and nature.

Ecofeminism

Nature is a feminist issue as there are important connections between the domination of women and the domination of nature. Ecofeminism wishes to make clear the links between women and nature and, where they are a source of harm, to overthrow them.

Link

For more on **Murray Bookchin**, see Section 2.3.

Key term

Decentralisation basing society around communes, villages or bioregions that can achieve sustainability through a high level of self-sufficiency, making them dependent on their natural environment.

Before the 17th century, nature was regarded as alive, female and nurturing, and this placed moral restraints on how nature should be treated. The scientific and cultural revolution made nature passive, inert and dead. Nature remained female but now as it was dead, the moral restraints were lifted. Modern science could endorse nature's exploitation in unrestrained economic growth and a society that subordinates women.

During this change in views, women were removed from their role in midwifery, lost control over their bodies and were removed from their role in production. They were made subordinate to men in science, socially and in the sexual division of labour. This patriarchal domination of nature and women needs to be overthrown and nature should no longer be seen in gender terms. This will lead to a more holistic view that sees humanity in partnership with nature.

Pause & reflect

What are the key features of social ecology? How does it differ from shallow green and deep green thinking?

Human nature	Ecologists, based on the principles of ecology and holism, do not see humans as separate from and superior to nature, and reject the anthropocentric ideas that humans are masters of nature. Shallow ecologists support a form of enlightened anthropocentrism, where humanity recognises itself as part of nature and should act as a steward, maintaining it to sustain human life. Deep greens take a more radical position, arguing that humans are fully interconnected with nature, giving rise to the principle of ecocentrism. This is expressed through the environmental ethics such as biocentric equality, or through the idea of environmental consciousness brought about by an inner revolution within individuals that fundamentally changes their view of human nature.
The state	There is agreement among ecologists that the state has been part of the problem as it has promoted industrialism, causing critical environmental issues. However, there is disagreement as to whether the state is part of the solution. Shallow greens argue that the state can take a managerial approach, using targets and regulations, or focus on green capitalism to tackle environmental problems. Deep greens and social ecologists do not see the state as part of the solution. Deep greens argue for living democracies that are decentralised and based around bioregions – not states – and that will be ecologically and socially responsible. Social ecologists argue that states and societies built on hierarchy, domination and class relationships must be overthrown so humanity can work in partnership with nature.
Society	Green thinking sees consumerism and materialism in society as driving ecological problems. For shallow greens, with a strong faith in technological solutions, the focus is on doing more with less in environmentally smarter ways. For deep greens and social ecology, there needs to be a clean break between consumerism and happiness. The future society will do less with less, focusing on the basic needs for all and building society around justice for all peoples, more rewarding work, greater care and compassion and deeper respect for the planet. This future society will be decentralised and community-based, and will use direct democracy.
The economy	Ecologists accept that there are limits to growth, which clash with the industrialism of mass production and limitless growth that has been damaging the sustainability of the planet. Shallow green thinkers support weak sustainability and would achieve it by managerialism or green capitalism. Deep greens and social ecologists support strong sustainability. This is a direct challenge to the mechanistic world view, which sees nature just as a pool of resources to be exploited. Deep greens argue for living economies that are built around principles like Buddhist economics, which will promote quality of life, provide vital needs and reconnect people with nature.

Table 2.1: Core principles and ideas of ecologism in action

2.3 Ecologist thinkers and their ideas

Aldo Leopold (1887–1948)

Key ideas

- The land ethic.
- The failure of conservation.

Leopold's work predates the rise of ecologism, but has become an inspiration particularly for deep green thinking.

Aldo Leopold: 'A thing is right when it tends to preserve the integrity, stability and beauty of the biotic community; it is wrong when it tends otherwise.'

- **The land ethic:** Leopold extended the biotic community to include the non-human world – 'soils, waters, plants, and animals, or collectively: the land'. Within this land community, humans are not conquerors but members and citizens, who should respect fellow members and the community as a whole. This creates the idea of biocentric equality, where all beings and the community itself have equal intrinsic value. Biocentric equality is a basis for a new form of ethics for society, changing how humanity sees its place in the world.

- **The failure of conservation:** Leopold argues that conservation fails as it is still based on an economic model, rather than moving beyond economics to a new human–land relationship. From his perspective, economics does not understand how to deal with or value concepts like wilderness, beauty or land health. Instead society has adopted a simplistic economic model based on growth and land degradation. He argued that the ideas of public ownership by the state or regulation of private ownership of the state was not enough to ensure conservation. For Leopold, what was needed was a new type of relationship with the land – his land ethic – which would require 'a new kind of people'. This would involve a real change in human nature, as well as in the structures of the economy, state and society. It turns on its head the mechanistic world view of science that sees nature as of no value in itself and only as a resource for humanity to exploit.

Rachel Carson (1907–1964)

Key ideas

- Gods of profit and production.
- Science and sustainability.

Rachel Carson's book *The Silent Spring* (1962), brought to public attention the issues around pollution while highlighting the science of ecology. It has served as a key inspiration to ecologism as it identified the issues that needed to be tackled without offering a political strategy to tackle them.

Rachel Carson: 'Man is a part of nature and his war against nature is inevitably a war against himself.'

- **Gods of profit and production:** *Silent Spring* (1962) is regarded as a key inspiration to the ecologism movement, and made many people aware of the science of ecology for the first time. The book investigated the use of pesticides in agriculture in the USA, which were promoted as economically beneficial by big business and the state through the Department of Agriculture. Carson's focus was the chemical DDT, used during the Second World War to kill lice on soldiers. Carson argued that an excess of DDT and out-of-work pilots encouraged the government and business to find other uses for the product, which led to it being used as a spray to control pests such as mosquitoes and fire ants. The big idea that Carson was able to get across was that 'the gods of profit and production' were the key destructive forces at work in modern society.

- **Science and sustainability:** Carson argued that humanity should not seek to dominate nature using science in the name of progress where the science is mechanistic and reductionist. The use of scientific and technological innovation could easily damage the Earth's fragile ecosystems. The continued use of DDT would lead to a time when 'the birds had disappeared and spring was silent'. She argued that humans were part of the vast ecosystems of the Earth, like all other living beings. If humankind continued to poison nature, it would lead to a time when nature would poison humankind.

E.F. Schumacher (1911–1977)

Key ideas

- Buddhist economics.
- The problem with traditional economics.

Schumacher's work has been very influential on green thinking through his attack on modern economics and globalisation. His ideas about human scale, decentralisation and appropriate technologies provided a criticism of existing practices and a blueprint for the future.

E.F. Schumacher: 'Any intelligent fool can make things bigger, more complex, and more violent. It takes a touch of genius – and a lot of courage to move in the opposite direction.'

- **Buddhist economics:** Schumacher argued for a form of Buddhist economics – economics founded on the principle that people matter – based on a maximum of well-being and a minimum of consumption. His thinking draws inspiration from the Buddhist principle of non-violence and applies that principle to the impact of economics on both society and the biosphere. He observes an increasing move to gigantism, where bigger is better. Global corporations mass-produce cheap products that damage the environment, using mechanised production lines that strip work of its satisfaction. Industrialised agriculture destroys local environments and causes mass unemployment and migration to cities destroying local communities. Schumacher focuses on small-scale organisations, using local resources and highly skilled labour to produce very high-quality products as the basis for sustainability in nature and human happiness.

- **The problem with traditional economics:** Schumacher launches a direct attack on traditional economics. He views the obsession with GDP growth as hugely damaging, as it sees natural resources as income (which is renewable) when it is in fact capital (it is depleted by being used). GDP also views growth as good, linking consumerism and materialism to happiness, so it fails as a measure. Schumacher argues that quality of goods should replace quantity and that spiritually fulfilling work based on human creativity should replace dehumanising work to earn money in order to consume.

Key term

Buddhist economics the idea that economics should be built on the principles of 'right livelihood' rather than on an obsession with economic growth.

EXTENSION ACTIVITY

Listen to the podcast at www.theguardian.com/commentisfree/audio/2011/nov/09/big-ideas-podcast-schumacher-small-is-beautiful-audio. What are the key principles of 'small is beautiful'?

Murray Bookchin (1921–2006)

Key ideas

- Domination.
- Ecotopia.

Bookchin coined the phrase 'social ecology' and was a pioneer of the ecologist movement that was anti-capitalist and pro-decentralisation.

- **Domination:** Bookchin argues that ecological destruction is the result of social structures of our society based on the domination of man by man. Sexism, racism and exploitation of the Third World are based on the same domination as the destruction of the rainforests. Capitalism, which drives materialism and consumerism in the name of corporate profits and the state that protects and promotes this market society are the social structures of this domination. Ultimately this domination of man by man needs to be destroyed through radical social change.

- **Ecotopia:** Bookchin argues that humanity can learn lessons from ecology. His new society – ecotopia – would be a confederation of self-governing communes based on the principle of direct democracy. This view has informed both eco-anarchism and the wider green movement. In economic terms, Bookchin proposes a version of '**anarcho-communism**' based on the abolition of private property, the principle of distributing goods according to need and a reduction in the time spent working. Ecotopia replaces domination with social solidarity and this would lead to a harmonious relationship with nature that would be deeply appreciative of the needs of non-human life.

Link

For more on **anarcho-communism**, see Section 1.2 of Anarchism.

Carolyn Merchant (1936–)

Key ideas

- Science and the domination of nature and women.
- Overthrow patriarchy.

Carolyn Merchant was one of the first thinkers to make the connections between the domination of women and the domination of nature. These connections led to a dramatic expansion in ecofeminism.

- **Science and the domination of nature and women:** Merchant challenged the consensus view that mechanistic science was a marker of progress for society, saying that instead the scientific revolution of Bacon, Descartes and Newton is implicated in the ecological crisis, the domination of nature and the oppression of women. Her core idea is that nature is cast in the female gender. In the scientific revolution, nature was portrayed as inert and passive, so could be dominated by science, technology and capitalism. Nature's 'womb' had symbolically yielded to the 'forceps' of science. Nature's womb hides the secrets of nature that technology takes to benefit humanity. She highlights the parallels between the violent approaches of controlling unruly nature and unruly women.

- **Overthrow patriarchy:** The scientific view that Merchant was arguing against, most closely associated with Bacon, was that nature should be bound into service by humanity; in the same way, women should be bound into service. Nature is turned into a vast pool of material resources to be exploited for the good of humanity, just as women would be made to forcibly breed more workers, all in the name of economic profit. Patriarchy, which is a relationship of domination in society, needs to be overthrown and a new spirit of partnership created between humanity and nature, where nature is no longer seen as mother, virgin or witch but rather as an active partner.

EXTENSION ACTIVITY

Arne Naess is regarded as laying out the principles of deep ecology. Research his principles at www.deepecology.org/platform.htm to find out what his understanding of deep ecology is.

Pause & reflect

Draw a grid with the key thinkers as the rows and the state, the economy, human nature and society as the columns. Add the key ideas of the thinkers where they apply.

Assessment support: 2.2.2 Ecologism

The non-core ideas question is on Paper 2, Section B. It is worth 24 marks and must be completed in 30 minutes. All ideas questions start 'To what extent', so you must look at both sides of the debate. You are given a choice of two questions in this format, of which you should answer one.

EITHER

3 (a) To what extent is ecologism more united than divided? [24 marks]

OR

3 (b) To what extent are ecologists in agreement over their view of the economy? [24 marks]

You must use appropriate thinkers you have studied to support your answer.

These questions each test all three Assessment Objectives, with marks divided equally between them. You must:

• set out the nature of the debate

• draw similarities and differences between the different strands or tensions

• use at least two relevant thinkers.

Your answer should make judgements based on evidence about the significance of the differences and similarities, leading to a clear and justifiable conclusion.

• Always plan before you write. What are the key similarities and differences between the main strands (deep versus shallow versus social ecology)? Expand these into the sub-strands (eco-anarchism or eco-socialism or eco-feminism if needed) to develop your answer. What ideas of key thinkers are valid for this answer? Try planning your answer to the two questions listed above.

• Your essay should include a brief introduction outlining the main arguments, four main points and a conclusion that should reach an overall judgement that naturally flows from the essay.

Here is part of a student's answer to question 3 (b) – the first paragraph after the introduction. The essay has laid out the main ideas, the agreement over their criticism of the existing economic model and this is developing the different approaches to the economy going forward.

Ecologists are divided over what the term sustainability means and the best methods that should be employed to achieve it. Shallow greens emphasise weak sustainability, which involves continued economic growth, but at a slower rate that works within limits of growth. Sustainability will involve meeting the means of the present generation without comprising the rights of future generations. This will be achieved by working within existing state and economic structures through a mixture of green capitalism, managerialism and ever-improving technology. However, social ecologists and deep green thinkers see this as merely treating the symptoms rather than causes, and argue for a more radical transformation of the economy. Deep greens such as E.F. Schumacher argue for an economy built around the principle of right livelihood, which would be based on strong sustainability.

• This reveals a clear understanding of the key ideas of shallow green thinkers and the key areas of disagreement.

• It defines the term sustainability and the methods to achieve it from a shallow perspective.

• It offers clear disagreement with the shallow and social ecologist view, which can be developed in the later paragraphs.

CHAPTER 3 Feminism

Feminism is an ideology that has at its core the belief that society and related institutions, as they currently stand, do not always work equally in the interests of women and men. However, feminism has many different strands, some of which are diametrically opposed to each other.

While it is impossible to date when the role of women first became an issue in society, it is widely accepted that the Enlightenment period brought this debate to the fore. Mary Wollstonecraft wrote her key work *A Vindication of the Rights of Woman* in 1792, and her ideas were supported by liberals Jeremy Bentham and John Stuart Mill.

The history of feminism is often described as occurring in waves. The 'crest' of each wave signifies the heights of feminist pressure, often resulting in some level of 'success' and then retreating to the background until further issues and problems arise, starting the next wave.

First wave	Second wave	Third wave	Fourth wave
1850s to 1940s	1960s to 1980s	1990s	2008 onwards

Figure 0.1: The waves of feminism

Link

For more on **suffrage**, see Section 1.2 of Democracy and Participation.

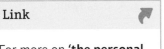

Link

For more on **'the personal is political'**, see Section 3.1.

- First-wave feminism focused on the legal and political rights of women, most famously in the UK through the suffragette movement, which culminated in equal **suffrage** with men in 1928.
- Second-wave feminism focused on the different roles that society expected of men and women. This was where the concepts of patriarchy, sex and gender, and **'the personal is political'** were discussed.
- Third-wave feminism, which emerged in the 1990s, was concerned with the idea that feminism had solely focused on white middle-class women, failing to recognise the concerns of women of other cultures.
- Fourth-wave feminism – Some suggest that a new wave of feminists are reacting against inequality based on media images of women, online misogyny and issues arising through the expansion of social media.

In this chapter you will learn about:

- the core ideas behind feminism
- different types of feminism
- key feminist thinkers and their contribution to the debate.

3.1 Core ideas and principles

The ideas discussed in this section are primarily associated with radical feminism – a type of feminism that arose in the second wave. Radical feminism introduced new words and concepts into our language to analyse, explain and challenge society's views of women. While it was not the first time the role of women was discussed in society, previous discussions had focused on the role of women using the language of liberalism or socialism.

Sex and gender

One of the main areas of focus for feminists has been why society has believed that women should focus on the domestic side of society, such as housekeeping and child-rearing. For many feminists, the answer can be found in the blurring of the concepts of 'sex' and 'gender'.

Sex refers to the biological differences between men and women – their body shape, size, and sexual and reproductive organs. Gender is used to explain the 'innate character' of men and women – for example, women are sensitive, emotional and caring while men are confident, logical and responsible. Feminists argue that, whereas biological differences are clear, there is no evidence or justification for gender roles being ascribed to people. From culture to culture, the biological differences between men and women do not change, yet different cultures have very different ideas as to what constitutes masculinity and femininity. This shows that gender is learned behaviour imposed by society.

In society, the terms masculine and feminine are used to describe an 'ideal' gender type for men and women to aspire to. Feminists argue that this is a key part of the way society seeks to keep women in a subordinate position. It is no surprise that the key characteristics for women to aspire to are to be calm and passive, compassionate and thoughtful, poised and elegant. Virginia Woolf gives a telling description in *A Room of One's Own* (1929), where she describes 'the Angel in the House':

> She was intensely sympathetic. She was immensely charming. She was utterly unselfish. She excelled in the difficult arts of family life. She sacrificed herself daily. If there was chicken, she took the leg; if there was a draught she sat in it – in short she was so constituted that she never had a mind or a wish of her own, but preferred to sympathize always with the minds and wishes of others. Above all – I need not say it – she was pure. Her purity was supposed to be her chief beauty – her blushes, her great grace. In those days, every house had its Angel.

Pause & reflect

Why do feminists find the use of the following words to describe men or women unacceptable?

• submissive	• clumsy	• passive	• sensitive
• logical	• aggressive	• athletic	• breadwinner

Patriarchy

The term patriarchy is used by most feminists to describe a society that is dominated by men and run in the interests of men. Most definitions identify patriarchy as a systematic oppression of women by men, suggesting that patriarchy is pervasive throughout society.

In *Theorizing Patriarchy* (1990), Sylvia Walby identified patriarchy's pervasive and systematic nature as 'a system of interrelated social structures which allow men to exploit women'. She argued that the six overlapping structures take different forms in different cultures and different times.

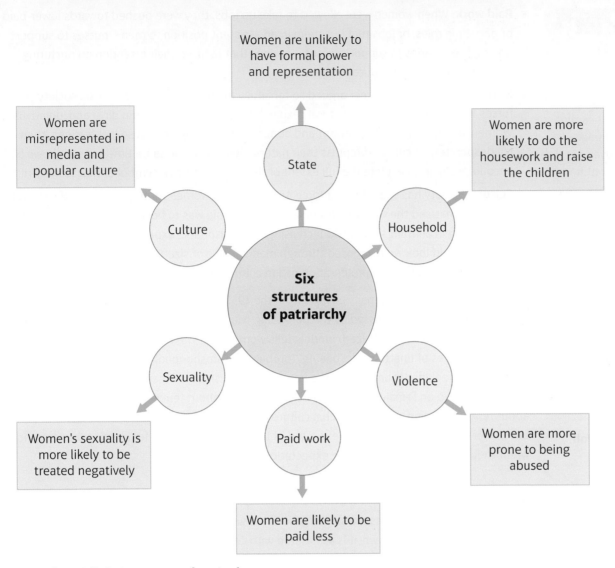

Figure 1.1: Sylvia Walby's six structures of patriarchy

Here is a closer look at Walby's six structures.

- **State:** Throughout history, women have been denied representation as well as being under-represented in the formal positions of power in the state. Even when they could take up these positions, they found the working hours to be anti-family, or the culture to be so sexist that they gave up these positions 'voluntarily'.

- **Household:** Women have been conditioned into believing that domesticity is destiny, and have been discouraged from pursuing occupations that take them out of the home. Many feminists agree with Kate Millett's view that 'the family is patriarchy's chief institution'.

- **Violence:** For many women, there is a 'dark side' to family life. Domestic abuse has only recently been taken seriously in society; in the past, it was not unheard of for police to consider it a private family matter and not for them to 'interfere'. According to statistics, two women are killed every week in England and Wales by a current or former partner (Office for National Statistics, 2015), one in four women in England and Wales will experience domestic violence in their lifetimes and 8 per cent of women will suffer domestic violence in any given year (Crime Survey of England and Wales, 2013/14).

- **Paid work:** When women were allowed to take up jobs, they were pushed towards lower-paid or part-time roles, or jobs that put them in an assistant position to men – nurses to support doctors, secretaries to support bosses – or ones that focused their attention on nurturing children, such as in the education sector.

- **Sexuality:** As Germaine Greer argued so forcefully in *The Female Eunuch* (1970), society forces women to repress their natural sexual desires and consider them dirty and 'unladylike'. Women spend years feeling deviant and abnormal for having normal sexual feelings, then try desperately to curb and repress their natural desires. At the same time society allows and encourages men to explore the full extent of their sexuality, as a symbol of masculine virility.

- **Culture:** Society has sought to reinforce its message to women through culture. Adverts in the 1950s emphasised the view that a woman's primary role was to be a good wife to her husband by excelling in all things domestic. Increasingly, unreasonable expectations of the way 'normal' women should look were imposed through media usage of size-0 models on catwalks and in advertising, as well as the proliferation of 'lad culture' magazines.

Feminists would argue that many adverts from the 1950s through to the 21st century clearly show how women are oppressed by the pervading values of patriarchy. They would argue that modern-day media usage of size-0 models tells women that the way they look is paramount, and these images of unattainable 'beauty' (probably photoshopped) seek to oppress women by making them feel inadequate about the natural, normal shape of their body. As **Naomi Wolf** said, 'a culture fixated on female thinness is not an obsession about female beauty; it is an obsession about female obedience'. So patriarchal culture uses the media (and now social media) to subtly, but powerfully, tell women what is expected of them and make them feel inadequate or abnormal when they are unable to meet these expectations.

Link

For more on **Naomi Wolf**, see Section 3.2.

The personal is political

'The personal is political' was the slogan associated with the rise of second-wave feminism. Although its origin is unknown, it is associated with Carol Hanisch and her essay of that name published in 1970.

Key terms

Public sphere
the area in society where relationships are public, specifically life outside the home, particularly society and work.

Private sphere
the area in society where relationships are seen as private, specifically home and domestic life.

Most feminists distinguish between the **public sphere** (society) and the **private sphere** (family). Traditionally, discussion about the subjugation of women had been limited to the public sphere. 'The personal is political' sought to convey the notion that all relationships between men and women are based on power and dominance, not just those in the public sphere.

The essence of this slogan was to highlight to women, and to wider society and politicians, that aspects of life that were considered 'personal' and therefore private (and no one else's business) were in fact part of a system that sought to repress women (patriarchy).

Take the extreme example of domestic abuse. In the 1960s and 1970s, domestic abuse was something that was largely ignored by society. When it was discussed, women were often blamed for provoking their husbands. Importantly, the pervading culture surrounding domestic abuse was that it was 'a private matter' and one that police and doctors should not intervene in. Today we can understand how flawed this thinking was.

Like domestic abuse, so many things in the 1960s and 1970s that oppressed women were considered 'normal' and 'private'. The message of 'the personal is political' aimed to raise awareness among women so that they could challenge the status quo. This brought feminism into the area of personal relations between men and women and in the family.

Women protest outside the Miss World competition in London, 1970.

Many feminists, including Kate Millett, have identified the family as a key area of women's oppression. They see the family as fulfilling several roles to keep women and girls 'in their place'.

- It socialises girls and boys to accept their different, hierarchic roles: daughters to show dependence, obedience, conformity and domesticity; boys to be dominant, competitive and self-reliant.
- It socialises women into accepting the role of housewife as a woman's only and most fulfilling role.
- Children see their parents acting out traditional gender roles and perceive these roles as natural and inevitable.
- Women are expected to carry out free domestic work, even when they are also doing paid work.
- Wives are expected to cater for the emotional, sexual and physical needs of their husband.
- Once married women have children, they sacrifice their career prospects and are expected to raise the children at whatever cost to their own paid work.
- Once women leave paid employment to raise their children, they find their promotion prospects blocked when they return.

Pause & reflect

How are the ideas of patriarchy and 'the personal is political' interrelated?

Equality feminism and difference feminism

Most feminists seek equality for men and women and believe that the biological differences between men and women are inconsequential in modern society. This view is known as **equality feminism**.

However, a small group of feminists, known as **difference feminists** or **essentialist feminists**, argue that men and women are fundamentally different from one another. This form of feminism, which arose in the 1980s and 1990s, is based on the belief that there are essential, biological differences between men and women.

Carol Gilligan's *In a Different Voice*, published in 1982, gave attention to the concept of difference feminism. She wrote that men and women think and speak in different ways and argued that women's voices and experiences had been ignored because they sounded so very distinct from men's. She argued that she was not making moral judgement about the differences, but just acknowledging they were there.

Difference feminists call for highlighting and valuing the differences between men and women, rather than encouraging women to deny their distinctiveness and seeking to be 'like men'. They believe that, by celebrating women's special and unique qualities, they will create a more female-oriented culture. They argue that traditional equality feminism has encouraged women to replicate men's behaviour and deny their own nature, which only alienates women from themselves. Difference feminism seeks to encourage women to accept and respect their own female qualities, which are (at the very least) as important as men's.

Some difference feminists go further, stressing the superiority of women's cultural values – such as compassion and pacifism – believing that these will overcome masculine qualities of selfishness, violence and lack of self-control in sexual behaviour. **Cultural feminism** also challenges the dominant cultural argument that women are inferior and subservient to men.

Key terms

Equality feminism
feminism that seeks equality for men and women in society and believes that the biological differences between men and women are inconsequential.

Difference feminism
feminism that argues that men and women are fundamentally different from one another.

Essentialism
for difference feminism this is the belief that biological factors are significant in the different behaviour of men and women.

Cultural feminism
a form of difference feminism that seeks to challenge the dominance of male culture in society by promoting 'women's values'.

Link

For more on **difference feminism**, see Section 3.2.

271

An extension of this view comes in the form of separatism and political lesbianism. Separatist feminism is not a unified view. Some separatists suggest that women should create permanent separate societies from men, while others suggest that women should, from time to time, create separate spaces and spend time without men in order to separate themselves from patriarchal society, allowing themselves to reconnect with their female values. Charlotte Bunch argued in *Learning from Lesbian Separatism* (1976) that 'in a male-supremacist society, heterosexuality is a political institution and the practice of separatism is a way to escape its domination'. This suggests that any relationship with a man is based on power and control, and the only equal relationship a woman can have is with another woman – so lesbianism is a political choice. Sheila Jeffreys was a proponent of this view and co-wrote *Love your Enemy?* in 1979.

It is worth noting that difference feminism has been extremely controversial among other feminist groups. They argue that suggesting that women have a passive, nurturing, caring nature takes women back hundreds of years and undermines all the progress that the women's movement has made.

Case study: Greenham Common Peace Camp

As well as the more prominent demonstrations, the protesters set up a permanent camp at Greenham Common.

The Women's Peace Camp was set up at Greenham Common in the 1980s.

A peace camp was set up in the 1980s at the RAF's Greenham Common base as a protest against the government's decision to site nuclear missiles there. What was unusual about this peace camp was its women-only nature. The protesters argued that women had a unique abhorrence towards missiles of mass-destruction as they were 'life givers' who had to protect their children and future generations – something that men could not understand.

Their mainly non-violent protest took the form of singing songs, linking arms to create a human chain around the base, sit-ins, lie-downs, camping, and chaining themselves to and cutting through the fencing. The women were a permanent fixture for 20 years. As they were legally trespassing, the police were called in to forcibly remove them. The scenes that followed were reminiscent of Gandhi and Martin Luther King's non-violent resistance. However, the media coverage was exceptionally hostile towards what was a largely innocuous protest.

The Greenham Common Peace Camp became a symbol of feminist protest against the male values of aggression and destruction.

Questions

- How is this an example of difference feminism?

- What explanations would feminists give to explain the hostile press coverage of the Greenham Common Peace Camp?

Intersectionality

The concept of intersectionality arose in the late 1980s and is associated with third-wave feminism. Intersectionality criticised previous forms of feminism for ignoring black and working-class women's experiences of patriarchy.

The term was coined by Kimberlé Crenshaw, when showing how black women were often marginalised by both feminist and anti-racist movements because their concerns did not fit comfortably within either group. She argued in 2015 that **intersectionality** 'has given many advocates a way to frame their circumstances and to fight for their visibility and inclusion'.

bell hooks in *Ain't I a Woman?* disputed the idea that 'women' were a homogeneous category essentially sharing the same life experiences. Her argument stemmed from the realisation that white, middle-class women did not serve as an accurate representation of women as a whole. Recognising that the forms of oppression experienced by white middle-class women were different from those experienced by black, poor or disabled women, feminists sought to understand the ways in which gender, race, religion and class combined to determine the female destiny. For example, the way Muslim women and working-class women experience patriarchy is different to the way middle-class white women experience it.

Intersectionality was aimed at widening the narrow focus that feminism traditionally had, to welcome the many different experiences that women from different cultures, classes and religions experience, and to give these women a voice.

> **Key term**
>
> **Intersectionality** an idea that challenged the notion that 'gender' was the singular factor in determining a woman's fate, arguing that black and working-class women's experiences of patriarchy are different from that of white, middle-class women.

3.2 Different types of feminism

Liberal feminism

Liberal feminism is probably best understood by taking the liberal values of individualism and foundational equality (all humans are of equal moral worth) and applying them to women. If all humans are of equal worth, and women are humans, women are entitled to the same rights and freedoms as men. Put simply, women should have all the freedom they need to become autonomous individuals in society.

Mary Wollstonecraft was one of the famous early liberal voices fighting for women's rights. When she published *A Vindication of the Rights of Woman* at the end of the 18th century, women's rights remained unconsidered. Wollstonecraft was determined to change this and to add a dissenting female voice to those demanding political emancipation.

> **Link**
>
> For more on **Mary Wollstonecraft**, see Section 2.3 of Liberalism.

Key terms

Gender equality
the belief that men and women are of equal value in society and should be treated the same.

Legal equality
no one is above the law and the law applies equally to all.

Political equality
equal right to vote and protest.

Equality of opportunity
all individuals have equal chances in life to rise and fall.

Link

For more on **Betty Friedan**, see Section 2.3 of Liberalism.

Key terms

Reformist
seeking to change society gradually and peacefully.

Gender stereotypes
the dominant and usually negative views in society on the different ways men and women should behave.

Discrimination
less favourable treatment of one group of people compared to other groups.

Liberal feminism was an early form of feminism primarily associated with the demand for women's suffrage. The assumption was that once women had a vote, they would have a voice, and politicians would need to listen to them if they wanted to be elected. Their aim after the vote had been achieved was equality in all areas of the law. Philosophically, they saw the individual as the basis for **gender equality**.

Liberal feminism is also concerned with the equal distribution of rights and entitlements in society, known as **legal** and **political equality**. Liberal feminists in the last century campaigned for educational equality, pay equality, abortion and divorce laws and freely available contraception for men and women. Liberal feminism also seeks to ensure equal access to the public sphere, which is connected to the liberal idea of **equality of opportunity**.

Betty Friedan is a clear exponent of this view. Her 1963 bestseller *The Feminine Mystique is* often credited with starting second-wave feminism. In it she outlined 'the problem that has no name', by which she meant the misery and frustration of middle-class women festering in domesticity, which was supposed to make them feel fulfilled but in fact trapped them. Friedan asserted that women were as capable as men in any career path and lobbied for the reform of laws that restricted women. Friedan believed that women were being held back from their full potential because they were limited to only a few jobs that were 'acceptable' for women.

Liberal feminism is **reformist**, believing that gender imbalance can be overturned primarily through democratic pressure. Further it believes that, once all barriers to women entering the workplace have been removed, it is merely a matter of time before women will enter all areas of industry. Liberal feminists believe that as women start doing traditional 'men's jobs', society will accept that there is no industry that women cannot work in. Also, the more young girls see women in all types of jobs and positions of responsibility, the sooner **gender stereotypes** of the past will start to disappear.

Unlike other types of feminism, liberal feminism does not seek to challenge the private, domestic sphere; it simply argues that society should give women (and men) the equal opportunity to stay at home or go out to work, or both. Thus liberal feminism does not believe that a fundamental restructuring of society is necessary. It rejects the idea of patriarchy as the pervasive and systematic oppression of women, instead highlighting **discrimination** against women – which, through the methods outlined above, will slowly disappear.

Pause & reflect

What links can you make between the liberal ideas you learned about in liberalism and liberal feminism?

EXTENSION ACTIVITY

Go online and look into 'Take your daughter to work' day. Why is this an example of liberal feminism in action?

Socialist feminism

Socialist feminism believes that gender inequality in society stems from economics and, more specifically, capitalism.

In 1884, in *The Origin of the Family, Private Property and the State*, Friedrich Engels noted that the move away from matriarchal societies to patriarchal ones coincided with the arrival of capitalism, and suggested that women were oppressed primarily by capitalism.

He argued that women served the needs of capitalism in several ways.

- Capitalism needed workers to be supported and looked after by unpaid helpers to enable them to carry out a proper day's work.

- Women were to be confined to the domestic, private sphere where their primary roles would be to take care of their husbands, have children and socialise those children into becoming the next generation of workers and carers that capitalism needed. This is sometimes known as reproducing the labour force.

- Women also acted as a **reserve army of labour** and could be used as part of the workforce when needed, then sent back home when their usefulness had ended.

- Because capitalism was based on the accumulation of private property, assuring the paternity of their heirs was vital to men, so women were therefore required to be virgins until marriage and monogamous throughout marriage.

> **Key term**
>
> **Reserve army of labour** the idea that women constitute a spare workforce that can be called upon as and when needed.

Women were encouraged to enter the workforce during the First World War as their patriotic duty, but had to leave their roles behind once the war was over.

Link

For more on **Charlotte Perkins Gilman**, see Section 3.3.

Socialists feminists such as **Charlotte Perkins Gilman** have envisaged socialist societies as revolving around alternative living arrangements whereby childcare would not be the concern of individual mothers. Instead, a more communal basis of living was imagined, with couples living alongside other couples, and perhaps also single people, allowing the responsibility of housework to be shared and companionship to be enjoyed by all.

> **Communal living and feminism**
>
> Charles Fourier, a utopian socialist, wanted to model society on communal living where people worked together for mutual benefit. He argued that traditional families were oppressive to women and that gender roles could be transformed from within the community. The kibbutz system established in the first half of the 20th century was set up based on these socialist ideals. They argued that women could only be liberated when they were separated from childcare and domestic responsibilities, introducing collective child-rearing as a way to escape patriarchal society.

Socialist feminists believe that capitalism creates patriarchy, so women should join together with men to fight capitalism and by doing so, remove patriarchy too. They see patriarchy as a consequence of capitalism and thus believe only a revolution, based on socialist values, will bring about women's liberation.

Whereas traditional socialist feminism prioritises class over gender, modern socialist feminism sees patriarchy and capitalism as interlocking systems of oppression, suggesting that patriarchy could survive the collapse of capitalism. In *Women's Estate* (1971), Juliet Mitchell criticised Marx and Engels for considering women's oppression to be nothing more than an aspect of the bourgeois family. She argued that the family is an independent source of female oppression as it keeps women hidden away and dependent on their husbands financially.

Mitchell argues that women are oppressed in four ways, through reproduction, through sexuality, through socialisation of children and through production. While recognising that capitalism is responsible for some of these, she argues that the others are unrelated to capitalism. Women should fight both capitalism and patriarchy to create a classless society where men and women can work alongside each other as equals. Only when all four areas are transformed will women be truly free.

Radical feminism

Radical feminists believe there need to be radical changes to society – a sexual revolution, to fundamentally change the structure and nature of society – not merely the redistribution of rights or wealth. Many of the core principles discussed earlier are primarily associated with radical feminism.

Radical feminism is not a single idea, but a collection of ideas by different feminists united by a belief that society can be defined purely as patriarchal. For them, gender inequality is the foremost system of oppression, and patriarchy is an independent system of oppression, separate from other ideologies. They think other strands of feminism are caught between their commitment to women's emancipation and other ideology, such as liberalism or socialism.

Radical feminism is associated with second-wave feminism and the slogan, 'the personal is the political'. Politics – power relationships – can be found in all relationships between men and women. Different radical feminists focus on different areas of the 'personal' to show how they are 'political', and how patriarchy pervades every aspect of life. They seek to challenge patriarchy by raising awareness of its existence among women as much as men.

In many ways, **Kate Millett's** *Sexual Politics* (1970) started the thinking process that we now call radical feminism, critiquing patriarchy with a particular focus on its role in the family. She also showed how, historically, society treated a women as the property of her husband. For example, if a woman committed adultery, her husband had the legal right to divorce her, keep any money or property that she may have brought to the marriage and prevent her from seeing her children. Until very recently, a marriage contract assumed an exchange of the right for the husband to have sex with his wife for the wife being supported by her husband.

Millett argues that the way women have been portrayed in art and literature was almost universally degrading or patronising. She references Norman Mailer and Henry Miller to show the way that dominant men and compliant women were considered completely normal in their books. She also studied the language of sexual activity in books and showed how women were the passive 'accepters' of sexual activity – mere commodities that men seek to 'possess'.

Germaine Greer continued this theme of the sexuality of women in her groundbreaking book *The Female Eunuch*, published in 1971. She argued that women's ability and interest in being satisfied sexually had been removed from them (by socialisation), much like eunuchs in ancient royal courts. Women had been socialised into believing that having sexual desires and wanting them satisfied was unfeminine and unacceptable. Women were encouraged to engage in sexual activity merely to procreate and should not expect sex to be enjoyable. Women who dared to show an interest in sex were heavily condemned by men and women alike. Greer sought to encourage women not to be embarrassed by their bodies or their sexuality:

> I'm sick of pretending eternal youth. I'm sick of belying (denying) my own intelligence, my own will, my own sex. I'm sick of peering at the world through false eyelashes, so that everything I see is mixed with a shadow of bought hairs. I'm sick of weighting my head with a dead mane, unable to move my neck freely, terrified of rain, of wind, of dancing too vigorously in case I sweat into my lacquered curls…

Another excellent insight was developed by Naomi Wolf in *The Beauty Myth* (1990), where she argued that beauty was 'the last, best belief system that keeps male dominance intact'. As women started to challenge men in education and the workplace, she wrote, additional pressures were brought to bear on their physical appearance. This notion of 'the ideal women' grew stronger as photoshopped images became the norm, making 'perfection' unattainable. Wolf argued that, as women broke into ever-higher ranks in industry, so did the number of women suffering from eating disorders and having cosmetic surgery.

The relevance of Wolf's book today cannot be denied. Social media puts huge pressure on girls. In 2016 the Children's Society reported that 34 per cent of 10- to 15-year-old girls are unhappy with their appearance. Researchers were told of girls feeling ugly or worthless – representing a sharp rise in unhappiness from when the same survey was done five years before – while boys' sense of happiness remained stable.

Link

For more on **Kate Millett**, see Section 3.3.

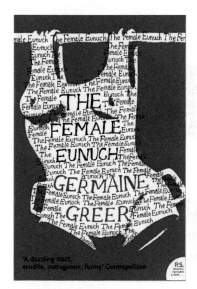

Germaine Greer's *The Female Eunuch* was a landmark in feminist thinking.

Pause & reflect ✔

Think about Naomi Wolf's comments about beauty. How does she see this view of beauty as connected to power and patriarchy?

In summary, radical feminism is not a cohesive ideological approach to the oppression of women in society. Radical feminists have different areas of interest, often disagree with each other and sometimes have diametrically opposite views on the same issue. However, they would all agree that patriarchy is alive and well in modern society.

Post-modern feminism

Post-modern feminism (also sometimes known as post-structuralist feminism) was associated with third-wave feminism, which is widely accepted as starting in the 1990s. If one were to try to encapsulate its essence in one word, it would be 'difference'. We have been introduced to the concept of difference feminism earlier in the chapter, but this idea of difference was arguing against the somewhat fixed notions of 'women' that had occupied the thoughts of many feminists previously. Feminists had initially been arguing with men that women weren't X, they were Y, and then with other feminists that some women weren't Y, they were Z.

Post-modern feminism argued for a more fluid understanding of being a 'woman'. It argued that there are as many differences between women's experiences as there are between men and women's experiences, arguing at times that there is no such thing as 'women' – i.e. that it is impossible to generalise about theoretical people called 'women' because women's experiences of life are so vastly different.

Equally, if there is no fixed understanding of a 'woman', then women could define feminism for themselves by integrating feminist values within their own core values and beliefs. Richards and Baumgardner argued in *Manifesta* (2000) that in each generation, young women would rediscover and re-establish what feminism meant for them.

Post-modern feminism also challenged the notion that gender alone was the primary factor affecting women in society. It argued that putting gender alongside race, religion or class was a more precise way of understanding the challenges that affect women. It criticised feminism for focusing on white, middle-class women and not recognising that black and working-class women had very different experiences of patriarchy. Women experience oppression in various configurations and to varying degrees of intensity. Examples of this include race, gender, class and ethnicity. Intersectionality is the term post-modern feminists use to describe the contention that there is no single basis for women's subordination and no single method of dealing with it.

bell hooks in *Ain't I a Woman* (1981) suggested that the combination of sexism and racism led to black women having the lowest status of any group in American society, and that this was compounded by the marginalising of black women's experiences from the mainstream feminist movement.

In *Feminist Theory: From Margin to Center* (1984), hooks criticised the idea of second-wave 'sisterhood', which sought to find a commonality of oppression among women, thereby excluding the experiences of minority women. By seeking connections between women, this immediately gave white, middle-class women a voice and a bond, while discouraging women of colour from speaking up about their different experiences. Instead, hooks argued, women should seek to understand the different cultures that women are brought up in and by recognising the different guises that oppression works under, a genuine sisterhood can be found.

Human nature	Feminists are divided on their view of human nature. The vast majority of feminists are equality feminists, who believe that the natures of men and women are the same, and that the distinction between sex and gender is artificial. They support gender equality, believing gender stereotypes to be a social construct. Difference feminists disagree, believing that men and women have fundamentally different natures stemming from biology, known as essentialism. Equality feminists believe patriarchy can be overthrown when gender roles and stereotypes are challenged. They believe that a woman's biology should not determine her social position; biology is thus not destiny. By contrast, difference feminists believe that liberation can only be achieved when women are encouraged to allow their different natures and creative spirit to flourish.
The state	Liberal feminists believe that the state can play a role in promoting female liberation by promoting legal and political equality. The state can also help to ensure equality of opportunity between the sexes. Radical feminists disagree, believing that providing an equal, legal framework is insufficient to overthrow patriarchy. They argue that the state primarily promotes the interests of patriarchy. Socialist feminists reject the liberal idea of state as a neutral body, suggesting instead that it works in the interest of capitalism and thus patriarchy. Liberal feminists believe that the state should concern itself only with correcting inequalities in the public sphere, by promoting equality of opportunity and outlawing discrimination. Radical feminists believe that the state has a role to play in eradicating patriarchal values in the public and private sphere by outlawing pornography and ensuring harsher punishment for domestic violence, rape and other crimes against women.
Society	All feminists believe that women are not treated equally in society. However, they differ in the extent to which they think there is a problem and the reason behind it. Liberal feminists argue that women are discriminated against in society, but focus their attention solely on the public sphere. Radical feminists believe that society is pervaded by patriarchal values that seek to preserve men's dominant position in society. They argue that 'the personal is political', in that all relationships between men and women, both in the public (society) and the private sphere (private relationships), are based on power and dominance. Radical equality feminists want a society in which gender ceases to structure a person's identity, whereas radical difference feminists believe this encourages women to be 'male identified' and perpetuates feelings of 'otherness'. Some difference feminists express this through cultural feminism. Post-modern feminists challenge the notion that 'gender' is the sole factor in determining female oppression in society, arguing that black and working-class women's experiences of patriarchy are different from those of white, middle-class women – this concept is known as intersectionality.
The economy	Socialist feminists believe that the economy is the key determinant of female oppression – that capitalism in the economic sphere, not patriarchy, determines the nature of female oppression in society. They argue that capitalism needs women to play a subservient role in the economy and society – as a reserve army of labour – because capitalism, not patriarchy, requires them to fulfil that function. Modern socialist feminists have argued that there is an interplay between capitalism in the economy and patriarchy in society that causes the oppression of women.

Table 2.1: Core principles and ideas of feminism in action

3.3 Feminist thinkers and their ideas

Charlotte Perkins Gilman (1860–1935)

Key ideas

- To be free, women need economic independence.
- Gender stereotyping in childhood is wrong.

Gilman was a prominent American feminist associated with socialist feminism. She is best known for her short story, *The Yellow Wallpaper* (1892), about a woman suffering from mental illness after three months of being closeted in a room by her husband for the sake of her health. Her story was inspired by her own postnatal depression and her treatment by her first husband, who demanded that she stayed in bed, confined to one room. This was the opposite of what she needed – mental stimulation and an escape from monotony.

Charlotte Perkins Gilman: 'In a sick society, women who have difficulty fitting in are not ill but demonstrating a healthy and positive response.'

- Gilman's main argument was that sex and domestic economics went hand in hand; for women to survive, they were reliant on their sexual assets to please their husband so that he would financially support his family.
- She also argued that from childhood, young girls are forced to conform to a domestic role and motherhood, and are prepared for this by toys that are marketed to them and clothes designed for them. She argued that there should be no difference in the clothes that little girls and boys wear, the toys they play with or the activities they do.
- Gilman believed economic independence was the only thing that could bring freedom for women and make them equal to men. She argued that motherhood should not stop a woman from working outside the home.
- She suggested that communal housing should be constructed that was open to men and women, which would allow individuals to live singly and still have companionship and the comforts of a home. Both men and women would be economically independent, with women taking their place in the workforce alongside men and being freed from their role as domestic slaves. This would allow for marriage without either the male or the female's economic status having to change.

Simone de Beauvoir (1908–1986)

Key ideas

- Women are taught and socialised into becoming 'women'.

- **Otherness** – men are the norm; women are 'other'.

Simone de Beauvoir was initially reluctant to call herself a feminist. She believed that socialist development and class struggle were needed to solve society's problems, not a women's movement. However, when she realised that socialist development had not left women better off, she publicly stated that she no longer believed a socialist revolution to be sufficient to bring about women's liberation.

Simone de Beauvoir: 'One is not born, but rather becomes, a woman.'

> ### Key term
>
> **Otherness**
> the idea that women were considered to be fundamentally different from men, who were seen as the 'norm'; women were deviants from this norm.

- Simone de Beauvoir famously stated, 'One is not born, but rather becomes, a woman.' She was arguing that women are taught and socialised to do and be what is perceived to be a 'woman'. She called motherhood a way of turning women into slaves as they were forced to focus on motherhood and femininity instead of politics, technology or anything beyond home and family.

- De Beauvoir also discussed the issue of 'otherness', which referred to the fact that women were considered to be fundamentally different from men in every sense. Men were thus the 'norm', while women were 'deviants' from the norm.

- De Beauvoir argued that women have accepted and internalised their otherness – not only had it been imposed on them by men, but women had also come to accept it for themselves. Thus, women were not just inferior in the eyes of men, but inferior in their own eyes too. Women needed to first become conscious of their domination before they could struggle against it.

- However, de Beauvoir was dismayed by the idea of a separate, mystical 'feminine nature'. She argued that the idea of 'a woman's nature' was an example of the further oppression of women. She did not think it was beneficial for women to refuse to do anything 'a man's way' or refuse to take on qualities deemed masculine.

- She recognised that the women's movement had done some good, but said feminists should not reject being a part of the man's world, whether in organisational power or with their creative work.

Kate Millett (1934–)

Key ideas

- The family is the key tool of patriarchy.
- Socialisation gives men power, and denies women power.

Kate Millett wrote *Sexual Politics*, the book that gave birth to radical feminism. It caused a storm when it was published in 1970.

Kate Millett: 'Because of our social circumstances, male and female are really two cultures and their life experiences are utterly different.'

- Millett argued that female oppression was both political and cultural, and suggested that undoing the traditional family was the key to true sexual revolution. She argued that the family was 'patriarchy's key institution'; it was a mirror of the larger society, a patriarchal unit within a patriarchal whole. It was where very young girls were taught 'their place' in relation to their brothers, and where they learned about the role of women by observing the hierarchical relationship between their mother and father.

- Traditionally, patriarchy granted the father nearly total ownership over his wife and children. Her status as his property continued in her loss of name and the legal assumption that marriage involved an exchange of women's domestic service and sexual consent in return for financial support.

- The chief contribution of the family to patriarchy was the socialisation of the young into patriarchal attitudes. Although there were slight cultural variations, this was achieved and reinforced through friends, schools, media and other aspects of society. This culture supported masculine authority in all areas of life, and permitted the female none at all.

- Millett also explored the treatment of women in art and literature. She showed how patriarchal culture had produced writers and literary works that were degrading to women. Millett demonstrated how the language used in describing sex demonstrated the subjugation of women. Millett suggested that in literature, women were never their own agents; they were commodities silenced by the freedom of men to sexually possess them.

- Millett also attacked romantic love and called for an end to monogamous marriage and the family, which she referred to as patriarchy's chief institution. She proposed a sexual revolution that would bring the institution of patriarchy to an end.

Sheila Rowbotham (1943–)

Key ideas

- Women are oppressed economically and culturally.
- Capitalism and sexism are closely linked.

Rowbotham argued that women's oppression was a result of both economic and cultural forces, so a dual response examining both the public and private spheres was required to work towards liberation. Rowbotham is most closely associated with socialist feminism, which combines a Marxist analysis with feminism.

Sheila Rowbotham: 'The revolutionary woman knows the world she seeks to overthrow is precisely one in which love between equal human beings is well nigh impossible.'

- Rowbotham presented her analysis of contemporary social conditions from a Marxist-feminist perspective. She argued that origins of sexism predate capitalism, and that the institution of marriage closely resembled feudalism. She suggested that wives were the equivalent of feudal serfs, contracted to serve their husbands.

- She argued that achieving women's liberation required a 'revolution within the revolution'. She maintained that capitalism and sexism are so closely linked that the only way to destroy both was a radical change in the 'cultural conditioning' of humanity regarding child-rearing, homes, laws and the workplace.

- Rowbotham argued that capitalism oppressed not only the proletariat, but also women. Women are thus doubly oppressed as they are forced to sell their labour to survive, but also forced to use their labour to support their husbands and children.

- Rowbotham maintained that the domestic work done by women allowed the reproduction of men's labour. However, she claimed that the family was not just an instrument for disciplining and subjecting women to capitalism, but was a place where men took refuge from alienation under capitalism.

bell hooks (1952–)

Key ideas

- Mainstream feminism excludes the concerns of women of colour.
- Solidarity is important, between genders, races and classes.

hooks adopted the pseudonym of her great-grandmother, creating an 'other self' linked to her female ancestors, which empowered her to fight back against the opposition that surrounded her. She chose to use lowercase letters to distance herself from the ego associated with names.

bell hooks: 'No black woman writer in this culture can write "too much". Indeed, no woman writer can write "too much"… No woman has ever written enough.'

- hooks argued that, from a very young age, boys and girls are constantly being knocked down and told to fit into the boxes of characteristics that are expected of them. hooks pointed out that the boy was denied his right to show or even have any true feelings, while the girl was taught that the most important thing she could do was change herself and her own feelings in the hope of attracting and pleasing everyone else.

- She is mainly known for her efforts to bring the cultural concerns of women of colour into the mainstream feminist movement. hooks found the mainstream feminist movement had focused mostly on the plight of white, college-educated middle- and upper-class women who had no stake in the concerns of women of colour.

- Historically, women of colour often found themselves in a double bind. By supporting the woman's movement, they had to ignore the racial aspect of womanhood, but if they supported the civil-rights movement they were subjected to the same patriarchal order that all women faced.

- hooks wrote about the need to articulate and recognise a feminist theory of empowerment that was accessible to people of colour. She argued that feminists have not succeeded in creating political solidarity with women of different ethnicities or socio-economic classes. hooks always argued for solidarity: between genders, between races and between classes.

Assessment support: 2.2.3 Feminism

The non-core political ideas question is on Paper 2, Section B. It is worth 24 marks and must be completed in 30 minutes. All ideas questions start 'To what extent' so you must look at both sides of the debate.

You are given a choice of two questions in this format, of which you should answer one.

EITHER

5 (a) To what extent do feminists agree that the personal is political? [24 marks]

OR

5 (b) To what extent do feminists identify patriarchy as a natural aspect of human nature? [24 marks]

You must use appropriate thinkers you have studied to support your answer and consider any differing views in a balanced way.

This question tests all three Assessment Objectives, with marks divided equally between them. You must:

- set out the nature of the debate

- draw similarities and differences between the different strands or tensions

- use at least two relevant thinkers.

Your answer should make judgements based on evidence about the significance of the differences and similarities, leading to a clear and justifiable conclusion.

- Always plan before you write. What are the key similarities and differences between the main strands (liberal versus socialist versus radical)? Expand these into the sub-strands (difference versus equality feminism, if needed) to develop your answer. What ideas of key thinkers are valid for this answer? Try planning answers to the two questions listed above.

- Your essay should include a brief introduction outlining the main arguments, four main points and a conclusion that should reach an overall judgement that naturally flows from the essay.

Here is part of a student's answer to question 5 (a), setting out the radical feminist perspective and how it differs from a liberal feminist one.

The personal is the political is a phrase often used by radical feminists, to describe the relationship between women and society. The personal is the political argues that the oppression of women in the public sphere stems from the way women are treated in their private life. Radical feminists are therefore concerned with the way women are treated in everyday life, which includes their role in the family, the distribution of housework and the other domestic responsibilities.

Kate Millett argues that female oppression stems from patriarchy, which operates in all walks of life, both public and private, and in many respects, originates in the family itself. Millett further argues that the roles of men and women within the family are used to define the roles of men and women in wider society. For all radical feminists, the fight against oppression suffered by women in the private sphere is the same fight as in the public sphere. Liberal feminists reject this and argue that politics stops at the front door, in other words, the fight for female equality should occur in the public sphere.

- The answer defines the term 'the personal is political' and why radical feminists believe it is important.

- There is good use of Millett, a key thinker – remember, you must use (at least) two key thinkers in your answer – to extend and deepen the explanation of the point.

- It shows clear disagreement between the radical and liberal feminist view, which can be developed in the later paragraphs.

Multiculturalism

Multiculturalism could become one of the main themes of the 21st century. It is arguably the only route to deal with the increased levels of migration and cultural **diversity** experienced in modern societies, and has been adopted widely across the USA, Canada and Western Europe. Yet, since the events of 9/11 it has come under increasing attack, with David Cameron declaring war on multiculturalism in 2011 and Angela Merkel, in 2010, asserting that it has utterly failed.

This chapter looks at:

- the core ideas of multiculturalism
- how these apply to human nature, the state, society and the economy
- the different views and tensions within multiculturalism
- the key ideas of some of multiculturalism's key thinkers.

4.1 Core ideas and principles

Multiculturalism is a contemporary political concept based on the idea that human beings see and understand the world from within the system of values they are brought up in. Diversity should be cherished by respecting and strengthening **cultures**, including those of minority groups. It is the necessary basis for social cohesion in the modern world. This is not just a political idea, but also can be an existing set of policies to tackle issues raised by cultural diversity in society. Perhaps the best example in the UK is the Parekh Report (2000), commissioned, but not implemented, by the Blair government, which proposed the idea of a 'community of communities and individuals', underpinned by human rights for all, a government commitment to identifying and tackling all forms of racism and the reduction of associated inequalities.

Politics of recognition

Acts of recognition – such as praise from a respected teacher or support from a friend – play an important role in our lives, shaping how we feel. Acts can also have negative impacts, such as the ten taxi-cabs refusing to stop for a male, African American Princeton professor on his way to a meeting in New York. The politics of recognition is based on the idea that recognition forms, and even determines, our sense of who we are and the respect society holds for us.

For multiculturalists, recognition is about how cultural identities are recognised in society and how that recognition impacts on the individual. Multiculturalists argue that minority groups, such as African-Americans in the USA, are at a disadvantage compared to the majority. This can take the form of legal and political discrimination, such as the Jim Crow laws in America. Multiculturalists aim to establish equal citizenship or **formal equality**, which removes political and legal discrimination by granting equal rights to all. This is known as the politics of equal dignity. Multiculturalists also argue that oppression goes deeper than political or legal oppression to a cultural oppression. Those who are 'different' are marginalised through stereotyping, stigmatisation and racism – forms of oppression that can only be overcome through equal recognition.

In essence, multiculturalists, such as Charles Taylor, contend that the politics of recognition is based on equal dignity and equal recognition; both are needed to stop oppression and for individuals and groups to feel part of society.

Key terms

Diversity
the view that different races and cultures within a state is possible, positive and should be celebrated, although the extent to which diversity should extend is contentious.

Culture
values, customs and beliefs that are passed on down the generations through learning.

Formal equality
everyone is entitled to legal and political equality, based on Aristotle's idea that things that are alike should be treated alike.

EXTENSION ACTIVITY

Canada is considered a multiculturalist state. Read its view of multiculturalism at www.cic.gc.ca/english/multiculturalism/citizenship.asp. How is multiculturalism defined and justified?

Equal dignity

Equal dignity means that all members of a society have an innate right to be valued, respected and treated equally; there should be no second-class citizens. This was the position adopted by Martin Luther King and the civil rights movement in the USA. King argued that, on the basis of common humanity, all citizens of the USA were entitled to the rights under the Constitution. Equal dignity was realised in the Civil Rights Act of 1964, which banned discrimination in public places, provided for integration in education and other public facilities, and made employment discrimination illegal, while the Voting Rights Act of 1965 banned discriminatory voting practices based on race, such as literacy tests.

The principle of equal dignity is based on the uniform set of rules for all individuals. However, equal dignity cannot tackle cultural oppression. For example, the holy days of the majority culture are given as public holidays and are celebrated publically, but those of the minority culture are not. To correct this cultural oppression, equal recognition is needed to give protection to minority cultures and to celebrate diversity.

Equal recognition

The idea of identity – an individual's sense of who they are – has introduced a new form of second-class citizen: someone who is fully a citizen but still feels an outsider. An individual's identity is crucial to the way they understand who they are and their fundamental characteristics. This identity is not formed in isolation, but in dialogue – and sometimes struggle – with others, by both the individual's self-perception and how others see

Martin Luther King's 'I have a dream' speech inspired millions globally.

them. When others misrecognise someone's identity by stereotyping, racism and discrimination, this is oppression. It harms individuals, imprisoning them in a false, inferior and demeaned sense of themselves. So recognition is more than just a courtesy; it is a human need, crucial to our sense of self.

Equal recognition involves state policies that allow different cultures to survive and flourish. By including recognition of minority identities in laws, minorities will finally achieve equal standing with the majority; all identities will be treated as first-class citizens. Specific rights and protections will be allocated to particular groups, but not others. Muslims in France have challenged rules that prevent them from wearing headscarves in schools; Sikhs have objected to motorcycle helmet laws that are incompatible with turbans; and in the USA, orthodox Jews have fought for the right to wear the yarmulke (skullcap) in courtrooms and the military. In the province of Quebec in Canada, it is not enough for the French language to just be tolerated. The French language has official status in Quebec – it is the main language of government departments and business within the province – and there are rules to ensure all those with French heritage learn the language in school. This has led to the language and culture flourishing. In all cases, the fair treatment of cultural practices and ways of life will allow all individuals and groups to feel part of the shared community.

Pause & reflect

Explain what is meant by 'the politics of recognition' and why it is justified. Use examples to illustrate your argument.

> **Case study: Education**
>
> Within education, there is a view that humanities courses in universities and schools are based around dead, white men. In *No Place Like Home*, Gary Younge talks about growing up black in the UK: 'I never learned one thing about black British history or culture at school (that) would have helped me navigate my way from my mother's past to my present.' The non-recognition of other cultures, races and indeed genders by the dominant culture can create a negative and demeaning image for students from minority groups. This must be challenged and the curriculum changed in order to change these self-demeaning identities.
>
> **Questions**
>
> - How important do you think the educational curriculum is to supporting the politics of recognition?
>
> - What would be the basis for a multiculturalist curriculum?

Key term

Identity
the sense that someone has of who they are and what is most important about them.

Link

For more on **liberalism**, see Liberalism chapter.

Link

For more on **feminism**, see Feminism chapter.

Link

For more on **Rawls**, see Section 2.3 of Liberalism.

Culture and identity

The politics of recognition fits into a wider discussion about the politics of culture and **identity**. Confidence and pride in your own culture, plus positive recognition of that culture from society, give a sense of belonging to society. A negative conception of culture and identity can lead people to feel rejected, ridiculed or alienated – and so feel disengaged from society. Cultural politics can be understood in two ways: communitarianism and identity politics.

Communitarianism

Communitarianism is a set of ideas marked out by its opposition to **liberalism** – especially the individualistic nature of liberalism. The individual does not come before community so cannot be understood outside society. Some multiculturalists, such as Taylor, argue that liberalism prioritises the individual over the community, which undermines society. Others, such as Parekh, argue that human beings grow up in a culturally structured world, so they are culturally embedded – individuals' identities are mainly formed by the culture they grew up in, which shapes the way they see the world and themselves. Their culture provides a sense of meaning and significance, and they view their world from within it. As culture is so significant for an individual's integrity and moral code, the state must recognise these communities and not force people to act against their own identity or moral beliefs, or it will alienate them from society.

Identity politics

Much of contemporary politics – such as second-wave **feminism**, the gay rights movement and multiculturalism – is based around the politics of identity. This places identity at the heart of political action and movements. Identity politics tackles the idea set out by **Rawls** that citizens are all essentially similar individuals. It is argued that this 'neutral citizen' idea is not neutral at all, but rather an expression of white, male, bourgeois, able-bodied and heterosexual identities. Individuals are oppressed due to their membership of a minority social group, which may suffer stereotyping, economic exploitation through lack of opportunity and group-based violence. Stereotyping often involves giving one single identity to particular groups. This has happened with the term Muslim in the UK, despite the fact that Muslims are not one single entity but a very diverse group. This creates a clear sense of 'us' and 'them' in society.

Identity politics sees culture as both a tool of oppression and a positive force. The minority group is being targeted, which requires a group response. Cultures can build up group pride and create positive images to challenge their oppression. The best example of this is where African Americans have turned the term 'black' into a positive statement of difference, identifying themselves as black and using the ideas of black pride and black power. Minority groups can also redefine how they have been oppressed as part of this positive-identity statement. This can be seen in the way British Asians have redefined their oppression. Many used to see their oppression in terms of racism based on colour, but now see racism as based on distinctive stereotyping and attacks on aspects of the culture. This positive sense of identity will free minorities from oppression and achieve real equality in society. This becomes crucial to a multicultural society where all feel a sense of belonging.

The black power salute at the 1968 Olympic Games.

The key criticism levelled at the politics of culture and identity is that it causes a form of cultural balkanisation (the emergence within the state of strong and competing cultures), with a series of different and competing cultural traditions within the state. The desire for cultural authenticity means that groups emphasise their differences from others, rather than seeking out what they have in common. In particular, immigrant groups may look to adopt narrow, inward-looking cultural identities that reflect the culture they came from, rather than working towards the culture into which they have migrated. These groups, as a result, view all other cultures with distrust, especially the majority culture. The issue may be worsened when the minority culture is based around a religious identity, where key elements of the belief system are held to be sacred.

Pause & reflect

Does the politics of culture and identity promote a sense of belonging to society or difference?

Case study: Black Lives Matter

In the 1960s, Martin Luther King recognised the history of oppression in the USA through slavery and the Jim Crow laws, but argued for a 'colour blind' approach. He wanted to see equal rights, equal opportunities and the end of discrimination. His campaign focused on the idea that people should not be judged by the colour of their skin but by the content of their character. This stance was seen by the radical movement as not claiming identity as a positive force. However, Malcolm X promoted the idea that black people had to no longer view their bodies, minds and souls through 'white lenses'. They needed to reclaim their identity and their destiny to create their own freedom. One issue that the identity politics of Malcolm X raised was whether the end goal was black separatism, rather than the integration that Martin Luther King desired.

In many ways, this need for identity politics has remained strong. Black Lives Matter is a current expression of identity politics that argues African-Americans are oppressed and victimised because of their identity in their encounters with law enforcement. This oppression is down to identity, so identity politics is needed to escape it and achieve equality – the basis for a cohesive society. This is made clear in one of the guiding principles of the movement, which states that the movement is 'unapologetically black' in its approach to justice, freedom and equality. Black Lives Matter sees itself as part of a 'global Black family'.

Questions

- Why were there divisions in the black liberation movement in the 1960s?
- Is Black Lives Matter likely to promote difference or a more cohesive society?

Minority rights

Minority rights address the specific needs of particular groups by granting special rights to them, based on their different needs as a culture. Multiculturalists promote this approach as the way for diverse cultures and beliefs to live together in liberal society, without imposing their cultural values on others.

> **Key term**
>
> **Tolerance**
> from a multiculturalist view, the willingness to accept values, customs and beliefs with which one disagrees.

The basis of liberalism is that individuals will only co-operate and work together within society if the state remains neutral between all 'conceptions of the good', such as cultures and beliefs. This can be seen in key features of the liberal state such as **tolerance**, religious freedom and the separation of church and state. Multiculturalists offer a number of criticisms of liberalism and aim to develop a case for minority rights within the liberal framework.

- **The idea of neutral liberalism is inaccurate**. States that have granted formal equality and have anti-discrimination laws in place do not ensure minority groups are treated as equal. In most societies, the dominant group has established the norms, rules and institutions of the state to suit their culture. The state promotes certain identities while disadvantaging others by:
  - placing some cultures above others and ensuring members of the dominant culture have advantages in education, employment and politics. For example, the state has to choose what languages are used in schools and state services. In California, bilingual education was banned in 1998 and re-established in 2016, and Canada has both French and English as official languages.
  - placing limits on some cultural groups but not on others through state laws. For example, there are laws that establish dress codes in public places, such as the 2010 French law that bans the public wearing of the niqab and burqa.

This means that, in order to make different groups equal, the liberal state must allocate different rights to different groups – known as **group-differentiated rights**.

- **Cultures are crucial to meet the liberal objectives of freedom and autonomy**. Culture lets the individual acknowledge and revise their beliefs and convictions. Beliefs are the basis for meaningful choices about the life the individual wants to lead, based on their interests, values and desires. Group-differentiated rights should be granted to allow individuals access to their own culture so that they can be free.

- **Minority rights are a way of countering the oppression that minority groups suffer** through the misrecognition of their cultural identities. This can include the idea that, due to unequal power relations between the majority and the minority, the minority has a right not to be profoundly offended.

Key term

Group-differentiated rights
rights that belong to a group, in contrast to a right held by individuals.

Case study: *The Satanic Verses* controversy

The issue of minority rights was brought to light in 1988 with the publication of Salman Rushdie's *The Satanic Verses*, a novel that was seen as blasphemous for its depiction of Islam and the prophet Muhammad. Muslim responses in the UK included protests and leaders calling for the book to be banned while abroad, death threats were made against the author. The main liberal view was that the fundamental principles of society in the UK were non-negotiable – no limits should be placed on free speech (except in the case of public order and safety), so the book could not be banned. Banning of the book would be an attack on tolerance that chipped away at the basic freedoms of liberal democracy. However, it was argued that the book and the way the media simplistically framed the debate as democracy versus fanatics placed a singular, inaccurate identity on Muslims in the UK. This stereotyping damaged individuals who identify with that group, leading to alienation and **segregation** in society. At the same time, this led many Muslims to think about their identity – Rana Kabbani in *Letter to Christendom* described herself as an underground Muslim 'forced into the open by the Salman Rushdie affair'. In addition, it led to the creation of the Muslim Council of Britain, to lobby on behalf of Muslims, which has achieved one of its key aims, which is to have Muslims as a group recognised separately from issues of race or ethnicity.

Protestors burn a copy of *The Satanic Verses* in Bradford, 1989.

Questions

- Should there be extra protection for groups against profound offence (a group libel law), where it significantly harms the individuals who identify with the group?

- Are there cases when free speech should be limited?

Key term

Segregation
multiculturalism has led to ethnic and religious groups becoming increasingly separated, inward looking and protective of their own cultures.

Link

For more on **Will Kymlicka**, see Section 4.3.

Having justified minority rights, multiculturalists such as **Will Kymlicka** put forward a set of group-differentiated rights that can be used to protect minority groups based on their differing needs, as shown in Table 1.2.

Self-government rights	These rights meet the claims put forward by national minorities or indigenous peoples who ask for political autonomy or territorial control. Examples include Native Americans in the USA, aboriginal communities in Canada or Catalonians in Spain. These rights are justified on two conditions. • The group has experienced historical and structural disadvantage, as it has effectively been colonised. • The claim for self-government reflects the will of the group membership, and the group is territorially concentrated to make political autonomy practical.
Polyethnic rights	These rights are policy responses to demands of immigrant groups who wish to maintain their cultural identity. Such policies can include: • anti-racism laws (for example, the Equality Act 2010 in UK) • changes to the educational curriculum (for example, Black History Month) • additional resources (for example, funding for minority language schools) • exemptions from the law (for example, exemptions for Jewish *shechita* and Muslim *zabiha* methods of animal slaughter). Immigrant communities do not receive self-government rights. The act of migration is seen as voluntary, so immigrants are expected to participate in the public institutions of the dominant culture. Claims for recognition of culture in these cases are to help individuals better integrate into society.
Representation rights	These rights use **positive discrimination** to tackle the historical exclusion from public life that disadvantaged cultures have experienced. Examples in the USA include affirmative action in education and employment, and majority-minority districts in the House of Representatives, which created districts in line with the Voting Rights Act where a majority of the population comes from minority communities. Positive discrimination is the way of ensuring full engagement in society and that the decision-making process in the state reflects the diversity of its groups.

Table 1.2: Kymlicka's three different types of rights

Key term

Positive discrimination preferential treatment for groups within society to correct structural inequality or to compensate for historical wrongs.

Minority rights have been highly controversial. Arguments against minority rights have included the following.

• **'Affirmative action' or positive discrimination is a form of reverse discrimination**, however good its intentions. These measures also send the message that success is down to representation rights, rather than people's own hard work, ability and determination. US Supreme Court Justice Clarence Thomas argues that affirmative action 'harms the very people it claims to be helping'. At the same time, it is viewed by the majority group as discriminating against them.

• **Minority rights isolate groups within society**, creating an inward-looking view and leading to strong divisions within the state. Minority rights lead to immigrant communities focusing more on the country and culture that they left, rather than their new country. The choice to wear the burqa has been seen as a symbol of difference, rather than an expression of cultural identity.

• **Minority rights can contradict individual rights**. This is raised to tackle the issue of how a liberal state should react to an illiberal culture that restricts the individual rights or freedoms of its members. For example, some argue that banning minority women's distinct clothing is a way of protecting women's basic freedoms and rights, while others see the ban as projecting the stereotype that Muslim women are oppressed and Muslim men are oppressive – a form of cultural misrecognition.

In the US court case *Fisher v University of Texas* in 2013, Supreme Court Justice Clarence Thomas wrote that 'racial discrimination is never benign' in voting against affirmative action.

Diversity

Diversity has become a fact of life for many countries with the rise of globalisation and international migration. The non-white population of most Northern European large cities now stands at between 15 and 30 per cent and this will continue to grow. These cities are now highly diverse in religious, racial and ethnic terms.

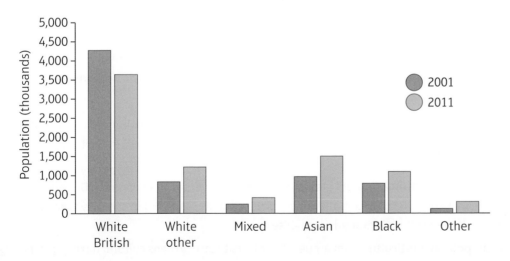

Figure 1.1: The changing nature of diversity in London (based on 2011 census data)

Some argue that multiculturalism offers the best platform to create a sense of shared community out of diversity. For example, multiculturalists such as **Bhikhu Parekh** argue that multiculturalism can find ways to reconcile diversity and unity, as a citizen cannot be fully committed to a political community unless that political community is fully committed to them by recognising their identity. This means society and its political structures, policies and conduct of public affairs must value difference and identity. Only then will individuals have a secure sense of identity and therefore the confidence to fully participate in and feel part of the shared community.

Pause & reflect

To what extent can minority rights be justified? Look at the different justifications and oppositions to minority rights.

EXTENSION ACTIVITY

To what extent have minority rights in the USA or UK been successful in achieving their aims?

Link

For more on **Bhikhu Parekh**, see Section 4.3.

However, conservatives have argued that political unity can only be achieved with cultural uniformity. This leads to two options.

- Ethnic and cultural minorities must be expelled in order to restore the original culture of the nation. This is both impractical and deeply unjust.

- Minorities must be encouraged to conform to the dominant culture and integrate, as this creates the strong, homogenised national identity needed for civic unity.

Multiculturalists say that this conformity is a form of cultural oppression that does not respect identity. It will lead to a sense of injustice, alienation and inequality among minority groups, and a breakdown of harmony in the state.

Some multiculturalists move beyond the argument that diversity is possible, to argue that diversity is a good in its own right, in two ways.

- Diversity benefits wider society, as well as migrant groups. The bubbling up of new ideas and new ways of doing things leads to creativity and energy in society, which help it progress, while intolerant societies will stagnate. For example, Canada is a very diverse and stable society with high levels of dynamism and social cohesion.

- Diversity creates and encourages creative discussion between different cultures and their moral visions. This encourages the tolerance and respect for difference that form the basis for political unity. A recent University of Oxford study showed that living in an area of high diversity rubs off on you, making you more tolerant of ethnic diversity.

EXTENSION ACTIVITY

How does the diversity of London affect voting patterns?

> **Pause & reflect**
>
> To what extent is diversity the basis for a politically stable society?

4.2 Different types of multiculturalism

The debate about how far diversity should extend highlights the tensions within multiculturalism. There are three main types of multiculturalism today.

- **Liberal multiculturalism** is based on liberal principles. It endorses cultural diversity, focuses on tolerance and personal autonomy, and promotes the idea of civic unity – all citizens being united and working together.

- **Pluralist multiculturalism** puts greater emphasis on diversity than on unity. Diversity is seen as a value in its own right. All cultures are equally legitimate, and people can only take part fully as citizens if their culture is properly recognised.

- **Cosmopolitan multiculturalism** argues that diversity strengthens cultural mixing, promoting global citizenship and undermining cultural identity as a driving force in society.

Liberal multiculturalism

Liberal multiculturalism developed out of debate within the liberal tradition about diversity and culture. Liberal multiculturalism uses three distinct ideas from liberalism to support diversity and integration.

- **The neutrality of the state:** In liberalism, the state does not try to promote any particular view, value or belief. In this sense, liberalism is 'difference blind' and treats all factors like race, religion and culture as irrelevant.

- This means that that there is a clear distinction between the private and the public spheres. In the private sphere, minorities can fully cultivate their identities based on religion, culture or language, and so celebrate diversity. In the public sphere, all are treated as individuals through formal equality and anti-discrimination laws. Everyone is expected to sign up to the values of the state, which may include speaking the official language, understanding the rights and duties of citizens and upholding democracy. This is **individualist integration** – migrants and minorities are integrated into the state only as individual claimants and bearers of equal rights, and this forms the basis for social cohesion. Institutional adjustments may be made for individuals, but minority communities are not recognised in the public sphere.

- The most radical form of this type of individualist integration can be seen in France. France exercises the principle of *laïcité* in public life. *Laïcité* refers to a strict separation of the church and state. In 2010, this led to the banning of the niqab and the burqa in all public spaces. Justice Minister Michèle Alliot-Marie said, 'The full veil dissolves a person's identity in that of a community. It calls into question the French model of integration, founded on the acceptance of our society's values.' The ban raises the question of whether the liberal state is in fact neutral or promotes certain identities while disadvantaging others.

- **The principle of tolerance:** Tolerance is the willingness to accept that others have values, customs and beliefs with which one disagrees. This has two key aspects.

  - You disapprove of what you are being asked to tolerate.

  - You must have the power to suppress that which you disapprove of, but choose not to suppress it.

Any suppression involves the removal of choice; tolerance allows the widest possible freedom and autonomy for individuals. However, tolerance is not morally neutral and only provides the foundation for shallow diversity, where diversity is only extended to cultures that are liberal and respect individual rights and democracy. Tolerance can only be extended to cultures, values and beliefs that are themselves tolerant and in keeping with the rules of the liberal state. This means that liberal multiculturalists cannot tolerate illiberal cultural practices, such as forced marriages, ritual scarring, female circumcision or female dress codes. President Sarkozy argued that the banning of the niqab and burqa in France was primarily in defence of women's individual rights, in particular their freedom and autonomy.

- **Liberal democracy** is regarded as the only legitimate political model by liberal multiculturalists. It is seen as the only political system that is based on the consent of the governed and which can uphold diversity and provide formal equality and freedom of choice and tolerance. This means liberal multiculturalism opposes other political models, such as theocracy. Within the liberal state, tolerance and respect will only be extended to groups that extend tolerance to others, and may include banning groups that wish to replace the liberal democracy with a state based on religious law.

However, within liberal multiculturalism, some thinkers have gone further. They have argued that group-differentiated rights are compatible with liberal democracy if they promote justice, personal freedom and autonomy. This can be found in the justifications for the politics of recognition and minority rights. So liberal multiculturalists support **multicultural integration**, which recognises difference, and argues that in addition to formal equality and anti-discrimination laws, the state must accommodate new group identities and cultures.

However, there is still the issue of what happens when group rights contradict individual rights. Can a group, whose right to act in line with its own cultural views has been recognised, compel an individual within that group to live by that right? For example, can a cultural group compel an

Key term

Individualist integration institutional adjustments for migrants or minorities as individual claimants and bearers of rights as equal citizens. Everyone is treated as an individual and not on the basis of difference.

E pluribus unum – meaning 'out of many, one' – on the Great Seal of the United States. Every immigrant wanting to become a US citizen must sign up to American values in the public sphere, as expressed in the Oath of Allegiance.

Key term

Multicultural integration integration in different ways for different groups and individuals, to create a new national identity where all citizens have not just rights, but a sense of belonging to the whole, as well as to their own group.

individual to accept a forced marriage, polygamy or particular forms of dress code? Secondly, can a cultural belief, value or practice that is unjust or limits autonomy be recognised or protected if it is central to the identity of that group? The answer here is clear. Group-differentiated rights can only apply to groups that allow members to question, adapt and even reject these practices, and recognition can only be advanced to groups that are themselves tolerant.

> **Pause & reflect**
>
> Is liberal multiculturalism compatible with individual rights? For example, does the group right to wear the burqa and niqab clash with individual rights, such as freedom and autonomy? Does the group right for Sikhs to wear the kirpan (ceremonial dagger) clash with the principle of equality before the law?

Pluralist multiculturalism

Pluralist multiculturalism is a broad ideology where diversity is a value in its own right, all cultures are worthy of respect and cultural recognition is the basis for civic participation. It moves beyond the liberal version where diversity only extends to cultures that are liberal and respect individual rights and democracy. Pluralists reject the idea that these liberal values are universal and support deep diversity, where all cultures have some worth and are due respect, not just those that meet liberal values. There are two justifications for this.

Link

For more on **Isaiah Berlin**, see Section 4.3.

Key terms

Value pluralism
the idea that there is no one absolute conception of the 'good life', but rather multiple competing and equally legitimate conceptions.

Universalism
the belief that certain values are applicable to all individuals and all societies, regardless of culture, history, geography or any other differences.

- Some pluralists support **value pluralism**, based on the work of **Isaiah Berlin**. There are many genuine values and they often come into conflict with each other. These conflicts are 'an intrinsic, irremovable part of human life' and are based in the world that we know and live in, and we recognise there is no general method for resolving them. When we choose values or ways of life, there is no right or wrong answer. They will inevitably come into conflict, but there is no way to resolve which is superior. So the values of liberal democracy, such as autonomy, freedom, democracy and tolerance, cannot be morally superior to other values, such as human solidarity, community, a sense of rootedness, selflessness, deep and self-effacing humility and contentment.

- Other pluralists attack 'liberal monism' or **universalism**, based on the work of Parekh. Liberalism sees its institutions, ideas and ways of living as the best, ignoring the claims of other value systems. These pluralists defend diversity based on three ideas.

  - Human beings are brought up and live in a culturally structured world. They are culturally embedded, so their values are deeply shaped by culture.

  - Different cultures have different meanings of the good life. Each culture can only grasp part of the totality of human existence and unlock a limited range of human capabilities. So each culture needs other cultures to understand itself better and expand its moral, creative and intellectual horizons. For individuals to have a richer life, their culture must have access to and dialogue with other cultures.

  - Liberalism is embedded in a particular culture, so can only offer a narrow and partial vision of the good life and cannot provide the sole basis for the good society. This is the basis for deep diversity and a deep recognition of difference.

Pluralist multiculturalism advocates a form of multiculturalist integration. On top of anti-discrimination laws, the state should accommodate the presence of new and existing groups in the public sphere through group-differentiated rights to protect their identities. As each group is marked by difference, integration must take many different forms so each group will have culturally differentiated applications of laws and policies.

Some pluralist multiculturalists also argue that there is a need to continuously review national identity. In the past, these identities may have been linked to nationalism and have been exclusionary, but countries like Canada have shown it is possible to create national identities that are inclusive. These identities and national stories should emerge out of debate and discussion between majority and minority groups in a way that will transform those groups to expand their horizons. The emerging and changing national identity will be inclusive, respectful and build on the identities that people value to create a sense of belonging and willingness to respect deep cultural differences.

> ### Pause & reflect
>
> How does pluralist multiculturalism go beyond liberalism? And why do pluralist multiculturalists reject liberalism?

EXTENSION ACTIVITY

Can a new form of national identity develop in the UK? Read Modood's article at www.theconversation.com/multiculturalism-can-foster-a-new-kind-of-englishness-60759 and think about this question.

Cosmopolitan multiculturalism

Cosmopolitan multiculturalists support cultural diversity and recognise difference while seeing it as the basis for the fading out of cultural groups. **Cosmopolitan integration** asserts that diversity is positive as it allows cultures to interact and learn from each other, and allows individuals the widest range of cultural choice. Individuals pick and mix traits from the different cultures to form new identities.

In the modern world, the growth of social mixing and cultural sharing is driven by globalisation, migration and internet technology. This is leading to the dissolving of old identities, such as race and nation. For example, it is argued that while it made sense to talk of Caribbean-origin Britons in the UK as a singular group in the 1960s, it now makes sense to see this group in a more plural way, with individuals creating and holding multiple identities based on picking and merging aspects of different heritages. This also changes how people identify themselves. People who self-identified as black in the 1980s might have identified as Bangladeshi ten years later, and might see themselves as British Muslims today. Identification with a group now no longer involves active participation in its practices and behaviours. For example, some Indians in the UK identify themselves as Indian but do not use an Indian language, attend a temple, gurdwara or mosque, or wear Indian dress.

This has led to individuals developing multiple, fluid identities that are constructed for themselves and are opposed to the idea of belonging to one particular culture. It is helping to create populations dispersed across different countries that have a greater sense of loyalty to each other than to their fellow citizens. This is the idea of cosmopolitan citizenship that goes beyond communal and national boundaries – individuals see themselves as global citizens. This global understanding expresses unity and dissolves cultural groups and therefore diversity.

The key difference between cosmopolitan multiculturalism and other forms of multiculturalism is that it is a direct challenge to the idea of communitarianism and the view that the individual is culturally embedded. Culture is instead seen as a matter of choice for individuals, based on their changing needs and situation. The key criticism levelled at this view by other multiculturalists is that its 'pick and mix' nature creates new identities that detach people from their own culture and cultural group. These identities may also be seen as inauthentic, which may weaken any sense of cultural belonging – something that could be damaging, both for the individual and for society.

> ### Key term
>
> **Cosmopolitan integration** integration that entails the maximum freedom for minority as well as majority individuals, to mix with, borrow and learn from all cultures.

> ### Pause & reflect
>
> Where does cosmopolitanism differ from other multiculturalist views?

The conservative criticism

Conservatives argue that multiculturalism has led to people from different cultural groups leading separate lives in segregated communities.

Conservative critics of multiculturalism argue that human beings are limited, dependent and security-seeking. By nature, they fear diversity and are drawn to others who share the same values, customs and lifestyles as themselves. The essence of a stable and successful society is shared values and a common culture, but multiculturalism is based on the recognition and celebration of difference, which directly clashes with human nature. There can be no diversity within unity, because multicultural societies will inevitably lead to segregation, conflict and instability. Immigration has increased this concern, with conservatives arguing that recent immigrants do not identify with the traditions and political culture of the state, leading to a weakening sense of national identity.

For conservative critics, an increase in multiculturalism will lead to a rise in resentment among the majority population. Treating all cultures as equal will damage the culture of the majority community, leading to hostility driven by fear. In the UK, this led David Cameron to argue: 'We have even tolerated segregated communities behaving in ways that run counter to our values.' In France, President Sarkozy made this point even more clearly in 2011, when he claimed: 'We have been too concerned about the identity of the person who was arriving and not enough about the identity of the country that was receiving him.'

Conservative critics are also deeply suspicious of the idea of multicultural integration, which argues for a constant revision of the national identity and story. Those who argue for a new, inclusive national identity that is not based on nationalism are demeaning the history and culture of the majority by associating it with colonialism, racism and exploitation. This is made worse by the fact that minority rights favour the interests of minorities while creating reverse discrimination for the majority.

The conservative solution to diversity is based on two main ideas: a strict immigration policy and, where minority communities exist, encouraging minorities to conform to the dominant culture – a process called **assimilation**. Assimilation creates the strong, homogenised national identity necessary for civic unity, flattening cultural difference by forcing minorities to adopt the values, customs and beliefs of the majority.

Key term

Assimilation
the processes affecting change and the relationship between social groups are one-way, with minorities adopting the values, customs and beliefs of the majority.

Pause & reflect

Why do conservatives oppose multiculturalism?

Human nature	For most multiculturalists, individuals are culturally embedded – the culture they grew up deeply shapes them, so it is not possible to isolate one aspect of the individual or a culture and say that it is human nature. For liberal multiculturalists, the importance of culture to the individual provides support for the politics of recognition, identity politics and minority rights. For pluralist multiculturalists, it is more about the central importance of cultural diversity than minority rights. For individuals to have a richer life, their culture must have dialogue with other cultures as this allows them to learn about themselves and humanity as a whole. For cosmopolitan multiculturalists, humans are not culturally embedded, but need different cultures to choose from to form new identities.
The state	The liberal state can provide a basis for diversity in society because it is neutral, there is a clear public–private divide and it is tolerant. It can provide individualist integration to ensure all minorities and immigrants have rights as equal citizens. However, liberal multiculturalists think that the liberal state is not neutral, so it must allocate group differentiated rights to meet the liberal objectives of freedom and autonomy to tackle cultural oppression and protect culture and identity. Pluralist multiculturalists agree that this approach is hospitable to diversity, but argue the state must move beyond just tolerating and accommodating diversity. Liberal universalism places one set of values, ideas and state institutions above all others, creating a 'West versus the rest' divide. As no culture is perfect, this is a mistake and dialogue within and between cultures is necessary for cultural diversity to be the central value. The state must allow and formalise dialogue between cultures, support minority rights and the politics of recognition to promote diversity.
Society	Society is culturally diverse, which gives rise to the question of how to balance diversity and unity. For liberal multiculturalists, this balance can be achieved by creating a sense of civic unity (granting equal rights to all citizens) and supporting new cultural groups (granting minority rights, to create a sense of belonging to their group and society as a whole). Pluralists support multiculturalist integration, including the creation of new national identities and inclusive stories to create a deeper sense of belonging and respect for diversity. Cosmopolitan thinking argues that, as individuals pick and mix from cultures, this will create global citizens with a sense of global unity, and will dissolve cultural diversity. The conservative criticism argues that diversity in society leads to segregation, leading to proposals for strong immigration controls and assimilation.
The economy	Multiculturalists recognise that minority groups can suffer multiple forms of marginalisation. Historically, many minorities have been excluded from public life. Positive discrimination is one way of ensuring full engagement in society and making sure that all aspects of public life reflect a country's diversity. This can include the provision of public resources to support minority groups to rebuild confidence, resist assimilation and enjoy equal recognition. This interaction of minority cultures with the majority culture will bring benefits to the whole of society.

Table 2.1: Core principles and ideas of multiculturalism in action

4.3 Multiculturalist thinkers and their ideas

Isaiah Berlin (1909–97)

Key ideas

- Value pluralism.
- Liberty as a primary goal.

Berlin developed the idea of liberal pluralism, which has influenced the development of pluralist multiculturalism.

- **Value pluralism:** This idea has been used to justify support for diversity and the politics of difference. Berlin argues that there is no singular conception of the good life but rather there are a number of views meaning that human beings will inevitably disagree over their ways of life. Based on experience of life, it is clear that these conceptions will conflict with each other and there is no general way of resolving these conflicts. This requires a society that will give people the space to hold different cultural and moral beliefs while ensuring that there is stability and peace.

Isaiah Berlin: 'Human nature generates values which, though equally sacred, equally ultimate, exclude one another, without there being any possibility of establishing an objective hierarchical relation among them.'

- **Liberty as a primary goal:** Berlin goes beyond the diversity and toleration of liberal multiculturalism. However, Berlin does remain a liberal to the extent he believes that the only type of society that can provide this space as well as the stability is a liberal one. Society must ensure liberty as a primary goal as it allows people to choose between different cultural and moral beliefs. This still leaves the question of how liberal and illiberal beliefs can co-exist peacefully in the same society.

Charles Taylor (1931–)

Key ideas

- Equal dignity.
- Equal recognition.

Charles Taylor is a Canadian philosopher who has influenced the politics of recognition, culture and identity.

- **Equal dignity:** The politics of recognition can be seen in equal dignity, which is difference-blind and based on the equalisation of all rights and entitlements. This equalisation of rights is based on the view that the existence of first-class and second-class citizens should be avoided at all costs. For some this has meant extending civil rights and voting rights to all, although for others this means tackling poverty through socioeconomic measures. These rights and benefits are defined by the dominant culture so the politics of difference is necessary as well.

Charles Taylor: 'Dominant groups tend to entrench their hegemony by inculcating an image of inferiority in the subjugated.'

- **Equal recognition:** Taylor argues that everyone should be recognised for his or her unique identity. The politics of difference is based on the universal right for the individual or the group to have their identity recognised and so is difference-friendly. The outcome is that certain rights will be allocated to particular groups but not others and this involves a positive endorsement of diversity. This form of multiculturalist integration involves both the granting of formal equality and differentiated rights as the basis for group integration into society and for social harmony.

Bhikhu Parekh (1935–)

Key ideas

- Rejection of liberal universalism.
- Cross-cultural dialogue.

Lord Bhikhu Parekh is a political theorist and Labour peer in the House of Lords. He sees liberalism as an inadequate basis for multiculturalism and has developed a form of pluralist multiculturalism.

Bhikhu Parekh: 'A community of citizens and a community of communities.'

- **Rejection of liberal universalism:** Parekh rejects liberal universalism as it sees difference as morally irrelevant by overplaying the significance of our shared human nature. Individuals are culturally embedded and so respect for the individual must entail respect for their cultures and values. No culture is perfect; rather each culture captures only one vision of human life and highlights one set of capabilities – so each culture is valuable but incomplete. Cultures are also internally diverse, so a continuing conversation both within the culture and between cultures is necessary to better understand itself and expand its horizons. This is the basis for deep diversity and the politics of recognition.

- **Cross-cultural dialogue:** There should be cross-cultural dialogue so that cultures can access the treasures from other cultures that are lacking in their own. Hence, diversity strengthens society. This does not mean, as sometimes alleged, that all cultures are equally rich and deserve equal respect. Rather it assumes that no culture is worthless, so all deserve some respect. The dialogue between cultures will be transformative for both the majority and minority cultures and will create common citizenship, based on a shared commitment to the political community. At the same time, the state must use measures such as culturally differentiated applications of laws and policies, state support for minority institutions, and a judicious programme of affirmative action to show that it accepts all cultures and deepens the sense of belonging.

Tariq Modood (1952–)

Key ideas

- Integration.
- National Identity.

Professor Tariq Modood is the founding Director of the Bristol University Research Centre for the Study of Ethnicity and Citizenship. He is particularly concerned with the need to include Muslims in contemporary conceptions of multiculturalism and how multiculturalism is necessary for social cohesion.

Tariq Modood: 'A sense of belonging to one's country is necessary to make a success of a multicultural society.'

- **Integration:** As society is multicultural and all cultures are internally diverse, there is no singular model on integration that fits all. In order to have a real chance of integrating the maximum number of minorities, no model for integration should be dismissed. So all four views of integration – assimilation, individualist, multiculturalism and cosmopolitanism – may be valid based on the context, provided it is the preferred choice of the individual or group and it is not imposed.

- **National identity:** Strong multicultural identities are a good thing and should be recognised as integral to society. Strong identities are not intrinsically divisive but they need a complement of a vibrant, national narrative that gives expression to national identity. This narrative needs to be woven out of debate and discussion between recognised cultural groups. This will ensure that all citizens have not only rights, but a sense of belonging to the whole as well as their own culture.

Will Kymlicka (1962–)

Key ideas

- Self-government rights.
- Polyethnic rights.
- Representation rights.

Will Kymlicka is a Canadian political philosopher who is often seen as the leading thinker of liberal multiculturalism. He develops a case for group-differentiated rights from within liberalism that links rights to personal autonomy. He argues for three different approaches for different reasons.

Will Kymlicka: 'If a culture is not generally respected, then the dignity and self-respect of its members will also be threatened.'

- **Self-government rights** for indigenous peoples or national minorities when geographically concentrated. Minorities did not choose this status but were coercively incorporated into the larger state.

- **Polyethnic rights** for immigrant minority communities – where they are religious or ethnic minorities – that may include legal exemptions from generally applicable laws or bilingual education so that they can maintain their cultural identity, providing fairer terms for integration.

- **Representation rights** for disadvantaged minorities to address the issues of under representation in all areas of public life. This positive discrimination can ensure the full and equal participation of all cultures in society, which protects civic unity.

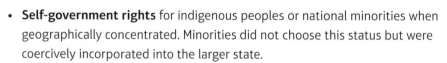

Pause & reflect ✔

For each thinker, summarise how multiculturalism can create social cohesion.

Assessment support: 2.2.4 Multiculturalism

The non-core ideas question is on A-Level Paper 2, Section B. It is worth 24 marks and must be completed in 30 minutes. All ideas questions start 'To what extent' so you must look at both sides of the debate. You are given a choice of two questions in this format, of which you should answer one.

EITHER

3 (a) To what extent do multiculturalists support diversity? [24 marks]

OR

3 (b) To what extent does multiculturalism create tension and conflict in society? [24 marks]

You must use appropriate thinkers you have studied to support your answer and consider any differing views in a balanced way.

This tests all three Assessment Objectives, with marks divided equally between them. You must:

- set out the nature of the debate

- draw similarities and differences between the different strands or tensions

- use at least two relevant thinkers.

Your answer should make judgements based on evidence about the significance of the differences and similarities, leading to a clear and justifiable conclusion.

- Always plan before you write. What are the key similarities and differences between the main strands (conservative criticism versus multiculturalists)? Expand these into the sub-strands (including pluralist, liberal and cosmopolitan multiculturalists) to develop your answer. What ideas of key thinkers are valid for this answer? Try planning your answer to the two questions listed above.

- Your essay should include a brief introduction outlining the main arguments, four main points and a conclusion that should reach an overall judgement that naturally flows from the essay.

Here is part of a student's answer – a middle paragraph – to question 3 (b). The answer has already laid out the conservative view that multiculturalism creates conflict and tension in society.

Liberal multiculturalism is widely viewed as a solution to cultural tensions and social conflict because it endorses diversity within a framework of liberalism, which is a form of shallow diversity. It confines diversity and difference principally to the 'private' sphere, while providing equal dignity in the public sphere. This enables individuals to integrate into wider society and preserves a sense of civic unity, as represented by the American oath of allegiance and the US ideal of 'out of many, one'. On the other hand, pluralist multiculturalists raise the issue as to whether the state, by relegating culture to the private sphere, is acting in a neutral way. The liberal state cannot be neutral as it promotes liberal monism according to Parekh, which still marginalises other cultures and identities, as seen in the case of the ban on the niqab in France. This only serves to deepen tensions in society by alienating cultural groups, whereas pluralists argue only deep diversity can provide the solution to social conflict.

- This paragraph reveals a clear understanding of how liberal multiculturalists believe multiculturalism can be a solution to conflicts and tensions in society.

- It makes the point that there is a clear disagreement between multiculturalists as to how to solve cultural tensions and conflicts, by contrasting liberal and pluralist multiculturalist views. Parekh is used here as the thinker to explore this difference.

- The last sentence allows the student to move on to the next paragraph where they consider whether pluralist multiculturalism solves the tensions or creates balkanisation.

Nationalism

Nationalism is an ideology that has at its core the belief that nations are the only genuine community in society. Because of this view, nationalists tend to see the world from the perspective of the nation.

There can be no doubt as to the significance of nationalism as an idea that motivates people to act, and that has the capacity to realign geopolitics. Across the globe, whether over the last decade, century or even millennium, world history and geography have been shaped by nationalist ideas.

However, nationalism is not one cohesive ideology. Different types of nationalism can be so widely defined so as to have no clear meaning. Brexit, the annexation of Crimea, Scottish independence and conflict in the Middle East are all recent examples caused by different interpretations of nationhood and self-determination. Further back, the war in the Balkans, the fall of the Berlin Wall and apartheid in South Africa are all connected to nationalism too. Most of the world's conflicts, including the two World Wars, are linked to the ideas of nationalism covered in this chapter.

This chapter looks at:

- the core ideas of nationalism
- how these apply to human nature, the state, society and the economy
- the different views and tensions within nationalism
- the key ideas of some of nationalism's key thinkers.

5.1 Core ideas and principles

With liberalism, socialism and conservatism, the core principles knit together to form a cohesive whole; however, with nationalism they do not. Instead this chapter covers ideas and principles that are vital to understanding the different types of nationalism.

Nations

All forms of nationalism recognise the nation as the basis of a community. However, there is much discussion about what a nation is.

A nation refers to people – or more specifically to 'a people'. Belonging to a nation means being part of larger group of people who share particular characteristics like language, culture, values, traditions, history or religion. Generally, a nation can be identified as a group of people who identify themselves as such – as long as people identify with the characteristics that they have in common, they can be considered as a nation.

Confusion arises in part because different nations have different characteristics. So, the British may consider themselves a nation, but many Scots identify instead with a Scottish nation. People from most of Spain may identify with Spanish nationhood, while those from Barcelona may see themselves as Catalonian.

Some people born in Spain would see the Catalonian flag (left) as representing their nation, rather than the Spanish flag (right).

The French consider their language to be a key part of their nationhood, and it might be argued that the love of food is an important part of national identity, while religion is categorically not a part of France's nationhood (unlike, for example, Italy).

By contrast, American nationhood has been forged on the idea of the 'American dream', which is the view that anyone, no matter what their background, can be successful if they work hard enough. The American nation is sometimes seen as a 'melting pot', where immigrants from other countries and other cultures came to America, and different cultures have merged to form a new culture. This is the opposite of the **multiculturalist** 'mosaic' or 'salad bowl' approach, which encourages different cultures to hold on to their unique cultures, but live alongside each other peacefully in one nation.

> ### Link ↱
>
> For more on **multiculturalism**, see Multiculturalism chapter.

Pause & reflect ✔

What do you think the shared characteristics of the Spanish nation are? What unifies them as a nation?

Self-determination

Self-determination can be defined as nations being able to decide how they are governed. Applied to individuals, this could be called autonomy or independence. The belief in self-determination is based on the view that nations are a genuine political association and that only they know what is in their own national interest.

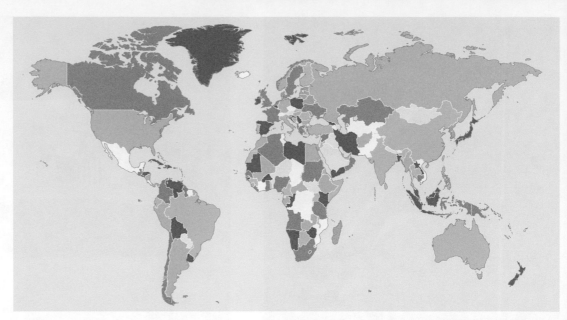

Figure 1.1: Compared to maps from earlier centuries, where nations had no right of self determination, this map from 2016 shows how important self-determination has become as a political aim. It shows 196 countries; in 1900 the figure was around 70.

Self-determination sounds relatively uncontroversial, yet different forms of nationalism have very different views about its benefits and desirability for other nations. Some nationalists rest on the belief that international order can only exist when all nations have the right of self-determination; others believe that only they, and no other nation, have the right to self-determination.

Many conflicts throughout history have existed because of self-determination. The Balkans war in the 1990s came after the collapse of the Soviet Union, when the Serbs, Croats, Slovenians and Bosnians – each of whom identified themselves as individual nations – fought to win self-determination.

*Autonomous provinces

*Kosovo is administered by the UN

Figure 1.2: Until the 1990s, Yugoslavia was one country, but the desire for self-determination from the different nations within it led to the violent and bloody Balkans conflict.

Pause & reflect ✔

How many nations are there in the UK? What are they? Why is the Union Jack called that? Do you know which flags it is composed of?

Nation-state

If a 'nation' is a group of people who identify themselves as such, a 'state' simply refers to a geographical area with clear boundaries – so the term 'nation-state' can be defined as a nation of people who rule themselves in their own sovereign territory.

The nation-state comes about through national self-determination, and the two concepts are closely related. In today's world – particularly in Europe – the nation-state is the usual organisation of a country. France is ruled by the French in their own geographical territory, Denmark is ruled by the Danes in their own geographical territory, and so on.

However, this has not always been the case. As recently as the 1970s, the nation of Germany was divided into two states, and Yugoslavia – which has now disintegrated, with its component states becoming nations in their own right – was one country (see Figures 1.2 and 1.3).

Figure 1.3: National boundaries in Europe in 1970 showed a divided German nation and Yugoslavia, which contained many nations all being ruled together in one state.

It has been the aim of mainly **liberal nationalists** to create a world of nation-states. However, other forms of nationalism, specifically **chauvinistic nationalism**, rejected this idea, believing that only some nations can benefit from nation-statehood, while other nations should accept their position as colonies of the 'stronger' nations.

EXTENSION ACTIVITY

Do some research to find other flags that represent 'blended' nations. For two of these, write notes on how the 'blend' came about.

Link

For more on **Liberal nationalism**, see Section 5.2.

Key term

Chauvinistic nationalism a form of nationalism that believes one nation is superior to others, regarding them as a threat to survival.

> **Pause & reflect**
>
> How is the Russian invasion of Crimea in 2014 an example of conflicting ideas of the nation-state?

Self-determination versus colonialism

Key term

Colonialism
also known as imperialism, the extension of control by one country over another by settlement or economic domination.

The further you go back in history, the fewer nation-states you will find. It used to be a sign of power and prestige for larger countries to rule other countries – known as **imperialism** or **colonialism** (although these two terms mean slightly different things).

Having an empire was the key aim of monarchs and countries throughout history. Citizens of European countries will be familiar with stories of historical figures finding 'new' countries and bringing back delights from far-flung shores, such as Sir Francis Drake bringing potatoes from South America back to England for Queen Elizabeth I. The 'newly discovered' countries actually already existed, with indigenous populations who had their own governments, cultures and economies.

EXTENSION ACTIVITY

What examples are there of 'newly discovered' countries that already had an indigenous population? Were these issues ever resolved? If so, how?

Key terms

Civic nationalism
a form of nationalism based on a shared vision of an individual's duty to observe given laws and, in turn, receive legal privileges.

Rational
using or being able to use reason or logic in making decisions.

Volksgeist
the 'spirit' of a nation; the unique identity of a people based on their culture.

Culturalism

Culturalism is a way of understanding nationhood. It is the view that people have an emotional connection with their country that draws them together. Whereas **civic nationalism**, like liberal nationalism, are based on a **rational** approach to nationhood, culturalism argues that people have a deeper, emotional tie to their country.

Proponents of culturalism believe that each nation has an essence that is tied up in its music, art, folklore and language. German intellectual Johann Gottfried von Herder wrote about culturalism in the 18th century, claiming that each nation has its own unique *volksgeist* – folk spirit, a culmination of its own unique experiences, history and culture. For Herder, no nation could be the same as any other, and each nation's culture was as valuable as any other's.

Herder is seen by many as the developer of culturalism, but his ideas have been used in a darker way by some to support the idea of **expansionist nationalism**. This is the idea that one nation's unique spirit can be superior to that of other nations, thereby justifying imperialism and domination. However, Herder himself rejected this idea, writing that 'notwithstanding the varieties of the human form, there is but one and the same species of man throughout the whole earth'.

Link

For more on **expansionist nationalism**, see Section 5.2.

Unlike civic nationalism, which argues that nationhood can be virtually instant, cultural views of nationalism say that membership of a nation takes time to develop. For example, a person may be able to become a French citizen, and be able to speak French fluently, but this does not necessarily make them truly French. They may technically be French, but they will only become 'genuinely' French after they have spent years living as a French person, absorbing themselves in French culture and the French way of life.

Culturalism is concerned with protecting a nation's unique culture, without necessarily focusing on specific ambitions for statehood. An often-used example of this is Wales. The Welsh are proud of their unique culture within the United Kingdom, and many wish to revive the Welsh language in schools and ensure that Welsh folklore and songs continue throughout the generations. However, compared to their Scottish counterparts, the Welsh have far less interest in self-determination and independence. Instead they see their devolution settlement as an acceptable way to gain the freedom to protect their culture, without needing total political independence.

Culturalism has strong links with the concept of patriotism – having a significant emotional connection with a country. Patriotism may even result in a willingness to make significant sacrifices to promote the country's best interests. In this way, patriotism is the embodiment of national cultural identity.

The Welsh take particular pride in their prowess as a rugby-playing nation.

Racialism

The Oxford English Dictionary defines racialism (or racism) as 'the belief that all members of each race possess characteristics, abilities, or qualities specific to that race, especially so as to distinguish it as inferior or superior to another race or races'.

Racialist ideas are rooted in the belief that humanity is not one single human race, but can be meaningfully divided into separate races. This view states that the differences between the races are biological and fixed. Racialist theories usually ascribe different traits to different races, with certain races being naturally 'good' or 'bad' at different things, which leads to a racial hierarchy. Racialist theories then usually advocate racial segregations, to avoid 'polluting' the blood stock of the races.

Case study: Hitler's racialist theories

Racialist ideas are more than mere bigotry or prejudice; many have used pseudo-scientific language to justify their theories. One of the most extreme examples of this are the racialist theories of Hitler's Nazi Germany. Using the views of Count Gobineau and H.S. Chamberlain, Hitler came to the view that history was a struggle between the races, with the principle struggle between the Jews and the Aryan race. For Hitler, the world was generally divided into three groups: founders, bearers and destroyers of culture. Founders were responsible for all creativity in the world, bearers were able to appreciate the greatness of the founders but destroyers were pitted in an unending battle with the founders of culture and responsible for all evil in society. The Aryans were the founders of culture; the bearers were the Slavs, Asians and the Latin people; the destroyers of culture were gypsies, black people and the Jews.

Questions

- Looking at the explanation of racialism, how well do Nazi race theories fit with the definition?
- Why were Nazi racial theories called pseudo-science?

Figure 1.4: Founders, bearers and destroyers of culture

Key term

Ethnicity
the sense of belonging to
a social group that shares
a common and distinctive
culture, religion, language
and history.

Race versus ethnicity

The word **ethnicity** has largely replaced the word race in everyday usage, but the two terms
do not mean the same thing. Race concerns a person's biological make-up. Ethnicity refers to a
variety of attributes about an individual: the culture they associate with, the culture their parents
were brought up in (their ancestry), the language they speak, the history of the region they were
brought up in and, in some cases, their religion.

Mo Farah proudly holding a Union Jack after winning a gold medal in London 2012.

Mo Farah is a British citizen, but that is just one way he could be described. Referring to his 'race',
he could be described as black, but this does not advance our understanding of Farah much
further. However, understanding his ethnicity gives a much fuller picture. Mo Farah was born in
Somalia and came to London at the age of eight to join his father (a British citizen). He barely spoke
any English when he arrived. He went to school in London where his talents were spotted and he
was encouraged to pursue athletics. He has gone on to become a double-double Olympic gold-
medal winner. Mo Farah is a devout Muslim and an Arsenal supporter. In 2016, he was honoured
with a knighthood. Exploring someone's ethnicity, as opposed to making simple judgements
on them based on their race, allows us to explore a variety of aspects of a person's experiences
and ancestry.

Internationalism

Generally, internationalism is the belief that the peoples of the world should unite and connect
across national boundaries, looking beyond what is best for individual nations to see what is
best for the world. Its aim is to secure a peaceful world. It may seem odd to see a discussion
of internationalism in a chapter on nationalism, but some types of nationalism also have an
internationalist perspective. This section will look at two main types of internationalism.

- Liberal internationalism.
- Socialist internationalism.

Liberal internationalism

Liberal nationalism is based on applying the core principles of liberal individualism to the nation. Nations have the right to self-determination as much as individuals have the right to individual autonomy and freedom. The liberal nationalist aim, therefore, is a world of independent nation-states.

Liberal nationalists also assume that independent nation-states will seek to co-operate with each other as and when they need to – economically, educationally and culturally. This will create interdependence as they trade goods and services, share ideas and exchange cultures.

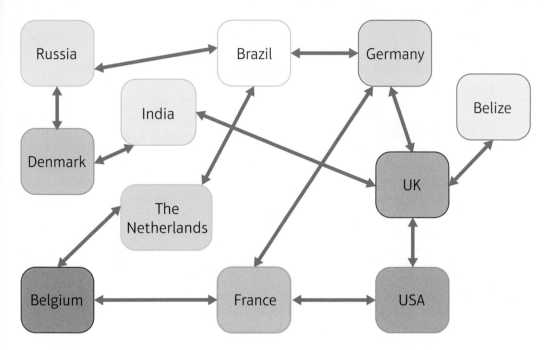

Figure 1.5: Liberal internationalism is based on the belief that interdependency between nations creates peace and stability.

The key aim of this co-operation and interdependency is to secure an internationally stable and peaceful world where disputes can be resolved rationally, without resorting to violence. This has led liberals to put their faith in supranational institutions – institutions that exist 'above' national institutions – such as the EU or the UN, to help resolve conflicts between nations. Just as sovereign individuals need to be kept in check by a state, so sovereign nation-states need to be kept in check by supranational institutions.

Socialist internationalism

The other well-known and more typical form of internationalism is **socialist internationalism**, which is largely incompatible with nationalism. Socialist internationalism is concerned with extending the idea of co-operation, community and humanity across the world, believing that humans are not naturally divided into nations and are instead connected to the whole of humanity, whatever country they happen to be living in.

Socialism is an internationalist ideology and rejects the concept of nationalism. Indeed, it was Karl Marx who said, 'The working man has no country'. Marx and Engels believed that nationalism and patriotism were part of 'false consciousness' and a way of keeping the truth hidden from ordinary people. Nationalism artificially divided the proletariat into the French, German and British nationalities to stop them from seeing that they were all exploited by the bourgeoisie. The point of 'false consciousness' was to stop the international proletariat from uniting and rising up against their (minority) bourgeoisie bosses.

Later, Lenin re-visited nationalism in his writings on imperialism. In his 1917 booklet *Imperialism, the Highest Stage of Capitalism*, Lenin's premise was that capitalism had avoided collapse (as predicted by Marx) by 'buying off' its indigenous population with proceeds made by exploiting the proletariats in its colonies. This gave the country's own workers improved wages and working conditions while ruthlessly exploiting workers in other countries it controlled. In this way Lenin extended Marx and Engels' analysis of nationalism as being a tool used by capitalism to prevent a proletarian revolution.

> ### Pause & reflect
>
> Can you explain the relationship between nationalism and the two different forms of internationalism?

Human nature	Civic nationalism is a rational form of nationalism, as it is based on citizens actively participating in society as equals. Liberal nationalism is rational, inclusive and progressive. It promotes mutual respect for rights and national identities, believing that sovereign nations should co-operate to create interdependency and avoid conflict. Culturalism, when nationhood is based on shared culture rather than civic loyalties, is a more emotional, irrational approach to nationalism, centred on *volksgeist* – the unique, cultural 'spirit' of a nation. It is an exclusive form of nationalism, as it takes time to be a part of the nation. Expansionist, chauvinistic forms of nationalism are the most irrational, believing a nation (and sometimes race) to be naturally superior to others, who threaten their survival. These forms often result in integral nationalism – an intense, hysterical form of nationalism in which the individual is absorbed into the nation. Some argue that all nationalism is based on irrationality, as all subscribe to patriotism, which is defined as having a significant emotional connection with a country. Some argue nationalism is part of their nature.
The state	All nationalists recognise the role of the state in the sense of a nation-state. Liberal and anti/post-colonial nationalists see the nation-state as the only legitimate unit of government, advancing freedom from oppressive imperialist domination and allowing nations to decide their own destiny within their own borders. Liberal internationalists seek a world of independent nation-states, as this offers the prospect of peace and international order if regulated by supranational law and states. Conservative nationalism values the nation-state as a socially and culturally cohesive unit, helping to bind the nation closer together. Expansionist, chauvinistic forms of nationalism reject nation-statehood for all, believing it is only for a privileged few nations that are sufficiently developed.
Society	Civic nationalism is based on a commitment to a shared vision of society based on civic loyalties where society requires people's active participation. This represents an inclusive vision of society, not based on shared experiences. Traditionally, civic nationalism is associated with a progressive society, where society is constantly improving and advancing. However, culturalism is based on people sharing cultural values in society. Often culturalism is based on defining the nation by ethnicity, when a nation shares a common distinctive culture, religion or language. This is a more exclusive vision of society. Extreme versions of culturalism are chauvinism and racialism, where society seeks a divide into 'us' and 'them'. These ideas can be seen as regressive, as they seek to revert society to a former or less advanced state.

| The economy | A nation-state can be defined as a group of people who control their economy. Liberal nationalists assume that independent nation-states want to co-operate economically, leading to a peaceful world where disputes are resolved rationally. Socialist internationalists argue that nationalism is based on economic exploitation of weak economies by strong capitalist ones. Lenin argued that capitalism had avoided collapse by 'buying off' its indigenous population with proceeds made by exploiting colonies, while Garvey argued that black people would be respected only when they were economically strong, and proposed an independent black economy. Chauvinistic nationalism sees other nations as a threat to their survival. As such they support autarky, which means being economically self-sufficient. Expansionist, chauvinistic forms of nationalism reject any reliance and co-operation with other nations. This need for economic self-sufficiency also creates an additional reason for colonialism. |

Table 1.1: Core principles and ideas of nationalism in action

5.2 Different types of nationalism

Many different types of nationalism have developed from the principles and ideas outlined above. Anthony Smith referred to nationalism as a 'chameleon ideology' because of its ability to adapt itself to virtually any ideology. There are examples of extreme right-wing nationalism and types of left-wing nationalism.

Heater wrote of three paradoxes contained within nationalism.

- It can be a force for peace or violence.
- It can be a force for democracy or dictatorship.
- It can be either **progressive**, moving towards improving society, or reactionary, opposing progress or reform.

Key term

Progressive
ideas, movements or groups that move towards improving society.

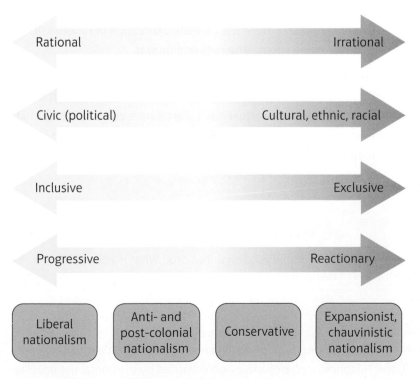

Figure 2.1: Nationalism shown as a sliding scale

Link

For more on **liberalism**, see Liberalism chapter.

Key term

Inclusive nationalism
a form of nationalism that believes that joining a nation is straightforward and quick as it is not based on shared previous experiences.

Liberal nationalism

Liberal nationalism can be understood by applying **liberal ideas** of individualism to the nation. Liberal nationalists see nations as entities with their own rights; if individuals are entitled to determine their own destiny, so are nations. The ideal form of government for liberal nationalists is the nation-state, which is seen as the only legitimate basis for political rule – the ideal political community. A state gives nations a meaningful and autonomous existence whereby they can fulfil their national ambitions.

For liberal nationalists, nationhood is **inclusive** and open. This is based on a civic understanding of nationhood – being committed and loyal to the nation's values is the primary requirement for membership, so anyone who identifies passionately with the values of a nation should be permitted to join it. This form of nationalism is also progressive – society is forward-looking, seeking to advance and improve to make itself better and fairer.

In the 18th century, the Enlightenment gave rise to the idea that the nation-state was the ultimate expression of rationalism; people of the same nation should rule themselves in their own state. For liberals, there is an intrinsic link between nationhood and statehood, so they seek the ideal of a world of independent nation-states. Liberals associate nationalism with freeing nations from colonial enslavement and creating democratic nation-states.

Liberals also believe that independent nation-states will co-operate with each other for mutual benefit, and that economics can play a key role in helping to create a stable and peaceful world order. Free trade between nations plays an important role in creating a culture of interdependency. The liberal ideal is a world of independent nation-states co-operating with each other economically, creating a level of interdependence that would reduce the possibility of conflict, as countries who trade with each other and are mutually interdependent will always seek peaceful ways of resolving areas of disagreement.

When the European Union was set up in the 1950s, it was not primarily for economic purposes. The fundamental purpose of the EU was to promote greater social, political and economic harmony among the nations of Western Europe, as nations whose economies are interdependent are less likely to engage in conflict. For liberal nationalists, this is the ultimate expression of rationalism – reason dominating irrationalism and discussion triumphing over waging war.

However, in the same way that liberals fear that a few powerful individuals may harm weaker ones if there is no rule of law enforced by a state so liberal nationalists have been concerned that more powerful nation-states may try to dominate less powerful ones. Liberals have come to accept that supranational institutions may be necessary to 'police' the international political world. This idea was the motivation behind the creation of the League of Nations and the United Nations. Liberals also support the idea of collective security as practised by NATO.

Pause & reflect

Why are the UN and the EU examples of supranational organisations? What is 'collective security' and how do the members of NATO use it to ensure peace?

Conservative nationalism

Conservative nationalism is an inward-looking form of nationalism that shows little interest in self-determination for other nations. Historically, conservatives were worried by the liberal nationalism that was associated with the French Revolution as it threatened the stability of the existing world order. However, conservatives came to appreciate other aspects of nationalism, which it shaped into its own unique brand of nationalism.

Conservative nationalism tends to exist in older nation-states, like the UK and France. It was seen as a way of creating a sense of cohesion and unity within society. When countries have existed for centuries and their existence has not come under threat for many decades or even centuries, creating a sense of national unity of purpose can be difficult. Conservatives saw that using nationalism to focus on shared traditions, history and culture could create a common bond within a nation, which could override issues that divided its people. They understand nationhood more in cultural terms, as people who share common traditions, history and heritage.

Conservatism is an ideology that is primarily concerned with conserving society as it is; conservative nationalism sees the nation as a focal point of national unity, helping to bind people together. Conservative nationalism seeks to remind its citizens of what they have in common and what past experiences they share – what historical catastrophes and political storms they have endured together. Essentially it uses nostalgia to create a cohesive society.

Conservative nationalists use the state and associated institutions – such as the monarchy – as a source of unity that embodies the spirit of the nation. National celebrations, such as anniversaries of historic victories or birth dates of significant figures from the past, commemorate the uniqueness of the nation's culture, while international sporting events foster a sense of national unity.

> **Link**
>
> For more on **conservatism**, see Conservatism chapter.

'Our' Queen

In the UK, nothing exemplifies using state institutions as a source of unity more than Queen Elizabeth II. Since she became heir to the throne in 1936, through to her becoming Queen in 1952 and up until the present day, she personifies the United Kingdom. National celebrations and commemorations revolve around her. She is a symbol of Britishness, of quiet strength in the face of adversity; even though the world has changed dramatically during her reign on the throne, and many of her subjects may feel frightened by such changes, she is constant. The Queen's birthdays and anniversaries are celebrated with pomp and ceremony, and she even became a highlight of the opening ceremony at the London 2012 Olympics.

Conservatives believe that humans seek security and tend to be drawn to their 'own' people. Conservative nationalism encourages an emotional, nostalgic view of the nation and uses rituals and ceremonies to appeal to people's deep cultural connection to their nation. In this sense, it is irrational – it is based on emotions, not reason and logic.

Conservative nationalists have understood the enormous power of patriotism as a unifying force in society and have used it as a basis for political order and stability. Instead of seeing society as made up of rich and poor, or old and young, conservative nationalists encourage us to see ourselves as one British nation – the **'one nation'** of Disraeli's strand of conservatism.

However, unlike liberal nationalism, conservative nationalism can tend towards **exclusiveness**. To feel part of the nation, you need to have shared the historical events that bind society together. For example, if you weren't living in the UK during the Blitz in the 1940s you cannot possibly understand the 'spirit of the Blitz' that existed. People are essentially excluded from feeling part of the nation until they themselves have shared experiences as part of the nation. Membership of the nation is thus not instant, but takes time.

> **Link**
>
> For more on **one-nation conservatism**, see Section 1.2 of Conservatism.

> **Key term**
>
> **Exclusive nationalism** a form of nationalism that believes that it takes time to be a part of the nation, as membership is based on shared history and/or language.

Conservative nationalism can also be inward-looking because it aims to defend its own national identity and way of life, rather than concern itself with the interests of other nations. To be part of the nation, you must be prepared to give up any customs and traditions of your own that go against the national character. Because of this, immigrants need to assimilate into British society and adopt its customs. Conservative nationalism thus stands against the notion of cultural diversity and multiculturalism, requiring an absolute commitment to the shared customs, values and beliefs of the host nation. If the stability and unity of society seem to be threatened by immigration, conservative nationalism can become hostile, suspicious and xenophobic.

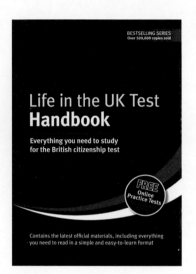

In 2002, David Blunkett, home secretary under Prime Minister Tony Blair, introduced citizenship tests and English-language tests to those wishing to become citizens of the UK.

Case study: The cricket test

In the 1980s, British Conservative politician Norman Tebbit came under heavy criticism over what came to be called 'the cricket test'. Post-war Britain had received many people migrating from ex-colonies in the West Indies and South Asia where cricket was a major sport. In an interview with the *Los Angeles Times*, Tebbit referred to these communities when talking about integration in the UK, saying: 'A large proportion of Britain's Asian population fail to pass the cricket test. Which side do they cheer for? It's an interesting test. Are you still harking back to where you came from, or where you are?'

Question

- What does the cricket test show about conservative nationalism's view on assimilation and multiculturalism?

Despite the fact that Tebbit's quote received widespread negative coverage, multiculturalism and lack of assimilation of immigrant populations continued to concern many in the UK. Anti-immigration sentiment was a key factor in the 2016 Brexit vote. Moreover, the national character and culture were also felt to be under assault by the European Union, a remote European bureaucratic elite trying to impose very different attitudes and culture on the UK. This could be seen as an issue related to culturalism.

Pause & reflect

Why did the Blair government introduce a citizenship test in the UK? What were its aims?

Anti-colonial and post-colonial nationalism

Anti-colonial and post-colonial nationalism are terms that have been used to describe countries that have gone through two historical phases, giving their experience of nationalism a dual character.

- Anti-colonial nationalism refers to the first stage, where the indigenous population of the colonies begin questioning and then rejecting the supremacy and authority of the colonial powers. This usually emerges alongside a rising sense of their own nationhood.

- Post-colonial nationalism refers to the second phase and the experiences of these nations once they have achieved their goal of independence.

The 'scramble for Africa' refers to a time period beginning in the 1880s when the European powers invaded, occupied and annexed Africa for their own interests. The Berlin Conference of 1884–85 aimed to regulate colonialisation and trade in Africa, and was the start of a period when European powers wiped out most forms of autonomous government in the African continent. Before this, only 10 per cent of Africa was under colonial rule; by 1914 the figure had risen to 90 per cent.

To European powers, Africa was an untapped natural resource with an undeveloped economy and the potential to bring in huge profits, along with the opportunity to spread their own culture, language and religion across the globe.

When colonial powers rule over an area, they encourage the indigenous populations they ruled over to reject their own culture and traditions and adopt the ruler's language, culture and religion. Today many African nations have English, French or Portuguese as their official language – a leftover from colonial days.

The Berlin Conference, with the German chancellor Otto von Bismarck about to divide up the 'cake' of Africa between the different powers of Europe.

Anti-colonial nationalism started when these oppressed nations began to recognise their oppression and reject the culture of their oppressors, wishing to follow their own traditional ways. It can be seen as a form of liberal nationalism – the desire for a nation to rule itself in its own sovereign territory. But anti-colonial nationalism is distinct as it refers to the experiences of African, Asian and Latin American nations, which were all subject to the same phenomenon over a similar period. The symbol of India's anti-colonial movement was Mahatma Gandhi.

Case study: India under British rule

Mahatma Gandhi was the main leader of India's independence movement. He advocated a form of non-violent resistance known as *Satyagraha* (truth and firmness) against the British: 'My ambition is no less than to convert the British people through non-violence and thus make them see the wrong they have done to India.'

One infamous event of this campaign was the Salt March. In protest over the Salt laws, Gandhi walked from his retreat near Ahmedabad to the Arabian Sea, 240 miles away, and was joined on the way by thousands of marchers. On arrival, they were confronted by British policemen. More than 60,000 were arrested including Gandhi, but the campaign continued. When an American journalist reported on policemen viciously beating a group of peaceful demonstrators, there was an international outcry over the injustice Indians faced at the hands of the British. Gandhi was named *Time* magazine's 'Man of the Year' for 1930.

India was granted independence in 1947. The history books identify Gandhi and his method of *Satyagraha* as the key reason for its occurrence.

Gandhi and his form of non-violent resistance were instrumental in India's move to independence.

Question

• What effect do you think the Second World War had on India's push for independence?

Post-colonial nationalism refers to the experiences of these nations once they have achieved their goal of independence. In post-colonial societies, colonial rule was often replaced by non-Western or anti-Western ideas. Often these nations wished to throw off the yolk of colonialism in every way, and certainly did not seek to replicate their oppressors by setting up capitalist, liberal democracies.

Many African and Asian nations saw the point of independence as being free to shape their own destiny, based on their traditional culture and practises. Often they looked towards socialist ideas to provide a framework. Post-colonial nationalism has found connections with socialism for a number of reasons.

• They related strongly to Lenin's analysis of imperialism as a form of capitalist oppression. For many colonies, Lenin's scrutiny gave them an insight into their oppression in economic terms. Lenin argued that rich, Western capitalist countries could 'buy off' the indigenous working-class of their colonies by exploiting and pillaging the raw materials and cheap labour.

• Former colonies could use Marxist–Leninism as a guide for developing their countries' national movements and as a focal, unifying force.

• Former colonies have been attracted to socialist values that resonate with their more traditional ways of life as communities, co-operating together and sharing ownership.

African Socialism

African Socialism was practised by Léopold Senghor of Senegal, Kwame Nkrumah of Ghana and Julius Nyerere of Tanzania. Nyerere is also associated with the concept of *Ujamaa* – 'familyhood' in Swahili – which he used as the basis for the rejuvenation of Tanzania after it gained independence from Britain in 1961. Wanting a system unlike that of the colonial masters, Nyerere created a one-party state, with the nationalisation of industry and the collectivisation of agriculture. He also insisted on free education, resulting in extremely high literacy rates, and medical facilities that helped halve infant mortality. Nyerere aimed to unite Tanzania by encouraging Tanzanians to reject tribal loyalties, creating a relatively cohesive nation. However, his economic experiment failed, leaving poor infrastructure and a crippled economy reliant on international aid.

Post-colonial nationalism has been linked with **black nationalism** through **Marcus Garvey** and the many movements that emerged from his ideas. Garvey was born in Jamaica but travelled to London and then the United States to extend his understanding. He saw black people returning from the Second World War, thinking that their war effort would lead to equal treatment by American society, only to see nothing change and losing hope of genuine equality.

Garvey believed that the answer was twofold.

- Black people should learn to be proud of their race and see beauty in themselves (for example, by leaving their hair naturally as 'afros', rather than straightening it to make it seem more like white people's hair).

- A second, more radical alternative, was for black people to go to Africa and set up an African nation in their ancient homeland. Only when black people could show white people that they could be successful economically, culturally and politically in their own homeland would they start to earn the respect of others and be treated as equals.

Expansionist nationalism

There is no clear unifying philosophy behind expansionist nationalism, but these forms of nationalism tend to exist alongside a belief in chauvinism. National chauvinism is the belief in the superiority of one nation, and the inferiority of other nations. It tends to be explicitly racialist, where membership of the nation is often restricted to those of a specific 'race'.

Expansionist nationalism is typically associated with the fascist regimes in 1930s and 1940s Germany, Italy and Japan, but could also be seen in the 'scramble for Africa' exercised by the European powers in the 19th century. All these nations believed themselves to be superior to and more deserving than other nations. Hitler's concept of *lebensraum* – a living space in the East, which he wrote about at length in *Mein Kampf* – outlines this idea perfectly: 'The National Socialist Movement must strive to eliminate the disproportion between our population and our area.'

Simply put, the Aryan race were the master race, superior to the Slavic race who occupied a huge area to the east of Germany, which was full of natural and mineral resources. It was therefore wrong that an inferior race should occupy such a large, plentiful area while the Aryan, master race were crowded into a smaller, less abundant land. To Hitler, the answer was as obvious as it was simple. The Aryan race should take the large expanse of land to their east – the Soviet Union – for themselves.

Another reason for expanding into other territories was for economic self-sufficiency (autarky), rejecting any reliance and co-operation with other nations. Germany suffered from trade blockades during the Second World War that caused food shortages, so the need for economic self-sufficiency via newly acquired land gave it an added impetus.

Key term

Black nationalism
a reaction to white oppression originating in the mid-20th century.

Link

For more on **Marcus Garvey**, see Section 5.3.

The UNIA (Universal Negro Improvement Association) became the flag of the Pan-African movement, which was influenced by Garvey's ideas.

Figure 2.2: Nazi Germany expands into Europe

Expansionist forms of nationalism are highly militaristic. They associate an empire with evidence of national greatness, based on the notion of 'survival of the fittest' nation – and the army is the tool through which this can be achieved. Attention is focused on remilitarising and expanding the army. The state, government and army become fused and the country's resources are devoted to the mission of world domination.

Expansionist nationalism is highly irrational in its outlook. Its belief in national chauvinism is a form of **integral nationalism**; the individual is swept away on a tide of intense, passionate patriotism, and is prepared to make any sacrifices for the good of the nation. As Charles Maurras said, 'A true nationalist places his country above everything.' These types of nationalism tend to use past periods of national greatness alongside myths, art, culture and folklore to create a highly emotional, anti-rational approach to nationalism.

These ideas are also highly **regressive**. Society returns to a former or less developed state, often by supporting ideas and values from previous times that may be seen as old-fashioned.

Key terms

Integral nationalism
an intense, hysterical form of patriotism in which the individual is absorbed into the nation.

Regressive
seeking to revert society to a former or less advanced state.

EXTENSION ACTIVITY

In what way were Mussolini's Italy or Japan in 1940s examples of chauvinistic as well as expansionist nationalism?

Nazi Germany is a good example of integral nationalism.

5.3 Nationalist thinkers and their ideas

Jean-Jacques Rousseau (1712–1778)

Key ideas

- The collective will of the community.
- Legitimate government requires active citizen participation.

Jean-Jacques Rousseau: 'Man is born free; and everywhere he is in chains. One thinks himself the master of others, and still remains a greater slave than they.'

Rousseau was born in Geneva and his political philosophy was highly influential during the Enlightenment as well as on liberal thought. He is seen as the father of modern nationalism – particularly liberal nationalism – despite the fact that his writings did not specifically discuss the issue of the nation.

- **General will:** Rousseau argued that governments should be based on the indivisible, collective will of the 'community'. This notion of community was based on the idea of a national community – a nation. He argued that these communities had the right to govern themselves, so he was associated with the idea of national self-determination.

- **Government:** For Rousseau, governments were obliged to listen to the collective will of the people and ensure that its laws applied universally. The government's function is to enforce the collective will of the people, not to direct it.

- **Civic nationalism:** Rousseau argued that the state can only be legitimate when it is based on the active participation of its citizens. He went on to write *The Social Contract* (1762), which expands on this idea. This forms the basis of civic nationalism.

Johann Gottfried von Herder (1744–1803)

Key ideas

- Every nation has its own unique character.
- *Volksgeist* – the special spirit of a nation.

Johann Gottfried von Herder: 'Each nationality contains its centre of happiness within itself.'

Herder was associated primarily with culturalism. He rejected the rational beliefs of liberal forms of nationalism, focusing instead on nations as cultural, organic groups invested with their own unique 'spirit'.

- **Culturalism:** Herder suggested that every nation was different, and that each had its own unique character and identity that it should pursue and enhance. Humanity was a single species but had developed different languages, cultures and ways of life because people evolved in different environments. Relations between nations allowed an understanding of other nationalities, and encouraged people to understand what was distinctive about their own nation.

- ***Volksgeist:*** Herder identified the people (*Volk*) as the root of national culture and special nature (*Volksgeist*) that each nation should try to express. The *Volk* could best be understood by studying their history – their language, culture, customs, religion, literature, law and folklore. Herder argued that nation-states are an expression of cultural differences, not the creator of them.

- **Patriotism:** Herder attached exceptional importance to the concept of nationality: 'He that has lost his patriotic spirit has lost himself and the whole worlds about himself.'

Giuseppe Mazzini (1805-1872)

Key ideas

- To be free, people need nations.
- Nationalism takes precedence over other causes.

Giuseppe Mazzini: 'Every nation is destined, by the law of God and humanity, to form a free and equal community of brothers.'

Mazzini was born in Genoa and is associated with the cause of Italian Unification – liberating the separate Italian states from foreign rule and fusing them into a free and independent republic. Mazzini is seen as a liberal nationalist, but this is only true to a certain extent.

- **Nationhood:** Mazzini believed that humans could only express themselves via their nation. People had to unite as nations to enjoy their rights; thus human freedom rested first and foremost on the creation of one's own state. For Mazzini, the nation-state was not merely a convenient form of government, but was a partnership of free and equal humans bound together in unity towards a single aim.

- **Patriotism and action:** For Mazzini, the nationalist cause had to take precedence over all other causes. He regarded patriotism as a duty, and love for the Fatherland as a divine mission. Mazzini rejected intellectualism and rationalism and created an idea known as 'thought and action', in which every thought must be followed by action.

- **Spirituality:** Mazzini's motto was *Dio e Popolo* – 'God and People' – and he believed that it was God who divided humanity into nations. Even though his writings can sometimes be understood as speaking out against the Catholic church, he remained deeply spiritual, distinguishing between religious sentiment and the Catholic church.

Charles Maurras (1868–1952)

Key ideas

- Nations come first, not individuals.
- Military might and expansion.

Charles Maurras: 'A true nationalist places his country above everything.'

Charles Maurras was born in France and his ideas were influenced by the turbulent aftermath of France losing the Franco-Prussian War in 1870, swiftly followed by the Paris Commune of 1871. Maurras was a key advocate of integral nationalism, a form of right-wing nationalism that influenced the ideas of fascism.

- **Integral nationalism:** Maurras' political ideas were based on integral nationalism, and some of its qualities include anti-individualism and aggressive expansionism. Integral nationalist states were usually totalitarian, where the state dominates all aspects of society. Mussolini's Italy was the first example of such a society; Japan in the 1940s would be another, as it often overlaps with fascism. A major tenet of integral nationalism is the total immersion of the individual in the interests of the nation.

- **Individualism:** Maurras rejected individualism as it led to individuals thinking only of their best interests, rather than the nation and their place in it. He believed that the French Revolution had contributed to this malaise.

- **Militarism:** Integral nationalism often results after a nation has achieved independence and established a state. Often these countries had a strong military ethos, which became entrenched through the struggle for independence. Sometimes the success of the struggle for liberation resulted in feelings of national superiority that led to extreme nationalism.

Marcus Garvey (1887–1940)

Key ideas

- People should be proud of their blackness.
- Africans are one nation, wherever they are.

Marcus Garvey was born in Jamaica, but travelled around Central America and lived in London and America. Garvey was an early advocate of Pan-Africanism, founding the Universal Negro Improvement Association (UNIA) as well as pioneering black nationalism.

Marcus Garvey: 'The Black skin is not a badge of shame, but rather a glorious symbol of national greatness.'

- **Black Pride:** Garvey encouraged African people around the world to be proud of their race and to see beauty in their own kind. His central belief was that African people in every part of the world were one people and that they would never progress if they did not put aside their cultural and ethnic differences. Garvey's ultimate dream was for the creation of a United States of Africa. Garvey set the precedent for subsequent black nationalist and Pan-Africanist thought.

- **Pan-Africanism:** Garvey advanced a Pan-African philosophy. He wished to inspire a global mass-movement and economic empowerment focusing on Africa, where he sought to end imperialist rule and create modern societies. He argued that black people would be respected only when they were economically strong and proposed an independent black economy. He connected black communities on three continents with his newspaper the Negro World and formed the Black Star Line shipping company to provide transport and to encourage trade among black businesses of Africa and the Americas.

- **Separatism:** Although Garvey was a supporter of racial separatism, he believed that humans were all equal and did not wish to create a hostile atmosphere with white people. The purpose of separatism was to empower black people and to enable them to find an identity.

Assessment support: 2.2.5 Nationalism

The non-core ideas question is on Paper 2, Section B. It is worth 24 marks and must be completed in 30 minutes. All ideas questions start 'To what extent' so you must look at both sides of the debate. You are given a choice of two questions in this format, of which you should answer one.

EITHER

7 (a) To what extent do nationalists promote instability and war? [24 marks]

OR

7 (b) To what extent is nationalism an exclusive ideology? [24 marks]

You must use appropriate thinkers you have studied to support your answer and consider any differing views in a balanced way.

This question tests all three Assessment Objectives, with marks divided equally between them. You must:

• set out the nature of the debate

• draw similarities and differences between the different strands or tensions

• use at least two relevant thinkers.

Your answer should make judgements based on evidence about the significance of the differences and similarities, leading to a clear and justifiable conclusion.

• Always plan before you write. What are the key similarities and differences between the strands (liberal versus anti-/post-colonial versus conservative versus expansionist)? What ideas of key thinkers are valid for this answer? Try planning your answer to the two questions listed above.

• Your essay should include a brief introduction outlining the main arguments, four main points and a conclusion that should reach an overall judgement that naturally flows from the essay.

Here is part of a student's answer to question 7 (b). This middle section outlines why liberal nationalism is not exclusive and introduces the conservative nationalist perspective.

The idea of exclusivity in nationalism refers to how a nation is defined and how easy it is to become a part of that nation. For example, civic forms of nationhood are very inclusive whereas nations based on the idea of race are completely exclusive. The type of nationalism least associated with the idea of exclusiveness is liberal nationalism. Liberal nationalism has a civic concept of nationhood, an idea originally associated with Rousseau, which means that in order to join a nation you simply have to support its values and want to be a part of it. Anyone who meets these criteria can join, making liberal nationalism highly inclusive, not exclusive.

This can be contrasted with conservative nationalists who believe that nations are formed in part due to a shared history, language and culture, as such this means that one cannot become a member of a nation overnight. Conservative nationalists would argue that it takes time to become part of a nation, to understand what Herder would call its 'volksgeist'.

• The term 'exclusivity' is defined well at the beginning of the paragraph allowing the student to develop it using the example of liberal nationalism.

• This paragraph shows a clear understanding of how liberal nationalism is not exclusive, with good use of key thinkers.

• It shows that there is a clear disagreement between nationalists by contrasting liberal and conservative nationalism. It also creates a link to conservative nationalist ideas, allowing them to be explored in more depth.

US Constitution and Federalism

This chapter explores the United States' Constitution. This document outlines the rules of the political game and the guiding principles that strongly influence the nature of the United States' political system today. It is these rules and principles that are central to an understanding of the topics covered in United States politics as a whole.

In this chapter you will learn about:

- the nature of the Constitution as a codified, entrenched document
- the key principles of the Constitution, including the separation of powers and federalism
- debates about the Constitution, including its strengths and weaknesses, and the extent to which state power is protected.

Key term

Constitution
a set of rules determining where sovereignty lies in a political system, and establishing the precise relationship between the government and the governed.

1.1 The nature of the US Constitution

The constitutional framework

The US **Constitution** was ratified by the colonies between 1787 and 1790, bringing the 13 separate colonies together into a new country: the United States of America.

The original Constitution contains seven articles.

- The first four deal with the four key institutions of government in the United States: Congress, the presidency, the Supreme Court and the states.
- Article V outlines the amendment process.
- The 'Supremacy Clause' in article VI established the US Constitution as the highest law in the land.
- Article VII outlines the ratification process – nine of the 13 colonies were required to agree the new framework for governing the US before it could begin.

Beyond this, the Constitution has only 27 changes, known as amendments. Most of these amendments can be seen as additions to the Constitution, creating new rules or requirements.

Some amendments – shown in Figure 1.1 – represent major social change or are the end product of huge conflict, violence and death. Others make extremely important alterations, such as the 25th amendment (1967), passed after the assassination of President Kennedy in 1963, at the height of the Cold War. This amendment allows the vice president to become the president on a temporary basis.

The Bill of Rights

The Bill of Rights is made up of the first ten amendments of the US Constitution. They were all passed in 1791, shortly after the Constitution was created.

A bill of rights is usually seen as a method of protecting the rights of the individual against government power. However, the US Bill of Rights also focuses on protecting the power of the states against federal government. Several colonies were reluctant to join the newly created Union, and a discussion of new provisions helped to reduce state concerns regarding the power of a new central government.

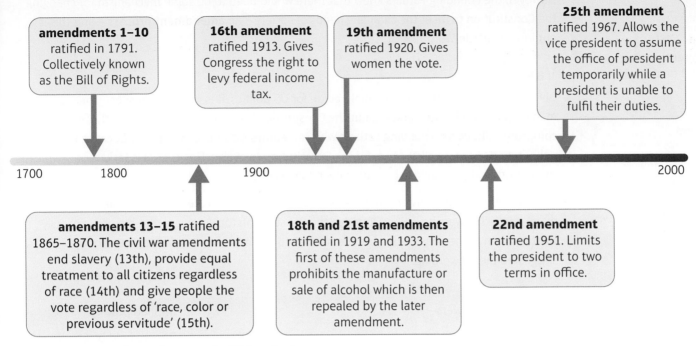

amendments 1–10 ratified in 1791. Collectively known as the Bill of Rights.

16th amendment ratified 1913. Gives Congress the right to levy federal income tax.

19th amendment ratified 1920. Gives women the vote.

25th amendment ratified 1967. Allows the vice president to assume the office of president temporarily while a president is unable to fulfil their duties.

1700   1800   1900   2000

amendments 13–15 ratified 1865–1870. The civil war amendments end slavery (13th), provide equal treatment to all citizens regardless of race (14th) and give people the vote regardless of 'race, color or previous servitude' (15th).

18th and 21st amendments ratified in 1919 and 1933. The first of these amendments prohibits the manufacture or sale of alcohol which is then repealed by the later amendment.

22nd amendment ratified 1951. Limits the president to two terms in office.

Figure 1.1: Timeline of amendments to the US Constitution

Some of the key rights of the Bill of Rights include:

- 1st amendment – freedom of expression and religion
- 2nd amendment – right to bear arms
- 4th amendment – no unreasonable searches or seizures of people or property
- 5th amendment – protection against double jeopardy and self-incrimination (ensures due process of law and just compensation)
- 8th amendment – right to provide freedom from cruel and unusual punishment
- 10th amendment – right of the states to have reserved powers, as opposed to the federal government.

Codification and entrenchment

The US Constitution is codified, meaning that it is written in one document.

A constitution that has been through the process of **codification** is:

- authoritative – it is on a higher level than ordinary law, so it sets out the basis for all political institutions, including those that create everyday legislation
- entrenched – **entrenchment** means it is hard to amend or abolish
- judiciable – as a higher form of law, other laws can be judged against it. The judiciary is responsible for this, judging whether other laws are constitutional or not.

The Founding Fathers deliberately entrenched the Constitution to prevent it being changed too easily by a single institution or political party in their own self-interest – for example, by centralising excessive power in the hands of the government of the day.

> **Key terms**
>
> **Codification**
> writing a constitution down in one document.
>
> **Entrenchment**
> a system by which a constitution is protected from change by law.

Since the Constitution came into force in 1789, 27 amendments have been added.

Link

For more on the **amendment process**, see Figure 1.2 on page 330.

Key term

Enumerated powers powers explicitly stated – such as article I, section 8 in the US Constitution, which provides a list of congressional powers.

However, the Founding Fathers knew that there would need to be some mechanism for changing the Constitution to meet the changing needs of society – an **amendment process** – and this is outlined in article V.

Vagueness

Given that the Constitution is the main guide for US politics, it is surprisingly short. There are many clearly enumerated powers, but the Constitution is often unclear. This is partly because it is a compromise between Founding Fathers who sometimes disagreed, and partly because there was a deliberate decision to allow room for the Constitution to evolve. However, this lack of clarity means there is often significant disagreement over its meaning.

The Constitution has many **enumerated powers**, some of which are shown in Table 1.1. However, many implied powers have been found in the Constitution too – powers that are not expressly written down in the Constitution but are needed to perform an enumerated power or are suggested by the wording.

Enumerated powers	Implied powers
Powers held by Congress • Collection of taxes and duties, which provide for the debts of the United States, as well as for the common defence and welfare of the country. • Borrowing money on behalf of the United States. • Regulation of commerce, both on the international and interstate levels. This also includes Native American tribes. • Establishing currency and coin money and fixing common weights and measures. • Establishing post offices. • Provision for and maintenance of an army and navy. • Organising, training and arming a militia. • Exclusive powers to legislative matters of the country. • Establishing courts that are subordinate to the Supreme Court. • Declaration of war. • Amendment of the Constitution (shared with states). • 16th amendment allows Congress to raise income tax. • A number of other powers are clearly laid out in the Constitution, but are given to one of the two chambers only.	Powers held by Congress • The necessary and proper clause • Interstate commerce clause
Powers held by the president • Heads the executive branch. • Nominates Cabinet members, ambassadors and the judiciary. • Proposes measures to Congress. • Vetoes legislation. • Grants pardons.	Powers held by the president • Commander in chief of the armed forces
Powers held by the Courts • Rule on cases arising under the Constitution, the Laws of the United States, or Treaties.	Powers held by the Courts • The power of judicial review

Table 1.1: Key enumerated and implied powers of the Constitution

The 'necessary and proper' or elastic clause

Article I, section 8 of the Constitution states that Congress has the power 'to make all laws which shall be necessary and proper for carrying into execution the foregoing powers'. This clause is also known as the 'elastic' clause because it allows Congress to stretch its powers. It has been a source of great controversy, being used to justify major expansion of the power of federal government. In *McCulloch v Maryland* 1819, the Supreme Court tested the necessary and proper clause and ruled that Congress has the power to create a national bank, even though the right to create a bank is not explicitly stated in the Constitution. It gave a broad interpretation using implied powers to allow Congress to act. The interstate commerce clause is often described as elastic because of the way in which it has been used to justify the expansion of federal power.

This vagueness could be seen as a considerable advantage. It has arguably allowed the Constitution to survive for such a long time as its meaning can be adapted without the need for formal amendments. A more detailed Constitution would perhaps have been harder to apply to the needs of modern society.

While some vagueness enables the Constitution to be applied to modern society, there are a number of concerns associated with it.

- **The Constitution could fail to regulate political practice:** The Constitution is meant to regulate politicians and set the rules of the political game. The vagueness of the Constitution can undermine its authority – and that of the Supreme Court – as people reject newly established rulings or political practices. For example, in *Obergefell v Hodges* 2015, in stating that gay marriage was a constitutional right, some politicians and even a member of the Supreme Court claimed that the Supreme Court was no longer following the Constitution, essentially making up new rules as it went along. A loss of respect for constitutional rules can have dire effects.

- **The Supreme Court could become too powerful:** The vagueness of the Constitution allows individual justices to apply their own ideologies when ruling on a case. Each of the nine justices is associated with a particular ideology, consistently ruling with a clear bias. For example, liberal justices typically interpret the Constitution to achieve liberal outcomes. A more detailed Constitution would give less room for this bias. For example, the 8th amendment 'cruel and unusual' phrase has been used by some justices to allow the death penalty, while others say the death penalty is unconstitutional.

- **There could be significant conflict:** The lack of clarity leads to strong disputes, with each side claiming that their particular view of the Constitution is more legitimate. This is often based on ideology and allows further divisions in US society. Conservatives and liberals continue to argue about how far the Constitution allows the federal government to control the states. For example, there is an increasing divide between the Democratic and Republican Parties over issues such as gay rights, race and policies such as the Affordable Care Act.

The amendment process

The amendment process has just two stages: first an amendment is proposed, then it is ratified.

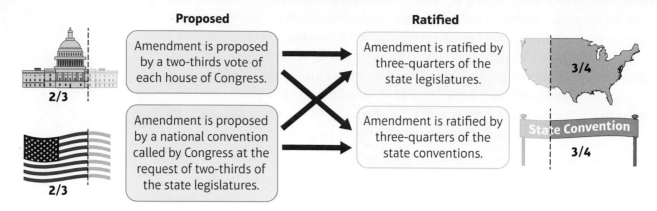

Figure 1.2: How the US Constitution can be amended

Either states or Congress can propose, but only states can ratify. In practice, all of the successful amendments to the US Constitution have been initiated by a congressional vote, and all but one were ratified by three-quarters of the states in state legislatures. Only the 21st amendment, which repealed prohibition, was ratified by state conventions. The Constitution makes no reference to time limits between congressional proposal and state ratification. Modern practice is for Congress to give a deadline for state ratification of proposed amendments, beginning with the 18th amendment (ratified in 1919).

Proposals passed by Congress that failed to receive sufficient state support	
The Equal Rights amendment Would have provided equality of rights by the federal or state governments on account of sex. Congress took it up again recently with a number of proposed measures that never came to congressional vote. Failed to reach required number of states in 1982.	**The District of Columbia Voting Rights amendment** Would have given District of Columbia full representation in the United States Congress as if it were a state. DC would also be able to participate in the amendment process. Failed in 1985.
Proposals voted on in Congress that did not receive a 2/3 majority in each chamber	
The Flag Protection amendment Would allow Congress to make it illegal to desecrate the US flag. Hotly disputed issue. Supreme Court in *US v Eichman* 1990 overturned the Flag Protection Act on the basis of 1st amendment freedom of expression rights. Constitutional amendment proposal was an attempt to overturn this. Successfully passed in the House six times up to 2006, but always failed to be voted on or gain enough votes to pass the Senate.	**The Federal Marriage amendment** Introduced into Congress several times between 2002 and 2013. Seeks to define marriage as exclusively between a man and a woman. Failed to receive the required votes in both the House and Senate in 2006. Issue seen as central in 2004 presidential elections, with George W. Bush strongly for the amendment and John Kerry arguing that individual states should decide. Introduced in 2015, without congressional vote, by Tim Huelskamp, a social conservative in the House.
Proposals introduced in Congress but not voted on by both chambers of Congress	
Right to vote amendment Introduced to prevent restrictions on voting. Would end felony voting restrictions and help protect voting rights after *Shelby County v Holder* Supreme Court ruling in 2013 overturned sections of the Voting Rights Act 1965. Representatives Mark Pocan and Keith Ellison reintroduced it in 2013.	**Saving American Democracy amendment** Proposed by Senator Bernie Sanders in 2011. Aimed to overturn *Citizens United v FEC* ruling of 2010 in which the court removed regulations on funding of elections. Aims to limit influence of corporate donors in United States elections.

Table 1.2: Six recently proposed amendments

Of particular importance is the US requirement that both federal government (Congress) and the states need to agree. This is a key principle on the protection of federalism. Federal government cannot restrict the power of states without state-level agreement.

Given that the first ten amendments were passed in 1791 – almost at the same time as the writing of the Constitution itself – and that the 18th and 21st amendments (prohibition and its repeal) cancel each other out, there have been only 15 operating amendments passed in over 200 years. In those 200 years the social, political and economic life of the US has transformed in a manner that was unimaginable at the time of writing the original.

This is not because there have been few ideas or demands for change. Members of Congress have introduced over 11,000 amendment proposals since the Constitution was first established. Congress has accepted only 33 of those proposals, with 27 making it past the states for constitutional inclusion.

Disadvantages of the formal process

✗ It is difficult to remove outdated aspects

When a part of the Constitution is outdated or unpopular, it is difficult to get wide support to make necessary changes. The original document is over 200 years old and US society has changed dramatically, as have key principles like democracy. An obvious example of this is the rules surrounding the election of the president, which make use of the electoral college. This mechanism was established when there were fears that the people would not make rational decisions, allowing the people only to vote for an electoral college of voters who would decide who the president would be. It is inconceivable that the electoral college would reject the will of the people today, but it has left the US with a number of undemocratic problems. The state-based system makes it possible for one candidate to get the most popular votes, but for another candidate to win (as happened with the election of Bush in 2000 and Trump in 2016). In addition, the system over-represents smaller states, so people in some states have greater voting power than in others. A lack of political quality in voting undermines core principles of modern democracy, yet the system cannot be changed due to a lack of support among over-represented states.

✗ It is difficult to incorporate new ideas

Views have changed dramatically since 1787, as have the needs of society, but it is difficult to incorporate additions that may improve the workings of the Constitution due to its entrenched nature. In a modern society there is huge consensus over the idea of gender equality. Despite the change in values regarding women's rights, the Equal Rights amendment failed as recently as 1982, with persistent attempts to reintroduce the ERA in Congress making little progress. An easier process would allow the United States to respect fundamental rights, show that the US politicians and the Constitution value equality, and enable the US to become a more modern, liberal democracy.

✗ The amendment process is undemocratic

The amendment procedure goes against the concept of majoritarian democracy. To block an amendment, only 13 of 50 states have to oppose it. It would be possible (even if unlikely) for the 13 smallest states to block an amendment proposal. This is also true in Congress where some amendments (such as the Flag Protection amendment) have received over 50 per cent of the votes in both House and Senate, but have not reached the super-majority threshold.

✗ It gives the Supreme Court excessive power

Entrenchment allows nine unelected judges to have the final say on key issues of institutional power and human rights. Rulings by Supreme Court justices are extraordinarily difficult to overturn, rendering their word final. This might be acceptable if justices were neutral interpreters of the Constitution, but they are not – they use their own personal biases. The ambiguous nature of the Constitution, outlined above, exacerbates this problem. This has led Edwin Meese to argue that the US has an imperial judiciary with no effective constitutional limits, because it is virtually impossible to change their rulings.

Case study: The Roberts Court

The Roberts Court arguably has an activist agenda to overturn any regulations that aim to limit the use of money in US elections. In cases such as *Citizens United v FEC* 2010, the majority overturned the Bipartisan Campaign Reform Act, and Obama explicitly denounced the ruling before it took place. The act was passed by the elected Congress of 2002 with the approval of the elected president and the support of the current president at the time of the Supreme Court case. Due largely to this level of entrenchment, the Supreme Court is above elected institutions.

Chief Justice Roberts

Question

- Why do you think President Obama was so outspoken about the ruling on the Bipartisan Campaign Reform Act?

Advantages of the formal process

✔It protects key principles of political processes

Some political principles are so important that it should be difficult to change them. Basic democratic ideas – such as elections every four years and separation of powers – could be seen as essential principles. The Founding Fathers made some ideals almost completely immune from change, such as the requirement for a republic to be a guaranteed form of government, going further than the entrenchment outlined in article V.

However, the Constitution does allow for change. These principles can be altered when there is very broad support, through the formal amendment process or by the Supreme Court setting precedents to the Constitution, without the need to pass amendments.

✔It protects states and upholds federalism

The US has a tradition of respect for states' rights, and entrenchment helps to maintain this. While this could be seen as an extension of the idea of protecting key principles of the political process, for many it is the key process. This is ensured through the 10th amendment and the amendment process, as well as small states receiving equal representation in Senate and the electoral college. Proposals to undermine the power of states have failed through the amendment process, such as attempts to remove the electoral college. The Supreme Court has successfully upheld state rights partly due to the entrenched nature of the Constitution.

✔It prevents abuse of power

An entrenched Constitution stops an individual from one political party changing constitutional rules for their own benefit. This was a key aim of the Founding Fathers. The current US process requires bipartisan support – a single party is highly unlikely to have a two-thirds majority in each chamber of Congress. President George W. Bush requested a line-item veto power in 2006, a measure that would have allowed him to veto just parts of a bill, rather than a whole bill. This enhanced power was not approved by Congress.

✔ It prevents ill-thought-through amendments

The amendment process involves several institutions and requires cross-party agreement. This prevents short-term or irrational thinking entering the Constitution. Several amendment proposals can be seen as knee-jerk reactions to a current event or Supreme Court ruling. Many commentators felt this about the proposed inclusion of gay rights into the Constitution or their proposed exclusion (as in the federal marriage amendment). Given how quickly values change, a federal marriage amendment passed in the early 2000s could easily be seen as outdated today.

Pause & reflect ✔

What is your overall judgement on the amendment process? How strong do you think each argument is? Make a judgement about each one by giving it a strength score out of 10 and then writing a very short justification for your view.

EXTENSION ACTIVITY

How would you establish the amendment process for the US? Would it be good to reduce the percentage of votes needed in the House, Senate and states? Can you increase the power held by politicians as elected officials representing public opinion, while also protecting key constitutional principles?

1.2 The principles of the US Constitution and their effectiveness today

The key **principles** of the Constitution can be seen as the values that drive its content. They show the underlying beliefs of the Constitution's authors, and should be reflected in US political practice today. There is one overriding principle behind the development of the Constitution, which is to ensure that power is shared among different political bodies. The five key principles of the Constitution can all be linked to this single idea of sharing power.

Key term

Principle
a fundamental and organising idea that runs throughout something.

Key principles
- Federalism
- Separation of powers
- Checks and balances
- Bipartisanship
- Limited government

Figure 2.1: The five key principles of the Constitution

Federalism

The US Constitution attempted to balance the need for central government control with the desire of the original colonies to protect their own interests. A system of **federalism** was created, with power divided between central government (the federal government) and regional government (the states). This means that citizens are ruled by two governments. Some policies are made at a federal level, by president and Congress, and other decisions are made by the state governments.

Each state is like a smaller version of the US, with its own Constitution, head of the executive branch (Governor), legislature (State Congress) and Supreme Court. Each state is subject to the constitutional rules of the US, but has a huge degree of control over its own affairs.

Key term

Federalism
system in which sovereignty is shared between a central government (federal government) and individual states, with each having their own specific rights.

Link

For more on **federalism**, see Section 1.3.

Key term

Separation of powers where the three key bodies of government – legislature, executive and judiciary – each have their own powers, personnel and buildings. The principle behind the separation of powers ensures that a system of checks and balances prevents too much power residing with any one body.

Key term

Checks and balances the division of power between the three branches of government, where each branch has a direct ability to prevent action from another branch.

The Constitution is particularly unclear in relation to **federalism** and the protection of state power. The power of the federal government has grown hugely as a response to economic crisis, increased demands for civil-rights protection and greater provision of social policy. The states are increasingly controlled by federal institutions, but the Constitution has barely changed in these areas.

Separation of powers

To fully understand United States politics, it is vital to understand the meaning and implications of the **separation of powers**.

The separation of powers refers to the complete division of a system of government into three branches: the executive, the legislature and the judiciary. In the case of the US, the Founding Fathers created a president, Congress and Supreme Court. In the US system, no one is allowed to be in more than one branch at the same time. So, for example, it is not possible to be both a member of Congress and work alongside the president in the executive branch. On becoming president in 2009 Barack Obama had to give up his Senate seat, and in becoming attorney general in 2017 Jeff Sessions had to give up his Senate seat to join the executive branch. This contrasts with the centralisation of power of an absolute monarchy, or the fusion of powers in which separate branches are created, but have significant overlaps.

The separation of powers is based on a desire to share power, preventing any one institution or politician from dominating the political system. For many of the Founding Fathers it was a guiding principle that allowed the preservation of the liberty of individuals in society.

Checks and balances

With the three branches separated in terms of personnel, the Founding Fathers created a series of **checks and balances** that each branch could impose on another. Each branch of government has exclusive power, limiting the ability of other branches to operate in an unrestrained manner.

These checks – or restrictions – ensure a high degree of balance between the three branches of government, so no one institution is dominant. Working alongside the separation of powers, they force the three branches of government to share power.

Power is balanced not just by the provision of checks, but also by the denial of certain powers to each of the three branches. For example, the president can propose legislation, but cannot amend legislation, lacking what is known as a line-item veto, which would allow the rejection of certain lines (or provisions) of a bill. Under the Constitution, it is Congress that can initiate, amend and reject legislative proposals. Fearing an unrestrained president, the Founding Fathers gave Congress significant checks, allowing them to restrain the president heavily.

Bipartisanship

While it makes no mention of political parties, the Constitution itself means that compromise is inevitable if decisions are to be made. The division of power between president, House and Senate means that parties need to co-operate in order to govern the country. In addition, the Constitution requires cross-party support through the need for super-majorities for amendments, and for the Senate to ratify treaties. The original Constitution makes it possible for rival political groups to control the three bodies with most legislative influence. As James Madison put it in his essay *Federalist 51*, 'Ambition must be made to counteract ambition.'

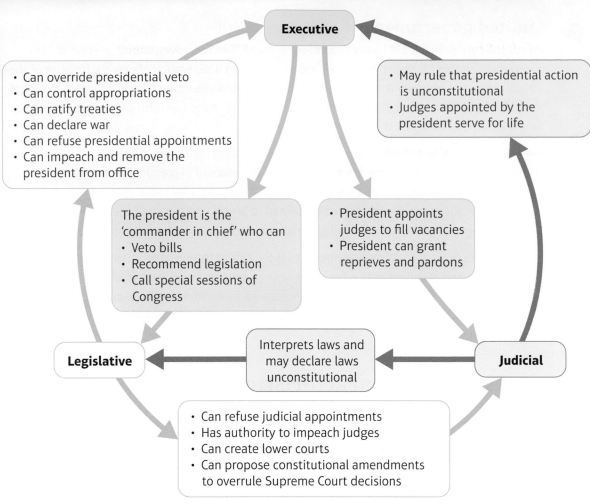

Figure 2.2: US government checks and balances

> **Pause & reflect** ✔
>
> Consider the differences between the separation of powers and checks and balances. Why does the separation of powers not **necessarily** ensure checks and balances?

In the US, bipartisan control between these institutions is common. When **divided government** occurs – when the House of Representatives, Senate and presidency are not all controlled by one party – parties have to work together to pass policy. This has worked effectively over the history of the US as parties have often found legislative compromises.

> 'There is nothing which I dread so much as a division of the republic into two great parties, each arranged under its leader, and concerting measures in opposition to each other. This, in my humble apprehension, is to be dreaded as the greatest political evil under our Constitution.' John Adams, Founding Father

Today, the constitutional requirement for **bipartisanship** has led to a major constitutional challenge. With parties becoming more polarised, there is less scope for compromise and Congress has been less able to legislate, leading to weak government. Some critics have questioned the desirability of a constitutional system, arguing that current constitutional arrangements are no longer suitable. Others see this as a crisis of political parties in which the parties themselves are the problem. A lack of willingness to compromise has meant that Adams's 'political evil' is present today.

> **Link**
>
> For more on **divided government**, see Section 2.3 of US Congress.

> **Key term**
>
> **Bipartisanship** attempts within the structure of the US Congress to try to ensure that the two main parties must work together in order to fulfil congressional functions.

Link

For more on **limited government**, see Section 2.1 of Liberalism.

Limited government

One of the core principles of liberal democracy is that of **limited government**: the role of government should be limited by checks and balances and a separation of powers, because of the corrupting nature of power. In the context of the US, limited government means that the power of the federal government is subject to limitations as laid out in the Constitution, so that it cannot simply impose its policy on the state and its citizens.

The Bill of Rights also prevents the federal government from restricting the rights of the individual or the rights of states. Amendments such as the 1st (freedom of expression) and 4th (freedom from unreasonable searches) can be seen as limiting government by protecting individual freedoms. The 10th amendment is clearly designed to protect the power of the states by stating that any power not given to the federal government is reserved for the states or the people.

Modern conceptions of limited government cover the extent to which the federal government plays a role in social and economic policy. For conservatives, and particularly for libertarians, there is a desire to reduce government involvement in areas such as expenditure (for example, on welfare provision). Social programmes are frowned on as being part of a 'big government' agenda, which is rejected by many in the US.

1.3 The main characteristics of US federalism

The nature of the federal system of government

Federalism grew out of a desire to protect the interests of each of the original colonies when the union was created, and to ensure that the power of the central (federal) government was limited.

Federalism has two essential features.

- **The power of regional governments or states is protected by the Constitution**. This means that the federal government is unable to reduce the power of the states without their consent. There is shared sovereignty between the federal government and the states. The amendment process prevents any change to state power without the consent of two-thirds of states.
- **Regional powers are equal**. All states are given the same level of power. This means that, for example, either all states can set their own tax rates or none of them can, or all states will determine electoral rules or none of them will. States are free to apply their powers differently to each other, but all states have the same level of decision-making power.

The Constitution is supposed to provide the US with a dividing line, explaining what is federal power and what is state power, but in reality the division is unclear. The relationship remains very fluid. This has been a major factor in allowing the power of the states to change hugely since the Constitution began.

The relationship of the federal system of government with the states

The nature of federalism means that in some areas there is a clear division between federal and state power. Each level of government operates relatively independently from the other.

Historically this has been the case with a reasonably clear division between the roles of the two. Arguably, state powers have had a higher level of impact on the lives of citizens than the federal government. The states would deal with most aspects of domestic policy, including education and economic policy (the original Constitution did not grant the federal government the right to levy income tax). Other than a few domestic essentials such as coining money, the federal government was limited to a foreign policy and security role.

There are a number of key aspects to this relationship.

- Over time the power of the states has been eroded. The major turning point was the economic crash of 1929 and the response of the Roosevelt presidency. Roosevelt's New Deal policies meant huge growth in the role of the federal government and greater federal control over the states. The dominant trend since then has been an erosion of state power.

- The federal government and states are interconnected, with the two having to work together in order to govern the US. Some individual policy areas are now controlled and carried out by both the federal government and the states. This creates interdependence, where they have to work together.

- Commonly this involves the federal government providing resources, usually in the form of money, to carry out policies that the federal government would like to see put in practice. In some cases states can voluntarily access this money if they would like to carry out a policy. These grants often come with criteria, however, allowing the federal government to restrict states. For example, in his Race to the Top initiative in 2009, Obama and Congress created $4.3-billion-worth of grants that states could compete for, but money was awarded according to which states met 20 educational goals set by federal government.

- In other cases the federal government passes laws that force states to comply. These are known as federal mandates and often lead to conflict between the federal government and the states. States can try to overturn these restrictions in the Supreme Court. In *Shelby v Holder* 2013, federal law was overturned when parts of the Voting Rights Act were declared unconstitutional. This gave states greater freedom in electoral law.

- States create a range of their own laws independently from the federal government. Sometimes this also creates conflict with the federal government challenging these laws. The federal government may be ideologically opposed to these laws and try to undermine them. The Obama administration attempted to ensure that North Carolina respected transgender rights by threatening to withhold some of the federal education funding it provides to the state. Alternatively, the federal government may feel that the states are carrying out roles that, constitutionally, belong to the federal government.

Case study: The commerce clause, federal power and marijuana

When California legalised marijuana, the federal government claimed that this was in fact a federal responsibility, not a state one. The ensuing Supreme Court case featured a battle between the federal and state government in *Gonzales v Raich* 2005. In this case the Supreme Court interpreted the power of Congress in a broad manner, stating that the interstate commerce clause allowed the federal government to regulate California. This was because, the court argued, the legalisation of production of marijuana in California would have an impact on the supply and demand of the drug across the US, thus affecting interstate commerce.

While the federal government has the ability to regulate marijuana, the situation is more complex. Despite this ruling, Congress has not acted to regulate marijuana on a national scale even though the Supreme Court has given it the constitutional authority to do so. Referring to the legalisation of marijuana for recreational use in Washington and Colorado (since joined by Oregon and Alaska), Obama decided not to intervene, saying that there were 'bigger fish to fry'.

State law has a huge variety of practices, with some states legalising marijuana for recreational use and many others only allowing it for medical purposes. In many states any sale of marijuana is a criminal offence, with Illinois making this a misdemeanour while its neighbour Iowa classes this as a felony. Florida law punishes sale of marijuana by up to six years in prison with very heavy fines for possession of small quantities.

On the other hand the clause protects the powers of the states to regulate business and trade within each state (intrastate commerce). There are court cases in which the federal government has lost, such as the Lopez case on gun controls.

Question

- Can you think of any other instances where there are big differences between the laws in different states?

1.4 Interpretations and debates around the US Constitution and federalism

The extent of democracy within the Constitution

To what extent can the US Constitution be seen as a democratic document? To answer this question, you must first consider what 'democracy' means. A starting point is to remember that democracy is anything that maximises the power of the people.

Elections

The US Constitution upholds fundamental principles of a representative democracy by creating free and fair elections. The system of separation of powers and federalism has led to a huge number of elections, allowing US citizens to vote more often than in any other country in the world. The Founding Fathers also created short two-year terms for the House of Representatives, who must exercise high levels of sensitivity to public opinion. With the Senate and president also elected, there is a significant representation.

However, a number of criticisms can be raised. The **electoral college** is an out-dated voting method, based on a reluctance to give power to the people. Many aspects of the electoral college offend fundamental principles of a representative democracy.

Checks and balances

Checks and balances, backed by the separation of powers, could be said to serve the interests of democracy by maximising the power of the people.

Checks and balances may prevent one person, party or institution from holding all of the power, with the potential to abuse their position for their own benefit, or for the benefit of limited groups in society. Checks and balances can be used to prevent such corruption by blocking any such attempts, as when President Bush requested a line-item veto power, but Congress denied him.

Checks can also ensure that everyone's interests are considered. In a separated system where it is common for different parties to control the main office of government, policy is more likely to be based on the consideration of the many, not the few. Collectively, when policy is eventually passed, there is a greater representation for all.

On the other hand, the system of checks and balances may damage US democracy. Democrat voters vote for Democrat policies, and Republican voters vote for Republican policies, but neither set may feel that they get any policies that reflect their wishes or interests. For example, in 2012, the public voted for a Democrat president who argued for comprehensive immigration reform. When immigration reform was introduced into the House, the then-Speaker John Boehner refused to allow the House to debate the full proposal.

Link

For more information on **criticisms of the electoral college**, see Section 5.1 of US Democracy and Participation.

Case study: The Affordable Care Act and electoral democracy

Obama received a mandate for health care reform in 2008, yet was forced to abandon major aspects of his policy in light of opposition from Congress, including Democrats. The elected House prevented the elected president from achieving his policy goals, as outlined in the 2008 campaign. In 2014 the Republicans took control of the Senate in the mid-term elections. When they subsequently sent legislation to the president to repeal health care laws, he vetoed it. In 2016 Republicans were elected, gaining control of the House, Senate and presidency, campaigning to repeal the ACA. The Republican Party did not, however, give a clear idea of what they would replace it with and could not agree on an alternative in March 2017, meaning that it failed to repeal and replace Obamacare. Conservative Republicans were arguably representing constituency views by rejecting the proposal that maintained many of the key aspects of the ACA, but ended by achieving no reform at all.

Is this positive or negative for democracy? In this case, some would argue that members of Congress were responding to shifting public opinion and that House members, with their two-year terms, were ensuring that policy was based on the latest views and values of voters.

Question

- Why do you think the issue of affordable health care causes so much division among the US electorate?

Rights protection

It is clear that the US has a very strong system of rights protection, with a powerful Supreme Court that is able and willing to promote liberties as outlined in the Constitution. The Bill of Rights, alongside the 14th amendment, gives legal protection to those in the US. Democracy, in seeking to maximise the power of the people, is based on a liberal idea of individual freedom. Rights allow people to have power, giving them control over their own lives, free from excessive government control. This can be seen in the religious freedom clause of the 1st amendment, the right to remain silent in the 5th and freedom from racial discrimination in the 8th. Rights also protect certain powers the people have, giving them the ability to have influence over the government.

Figure 4.1: The 1st amendment of the Constitution protects freedom of speech

On the other hand, there is plenty of evidence of a lack of rights protection in the United States, and thus the undermining of the political power of the people. The Shelby ruling has allowed states to create laws that undermine the opportunity for poor or racial-minority voters to participate. In addition, rights protection itself may contradict principles of democracy. If the electorate vote for a policy, arguably the laws of democracy say they should have it. If voters choose politicians who want to introduce voter ID laws, support laws to prevent the burning of the flag or prevent anti-immigrant marches, then arguably, the rules of democracy should allow those politicians to carry out the will of the people. Much depends on which type of democracy is most highly valued.

Liberal versus conservative views

Further to this, a criticism from liberals suggests that the system of checks and balances deliberately protects the interests of the few, not the many. Creating any change is made extremely difficult, which means that the conservative nature of the Constitution protects the status quo – the economic elite hold all of the power. The failure of those such as Sanders to change such rules or the extremely limited nature of banking reform passed by Congress after the banking crash of 2007–08 provide evidence of this view of the Constitution. Conservatives argue that the system is fair because all groups have equal democratic rights to participate in the system through the right to vote, and the protection of rights such as freedom of speech.

Types of democracy

There are several different types of democracy. Consider the two alternatives below.

Majoritarian	Pluralist
The 'majoritarian' principle is the one that most people commonly associate with the word democracy. In simple terms, the majority gets what the majority wants. People select representatives to act on their behalf; if over 50 per cent of those representatives vote for more tax, this is what the people get. This principle is present in majoritarian electoral systems in which the 'winner takes all' in a constituency. This creates a national parliament in which one party typically has over 50 per cent and the majority of voters get what they have voted for. It maximises the power of the people by giving the largest group what they have voted for.	The 'pluralist' principle sees majoritarian democracy as over-simplistic. Instead there is an attempt to base policies on a compromise of different views and interests. This can be seen in, for example, the use of proportional representation (PR) electoral systems, which allow those who are not in the majority to gain some political influence. PR tends to create multi-party politics and coalition governments where compromise is required. The power of the people is maximised by attempting to give all or most groups an influence in determining any final outcomes.

Table 4.1: Alternative types of democracy

Strengths and weaknesses of the Constitution

Criterion	Key questions	Links
Effective guide to political practice	Does contemporary political practice reflect the rules? Do politicians follow the requirements of the Constitution?	See Section 4.6 of US Supreme Court and Civil Rights.
Flexibility	Can the Constitution adapt to new social, political and economic circumstances? Is it easy to amend? Is it too easy?	See Section 1.1 of this chapter for more on the amendment process and vagueness of the Constitution.
Strong government	Is the government able to function? Can it provide effective leadership? Is government too strong? Can it make decisions so that it can govern the country?	See Section 3.4 of US presidency for more on the imperial presidency. See also Section 1.2 of this chapter for more on the key principles of the Constitution.
Democracy versus tyranny	Does the Constitution maximise the power of the people? Are there sufficient checks and balances? Does one politician or institution have too much power?	Discussed in the section above.
Civil liberties	Are the right rights being protected?	See Section 4.4 of US Supreme Court and Civil Rights.

Table 4.2: Criteria for assessing the strengths and weaknesses of the Constitution

EXTENSION ACTIVITY

What evidence and arguments can you find that the US is a pluralist or a majoritarian democracy?

Conservatives and liberals will disagree over the criteria and the relative importance of each of them. This, then, is a debate about what makes a desirable constitution, as much as the US Constitution itself. Liberals will accept the need for checks and balances and for power to be shared. Their liberal vision, however, is of a society in which government has a key role to play in bringing about social justice.

The desirability of the Constitution has been disputed by liberals and conservatives, with different views regarding which rights are prioritised by the Constitution. Liberals will tend to emphasise the 14th amendment and conservatives will tend to emphasise the 2nd. In addition, there can be conflict between state rights (which are constitutional rights) and individual rights. Conservatives have often challenged developments in individual rights as a restriction of the rights of the states.

It is clear that the Founding Fathers emphasised checks and balances as a key criteria. The chapters on the three main institutions, as well as political parties, will explore the extent to which these checks and balances operate effectively. There are many reasons to believe that those checks and balances are not functioning properly. The imperial presidency theory, for example, argues that there are no significant constitutional restraints on the president. On the other hand, in the age of polarisation of parties, there is a view that these checks and balances are now excessive, leading to legislative sclerosis and a lack of political leadership.

Impact of the Constitution on the US government today

This section examines the impact on government in particular and not the wider advantages and disadvantages of the Constitution.

Much of the debate surrounding the impact of the Constitution relates to the following key areas. It can be assessed by looking at the ways in which the Constitution affects government processes in terms of:

- democracy
- civil rights
- federalism/state power
- the power of political institutions, especially in preventing tyranny
- making laws – effective government and the role of political parties in it.

Positive impacts	Negative impacts
Frequent elections, short terms for the House and the separation of powers creates a highly representative government.	The electoral college can produce a government that does not reflect the wishes of the majority.
Checks and balances ensure that branches work together. This prevents tyranny and means that policy is based on a compromise of different interests.	Policy-making is very difficult, leading to ineffective government in the form of gridlock. Partisanship in Congress has made this considerably worse.
A powerful Supreme Court alongside constitutional rights ensures a high level of protection of civil rights.	The power of the Supreme Court means that the government may be prevented from carrying out policy, leading to ineffective government and claims of limited democracy.
The amendment process prevents politicians from changing the rules to award themselves more power.	The amendment process prevents necessary changes. This might mean that government is not responsive to the needs of modern society.

Positive impacts	Negative impacts
The vagueness of the Constitution has allowed government to operate effectively by allowing changing political practice to suit the needs of modern society.	The vagueness of the Constitution has meant 'loopholes' have been exploited, such as executive orders, which has allowed for the dominance of one branch over another.
The states are well protected, allowing government to meet the needs of each state.	There is insufficient protection of state power. The federal government therefore dominates policy-making.

Table 4.3: Impact of the Constitution on the US government today

The debates around the extent to which the US remains federal today

This debate centres around the idea that states can no longer protect their powers from an increasingly powerful federal government. For federalism to still exist and to be thriving, it must be evident that states are making a significant amount of laws/polices for themselves and that their powers are protected by the Constitution and the Supreme Court.

States have a great deal of control over health, education, law and order and even economic policy. For example, states set their own sales tax, with some states like Montana having no sales tax and California having the highest rate at 7.5 per cent. Further differences can be seen in the case study below.

For some commentators the power of states has been eroded so much that the US cannot be considered to be a true federal system. This argument is based on the idea that constitutional protections of state power are largely meaningless, with the federal government able to take control in virtually any policy area, with limited likelihood that they will be blocked. The federal government has taken more control by imposing national policies on all states, with laws such as the Clean Air Act 1970 and the Affordable Care Act 2010 which requires all states to set up health exchanges to ensure that everyone has insurance.

For others, federalism is alive and kicking, with states that have huge policy control, which is well protected by the Constitution. For example, states have different laws on marijuana. In 2016 California, Nevada and Massachusetts joined a growing list of states that have legalised personal use of marijuana. Other states, including Florida and Georgia, only permit its use if prescribed by a doctor, whereas in Idaho, marijuana is not legally permitted for any use at all, with fines of up to $1,000 or one year in prison.

Case study: Liberals versus conservatives and the federalism debate

The conflict over transgender bathroom laws shows a division between liberal (typically Democrat) and conservative (typically Republican) views on federalism. North Carolina restricted transgender individuals from using bathrooms of their adopted gender, and New York State took the opposite approach, providing legal protections. At the start of 2017, 14 states had restrictive laws while many others were in the process of passing such laws. This can be seen as federalism in action with a diversity of state laws. When in office, President Obama had attempted to place restrictions on states by threatening to withhold federal education funding if discriminatory practice was present. On the other hand, President Trump lifted all attempts at federal regulations on this issue. He argued that he was not opposed to transgender rights, but that this was a states' rights issue.

Liberals criticise the states' rights argument as an excuse to restrict civil rights. Typically they have been supportive of greater centralisation of state power. Many central government controls have had liberal goals, which have typically promoted the interests of poorer sections of society, racial minorities or individual liberty. They claim that this does not destroy the concept of federalism as states are still free to pursue a huge range of policies for themselves.

Conservatives have tended to resist such programmes, claiming that they restrict federalism. On moral issues such as abortion, gun control or gay rights, conservatives will typically oppose federal standards, arguing that it should be a state's responsibility to choose. Conservatives often criticise such interventions as a limit to states' rights. The conservative case argues that the intent of the Founding Fathers and the fundamental meaning of the Constitution are being ignored.

Question

- Why do you think there is often such a divide between northern states and southern states when it comes to state-level legislation that restricts civil liberties?

The development of 'rainbow federalism' in recent years has seen a huge range of state initiatives, leading to the development of a diversity of state-based policies.

To understand the extent to which the US remains federal, it is important to consider the powers and limits on the states in practice today.

How does the Constitution protect state power?

The Constitution does not mention the word 'federalism', and there are very few specific sentences that seek to outline the power of the states. The Constitution covers some details of the enumerated powers of Congress, such as the power to coin money, declare war and regulate business relationships between states. It also forbids the federal government from certain practices, such as using titles of nobility or abandoning republican principles. However, rather than enumerating the power of states, it simply gives a statement that all other powers reside with the states or the people.

Constitutional protection of states

Powers denied to Congress

The Constitution provides limitations on Congress, allowing freedom for state power. The interstate commerce clause implies that states are free to regulate their own internal business policy. In addition, constitutional amendments such as the 2nd amendment (the right to bear arms) can prevent the federal government from imposing gun regulations on the states.

In *US v Lopez* 1995, the federally imposed Gun Free School Zones Act of 1990 was successfully halted by states that objected to its imposition. The court ruled that the commerce clause did not allow Congress to ban possession of a gun near a school because gun possession by itself is not an economic activity that affects interstate commerce. This was the first time since Roosevelt's presidency that the Supreme Court found in favour of state rights under the commerce clause.

The 10th amendment

The 10th amendment states that any powers not reserved for the federal government should be considered a state power. This implies that Congress only has those powers that the Constitution awards it; all other powers belong to the states. States have successfully taken a number of cases to the Supreme Court allowing them to overturn federally imposed policy. In *Printz v United States* 1997 the Supreme Court overturned the Brady Act requirement that state officials must perform background checks on those wishing to purchase a gun. The 10th amendment meant that this was a state, not federal, policy.

The amendment process

The amendment process protects state power because it is impossible to reduce the power of states without their consent. States can also block amendments they are ideologically opposed to. Any proposed amendment to the Constitution requires three-quarters of states to agree. The failure to remove the electoral college through constitutional amendment shows how smaller states can protect their political influence. This is the main reason why amendments relating to the electoral college system are unlikely to be passed. The current voting system over-represents smaller states such as Wyoming and Alaska, which will not vote to amend the Constitution on this practice.

Limits to state power

Some provisions of the Constitution award powers to the federal government and allow for clear limits on state power. These enumerated powers of the federal government represent areas where states have little or no control, including the power to collect tax and coin money. Key constitutional amendments have contributed to an erosion of state power. The 14th amendment applies the standards of the Bill of Rights to the states – previously it only restricted the federal government. The 16th amendment allowed the expansion of federal power through its right to impose federal income tax. There have also been several areas where the power of the states has been eroded.

The erosion of state power

Federal mandates

Federal mandates are federal laws, in the forms of Acts of Congress, which impose national standards on the states. These laws limit state power because all states are required to comply. There has been an increasing number of federal mandates since President Roosevelt's New Deal in the 1930s. Not only do federal mandates create policy restrictions on the states, they can also limit states financially. In some cases states are required to pay for the policy imposed upon them, taking up valuable resources that could have been spent elsewhere.

The Affordable Care Act 2010, President Obama's flagship policy requiring everyone to have health insurance, limits state choice in health care. All states are required to set up health exchanges (or allow citizens to use the federal health exchange) in which they can purchase health insurance.

Fiscal power of the federal government

With the creation of the 16th amendment allowing federal income tax and the expansion of the role of the federal government, states become increasingly reliant on the federal government for funding.

Central government provides states with approximately a quarter of their total expenditure in the form of federal grants, sometimes referred to as federal aid. In itself this is not necessarily a restriction on state power, as states may simply be receiving more financial benefits. The restrictions mainly come from the conditions imposed upon such federal funding of the states. If states are to maintain access to this huge financial resource they often have to adhere to policy requirements imposed by the federal government.

Interstate commerce clause

Article I, section 8 gives power to the federal government to regulate commerce with foreign governments and between the states. So what is covered by interstate commerce (in other words, the buying and selling of goods across state borders)? Would this allow Congress to regulate home-grown marijuana (which, for example, is allowed in California for medical purposes) or the sale of marijuana for medical purposes? Can it be used to allow the federal government to force motels to accept guests from all racial groups? The answers to these questions is yes, yes and yes.

This clause has been used to justify a huge range of federal laws that go beyond the intentions of the Founding Fathers. This includes many areas that arguably exceed the basic idea of commerce.

Pause & reflect

States have clearly lost a great deal of power over the last century. How powerful do you think states are today? Which side of the debate has stronger arguments and evidence?

Case study: State power and the environment – the Trump effect

The Trump presidency has made major cuts to federal regulations, notably in environmental areas, meaning that states no longer have to comply to the same standards on carbon emissions, preventing coal mining waste being dumped in rivers or complying with fuel efficiency standards for cars. All of this can be seen as returning power to states. On the other hand, the major cuts in environmental funding under Trump have left many states unsure whether they still have to comply with federal environmental regulations (or wanting to maintain high environmental standards, but being unable to do so due to a lack of financial resources). Trump has proposed cutting the Environmental Protection Agency budget by a third. To make things even more complicated, many states are now more directly involved in trying to meet international climate change targets, albeit on a voluntary level. When Trump withdrew the USA from the Paris climate change agreement in June 2017, many US cities and states committed to continuing to honour the goals of the agreement. It thus appears that the level of state power can be positively or negatively affected when the federal government reduces its role.

Questions

- To what extent has the Trump environment agenda increased state power?

- Does the case study suggest that the US remains federal?

Assessment support: 3.1.1 US Constitution and Federalism

Question 3 on A-Level Paper 3 requires you to answer two questions from a choice of three, each of which is worth 30 marks.

Evaluate the extent to which the Constitution protects state power. [30 marks]

You must consider this view and the alternative to this view in a balanced way.

These questions require an essay-style answer. They test all three Assessment Objectives, with 10 marks available for each. These questions always ask you to **evaluate**. The requirement for **balance** means that you have to show an awareness of different arguments and viewpoints. It is essential to go beyond simply explaining what those different arguments and viewpoints are. Evaluation requires you to make a judgement about the strength of arguments rather than just stating them. You will need to do this throughout your answer and not just in a conclusion. You will need to show an awareness of different perspectives and to outline different arguments, typically using three or four well-evaluated arguments with counter-arguments. You will also need an introduction and a conclusion.

To evaluate the extent to which the Constitution protects state power you could make judgements about different constitutional protections (10th amendment, the amendment process, the interstate commerce clause) and ways in which state power has been limited (federal mandates, financial power of the federal government, the vagueness of constitutional protection).

Here is part of a student's answer.

The argument that the interstate commerce clause protects the states is weak, however. This clause has been used to protect state power but it has commonly been interpreted by the Supreme Court to allow greater restrictions on the states. If the Constitution had a clearer statement, defending state power, federalism would be better protected. In the NFIB v Sebelius case, the court rejected the argument that Obamacare was unconstitutional – the interstate commerce clause did not prevent erosion of state power. Since the New Deal there has been a major increase in federal power at the expense of the states. The evidence, therefore, does not support the view that the states are well protected by the interstate commerce clause.

- The student states that an argument is weak and then gives a theoretical idea to challenge this argument (the lack of clear protection in the Constitution). This is good evaluation.

- The student uses examples in their evaluation, and suggests that the evidence does not support the argument.

Here is another part of a student's answer.

The federal government uses conditions of aid, only giving money to states if they comply with certain federal regulations. This allows them to direct state policy without breaking any constitutional rules because states are not forced to accept the regulations or the money. Obama, in his Race to the Top education programme, provided $4.3 billion worth of grants which states could compete for. Money was only awarded to the states that could best show that they met 20 educational goals set by federal government. While President Trump has removed many environmental regulations on states, he has also cut state funding for environmental projects. States cannot use the Constitution to protect this aid and are therefore limited in achieving green policy goals.

- The student shows a good understanding of relevant processes and how they relate to the question. They also make it clear that they appreciate the key aspects of federalism, such as the powers of and limits on states.

- This answer makes good use of two recent, detailed examples – using contemporary examples is important throughout Paper 3.

CHAPTER 2 Congress

In this chapter you will learn about:

- Congress's structure and functions
- some of the debates surrounding its role and powers.

2.1 The structure of Congress

A bicameral institution

Congress is a bicameral legislature, with two equal legislative bodies. The House of Representatives (or simply 'House') awards political representation to states in proportion to their population – so larger states have more seats. In the Senate, there are two politicians per state, regardless of population, giving a degree of protection to the interests of smaller states.

The Senate and the House of Representatives

Senate		House
Senator	**Title**	Congressman Congresswoman
6 years	**Term length**	2 years
100	**Total number**	435
2 per state. Each Senator represents the whole state	**Number per state**	Proportional to population Wyoming = 1 California = 53
$174,000	**Salary**	$174,000
President Mike Pence **Majority Leader** Mitch McConnell **Minority Leader** Chuck Schumer	**Senior figures 115th Congress 2017**	**Speaker** Paul Ryan **Majority Leader** Kevin McCarthy **Minority Leader** Nancy Pelosi
46 Democrats 52 Republicans 2 Independents	**115th Congress 2017/2018**	194 Democrats 241 Republicans

Table 1.1: How Congress is organised (information correct as of early 2017)

The election cycle

Congressional elections take place every two years in November. All members of the House are on the ballot, but only one-third of Senators, so the party majority in either chamber can change every two years. Some congressional elections take place at the same time as the presidential election. However, **mid-term elections** take place in the middle of a presidential term and occur every four years.

Link

For more on **mid-term elections**, see Section 2.2.

Key term

Mid-term elections
Congressional and state-based elections held mid-way through a president's four-year term.

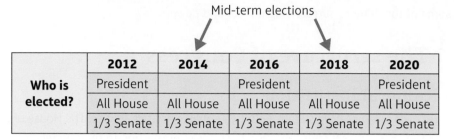

Mid-term elections

Who is elected?	2012	2014	2016	2018	2020
	President		President		President
	All House	All House	All House	All House	All House
	1/3 Senate	1/3 Senate	1/3 Senate	1/3 Senate	1/3 Senate

Figure 1.1: The election cycle

The distribution of power within Congress

Powers given to Congress in the Constitution

The Constitution awards a number of roles and powers to Congress. Concurrent powers are those given to both the House and Senate, creating yet more checks and balances and power sharing within the Constitution.

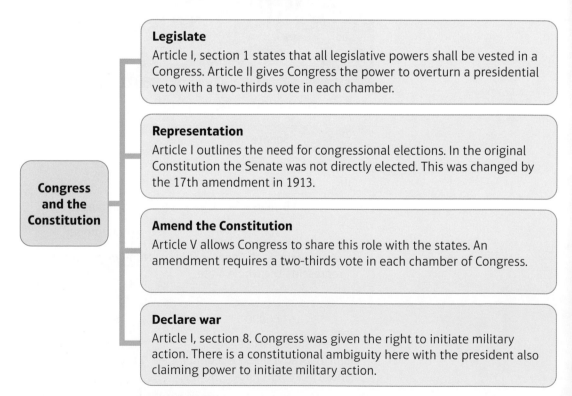

Congress and the Constitution

Legislate
Article I, section 1 states that all legislative powers shall be vested in a Congress. Article II gives Congress the power to overturn a presidential veto with a two-thirds vote in each chamber.

Representation
Article I outlines the need for congressional elections. In the original Constitution the Senate was not directly elected. This was changed by the 17th amendment in 1913.

Amend the Constitution
Article V allows Congress to share this role with the states. An amendment requires a two-thirds vote in each chamber of Congress.

Declare war
Article I, section 8. Congress was given the right to initiate military action. There is a constitutional ambiguity here with the president also claiming power to initiate military action.

Figure 1.2: Congress and the Constitution

The exclusive powers of each chamber

The House has exclusive power to...	The Senate has exclusive power to...
Impeach Impeachment does not mean removing a politician from office. Rather it means the House wanting to bring formal charges against a public official because, in their view, there is sufficient evidence of 'Treason, Bribery, or other high Crimes and Misdemeanors.' (Article II, section 4). Two US presidents (Andrew Johnson in 1868 and Bill Clinton in 1998) and one Supreme Court justice (Samuel Chase in 1804) have been impeached.	**Try an impeachment case** If the House impeaches a public official there is a trial in the Senate. A two-thirds Senate vote is then required to remove someone from office. Clinton was impeached but not removed from office, mainly because of the result of the mid-term elections in 1998, which saw the Democrats increase their share of seats in the House. The Republican failure to gain seats in the Senate was largely seen as public reaction against the ongoing Republican pursuit of Bill Clinton over the Lewinsky affair. Johnson and Chase survived the attempt to remove them in the Senate.
Elect the president if no candidate has over 50% of Electoral College Votes (ECV) With only two parties seriously contesting presidential elections, it is possible (though unlikely) for each candidate to get 269 ECVs. This power has only been used twice: in 1800 and 1824. Each state has one vote in the House, voting as a bloc.	**Elect the vice president, if no candidate has over 50% of ECV** Much like the House power to select the president, this power has rarely been used.
Begin consideration of all money bills Most legislation can begin in either chamber (many bills effectively pass through both at the same time), but all revenue-raising bills (those imposing taxes) must pass through the House first. Given the sensitivity of taxing people, the Founding Fathers wanted to give the House, the only elected chamber at the time, more influence over taxation than the Senate. This power is not very significant today as all House decisions still have to be accepted by the Senate, which can amend or reject House decisions.	**Ratify treaties** All treaties negotiated by the president are subject to confirmation by the Senate, requiring a two-thirds vote. Obama achieved ratification of the START treaty in 2010, a deal with Russia to scale back nuclear arsenals. The last Senate rejection was in 2012, of an Obama-backed treaty on disabled rights, which gained the support of only 61 Senators. The role of treaty ratification has been eroded by the president's use of **executive agreements**.
	Confirm executive appointments Over 1200 senior appointments – Cabinet members, some senior members of the EXOP and all federal judges, including **Supreme Court** justices – are scrutinised, usually through Senate committee hearings, with the Senate having the right to confirm a presidential nomination by a 50% + vote. This appointment process has become more politicised in recent years, although a president can expect almost all of his or her Cabinet members nominated. The extent of scrutiny depends partly on the nature of party control of the presidency and the Senate.

Table 1.2: Exclusive powers of the House and the Senate

> **Link**
>
> For more on **executive agreements**, see Section 3.4 of US Presidency.

> **Link**
>
> For **Supreme Court examples**, see Section 4.2 of The Supreme Court and Civil Rights.

EXTENSION ACTIVITY

Using the internet, find examples of President Trump nominations that have been subject to Senate ratification. Were some nominations harder to pass than others? Take notes on the reasons why.

2.2 The functions of Congress

Representation

Congressional elections

The frequency of elections means voters' voices are heard every two years, offering high levels of representation. Congressional elections use the first-past-the-post voting system (FPTP), in which members of both the House and the Senate are elected in single-member constituencies. These are whole states for the Senate (one Senator is usually elected in a state at any one time) and districts for the House.

Link

For more on **primaries**, see US Democracy and Participation chapter.

Congressional elections are also subject to **primaries**, much like presidential elections. A primary contest will only occur within a party when more than one candidate wants to represent the party for that seat.

The importance of mid-term elections

Mid-term elections are often effectively a referendum on the first two years of a presidential term. The results can have a major impact on presidential power, as the president's party can lose a majority in either chamber, or in both, making it harder to pass legislation. There is a clear pattern: the president's party loses seats in mid-terms, with voters often trying to curtail presidential power. The presidential party has only ever gained seats in the House three times: under President Roosevelt in 1934, President Clinton in 1998 and President Bush in 2002.

The nature of these elections has changed hugely. In mid-term elections, each party runs a national campaign based around a common party platform, usually under the leadership of the House speaker and the House minority leader. There has been a tendency for congressional candidates to develop their own individual policy platform, but this has been eroded by an increase in nation-based agendas. This came to the fore in 1994 when Newt Gingrich successfully moved from minority leader to speaker, based on his 'Contract with America', a fiscally conservative package presented to voters, which President Clinton was forced largely to accept. More recently, Nancy Pelosi and the '100-hour agenda' in 2006 and John Boehner and 'The Pledge to America' in 2010 gave a national mandate to the incoming speaker as their party took a House majority. This mandate allows speakers to become more powerful, often setting the legislative agenda as much as the president. However, this is only true when the president's party loses a mid-term and the opposing party takes control of one or more chambers.

President	Year	Party control	Notes
Clinton (D)	1994	Republicans gain seats and take the majority in both chambers from Democrats	Newt Gingrich and the 'Contract with America'. Clinton experienced a major decline in his power.
Clinton (D)	1998	Democrats gain seats but Republicans still maintain overall majority in both chambers	The Republicans tried to make this into a referendum on the Lewinsky affair. This backfired with Democrats gaining House seats, effectively ending the aim to remove Clinton from office.
Bush (R)	2002	Republicans gain seats and take majority in both chambers from Democrats	One of only three elections where the president's party has gained seats in the House. Came from a desire to unify around the president after 9/11, making George W. Bush one of the most powerful US presidents for the next four years.
Bush (R)	2006	Democrats gain seats and take majority from Republicans in both chambers	Nancy Pelosi and the '100-hour agenda'. As with Clinton in 1994, Bush experienced a major decline in power with the Democrats successfully setting their own agenda over the next year.
Obama (D)	2010	Republicans gain seats and take majority from Democrats in House only	Obama lost his majority in one chamber – a significant blow leading to legislative gridlock, with a federal government shutdown in 2013
Obama (D)	2014	Republicans gain seats and take majority from Democrats in the Senate, retaining House control	A further decline occurs as the Republicans take control of both chambers and act in a very partisan way, making it almost impossible for Obama to enact any policy. Obama resorts to executive orders to achieve key policy goals.

 President's party loses control of one or more chambers

 President's party gains seats in at least one chamber but does not gain a majority in either chamber

 President's party gains seats and a majority in both chambers

Figure 2.1: Recent mid-term elections

The significance of incumbency

A notable feature of congressional elections is that the **incumbent** typically wins their seat again in the next election. In 2016 incumbency re-election rates were 97 per cent for the House and 90 per cent for the Senate.

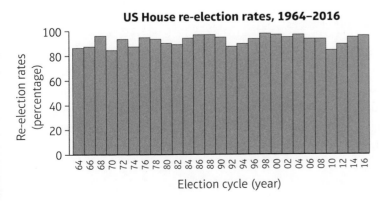

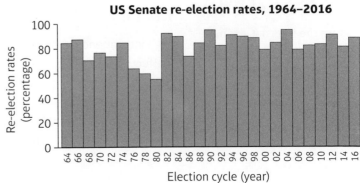

Figure 2.2: Incumbency re-election rates for House and Senate (1964–2016)

There are several factors responsible for high incumbency re-election rates.

Link

For more on **gerrymandering**, see the case study later in this chapter.

- **Use of office:** Congresspersons and Senators can use their place in office to establish popularity and attract major donors. A proven track record inspires trust among voters and donors.

- **Safe seats and gerrymandering:** The winner-takes-all system has allowed a huge number of safe seats, where a candidate wins so convincingly that they are expected to keep the seat at the next election. An appropriate system of proportional representation would end this. However, this problem is made worse by **gerrymandering** – drawing electoral boundaries to favour a certain social group or party. This lets the dominant party draw district boundaries in their favour, at the expense of the opposition. Racial gerrymandering was common before the civil rights era as many state boundaries are drawn up by the politicians elected at state level.

- **Pork-barrel legislation:** This is when a member of Congress proposes an amendment to legislation that will bring benefits (especially financial ones, such as infrastructure projects or service provision) to a particular group. An amendment added by a politician to add expenditure to a bill that benefits their constituency is referred to as an 'earmark', which is often criticised for promoting unnecessary spending and contributing to the budget deficit. Even fiscal conservatives will engage in such proposals to improve their re-election chances. Some see pork-barrelling as evidence of the highly representative nature of Congress; others see it as a form of over-representation, in which financial benefits are not spread evenly around the country or constituency. In 2010, Republican leaders placed a moratorium on earmarks in order to restrict pork-barrel legislation, but this did not stop the practice altogether. In 2016, Congress passed legislation to spend $475 million on a new navy ship that the defense secretary and navy did not want, especially after a Pentagon report showing its unreliability. The project was supported by Representatives Byrne from Alabama and Ribble of Wisconsin, who represent districts with major shipbuilding companies.

- **Financial advantage:** Incumbents can attract more money than challengers, allowing them to run more successful campaigns. Challengers can struggle to gain name recognition and often find themselves under attack through well-funded negative adverts.

Candidate type	Total raised (millions)	No. of candidates	Money raised per candidate (millions)
Incumbent	$627.3	417	$1.50
Challengers	$135.3	631	$0.21
Open seats	$198.4	334	$0.59
Total	$961.0	1382	$0.69

Source: www.opensecrets.org

Table 2.1: House election funding in the 2016 elections

EXTENSION ACTIVITY

Using the internet, examine the impact of the 2010 ban on pork-barrel legislation. What are the advantages and disadvantages of such a ban?

High incumbency re-election rates can be seen as a threat to US democracy, suggesting an ineffective level of representation. Some states tried to resolve this by creating term limits for their Congresspersons and Senators, but this was struck down by the Supreme Court. Term limits would end the stagnation of politicians in Congress, but they would only be attacking a symptom of incumbency. The major underlying causes, such as funding and gerrymandering, would remain, along with significant concerns about how representative members of Congress were.

Case study: Gerrymandering and Operation REDMAP

After Obama's election victory in 2008, a group of Republican tacticians developed a plan to increase their chances of winning congressional seats. They targeted Democrat states due to re-draw their House-district boundaries, and concentrated resources to make sure Republicans could take control of the state legislature. After this, new Republican-held state legislatures changed constituency boundaries to maximise Republican success in House of Representative elections.

Political writer David Daley has shown how in various states, such as Pennsylvania, the Republican Party spent significant campaign finance to attack a small number of Democrat state politicians, giving the Republicans a majority that they used to change boundaries for that state. The impact of changing just one state seat from Democrat to Republican was enormous. In 2008, Obama won Pennsylvania and 12 Democrat Congresspersons won seats from this state. In 2012, Obama won again, but only five Democrats won House elections because the constituency boundaries had changed. In 2012 – the first election using the new maps – Democratic congressional candidates received 100,000 more votes than Republicans, but Republicans won 13 of the 18 seats: 51 per cent of the vote translated into just 28 per cent of the seats. Democrats won by huge margins in just five areas, but more Republicans dominated House elections, with few changes in overall voting patterns.

Question

- Why do you think Democrats have not effectively challenged anomalies that allow a minority of votes to win a majority of seats?

Factors affecting voting behaviour within Congress

Members of Congress vote frequently on legislation and legislative amendments. They also hold a range of other important votes, including constitutional amendments, initiation of military action and, in the Senate, ratifying presidential appointments.

Congressional politicians are subject to a number of pressures that determine how they vote.

- **Public opinion/constituency:** Representatives must take into account public opinion or run the risk of being voted out of office. Congresspersons and Senators are subjected to frequent elections, which provide public accountability due to the threat of removal. It can be argued that this factor is more important in the House, as elections to the House take place every two years, compared to six years to the Senate. However, separation of powers means that there are strong levels of representation in both chambers, creating an individual mandate for each politician. People are likely to vote for a certain candidate due to their individual policies rather than because of their party label or party leader. In 2009, several Democrats switched their position, dropping their support for Obama's Affordable Care Act, after meetings with constituents and rising opposition to the bill. *The New York Times* stated that ten moderate Republicans opposed the Republican plan to repeal this act in March 2017. Some of these moderates represent districts which voted for Clinton in 2016. Politicians in the House and the Senate are clearly more accountable to public opinion than their own president.

- **Party/party leaders:** By being members of a party, representatives are pressured to vote according to the majority party view. There is a sense of belonging to a party that encourages politicians to vote together. Team competition – the desire to stop the opposing party – contributes to higher unity. It is the sort of message that can be driven home during weekly caucus meetings, where all members of a party in congress gather together, usually led by senior members of the party. Party leaders also have limited use of patronage power with promises of committee chairmanships or membership to induce politicians to vote a certain way.

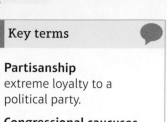

Key terms

Partisanship
extreme loyalty to a political party.

Congressional caucuses
groups of legislators who share special interests and meet to pursue common legislative objectives, such as black caucus, women's caucus, Hispanic caucus.

Link

For more on **Blue Dog Democrats**, see Section 2.3.

Link

For more on **professional lobbyists**, see Section 5.3 of US Democracy and Participation.

No Republicans voted for Obama's stimulus budget in 2009, arguably due to **partisanship** rather than an ideological belief that the economy should self-stabilise and the government should not interfere. However, the fact that local opinion led 11 southern Democrats to vote against Obama's 2009 economic stimulus package suggests that public opinion has a greater impact on the way Congresspersons vote.

- **Caucuses:** There are many factions within Congress, often called **congressional caucuses**. Some are based on ideology (such as the conservative **Blue Dog Democrats**). Other factions are based on social characteristics, such as the congressional black caucus, which has approximately 40 members. While it is dominated by Democrats, it is officially non-partisan: Mia Love, the first Republican black Congresswoman, is part of the group. Yet others are based on economic interests and are not set along party lines, such as the Congressional Steel Caucus containing approximately 100 members who mainly represent districts with steel manufacturers. These groups often vote together on legislative issues.

- **Interest groups and professional lobbyists:** These groups can influence voting through means including donations, which may influence a Congressperson or Senator to vote for policies that favour that group. Some interest groups, such as the AFL-CIO (American Federation of Labor and Congress of Industrial Organizations) and the AARP (American Association of Retired Persons), also have large, active memberships, so members can mobilise to create the threat of removal of members from Congress. After the 2012 Newtown shootings, Obama was unsuccessful in passing legislation to limit guns, despite clear majority public support. Pressure from the National Rifle Association and the vocal (and sizeable) minority apparently carried more weight than public opinion. Politicians may also be strongly influenced by professional lobbyists and big businesses. Members of Congress, once they leave Capitol Hill, can command a much higher salary within such an organisation.

Pause & reflect

How important are these different factors?

The legislative function

How Congress legislates

Figure 2.3 outlines the complex US legislative process. The easiest (and most interesting) way to appreciate the details is through understanding the most important features and their implications.

Four key features of the legislative process

- **Initiation:** Presidents can dominate the political agenda, but leaders in the House or Senate – and individual members of Congress – regularly initiate policy. Congress may be more active in setting an agenda if the president's party has recently lost control of Congress in a mid-term election or if bipartisan control exists.

- **Compromise:** The separation of powers and the checks and balances, including the co-equal legislative power of the House and Senate, make compromise between parties or chambers necessary. Successful legislation will usually be a result of huge concessions and additions to a bill. Legislation does not pass in a linear manner, travelling from president to House to Senate. A proposal may travel through both chambers at the same time, with the House and Senate then producing alternative versions of a law, which they then have to reconcile. This can be done through a conference committee, in which members of both chambers try to come to an agreement.

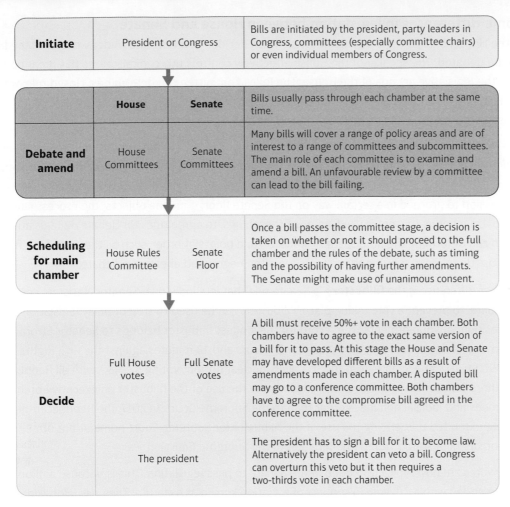

Initiate	President or Congress		Bills are initiated by the president, party leaders in Congress, committees (especially committee chairs) or even individual members of Congress.
	House	**Senate**	Bills usually pass through each chamber at the same time.
Debate and amend	House Committees	Senate Committees	Many bills will cover a range of policy areas and are of interest to a range of committees and subcommittees. The main role of each committee is to examine and amend a bill. An unfavourable review by a committee can lead to the bill failing.
Scheduling for main chamber	House Rules Committee	Senate Floor	Once a bill passes the committee stage, a decision is taken on whether or not it should proceed to the full chamber and the rules of the debate, such as timing and the possibility of having further amendments. The Senate might make use of unanimous consent.
Decide	Full House votes	Full Senate votes	A bill must receive 50%+ vote in each chamber. Both chambers have to agree to the exact same version of a bill for it to pass. At this stage the House and Senate may have developed different bills as a result of amendments made in each chamber. A disputed bill may go to a conference committee. Both chambers have to agree to the compromise bill agreed in the conference committee.
	The president		The president has to sign a bill for it to become law. Alternatively the president can veto a bill. Congress can overturn this veto but it then requires a two-thirds vote in each chamber.

Figure 2.3: The legislative process in the US

- **Weak parties and party leaders:** Due to the separation of powers and federalism, parties tend to be weak, with many factions. Party leaders also have limited power over their own party, with ineffective patronage and whipping – many Congress members are more interested in listening to the 'folks back home' and prioritising the concerns of their own state or district over the national agenda. As a result, parties do not act as a single unit in passing legislation, making it difficult to pass laws. The rise in partisanship can help the passage of legislation through Congress, but this is of little use if the presidency is controlled by a different party or the House and Senate have split control (as in 2010–14). Here partisanship can cause high levels of **gridlock**, where president, House and Senate fail to agree and legislation cannot be passed.

- **Obstacles to success:** It is far easier to prevent change than to bring it about. Here are some of the main impediments to passing laws.

  ○ Senate and House roughly share power and have equal law-making powers. Each chamber may have different legislative priorities due to differing term lengths. There may also be differences in party majority, leading to major legislative conflict.

  ○ Legislation has to pass through several congressional committees, each of which can amend or obstruct a bill. Many committees are policy-based and will make decisions regarding the efficacy of a proposal. All bills requiring spending also have to pass through an appropriations committee, which determines whether there is sufficient funding. Separate committees cover the same or similar functions in each chamber.

  ○ Overriding a presidential veto requires a supermajority of two-thirds in both chambers.

Key term

Gridlock
a situation in US politics where the president and Congress are equally powerful and constantly prevent each other from acting, resulting in difficulty passing legislation.

Some differences in legislation between House and Senate

In the House, bills go to a Rules Committee, which decides how long and under what rules the bill will be debated. The speaker of the House effectively controls this committee, so has great power over the legislative agenda of the House. The Rules Committee can determine a closed rule, where a bill can be discussed but no amendments can be offered. This is unusual, but can speed up passage of a bill. The Senate does not do this; all bills are fully debated.

The Senate is much less structured than the House, does not have a Rules Committee and gives unlimited debate time for a bill. The Senate also often uses a process called **unanimous consent**, where all Senators involved agree on a decision being made. A member of the Senate requests permission to proceed in a certain way on the Senate floor; if no one objects, the process can begin. Unanimous consent is used, among other things, to agree rules for debate on legislation, which can determine the time spent or waive certain points of order, such as the need for a full reading. Unanimous consent agreements are often negotiated ahead of a debate.

Another difference is the **filibuster** – a Senate rule that lets individual Senators insist on continuing to debate, to prevent a vote taking place. Filibusters can be used to stop or delay legislation or presidential appointments. The record for the longest filibuster belongs to Senator Strom Thurmond of South Carolina, who spoke for 24 hours and 18 minutes against the Civil Rights Act of 1957. In 2013, the Senate used the so-called 'nuclear option', voting 52–48 – with all Republicans and three Democrats voting against – to eliminate the use of the filibuster on executive branch nominees and judicial nominees other than to the Supreme Court. In 2017, the Republican-held Senate extended this, ending the use of the filibuster for Supreme Court nominations after Democrats filibustered Trump's nomination to the Supreme Court.

Sixty votes are now typically needed in the Senate to pass legislation. This is because a filibuster can be ended with a 3/5 vote in support of a motion known as a cloture. Their use, alongside the use of filibusters, has increased hugely in recent years. In 2010, the DREAM Act, having passed the House, failed to gain the 60 votes needed to overcome a Republican filibuster.

Key terms

Unanimous consent
a Senator or Congressperson may request unanimous consent on the floor to set aside a specified rule of procedure so as to expedite proceedings.

Filibuster
a process in which a Senator gives a prolonged speech on the floor of the Senate to obstruct legislative progress of a bill or confirmation of appointments to the executive or judiciary.

Link

To see how filibustering affects the nomination of Supreme Court justices, see Alito and Garland case study in Section 4.2 of The Supreme Court and Civil Rights.

Case study: Chris Murphy's unconventional filibuster

Democrat Senator Chris Murphy took the unusual step of using a filibuster to force a vote, rather than to prevent one taking place. Murphy represents the state of Connecticut, where 26 children and teachers were shot and killed in Sandy Hook Elementary School, Newtown, in December 2012. Senator Murphy began a filibuster that he said he would only end once the Senate agreed to vote on two key gun control measures. The first would expand background checks required for weapons purchases, and the second would allow the US to ban sales of guns and explosives to people listed on government watch-lists of suspected terrorists. Senate leaders eventually agreed to a vote, and Murphy halted his filibuster after 14 hours and 50 minutes.

The amendment to ban weapons sales to those on terrorist watch-lists failed with a vote of 47–53; just two Republicans supported the ban, and one Democrat opposed it. The background checks amendment was also rejected by 44–56, with one Republican Senator in support and three Democrats opposing.

Question
- Why do you think the issue of gun control is such a divisive issue in US politics?

Strengths and weaknesses of the legislative process

Strengths	Weaknesses
Checks and balances prevent tyranny, forcing compromise between different interests. In this sense the United States creates a pluralist democracy in which power is shared.	**Inefficiency/low output** results from the excessive need to compromise. Congress cannot act quickly and often fails to agree on legislation to address key needs.
Quality policy comes from detailed consideration of bills and filters to remove undesirable aspects. This limits the danger of a bill being poorly thought through.	**High levels of partisanship** mean parties are unwilling to compromise, leading to more gridlock. The Constitution requires compromise for laws to be passed.
Individual and states' rights are protected, as Senators can insert amendments or filibuster on the basis of their equal state power and interests.	**Poor-quality legislation** can come from too much compromise. A bill may lack coherence due to many amendments and interests. Prevalent pork-barrelling can create financially wasteful policy not based on rational decisions.

Table 2.2: Strengths and weaknesses of the legislative process

The policy significance of Congress

Congress is clearly able to have a huge impact on the United States through major legislation that has brought about major social change, determines the spending priorities of the federal government and determines the nature and extent of individual liberty.

The section above on the strengths and weaknesses can be used to judge the effectiveness of laws passed. In addition, any assessment of the effectiveness of laws passed will clearly be affected by ideological judgements. In other words, liberals and conservatives will disagree over the effectiveness of laws that are passed. Furthermore, conservatives may support the current complex legislative process because it makes it difficult to bring about change and can be used to stop the federal government from imposing new requirements on US citizens and the states. Many acts of Congress restrict states' ability to control their own affairs, causing conflict between federal and state government. It has often been conservatives who have objected to federal laws – such as the Voting Rights Act or the Affordable Care Act – because they undermine federalism. On the other hand, liberals may prefer a more efficient process in order to increase their chances of developing socially progressive legislation. Much depends on the nature of party control, however. Democrats who want the president to have greater power to make policy, arguing that the filibuster has been misused by the Senate during the Obama presidency, might be the same Democrats who strongly support the use of the filibuster to prevent the more conservative elements of President Trump's legislative agenda from coming to fruition.

Quorum state that Congress introduced 10,078 bills in the 114th Congress (2015–17) and sent 329 of those to President Obama (just three per cent). The 113th Congress saw 8911 introduced bills and only 282 bills sent to the president (again just three per cent).

Passed	Failed
American Recovery and Reinvestment Act 2009 • Gave the economy a $787 bn injection to protect jobs and stimulate the economy. • Covered infrastructure, aid to low-paid workers, education and tax breaks. • Effectiveness strongly disputed; Congress vote split almost entirely on party lines.	**DREAM Act** • Advocated by Obama in 2008 and 2012 election campaigns. • Aimed at allowing all illegal immigrants who arrived in the US before 18th birthday to have a right to remain. • Filibustered in Senate, with Obama using temporary executive orders to achieve some of his policy goals.

Passed	Failed
Patient Protection and Affordable Care Act 2010 • Requires almost all Americans to have health insurance, with provisions for those on low/no income. • Requires insurance companies to insure those with pre-existing conditions. • Support in Congress based mainly on party affiliation.	**Gun regulations** • Proposed in various forms by president and Congress. • Legislation developed by Vice President Biden, after Sandy Hook Newtown shootings, was defeated in the Senate. This would have banned some assault rifles, limited the size of magazines and increased the use of background checks.
The Freedom Act 2015 • Created after Edward Snowden revealed how the Patriot Act was being used to monitor US citizens. • Reauthorised many provisions of the controversial Patriot Act (2001) until 2019, including giving the government powers to collect bulk communications data via surveillance (gathering data but not contents of calls/emails). • Continued the suspension of 'probable cause' to suspect that someone is involved in terrorism before a search takes place. • Led to a major dispute between House and Senate in which Mitch McConnell held out for full re-authorisation of the Patriot Act.	**Budget shutdown in 2013** • Legislative gridlock due to lack of agreement on Continuing Appropriations Resolution (to settle key budget policies). • Disagreement centred on spending levels, budget deficit and the Affordable Care Act which the House insisted on defunding. • Lasted 16 days at an estimated cost of $24 bn. Over a million federal employees worked without knowing their pay dates; many others were told not to go to work. • Inability of president and Congress to agree on annual budget plagued Obama's presidency.

Table 2.3: Some major legislative proposals since 2008

Pause & reflect ✔

What do the above examples suggest about the impact of congressional laws and the effectiveness of laws passed?

EXTENSION ACTIVITY

Do some research to find out more about the leaks made by former CIA member Edward Snowden in 2013, which exposed the levels of US surveillance. What were the political and constitutional impacts of this leak?

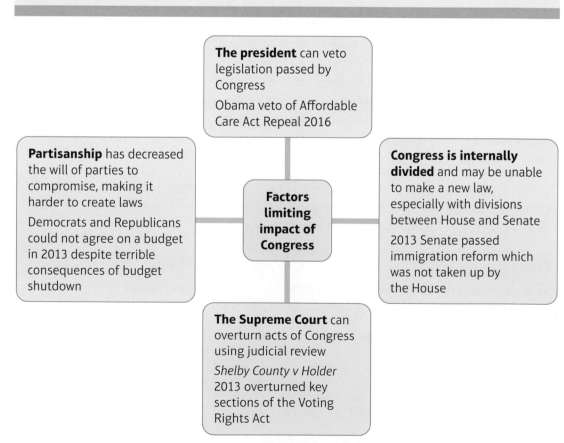

Figure 2.4: Factors that limit the impact Congress can have

Oversight

Checks and their effectiveness

The separation of powers and high levels of checks and balances in the Constitution put Congress in a strong position to provide checks on the executive branch in particular. **Oversight** of the executive branch occurs when Congress scrutinises or limits its actions.

Key term

Oversight
the ability of one branch of government to supervise the work of another.

Vote on presidential proposals
On a daily basis this is the most significant check that Congress can place upon the president. Congress can and does use this power in a number of ways to restrict presidential policies.

- **Vote against laws initiated or supported by the president**
  In March 2017 Trump was frustrated by his inability to pass the American Health Care Act despite holding a Republican majority in both chambers.

- **Amend laws initiated or supported by the president**
  Obama was restricted by amendments to budget policies, which he was forced to accept. Congress also passed amendments to National Defense Authorization Acts, both limiting presidential power (Obama had to give 30 days' notice to relevant congressional committees before moving anyone from Guantanamo) and giving him powers he did not want (Obama said he would never use the power given to him to order the killing by drone strike of United States citizens within the United States territory suspected of terrorism).

- **Determine funding for presidential projects**
  By failing to allocate funding, Congress can restrict or cancel a policy from being put into practice. In 1995 Congress withdrew funding for US military involvement in Bosnia, forcing President Clinton to withdraw troops. Congress has repeatedly attempted to defund many of Obama's domestic policy priorities.

- **Proposing legislation**
  Actively developing their own congressional agenda will contrast or strongly conflict with the goals of the president. The policy platforms developed by Speakers Pelosi, Boehner and Ryan all provide evidence of a president being limited by the agenda of Congress.

Overturn presidential veto Using a two-thirds vote Congress can stop the president from overriding its legislative goals. Obama issued his 12th veto against the Justice Against Sponsors of Terrorism Act in 2016, a bill which would allow families of victims of 9/11 to sue the Saudi Arabian government for any involvement they may have had. This was easily overturned 97-to-1 in the Senate and 348-to-77 in the House.	**Senate ratification of appointments** Critical to the president achieving their policy goals is their ability to appoint their favoured people to executive and judicial positions. The failure of the Senate to vote on Obama's nomination of Merrick Garland to the Supreme Court in 2016 allowed President Trump to nominate Justice Gorsuch and influence the ideological balance of the Court.
Declare war In theory this power is given to Congress, thus limiting the president's ability to initiate military action. Most presidents have requested permission for military action, such as George W. Bush seeking approval for the Iraq War in 2003.	**Senate ratification of treaties** The president is not free to enter into agreements with other countries without seeking approval from the Senate by a two-thirds vote. In 2014 the Senate blocked a United Nations disability treaty, which Obama had pushed for.

Impeachment and removal of members of executive branch
The House can impeach a member of the executive branch and the Senate can then hold a trial in order to decide whether or not to remove them. While President Clinton was impeached in 1999, he was not removed from office.

Figure 2.5: Main congressional checks on the executive provided by the Constitution

As well as congressional checks, which are created by the Constitution, a major part of the oversight process comes from the committees created by Congress. They can check the executive in a number of ways.

- Most committees are policy-based and conduct oversight based on their policy expertise. Typically they investigate a department and hold hearings for executive members.
- The House Committee on Oversight and Reform has the sole role of scrutinising the executive. In the years before the 2016 election, Committee Chair Jason Chaffetz used the committee to investigate Hillary Clinton's use of a private email account for her work as secretary of state.
- Congress can create temporary committees to provide oversight if an event of concern arises. Congress created the House Select Committee on Benghazi in 2014, after the US ambassador to Libya was killed there.

Key term

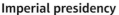

Imperial presidency
a dominant presidency with ineffective checks and balances from the other branches.

The effectiveness of congressional checks may be limited. Congress may be restricted by the extent of presidential power. Congress may be unable to provide checks on the president where the president makes use of certain presidential powers. The theory of the **imperial presidency** suggests that the president has a number of tools to bypass these checks. For example, by using executive orders directing the executive branch to carry out a policy in a certain way, the president can effectively create new policies without passing legislation through Congress. Congress has criticised President Obama for his many executive orders on gun control, immigration and federal pay. President Trump was criticised for the high number of executive orders he issued in his first weeks in office, making it difficult for Congress to examine the implications of each one.

Figure 2.6 shows that there are also a number of factors that influence the relationship between the president and Congress, such as the policy area itself. The extent to which these checks are effective changes according to political circumstances. In other words, the power to vote against presidential proposals is more likely to be used if the president or policy is unpopular. In addition, if the president and Congress are of the same party, given the increasingly partisan nature of Congress, oversight might be limited. In 2017 Devin Nunes, chair of the House Intelligence Committee charged with investigating alleged Russian involvement in the US elections, was criticised for his lack of independence from Trump. Nunes travelled to the White House to view security documents rather than having these documents open to scrutiny by the whole committee. He drew criticism from both Democrats and Republicans with Senator John McCain saying, 'You've got to have a bipartisan approach to an issue such as this if you want to be credible.' Congress is supposed to act as a watchdog on the executive branch, but can go from attack dog to lap dog, depending on which party is in control.

Link

For more on **the extent to which Congress can check the president**, see US Presidency.

Factors influencing the relationship between Congress and the presidency

EXTENSION ACTIVITY

Using the internet, find examples of conflict between president and Congress this year or last. Take notes to show who was more successful in this relationship and take account of the influence of any of the factors here.

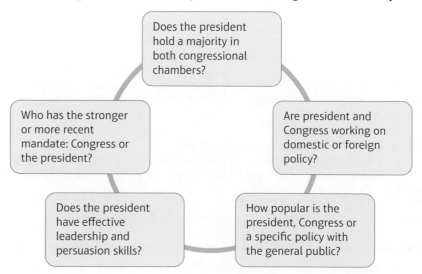

Figure 2.6: Factors influencing the relationship between Congress and the presidency

Congress's limits on the Supreme Court

The ultimate power Congress holds over the Supreme Court is to overturn a decision. Using an amendment to the Constitution, Congress can reverse or amend a Court ruling. When Congress and the states lowered the voting age to 18 in the 26th amendment of 1971, it effectively overturned the *Oregon v Mitchell* 1970 ruling, which allowed states to retain the age of 21 as the voting age for state elections if they wished to. However, this restriction on the Court is limited by the difficulty of amending the Constitution. The vast majority of Supreme Court rulings are not subject to an amendment effort; those that are, usually fail.

The other key aspect of the relationship between Congress and the Supreme Court is the Senate's role in ratifying presidential nominations. This is a contentious area, but the Senate cannot check the Court as a whole, nor does it have control over a justice. The Senate's role is limited to conducting hearings and then voting on a nominee. Once that person becomes a justice, there is no threat of removal from the Senate.

Congress has two other powers in relation to the Supreme Court, neither of which has any impact on the Court as a whole on a year-to-year basis.

- Individual justices can be impeached and removed by Congress. The last such attempt to remove a justice was in 1804, when Justice Samuel Chase was impeached by the House but acquitted by the Senate.
- The Constitution gives Congress the authority to determine the total number of justices on the Court. The number has been settled at nine since the Civil War. Congress could increase this number to allow a president to appoint new members of the Court and establish a majority, but this has neither been used nor threatened since the Roosevelt presidency.

2.3 Interpretations and debates

The changing significance of parties in Congress

One of the most important developments in recent years is the polarisation of parties, as the Democratic and Republican Parties have moved further apart in terms of values and policies. This fits closely with another important development – increased partisanship, in which each party is becoming more internally united, in opposition to the other party.

To what extent does partisanship exist?

Since the 1970s, both Democrats and Republicans have become increasingly unified (see Figure 3.1). The Republican Party was criticised for excessive partisanship during the Obama presidency, with some politicians seeming to oppose any policy supported by Obama. For example, the then-House Budget Committee Chair Tom Price refused to begin committee consideration of Obama's final $4 trillion budget proposal.

Party unity scores are calculated by looking at the number of times a member of Congress votes with the majority in their own party. In Congress, the average unity in the 113th Congress (2013–14) was 92 per cent for the Democrats and 90 per cent for Republicans – 'a record for sustained party discipline unmatched in the House in the history of our party unity studies', according

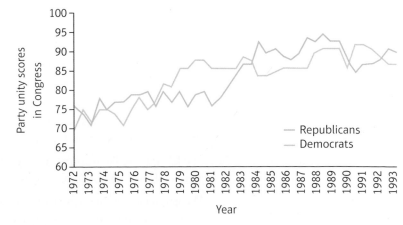

Figure 3.1: Party unity scores in Congress since 1972

to the *Congressional Quarterly.* Voting between parties has become more divergent than at any other period since the Second World War. In addition, the political middle has disappeared, with declines in moderate conservatives and Blue Dog Democrats, who represent a crossover between the two parties.

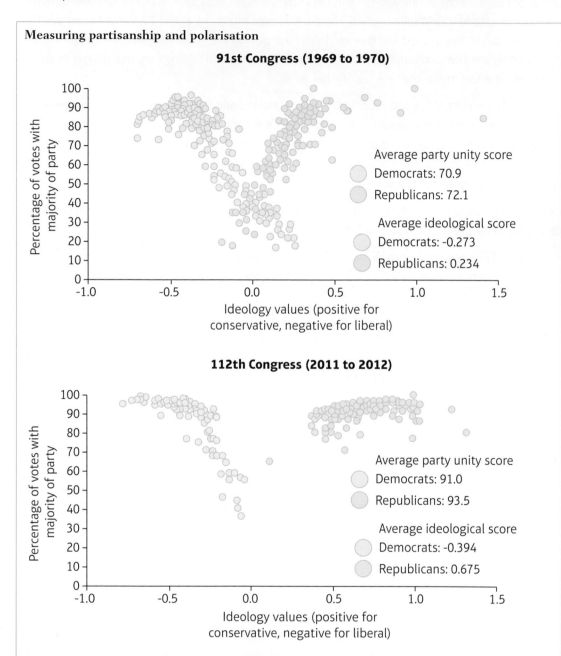

Measuring partisanship and polarisation

91st Congress (1969 to 1970)

Average party unity score
Democrats: 70.9
Republicans: 72.1

Average ideological score
Democrats: -0.273
Republicans: 0.234

112th Congress (2011 to 2012)

Average party unity score
Democrats: 91.0
Republicans: 93.5

Average ideological score
Democrats: -0.394
Republicans: 0.675

Figure 3.2: Partisanship and polarisation

Figure 3.2 gives a clear representation of both partisanship and polarisation. Each dot represents the voting pattern of a single member of Congress (yellow for Democrats, green for Republicans).

The vertical scale measures party unity, expressed as a percentage. If a member of Congress votes with the majority in her party, say, 9 times out of 10, she will have a score of 90 per cent. The higher the dot on the graph, the stronger the party unity.

The left-right scale measures ideology. The further left the dot is, the more liberal/left-wing the voting pattern of that member of Congress.

The graph clearly shows increased partisanship with much higher levels of party unity. It also shows polarisation – the two parties are moving further apart.

Partisanship is not absolute; there are instances of bipartisan agreement and compromise. Democrat and Republican Senators worked together after the 2012 election in the 'Gang of 8' to pass immigration reform (which was blocked by the House). Democrats and Republicans have eventually arrived at compromise measures allowing budgets to be passed, and the two sides have even agreed on the removal of Senate filibusters for judicial nominations – a move Democrats may now regret given the election of Donald Trump in 2016. In some cases there has been significant cross-party agreement. In 2016 there was a convincing vote to overturn Obama's Saudi Arabia legislation veto. This upheld Congress's original law to allow families of the victims of 9/11 to sue the Saudi Arabian government. In addition, the existence of caucuses, within or between parties, reveals that a party is not fully united.

Implications of partisanship

Legislation and gridlock

The increased operation of parties as collective units has hugely reduced Congress's ability to pass legislation in recent years. The last two congressional sessions were the two least productive in its history, passing 208 (112th Congress) and 212 (113th Congress) substantive laws (ones that had an impact on an aspect of US society, as opposed to ceremonial laws such as post-office renamings or commemorative coin authorisations) in each of these two-year periods, although more laws were passed in 2015 than in each of the two years before that.

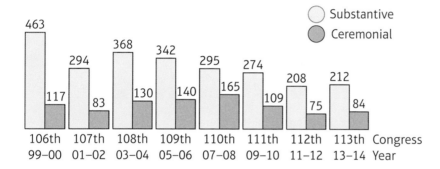

Figure 3.3: Public laws enacted by each Congress, by category

Those fearing over-powerful leadership may see this as a healthy sign that government cannot enforce too many policies on the people. This perhaps reflects the vision of the Founding Fathers in creating constitutional procedures to ensure limited government. On the other hand, it could be seen as a failure of Congress to address the specific needs of the nation. Gridlock between parties in the executive and legislature, over the budget and health care, led to the financially disastrous budget shutdown of 2013.

Case study: Gridlock and the Zika virus 2016

Democrats and Republicans were unable to agree on federal funding to tackle the growing Zika virus crisis in the United States. When the virus affected people in Florida, Democrats and Republicans argued about levels of spending to tackle the problem. Obama requested $1.9 billion in Zika funding, but the Republican-led Congress wanted to cut this to $1.1 billion, with Senate Democrats stopping the bill because they argued it was insufficient to deal with the outbreak. As a result, no agreement was reached. Obama blamed the Republican Party for the impasse, and Democrat Senators called on the Republican Senate Majority Leader to cut short a recess so that they could attempt to resolve their differences. Republican House Speaker Paul Ryan accused Obama of partisanship: 'We need the White House and Senate Democrats to drop politics and put the public's health first.'

Question

- What characteristic of US politics makes its federal government particularly prone to gridlocks?

Checks on the president

The increase in partisanship has had a major impact on presidential power. Under **divided government** the president might fail to provide significant leadership; Congress could obstruct a president's policy initiatives, adopting an aggressive oversight role. This characterised presidential congressional relations between Obama and the Republican-led Congress (2011–16) and Bush and the Democrat-led Congress (2007–08), and reduced presidential power significantly.

On the other hand, if there is **unified government** with one party holding the presidency, House and Senate, partisanship may lead to a major increase in the power of the presidency. Driven more by party loyalty, Congressional politicians may overlook oversight and fail to provide significant checks on the executive. Congress was accused of 'forgetting' to provide oversight of the Bush administration when the president held a Republican majority between 2003 and 2008, despite controversies over the Iraq War, the Patriot Act and the creation of the Guantanamo detention camp.

Lower party unity	**Higher party unity**
• Weak leadership due to limited patronage power of leaders means individuals do not always vote with their party • Constituency opinion has stronger influence than party • Members of Congress may be strongly allied to an interest group or congressional caucus or faction	• Leaders in Congress have become more powerful, with nationalisation of mid-terms and speaker's increased power • Increased partisanship has led to high levels of party unity

Figure 3.4: Impact of party unity levels on the role of Congress

The changing powers of Congress

Congress has undergone some long-term constitutional and structural changes that have increased its powers. The 16th amendment (1913) gave Congress the power to levy federal income tax, marking a major increase in the power of federal government in general. The move to directly elected Senators with the 17th amendment (1913) increased the legitimacy of the Senate and allowed it to increase its power relative to the House.

Three changes in recent years have led to a change in congressional power.

- **The rise in importance of foreign and military policy** has arguably undermined congressional power as international affairs became increasingly controlled by the presidency. As military action became faster, more complex and more deadly, the president, surrounded by superior executive resources, has been able to exert greater control over **military policy**. Congress has attempted to exert authority with the War Powers Act of 1973.

- **The nationalisation of mid-term elections** has centralised greater power in the hands of the House speaker. Under divided government this has allowed the speaker to act as a significant rival to the president, suggesting an increase in the collective power of Congress.

- **Partisanship** has created greater extremes in Congress's reaction to the presidency and the extent to which they have attempted to restrict the executive branch. Under divided government, partisanship has arguably strengthened the power of Congress as it becomes more determined to challenge presidential power.

There are also many short-term changes, where the power of Congress is constantly in flux, with frequent elections changing the party majority in each chamber, as well as changing the party in control of the executive. It is tempting to see an election result that produces divided government as one that creates a more powerful Congress. Certainly, Congress tends to become more assertive in these situations and will often vote against presidential proposals or apply intense scrutiny. On the other hand, if president and Congress are from the same party, Congress will be able to achieve more of its policy goals.

What is power?

This concept is commonly used in politics but its exact meaning is not always clear. In the paragraph above there are two different ways of measuring power. The first is based on the idea of blocking the president, by stopping him or her from passing policies. The second is based on achieving desired aims, where power is measured by the ability to get what you want. If you apply this second understanding of power, Congress is more powerful under united, not divided, government.

Pause & reflect ✔

In this section you have examined the changing power of Congress, rather than the power of Congress. Look over this section again and identify all of the words and phrases that suggest change.

EXTENSION ACTIVITY

The **imperial presidency** theory can be applied to the idea of changing power, but this involves showing how the president has become more powerful over time – and Congress less so. What aspects of the imperial presidency could easily be described as a change? How has the president become more powerful over time?

Congress and representation

The concept of representation has much in common with the idea of (representative) democracy. To put it simply, representation occurs when the people get what the people want. There are also different types of representation (see Figure 3.5). When looking at the main arguments for and against the idea that Congress is representative, these two forms of representation can be applied to assess which type Congress is most (or least) able to offer.

Link ↗

For more on **imperial presidency**, see Section 3.4 of US Presidency.

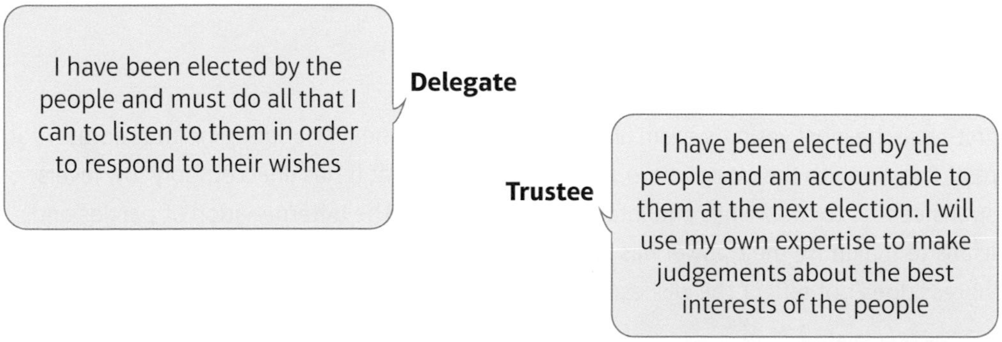

I have been elected by the people and must do all that I can to listen to them in order to respond to their wishes — **Delegate**

Trustee — I have been elected by the people and am accountable to them at the next election. I will use my own expertise to make judgements about the best interests of the people

Figure 3.5: Two different types of representation

Congress is representative

Separate elections for president and Congress

The separation of powers arguably provides the most significant contribution to high levels of Congressional representation. Unlike parliamentary systems, it allows voters to have separate votes for the executive and the legislature. This maximises voter choice and allows the electorate to select a member of Congress according to their ability to respond to the wishes and interests of the constituency.

The lack of executive influence over members of Congress ensures accountability to the public, not the president. One of the most moderate Republican Senators, Susan Collins of Maine, represents a moderate constituency and often votes against her own party. The prevalence of split-ticket voting – in which a voter selects two (or more) different parties in the same election – suggests that Americans value this opportunity to vote according to the specific views and policies of the politician, not simply for a broad party platform.

Two elected chambers – complementary representation

As both chambers are elected, voters have two choices rather than one, with the benefit of alternative or complementary representation. By providing both delegates (Congresspersons on two-year terms) and trustees (Senators on six-year terms), Congress can maximise representative levels in a way that alternative systems with two chambers, both elected every four years, cannot. Owing to the different term lengths, Congresspersons and Senators normally react to legislation differently. By staying in power longer, the Senate arguably makes decisions based on rationality by considering long-term effects; the two-year term forces Congresspersons to issue policies rapidly and emotionally, to respond to public opinion. Taking different types of representation into account, Congress is an effective representative body. This can be seen in the response to the demand for a flag protection amendment, in which the House regularly voted to support this populist measure, whereas it failed to reach the required votes to change the Constitution in the Senate.

Frequent elections and short House terms

Congressional elections take place every two years, causing Congress to be a highly representative body – changes in public attitudes can be quickly reflected through the composition of the Congress. In the 2014 mid-term elections, the unpopular Democrats lost control of the Senate, allowing Republicans to take control. If all Senators were elected in, say, 2012, the majority in the Senate would not have been open to change until 2018. As the House is elected every two years, Republican Congresspersons have to keep responding to public opinion; otherwise, they can easily be removed at the next election. The high level of sensitivity to public opinion directly pushes Congresspersons to be highly representative of constituency views, and a strong level of accountability means that public opinion is reflected in the House.

Congress is not representative

FPTP and gerrymandering

The first-past-the-post voting system and **gerrymandering** heavily undermine the representative nature of Congress, to the point where some might argue that it has unacceptably low levels of responsiveness to the wishes and interests of the public. The determination of parties and politicians to maximise their power has led to a major distortion of public opinion, in which power in Congress does not reflect the wishes of the people.

Social representation

Even if Congress is elected frequently and separately from presidential election, the composition of Congress still does not reflect the make-up of society, particularly in terms of race and gender. Congress does not look like the United States.

There is a debate about the extent to which this matters. Conservatives emphasise the idea that white people can represent Hispanics and vice versa, and that minority representation has grown rapidly. The 115th Congress starting in 2017 is the most racially diverse ever. Liberals, on the other hand, point to the under-representation of minority groups, especially in the Senate. In 2017 non-whites make up 38 per cent of the population but 19 per cent of Congress. This figure is only 10 per cent in the Senate. In 2017 the number of women in the House fell slightly but increased in

Link

For more on **gerrymandering**, see Section 2.2

the Senate. White people may not fully understand the wishes and interests of other racial groups, so that they might not be able to directly respond to their constituents. The liberal argument suggests that, without intentional bias, there is still an over-representation of white, male, wealthy interests, limiting the US's claim to be a pluralist, representative democracy.

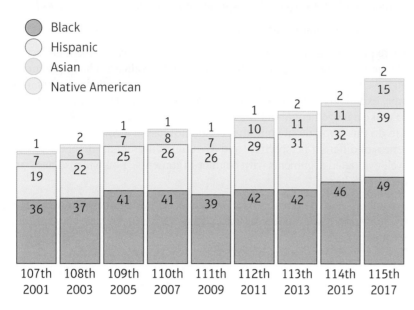

Figure 3.6: Number of non-white members of Congress by racial group

Influence of pressure groups

Congress is influenced by **pressure groups** in a manner that arguably distorts the wishes of the public. In some cases, politicians respond to the interests of unelected pressure groups, which then gain disproportionate representation in Congress. The significance of money means that richer pressure groups dominate, gaining over-representation of their wishes and interests at the expense of others. Elite theory suggests that Congress is not at all democratic because it responds only to the wishes of a small group in society.

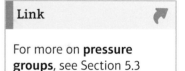

Link

For more on **pressure groups**, see Section 5.3 of US Democracy and Participation.

> **Pause & reflect** ✔
>
> How could you apply the idea of delegates and trustees to the question of representation? Do the above arguments suggest that members of Congress are delegates or trustees?

Assessment support: 3.1.2 Congress

Question 3 on A-Level Paper 3 requires you to answer two questions from a choice of three, each of which is worth 30 marks.

Evaluate the extent to which Congress is a representative institution. [30 marks]

You must consider this view and the alternative to this view in a balanced way.

These questions require an essay-style answer. They test all three Assessment Objectives, with 10 marks available for each. These questions always ask you to **evaluate**. The requirement for **balance** means that you have to show an awareness of different arguments and viewpoints. It is essential to go beyond simply explaining what those different arguments and viewpoints are. Evaluation requires you to make a judgement about the strength of arguments rather than just stating them. You will need to do this throughout your answer and not just in a conclusion. You will need to show an awareness of different perspectives and to outline different arguments, typically using three or four well-evaluated arguments with counter-arguments. You will also need an introduction and a conclusion.

This question requires you to demonstrate an awareness of the arguments and evidence for and against the view that Congress is representative. You will have to evaluate these arguments by judging how strong they are.

Here is part of a student's answer.

Congressional representation is limited by the gerrymandering of House districts. This is a deliberate attempt to fix electoral boundaries in order to favour one party. This means that the number of politicians elected for a party does not accurately reflect voting patterns. If the people are not getting what they voted for then it is clear that Congress is not particularly representative.

- This covers a limit to the levels of representation in Congress, evaluating that argument in the final sentence by making a judgement about the strength of the argument.

Here is another part of a student's answer.

The House of Representatives is far more representative than the Senate. It has the advantage of short terms making it more responsive to public opinion. It also has smaller constituencies which allows the Congressperson to respond to the needs of the constituency. It is virtually impossible for a Senator to represent the diverse wishes and interests of the whole state.

- The student makes a useful distinction between the House and Senate and analyses these two parts separately, resulting in a clearer, more detailed insight into the issue of congressional representation. You can apply this to other topics and questions. For example, questions about presidential power could be answered by breaking power up into separate areas – perhaps the president is more powerful in foreign policy than domestic policy.

- Questions on representation benefit from accurate data, so including representation figures that show majorities in Congress of individual representatives would be a major boost.

CHAPTER 3

US Presidency

This chapter explores the office of the president. It examines:

- key roles of the president
- the internal organisation of the executive branch
- the constitutional powers and limits of the president.

3.1 Formal sources of presidential power as outlined in the US Constitution and their use

The president of the United States holds what is arguably the most significant political office in the world. But there are many controversies about presidential power, including ways in which presidents have arguably bypassed constitutional limits.

The role as the head of state

A head of state is the chief public representative of a country. As head of state, the president has diplomatic and ceremonial duties, such as receiving visiting dignitaries and other heads of state, or travelling to other countries to represent the US. The president is often a central focus-point in times of national crisis and it is common for the president to make speeches or visits in relation to national disasters.

While this does not give the president any formal powers (such as making an appointment or vetoing legislation) it does allow him or her to exert a huge amount of authority. The respect that can come from this role allows the president to be seen as a national leader, with the opportunity to direct US policy in both national and international affairs. The rise of national media, particularly television, has allowed the president to deliver a US-wide message and exert greater influence over both public opinion and Congress. This has helped to give the president a national mandate to carry out policy goals.

In the aftermath of 9/11, President Bush was seen as a symbol of American resolve and pride, taking a strong, tough stance. However, Bush was heavily criticised for not personally visiting areas hit by Hurricane Katrina in 2005, providing evidence of the importance of the symbolic role.

Case study: The Newtown shootings

In 2012, Adam Lanza shot and killed 26 people at the Sandy Hook Elementary School in Newtown, Connecticut. 20 children – aged six and seven years – and six adult staff members died. Lanza committed suicide at the school. More people were killed in this incident than in any other high-school shooting in US history. President Obama immediately gave an emotional public address followed by a number of speeches, both in Connecticut and from the White House, about the killings. He also met with families of school shooting victims. He used this visit as a springboard to push gun-control legislation. He created a gun violence task force headed by his vice president, Joe Biden. Legislative proposals sent to Congress included maximum ammunition magazines of ten rounds and the reintroduction of an assault-weapons ban, which existed under the Clinton presidency. This legislation was soon debated in Congress but failed

Key terms

Executive order
a direction to the federal bureaucracy on how the president would like a piece of legislation to be implemented.

Executive branch
headed by the president, one of the three branches of government, alongside the legislative branch (Congress) and the judiciary (headed by the Supreme Court).

to pass. Obama then pursued a number of **executive orders**, bypassing Congress and achieving some of his policy goals. This role, therefore, heavily feeds into the description of the president as chief legislator.

Questions

- What were the main policies that Obama proposed?
- How did Obama's role as head of state affect his ability to achieve his policy goals?

The role as the head of government

'The Executive Power shall be vested in a President of the United States of America.'

Article II, section 1, Constitution of the United States of America

This single sentence encompasses a huge amount of roles and responsibilities, as well as a vast series of offices. The president has absolute constitutional control of the **executive branch**. As the ultimate decision-maker, the president is able to use the executive branch to develop their political goals and use a complex network of departments and agencies to take control of policy-making and put that policy into practice.

Under his direction are the Cabinet (mainly the heads of government departments with the title Secretary) and each of the 15 Cabinet departments. In addition, the president can utilise the Executive Office of the President (EXOP). Created in 1939, it originally contained two offices but has since grown enormously in size and scope in order to assist the president in decision-making.

As head of the executive the president makes approximately 3000 appointments to federal posts. They all 'serve at the president's pleasure'. In other words they are expected to serve the wishes of the president and can be appointed or dismissed by him at any time.

They include:

- nearly 500 Cabinet and sub-Cabinet posts, subject to Senate confirmation
- 2500 additional appointees, mainly within the EXOP.

Posts requiring Senate approval include:

- Cabinet and junior Cabinet posts
- ambassadors
- agency heads, including Environmental Protection Agency (EPA), Federal Emergency Management Agency (FEMA), Central Intelligence Agency (CIA), Federal Bureau of Investigation (FBI)
- members of regulatory commissions, for example, Federal Communications Commission (FCC), Federal Energy Regulatory Commission (FERC), Securities Exchange Commission (SEC)
- all federal judges (supreme, federal district and circuit courts).

As well as being able to use the executive branch to determine government policy, the president can use the executive to influence the rest of the political system, particularly in relation to Congress.

Case study: Trump and Obama as head of the executive branch

In 2013, Obama created the White House Council on Native American Affairs, which meets at least three times a year, and includes a range of Cabinet-level posts, chaired by the secretary of the interior. This was part of many initiatives created by Obama, such as the Annual White House Tribal Youth Gathering. Obama made much of this in his 2008 election campaign when he said of Native Americans, 'You will be on my mind every day I am in the White House.'

In 2017, Democrats appealed to President Trump to retain these Obama initiatives with no statements or appointments from the White House in the early months of the Trump presidency. There are criticisms that Trump's agenda is harmful to Native American interests, given, for example, Trump's signing of an executive order to continue building the Dakota pipeline without consultation with this minority group.

Trump made other major changes in restructuring the White House. He installed his chief political strategist Steve Bannon as a permanent member of the National Security Council, the first time a political appointee has been a member of the body which provides security advice and information to the president. *The New York Times* has since found evidence that this was done accidentally! Bannon was removed in April 2017. In addition, Trump has created the Office of Innovation and appointed his son-in-law Jared Kushner to reform the federal bureaucracy, including government departments, by applying business principles to the running of government.

Questions

- How have Trump and Obama used their position as head of the executive branch to achieve their policy goals?
- Are there any differences in the types of change they made to the organisation of the executive branch?

As the head of the executive branch the president has also been entrusted with other critical roles, particularly relating to foreign policy. The president is known as the chief diplomat responsible for relations with other countries, as well as for nominating ambassadors and diplomats. The Constitution also makes the president the commander in chief of the armed forces. This clearly gives the president power to direct the military during times of war. There is a lack of clarity in the Constitution, however, as Congress is given the power to declare war. This has led to major conflict over who has the right to initiate military action. Obama created controversy over extensive bombing in Libya, leading to the downfall of the Gaddafi regime, again without any congressional approval. He followed a long line of presidents who are apparently over-stretching their commander in chief powers, including Bill Clinton, who ordered the bombing of Kosovo in 1999.

Link

For more on the **relative powers of president and Congress**, see Section 2.2 of US Congress.

3.2 Informal sources of presidential power and their use

The president has an array of formal powers outlined in the Constitution, which help him or her to take control of United States policy-making and practice. Beyond this, there are a number of other **informal powers** and sources of power that the president may be able to wield. Some of the informal powers are as important as, or even more important than, the powers delineated in the Constitution. These sources change over time, which can result in dramatic fluctuations in presidential power within and between presidencies. Informal sources of presidential power include all powers that are not explicitly taken from the Constitution. They include the electoral mandate, executive orders, national events, the Cabinet, EXOP and the president's own powers of persuasion.

Key term

Informal powers powers of the president not listed in the Constitution but exercised anyway.

The electoral mandate

Presidents can be affected by the extent to which they have an **electoral mandate** to govern. Some presidents are elected on a strong wave of support in which they outline a clear policy vision. Most presidents achieve their most important goals in the first two years of office while their mandate is fresh. Presidential success rates typically fall as the term progresses, partly as the president moves further from their original mandate. Obama achieved some of his most important policy goals in his first two years, including the budget stimulus, health care reform and beginning the process of moving troops from Iraq.

Other factors related to the electoral mandate can be just as important. The nature of partisan control is arguably a more important source of presidential power than their public mandate. Armed with a majority in Congress, a president is likely to be able to overcome limits to their mandate. It is a party majority that will have a larger impact on their power.

	Mandate	House control	Senate control	Major issues
Clinton (D) 1993–2001	43% popular 370/538 ECV	D 1992–94 R 1994–2000	D 1992–94 R 1994–2000	• Oklahoma bombing • Balanced budget politics and government shutdown • Monica Lewinsky scandal • Failed attempts at health care reform
Bush (R) 2001–09	47.9% popular 271/538 ECV	R 2000–06 D 2006–08	R 2000–06 D 2006–08	• 9/11 and the 'war on terror' • Iraq and Afghanistan Wars • Hurricane Katrina • Banking crisis
Obama (D) 2009–2017	52.9% popular 365/538 ECV	D 2008–10 R 2010–16	D 2008–14 R 2014–16	• Health care reform – the Affordable Care Act • Budget crisis and stimulus package • Osama bin Laden • Government shutdown
Trump (R) 2017–	46.0% popular 304/538 ECV	R 2017–	R 2017–	• 'The wall' and immigration • Russia connections and Comey firing • Trillion dollar infrastructure plan • Repealing Affordable Care Act

Table 2.1: Political context of presidents since 1992

Executive orders

Executive orders are an implied power of presidents based on their role as head of the executive branch. A president can create a legal order without a vote in Congress, then use it to direct the executive branch in carrying out policies. Many of these executive orders can be traced directly to an Act of Congress, with the president issuing instructions to ensure these laws are carried out. In theory this is a legitimate tool under the Constitution and many executive orders are uncontroversial. For example, Obama issued an executive order to create the White House Council on Native American Affairs. The authority to issue such orders is a powerful tool. Bush refused congressional pressure to end certain interrogation methods, but Obama swiftly achieved a key policy goal, issuing an executive order to stop CIA operatives carrying out what he saw as methods of torture as one of his first presidential acts.

Link

For an example of Donald Trump's difficulties with executive orders, see case study later in this section.

Unilateral presidential action such as this dates back to the formative years of the modern presidency with the New Deal in the 1930s. However, it can be argued that the scope of these orders has changed. If issuing an order is seen as identical to making a new policy or law, then constitutionally Congress could have the right to vote on the proposal.

However, there are limitations on these powers.

- The president has to show that their use is directing the executive branch in a manner that does not fall under the legislative role of Congress. This can and has been reviewed by the courts. While the vast majority of executive orders remain intact, some are blocked, as the 2016 case study below shows.

- There can be strong public and congressional outcry – and presidents have to be mindful of their popularity if they are to maintain power. Excessive use of executive orders may actually undermine a president's ability to make deals with Congress.

National events

National events, especially natural disasters, economic crises and terrorist attacks, can play a significant role on presidential power, directly or indirectly. They can reduce the time the president has to devote to other policies, and have an impact on public opinion. If a president or their policies are popular then Congress is likely to show more deference to the president.

Obama was almost blown off course in his bid to pass his flagship health care policy. The 2008 banking crisis and economic collapse meant that Obama had to prioritise an economic stimulus package, steering this through Congress before he could push his initial agenda. Opposition to his health care policy increased, forcing Obama to water it down – something he might not have done if he could have introduced legislation earlier.

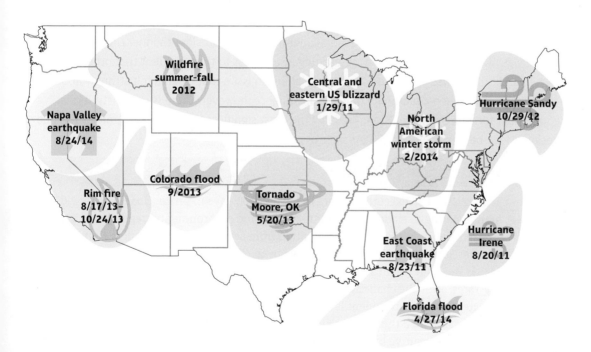

Figure 2.1: Natural disasters that the Obama presidency had to contend with

The 9/11 attacks had a profound effect on US politics, including on George W. Bush. His power surged dramatically after this event, as the unity of public support for the president increased. At the same time, given the extreme nature of these attacks and a rise in patriotism, a spirit of unity dampened any Democrat opposition to the president. In the following years, Bush was able to exert huge control over both **domestic politics** and foreign policy. This had a knock-on effect of allowing the Republican Party to take control of both chambers of Congress in the 2002 mid-term elections.

> **Key term**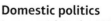
>
> **Domestic politics**
> issues within the USA that directly concern citizens, such as health care, gun control and race issues.

The Cabinet

The Cabinet includes the vice president and the heads of 15 executive departments, as well as Cabinet-level officials such as the chief of staff and the head of the Office of Management and Budget. Cabinet members can play an important role in helping the president to make and execute policy. Individual members of the Cabinet can act as key policy advisers, with senior Cabinet positions such as the secretaries of state and Treasury often having a major impact on policy. They can form part of a president's inner circle alongside other key advisers.

As a collective group the Cabinet has very limited power, however, with a limited number of meetings taking place each year. Its main influence lies with key individuals in the Cabinet. Under the Obama presidency, John Kerry as secretary of state took a central role in developing foreign policy alongside the president. He worked on the Israeli-Palestine peace accords, having visited 11 times in just over a year in 2013/14, as well as taking a key role on approaches to Syria.

The Cabinet has no constitutional status that would allow it to control policy and it cannot claim any kind of national mandate with a right to govern. As such the president has the final say on executive policy, with Cabinet members serving at the president's pleasure. Presidents may sideline individual members and seek advice and support from elsewhere. Often, advisers from EXOP (discussed below) who are closest to the president are the most influential figures. Much depends on the individual president, however. While Cabinet members have a great deal of authority, it is the president who can determine who to work with most closely.

The vice president is a case in point. While they are a member of the Cabinet, their main power lies with their ability to influence presidential thinking. The last three vice presidents – Pence, Biden and Cheney – have all been seen as influential members of the president's inner circle. Biden said that he was 'the last guy in the room', suggesting a closeness to the president that others did not have. In addition, he was used to draft gun legislation, an issue that Obama felt strongly about. The vice president has no guarantee of political influence, however. There is no constitutional requirement for a president to listen. Arguably the most significant constitutional role of the vice president is to be next in line to the president.

Case study: Trump and the immigration ban

President Trump issued 32 executive orders in his first 100 days in office (Obama averaged 35 per year), many relating to trade and business reform, and environmental regulations. In 2017, he issued an executive order banning immigration from seven countries, arguing that this would limit terrorist threats to the US. There have been many conflicts within the executive branch over this issue. President Trump dismissed a member of the Cabinet, the US Attorney General Sally Yates, after she challenged his immigration ban. Yates, appointed by Barack Obama, instructed Justice Department lawyers not to enforce the president's executive order. Trump apparently sidelined the Defense and Homeland Security Departments when making a decision to create an executive order, with members of EXOP secretly consulting staffers on the House Judiciary committee to help create it. The order was signed by Trump with Secretary of Defense James Mattis, standing at Trump's shoulder at the Pentagon, even though the Defense Department was not consulted on its contents. The executive order was halted by a federal judge after it was challenged over concerns regarding religious discrimination as well as green-card holders who already have a legal right to enter the US.

Questions
- What does this case study say about presidential power within the executive branch?
- What limits occur from (a) the rest of the executive branch and (b) from beyond the executive branch?

Powers of persuasion including the nature/characteristics of each president

Another major presidential resource is the president themselves. Presidential personality and leadership skills are incredibly important for presidential success. Presidents have to draw on their political skills, and particularly their **powers of persuasion**, to achieve their policy goals. Presidents can use their position to attract media and congressional attention. The president's position as the head of state and head of executive branch gives them high degrees of authority, allowing them to be persuasive.

The personal ability of each president affects the extent to which they are successful persuaders of both Congress and the public. Different presidents have different natures or characteristics that influence their approach. President Trump's aggressive approach can be contrasted with the more conciliatory style of Obama. Trump has been quick to denounce most people who oppose him, often in personal terms. After the failure to pass the American Health Care Act in March 2017, Trump threatened both Democrats and conservative Republicans in the Freedom Caucus saying that they should be removed in the 2018 mid-term elections. There is a debate about the effectiveness of these approaches in terms of gaining influence, which is further addressed in the case study below.

> ### Key term
>
> **Powers of persuasion**
> the informal power of the president to use the prestige of their job and other bargaining methods to get people to do as they wish.

> ### Richard Neustadt and the power to persuade
>
> In 1960, in his book *Presidential Power*, Richard Neustadt suggested that 'presidential power is the power to persuade'. This suggests that the president has extremely limited constitutional power to enforce political change, unlike prime ministers in European democracies or dictatorships. The president can ask Congress to accept his views, but has little power to back this up. Due to the separation of powers and checks and balances, Congress has the ability – and often the will – to say no.

Case study: Obama's personal powers

There are different schools of thought about Obama's presidency. Many critics argue that, while he had strong oratorical skills, he was not decisive or forceful enough in pushing his own agenda. Obama's governing style has been criticised for being too aloof, perfectionist and passive toward key issues, rather than pragmatic and commanding. Over the budget negotiations after budget shutdown in 2013, some (including Senator Bernie Sanders) complained that he was not taking charge. In this sense Obama could be accused of not being 'presidential' enough and forcing the two sides to form a compromise.

Others suggest that Obama's willingness to devolve responsibility to Congress for developing legislation was a better way to gain congressional support. Obama was merely reacting to a hostile Congress with polarised parties. If Obama had been too aggressive, he might have achieved nothing other than irritating Congress. His willingness to compromise, even when he held a Democrat majority, helped him achieve some of his policy goals, such as health care, where a more stubborn Bill Clinton failed.

Question

- Do you think Obama's style of governing would have been better suited to a different type of political structure?

Executive Office of the President including the role of the National Security Council, Office of Management and Budget and the White House Office

The president relies on those around them in order to have control. They rely on support (but in some cases get opposition) from the Cabinet, the EXOP and the vice president.

The Executive Office of the President (EXOP)

The president's closest advisers are usually found in the EXOP – the general term for the presidential agencies and staff that provide advice and administrative support. The EXOP began in 1939, when the Brownlow Committee reported that the president was seriously understaffed and needed substantial administrative support. Since then EXOP has grown enormously, paralleling a huge increase in the size of the federal government, and now comprises more than 1800 people.

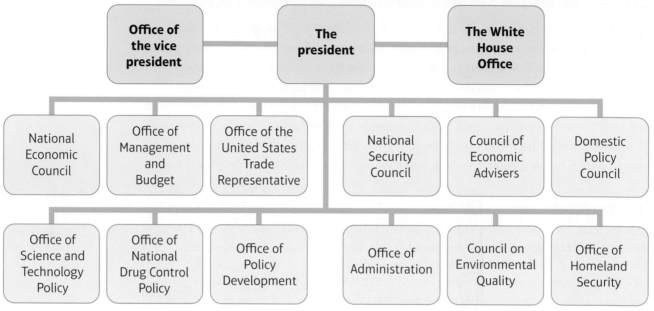

Figure 2.2: The structure of the EXOP

The EXOP is commonly referred to as the 'West Wing' of the White House, which is home to the president's Oval office and the offices of the closest advisers. However, the EXOP is actually housed in more than a dozen offices, in the West and East Wings and the Eisenhower building. Few Americans have heard of the members of EXOP, but they include some of the most powerful people in the United States.

Role of EXOP	Explanation
Policy advice	The EXOP consists of presidential (executive branch) agencies that provide advice, help, co-ordination and administrative support. For example, the OMB advises the president on mainly budgetary issues, while the NSC helps the president consider national security and foreign policy matters.
Manage the president	The chief of staff oversees the actions of the White House staff and manages the president's schedule, deciding who the president can meet and what policies to prioritise. The chief of staff is often called 'the gatekeeper', 'the co-president' or 'the lightning conductor'.
Oversee departments	Some EXOP offices oversee different departments of state and agencies. Senior members of the EXOP are often charged with taking control of Cabinet and government departments to make sure they follow presidential priorities. Most obviously the OMB reviews the spending of all federal departments and agencies, and the director of national intelligence oversees the work of the intelligence agencies, such as the CIA and FBI.
Relations with Congress	Specialist advice and support in dealing with Congress is a critical part of the president's success in achieving policy goals. The Office of Legislative Affairs develops strategies to advance the president's legislative initiatives. Recent presidents have made use of their vice presidents, who assume some of the responsibilities of the president or EXOP.
Specialist functions	Some presidents have created offices with a specific mandate related to their special interests. For example, Obama sponsored the Office of Faith-based and Neighborhood Partnerships to work with community groups to end poverty, support women and children, and encourage fathers to remain in the home.

Table 2.2: Roles of the EXOP

The National Security Council (NSC)

The NSC, established in 1947 at the beginning of the Cold War, is the principal body advising the president on national security and foreign policy issues. The workings of the NSC are somewhat secretive; however, the close proximity of the NSC office to the Oval office suggests strong levels of influence.

The president gets a daily briefing from the NSC and consults the national security adviser (NSA) over major security issues. The NSA's role potentially puts them into conflict or rivalry with the secretary of state, who will not normally have such regular contact with the president.

Given the global importance of the US, the NSC and the NSA are incredibly important roles, as they help shape the president's thinking on major issues. Even so, the president can bypass or ignore them. President Trump was heavily criticised for the politicisation of this office by including Steve Bannon as senior counselor in the NSC, eventually removing him from this sensitive security position. As a national security body, the Council is supposed to provide advice to the president based on its intelligence, and the inclusion of Bannon may distort this advice. Susan Rice, the former NSA, tweeted, 'This is stone cold crazy. After a week of crazy.'

As national security adviser, Susan Rice (left) was President Obama's closest aide on national security and foreign policy issues. She reportedly played a key role in the progress of the Iran nuclear deal. The previous NSA, James L. Jones (right), was sidelined by Obama and was not part of his inner circle.

EXTENSION ACTIVITY

Research the current membership of the US National Security Council. How many of the roles do you recognise? How many of the individuals have you heard of? Who are the most influential members and what evidence do you have for this?

Office of Management and Budget (OMB)

The OMB is the largest office with 500 employees. It is the only EXOP office in which the head needs to be confirmed by the Senate.

It has two main functions:

- to advise the president on the allocation of funds for the annual budget
- to oversee spending in all federal departments and agencies.

The OMB is another body that is critical to the president achieving their policy agenda. It makes macro-economic decisions that affect the future development of the US economy, and prepares the annual budget – a huge and complex document that enables the president to fund policy priorities. In 2015, the budget amounted to almost $4 trillion. In 2017, Mick Mulvaney, the head of the OMB, was given a central role in co-ordinating attempts to repeal Obamacare. Partly because of the huge financial implications he was seen to have a greater role than the health and human services secretary, Tom Price.

White House Office (WHO)

The White House Office includes the president's closest aides and advisers. Senior EXOP staff have the title 'assistant to the president'. The head of the White House Office, the chief of staff, is usually the president's most important adviser, as they have an overview of all EXOP offices. They are the connection between presidential advisers, Cabinet officers and the president. In this role, the chief of staff must be flexible, open-minded and an 'honest broker' – someone who allows people with a variety of different perspectives and ideas to gain access to the president.

In many ways Reince Priebus was a surprise pick for Trump's position of chief of staff, given his position as chair of the Republican National Committee, as a Republican insider. On the other hand, Priebus gives President Trump a greater opportunity to make connections with senior Republican figures, increasing his chances of gaining congressional support.

Some chiefs of staff have struggled to play a major or effective role. Bill Daley was seen as a failure as Obama's chief of staff. He struggled to gain command and respect of the West Wing, perhaps as a result of his hands-off style. He was criticised for giving too much ground to Republicans in budget negotiations. Denis McDonough prioritised improving Obama's relationships with the Cabinet. He acted as a firefighter, dealing directly with the press in public-relations exercises, and he acted as a close confidante when Obama decided not to attack the Assad regime in Syria.

Denis McDonough, Obama's final chief of staff.

How is the White House organised?

There are two main models of organisation that presidents use for the functioning of the White House.

- **'Spokes in a wheel'** The president acts as the hub, and the advisers and Cabinet officials are the spokes. The president is available to a relatively wide range of advisers; most have permission to see the president. This typified the Clinton presidency, allowing him to take a hands-on approach and have greater control over policy. However, this made it difficult for Clinton to delegate details and focus on the bigger picture. Ultimately this model can be less efficient.

- **Pyramid system** A hierarchical system, with the president at the top. Only a few key advisers have direct access to the president; the chief of staff acts as the ultimate 'gatekeeper'. Most presidents adopt this model, including Obama and Bush. Obama was sometimes accused of needing to understand too much policy detail, but he relied on an inner circle of advisers, mainly from the EXOP but also including the vice president and a few key Cabinet members.

Pause & reflect

Which of the three main sections of the executive is the most important source of presidential support? Why? Looking over the evidence, which of the Cabinet, EXOP and vice presidency is the most powerful?

3.3 The presidency

Relationships between the presidency and Congress

The most important political relationship in the US is the one between president and Congress. The annual struggle between the two largely determines the shape of US domestic and foreign policy.

	Domestic	Foreign
Term 1	• Stimulus package 2009 • Affordable Care Act 2010 • DREAM Act • Nominations – Sotomayor and Kagan	• Afghanistan surge 2009 • Russia treaty 2010 • Libya 2011
Term 2	• DREAM Act and immigration reform, Gang of 8 and executive orders 2013 • Gun regulation – 2013 State of the Union and executive order • Budget shutdown, Path to Prosperity and Affordable Care Act 2013 • Keystone Pipeline veto 2015 • Garland nomination 2016 • Veto of health care repeal 2016 • Zika virus gridlock 2016	• NDAA veto threat and compromise/ failure to close Guantanamo 2015 • Defence budget veto 2015 • Syria-Assad 2013 and Islamic State strikes 2015 • Iran deal 2015 • NDAA veto 2016 • Saudi Arabia right to sue legislation, veto and overturn 2016

Table 3.1: Examples of clashes between Obama and Congress

It is debatable which institution is the most powerful. The Founding Fathers used the **separation of powers** and **checks and balances** to ensure that power was shared between the two branches. In practice this was to prevent the executive branch dominating in the way that it can do in parliamentary systems. All of this suggests that power is balanced.

The power relationship between the presidency and Congress can be examined by looking at three key areas:

- the separation of powers and presidential-congressional relations
- agenda-setting and legislation
- votes and vetoes.

The separation of powers and presidential-congressional relations

The separation of powers allows checks and balances to operate effectively, suggesting that president and Congress share power in roughly equal measures.

The separation of powers significantly limits the president for three main reasons.

- **The president and Congress receive separate mandates:** Both branches feel that they have the right to govern, which means Congress is likely to be an active legislative branch, unwilling to simply respond to presidential demands. Indeed Congress can often claim a stronger mandate, as House elections renew its mandate every two years. Congresspersons and Senators tend to vote according to their constituencies' views, rather than the wishes of the president. They will be reluctant to toe the party line in the face of hostile constituency views.

- **The president has limited patronage power over individual members of Congress:** Because the two branches are kept separate, the president does not work alongside a team within Congress, so cannot regularly promote or demote them. Unlike a British prime minister, the president will typically choose a Cabinet that lasts for the full four years of their presidency. If a congressional member of their own party will not support presidential policy requests, there is little a president can do.

Link

For more on the **separation of powers** and **checks and balances**, see Section 1.2 of US Constitution and Federalism.

- **There is a possibility of bipartisan control or divided government between president and Congress:** It is common for the president to be controlled by one party, while at least one chamber of Congress is controlled by the other. The separation of powers creates the likelihood of conflicting agendas, where compromise is inevitable if either side is to achieve their policy goals.

Agenda-setting and shaping legislation

As a single executive office holder who is nationally elected, the president is in a stronger position than Congress to claim a national mandate to set the national policy agenda. This has become increasingly the case as radio and television have strengthened presidents' mandates. In 2016, President Trump ran a national campaign, selling his ideas to the country based on his political agenda, including the repeal of the Affordable Care Act, immigration reform and infrastructure expenditure. The mandate received made it easier for Trump to ensure that Congress debated his political priorities in 2017 and beyond.

Agenda-setting is very important. It allows the president to act as the driving force of US politics. This is re-enforced by the president's position as both head of state and head of the government. It is this aspect of power and decision-making that led to the description of the president as 'Chief Legislator' – the dominant force in the legislative process. The president can dominate the agenda of US politics and can further influence legislation through veto power, signing a bill, speaking directly to Congress and meeting with individual members of the legislative body. The growth of the EXOP has helped the president to have high levels of authority, with access to arguably superior sources of information and advice. This has helped modern presidents to become the dominant force in the legislative process.

However, the president is not all-powerful in setting the political agenda. Congress is the sole legislative body with a mandate of its own, so it can set a national agenda. It is increasingly common for Congress, under the direction of a powerful House speaker, to develop a set of policy priorities of its own. This is particularly the case when the opposing party to the president wins a mid-term election.

Case study: Presidents Obama and Trump versus Congress

In the 2010 mid-term elections, the Republican Party took control of the House of Representatives. This led to the new speaker, John Boehner, setting an alternative political agenda to the president's, based on economic austerity and major budget cuts.

The rival agendas of president and Congress clashed, resulting in gridlock, leading to the federal government being shut down in 2013. There was no agreement on the budget and many federal offices were closed until agreement could be found. Obama eventually had to accept budgetary cuts he would not have otherwise proposed.

While Obama set a political agenda of immigration reform after the 2012 election, Congress did not have to accept this agenda. Speaker Boehner refused to debate the immigration reform package, even though it had been passed by the Senate with the president's support.

In 2017, Trump struggled to pass the American Health Care Act through the House of Representatives, withdrawing the bill in March due to lack of congressional support. After much compromise and a shift to the right to please conservative Republicans, the bill narrowly passed the House in May 2017. This shows that, even when a president has a majority in Congress, he cannot easily achieve legislative success. Opposition came from both conservative Republicans in the Freedom Caucus (who felt that the law did not go far enough in removing insurance regulations and cutting the deficit) and moderate Republicans, some representing districts which voted for Clinton as president (who were concerned about the loss of health insurance coverage for many people, as well as the projected increase in premiums). Trump and Speaker Paul Ryan were able, eventually, to build a coalition of Republicans in the House. The bill then had to be sent to the Senate, where it faced even greater obstacles in succeeding due to the slim Republican majority there.

Question

- What are the reasons why the US system suffers from such gridlock in which bills gets stuck, often failing to become law?

Once legislation is underway, Congress can shape legislation in a way that a president cannot. Congress amends legislation put before it, and can alter presidential proposals – even adding major aspects that the president does not support. The president has no such luxury. If presidents are to see their own legislation pass, they must accept such legislative compromises.

Relationships between the presidency and the Supreme Court

The president's only formal power over the Supreme Court lies with nominations at a time of vacancy. This gives the president influence over the ideological balance of the Court. The nomination of Merrick Garland by President Obama in 2016 may have had a huge impact on the rulings of the Court. Before this, the Court had a 5-4 conservative majority but with the death of one of those five, a strong conservative, Antonin Scalia, Obama had the opportunity to tip the balance in favour of liberals. Another major tipping in the overall ideological balance of the Court occurred with the appointment in 1991 of conservative Justice Clarence Thomas to replace the devoutly liberal Thurgood Marshall.

The extent to which this gives power to an individual president is arguably very limited, however. Most presidential appointments make little or no difference to the overall ideological balance of the Court. This is partly because justices choose when to retire and typically do so when they are ideologically aligned with the current president.

It is difficult to see these appointments as a significant limit on the Supreme Court. Presidents may influence the composition, but they have virtually no influence over any one of the nine justices who make a decision, including the ones they have appointed. Justices have life tenure, so the president can make no threat of removal against them. Also, most presidents only make one or two appointments, with limited overall impact during their presidency.

The role of the presidency is to defend the law and the Constitution, which means executing Supreme Court decisions. Presidents sometimes give a hostile response to Court rulings, however. Obama criticised the Court for its Citizens United ruling, while many of them sat in the audience of his 2010 State of the Union address. More controversially, there have been some occasions when presidents have challenged the legitimacy of a Court ruling and attempted to undermine it. Trump immediately clashed with the judiciary in 2017, attacking the judge who halted his immigration ban. Referring to District Judge Robart as a 'so called Judge,' Trump instructed the US public to blame the judge if anything went wrong. Even Senior Republicans such as Mitch McConnell were critical of Trump's approach.

Limitations on presidential power and why this varies

The changing nature of presidential power over their term in office

The level of presidential power is not static, but instead changes over their time in office according to a number of different factors.

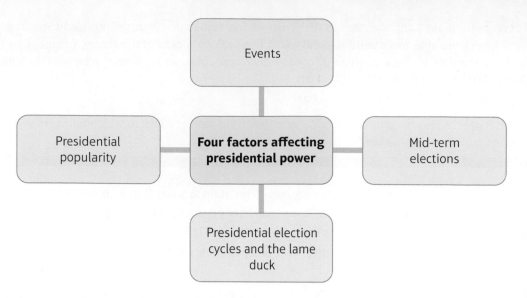

Figure 3.1: Four factors affecting presidential power

Presidential popularity

A well-supported president is likely to receive less resistance from Congress than an unpopular one. Presidential popularity and/or the popularity of their key policies often decline over the term of a presidency. Where this is the case it makes it more difficult for a president to persuade Congress to support their measures.

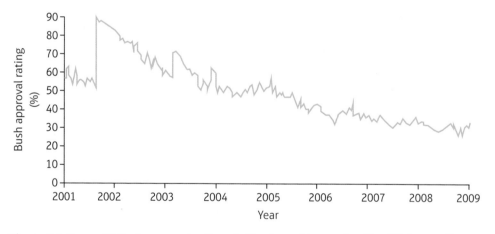

Figure 3.2: George W. Bush approval ratings declined over his term in office. While not all presidents have such a clear downward trend, this is a common pattern for post-war presidents.

Events

A president can be strongly affected by major events that they may be unable to control. Natural disasters, acts of terrorism, war and economic crisis have all affected presidential power. Different events have different effects and can be positive or negative for presidential power. President Bush experienced a huge increase in his power after 9/11. On the other hand, the Iraq War and the failure to find the 'weapons of mass destruction' that formed the basis for going to war increasingly led to reductions in the power of President Bush, with increased resistance from Congress and the public.

In addition, mid-term elections and subsequent presidential elections often alter presidential power. This is discussed in the election cycle section below.

The president, the Constitution and the Supreme Court

The written, entrenched and sovereign Constitution aims to place stringent limits on presidential action in a variety of ways.

This section begins with an exploration of how the president can be influential over the Supreme Court. However, presidents are strongly limited by the Supreme Court, which can and does uphold constitutional rules against them. Presidents typically 'lose' Supreme Court cases in every year of their presidency.

There is an array of constitutional regulations on presidential power. Some rules are so clear that it is unlikely any president would break them – for example, the maximum two-term rule or the ratification of justices by the Senate. In other cases, the Supreme Court can use its considerable power of **judicial review** to overturn either the actions of the president or the president's favoured policies.

> **Key term**
>
> **Judicial review**
> the ability of the Supreme Court to review the actions or laws of any other body (including president, Congress and state) and overturn those actions if they break the Constitution.

The election cycle and divided government

Presidential power is also affected by both mid-term elections and the next set of presidential elections.

Mid-term elections: Congressional elections in the middle of a president's term typically bring defeat to the president's party, which may lose seats and even their overall majority in one or more chambers of Congress. As a result, presidents often experience a decline in power mid-way through their term. The presidential party of Clinton, Bush and Obama all lost its overall majority in Congress during a mid-term election.

Lame duck presidency: With presidents being elected in November but not replacing the incumbent president until January, the president in office finds it difficult to achieve policy goals. Politicians and the public often focus on the new president and their policy agenda. The term 'lame duck presidency' has been applied to the period before the election, especially in a president's final term when there is a great deal of focus on the presidential elections.

3.4 Interpretations and debates of the US presidency

How effectively have presidents since 1992 achieved their aims?

There are several key considerations that help us to assess the extent to which presidents have achieved their policy goals.

1. Using the separation of powers and strong checks and balances on presidential power, the US Constitution deliberately restricts the ability of the president to achieve their aims. If presidents achieve their policy goals, they are often required to make major compromises.
2. The rise of partisanship has had a major impact on the effectiveness of presidents. When presidents govern under divided government, the opposing majority in Congress makes it even more difficult to achieve policy goals (compared to an era when party unity was lower). This has led to legislative gridlock with presidents struggling to reach their desired goals.

3. There is arguably a distinction between foreign policy (where the president is more easily able to achieve policy goals) and domestic policy (where he/she is not). This is addressed in detail below.

4. Presidents may bypass constitutional checks and balances using the tools of the imperial presidency, which is the subject of the next section.

Looking at the aims and achievements, as well as the failures, of the Clinton, Bush and Obama presidencies helps to illustrate these four points.

Clinton presidency's policy aims:

- Clinton is viewed as a very moderate Democrat, allowing him to gain support from some Republicans and independents but causing some on the progressive left of the party to be concerned about his centrist policies.

- **Reducing budget deficit:** This could be seen as a major success of the Clinton presidency, given that deficits have occurred in virtually every year since 1945. On the other hand, others would see this as the success of the Republican-led Congress in which Speaker Newt Gingrich helped cause budget shutdown as part of a battle to further reduce government expenditure.

- **Health Care Reform:** This bill was similar to the one eventually passed under Obama, with Clinton failing to get his priorities passed despite a clear mandate for the policy when he was elected in 1992 and a Democratic majority in both chambers of Congress.

- **Greater gun control:** Clinton supported this during the 1992 election campaign and supported the Brady Bill which he signed, creating background checks and waiting periods for gun purchases.

- **Greater protection for civil rights:** Clinton advocated the end of the ban on lesbian and gay soldiers in the military during the 1992 campaign. Facing strong opposition from the military as well as some Republicans, he passed a compromise policy known as Don't Ask Don't Tell, which effectively ended the ban. It was criticised by progressive Democrats and gay rights groups because it was not an absolute end to the ban but a requirement that military officers did not investigate someone's sexuality.

- **Foreign policy:** Clinton became president at the end of the Cold War and had to find a new policy approach. He emphasised a stronger moral dimension to foreign policy, arguing for US involvement in Bosnia, Rwanda and Somalia to prevent civil war and genocide. Clinton struggled to achieve these aims and had to issue an executive order to launch airstrikes in Bosnia after congressional opposition. Congress also forced Clinton to withdraw troops from Somalia.

Bush presidency's policy aims:

- Bush was elected as a 'compassionate conservative', attempting to take the centre ground in the 2000 election.

- **Major tax cuts:** Bush successfully steered his budget plan through Congress, although it required Vice President Cheney's vote to overcome a Senate tie. This led to major reductions in tax, mainly for the wealthy.

- **Commitment to public education:** Bush successfully passed the No Child Left Behind Act, imposing federal standards of education on states. This was criticised by some Republicans as evidence of Bush's lack of conservative credentials, as he increased federal intervention in state policy.

- **Social security reform:** Bush attempted to reform social insurance for the elderly, describing the existing system as 'heading for bankruptcy'. His plans, including the idea of privatising this provision, were controversial among Democrats and Republicans and failed to make progress in Congress.

- **9/11 and 'war on terror':** 9/11 is the defining moment of the Bush presidency, helping him to increase his power hugely and set a 'war on terror agenda'. This led to the easy passage of votes to begin the Iraq War, create the Homeland Security Department and introduce the Patriot Act, which led to an increase in security powers, including mass surveillance of internet/phone communications. It also led to an executive order to create Guantanamo Bay detention centre. The events of 9/11 helped Bush to increase the Republican share of seats in Congress. The war on terror moved Bush away from fiscal conservatism with huge increases in federal expenditure.

Policy aim presented during election campaign	Policy achieved?
Introduce health insurance for all (2008 campaign)	Partially achieved with the passing of the Affordable Care Act. Obama compromised on the public option, dropping his desire for a federal health insurance company to compete in the marketplace.
Close Guantanamo detention centre (2008 and 2012 campaigns)	Failed. At the end of the Obama presidency, Guantanamo still held 41 people. The number did decline hugely however, with 242 detainees at the start of the presidency and 197 being transferred, repatriated or resettled by January 2017.
Remove US troops from Iraq and increase US involvement in Afghanistan (2008 campaign)	Largely achieved with troops being removed from Iraq, and Congress agreeing to a troop surge in Afghanistan in Obama's first term.
Stimulus package for the economy (2008 campaign)	Achieved with legislation being passed in 2009 that led to additional spending of $787 billion.
Immigration reform to allow more people to have a path to citizenship (2008 and 2012 campaigns)	Failed to pass Congress in the first and second terms. Obama had partial success using executive orders to achieve some of his goals, although some of these were struck down by the Supreme Court.

Table 4.1: Key policy promises of President Obama and the extent of their success

EXTENSION ACTIVITY

Judging the extent of presidential success is not simply a case of stating that a policy passed or failed. Use the internet to research Obama's policies listed in the table above. To what extent was Obama able to achieve exactly what he wanted? How do different politicians or news organisations disagree over the extent to which Obama was successful in getting what he wanted?

The imperial presidency

An imperial presidency is one in which the president stretches the Constitution in the exercise of constitutional roles, such as chief executive and commander in chief, and may ignore the wishes of Congress.

The term 'imperial presidency' was used by Arthur Schlesinger Jr in 1973, when he attacked what he viewed as the unconstitutional extension of executive power under President Nixon. Schlesinger argues that presidents wield huge amounts of power with little or no constraints. In particular, he suggests a failure of the constitutional restrictions to restrain the presidency.

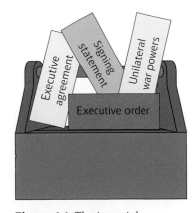

Figure 4.1: The imperial presidency toolkit

Successive presidents have acquired powers that go beyond the intended checks imposed by the Founding Fathers, or such regulations fail to operate. The president can evade constitutional regulations, using a 'toolkit' of methods to exert huge power.

Executive order

What is it? The president can instruct the executive branch to carry out/not carry out certain practices without consulting Congress. This could be seen as effectively creating new policy without the need for a congressional vote.

Link

For more on **executive orders**, see Section 3.2.

Evidence: Immigration, including Obama policies on DAPA and DACA and Trump's 2017 executive order banning immigration from seven specified countries. In 2001 Bush signed an executive order that allowed the creation of military tribunals in language that covered the detention, treatment and trial of non-US citizens involved in terrorism, leading to the creation of the Guantanamo detention camp.

Limits: The scope of these orders is limited. In theory the president cannot pass new laws but only enforce existing ones or use his/her power to govern the executive branch. Obama's planned extension of DAPA and DACA was halted by a Court ruling in 2016, as was Trump's immigration executive order in 2017.

Signing statement

What is it? A statement written and signed by the president at the same time as signing a piece of legislation. When signing a bill the president may state that they will not enforce certain sections (for example, because they deem them to be unconstitutional). This gives the president the power to effectively hold a line-item veto, allowing them to strike out individual lines of a bill. The Supreme Court has declared the line-item veto unconstitutional in *Clinton v New York* 1998, stating that a president can either accept or reject a whole bill only. Many signing statements (or parts of them) have limited constitutional significance.

Evidence: In 2014, Obama signed the National Defense Authorization Act, which contained a clause requiring the defense secretary to notify congressional committees at least 30 days before moving someone from Guantanamo Bay. Obama issued a signing statement rejecting congressional authority here. Obama did not comply with the act when he secretly traded a captured US soldier, Bowe Bergdahl, for five Taliban members detained at Guantanamo.

Limits: The president can issue such words but may find it difficult to actually bring about any change. For most laws, such as budget agreements, there is little a president can do with a signing statement. Also, a signing statement is only words on a page. Congress may insist on the laws it has passed, and the Supreme Court could force the president to follow the intentions of congressional law. Future (and current) presidents are not obliged to follow suit. Obama signed a statement saying he would not use drone strikes to kill US citizens in the US, even though he signed a law permitting it. There is no reason why President Trump needs to follow this interpretation of the law in existence.

Executive agreement

What is it? A piece of constitutional magic conjured up by the president in making an agreement with another country. This agreement does not require Senate ratification. This could be seen as replacing treaties and allowing the president to bypass traditional constitutional relations to achieve **foreign policy** goals. It is the president who decides what is a treaty and what is simply an 'agreement'.

Link

For more on **foreign policy**, see later in this chapter.

Examples: Obama's Iran deal in 2015, agreeing on lifting some trade embargoes and freezing Iranian assets in return for Iranian efforts to end their aims to be a military nuclear power; 2015 China environment deal, negotiated in secret, agreeing to US and Chinese attempts to reduce CO_2 emissions.

Limits: An executive agreement is only an agreement with the incumbent president, not with the US government in general. In theory, it could be ignored by future presidents, although there could be legal and political complications. Any agreement is arguably unconstitutional. In 2015, Senators wrote an open letter to Iran saying they did not recognise the Iran deal as having any force in US law.

Unilateral war powers

What is it? Presidents have made military decisions without consulting Congress – something that has become increasingly important since the Second World War, marking a major change in presidential power. The requirement for greater speed, secrecy and expertise in decision-making has allowed the president increasingly to take control of military and security policy. Ordering military action without consultation or consent from Congress can be seen as bypassing key requirements of the Constitution.

Evidence: Libya 2011, when Obama ordered air strikes – without consulting Congress – helping to destabilise the Libyan government.

Limits: Presidents are particularly powerful over short-term action; longer term action is more easily regulated by Congress using the War Powers Act or funding restrictions. The president may be heavily limited by strong public opposition, a consideration that may have held Obama back over what appeared to be his inevitable orders to attack the Syrian Assad regime.

The imperilled presidency

The theory of the **imperilled presidency** suggests that the president is not simply restricted, but is the holder of a weak office, without sufficient power. This contrasting theory to that of an imperial presidency was put forward by former President Gerald Ford. He found that the federal bureaucracy was too big to manage effectively, and complained of the president's lack of control over an increasingly complex executive branch.

The phrase has since been adapted to argue that there are excessive limitations on presidential power, which cause ineffectual political leadership. The rise of polarised parties could be applied to this idea, with a recalcitrant Republican Party proving unwilling to co-operate and compromise with elected Democrat presidents, such as Obama.

> 'There is nothing more frustrating for a President than to issue an order to a Cabinet officer, and then find that, when the order gets out in the field, it is totally mutilated.'
>
> President Gerald Ford

The role and power of the president in foreign policy

Foreign policy is arguably an exceptional area in which the president can dominate, evading constitutional limitations. This is an idea developed in the 'dual presidency' theory put forward by Wildavsky during the Cold War. Wildavsky analyses presidential power by considering that the president has two major concerns: domestic and foreign policy. He argues that presidents prefer to focus on foreign policy because the US political system gives them greater control in this area. This gives rise to the idea that there are effectively two presidents: a foreign policy president who is powerful, with strong ability to achieve their policy goals, and a domestic policy president who is severely constrained.

Who controls foreign policy: president or Congress?

Possible presidential advantages in foreign policy can be examined in constitutional, political and practical terms.

Constitutional

- **Presidential advantages:** The Constitution gives the president significant foreign policy powers that might enable them to dominate policy in this area, especially in overcoming potential checks from Congress. In particular, the commander in chief role gives the president huge constitutional

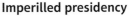

Key term

Imperilled presidency a presidency where the president does not have enough power to be effective, particularly because of complexity or direct resistance in the executive branch – the opposite to an imperial presidency.

EXTENSION ACTIVITY

Read the first chapter of G. Calvin Mackenzie's *The Imperiled Presidency: Leadership Challenges in the Twenty-First Century.* Mackenzie argues that the major problem for the US is that the president is too weak to exert effective leadership. The first chapter summarises his argument, and outlines both the constitutional and the recent historical context of presidential power, using the Bush and Obama presidencies as case studies.

authority over military policy. Presidents have used this to act unilaterally, initiating military action without a congressional vote. Evidence of this can be seen in Obama's actions in Libya in 2011 as well as strikes in Iraq and Syria in the fight against Islamic State. With legal attempts to limit the president in this area failing, it appears that presidents can initiate military action at will.

The president's position as head of state and chief diplomat allows them, rather than Congress, to conduct foreign relations with other countries. International co-operation (or conflict) and formal agreements with other states in the form of treaties are all in the hands of the president. Obama and his team worked with countries such as Iran, China and Cuba without congressional leaders. Again the president appears to be the driving force in these aspects of foreign policy.

Presidents can use **executive agreements** to bypass traditional constitutional restrictions. In terms of foreign policy, presidents can ignore the requirement for Senate ratification of treaties, often with much anger from Congress. Presidents are, therefore, in a powerful position to achieve foreign policy goals.

Link

For more on **executive agreements**, see above.

- **Presidential limits:** Congress holds a number of important constitutional powers that can restrict the president. Firstly, the Constitution gives Congress the power to declare war – so there is an apparent constitutional ambiguity, which has led to a major constitutional dispute. Who has the right to initiate military action – president or Congress? In practice, presidents have committed military action without a congressional vote. On the other hand, there are instances when presidents have deferred to congressional authority by putting proposed attacks to a vote of both legislative chambers. This was the case with the Iraq War in 2003, when President George W. Bush requested and was given approval for military action. In 1973, Congress tried to clarify the situation and assert its constitutional control by passing the War Powers Resolution, which arguably further restricts the president.

The War Powers Act 1973

In order to clarify presidential congressional relations and to stop Nixon continuing the war in Vietnam, Laos and Cambodia, Congress passed the War Powers Resolution in 1973. This became the War Powers Act 1973 after Nixon's veto was overturned. The act stated the president can only commit troops in what it describes as 'hostilities' abroad with congressional approval unless there is a national emergency. Congress has the right to withdraw troops, and the president must withdraw troops after 60 days of notifying Congress of the start of hostilities if Congress has not voted to approve military action. Clinton was forced to withdraw troops from Somalia (in a military intervention initiated by the previous president, George H.W. Bush, to prevent genocide in a brutal civil war). Congressional pressure from both parties ended US involvement in 1994.

However, the War Powers Act has been largely unsuccessful in preventing presidential action. Presidents have asserted that it has no constitutional authority and restricts the president's constitutional duties. Some have argued that the act itself means that Congress has ceded ground to the president compared to the intentions of the Founding Fathers, allowing the president 60 days to complete short-term military action without the need to consult Congress. There have also been cases of military action where presidents (and their lawyers) have stated that the War Powers Act does not apply. To the dismay of congressional leaders, Obama denied that his Libya actions could be limited by the act. The White House sent a 38-page letter to Congress explaining why the Libya actions did not cover the sort of 'hostilities' referred to in the act, stating: 'US operations do not involve sustained fighting or active exchanges of fire with hostile forces, nor do they involve US ground troops.'

Congress also has funding power, which it can use to control military action. By refusing to fund (or even by defunding), Congress could prevent action abroad. When Clinton took executive action in Bosnia despite protests from Congress, the House voted to withdraw funding for the conflict in 1995, a measure that was only narrowly defeated.

Finally, the Senate has the power to ratify treaties, which can restrict presidential goals. In 1999, the Senate easily defeated the Comprehensive Test Ban Treaty on nuclear weapons, with Clinton failing to get the two-thirds of votes needed. A UN disability-rights treaty was also rejected by the Senate in 2012, despite Obama signing the treaty in 2009 and campaigning heavily for it.

Political

- **Presidential advantages:** The president, with a national mandate, is arguably best placed to make decisions for the whole US. As the only nationally elected body, the presidency has more authority than individual members of Congress. As a result of this and of the president's constitutional prowess, US citizens tend to look to the president, not Congress, for foreign-policy initiatives. Congress is, therefore, arguably a more passive institution in this area and at times defers to the president. This might be seen in former Speaker John Boehner's response to Obama's campaign to overthrow Libyan leader Muammar Gaddafi in 2011.

  Boehner wrote a strongly worded letter to Obama asking him to answer key questions, stating: 'I respect your authority as commander in chief and support our troops as they carry out their mission.' This is clearly not a significant attempt to invoke constitutional control over these actions, although later Boehner did propose a resolution to end US involvement.

  When congressional leaders have attempted to take control of foreign policy they have often received widespread criticism for usurping the traditional roles of the president. House Speaker Nancy Pelosi was strongly criticised for her decision to visit President Assad in Syria in 2007. Speaker John Boehner's decision to invite Israeli Prime Minister Netanyahu to speak before a joint session of Congress was seen by many as overstepping his authority, with criticism even from some US Jewish lobby groups.

- **Presidential limits:** Congress may feel that it has a legitimate right to determine US foreign policy on behalf of US citizens as an elected body. Congress has a collective national mandate but, more importantly, the separation of powers encourages individual members of Congress to respond to constituency views. If the public in a state or district oppose presidential foreign policy goals, members of Congress are likely to challenge them. This can be seen in the Democrat attempts to end the Iraq War after the mid-term election of 2006, in which Nancy Pelosi and Harry Reid created legislation that gave a timeline for troop withdrawal. Far from being inactive, Congress can and will challenge presidential policy. This is likely to be particularly in evidence under situations of divided government, where the president faces a hostile majority in Congress.

Practical

- **Presidential advantages:** It can be argued that changes in practical considerations have led to a huge surge in the president's control of military policy in recent years. Changes in technology have fundamentally altered the power relationship between president and Congress. As war has become faster and more deadly, in a way that was unimaginable at the start of the 20th century, the public and Congress have put more faith in presidential decision-making.

  Nuclear weapons, fighter jets, drone strikes, satellites and computer technology all require decisions to be made with greater speed, secrecy and expertise. The office of the presidency is far more suited to these requirements than Congress. The rise of the EXOP, and especially the National Security Council, gives the president a key advantage over Congress: the president holds critical information that is classified. Congress is often in a position where it has to trust the president. This can be seen with the Iraq War in 2003, in which Bush sought congressional approval while telling them of the imminent dangers of Saddam Hussein's use of 'weapons of mass destruction'. Many members of Congress, including Senator Hillary Clinton, were extremely sceptical of the case for war, but still voted for it.

- **Presidential limits:** Much depends on the type of foreign policy being conducted. The president cannot claim the need for speed and secrecy in all cases. Attacks on Libya, Syria, Bosnia or Somalia could be placed in this category, where it is arguably militarily acceptable to consult Congress. Nor do these advantages apply to other aspects of foreign policy, such as treaty-making and trade deals. Furthermore, Congress has its own expertise in foreign affairs, which helps it to question the authority of the president. The US Senate Committee on Foreign Relations has included many Senators with huge experience of foreign policy, such as Joe Biden and John Kerry, who arguably had greater knowledge than the presidents they were checking. Closed sessions of Congress also allow congressional committees to receive sensitive information in which they can challenge executive action. Committees such as the House Intelligence Committee often have such closed sessions.

Pause & reflect

Why do presidents sometimes ask for permission for military action, and sometimes act unilaterally? Consider two or three reasons. It would help to compare three or four different examples and consider the broader context of US politics at the time.

Assessment support: 3.1.3 US Presidency

Question 3 on A-Level Paper 3 requires you to answer two questions from a choice of three, each of which is worth 30 marks.

Evaluate the extent to which the president controls foreign policy. [30 marks]

You must consider this view and the alternative to this view in a balanced way.

These questions require an essay-style answer. They test all three Assessment Objectives, with 10 marks available for each. These questions always ask you to **evaluate**. The requirement for **balance** means that you have to show an awareness of different arguments and viewpoints. It is essential to go beyond simply explaining what those different arguments and viewpoints are. Evaluation requires you to make a judgement about the strength of arguments rather than just stating them. You will need to do this throughout your answer and not just in a conclusion. You will need to show an awareness of different perspectives and to outline different arguments, typically using three or four well-evaluated arguments with counter-arguments. You will also need an introduction and a conclusion.

This question requires you to have an awareness of the reasons why the president might have particular power in foreign policy. You could cite constitutional, practical and political reasons. You should also use examples of limits on presidential power to try to evaluate these powers and limits throughout your whole answer.

Here is part of a student's answer.

Presidents can be limited in foreign policy by the need to gain congressional support for military action and funding. Congress has the power to declare war and, at least in theory, the power to authorise or deny military action. The extent to which the president controls foreign policy depends on their relationship with Congress however. A president with a majority in Congress is more likely to achieve their military goals than one facing divided government.

- The student uses the technique of establishing an argument then showing how the strength of this argument depends on certain factors (in this case, which party controls Congress, showing that power will be different in different circumstances). The student shows they understand that power tends to be dynamic, not static, so presidential power can change over time.

Here is another part of a student's answer.

It is true that presidents are more likely to achieve foreign policy goals when they have a majority in Congress. This, however, is not necessarily the case as presidents often commit military action without consulting Congress. In 2011 Obama ordered military attacks in Libya without asking Congress, claiming that the War Powers Act did not apply to airstrikes. He was able to have power in foreign policy despite the Republican majority in the House of Representatives. The evidence suggests that the factor of party control is not always important in this area.

- Here the student uses evidence that contradicts the argument to make a judgement about the strength of that argument. It is important to summarise evidence in order to explain what it does (and does not) reveal about an argument or idea. This judgement means that the student is following the all-important requirement to evaluate.

The Supreme Court and Civil Rights

The Supreme Court is a powerful institution in which nine unelected justices can overturn the decisions of president and Congress, and have a major impact on the daily lives of those who live in the US. As a constitutional court, it deals with highly contentious issues covering areas such as civil rights, the balance between federal government and states, and presidential power.

In this chapter you will examine:

- the role and extent of power of the Supreme Court
- the appointment process and the debates surrounding it
- the theories and significance of different approaches to interpreting the Constitution
- the impact of Supreme Court decisions
- the role of the Court in protecting civil rights.

4.1 The nature and role of the Supreme Court

The US Constitution

The central role of the Supreme Court is to uphold the Constitution, as outlined in article III. As a constitutional court (rather than a criminal one) it is not trying to ascertain innocence or guilt. Instead it determines the acceptability (or otherwise) of actions within the rules of the Constitution.

'The judicial Power of the United States, shall be vested in one supreme Court, and in such inferior Courts as the Congress may from time to time ordain and establish.'

Article III, Constitution of the United States of America

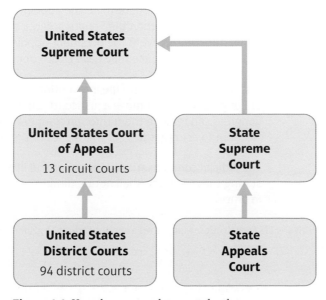

Figure 1.1: How the courts relate to each other

Established by the Constitution	Implied by the Constitution
• **Establishes a Supreme Court** (art. III, sec. 1) • **Extent of judicial power** 'to all Cases in Law and Equity arising under the Constitution' (art.III, sec. 2). The Supreme Court cannot initiate cases but must wait for a constitutional dispute to arise. • **Life tenure for judges** during 'good behavior' (art. III, sec. 1) • **Original jurisdiction** – a case is tried at the Supreme Court and does not have to be heard first in a lower court, in cases such as those involving constitutional disputes between states and between federal government and the states (art. III, sec. 2). • **Appellate jurisdiction** – most cases must go to another court before being presented to the Supreme Court on appeal. The losing side in a lower court can appeal to the next court level until finally reaching the Supreme Court. • **The appointment process** (art. II, sec. 2) – all justices are nominated by the president and ratified by the Senate.	**The power of judicial review** is the central power of the Court, allowing it to overturn any other institution because the Court declares its actions to be unconstitutional. The Court gave itself this power in *Marbury v Madison* 1803 when it first overturned an Act of Congress. This power was further defined in *Fletcher v Peck* 1810 in which the Court overturned state law for the first time. Some argue that this power is apparent in the Constitution, as the Supreme Court is charged with upholding matters arising under the Constitution. Others argue that the power of judicial review is not a legitimate power, as it is not awarded to the Supreme Court by the Constitution.
	Established by Acts of Congress under constitutional authority
	Congress has the power to: • **establish 'inferior courts'** – Congress determined a series of federal courts with constitutional power. There are 13 circuit courts (or appeals courts) below the Supreme Court, the final court of appeal • **determine the number of justices on the Court**, which has long been set at nine, originating from post-Civil War legislation.

Table 1.1: The Constitution and the Supreme Court

The independence of the Court

The Constitution ensures that the highest court in the United States is independent from other political institutions. This is particularly important for a constitutional court because it has the role of determining the constitutional acceptability of the laws and actions of president and Congress. A court that is accountable to these institutions may be unable to give a ruling that regulates the president or Congress.

Separation of powers	The separation of personnel means that no one in the executive or legislature works closely with judges, so there is little chance of close connections or pressure. (By contrast, in the UK, the highest court, the Law Lords, was until recently placed inside a legislative body, the House of Lords.)
Appointment process	The president cannot determine the appointment of justices alone, but instead nominates, then the Senate accepts or rejects, having the power to ratify. This could prevent the president appointing someone who will not act independently, because they have close connections to the president.
Life tenure	Justices are appointed for life, preventing a threat of removal. President or Congress cannot remove a justice (though if a justice has acted illegally, Congress can remove them through a supermajority). This gives justices the freedom to act regardless of the wishes of the president of the day.
Salary	The judicial compensation clause of article III protects the pay of judges, stating that their pay 'shall not be diminished during their continuance in office'.

Table 1.2: How the US Constitution establishes an independent Supreme Court

The judicial review process

The Supreme Court cannot initiate a case. Cases are presented to court by an individual or institution who feels that the Constitution has been broken. The Supreme Court receives between 7000 and 8000 cases a year. The Court has no duty to hear a case and currently opts to hear more than 100 cases per year. In the 2015–16 term, the Court dealt with 80 cases. The Court has some discretion in determining its own constitutional priorities.

The Roberts Court – as the Supreme Court under Chief Justice John G. Roberts is sometimes known – before the death of Scalia

The Supreme Court operates in a similar way to a criminal court. There is a plaintiff and a defendant. Lawyers make arguments on either side, being given just 30 minutes to present their oral arguments. All nine justices usually hear a case; the justices can ask questions or make points during these hearings.

Once a case is heard, the Supreme Court discusses the case in private in order to reach a majority opinion of five or more. A justice in the majority is tasked with writing the opinion, with input from other justices. The opinion of the Court is a written document detailing how the Constitution has or has not been broken, at some length – for example, the Affordable Care Act ruling, *NFIB v Sebelius*, runs to 193 pages.

A majority opinion is an agreement by five or more members. It helps set a precedent for future cases, particularly for political institutions, organisations and individuals. The Supreme Court could choose to have a narrow and limited impact, or a broad-ranging one, when writing their opinion. In split decisions, a minority opinion is also written.

In hearing a case, the Supreme Court has the power to declare that the actions or laws of other institutions are unconstitutional. This allows the Court to overturn those actions or laws using the power of judicial review.

4.2 The appointment process for the Supreme Court

The appointment process and its strengths and weaknesses

A single change to the Supreme Court can affect the nature of the rulings it delivers. In some cases, but certainly not all, replacing just one justice can have a critical impact on the lives of millions of people.

Link

To find out how the addition of a new judge can affect the balance of the Supreme Court, see Alito and Garland case study later in this section.

Step one

A vacancy occurs

Vacancies are caused by the death, resignation or impeachment of a justice. Justices are protected from threat of removal by life tenure.

Step two

The president nominates a new justice

Presidents, with the aid of White House officials, will typically draw up a shortlist of nominees. The nominees' public records and private lives are scrutinised, including FBI reports, before a president settles on a single nominee.

Step three

The Senate decides

The Senate Judiciary Committee holds hearings, including an interview with the nominee, and makes a recommendation to the full chamber. The American Bar Association issues a report on the extent to which the justice is qualified, which may or may not influence the final decision. The full Senate votes with over 50 per cent required for the nominee to be appointed.

Figure 2.1: The process for appointing a new justice

Nominations to the Supreme Court are not always successful. Here are some examples of failed nominations.

Key term

Conservative justice
a justice who interprets the Constitution and produces conservative outcomes. This might mean favouring the authority of the government over civil rights, overturning liberal policies of law-makers or upholding conservative ones, or protecting freedoms championed by conservatives, such as the right to bear arms or the right to life.

- **Robert Bork 1987** was nominated by Reagan and was the last nominee to fail a vote in the Senate, 42–58.

- **Harriet Miers 2005** was nominated by George W. Bush. Her moderate conservative nature and lack of judicial experience were both used as criticisms of her nomination. With a Republican Senate majority, Bush could have proposed a more **conservative justice**. Democrats chose to attack Miers, focusing on her lack of experience and connections to the president. This could be seen as irrational partisanship: after Miers withdrew, Bush nominated the far more conservative Justice Alito – a political own goal for the Democrats.

- **Merrick Garland 2016** was nominated by Obama to replace conservative Justice Scalia. The Senate blocked any nomination by refusing to hold a vote. This can be seen as extreme partisanship: the Senate did not fulfil its constitutional duty to advise and consent. This is of major importance because it allowed President Trump to fill the vacancy instead – with Justice Gorsuch – and prevented the Court from switching to a 5–4 liberal majority.

Strengths

✔ It ensures independence

The life appointment and the use of separation of powers and checks and balances, after careful scrutiny, prevent a justice feeling under obligation to any one political institution or public opinion.

✔ It ensures judicial ability

As nominations are carefully scrutinised by the Senate Judiciary Committee and rely on a full Senate vote, they are vetted for their ability to operate as a justice on the highest court in the United States. Justices without significant legal experience are unlikely to be successful. Since the start of the Clinton presidency, seven of the nine nominations to the Supreme Court worked in the US circuit courts. Harriet Miers, nominated by President George W. Bush in 2005, withdrew her nomination after heavy Senate opposition.

✔ It ensures personal suitability

The intensive nomination also ensures that there are no historical concerns or character flaws. Sonia Sotomayor was questioned by some members of the Senate Judiciary Committee who were concerned about apparent racial and gender bias, especially her publicly expressed view that a 'wise Latina' might make a better judge than a white male. Reagan also experienced failure with the nomination of Douglas Ginsburg who was withdrawn after evidence emerged of previous marijuana use.

Weaknesses

✘ The nomination process is politicised

The president's own policy preferences infect the Court. This makes the Supreme Court a highly political body; justices are even described as liberal or conservative. This threatens the neutrality of the Court and its rulings.

There are constant criticisms that a justice has not based a decision on the Constitution. This threatens the Court's authority – and the Constitution itself – with the risk that rulings are not respected. The decision of justices to retire can also be seen as a political decision, with a justice choosing to retire at a point where a like-minded president is in office.

✘ The ratification process is politicised

Increasingly the Senate appears to be acting in a partisan manner, supporting or opposing the nomination according to which president made it. The appointments in the 1980s of Kennedy and Scalia passed with huge bipartisan support and no votes against them. The nomination of Bork in 1987 appears to be something of a turning point. The Bork nomination was rejected, by Democrats in particular, who tried to prevent a strong conservative influencing the outcome of Court decisions. Since then, hearings have become more politically charged. This affects the neutrality of the Court as justices become entangled in a political dispute between Democrats and Republicans. Of the last four justices eventually nominated, all were opposed by more than 30 Senators.

✘ It is ineffective

As a result of this politicisation, nominees tend to avoid giving much detail of their views of the Constitution and recent constitutional issues, so the process fails to provide adequate scrutiny of the nominee. Nominees avoid what was arguably Bork's mistake of being very open about their views (for example, Bork said that *Roe v Wade* had little or no legal basis). Instead they simply argue, as Gorsuch frequently did in 2017, that they can only be expected to give a ruling on a case in front of them where they have all of the facts. Gorsuch regularly cited the need to maintain his public neutrality before he heard cases and said that he could not even say which precedents of the Court he particularly supported. In the Sotomayor nominations, Judiciary Committee Senators spoke twice as many words as Sotomayor, making this less of a hearing and more of a 'talking'.

The level of criticism is often affected by the political context and details of the nomination. Some nominations will have limited impact on the Court and the process tends to be less controversial – for example, when the nominee has similar values to the one being replaced. The nature of party control will also have an impact on how the nomination process plays out, with presidents more likely to secure a successful nomination if their party has a majority in the Senate (see case study below).

Key term	

Swing justice
informal name for the justice on the Supreme Court who falls ideologically in the centre of the nine current justices and sometimes swings towards a liberal interpretation and at other times acts more conservatively.

Case study: The nominations of Alito and Garland

When Justice Alito, a strong conservative, was nominated to replace Sandra Day O'Connor (a moderate **swing justice**), this led to strong opposition from the minority Democratic Party, with the late Senator Kennedy referring to it as a vote of a generation. The eventual appointment of Alito tipped the ideological bias on the Court, firmly establishing a conservative majority. This can be easily illustrated with their change in attitude to campaign finance regulations and 1st amendment freedom of expression. In *McConnell v FEC* 2003, the majority delivered a 5–4 opinion, upholding the Bipartisan Campaign Reform Act 2002 and limiting campaign expenditure in US elections. After Alito replaced O'Connor, the Court reversed this decision in *Citizens United v FEC* 2010, undermining the regulations.

The death of conservative Justice Scalia gave Obama the chance to replace a conservative with a liberal, and to tip the ideological balance on the Court from a 5–4 conservative majority to a 5–4 liberal one. The subsequent refusal of Senate majority Republicans to hold confirmation hearings, thus blocking the nomination until President Trump was in office, is evidence of both the importance of this particular nomination as well as the polarised nature of the process. Trump's nomination of Gorsuch had less significance in changing the composition and outlook of the Court than Obama's nomination would have done. Gorsuch has a similar conservative ideology to Justice Scalia whereas Garland, the choice of Obama, was far more liberal. The nomination of Gorsuch led to a radical departure from traditional practice, where Senate Democrats for the first time led a successful filibuster against a Supreme Court nominee. As such, Gorsuch required 60 votes in order to end the filibuster (and not the 50%+ vote required by the Constitution). The Republicans then decided to change Senate rules to end the filibuster so that the Gorsuch nomination could pass.

Questions

- How did the Alito appointment affect the ideological balance of the Court?

- How important was the prevention of the Garland nomination?

- What is the difference between an appointment and a nomination?

Factors influencing the president's choice of nominee

Judicial ability

First and foremost, presidents are picking from a pool of qualified people with legal expertise. The vast majority of recent justices worked in the circuit courts, one level below the Supreme Court. Those with a lack of judicial experience have arguably faced tougher confirmation hearings. In his opening remarks to the Senate Judiciary Committee hearings on Kagan, Senator Jeff Sessions expressed concern at her background in legal academia rather than judicial practice: 'Ms. Kagan has less real legal experience of any nominee in at least 50 years, and it is not just that the nominee has not been a judge. She has barely practiced law and not with the intensity and duration from which I think real legal understanding occurs.'

Ideology

Presidents are undoubtedly influenced by the ideological bias shown by the nominee, usually in the way in which they have interpreted the law or the Constitution in the past. Presidents are highly unlikely to nominate someone of an opposing political view; a Republican president is likely to choose a conservative justice.

Presidents have acknowledged as much, often highlighting other important qualities. Obama, appointing Sotomayor, said that judicial experience alone was insufficient. He said: 'Experience being tested by obstacles and barriers, by hardship and misfortune, experience insisting, persisting, and ultimately, overcoming those barriers. It is experience that can give a person a common touch and a sense of compassion, an understanding of how the world works and how ordinary people live.'

Social characteristics

Geographical background has long been a consideration (Washington was careful to award his six court appointments to different states), but there is an increasing racial and gender diversity on the Court. The Supreme Court in 2017 has three women sitting; only four women have served in total in its entire history. The Court has one black (two in total) and one Hispanic justice. It could be that presidents are making a value judgement about the desirability of diversity in positions of power. This is something that might be expected in a liberal president such as Obama replacing two white males with two females, including the Court's first Hispanic justice. George H.W. Bush nominated Clarence Thomas, the second black justice on the Court, in 1990 (although Bush was also replacing the first black justice, Thurgood Marshall).

Political motivations

Presidents may be concerned more with personal political gain than with fulfilling ideological goals. A nominating president has to consider the likely response of the Senate. A president facing a hostile majority in the Senate might make a more moderate choice to limit opposition. Conversely, a president may choose a justice to maintain support from key voting groups. After choosing Sotomayor, Obama was able to use this to increase his support among Hispanic voters between 2008 and 2012.

The composition and ideological balance of the Court

Periods in the Court's history are often defined by the name of the chief justice of the time. For example, the Burger Court is the name given to the Court while Warren Burger acted as the chief justice between 1969 and 1986. Some courts are known for a certain focus, action or approach. The chief justice does not have any significant power compared to each of the other justices.

The Warren Court 1953–69	The Rehnquist Court 1986–2005	The Roberts Court 2005–
Known for hearing a series of civil rights cases delivering liberal opinions. Cases such as *Brown v Board of Education* 1954 and *Miranda v Arizona* 1966 are seen as landmark liberal rulings. Described as activist by those who claim it overturned established practices to achieve its own political goals.	Seen as a more restrained rather than active court. It heard fewer cases, dealing with fewer than 100 per year, reducing its political impact. Associated with a states' rights agenda with several rulings that protected the power of the states, halting decades of expansion of federal power.	Arguably more conservative than the Rehnquist Court with the nomination of Justice Alito to replace the moderate conservative swing justice, Sandra Day O'Connor. Has delivered a series of conservative rulings undermining campaign finance regulations such as *Citizens United v FEC* 2010 and *McCutcheon v FEC* 2014. Has disappointed conservatives in other cases such as *NFIB v Sebelius*, which upheld Obama's Affordable Care Act.

Table 2.1: Three recent Supreme Courts, named after the chief justice at the time

The Roberts Court				
Nominee	Year	President	Senate vote	Ideology of justice
Kennedy	1987	Reagan	97–0	Moderate conservative/swing
Thomas	1991	Bush Snr	52–48	Conservative
Ginsburg	1993	Clinton	96–3	Liberal
Breyer	1994	Clinton	87–9	Liberal
Roberts	2005	Bush Jnr	78–22	Conservative
Alito	2006	Bush Jnr	58–42	Conservative
Sotomayor	2009	Obama	68–31	Liberal
Kagan	2010	Obama	63–37	Liberal
Gorsuch	2017	Trump	54–45	Conservative

Table 2.2: The make-up of the current Supreme Court – the Roberts Court

The Roberts Court is finely divided, with a 5–4 conservative majority, as reflected in the votes in several key cases. It is typically seen as conservative, interpreting the Constitution to give conservative outcomes.

It would be simplistic to view all rulings being based on these strict ideological lines. The Court is finely balanced. Justice Kennedy acts as a swing justice who is typically conservative but sometimes joins the liberal group. He could be seen as the Court's deciding voice. Furthermore, Chief Justice Roberts argued for the importance of consensus on the Court in order to give clarity as well as guidance to lower courts. Two-thirds of the 72 cases heard in the 2014 session were unanimous. However, several 9–0 decisions may have much less significance than one 5–4 decision. While most cases have not been 5–4 rulings, the most important ones almost always are (see case study below).

Case study: The conservative agenda of the Roberts Court

The dominant outcome of the Roberts Court has been conservative in its impact. This can be seen in a number of 5–4 cases that have angered liberals. In *DC v Heller* 2008, the Court departed from judicial precedent, stating for the first time in its history that the 2nd amendment gave individuals (as opposed to those joining militias as a form of protection of state power) the right to bear arms. This overturned one of the most restrictive gun laws in the US, favoured by liberals, in which handguns were banned from homes. The Court's conservative credentials were further established in *Citizens United v FEC* 2010 and *McCutcheon v FEC* 2014. These cases overturned congressional restrictions on the use of money in US elections, making it easier for the wealthy to donate unlimited dollars. One of the most controversial rulings was *Shelby County v Holder* in 2013, which undid some of the major aspects of the civil rights movement by critically undermining the Voting Rights Act. This means that states cannot be checked by the federal government to ensure that their voting practices are not discriminatory. According to the NAACP (the National Association for the Advancement of Colored People), this ruling has led to an explosion of restrictive practices in the 2016 elections.

However, conservatives have been disappointed and in some cases angry at some of the most important decisions made by the Court. In *NFIB v Sebelius*, the Court was given an opportunity to review Obama's Affordable Care Act with only four of the conservative justices arguing that it restricts state power, breaking the interstate commerce clause. Chief Justice Roberts, in a surprise interpretation, stated that the act was constitutionally acceptable because the health care provision was a form of tax, which Congress had the right to impose. The four liberals also ruled in favour of the act but for different reasons, meaning the Court upheld Obama's flagship policy. This interpretation shows how much control justices have over their rulings. In *Obergefell v Hodges* 2015, the Court issued a landmark liberal ruling by stating that gay rights were protected by the 14th amendment.

Questions

- What is the dominant ideology of the current Court? In other words, which ideology has a majority?
- How have recent nominations changed the balance of ideology on the Court?
- Which justices did Obama appoint and to what extent are they similar?

4.3 The Supreme Court and public policy

The Supreme Court has a major impact on public policy through its use of judicial review. By giving rulings in areas such as health, education or the environment it can impact on **public policy** by removing it or upholding it.

Significant public policy cases of the Roberts Court

Key term

Public policy
legislation and judicial decisions made on any policy that affect the US populations.

DC v Heller **2008**	2nd amendment case overturning a ban on handguns in the home in Washington DC
Citizens United v FEC **2010**	1st amendment case overturning public policy regulating money in elections, declaring that parts of the Bipartisan Campaign Reform Act were unconstitutional
NFIB v Sebelius **2012**	States' rights/interstate commerce clause and the 16th amendment right of federal government to impose income tax, which upheld a major piece of public policy in the Affordable Care Act
Shelby County v Holder **2013**	Overturned longstanding public policy of Voting Rights Act 1965, arguing that there was no case for it under the 14th amendment, equal treatment, thus protecting states' rights to decide election laws
Riley v California **2014**	4th amendment case that unanimously protected people from unwarranted police searches of their mobile phone
Obergefell v Hodges **2015**	Created a constitutional guarantee of the right to gay marriage under the 14th amendment, covering both the due process and equal treatment clauses, forcing many states to change their public policy
Whole Woman's Health v Hellerstedt **2016**	Overturned Texas state regulations on abortions (which required health compliance leading to the closure of most Texas clinics) on the grounds of 14th amendment restrictions on equal protection, placing an undue burden on women.

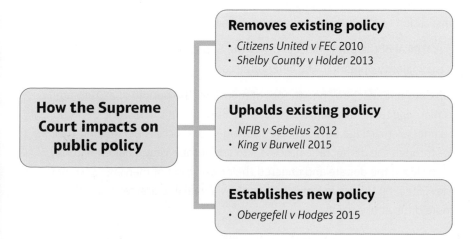

Figure 3.1: How the Supreme Court impacts on public policy

The role of judicial activism and judicial restraint

Judicial activism is an approach to interpretation of the Constitution. It has two key components:

- justices use their own views and values in order to achieve their own social or political goals
- activism involves the Court overturning other political institutions or the precedent of previous courts.

This activism might reflect itself in the approach of an individual justice who is associated with a particular stance, which they use to challenge political institutions. However, it is most forceful when used by the majority on the Court, and is most easily seen over a series of cases where justices consistently appear to be attempting to challenge political institutions.

A judicially active court is likely to have a major impact on public policy. Judicial activism is associated with the Warren Court 1953–69, which gave a series of rulings that promoted civil rights, typically at the expense of state law. This civil rights agenda can be seen in cases such as *Brown v Board of Education* 1954 and *Miranda v Arizona* 1966. The Roberts Court has consistently ruled against campaign finance regulations – for example, in the Citizens United and McCutcheon cases – suggesting it is using its interpretation of the 1st amendment to promote conservative judicial activism.

Judicial restraint is the opposite of judicial activism. Justices may or may not have a personal bias, but their approach to judicial interpretation is to limit the extent to which they overturn political bodies. This could be based on a view that, as an unelected body, the Supreme Court should defer to institutions with greater democratic legitimacy. It is an approach to the interpretation of the Constitution in which courts show deference to wishes of political institutions. It suggests political institutions such as Congress should only be overturned if there is clear evidence that the Constitution has been broken. This judicial philosophy limits the impact the Supreme Court has on public policy.

Pause & reflect

Is judicial activism liberal or conservative? What evidence do you have for this view?

Judicial activism has been criticised for giving justices excessive power over elected politicians. Restraint could be seen as more suited to a democratic society as it restricts the likelihood of unelected justices denying a majority view as expressed by elected politicians, at national or state level. Activism also suggests a political agenda in which courts abuse their power, using the vagueness of the Constitution to reach their own personal goals.

Chief Justice Roberts is critical of the public policy role of the Supreme Court. Here he attacks the apparent activism in the majority opinion in the Obergefell case:

> our Constitution does not enact any one theory of marriage. The people of a State are free to expand marriage to include same-sex couples, or to retain the historic definition... Supporters of same-sex marriage have achieved considerable success persuading their fellow citizens – through the democratic process – to adopt their view. That ends today. Five lawyers have closed the debate and enacted their own vision of marriage as a matter of constitutional law. Stealing this issue from the people will [make] a dramatic social change that is much more difficult to accept.

Conservatives in particular have been critical of judicial activism because of the way in which it has been used by the Court to 'find' new rights, such as abortion and gay rights, in the Constitution. Supporters of judicial activism will often base their argument on the need to protect civil liberties, based on the idea that the Constitution has to evolve with the changing values of modern society. In some cases, the Court has enhanced civil liberties that some would see as fundamental.

Judicial restraint has been attacked because it could be seen as a dereliction of duty. In deferring to elected politicians, the Supreme Court is failing to enforce the Constitution. The United States Constitution is not based on the desire for majoritarian democracy to prevail but instead prioritises checks and balances and the protection of individual liberty. If the Court is restrained it may fail to protect such **principles**.

Conservatives, while supporting Chief Justice Roberts's application of the Constitution in his majority view in Obergefell, were nonetheless enraged by his apparent restraint in the Affordable Care Act case, in which he was apparently reluctant to overturn the flagship policy of the elected president. What does this tell us? Support or criticism for one approach over the other is not necessarily based on some fundamental argument about these judicial philosophies. It is often a reflection of whether activism or restraint gives an individual what they want, based on their own personal ideology. In other words, a conservative might criticise the Court for its liberal activism in Obergefell but then support conservative activism when it was used in cases such as Citizens United.

> **Link**
>
> For more on the **principles of the Constitution**, see US Constitution and Federalism.

4.4 The protection of civil liberties and rights in the US today

The entrenched Constitution, the power of judicial review and the high priority given to enumerated rights in the Bill of Rights all allow the Supreme Court to have what is usually the final say on the issue of rights. This power is magnified by the vagueness of these rights, allowing the justices to have great freedom in deciding when and how civil liberties should be protected. The first ten amendments contain protections not only for individual rights but also for states' rights. The United States has long experienced major conflict over the issue of civil liberties, with political battles both to protect and deny certain rights. Which rights should be protected and which rights are protected by the Constitution?

> **Pause & reflect** ✔
>
> What is the difference between civil liberties and constitutional liberties?

Freedom of religion (1st amendment)	• Sought to protect people from religious discrimination by preventing the establishment of an official and therefore dominant religion. • Has been used to prevent school prayer in government schools in order to protect all religions.
Freedom of speech (1st amendment)	• Freedom of expression (protest/organisation and speech) seen as a cornerstone of liberal democracy. • Several controversial cases, such as those involving flag burning and campaign finance.
The right to bear arms (2nd amendment)	• Meaning much disputed, with disagreement over whether this gives the individual a constitutional right to a gun. • Many argue that the original intent was to promote the power of *states* to protect themselves from the federal government or foreign invasion. • Supreme Court case *DC v Heller* in 2010 overturned the state law banning handguns in Washington DC, setting a precedent of applying the right to an individual.

Freedom from unreasonable searches and seizures (4th amendment)	Warrants are required to search private property, and there must be a reasonable and specific reason for doing so. The Constitution is vague here when it says that government agencies require 'probable cause' to hold a search. This implies that there must be factual reasons for believing that an individual has committed a crime before searching. This right was upheld in *Riley v California* 2014 which prevented a warrantless search of a mobile phone for those who have been arrested. The 2001 Patriot Act has been highly controversial because it suspends probable cause for some searches with federal courts issuing rulings that did not challenge this aspect of the act.
Freedom from cruel and unusual punishment (8th amendment)	<ul><li>Hard to distinguish what is cruel and unusual. Subject to discretion of the Supreme Court.</li><li>The death penalty is not currently deemed cruel and unusual, although a few justices have implied this.</li><li>Most recent cases focus on death-penalty methods. In *Glossip v Gross* 2015, petitioners challenged the use of a three-drug method, arguing that the first drug, midazolam, does not sufficiently prevent the pain of the other two. The Court refused the arguments in a 5–4 ruling.</li></ul>
The reserved rights of states (10th amendment)	<ul><li>Designed to protect federalism and state power.</li><li>States that any power not possessed by federal government is reserved for the states.</li><li>Used successfully in *Printz v US* 1997 to protect states from requirement to create gun restrictions under the federal Brady Act of 1993.</li></ul>

Table 4.1: Some major rights protected by the Bill of Rights (1st to 10th amendments)

Equal protection (14th amendment)	Preventing racial discrimination
Due process (14th amendment and 5th amendment)	Preventing people's life, liberty or property from being restricted without fair legal processes
Right to vote (race) (15th amendment)	Protects voting regardless of race
Right to vote (gender) (19th amendment)	Protects voting regardless of gender

Table 4.2: Rights protected by further amendments

Rights protected by Supreme Court rulings

All of the above rights have formed the basis of Supreme Court cases in which, arguably, there is evidence of the protection of rights. However, there is a dispute about which rights are covered by the Constitution.

In 1907, Chief Justice Hughes said: 'We are under a Constitution, but the Constitution is what the judges say it is.' Many rights are enumerated in the Constitution, but there is a dispute about the way in which the Court has chosen to apply these to certain circumstances. This is illustrated by cases involving individual versus states' rights, in which some justices have prioritised the former and some the latter.

By overturning the section of the Voting Rights Act in *Shelby County v Holder*, the majority is protecting states' rights; the minority of justices on the Court see this as unjustified because it ignores the ongoing importance of protecting racial minorities. This ruling gives states greater control over their electoral laws, ending the requirement that the federal government scrutinises any changes to ensure there is no discriminatory outcome.

While all Supreme Court cases have to be based in the Constitution, some rulings have been particularly controversial because the Court has been accused of 'finding' rights that are not there.

- *Roe v Wade* 1973 protected the right to an abortion under the right to privacy under the due process clause of the 14th amendment. Both of the dissenting justices openly criticised the majority in establishing a right that they felt had no constitutional basis.

- In *Obergefell v Hodges* 2015 the 5–4 majority ruled that gay marriage bans were unconstitutional under the due process and equal protection clauses of the 14th amendment. Kennedy, in his majority opinion, wrote that the due process clause should 'extend to certain personal choices central to individual dignity and autonomy, including intimate choices that define personal identity and beliefs'. He also stated that a ban on gay marriage broke the equal treatment clause because of the discrimination it created.

The effectiveness of the Supreme Court in protecting rights

The effectiveness of the Court in protecting rights can be viewed from three perspectives.

- **Power:** How much power does the Supreme Court have to protect civil liberties?

  The Court is in an extremely powerful position as a result of the entrenched Constitution and its power of judicial review. The many rights placed in the Constitution allow the Court to play a prominent role in protecting civil liberties. However, the Supreme Court can be constrained, for example, by constitutional amendments that overturn its rulings (although this is rare). In addition, in the *Brown v Board of Education* case, their landmark ruling was ignored, with states failing to desegregate until Congress passed the Civil Rights Act in 1964.

- **Will:** How much willingness does the Supreme Court have to protect civil liberties?

  The vagueness of the Constitution gives a huge amount of personal control to justices. Justices often interpret the Constitution in a manner that may not promote liberties apparent in the Constitution. In *Plessy v Ferguson* 1896, the Supreme Court ruled that separate facilities did not break the Constitution (later interpreted as separate but equal). The Shelby ruling of 2010 could be seen as a failure to protect racial minority rights, a view taken by the four justices in the minority on the Court.

- **Ideology:** Which ideological perspective are we adopting?

  In an individual case there may be competing views about whether or not a right exists in the Constitution. There is a difference between rights (as a moral imperative or belief) and **constitutional rights**. It is possible to argue that both Roe and Obergefell uphold rights but not constitutional rights, because gay marriage and abortion are in no way mentioned in the Constitution. Liberals and conservatives make competing claims here, according to which rights they value. Each ideology claims that their preferred rights are apparent in the Constitution. Liberals can and have claimed that gay rights and abortion are constitutional rights (a view currently supported by the majority on the Court). Conservatives claim that the 2nd amendment gives an individual a right to a gun; liberals argue this is not based on the intentions of the Founding Fathers, who saw the right to bear arms essentially as a state right to organise a militia.

> **Link**
>
> For more on the **power of the Court to protect civil liberties**, see Table 6.1.

> **Key term**
>
> **Constitutional rights**
> the rights specifically outlined for citizens within the US Constitution, Bill of Rights and subsequent amendments.

4.5 Race and rights in contemporary US politics

Racial rights campaigns form a key part of the political and social history of the United States. Race has been a major issue given both the treatment of the original Native American population by colonial Europeans and the central role that slavery and racial segregation have played.

Two key developments in racial rights were the end of slavery after the Civil War (1861–65) and the civil rights movement of the 1950s and 1960s, which saw the end of legally supported separate facilities. Other important milestones include use of affirmative action and the election of Barack Obama, America's first black president.

Despite this, major concerns and conflict occur, with persistent levels of racial inequality and overt racism. There are still calls for desegregation and voter registration in the South, and better jobs, housing and school integration in the North. Voting rights, representation and affirmative action represent some of that ongoing political conflict.

Methods used by racial rights campaigners

Demonstrations and civil resistance

Grassroots movements to end discrimination and promote **racial equality** became prominent in the 1950s and 1960s. The protest of Rosa Parks and the Montgomery bus boycott in 1955, while not the first act of resistance, was followed by an array of actions across the South as momentum built to overcome restrictions on minority rights.

Demonstrations are still in use today, particularly since the *Shelby County v Holder* ruling and major concerns over the words and policies of President Trump. The NAACP has held a series of demonstrations across southern states in particular. Their Moral Mondays demonstrations, focused particularly in North Carolina, campaign against a variety of concerns including state-based restrictions on minority voting, such as the introduction of photo ID laws and felony voting restrictions. In 2014, the NAACP organised a peaceful sit-in at a Republican Party leader's office in the state legislature in Raleigh, in which 14 people were arrested.

Legal methods

Racial rights groups have regularly used the Court system to achieve their aims, utilising the 14th and 15th amendments of the Constitution, the Civil Rights Act of 1964 and the Voting Rights Act of 1965. The National Council of La Raza, a Hispanic rights group, successfully litigated against the state of Nevada in 2016 for its failure to register voters according to federal law principles. By taking legal action (litigation), pressure groups can challenge federal or state governments by initiating a court case themselves. Alternatively, pressure groups can submit amicus briefs, in which they provide written evidence and argument to the Court in a particular case.

Voter registration drives

The early 1960s saw the first voter-registration campaigns, which expanded quickly, supported by groups such as the NAACP. This involved educating the public in their voting rights, explaining voting processes and helping people with registration. Despite fierce resistance, with violence, death threats and lynching, the campaign continued to gather pace through the 1960s. In the 2016 elections, Native American groups were involved in organising and maximising voting under the banner of nativevote.org (assisting with voter registration) and Get-Out-The-Native-Vote (GOTNV) (election protection and education).

The effectiveness and influence of racial rights campaigns

Voting rights

The right to vote, regardless of race, was established by the 15th amendment of the Constitution. Despite this, southern states in particular acted to prevent racial minority voting. Using Jim Crow laws – the collective name given to any laws which continued to restrict minority rights – voting was heavily restricted for the black population. States typically used literacy tests and felony voting restrictions to prevent black voting. A grandfather clause was applied in many states, including Oklahoma and North Carolina, in which anyone qualified to vote before the Civil War (or related to someone who was allowed to vote) were exempt from literacy tests. The restrictions were so effective that, in many southern states at the start of the 20th century, black voter registration was close to zero. With many states requiring voter registration to stand for public office, millions of people were locked out of the process of representative democracy.

When the Civil Rights Act of 1964 ended separate facilities, black rights groups focused on ensuring voting rights. This culminated in the Voting Rights Act of 1965, which overturned the Jim Crow laws inhibiting minority voting. It prevented any state or local government from creating practices that led to racial discrimination in voting. In addition, the Federal Justice Department would vet all state laws to prevent any discriminatory practice. It is difficult to conceive of the election of Barack Obama without the civil rights movement of the 1950s and 1960s and the changes in voting rights. The impact has been enormous, with the number of black voters registered doubling within two years. In 2008, black turnout exceeded average turnout for the first time (source: Pew Research Center).

Hispanic voting power was seen as crucial in allowing Obama to be re-elected in 2012; his share of the Hispanic vote increased from 67 to 71 per cent with an increase in turnout. Hillary Clinton was unable to hold on to this share of the vote, falling back to 65 per cent – possibly a major factor in her failure to win the presidency. The Hispanic influence on voting is rising, with 27.3 million Latinos eligible to vote in 2016 – an increase of 4 million from 2012. This is particularly strong in a number of swing states such as Florida, where a huge rise in Puerto Rican voters was expected to help Clinton win a crucial state.

Despite this, there are still major restrictions on minority voting in the United States. There was a rise in state-based restrictions during the Obama presidency, and the Shelby ruling restricted the ability of the federal government to intervene to stop them. The NAACP is struggling to score victories at state level and is not receiving support from the Trump administration, significantly reducing its impact on public policy.

Representation
Policy and parties
Legal changes and major interest group efforts have allowed a huge increase in black candidates for public office and huge increases in representation at both state and federal level. Arguably the increased diversity among elected politicians has led to greater focus on minority issues in the creation of public policy. The enfranchisement of racial minorities has contributed to the realignment of the Democratic and Republican Parties and the formation of their current ideological identity. With Democrat Presidents Kennedy and Lyndon Johnson supporting minority rights, southern conservative Democrat voters switched their allegiance to the GOP. The Republicans, especially under Nixon, responded to this with their 'southern strategy' in which they attempted to attract white southern voters. The modern parties therefore are ideologically polarised with a typical north/south divide.

Positions of power
There has been a sea change in the representation of minority groups in terms of holding positions of power. The 115th Congress (2017–18) has the highest level of minority representation in the history of the United States. This is the product of the racial rights campaigns of previous decades.

Despite these major gains, Congress still does not look like the US. Black, Hispanic and Native American groups are all under-represented in both the House and the Senate. Racial minority representation is particularly low in the Senate. This is partly because there are many majority-minority districts in the House whereas the majority in each state representing a Senate seat is white.

House	Racial minority group	Senate
46	Black	3
34	Hispanic	4
2	Native American	0
83	Women	21

Table 5.1: Composition of the 2017–18 Congress for selected groups: numbers in each chamber by group

Key term

Affirmative action
a policy of favouring historically disadvantaged members of a community.

Affirmative action

Affirmative action (AA) was introduced by President Kennedy as a way of going beyond the legal and constitutional equality that was established by the 14th and 15th amendments and *Brown v Board of Education* 1954. It provides additional benefits to groups who have been historically discriminated against. It is common in areas such as awarding of places at university, the awarding of federal contracts and employment by governments. This can include milder forms such as Kennedy's instruction to the executive branch to take care to employ racial minorities. In stronger forms it includes the use of quotas in which a university might reserve a certain percentage of places for black or Hispanic students, usually to reflect the population at large. This approach was based on the idea that legal and constitutional equality would not lead to social and economic equality. In order to allow racial minorities to compete more effectively, proponents of affirmative action wanted to give better opportunities to minority groups.

> You do not take a person, who for years, has been hobbled by chains and liberate him, bring him up to the starting line of a race and then say "you are free to compete with all the others", and still believe that you have been completely fair.
>
> President Lyndon Johnson, 1965

The public policy of affirmative action provision could be seen as a major factor in the rise of educational standards and the growth of black middle classes in the United States. Without this assistance, arguably patterns of inequality would continue to repeat themselves much more strongly. The impact of racial rights groups in protecting affirmative action has started to wane, however, as such programmes are being challenged by state governments. Many states, such as California, Texas and Michigan have ended affirmative action. In several states the provision of affirmative action has been challenged by state initiatives. This is seen in the American Civil Rights Institute case study below.

Case study: The decline of affirmative action

The American Civil Rights Institute is a pressure group, created in 1996 by Ward Connerly, a black opponent of affirmative action. It has been responsible for initiating and funding state campaigns arguing that affirmative action constitutes unequal treatment. Despite strong opposition from groups such as the NAACP, the Institute has been highly successful. Five states – Arizona, Colorado, Missouri, Nebraska and Oklahoma – held votes in 2008, with only Colorado voting to maintain affirmative action.

There has also been a series of challenges to this policy in the Supreme Court, arguing that it breaches the 14th amendment. While affirmative action has not been declared unconstitutional, it has been increasingly restricted by successive court cases.

Court cases that have undermined affirmative action:

- *University of California v Bakke* **1978** – effectively ended the use of quotas

- *Fisher v University of Texas* **2013** – ordered strict scrutiny of the University of Texas's use of affirmative action (although the University policy was upheld in Fisher II in 2016)

- *Schuette v Coalition to Defend Affirmative Action* **2014** – rejected a challenge to Michigan's right to end affirmative action using a state initiative.

Question

- Can you think of examples of affirmative action that are used in other countries?

Ward Connerly, president of the American Civil Rights Institute.

There are a number of arguments surrounding affirmative action beyond the extent of its success. There are many criticisms about its desirability, regardless of its effectiveness in creating equality.

For some racial minority members, AA is patronising. Others argue that it is misplaced and measures to improve equality should focus on race, not class. When Obama was asked if his daughters should benefit from AA, he said they should not – but he still defended AA.

Arguments for AA	Arguments against AA
It was needed to improve the socio-economic status of minorities. It's helped close the gaps in education and income between racial groups.	It's a form of racial discrimination – a cause of racism, not a solution to it. And you could argue it's unconstitutional, breaking the 14th amendment.
It helps reduce racist attitudes by helping overcome de facto segregation. Greater interaction between racial groups can overcome prejudice.	It has the wrong focus – on college education and jobs, not on early years. By the time kids grow up their life chances have already been damaged by poor education and social surroundings.
It works. Where AA has been ended, there's has been a decline in racial minority enrolment in top colleges.	AA has not worked. Racial inequality still persists today. Despite AA, there is a major gap between racial groups in the top colleges (those which are selective).

Figure 5.1: Arguments for and against affirmative action

4.6 Interpretations and debates of the US Supreme Court and civil rights

The extent of Supreme Court power

The power of judicial review allows the Supreme Court to effectively amend the Constitution without any formal changes, having a profound effect on US politics and society. Judicial interpretations can create new political and constitutional expectations, seen as updating the meaning of the Constitution even though they are not actual amendments. These 'interpretive amendments' help to shape both the meaning of the Constitution and the powers, roles and limits of political institutions, as well as the rights of individuals. The Supreme Court does not simply give a yes or no answer to a constitutional dispute, but issues a detailed written opinion in which it explains how the Constitution is to be applied. Rulings can be seen as introducing an interpretive amendment, such as Obergefell, which established a principle of gay rights not mentioned directly in the Constitution.

Powers	Limits
Judicial review • Can overturn any other institution if it views actions as unconstitutional • Based on idea of constitutional sovereignty • Can overturn elected bodies, such as president or Congress • Especially powerful if the Supreme Court applies judicial activism	**Wording of Constitution** • Court is limited to this wording • Limits extent to which justices can interpret even ambiguous parts – limits the elasticity of the Constitution • Weaker if it applies judicial restraint

Powers	Limits
Interpretation • Constitution is vague, giving justices great latitude in applying personal views • A more detailed Constitution would undermine their power • Vagueness magnifies power of judicial review	**Limited jurisdiction** • Can only deal with constitutional issues • Weaker than other branches in controlling policy and influencing people's daily lives • Does not deal with annual budget, foreign policy decisions (for example)
Independence • Court protected from external pressure • Protects judicial review and interpretation powers, allowing justices to make judgements based on Constitution (or own values) • Hard to overturn decisions due to amendment process	**External pressure** • Subject to external influence or restraint • Justices influenced by public opinion or pressure groups • President's authority may undermine Court • Can ultimately be overturned by constitutional amendment

Table 6.1: Main powers and limits of the Supreme Court

EXTENSION ACTIVITY

Using the internet, research two or three Supreme Court cases from this year or last. Which powers and limits can you apply your evidence to? Which do you think are stronger: the powers or the limits?

The political versus the judicial nature of the Supreme Court

The Supreme Court has long been accused of acting like a political rather than a judicial body, with justices being described as politicians in disguise. Its very nature as a constitutional court, with a sovereign-entrenched constitution means that it is inevitably caught up in the political process. The Citizens United case, for example, had a clear political impact, overturning a congressional law and allowing more money in elections, increasing the impact of corporate donors. Some have accused the judiciary of using the power of judicial review when it was not constitutionally given and attempting to use this power to achieve their own policy goals. Unrestricted by the Constitution, an **imperial judiciary** has developed in which justices are largely unconstrained.

Key term

Imperial judiciary
an all-powerful judiciary on whom checks and balances are weak and ineffective.

Pause & reflect

The Supreme Court will always have a significant political impact – but is this the same as saying that the Court is a political body? From what you have read so far, what are the defining features of political bodies, and how do these differ from those of a judicial body?

Supreme Court is judicial	Difference	Supreme Court is political
Justices' decisions have to be based in the Constitution. Majority opinions must explain how the Court has applied the Constitution to a specific case to specific articles or amendments. 9–0 decisions suggest that justices are not applying personal values but enforcing constitutional rules. Justice Kennedy indicated that he did not support flag burning but nonetheless interpreted the Constitution to overturn the Flag Protection Act saying 'sometimes we must make decisions we do not like… because they are right, right in the sense that the law and the Constitution… compel the result.'	Ideologically motivated or neutral decision-making?	Justices apply their own values when applying the Constitution. The vagueness of the Constitution exacerbates judicial bias. This can be seen when an individual justice consistently gives rulings that please one ideological group. While 9–0 rulings are common, the Roberts Court has typically split 5–4 on the most significant cases. Chief Justice Roberts accused the Court of political bias in the Obergefell case. Justice Marshall, the first black justice on the Court, even appeared to declare a lack of neutrality, making his civil rights agenda clear: 'You do what you think is right and let the law catch up'.

Supreme Court is judicial	Difference	Supreme Court is political
Justices can avoid being political because the Constitution protects them from political influence. This allows them to maintain their neutrality, free from political interference. This can be seen in the *US v Nixon* case in which three Nixon appointees ruled against him. Justices are also careful not to stray into the world of politics. When **liberal Justice** Sotomayor was asked if she was 'apprehensive' about President Trump, she was careful not to show her own views, saying that she would answer the question in a different way adding that 'we can't afford a president to fail'.	Politically influenced and active or independent from external pressure and political processes?	Politicians try to put pressure on justices. For example, presidents may attack a ruling or even give speeches appealing to public opinion before a ruling is given. In his State of the Union address in 2010 President Obama attacked the Citizens United ruling with justices of the Court in front of him, prompting Justice Alito to mouth the words 'not true'. It is difficult to determine whether justices are swayed from their constitutional opinion by strongly held public views. Court rulings do often reflect changes in societal values: *Brown v Board of Education* 1954, *Roe v Wade* 1973 and *Obergefell v Hodges* 2015 are all very much of their time.
The Supreme Court is judicial because it can only apply the law and the Constitution, unlike political institutions, which can create policy in any area they wish. Justices are not free to initiate cases but must wait for a constitutional claim to be presented. There are many policies in which the Court has no role; these are left to political bodies to decide. It is inconceivable that the Supreme Court would review the whole annual federal budget or the president's military strategy. In areas such as foreign and security policy, the Court seems reluctant to get involved. During his confirmation hearings, Gorsuch said that there are no such things as Democrat or Republican judges, there are only judges.	Unlimited jurisdiction in policy-making or restricted to enforcing politicians' rules?	Justices have a big political impact, affecting the power of political institutions, the rights of the individual and the fate of a great deal of public policy. Like political bodies, the Court can deal with any issue it chooses due to the ambiguity of the Constitution. The Supreme Court has been likened to a policy-maker because it appears to use personal values to achieve its own public policy goals. With the Supreme Court ruling on health, education, defence, the environment, immigration reform and economic policies, it is hard to see that it has a limited remit kept within the judicial sphere. The *Bush v Gore* 2000 ruling was criticised as politically motivated, with the justices appointed by Republican Presidents Reagan and George H.W. Bush giving an interpretation that prevented Al Gore from becoming president. This ruling paved the way for George W. Bush to become president, having a huge impact on the policy direction of the US.

Table 6.2: Key differences between a political and a judicial body

Key term

Liberal justice
a justice who interprets the Constitution more broadly in order to give the people more freedom and bring about social change.

EXTENSION ACTIVITY

'I don't think any of my colleagues, on any cases, vote the way they do for political reasons. They vote the way they do because they have their own judicial philosophy.' Justice Antonin Scalia

Find articles in which the judicial philosophies of different justices are discussed. Note your findings on two or three justices who appear to have different approaches.

Pause & reflect ✔

Consolidate your understanding of the judicial versus political argument. Apply the approaches of judicial restraint and judicial activism above. Do judicial activism and judicial restraint suggest that the Court is political or judicial?

Originalism
the idea that the meaning of the US Constitution is fixed and should not be subject to interpretation.

Living Constitution
the idea that the Constitution is an evolutionary document that can change over time through reinterpretation by the Supreme Court (linked to **loose constructionism**).

Living Constitution ideology versus originalism

How do justices interpret the constitutional document? It was written over 200 years ago, in a society very different to modern-day America. How can justices apply those words in a modern context?

There are broadly two distinct approaches to judicial interpretation: **originalism** and the **Living Constitution**.

Originalism

Justices may interpret the Constitution based on the intended meaning of the authors of the Constitution, or on what the average person would understand as the meaning at the time of writing. Justices who practise this approach will verse themselves in the history of the writing of the Constitution, in particular the arguments presented at the Philadelphia convention, as well as the writings of some of the authors of the Constitution.

This approach is associated most closely with Justice Thomas, who often cites not only the values of the Founding Fathers but also the values of the people in US society at the time of writing. In 2011, he dissented in a 1st amendment case that struck down a California law regulating violent video games for minors, because minors were not seen by 18th-century society as having 1st amendment rights. He argued: 'The practices and beliefs of the founding generation establish that "the freedom of speech", as originally understood, does not include… a right of minors to access speech without going through the minors' parents.'

The Living Constitution

This alternative approach is based on the idea that the Constitution has to be applied to modern circumstances. In part, this is based on a view that the Founding Fathers intended the Constitution to be an organic or living document. The Living Constitution approach, or **loose constructionism** (the opposite of which is **strict constructionism**), recognises the practical difficulty of applying an originalist position. What did the Fathers think about video games or mobile phones? It can also be based on the idea that originalism may yield unacceptable rulings in modern society. For example, it may have been acceptable in the past for the president to consult Congress before military action. The advent of nuclear missiles and jet engines may make such requirements less palatable. One majority opinion of the Court has asserted the necessity of the Court to 'draw its meaning from the evolving standards of decency' in applying the vague 8th amendment. The Living Constitution approach tends to ignore the practice of **stare decisis** in which court rulings are based on precedent. The use of stare decisis would restrict the Living Constitution approach.

Loose constructionism
a legal philosophy that favours a broad interpretation of a document's language.

Strict constructionism
a philosophy that favours looking solely at the written text of the law.

Stare decisis
doctrine built on the idea of standing by decided cases, upholding precedents and maintaining former adjudications – it tends to favour status quo.

In favour of originalism

- It restricts the extent to which justices can force their own personal values on the Constitution and important constitutional disputes.
- It gives greater authority to the Constitution, which can be seen as a more objective document.
- If new principles or values are to be placed in the Constitution, this should be done through the democratic process, not enforced on society by unelected justices.

In favour of the Living Constitution

- It stops the Constitution becoming an outdated irrelevance, and lets it reflect the values and practical needs of modern society.
- It is virtually impossible to discern the exact views and values of the Founding Fathers and how this applies to modern society. Originalists are no more objective than Living Constitutionalists.
- The Founding Fathers may have been deliberately vague, allowing judicial discretion.
  Is originalism, basing a ruling in the intent or meaning of the Founding Fathers, something that the Founding Fathers intended the Supreme Court to apply?

The protection of rights

Legal and constitutional	Political	Socio-economic
Measures created by the Constitution or acts of Congress that try to enforce racial equality.	Actions by politicians, parties and pressure groups aimed at overcoming inequality. This could include voter mobilisation, publicity campaigns and demonstrations, as well as initiatives by the president.	This can involve policies that are targeted at helping racial minorities specifically in social or economic areas, such as affirmative action or funding. There are also many policies that are beneficial to low-income groups regardless of race, but have a disproportionately positive effect on racial minority groups.
• 14th and 15th amendments • Civil Rights Act • Voting Rights Act • Immigration reform (DREAM Act)	• NAACP and Nativevote.org voter participation • NAACP Moral Mondays • Obama creation of annual White House Tribal Nation summit	• Affirmative action • Affordable Care Act • Race to the Top $4.3 bn education plan • My Brother's Keeper Initiative

Table 6.3: Measures to promote equality

EXTENSION ACTIVITY

Using the internet, find examples from this year using the three headings in Table 6.3.
What measures have taken place that have promoted **or** undermined equality in each area?
To what extent?

Assessment support: 3.1.4 The Supreme Court and Civil Rights

Question 3 on A-Level Paper 3 requires you to answer two questions from a choice of three, each of which is worth 30 marks.

Evaluate the extent to which the Supreme Court has protected constitutional rights in recent years. [30 marks]

You must consider this view and the alternative to this view in a balanced way.

These questions require an essay-style answer. They test all three Assessment Objectives, with 10 marks available for each. These questions always ask you to **evaluate**. The requirement for **balance** means that you have to show an awareness of different arguments and viewpoints. It is essential to go beyond simply explaining what those different arguments and viewpoints are. Evaluation requires you to make a judgement about the strength of arguments rather than just stating them. You will need to do this throughout your answer and not just in a conclusion. You will need to show an awareness of different perspectives and to outline different arguments, typically using three or four well-evaluated arguments with counter-arguments. You will also need an introduction and a conclusion.

You can apply the powers and limits to the Supreme Court to show how it has been able or unable to protect rights. The key to this question is understanding what constitutional rights are. Make sure you focus on the exact wording of the question.

Here is part of a student's answer.

The Supreme Court has provided significant protection of constitutional rights in recent years using its power of judicial review to enforce the sovereign constitution. The Bill of Rights and other notable rights such as the 14th amendment have been used in court to ensure high levels of liberty. The Court protected rights in *Riley v California* 2014 when it prevented police from searching the contents of mobile phones without a warrant (4th amendment). In addition it protected the right to abortion in *Whole Woman's Health v Hellerstedt* 2016 by overturning Texas state restrictions which had led to the closure of the majority of clinics in the state (14th). In addition it has protected 1st amendment freedom of expression rights in *Snyder v Phelps*, allowing the Westboro Baptist Church to protest at funerals.

- The student shows good knowledge and understanding of a range of contemporary cases – something that is important throughout your answers. There are many important historical cases with landmark decisions, but you should be able to apply cases from the last three or four years to your answers. As a guide, 'recent years' could relate to the two most recent presidents.

Here is another part of a student's answer.

There is disagreement about the extent to which constitutional rights have been protected. There is a dispute about which rights are actually in the Constitution. Liberals have typically argued that abortion and gay rights are laid out in the Constitution, but conservatives have argued that they are not. In the Obergefell case, 2015, protecting gay rights, the Chief Justice Roberts accused the majority of basing their ruling in morality not the Constitution. Similar arguments have been made about *Roe v Wade* and Whole Woman abortion rights. In these cases conservatives argue that rights may have been upheld, but not constitutional ones.

- Students often lose sight of the question, but here the student shows clearly that they understand the question is about constitutional rights. Discussing rights that are clearly not in the Constitution would gain little or no reward.

- Writing plans for exam-style questions can help a great deal.

Democracy and Participation

As you read in UK Politics, democracy refers to political systems in which the people are involved in decision-making in some way, either directly or indirectly. Participation concerns the methods and levels at which people take part in the democratic process.

In this chapter you will look at the following areas:

- electoral systems in the USA, including presidential elections and campaign finance
- the key ideas and principles of the Democratic and Republican Parties
- interest groups in the USA and their impact on democracy.

5.1 Electoral systems in the USA

While the Founding Fathers wanted the public to have control over their government, they feared that the uneducated masses would not make the right decisions. In the original Constitution they ensured that only the House of Representatives was directly elected by the people, with Senators being appointed by the state government. They created a presidential election in which they inserted a safety mechanism: voters would choose a small group of people who would decide who the president is. This is the system that is still in existence today. In the 1960s, another election was added (primaries and caucuses) in which the public select which candidate will represent a party at elections. This system is not part of the Constitution but has been created by internal party rules. This means that the presidential elections, which do so much to determine the fate of America and the world, are – compared to most modern democracies – long and controversial.

Presidential elections and their significance

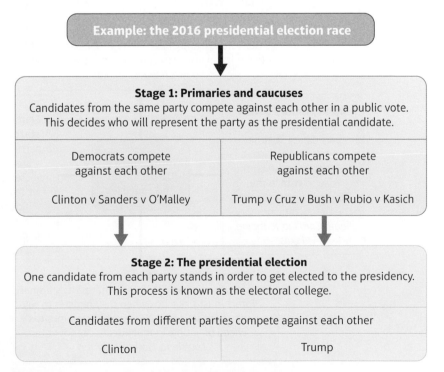

Figure 1.1: The two main stages of presidential elections

Primaries and caucuses

In the first stage of voting, candidates from the same party compete in a public vote. The whole process is often referred to as 'primaries', even though some states use primary voting and some use caucus voting. There are two primaries: one Democratic and one Republican.

Rather than having a national contest, there are separate contests for each state. This is a public vote, but each voter can only vote in one party's primary.

Candidates compete in a state to win delegates. Each state is given a number of delegates that broadly reflects its population. Delegates are party activists who agree to go to a party convention to vote for a specific candidate, according to how the voters in that state have voted.

In the 2016 Republican Party primaries, South Carolina had 50 delegates. Donald Trump received 33 per cent of the vote, beating Rubio (22 per cent), Cruz (22 per cent) and Bush (8 per cent). In doing so, Trump got 100 per cent of South Carolina's delegates. As a result, all 50 delegates then pledged to vote for Trump when they attended a national meeting of delegates from all states. This meeting is known as the 'national party convention'.

Different states and different parties have different rules regarding who can vote and how delegates are apportioned.

- **Republican primaries** traditionally used a winner-takes-all system (the candidate who came first got all of the state's delegates). Now some states use a proportional system (if a candidate gets 20 per cent of the vote, they get 20 per cent of the delegates).

- **Democratic primaries** award delegates to candidates in proportion to their vote totals in that state.

Voters cast a secret ballot into a ballot box, making a single choice. For either party, the candidate with 50 per cent or more of all delegates becomes the official presidential candidate.

Different parties elect different totals over the whole campaign. To win in 2016, a Democrat required 2,383 and a Republican 1,237 delegates. In theory the delegates make the decision at the

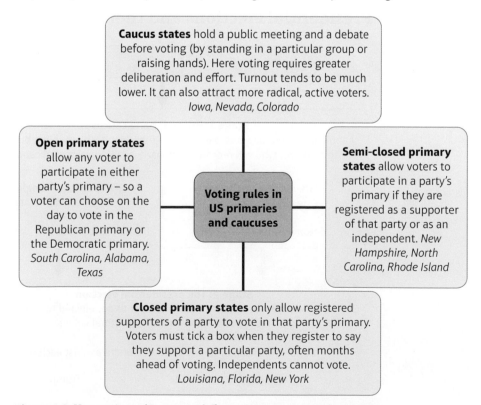

Caucus states hold a public meeting and a debate before voting (by standing in a particular group or raising hands). Here voting requires greater deliberation and effort. Turnout tends to be much lower. It can also attract more radical, active voters. *Iowa, Nevada, Colorado*

Open primary states allow any voter to participate in either party's primary – so a voter can choose on the day to vote in the Republican primary or the Democratic primary. *South Carolina, Alabama, Texas*

Voting rules in US primaries and caucuses

Semi-closed primary states allow voters to participate in a party's primary if they are registered as a supporter of that party or as an independent. *New Hampshire, North Carolina, Rhode Island*

Closed primary states only allow registered supporters of a party to vote in that party's primary. Voters must tick a box when they register to say they support a particular party, often months ahead of voting. Independents cannot vote. *Louisiana, Florida, New York*

Figure 1.2: How voting rules vary in different US primaries and caucuses

party convention at the end of the process. In practice, one person usually has more than 50 per cent, so therefore the winner is known before the convention.

Different states hold their primaries on different dates. In 2016 primaries began on 1 February, with 12 states holding votes on 1 March, six states on 7 June, and finishing on 14 June. Some states hold their primaries on the same day, with the largest collection of states all holding votes on what is known as Super Tuesday.

Pause & reflect

In 2012 only one party held a national primary as Obama was an unchallenged incumbent, whereas in 2016 both parties held primaries. How does this affect the extent to which the primaries help or hinder democracy? How would things operate differently depending on whether a state was open or closed?

Case study: The curious case of Nevada, 2016

The Democratic Nevada caucus held votes in three stages, with only the last stage allocating delegates to the convention. Stage 1 allowed public voting in February, and Clinton beat Sanders with 52.6 per cent of the vote. A majority of delegates was allocated to Clinton. Only the delegates chosen for Sanders and Clinton are then allowed to vote in the next stage. This stage, Stage 2, was surprisingly won by Sanders, because many Clinton supporters failed to turn out. This vote determined who would attend the third stage, a state-wide convention in May. At Stage 3, Sanders was then expected to win, but the party took the rather bizarre step of changing the rules to disregard the second stage of voting. As the meeting started, with many delegates still queuing to get in, the chair took a voice vote on the change. Despite loud shouts on each side, he decertified 64 of Bernie Sanders' delegates and denied them entry. As a result Clinton won and was given 20 delegates to the Democratic National Convention in Philadelphia; Sanders took just 15.

Questions

- Was the result of this election fair?
- What are the criticisms of the Nevada process?

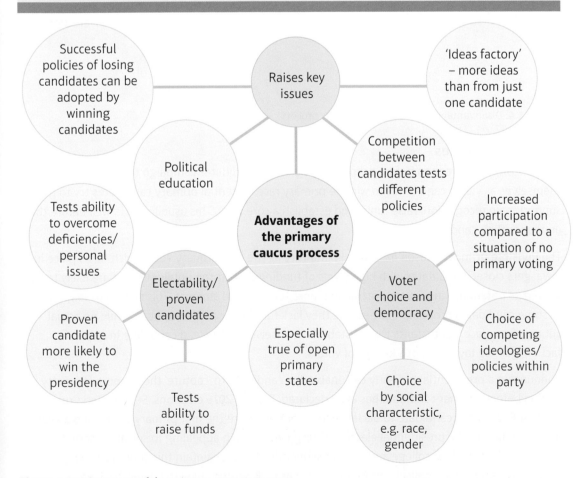

Figure 1.3: Advantages of the primary caucus process

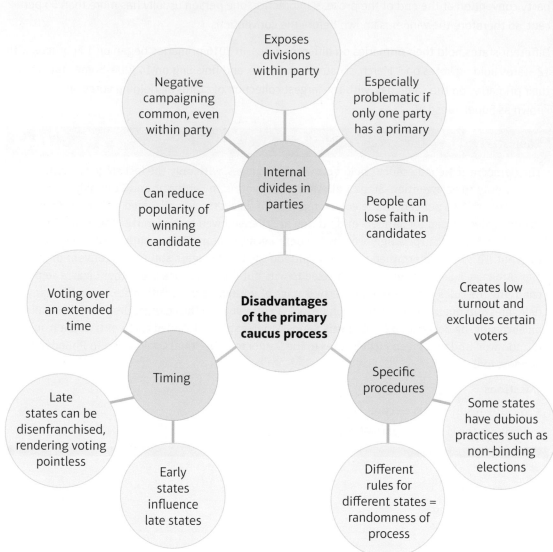

Figure 1.4: Disadvantages of the primary caucus process

Key term

Invisible primary
the period before the primaries take place, in which candidates attempt to establish their ability to be successful in the primaries. It is also sometimes called the 'money primary' as candidates spend most of their time raising money in an effort to show their political strength.

Invisible primaries

Invisible primaries happen before primary voting when candidates campaign to establish themselves as viable candidates to win the primary race. Potential primary candidates try to gather support, gain recognition, raise funds and establish a core staff. This usually starts well before they announce their candidacy.

The **invisible primary** season increases in intensity as the first primary vote, which takes place in Iowa, gets closer. Candidates with high levels of funding and strong public support are likely to be viewed as potential winners, thus attracting more funding and support. This season usually leads to some candidates dropping out because they lack funding or public support. While no actual voting takes place, contestants try to establish themselves as the lead candidate in a specific faction, gaining loyalty from a key set of voters.

Announcing a presidential bid early can enable the candidate to 'capture' the support of a party faction before another candidate has even declared. For the 2016 elections, Senator Ted Cruz was the first Republican candidate to declare, nine months before the first primary voting and a year and a half before the presidential election. Cruz gave a speech appealing to social conservative voters at an Evangelical college and was subsequently able to maintain this support, leaving previously popular Evangelical Republicans (such as Rick Santorum) with limited backing.

Invisible primaries can have a major effect on a candidate's chances of success. As well as being a key period of fundraising, invisible primaries are when candidates can spend a great deal of money, mainly on publicity campaigns, adding to the financial burden of running for the presidency. The process is also significant because it provides an opportunity for lesser-known candidates to establish themselves as realistic challengers to perceived frontrunners. This was the case with Barack Obama in 2007, who used solid performances in pre-voting debates to establish himself as the main rival to Hillary Clinton. Clinton 'won' the invisible primaries, thanks to higher fundraising and greater popularity, but Obama's ability to get close to her put him in a position to win the nomination. Sanders's invisible primary performance in 2015 helped him to gain funding and support, allowing him to run a fairly close primary race against Clinton.

Case study: Republican invisible primaries, 2015

In 2015 the Republican invisible primaries contained a record number of candidates who had declared their intention to run. This included seven televised debates between the candidates before the first votes were cast in Iowa. With 17 candidates the invisible primaries played an important role in narrowing the field with two governors, Rick Perry and Scott Walker, being forced to drop out. Walker, a one-time front-runner, announced his departure from the race in September 2015. His campaign team blamed a lack of media focus on his bid as well as a lack of funding. The invisible primaries could also be seen as the point at which Jeb Bush was effectively pushed out of the race. While Bush departed after the third primary contest in South Carolina, his lack of public support became apparent during the invisible primaries. Starting as a favourite to win, with name recognition, strong connections and a huge fundraising machine (in the first half of 2015 the Bush campaign raised a record-breaking $114 million, with Hillary Clinton being a distant second at $69 million and other Republican rivals well below that). Bush was eclipsed in terms of media focus and popularity with the entrance of Donald Trump into the race in June 2015, relatively late. With few commentators giving Trump any serious chance of winning, the Republican outsider soon took the lead in the polls at the same time that Bush experienced a serious decline in support.

Questions

- What does this case study say about the role of money in primaries and invisible primaries?
- What role did the invisible primaries play in 2015 in particular?

The party conventions

Figure 1.5: The place of party conventions in the presidential electoral process

National party conventions take place for each party in a presidential election year, usually lasting over three or four days. Modern conventions are attended by the delegates selected through the primary process. As such, they mark the end of the primary process and kickstart the presidential election campaign.

With the creation of national primaries in 1968, the role of conventions has changed. Their role in determining who wins the nomination and the party platform has now been lost mainly to the primary process itself.

Significant roles	Superficial roles
1. Select the presidential and vice presidential candidates for the party Delegates vote to decide who is the presidential nominee. The rules of each party require that a candidate gains more than 50 per cent of delegates. If no candidate achieves this, a brokered convention takes place requiring more rounds of voting.	**3. To act as publicity for the candidate** Conventions mark the start of the campaign and are a key part of the process. The winning candidate can sell their message to the public, often through attacks on the other party, stage-managed speeches by other politicians and endorsements by celebrities. The choice of state is also important: party conventions are often held in swing states.
2. Decide the policy platform Delegates debate and vote to determine the policy of the party (and therefore the candidate) for the presidential election. The convention takes place over several days, allowing for detailed policy debate.	**4. To reunite the party** Conventions can be very important for parties after the divisive primary process. The battle between candidates from the same party can be put aside. Losing candidates often give speeches endorsing the winner. This can create positive publicity and help win the election. **5. To rally party activists** Conventions are attended and watched by party activists who are crucial in helping a candidate win. They organise events, contact voters and raise funds. A good convention will address these people, as well as the general public, to thank and enthuse them.

Figure 1.6: Significant and superficial roles of party conventions

Republican National Convention 2016	Democratic National Convention 2016
July 18–21, Ohio (a state won by Trump)	July 25–28, Pennsylvania (a state won by Trump)
Many prominent Republicans did not attend. Trump gained endorsements from some losing primary candidates, such as Chris Christie and Ben Carson, who spoke at the convention.	A united convention with progressives such as Warren and Sanders giving highly supportive speeches. Barack Obama, Michelle Obama and Bill Clinton also gave speeches. Sanders' team was given a role in drafting the party platform.
Melania Trump gave a speech, but was accused of plagiarising a speech by Michelle Obama.	Some Sanders supporters organised protests, accusing the DNC of bias against Sanders in both the primaries and planning of the convention.
Ted Cruz's speech was perhaps the most remarkable as he used it to snub Trump. Rather than giving an endorsement, Cruz urged voters to 'vote your conscience'.	The convention made use of music stars including Paul Simon, Alicia Keys, Katy Perry and Lady Gaga.

Republican National Convention 2016	Democratic National Convention 2016
The official party platform opposed gay marriage. However, Peter Thiel, PayPal's co-founder, gave a speech on the importance of economic strategy, saying issues of who should use which bathroom should not dominate their thinking. He was the first Republican convention speaker to refer to his homosexuality.	A rule change was adopted to reduce the role of 'superdelegates'. The Sanders team wanted superdelegates to be bound to public voting, but a compromise meant that about two-thirds of superdelegates are bound to state results.
Trump's final-night speech appealed to his populist base, talking about immigration and his proposed wall at the Mexican border, terrorism and withdrawal from trade deals. He pledged to protect LGBT rights from a 'hateful foreign ideology'. Some pollsters reported a 3–4% bounce in ratings. **Final night broadcast audience: 34.9 million**	Clinton's final-night speech focused on her experience, judgement and compassion based on experience. Clinton prioritised job creation, appealing to Trump's key demographic support, as well as climate change and college affordability. She also attacked 'little men' like Trump. **Final night broadcast audience: 33.7 million**

Table 1.1: Comparison of the two national conventions in 2016

Pause & reflect

Look at Figure 1.6 and Table 1.1 together. How are the roles in Figure 1.6 reflected in Table 1.1?

The electoral college

Article II of the Constitution outlines the need for the president to be elected every four years using an electoral college, with the electorate in all states voting on the same day. The Founding Fathers feared popular sovereignty, so they created the electoral college to act as a filter or check on public opinion.

How does it work?

- Each state has a value of electoral college votes (ECV) based on the number of Congresspersons plus the number of Senators (in other words, +2) for that state. In addition, the 23rd amendment gives Washington DC three ECV.
- Candidates compete on a state-by-state basis, with the winner receiving all the electoral college votes in that state.
- All states use a winner-takes-all system (even though the Constitution lets states decide how to allocate ECV).
- To win the presidency a candidate requires more than 50 per cent of ECV: 270 of the 538 votes available.
- The ECV is not simply a points-based system. In each state, the ECV number represents the number of delegates (or electors) who are selected.
- Larger states have a larger number of delegates, although this is not proportional to population. The Constitution says that the value of each state is equal to the number of Congresspersons plus the number of Senators.
- The 538 delegates who make up the electoral college vote to decide who the president will be.
- Most states require their delegates to vote according to state opinion, but 21 states make no such requirement.
- Maine and Nebraska use a winner-takes-all system, but two of their ECV are allocated to the winner of the whole state, and further ECV are awarded to the winner in each district within the state.

- The system is based on a respect for the principle of federalism, with voting taking place in each state and smaller states being protected, as they are over-represented by the allocation of ECV.

- If no candidate wins an absolute majority of electoral votes, the Constitution states that it is up to the House of Representatives to choose the president. Each state receives one vote. Therefore the representatives of each state must first decide between themselves who they support, and then they would vote as one. Thus, the winner would require an absolute majority of 26 or more out of the 50 votes.

- If no candidate wins an absolute majority of electoral votes, the vice president is chosen by the Senate. Each Senator gets one vote, and an absolute majority is necessary: 50 per cent +1 vote.

- Only twice in the history of the country has a candidate not received an absolute majority of electoral votes: in 1800 and in 1824.

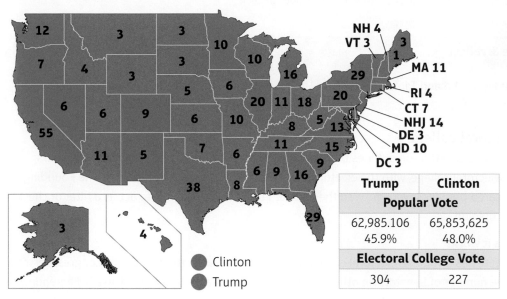

	Trump	Clinton
Popular Vote		
	62,985.106 45.9%	65,853,625 48.0%
Electoral College Vote		
	304	227

Figure 1.7: The 2016 presidential election result

'Rogue' or 'faithless' electors

There are 21 states with no requirement that the electors follow public voting, so some delegates occasionally vote contrary to the wishes of the people. This has happened in the majority of elections since 1960, although it has never changed a result. In 2016 there were seven rogue delegates. Clinton lost five delegates who should have voted for her; three of those votes went to Colin Powell, a Republican politician, while Bernie Sanders and Faith Spotted Eagle – a Native American activist – received one each.

The party system

A **party system** refers to the number of **parties** that have a realistic chance of forming a government within a political system. It is easy to argue that the United States is a two-party system, but there has been much debate about the extent to which each party works as a collective unit. Parties are so weak, it is argued, that they are not key actors within the political system.

The two-party system can easily be seen in the dominance of the Democratic and Republican Parties at all levels. All modern presidents have been Democrats or Republicans, and third parties typically have no seats in Congress. The 2016 elections were entirely dominated by two

Link

For more on **parties**, see Section 2.3 of US Congress.

Key term

Party system
the number of parties that have a realistic chance of forming government within a political system.

parties – there are only two parties in Congress; there are no third-party governors. Despite declaring himself to be an Independent, Sanders stood as a Democrat in the 2016 presidential primaries, caucused with Democrats in Congress, attended Democrat meetings and worked with Democrat leaders.

Third parties have had limited success through indirect influence:

- **The spoiler effect:** When a third-party candidate helps to prevent one of the Democratic or Republican Party from winning. In 2000, the Green Party candidate, Ralph Nader, may have prevented Al Gore (the Democratic nominee) from winning the presidency against Bush by taking votes away from Gore. If Gore had won Florida he would have won the presidency but lost the state by just 537 votes. Nader, whose supporters were much more likely to support Gore than Bush, received 97,000 votes.

- **Influencing the policy of Democratic or Republican Parties:** The last third-party candidate to receive significant votes for the presidency was Ross Perot in 1992 and 1996. While he failed to win the presidency, his popular economic policy of a balanced budget was embraced by Republicans and accepted by President Bill Clinton, with Perot's policy being successfully executed.

- **Infiltrating the two main parties, using primaries to gain prominence within a party:** Arguably, President Trump is an example of a successful third-party candidate, using the Republican primaries to run under their banner, even though the Republican establishment opposed his bid.

Incumbency

In the past ten presidential elections where the incumbent is in the race, only three presidents have lost. One of these, Ford, is a special case, as he rose to office as vice president to the discredited President Nixon, who resigned as a result of the Watergate scandal. This leaves Carter and Bush Snr as recent incumbent losers. Presidents Reagan, Clinton, George W. Bush and Obama each secured two election victories. In the last 57 US presidential elections, 32 have involved incumbents and 22 of those candidates have won – a win rate of 68.7 per cent.

	Incumbent: win or lose	2nd term challenger	Previous political office
Carter	lose	Ronald Reagan	Governor
Reagan	win	Walter Mondale	Vice president
Bush Snr	lose	Bill Clinton	Governor
Clinton	win	Bob Dole	Senator
Bush Jnr	win	John Kerry	Senator
Obama	win	Mitt Romney	Governor

Table 1.2: Wins or losses for recent incumbents

There is evidence, then, that it is beneficial to be in office when challenging for the presidency. The history of US presidential elections suggests that incumbency advantage exists, but it is not a cast-iron predictor of victory, as Table 1.2 shows. Presidents can and do exploit the powers of their office to increase their prospects for re-election, but a number of other factors influence the result, such as the personality, character and personal history of candidates, their ideologies and policies. Unexpected events can also tip the election in favour of one candidate over another.

Incumbency advantages	Limits to incumbency advantage
Executive control and experience	
Presidents can bring benefits to key groups and swing states or make popular policy shifts before an election. In 2011, Obama announced the main withdrawal of troops from Afghanistan. He could claim a major success in the killing of Osama bin Laden in 2011. In office, he rewarded key voting blocs, such as Hispanics, with executive orders on immigration and the appointment of the first Hispanic Supreme Court justice. Mitt Romney could do none of this.	Being in the White House can be double-edged. Presidents can receive praise, but also blame when things go wrong. Obama had to counter accusations of leadership failure over health care reform. The failing economy under President George H.W. Bush and his subsequent willingness to compromise on his famous campaign promise ('Read my lips: no new taxes') helped his demise.
Name recognition and media attention	
Presidents can attract publicity and sell their message. The Rose Garden strategy, in which the president addresses the nation, highlights the importance of the incumbent's work. Obama's speech on the death of US officials in Benghazi in 2012 highlighted his role as commander in chief at a time of great national significance.	Others can exploit the media. Presidential television debates allow challengers to impress on voters their advantages over a president. Reagan put Carter in his place in a television debate performance, asking the audience if they were better off than they were four years ago, and commenting 'There you go again'.
Electoral resources and experience	
The incumbent has an established campaign team with a proven track record. Incumbents also typically outspend their opponents. A rare exception was in 1992 when Clinton outspent the incumbent Bush. Here, however, it was Clinton the challenger who won the election.	Money does not guarantee success. Jeb Bush raised record sums in the 2016 Republican primaries, but still lost. Clinton outspent Trump in 2016. Also popularity may raise money, not the other way around. Perhaps Obama raised more than Romney because he was more popular.
Lack of primary challenge	
Incumbent presidents do not usually face a primary challenge. Challengers often face a long, bitter and expensive battle in which they are attacked by members of their own party. Romney faced this in 2012 when one of his defeated opponents, Ron Paul, continued to attack Romney at the party convention.	If incumbents do face primary challenges, this can be a bad omen for presidential bids. In 1992, George H.W. Bush won a primary challenge, but lost the election. Primaries may give a challenger the opportunity to show political strength and to take media focus away from the incumbent president.

Table 1.3: Advantages and disadvantages of incumbency

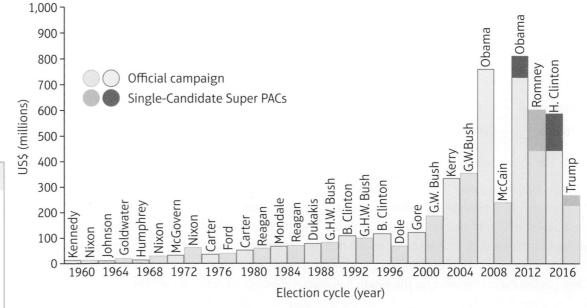

Pause & reflect ✔

What does incumbency advantage mean? Does it refer to an advantage for the person in office or for the party in office? What is the difference?

Figure 1.8: Presidential campaign spending 1960–2016

Campaign finance

Campaign finance refers to the funding of election campaigns. Expenditure can come from individuals, interest groups and businesses who are donating to campaigns, as well as the money spent by parties and candidates to try to ensure electoral victory. It can also include expenditure by other organisations (such as interest groups and corporations) that is not donated to a candidate but is spent, usually in the form of publicity, by that group to influence the outcome of elections. Candidates raise large amounts of money in order to run an effective campaign, with most of this money being spent on advertising. Money is also spent on an expensive campaign team, including technology advice and support. Without high levels of spending it is extremely difficult for a candidate to compete against other, better funded candidates.

In *McCutcheon v FEC* 2014, the Supreme Court struck down limits on individual campaign contributions, ruling that federal limits on combined donations to candidates, parties and **Political Action Committees** were an unconstitutional infringement on free speech. Chief Justice John Roberts ruled that Congress 'may not… regulate contributions simply to reduce the amount of money in politics, or to restrict the political participation of some in order to enhance the relative influence of others'.

Where campaign finance goes

Campaign donations can go to three different places:

- national parties
- presidential candidates
- Super PACs.

There have been major concerns over the role of money in US elections. The three main concerns are:

- excessive influence of major donors
- secrecy surrounding who is donating and receiving cash
- inequality of expenditure between candidates or parties.

Various laws called 'campaign finance regulations' have been passed to regulate money in elections. The two major regulations on presidential elections are the Federal Election Campaign Act (1974) and the Bipartisan Campaign Reform Act (known also by its sponsors, The McCain-Feingold Act) 2002. This was followed by the *Citizens United v Federal Election Commission* ruling in 2010.

FECA: the Federal Election Campaign Act (1974)

This law was introduced to regulate money in elections.

> **Main impacts of FECA**
>
> - Places legal limits on campaign contributions – a private individual can only donate $2,700 and a group can only donate $5,000 to an individual candidate.
> - Creates a maximum expenditure limit for each candidate in the presidential election.
> - Requires candidates to disclose sources of campaign contributions and campaign expenditure.
> - Created federal funding of presidential and primary elections, which works on a matching funds basis (for every dollar a candidate raises, they are given a dollar by the federal government). To qualify, a party must receive 5 per cent or more of the vote in the previous election.

- Created Political Action Committees. A PAC has to be created by any group wanting to donate money to a campaign. Businesses and interest groups create a PAC that is legally registered with the Federal Election Commission (FEC), a six-member bipartisan committee to oversee finance rules.

The law had many flaws, which severely reduced the effectiveness of the regulations.

- **Soft money**
Soft money is money donated (by interest groups or individuals) or spent (by parties or candidates) that could not be regulated under the law. Loopholes allowed for continued donations or spending without regulations. Business or interest groups spend money on campaign advertising for or against a candidate, without directly donating money to a candidate's campaign, for example.

- **Supreme Court**
Various Supreme Court rulings, often based on the 1st amendment, undermined legislation, making it harder to restrict donations and expenditure. For example, the restrictions cover funding of candidates, but not funding of parties. A party can spend money supposedly for the purposes of party building and voter education, but in fact use this to support a candidate. The Supreme Court also decided that the candidate's own money was exempt from restrictions.

- **The end of federal funding**
Candidates became increasingly effective at raising money. In 2000 George W. Bush raised more than the campaign limit (approximately $120 million) without using federal funds. By rejecting federal funds he was not constrained by campaign expenditure limits. This made it much harder for Al Gore, who took matching funds, to compete. In 2004 Bush repeated the feat against Kerry, who took matching funds. 2012 was the first election when neither candidate accepted matching funds; this was repeated in 2016.

These failures led to the creation of the Bipartisan Campaign Reform Act 2002, which:

- banned soft-money donations to national parties (all money raised or spent was now subject to federal limits)

- said that soft-money donations to local parties could not be used to support federal candidates, but only for genuine party-building activities

- said that issue adverts could not be funded directly by unions or corporations

- said that issue adverts mentioning a candidate's name could not be shown within 60 days of an election, or 30 days of a primary, unless approved by one of the candidates, with money spent being covered by spending regulations.

Difficulty in achieving effective reform

Campaign finance laws have had limited effectiveness for a variety of reasons. In addition, it has proven difficult to overcome these limitations:

- the ability of groups to find loopholes (soft money)

- the 1st amendment and the ideological balance of the Supreme Court in striking down key provisions

- the lack of legislation on the issue, which occurs both because it is difficult to pass legislation through Congress and perhaps due to unwillingness for politicians to regulate themselves

- the difficulty in amending the Constitution to regulate elections, such as Sanders' failed 'Democracy for all' amendment.

Super PACs

The Bipartisan Campaign Reform Act 2002 was dealt a major blow with the *Citizens United v Federal Election Commission* ruling in 2010, which struck down key parts of the legislation. The 5-4 ruling declared that the BCRA infringed 1st amendment rights.

This gave rise to new organisations set up solely to influence electoral outcomes without directly working with or donating to a candidate. These '**Super PACs**' raise funds from individual and group donors and spend this mainly on campaign advertising, without any campaign finance restrictions. Super PACs are typically created to support a particular presidential candidate.

Since the 2010 mid-term congressional elections, campaigns have been dominated by these organisations. Opensecrets.org reported that by 2016 there were 2398 Super PACS, raising over $1.5 billion during that year's elections.

Name	Rank	Supporting	2016 total	Ideology
Priorities USA Action	1	Clinton	$132,284,461	Liberal
Right to Rise	2	Bush	$86,817,138	Conservative
Senate leadership fund	3	Republican Senate	$85,964,625	Conservative
Conservative Solutions	5	Rubio	$55,443,483	Conservative
Rebuilding America Now	13	Trump	$19,846,597	Conservative
League of Conservation Voters	20	Environment	$14,043,293	Liberal
Make America Number 1	21	Cruz	$13,332,395	Conservative

Table 1.4: Some Super PACs in the 2016 election (Source: www.opensecrets.org)

Right to Rise was actually created by Jeb Bush, who raised funds for it until he declared his candidacy, when control was passed to Mike Murphy, a former political adviser to Mitt Romney. The Super PAC was also criticised for focusing negative advertisements mainly on the perceived main rival, Marco Rubio, rather than on now-President Donald Trump.

EXTENSION ACTIVITY

Super PACs are criticised for encouraging:

- inequality of funding
- negative campaigning
- excessive influence of major donors.

Do some research to find out more about these criticisms. Make notes on specific arguments or examples you find.

5.2 Key ideas and principles of the Democratic and Republican Parties

United States politics is dominated by two political parties: the Democrats, representing more liberal, left-wing policies and the Republicans, representing the right.

While the Democrats are on the left of the political spectrum in the United States, they might not be on the left in other countries, such as in Western Europe. There are many Democrat policies that the modern UK Conservative Party would embrace, and many Republican policies that Conservatives might reject. The Affordable Care Act, a move to ensure that all Americans have health insurance, has been attacked as a socialist or even communist policy in the United States, but is something most Conservative MPs would easily support.

Social and moral issues

Democrats are described as progressives on social and moral issues, while Republicans typically take a more conservative approach. Democrats tend to support greater protection of individual liberty and the prevention of discrimination. Modern Democrats have supported stronger rights for racial minorities, women and the LGBT community; Republicans have often resisted such changes.

Republicans tend to promote more traditional values, sometimes arguing for religious choice or states' rights to be given priority over other rights – for example, with gay rights or abortion.

- The two parties clashed over the civil rights movement, especially the passing of the Civil Rights Act in 1964, with continued conflict over racial issues, such as state voting regulations and the Voting Rights Act.

- The congressional vote to ban partial-birth abortion in 2003 was supported almost unanimously by Republicans, with a clear majority of Democrats opposing the bill.

- Democrats have been very supportive of LGBT rights, including the right to be allowed to use the bathroom (toilet) of their chosen gender; Republicans have typically opposed this. Obama cut federal funding to Republican-dominated North Carolina for its rejection of this right.

In 2016 Democrat Congressman Sean Maloney proposed an amendment to legislation: if a company did not comply with President Obama's executive order banning federal contractors from discriminating against LGBT workers, it would not receive federal funds. Forty-three Republicans voted for the Maloney legislation, while the vast majority of Republicans voted against it. Republicans proposed a further amendment to stop the Obama administration blocking North Carolina from receiving federal funds. Other Democrat initiatives included their 'no bill, no break' stance in 2016 when they organised a 16-hour sit-in at the House of Representatives, disrupting normal House business and urging greater gun control. Sitting on the House floor, they continued to live-stream their protest using their phones after 10 p.m., when the cameras were turned off in the room.

Economic policy

Democrats tend to call for greater governmental intervention in the national economy, mainly as a way of providing social justice, bringing social and economic benefits for those on lower incomes. Democrats generally see capitalism and free-market economics as positive, but they emphasise the need for protection for those who most need it. This could involve higher government expenditure to provide welfare services and regulations.

Republicans have a much more restricted view of governmental intervention in the national economy. Republicans emphasise the idea of personal responsibility and personal freedom from government control, with Democrats arguing for greater protection for lower socio-economic groups who have little control over the economic situation they find themselves in.

On taxation, Republicans have tended to favour tax cuts more than Democrats; Republicans focus those tax cuts on wealthier groups. In the 2016 election Clinton proposed a rise in the top rate of income tax, while Trump proposed major tax cuts for the wealthy.

Democrats typically support an increase in the federal minimum wage. In 2007, the new Democratic majority in the House initiated a rise to $7.25. All Democrats voted for the increased figure, while most Republicans opposed it. In 2016 the Democratic Party platform included a pledge to raise the figure to over $15; Republican Speaker Paul Ryan said this would 'do more harm than good'.

Provision of social welfare

Democrats have long favoured government provision of social welfare. They argue that the economic system provides a structure that does not promote the interests of everyone, so the government has a responsibility to intervene to provide a better life for everyone. This involves higher levels of benefits and funding for social programmes to help those who are less well-off, and to resolve social problems.

Republicans, emphasising personal responsibility and criticising the government's role as an infringement on individual freedom, have accepted the need for some welfare provision but have been more likely to restrict its use.

The Affordable Care Act was particularly aimed at the 46 million Americans, typically on lower (or no) incomes, who did not have health insurance. This act was eventually passed through a Democrat Congress in 2010, with all Republicans in the House and Senate voting against it.

While Republicans accept some need for food stamps for those in financial difficulty, they have generally pushed for cuts in the Supplemental Nutrition Assistance Program (SNAP), which gave $45 billion in food assistance to 43 million Americans in 2016. Democrats have strongly opposed these cuts. Jim McGovern, ranking member of the House Agriculture Committee, supported the programme, arguing that it keeps five million children out of poverty. Paul Ryan's 2016 poverty review proposed a $27-billion cut in food stamps over 10 years.

Conflicts and tendencies

The two main parties in the United States are weak, in the sense that:

- they lack strong leadership, which can create party unity
- they tend to have a great diversity of views and policies.

This has led some to claim that parties have a limited role in United States politics, which is better viewed as a battle of individuals who use party labels.

Another view emphasises the importance of **factions** within parties and the rivalry between them. These factions show the overlap between the two parties, with liberal Republicans sharing common ground with conservative Democrats.

Factions in the Democratic Party
Moderates
Sometimes known as centrists, moderate Democrats identify with centrism and compromise. It is typically the areas of the economy and welfare in which these moderates take a middle-ground approach. Moderate Democrats are more willing than others to end or reduce government-sponsored initiatives, as indicated by their support for welfare reform and tax cuts. On moral issues, there are areas where they may accept limitations to civil liberties to an extent that liberal Democrats would not. This might include greater restrictions on abortion or the acceptance of anti-terror laws.

This faction was organised around the Democratic Leadership Council, created in 1985 as a reaction to a second defeat in presidential elections to Ronald Reagan. They argued that a more moderate approach was needed to gain electoral success. They became more important in the 1990s as Democrats tried to overcome several presidential election defeats.

While the group dissolved in 2011, moderates represent the dominant force in the Democratic Party. Many members of Congress hold moderate views, and recent Democratic presidential candidates all reflect the moderate wing. Obama did not fit easily into either wing of the party, but there was a lot of evidence of his moderate approach, such as his willingness to compromise on health care reform and the federal budget.

Liberals
Liberals, or progressives, represent the more radical, left-wing elements of the party. Liberals are more determined in using the federal government to achieve social justice, by providing welfare, health and education for those who are disadvantaged and by increasing taxes on the wealthy. They support more government intervention in the economy and less intervention in deploying the

Pause & reflect

Do some research to find specific examples of current policies that fit the headings above.

EXTENSION ACTIVITY

Using the internet, research the latest policy battles between the two parties, using the three headings above. Look at legislation being debated in Congress and at the key political figures associated with a policy. What areas of overlap can you see between the two parties?

Key term

Factions
subgroups – ideological wings, particular age and occupation groups, and citizens concerned about particular issues – that make up political parties.

American military abroad. Liberals generally supported Obama, while at times feeling frustrated by him. They have been the faction most critical of the Republican Party, and most supportive of social and economic equality.

The more liberal elements of the party pushed Obama to reject the Trans-Pacific Partnership and reject certain Republican budget agreements in order to protect welfare expenditure. For example, Senator Elizabeth Warren, a leading liberal Democrat, publicly criticised Obama on issues including TPP, which she attacked for strengthening a system rigged to favour corporations over workers. Liberal Democrats have often opposed military intervention and were pleased to have Obama as their president, given his anti-Iraq War views. However, they opposed Obama on a number of defence issues, with 85 House Democrats opposing plans for the United States to arm Syrian rebels.

Conservatives

Conservative or 'Blue Dog' Democrats are a dying breed. The Democratic Party was once very conservative, with an influential Southern wing dating back to the end of slavery after the Civil War (1861–1865). While this changed, there remains a viable conservative wing of the Democratic Party.

Blue Dogs are conservative on moral issues, such as religion and guns, while disagreeing with the Republican Party's conservative views on trade and tax. In 2015, 47 House Democrats voted in favour of a Republican-led measure to have additional screening of Iraqi and Syrian refugees, despite Obama's opposition.

Despite the apparent demise of conservative Democrats, some progressives view Hillary Clinton as one. The *Huffington Post* ran an article stating that there was a moderate Republican in the 2016 primaries but she was running in the Democratic party.

Factions in the Republican Party
Social conservatives

Social or moral conservatives support traditional norms and values as part of the **religious right**. They focus on morality according to their religious beliefs (mainly Protestant and Evangelical Christianity). Social conservatives generally have a negative view of illegal immigration and oppose gay rights and abortion rights. On the economy and foreign affairs, they tend to support the official conservative Republican platform. This faction has grown to be a dominant force in the Republican Party, with a huge rise in support from Evangelicals.

The rise of social conservatism can be seen in Congress. In 2003, an overwhelming majority of Republicans supported the ban on partial-birth (late-term) abortion, and in 2016 only a few Republicans voted for the gay-rights legislative amendment. The failure of an immigration reform bill in 2013 could also be seen as a success for social conservatives.

Fiscal conservatives

Fiscal conservatives drive a conservative economic agenda, advocating a smaller government, especially one that follows a laissez-faire economic policy. Most fiscal conservatives support the abolition of the estate tax (inheritance tax) and reductions in other tax rates, as well as a cut in federal expenditure. This group became dominant in the 1990s, when Speaker Newt Gingrich led the Contract with America – a manifesto focusing on economic responsibility and a balanced budget.

Fiscal conservatism can be seen in the rising influence of the Republicans' Freedom Caucus. The defeat of moderate conservatives by Tea Party candidates in primaries in 2010, 2012 and 2014 helped push the party to the right. This sparked the development of the Freedom Caucus, containing approximately 40 members of the House, which has pushed a conservative fiscal and social agenda with a 'no compromise' attitude. It refused to support Obama's economic packages or seek compromise in any way, and prevented moderate and even conservative Republican plans

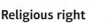

Key term

Religious right
an ultraconservative religious response to the sexual revolution, promoting family values, opposing abortion and the 1973 *Roe v Wade* judgment, same-sex marriage, civil partnerships and non-discrimination laws.

to compromise on legislative deals. In 2017 the Freedom Caucus attempted to exert influence over the Trump presidency by sending him a list of 228 regulations that it wants removed, including environmental regulations, nutrition rules for school meals and corporate regulations. It has largely replaced the Tea Party as the main right-wing faction of the Republican Party.

Moderates

Moderates support traditional conservative economic policies, such as low taxation and small government. However, they are typically more socially liberal than social conservatives – for example, they support civil-rights issues including gay rights and abortion. Moderates will accept higher taxes or more government programmes in order to support greater social harmony.

Moderates have gained positions of power in the party. For example, President George W. Bush horrified conservatives with major increases in government expenditure and his push for more liberal immigration reform. Relative moderates John Boehner and Paul Ryan have resisted attempts by others to push the party further to the right.

The most moderate are sometimes referred to as RINOs (Republican in Name Only). Senator Susan Collins of Maine was one of only three Republicans to support Obama's 2009 stimulus package budget. She supports gay rights, and she tried to broker a compromise deal over Obama's plans to increase the federal minimum wage. This RINO faction is more willing to compromise with Democrats in order to allow policy to pass.

Moderates are organised into the Main Street Partnership, a caucus created in 1994 as a reaction to the rise of conservative Republicans. Following the 2016 elections, the moderates made up a larger group of congressional politicians than the Freedom Caucus. They have lost power, however, as they have shown a lack of willingness to compromise and build a coalition with moderate Democrats as the two parties have moved further apart. However, their website lists many bills initiated by their members that have successfully passed into law.

EXTENSION ACTIVITY

Using the internet, find examples of the power and limit of any of the factions above. Is there any evidence of growing factions in Congress? How has the relationship between Trump and senior congressional Republicans like Ryan and McCarthy developed?

Case study: President Trump and the Trumpistas – America's first independent president?

President Trump is officially a Republican president, but many aspects of his views and policies put him at odds with the Republican Party – and give him common ground with Democrats. President Trump has no direct political experience, entering the presidential race directly from business and media. He used the Republican primaries to launch a hostile takeover of the party: voters selected a candidate whom most senior Republicans strongly opposed, especially in private. Reince Priebus (then head of the RNC) refused to campaign with him, Paul Ryan initially refused to endorse him, and Senator McCain and Mitt Romney openly attacked the Trump candidacy.

Trump's policies are met with both horror and delight by those on the Republican right. His populist attacks on racial minorities and abortion rights please the social conservatives, and his desire to cut financial regulations and reduce corporation tax is welcomed by fiscal conservatives. However, many of his policies are what would be expected from more radical, progressive Democrats, such as opposition to international trade deals like the TPP. In particular, Trump's trillion-dollar infrastructure plan could be seen as the opposite of fiscal conservative traditions.

Trump and Speaker Paul Ryan pulled the American Health Care Act (to reform the Affordable Care Act) in March 2017. Trump, despite concerted efforts, was unable to persuade any Democrats or enough Republicans to support the bill. Donald Trump's presidency is likely to have a major impact on both Republican and Democratic factions as congressional politicians work out how to work with him. Importantly, in Congress there is no Trump faction that backs all his policies and will fight for their passage in the legislature. Trump does have loyal 'Trumpistas', many of whom are ex-members of Congress or people who have left the Capitol to join his Cabinet – such as Jeff Sessions, Trump's pick for attorney general. Kevin McCarthy, Majority leader of the House is seen as a key Trump ally in Congress with the two having regular meetings both before and after the presidential election.

Questions

- What are the main reasons why Trump may be seen as an independent president and not a Democrat or Republican?
- What are the political advantages for Trump as someone who is not traditionally associated with either party?

Coalition of supporters

The Democratic and Republican Parties can usually rely on core voting groups for support in elections. Long-term factors based on the ideological heart of political parties and their policies have created long-term trends in voting patterns. However, short-term factors – such as economic or world crisis, or the race or gender of the candidate – may lead to fluctuations in these patterns.

As Figure 2.1 shows, race, religion, gender and education are all likely to influence voting patterns.

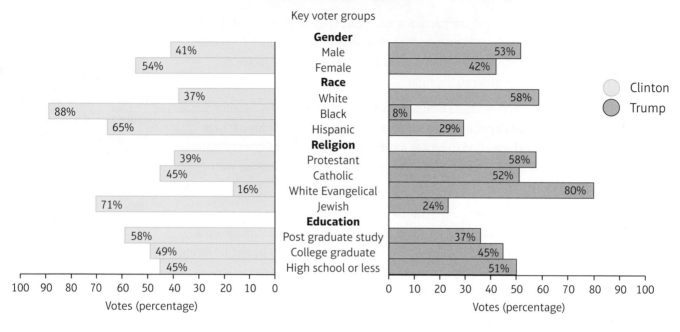

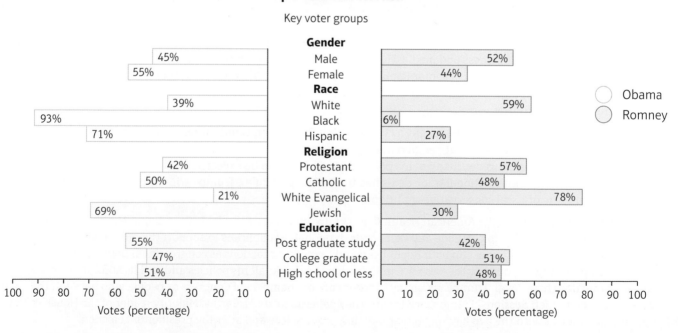

Figure 2.1: Voting patterns of key voter groups in the 2012 and 2016 presidential elections (Source: CNN exit polls)

Race

Here there are some consistent patterns, the most polarised being black voters strongly supporting the Democrats. This core voting group emerged in the 1960s, when Democrat President Johnson created the Civil Rights Act and Voting Rights Act. The Democratic Party has since championed racial-minority causes, supporting measures to end discrimination and give greater opportunities. For many black people the Republican Party is a toxic brand that has slowed the fight for equality. There is also an 'Obama effect', with record black turnouts in 2008 and 2012. In 2012, increased black voter turnout in marginal states made a major contribution to Obama's re-election.

The Hispanic vote is more volatile. In 2004 Republican George W. Bush secured 44 per cent of the Hispanic vote, but generally most Hispanic voters support the Democratic Party, because of its stronger stance for equality and against discrimination. With the recent focus on illegal immigration, Democrats have been far more supportive of liberal immigration reform, while Donald Trump's comments have angered many Hispanics. However, many Hispanic voters are social conservatives and support Republican views on abortion and gay marriage. Others have particular reasons for voting Republican, such as Hispanics who fled Castro's communist government and appreciate the party's hardline approach to relations with Cuba.

White voters are more evenly split, although most always select the Republican Party. Even when the Democratic candidate takes the White House, they do not get a majority of the white vote.

There are also more general socio-economic policies to consider. For example, statistically racial minorities are likely to be poorer than white people in the US, so are more likely to vote Democrat.

Religion

The clearest division here is with Jewish voters, who typically strongly support the Democratic Party. American Jews are usually strongly liberal, sympathising with the less fortunate and with minorities, and support greater government assistance for those with low socio-economic status. Despite issues with Israel and Palestine, Jews are far more likely to say that Muslims in America are discriminated against compared to the general population. However, Jews only make up around two per cent of the population.

Among Christian Protestants, there is stronger support for the Republican Party, particularly among white Evangelicals who identify with the strong streak of social conservatism running through the party. Many Republican politicians, such as Senator Ted Cruz, strongly oppose gay rights and attack immigration reform. Several Republicans take an Evangelical approach, saying that God is guiding them and they have a religious duty to influence the political process. Sarah Palin, a former Republican governor, said of the 2016 election: 'No doubt, divine providence played a huge role in this election… I saw it first-hand.'

Gender

Each group, men and women, is reasonably evenly split between the two main parties. However, there is a long-standing pattern in which most men support the Republican Party and most women support the Democrats. This is partly for broad ideological reasons: men have a more conservative outlook than women. Women may have a marginal preference for the Democrats because the Democratic Party has done more to fight for women's rights. Typically Democrats supported the failed Equal Rights amendment, with the greatest opposition coming from Republicans. There was bipartisan support for the Violence Against Women Act, but it was created and passed under Democratic control of the presidency and Congress in 1994. More recently Obama introduced the Lilly Ledbetter Fair Pay Act, attempting to secure equal pay for women, which was opposed by almost all Republicans in Congress. The Democratic Party also has significantly more congressional female politicians than the Republican Party.

Education

There is a clear trend in educational voting patterns: the less educated a voter is, the more likely they are to vote Republican. This is counterintuitive, given that lower income groups tend to vote Democrat. However, many people with relatively high incomes do not have a college degree.

The tipping point for those below college-level education came in 2016, when Trump won a majority of this group. Trump's populist anti-elitist agenda attracts those who may view those with higher education as part of a liberal elite protecting their own agenda.

'We won with young. We won with old. We won with highly educated. We won with poorly educated. I love the poorly educated.' Donald Trump 2016

Some people argue that education tends to produce more socially liberal values – such as greater acceptance of different racial groups and religions, and support for civil liberties – so more educated voters are more likely to reject the socially conservative elements of the Republican Party. However, some have argued that there is a tendency for liberals or Democrats to value education more, so they stay in education for longer – so being liberal leads to higher education, not the other way around.

EXTENSION ACTIVITY

Women are more likely to vote Democrat – but in 2016, female support for Clinton was lower than that for Obama in 2012, and most white women voted for Trump. Do some research to find out why this might have happened.

Key terms

Policy group
a group that attempts to influence a whole policy area.

Professional group
a group that represents the economic interests of its members.

Single-interest group
a group that advocates policy surrounding a limited, specific issue.

5.3 Interest groups in the USA

The term 'interest group' covers a multitude of different organisations in the United States with one thing in common: they are non-elected groups, with their own interest or cause, that try to influence government policy.

There are three types of interest group:

- **policy groups** that attempt to influence a whole policy area (such as the American Israel Public Affairs Committee, or AIPAC)
- **professional groups** that represent the economic interests of its members (such as the American Medical Association)
- **single-interest groups** that advocate policy surrounding a limited, specific issue (such as the National Rifle Association).

The significance of interest groups

Interest groups are highly influential partly because of the specific constitutional and political arrangements of the United States, which arguably allow them to have more influence than in any other country. Most groups can exert influence somewhere within the political system, so interest groups have a significant impact on policy-making.

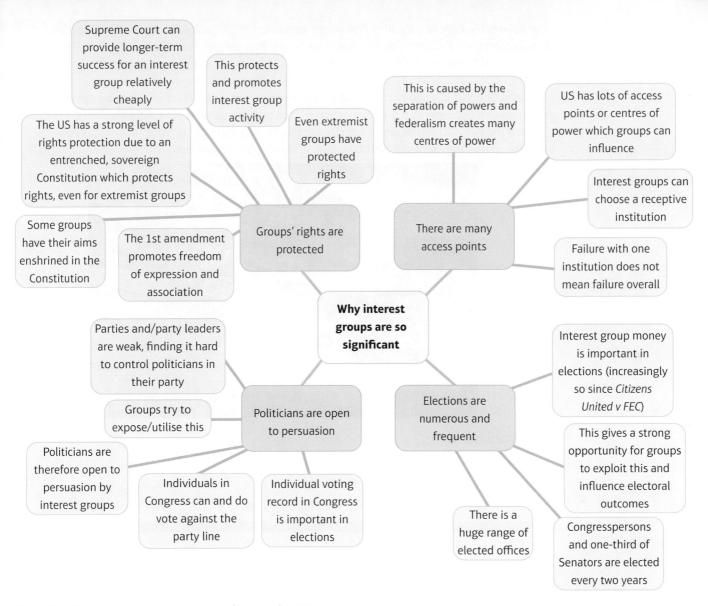

The four factors shown in Figure 3.1 suggest that power is inevitably shared in the United States system; interest groups are part of a pluralist system in which policy is made as a result of the compromise of different interests.

Figure 3.1: Why interest groups are so significant in the USA

> **Link** ↗
>
> For more on campaign finance, see Section 5.1.

> **Pause & reflect** ✔
>
> What is meant by access points? Why does the US have so many of them and what are the main ones? It may help to consider the differences between the US political and constitutional system and that of a dictatorship. Why do interest groups have so much power in the US but not in a dictatorship?

> **Link** ↗
>
> For an alternative view, arguing that the United States is in fact elitist, see the Policy Networks case study on page 439.

Case study: Professional group – AFL-CIO

The American Federation of Labor and Congress of Industrial Organizations (AFL-CIO) is the largest trade union in the United States with over 12 million members. It has close links with the Democratic Party. Its president, Richard Trumka, visited the White House six times in Obama's first six months in office and met with Obama in 2016 to lobby over concerns about the Affordable Care Act, a policy it strongly supported. With such a large membership, the group can be very effective at election time, organising volunteers to help influence electoral outcomes. It registered 450,000 new voters in 2012 and made 80 million phone calls during the election campaign. It has also had conflict with the Democratic Party – for example, it strongly opposed Obama's signing of the Trans-Pacific Partnership (TPP). Trumka wrote an open letter to Obama on the issue and publicly criticised him over the deal, saying it threatened US jobs. In 2016 the AFL-CIO campaigned heavily against Trump, focusing on marginal states such as Florida, where they sent out 120,000 copies of an anti-Trump leaflet.

Global Justice leaflet.

Questions

- What are the main methods of the AFL-CIO?
- What is the evidence of their influence and their limited influence over public policy?

Membership	An active membership can undertake grassroots lobbying to influence their members of Congress to support or oppose certain measures. Large groups can create an electoral threat to individual politicians. Members are often used at election time to contact potential voters to affect electoral outcomes, including turnout. This often targets swing constituencies or areas where the group knows it has strong support.	**Interest group resources**
Money	Strong financial resources allow interest groups to run more effective publicity campaigns. Many interest groups spend huge amounts of money on lobbying, which is expensive in the US. Interest groups also donate money to political campaigns.	
Contacts	Interest groups try to maximise their political contacts, often employing professional lobbyists who are former politicians or advisers. This creates contacts between some interest groups (especially major corporations) and politicians. A policy network develops in which at least some groups have high levels of influence.	
Expertise	Most groups establish expertise in their area, so they can lobby Congress and appeal to the public with greater authority. The importance of the Constitution and the law means that interest groups often employ legal experts to advise on how laws can be changed and provide constitutional lawyers to litigate in support of their cause.	

Table 3.1: Factors affecting the influence of specific groups

Interest group tactics

Publicity

Interest groups may use publicity to change public opinion, and may try to influence actual voting behaviour of the public – for example, by contacting potential voters who are likely to support the aims of the group.

Interest groups can run advertising campaigns through magazines, billboards or television, or can attract media attention with publicity stunts. For example, the National Rifle Association used television adverts to stop Obama and Congress from passing new gun regulations after the fatal shooting of school children and staff at the Sandy Hook Elementary School in 2012. One NRA television advert called Obama an 'elitist hypocrite', making reference to the fact that the president's own children had armed guards while at school, while Obama was reluctant to put armed security guards in schools in general.

Grassroots activity

Members of interest groups (rather than their leaders) can take part in email writing campaigns, demonstrations and direct action. The rise of the internet and social media has made this even easier for the general public. Most interest group websites have a 'take action' section, with model letters and a 'zip code engine' to find the address of someone's Congressperson or Senator. Demonstrations are common even among more powerful interest groups as a show of strength of feeling and to generate publicity, motivating others to act.

Legal methods

Many interest groups use the legal system to promote their cause or interest. Using the law and the Constitution can be powerful, especially to stop certain policies or practices. Some interest groups are strongly supported by the Constitution because it protects their aims. The NRA have had their cause protected in 2nd-amendment (the right to bear arms) Supreme Court cases such as *DC v Heller* 2008, which ruled that the 2nd amendment gives an individual a right to a gun.

The three main ways interest groups can influence the legal process are:

- through litigation – initiating a case by taking something to court
- through amicus briefs – in which the Supreme Court allows interest groups to provide information during a court case
- by influencing Supreme Court nominations – by lobbying the Senate.

Lobbying

Interest groups will often contact and persuade those in power. The separation of powers creates different access points, with a range of ways to find a responsive institution. An interest group that fails with one institution may have influence through another. Interest groups often concentrate on moderate or marginal politicians in order to influence legislative outcomes in Congress. Some interest groups even develop legislation or persuade members of Congress to do so. In addition, there are many professional lobbyists.

For example, AIPAC wanted to overturn the Iran deal that Obama had successfully negotiated, in which Iran agreed to halt its nuclear program. AIPAC attempted to pass a Senate resolution to block the deal, lobbying key Democrats such as Chuck Schumer (New York). AIPAC despatched 60 activists to his office to hold a meeting with Schumer, and he later opposed the Iran deal.

Link

For examples of how the NAACP use **grassroots activity** in their Moral Monday campaign, see Section 4.5 of US Supreme Court and Civil Rights.

Link

For more on the use of **legal methods**, see the case study on the American Civil Liberties Union on page 438.

Electioneering

Interest groups use elections to gain influence, through publicity, donations or canvassing. Interest groups can use elections to highlight key issues, but often try to influence electoral outcomes, sometimes campaigning for or against particular candidates. One main strategy is to maximise turnout among certain voters.

This has led to the creation of some interest groups specialising in affecting electoral outcomes, as can be seen in the case study of the League of Conservation Voters.

> ### Pause & reflect
>
> How successful are these tactics? Consider why one interest group featured in this section chooses certain methods and not others.

Case study: Policy group – The League of Conservation Voters (LCV)

The LCV is an environmental protection group interested in all aspects of environmental policy. It specialises in affecting electoral outcomes, to hold politicians accountable for the policies they make. It has campaigned to protect legislation such as the Clean Air Act and the Endangered Species Act. The LCV's top priority is climate change, and it works to publicise the negative impact global warming is having on the US (for example, by linking it to the $485 billion annual cost of extreme weather events in the US alone).

League of Conservation voters, a pro-environmental group, which targets US elections to achieve its aim.

The LCV funds the campaigns of pro-environment politicians, but its trademark campaign is 'The Dirty Dozen'. In each election, it selects 12 politicians who it views as posing the biggest threat to the environment. It then campaigns heavily against these 12, running poster, television and internet campaigns to expose connections between them and groups that may want harmful environmental policies. The LCV usually chooses more marginal races where it can have a greater impact. In 2012, 11 of the 12 were defeated, and in 2014, seven of the 12 were defeated. However, in 2016 only four of the 12 (including President Trump) were defeated.

Questions

- What are the main policy goals of the LCV?
- How successful have the LCV been in election campaigns?

Presidency	Congress	Supreme Court
• Lobby the president in order to bring about policy/legislative change. • Electioneer to change electoral outcomes and gain influence with candidates. • Publicise issues to generate positive or negative publicity for the president and their policy. • Super PACs are involved in raising funds and generating publicity for or against presidential (and congressional) candidates.	• Lobby congressional leaders or committee chairs especially over specific legislative requirements. • Lobby individual members of Congress, especially using constituents, to support or oppose a bill. • Propose and introduce legislation via a member of Congress. • Electioneer to change electoral outcomes and gain influence with candidates.	• Litigate by taking a case to the Supreme Court, often to challenge presidential action, congressional law or state law. • Lobby the court using an amicus brief. • Attempt to influence Supreme Court nominations by influencing the ratification vote in the Senate.

Table 3.2: How interest groups influence the three branches and policy creation

Interest groups and democracy

Interest groups clearly have a major impact on democracy in the United States, but it is hard to assess their overall impact. The central issue here is that democracy is not about moral right or wrong or producing good quality policy; it is simply the will of the people. If interest groups are increasing the political power of the people, they are improving democracy.

Arguments for interest groups enhancing democracy

Participation

Interest groups let the public get actively involved in US politics and increase their influence over politicians. Interest groups organise demonstrations, direct action and grassroots campaigns. Interest groups also raise awareness of issues and government responses, allowing people to understand key issues and to react. Interest groups add democratic value, partly because of low participation rates in United States elections. Many citizens are fed up with the two-party system, viewing themselves as independents. These people can use interest groups as a way to be involved in the political process. In 2016 the AFL-CIO said that it had used 2000 volunteers to contact six million voters in swing states to deliver an anti-Trump message.

Checks on government

It can be argued that interest groups enhance democracy by restricting the government. This can help stop government corruption or self-interest, maximising the wishes of the people. Groups can also help force the government to carry out their policy promises. Some groups such as the American Civil Liberties Union (ACLU) specialise in rights protection, encouraging the promotion of liberal democracy.

There is an argument that interest groups add little democratic value through checks. There are extensive checks in the system already, particularly through the separation of powers, so democracy is already highly protected from self-interest and abuse of power. Any group can use the system to have their interests considered. The NRA campaigned against Obama's gun laws by arguing that they are protecting individual freedom in the face of a self-interested president.

However, much depends on the nature of the group. It could be argued that interest groups are critical to democracy by protecting individual and minority groups when their rights are threatened. The **NAACP** protect voting rights by checking politicians who want to change electoral laws to reduce black people's ability to vote. Given concerns over the power of the state to maintain security, especially since 9/11, groups such as the ACLU (see case study below) play an important role in protecting liberal democracy.

Representation

Interest groups represent specific groups or interests in society, promoting their wishes and maximising their power. In particular, they can help represent a group whose interests may otherwise be overlooked – perhaps because that group is small or is ideologically incompatible with the government.

Again, it is possible to argue that interest groups cannot add much democratic value here. High levels of representation already exist as a result of the separation of powers and frequent elections, so interest groups are not needed. However, interest groups may become more important when one party controls the presidency, House, Senate and Supreme Court, as after the 2016 elections. Interest groups can also help overcome the limited representation in the US that results, in part, from the electoral college system and the use of a majoritarian voting system for Congress.

> **Link**
>
> For more on the **NAACP**, see Section 4.5 of US Supreme Court and Civil Rights.

Case study: Single-issue group – The American Civil Liberties Union

The ACLU aims to protect civil liberties, especially those protected by the Constitution. The group has focused on 1st amendment rights of freedom of expression. Founded in 1920, it has more than a million members. One of its main methods is litigation, launching court cases to protect individual freedom. In the two weeks after Trump was elected, the ACLU reported a huge increase in membership, with more than 120,000 new members.

American Civil Liberties Union, a group that specialises in the protection of constitutional rights.

The group strongly opposes many aspects of Trump's presidency, including Trump's nomination of Senator Jeff Sessions as attorney general. The ACLU takes issue with Sessions' position on LGBT rights, capital punishment, abortion rights, and presidential authority in times of war. Shortly after Trump's victory its website carried a picture of President Trump headed 'See you in court'. The ultra-liberal group has provided legal argument for groups regardless of their ideological stance, including the KKK and the Westboro Baptist Church (for example in its 37-page amicus brief in the *Snyder v Phelps* case 2011, involving homophobic demonstrations at funerals).

In 2016 the ACLU litigated on behalf of Suleiman Abdullah Salim, Mohamed Ahmed Ben Soud and Gul Rahman, who were tortured using methods developed by CIA-contracted psychologists James Mitchell and John 'Bruce' Jessen. Rahman died during his torture. The court was told that the CIA was operating on the orders of the president. The lawsuit against the private company is based on US law preventing gross violations of human rights.

Questions

- What are the different methods used by the ACLU?
- How influential have they been over public policy?

Arguments for interest groups restricting democracy

Violent and illegal activity

Some interest groups use violence or break the law as part of their campaign. This can undermine democracy in a number of ways. Firstly, breaking the law is a challenge to representative democracy, as laws have been passed using a democratic process. Secondly, violent and illegal activity can restrict the rights of others, limiting individual freedom. Interest groups may cause damage to property or life, attacking a key principle of democratic liberty. When the NAACP occupied the offices of a senior Republican politician in North Carolina, they were disrupting the representative process, arguably undermining democracy. This raises the question of whether illegal activity can ever benefit democracy. Some argue that the actions of the NAACP were promoting democracy by directly challenging laws that were already undermining democratic principles.

Restriction of elected government

Unlike politicians, interest groups have no elected mandate, yet they attempt to stop politicians making decisions. This can be seen as undermining the representative process. This is particularly the case if they prevent those in office from executing policy promises made at election time. When a range of groups, such as health insurance companies and the AARP (an interest group representing retired people that opposed sections of the proposal), lined up to stop Obama passing his Affordable Care Act – a key aspect of his electoral campaign – this arguably undermined democracy.

Inequality of representation

Interest groups contribute to the over-representation of minority groups and the marginalisation of other groups. Many argue that power is based on money: those with resources dominate decision-making, ensuring that policies favour that particular group. Professional lobbyists and the revolving door create a closed network of decision-making, magnifying the power of groups that already have political influence. The extent to which interest groups promote democracy can be based on whether they:

- promote pluralism, in which all interests in society have some policy influence, and policy is based on a compromise between different interests (even if it is largely based on the majority view)
- promote elitism, which is undemocratic, with policy being made in the interest of a small, powerful group or an elite.

Case study: Policy networks – corporations, professional lobbyists and politicians

John Boehner ran a business before he joined Congress. In 2016, he left his position as the speaker of the House of Representatives, and returned to the private sector, advising Squire Patton Boggs. SPB is one of the most influential professional lobbyists in the United States, with major clients such as Amazon, AT&T, Goldman Sachs and the Turkish government. SPB employs many former politicians and advisers with insider knowledge and contacts with the current Congress. It uses its expertise and connections to influence the legislative process on behalf of its clients. Given the expense of using professional lobbyists, many individuals and interest groups will not be able to afford these services.

Politicians' family members often work for – or create – professional lobbyist organisations. The lure of future million-dollar salaries encourages politicians to work closely with these organisations when in office. This brings a significant danger that politicians will work for the interest of themselves, their family and big business, but not the public.

Politicians, former politicians working for professional lobbyists and corporations can create a policy network that strongly influences law-making while excluding other interests. This community of decision-makers often excludes environmental groups, health groups and workers. Evidence for this can be seen in policy outcomes. For example, professional lobbyists working with the gambling industry used their connections with then Senate Minority Leader Harry Reid to add just 54 words to a spending bill in 2015, which saved the industry almost $1 billion in taxes. Despite the Republican Party's emphasis on economic austerity, it is willing to allow such tax cuts, pushed by lobbyists such as David Lugar, son of former Senator Richard Lugar, while cutting expenditure in other areas, such as welfare.

Questions
- What are the different ways in which the case study suggests that policy making is based on elitism?
- What are the possible counter-arguments to this view?

5.4 Interpretations and debates surrounding US democracy and participation

Advantages and disadvantages of the electoral college

Advantages

✔ **Respects the tradition of federalism:** By basing voting in individual states, the Founding Fathers emphasised the importance of states and state identity. Candidates are required to win the support of states. Smaller states are deliberately over-represented to make sure they are not intimidated by larger states; California has 63 times the population of Wyoming but only 18 times the ECV.

✔ **Produces a clear winner:** The winner-takes-all system helps to ensure that one candidate receives more than 50 per cent of the electoral college votes. This gives the elected president greater legitimacy, allowing them to govern more effectively. In 2012, Obama won 51 per cent of the popular vote, but received 332 of the 538 ECV – nearly 62 per cent. Even when there is a strong third-party candidate, one candidate typically receives an absolute majority. Despite the strong showing of Ross Perot in 1992 with 18.9 per cent of the popular vote, Clinton received 370 electoral college votes.

✔ **Protects low-turnout areas:** States are protected because they have a fixed value. In 2016 Minnesota had the highest turnout (74.2 per cent) and Utah and Hawaii had the lowest (57.7 and 42.5 per cent). Despite this, those who vote in Utah and Hawaii can still have an impact as their ECV values of 4 and 6 remain intact.

Disadvantages

✘ **The loser wins:** It is possible for one candidate to get the most votes, but for the other candidate to get elected by winning the most ECV. The United States has elected a president who the majority did not support five times in total, twice of those in recent years. President George W. Bush received almost half a million fewer votes than Al Gore in 2000, and in 2016 President Trump was easily beaten by Hillary Clinton, who received almost 3 million more votes.

✘ **Small states are over-represented:** Regardless of its size, each state has two Senators, and a minimum of one Congressperson – so a vote in Wyoming has greater value than one in California. This restricts the fundamental democratic principle of political equality.

✘ **Swing states are over-represented:** Most states are normally safe Republican or Democrat states, so the remaining marginal states are the decisive ones – the 'swing' or 'battleground' states. Candidates concentrate time and money on these swing states where winning could give them the ECVs that push them over the 270 mark. This gives the swing states disproportionate influence in selecting the president, and encourages candidates to offer greater political benefits to those states. Non-competitive elections in California and Texas mean that there is little point voting as the result is already decided. This can depress turnout rates.

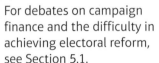

Link

For debates on campaign finance and the difficulty in achieving electoral reform, see Section 5.1.

Link

For debates on the role of incumbency in elections, see Section 5.1.

Link

For debates on the way in which interest groups can influence the three branches of government and policy creation, see Section 5.3.

Assessment support: 3.1.5 Democracy and Participation

Question 3 on A-Level Paper 3 requires you to answer two questions from a choice of three, each of which is worth 30 marks.

Evaluate the extent to which there is agreement on key ideas and principles between the Democratic and Republican Parties. [30 marks]

You must consider this view and the alternative to this view in a balanced way.

These questions require an essay-style answer. They test all three Assessment Objectives, with 10 marks available for each. These questions always ask you to **evaluate**. The requirement for **balance** means that you have to show an awareness of different arguments and viewpoints. It is essential to go beyond simply explaining what those different arguments and viewpoints are. Evaluation requires you to make a judgement about the strength of arguments rather than just stating them. You will need to do this throughout your answer and not just in a conclusion. You will need to show an awareness of different perspectives and to outline different arguments, typically using three or four well-evaluated arguments with counter-arguments. You will also need an introduction and a conclusion.

This question requires you to explore similarities and differences between the two main parties. The three policy areas covered in the specification (social and moral, economic and welfare) make a useful plan for many different questions on political parties.

Here is part of a student's answer.

Democrats and Republicans are in strong disagreement over moral policy. They usually have opposing views on abortion, gay rights and guns for example. Democrats have promoted greater civil rights for social groups such as women, racial minorities and members of the LGBT community. The Republicans have opposed transgender rights, coming into conflict with President Obama over his executive orders to attempt to give greater bathroom choice to transgender individuals. Almost all Republicans in Congress voted to undermine this order, which was repealed by Republican President Trump. There is therefore little or no sign of agreement in this area.

- Importantly, this answer states a difference then goes on to give specific policy details. In examinations a common mistake is to only write about general ideas (the Democrats support transgender rights) rather than specific contemporary evidence as above.

Here is another part of a student's answer.

It would be wrong to state that there is complete disagreement between the two parties. In some policy areas there are overlaps between the moderates in both parties. Moderate Democrats and Republicans have shown an ability to agree or compromise on economic policies such as the budget. Democratic Senate Majority Leader Chuck Schumer said that he could work with President Trump on economic policy, especially Trump's trillion dollar infrastructure plan. In immigration policy there was significant overlap with the Gang of 8 (4 Democrat and 4 Republicans) who agreed on immigration reform. There is a range of evidence, therefore, to show that there are some important points of agreement between the two parties.

- This makes good use of contemporary, detailed evidence. Showing knowledge of key political figures in Congress (such as Schumer) is important.

- Here the student also uses evidence to evaluate an argument, arguing that a range of evidence supports the view that there are some important points of agreement.

CHAPTER 6

Comparative Approaches

A stronger understanding of the US system of government can be gained by comparing it with the system in the UK. There are three different theoretical approaches you can apply to explain similarities and differences between the two systems.

In this chapter you will:

- look at the rational, cultural and structural approaches
- compare different aspects of the US and UK systems
- apply the different approaches when explaining similarities and differences.

6.1 Theoretical approaches

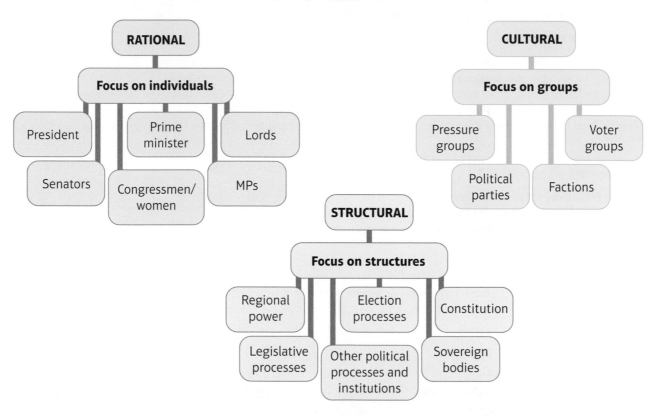

Figure 1.1: Three theoretical approaches

Rational

This approach focuses on individuals. It suggests that individuals' actions are guided more by consideration of their own interests than influence from groups or structures. By acting rationally, individuals judge how best to realise their own goals. These goals may be maintaining power within a political system or attempting to achieve ideological or policy goals, to make sure their views are put into practice.

This approach can be most effectively applied when looking at individuals within political systems such as president, prime minister, legislative politicians and voters.

- Comparing the power of the president and the prime minister, it could be noted that both act in a rational manner, using their own powers to achieve their policy goals. Both the president and prime minister have considerable authority as leaders of the government to set a political agenda for the country, based on their personal views. They also have power, particularly within the executive, to appoint people to key decision-making positions.

- Focusing on the power of a Congressperson and a Member of Parliament (MP), both might vote in Congress or in parliament, acting rationally to maintain their own position of power. They might resist structural and cultural factors. Members of Congress and parliament might ignore executive patronage-power or the dominant view of their party because they are trying to maintain their own political power by pleasing constituents.

Cultural

A cultural approach highlights the influence of groups, such as political parties, pressure groups, factions or groups of voters. It suggests that people operate as they do because of the group they are in. The group has a culture – shared ideas, beliefs and values – to which members conform, and which influences individual members' actions. While individuals often choose to join a group, this group can still influence or restrict their behaviour. Culture is habitual and perceived as natural, giving it power over individuals that they may not be aware of.

- Comparing the prime minister and president using a cultural approach, both may alter their policy goals because of the culture of their party. This can happen when their own views are out of step with the views of their party and the prime minister or president feels the need to adjust their aims.

- Looking at parties, with the high levels of party unity in the UK and increasingly in the US, there may be a dominant value system that leads to tribal politics, influencing the behaviour of politicians. Politicians are acting on the basis of party culture, without considering their own rational self-interest or structural influences.

Structural

Comparing the main political institutions or processes of the UK and US political systems involves a structural approach – a 'big picture' perspective. It often involves understanding the main constitutional roles, powers and limits of a political process or institution. The structural approach suggests that political actions are determined by these wider structures, and that the people who operate within politics are strongly influenced by them. The actions of individuals and groups are limited and largely determined by structures. The structural approach can be applied readily to all topics because major political structures, such as constitutions, influence or determine political processes in every area.

- Comparing the prime minister and president using the structural approach, the constitution provides a structure that restricts the office-holder's political actions. Both are subject to constitutional rules and may find that their powers or policy goals are restricted (for example, by the courts). Both presidents and prime ministers have seen some of their key policy goals restricted by court decisions.

- Looking at politicians in Congress and parliament, they have different levels of power from each other. Arguably, UK MPs are more limited because of the power of the executive (prime minister and government), whereas US members of Congress have greater ability to act as they wish because there is less pressure from the executive (president).

> **Pause & reflect**
>
> It is important to understand the three comparative approaches. Which of these three theories could you use to explain political institutions (such as president, Congress, parties, interest groups) and processes (such as voting, passing legislation, interpreting the constitution)?

6.2 Constitutions

The UK and US systems have a great deal in common – including being seen by some as models of democracy – but they have hugely different constitutional arrangements. These differences are the main reason behind the very different political processes and actions in the two countries. Here the structural approach is the most useful form of analysis. Constitutions are structures that affect so much of the rest of the political system and help to explain the main similarities and differences between the UK and US systems.

Similarities and differences

Codification and sources

The main function of a constitution is to set out the rules of the political game, by regulating the powers, roles and limits of all individuals and institutions involved in the political process. One fundamental difference is that the US Constitution is codified, while the UK constitution is not.

The UK constitution has a range of sources covering statute law, common law, conventions, authoritative works and treaties. The US Constitution has a single source, which could give it greater clarity and enable people to appreciate the rules more easily. The UK constitution does not have the same power as an idea over individuals and politicians, and it is less apparent what the rules are. This may mean that the US Constitution is a better guide to political practice. However, the US Constitution is still ambiguous. There are many debates about how the US Constitution should be applied, restricting its ability to be an effective guide.

In both countries, politicians may be able to evade rules by simply saying they do not apply in a particular case. For example, US presidents have claimed authority to initiate military action as commander in chief, despite Congress having the constitutional power to declare war. The vagueness of the US Constitution on the powers of states has led to huge transformations in federal–state relations, without any changes to the Constitution. This suggests that the Constitution has provided a very weak set of regulations in determining the power of the states.

Key principles and provisions of the US and UK constitutions
Provisions

UK		US
Parliamentary system Three separate branches (executive, legislature and judiciary), but they overlap or fuse power. At elections, people vote for the legislature (parliament) only. The government is drawn from and sits in parliament.	Separation of powers	**Presidential system** Separation of powers between executive, legislature and judiciary – no one can be part of two branches at the same time. Separate elections for the legislature (Congress) and executive (president).
• System of checks and balances exists between the three branches. • Parliament can check government by voting on government proposals and using a vote of no confidence. • House of Lords is unelected and cannot reject decisions made by the Commons. • Prime minister, as head of government, commands a majority in the House of Commons.	Checks and balances	• High premium placed on effective checks and balances between the three branches. • President can propose legislation, veto legislation, nominate to the executive and judiciary, and is commander in chief. • Congress can propose, amend and pass legislation, ratify treaties and appointments and declare war. • Both House and Senate provide powerful checks on the executive and each other.

UK		US
• Regional power given in the form of devolution. Parliament can give power to regions, but this power is not constitutionally guaranteed. • Different regions have different levels of power. Scottish parliament holds highest level; England has no devolved power at all.	Regional power	• Regional power created through the provision of federalism. • Power of states cannot be reduced without their consent through a 75% vote to amend the Constitution. • Regional power is even: each state has the same powers. • Regional power of states is more extensive than in the UK.
Parliamentary sovereignty: • Parliament has absolute power • Parliament can amend the constitution with a simple 50%+ vote in the House of Commons.	Location of sovereignty	Constitutional sovereignty: • Constitution is sovereign; its sovereignty is upheld by the Supreme Court • Constitution is entrenched, so is protected from change. Amendment requires supermajorities in House, Senate and states.
Main protection through the Human Rights Act 1998 and membership of the European Convention on Human Rights, which the UK joined in 1951.	Rights protection	Main protection through constitutionally entrenched rights, particularly in the Bill of Rights and the 14th amendment.
The constitution is easy to change with a 50%+ vote in the House of Commons.	Amendment process	The Constitution is entrenched and therefore difficult to change.

Table 2.1: Provisions of the US and UK constitutions

What are the significances of these differences?

Separation of powers

The fusion of powers in the UK provides the basis for greater executive domination. The parliamentary system means that the prime minister must command a majority in the House of Commons – a majority they can deploy to achieve their policy goals. US presidents are often in a situation where they lack a congressional majority, so are more subject to legislative opposition than a prime minister. Also, Congress and the president can claim an equal mandate and right to govern, which creates 'an invitation to struggle'. The awarding of a mandate in the UK is usually claimed by the winning party in government, in which the prime minister claims a right to put manifesto promises into practice.

Checks and balances

Both political systems provide checks and balances, with legislatures able to provide checks on the executive branch (for example, through voting on their legislative proposals). The UK's fusion of powers limits the effectiveness of checks and balances due to executive domination of the legislature. By contrast, the US president and Congress are interdependent; each finds it difficult to act without agreement from the other.

In the UK, while parliament can vote against the government, checks and balances are not particularly powerful. Power tends to be concentrated in the hands of the government or prime minister, and the powerful whip system and patronage ensure a loyal majority in the Commons.

The US Constitution provides extensive checks and balances, which prevent such executive domination. The president lacks ongoing patronage power. Members of Congress, even within the president's own party, may be more loyal to constituents than to their own party leader.

Location of sovereignty

This has a major impact on the relative power of the US and UK judiciaries. The UK Supreme Court is significantly weaker than its US counterpart, because UK justices have no codified constitution to uphold and cannot declare acts of parliament to be unconstitutional. However, in the US the Supreme Court can overturn acts of Congress.

Rights protection

Both political systems have strong mechanisms for rights protection, but it could be argued that the US Constitution provides much stronger protection than the UK constitution. The sovereign entrenched Constitution means that individuals can challenge powerful institutions that restrict liberty. There are many cases of individuals and groups protecting their rights in the US. In the UK, those rights are more vulnerable to executive and parliamentary attack, partly because they can be amended or overturned with a new act of parliament.

There are many counter-arguments that rights are not necessarily better respected in the US. Despite the lower level of structural protections, the UK has shown a relatively high level of **rights protection**. In the US there have been a number of rights concerns, including concerns about the power of the US security state after 9/11 (exemplified by the creation of the Guantanamo detention camp) and continuing major concerns about the rights of racial minorities.

Link

For more on **rights protection**, see Section 6.5.

The amendment process

The amendment process provides a much stronger structure in the US than the UK, restricting politicians more because they find it harder to change the rules of the political game. In the UK, any judicial interpretation can be overturned by a new act of parliament. If the government dislikes the way a law has been interpreted, it can easily change it. In the United States, the courts have the power of judicial review, through which they can overturn the actions of any institution, including Congress. The entrenched Constitution means that their decisions are unlikely ever to be overturned by politicians.

The US federal system and the UK system of devolution

Regional power

Devolution in the UK means that the power of regions is less protected than in the federal US. To reduce the power of a region in the UK, the House of Commons requires only a 50 per cent plus vote; in the US, a more difficult constitutional amendment is required. This is not to say that the level of regional power has to be higher in the United States. Federalism does not necessarily give regions greater power than devolution does, but simply protects that regional power from the central government. However, currently the UK constitution does award less power to regions than the US Constitution does.

Federalism is supposed to ensure greater protection of regional power, but whether it succeeds is open to question. In the US, the federal government and the Supreme Court have gradually allowed significant erosion of state power. In the UK, the structure of parliamentary sovereignty allows for the reduction of the power of devolved regions, including the Welsh or London Assembly.

Similarities	Differences
Power is divided between regions and central government.	Regional power is constitutionally protected in the US, but not in the UK.
There have been attempts to increase regional power in both countries in recent years.	Regional power varies in the UK, but is uniform in the US.
In practice, both systems provide similar levels of protection because: • UK devolution is protected by high expectations that regions should have significant levels of power – devolution is therefore unlikely to be reduced or removed. • US federalism has been eroded by federal intervention and Supreme Court interpretation.	Higher level of regional power in the US, with states having more power to determine policy than regions in the UK.

Table 2.2: Comparison of regional powers in the UK and US

Rational, cultural and structural approaches

The rational approach can be applied to the constitution, especially where the constitution is limited in regulating individuals. It can be used to show the different extents to which individuals can operate rationally by being able to pursue their own self-interests.

- Justices in the US have a strong ability to act according to their own ideology. The vagueness of the Constitution gives much discretion to judges in the US and allows self-interested judges to apply their own interpretations. In the UK, judges are involved in applying detailed parliamentary acts rather than a vague constitution, so are less able to use their own views.

- The rational approach suggests that US voters are more able to pursue their own rational self-interest than UK voters because they have greater choice. The separation of powers and short electoral terms means more voting and greater sensitivity to public opinion.

The cultural approach can be applied to the constitution by looking at the way in which group culture, rather than the constitution, determines political behaviour – where the attitude of groups is most important.

- In both countries the cultural approach reveals a similarity: in both the UK and US there are high levels of expectation of strong regional power. This may deter the central government from attempting to restrict regional power. It is possible for the UK government to reduce the power of regions but it is unlikely to do so for cultural reasons. Each main party feels devolution is highly desirable. In the US, the ideological cultures of the Democrats and Republicans are at odds over the desirability of regional power. There is a stronger culture of states' rights protection among Republicans and therefore greater desire to respect state power among Republican governments. However, the culture of states' rights is dominant in the US, so most politicians conform to this cultural expectation.

- The cultural approach might explain a key difference between the US and UK in relation to the actions of individual politicians. As there is no single document and fewer clear guidelines, the constitution has a lower impact in the UK, so there is more reliance on convention. Cultural expectations play a bigger role in regulating the activities of individual politicians.

- Cultural explanations could also be used to examine the level of rights protection. The US has stronger structures to protect rights than the UK, but rights are still well protected in the UK despite the lack of an entrenched bill of rights and sovereign constitution. There are cultural expectations of rights protection, within parties and the country. In proposing the right to gay marriage, David Cameron was responding to a dominant cultural belief of equality. This might suggest that the structural approach is central to understanding the US Constitution, where everything is laid out in a single document, while in the UK the cultural approach is equally important.

The structural approach is of particular importance in examining the constitutions of the US and UK. A full understanding of the constitutional differences is particularly important because it affects so much of the comparisons for the other topics.

All of the key provisions in Table 2.1 are structures that affect the workings of the two political systems. In particular they explain similarities and differences when comparing the executives, legislatures and judiciaries of the two countries.

Separation of powers and checks and balances

- The executive in the US is far more restricted than in the UK. There are effective structures limiting the president because he may lack a congressional majority and has limited patronage power over members of Congress, which means they are willing to resist his policies. In the UK, the prime minister is restricted by the structure of parliament, but less so than in the US system. The prime minister has a majority in parliament and strong patronage power, meaning that parliament is less likely to use the checks available to them.

- These structures also mean that Congress is more powerful than parliament in limiting the executive branch. In addition, the Constitution awards specific powers to Congress – such as ratifying treaties and appointments – which parliament does not have. These powers are structures that can be used to limit the president.

- The creation of checks and balances in both countries means that both have structures (legislatures) that can restrict the executive branch.

The location of sovereignty

- Constitutional sovereignty in the US has created a strong structure that limits the power of the executive and legislature considerably. The courts have a high degree of power, providing a structure that can be used to overturn president and Congress. In the UK, parliament is not limited by this structure, because it is parliament itself that is sovereign.

- Similarities can be found because both countries have a relatively independent judiciary, which provides structural limits on other political institutions.

The amendment process

- The UK constitution is more easily changed and therefore is a much weaker structure in restricting politicians than the US Constitution. Politicians are less bound by the constitution because they can more easily change it.

Regional power

- Devolution and federalism both provide structures that determine that power is shared between central and regional government.

- The structure of the US Constitution imposes a much more even sharing of power between central and regional government. While devolution provides a structure, the power levels of the regions are much lower and could be reduced by parliament as the sovereign body.

Pause & reflect

It is possible to argue that the US Constitution encourages power to be shared much more than the UK constitution. What are the main constitutional differences that might be used to support this view? Are there any counter-arguments?

6.3 Legislatures: Congress and parliament

The powers, strengths and weaknesses of each of the Houses

There are several similarities between parliament and Congress in terms of their powers and limits. Both Congress and parliament:

- can initiate and amend legislation, and have the power to vote on legislation to determine whether or not it is enacted
- place similar checks on their executives. Parliament and Congress can restrict the executive by voting against their proposals, and executive scrutiny takes place, especially via committees
- have a high degree of control over foreign policy, including military action, typically voting on executive proposals in these areas
- have a role in determining constitutional rules
- are accountable to the public, which might force politicians to respond to public opinion and reject executive proposals.

Capitol Building in Washington DC houses the House of Representatives and the Senate.

London's Palace of Westminster is home to the House of Lords and House of Commons.

Despite these similarities, a good case can be made for either body being more powerful than the other. Tables 3.1 and 3.2 present each of these arguments.

Comparing Congress and parliament

Separation and fusion of power	Parliament is dominated by the executive branch, so is less able to control legislative outcomes or restrict the executive branch.
	Congress is not dominated by the executive, which is elected separately. The president lacks patronage power and may lack a congressional majority, so Congress is a more active law-maker than parliament.
	However… Much depends on which party is in power. Congress may be more aggressive or very passive if the president has a majority in both chambers.
Checks and balances	The US Constitution gives Congress stronger checks than parliament has. The ratification of treaties and appointments and the ability to declare war rests with Congress, not the president.
	The royal prerogative, in theory, gives these powers to the prime minister. Executive appointments are not subject to parliamentary approval.
	However… It is unlikely that a prime minister would sign a treaty or declare war without a House of Commons vote. Again, much depends on party majorities.
Power of second chambers	Congress has a lot of power over the executive. It has two equally powerful chambers that can both provide significant checks on the president, making restrictions on the executive branch much more successful.
	The House of Lords is a relatively weak legislative body.
	However… Arguably there has been a resurgence in the House of Lords, with a more aggressive chamber based on greater legitimacy after the removal of hereditary peers. There was a short-term increase in power during the coalition government when the Salisbury convention was effectively suspended.

Table 3.1: Arguments for Congress being more powerful than parliament

Location of sovereignty	Parliamentary sovereignty means that parliament is far more powerful than Congress. Parliament can make constitutional laws at will, so it can more easily project its power throughout the UK system. Parliament can also make major constitutional changes, such as leaving the EU, removing the Human Rights Act and reducing the power of devolved regions.
	Congress is constrained by the Supreme Court and the Constitution. It cannot overturn judicial decisions or alter fundamental constitutional practices unilaterally.
Imperial presidency	This theory suggests that constitutional restraints on the president fail to operate, leaving Congress in a weak position to take control over US policy. Presidential use of executive orders, signing statements and executive agreements all have the effect of bypassing Congress, allowing the president to act unilaterally. This means that the president is able to act in much the way that a UK prime minister can. It may be that UK prime ministers are more limited, however, because they are more limited by their Cabinet in making decisions.
Bicameralism	The supremacy of the House of Commons means that parliament can act decisively and exercise its power by exerting influence within the system as a whole.
	By contrast, the equal nature of the two US legislative chambers can weaken rather than strengthen their power. If there is conflict within Congress, with the House and the Senate disagreeing over policy, it may be unable to act.

Table 3.2: Arguments for parliament being more powerful than Congress

Strengths and weaknesses of Congress and parliament

Congress	Role	Parliament
• Highly representative due to the separation of powers, with both chambers elected separately from the executive. • Complementary representation of two years (delegates) and six years (trustees).	Representation	• The elected Commons is responsive to public opinion with a mandate from the people. • Complementary representation in which the Commons can respond to the wishes of the people and the Lords can take a more reasoned view and consider the interests of the people.
• A powerful legislative body that is able and willing to restrict executive proposals. • Proactive in initiating its own legislation. • High-quality legislation due to detailed scrutiny of bills, especially in powerful committees in both chambers.	Legislation	• Has the power to scrutinise and block bills, providing quality legislation. • Government majority and influence in parliament ensure an efficient process in which bills can be passed and are agreed in timely fashion.
• Very high level of checks on the executive due to the separation of powers and checks and balances. • Important role given to Congress in declaring war, removing a president from office and in ratifying treaties and appointments (Senate).	Checks	• Effective checks of the executive through voting on legislation, select committees and question time. • Can remove a failing government through a vote of no confidence. • Checks are not excessive, allowing for strong, effective government.
House of Representatives	**Lower chambers**	**House of Commons**
• Two-year terms and separation of powers leads to high sensitivity to public opinion. • See congressional strengths for representation above.	Representation	• Elected chamber with a tradition of MPs representing all constituents, regardless of who they voted for.
• See all of the congressional legislative strengths above.	Legislation	• See all of the parliamentary legislative strengths above.
• Specialist function of impeachment. • See all of the congressional strengths for checks above.	Checks	• See all of the parliamentary strengths for checks above.
Senate	**Upper chambers**	**House of Lords**
• Representative due to separation of powers. • Six-year term allows Senators to take a more rational/long-term view of public interests.	Representation	• Serves the interests of the people because it can use its own judgement. • Not strongly affected by the government/patronage/whips and therefore can represent the people if the government is carrying out unpopular/undesirable policies.
• See all of the congressional legislative strengths above.	Legislation	• Lords have influence over legislation via their ability to amend and delay bills. • Their expertise gives Lords authority over legislative matters.
• Specialist function of removal from office after impeachment.	Checks	• Expertise gives authority in scrutinising government actions and policies. • Limits to checks (cannot block bills) ensures scrutiny but not weak government.

Table 3.3: Strengths of Congress and parliament

Congress	Role	Parliament
• Use of FPTP elections leads to lack of voter choice and safe seats in the US. • The party with the most votes does not necessarily get the most seats.	Representation	• Use of FPTP elections leads to lack of voter choice and safe seats in the UK, as well as disproportionality between votes and seats. • The party with the most votes does not necessarily get the most seats.
• Power is shared in Congress, making it extremely difficult to pass legislation. • Some legislative procedures such as 'pork barrel legislation' are undesirable.	Legislation	• Is mainly a reactive body considering government proposals with limited significant initiation of bills. • Has a fairly limited ability and willingness to challenge government proposals.
• Provides excessive checks leading to weak government, for example through legislative gridlock. • Partisanship in Congress has led to unacceptably high levels of checks under divided government.	Checks	• Insufficient checks on the government due to government majority/whip system and patronage. • Only one chamber with significant checking power.
House of Representatives	**Lower chambers**	**House of Commons**
• See all representative weaknesses of Congress above.	Representation	• See all representative weaknesses of parliament above.
• See all legislative weaknesses for Congress above.	Legislation	• See all legislative weaknesses of parliament above.
• See weakness in checks for Congress above.	Checks	• See weaknesses in checks for parliament above.
Senate	**Upper chambers**	**House of Lords**
• Six-year terms are arguably too long. • Two Senators per state leads to over-representation of small states. • Also see all representative weaknesses of Congress above.	Representation	• Unelected and unaccountable, Lords lack democratic legitimacy.
• Use of filibuster can be seen as undemocratic and leads to ineffective government. • Also see all legislative weaknesses for Congress above.	Legislation	• Has limited legislative power with no power to block legislation. • Amendments can be overturned by Commons. • Limited by Salisbury convention in blocking bills.
• See weakness in checks for Congress above.	Checks	• Has limited power to check government because it cannot overturn legislative proposals or insist on amendments.

Table 3.4: Weaknesses of Congress and parliament

Rational, cultural and structural approaches

The rational approach can be usefully applied when looking at the role of individual politicians in Congress and parliament. Politicians in Congress are less subject to pressure from the executive than those in parliament, which allows them to act more rationally pursuing their own beliefs or self-interest. This can help to explain why there are lower levels of party unity in the US than the UK, and greater checks on the president.

The rational approach is particularly useful in examining second chambers, explaining key differences between the Senate and the Lords. Members of the Lords are not elected and are barely subject to any patronage power. Party unity is low, with a high number of independent crossbenchers. This allows them to be relatively free from structures and cultures. Therefore individual Lords are more able to use their own judgement than Senators, who are limited by party and constituency expectations.

The cultural approach is useful in considering the role of parties in Congress and parliament and how that affects their powers, as well as the desirability of the legislative branches. There are high levels of party unity in both countries, especially since the US experienced a major increase in partisanship. This suggests that a desire to work with common values influences their political behaviour.

The cultural approach can also explain the importance of conventions in Congress and parliament. In particular, the Lords is governed by cultural expectations about roles. The unelected nature of the Lords often means that they are restrained in opposing government policy, especially when this is carrying out the express will of the people. Such cultural expectations can be seen in both countries. For example, in the US there is arguably a culture of deference to the president in foreign policy, with members of Congress being less aggressive than in domestic policy.

The structural approach is particularly useful in explaining key differences between the two countries' legislatures. It can be used to show how Congress is generally far more powerful than parliament when checking the executive. The US Constitution (separation of powers and high levels of checks and balances) means that Congress cannot be dominated by the executive in a way that parliament (fusion of powers and lower level of checks) can.

> **Link** ↱
>
> For more on comparison of constitutions, see Section 6.2.

The different constitutional rules regarding elections ensure that there are structural differences that can be used to compare the two countries. The constitutional requirement for elections in the Senate and life appointment in the Lords creates a major difference. It allows the Senate to be more powerful than the Lords, and also means that Senators tend to be far more aggressive in the desire to check the executive than peers are.

6.4 Executives

The roles and power of the president and prime minister are heavily influenced by the constitutional arrangements for each country. To understand the president and prime minister, it is important to understand how the constitution of each country affects their position.

> **Pause & reflect** ✔
>
> What does the comparative constitutions section say about the role and power of the president and prime minister? Which parts of the US and UK constitution have the most impact on these two offices?

President and prime minister: five key constitutional differences

These five differences can be applied to assess the roles and powers of the president and prime minister, as well as the extent to which they are accountable to the legislature.

Theresa May was chosen as leader of the Conservative party, and therefore prime minister, in 2016, after David Cameron's unexpected mid-term resignation following the EU referendum.

President Donald Trump won a surprise victory in the 2016 presidential elections, polls having predicted a narrow win for Hillary Clinton.

UK prime minister (PM)	US president
The PM is drawn from parliament after an election, and is usually the head of the largest party in parliament. PMs can take this position without the need for an election (as Theresa May, Gordon Brown and John Major all did).	Presidents are elected directly by the whole country. They have a direct mandate from the people.
There is only a vote for the legislature (parliament) and not the executive (government). Although people legally vote for their local MP, they are often strongly influenced by the PM, party or their preference for government.	There are separate elections for the president and Congress.
Fusion of power – the PM and the Cabinet are also members of parliament.	Separation of powers – members of the executive and legislature are kept separate. The president cannot be part of Congress.
The prime minister only retains their position as long as parliament has confidence in the government. Parliament can vote to remove the government, including the prime minister, in a vote of no confidence. Prime ministers will typically have a majority in parliament, even if that requires a coalition government.	The president's position is not dependent on holding a congressional majority. It is common for the president to govern under divided government, in which their own party lacks a majority in at least one of the two chambers of Congress.
Cabinet plays a prominent role in restricting the PM's power. The PM heads the executive branch, but their power relies on support from their parliamentary base. If leading members of that base withdraw support, it is hard for the PM to retain office. The constitutional convention is for Cabinet government, in which Cabinet and the PM make decisions collectively and Cabinet members may act as rivals to the PM.	The Constitution gives the president sole authority to head the executive branch. The people's direct mandate and the Constitution's wording mean that the president's position in the executive should go unchallenged. Everyone in the executive branch serves at the president's pleasure, always giving the president the final say within the executive.

Table 4.1: Five differences between UK prime minister and US president

Pause & reflect

Does the executive in the UK or the US hold more power over the legislature? What are the main reasons for this? Are there any valid counter-arguments to your view?

Roles of president and prime minister
Head of executive branch

- Both president and prime minister are head of their executive branch.
- There are significant differences in their constitutional position and power within the executive branch (see Table 4.1).

Head of state

- This role is held by the president in the US. The presidency combines a larger set of roles and responsibilities than the position of prime minister.
- This role is held by the monarch in the UK, not the prime minister.
- Gives the president a stronger ceremonial role in the United States and arguably greater authority as a symbol of their nation.

Chief diplomat

- Both president and prime minister are main negotiators with other countries, taking a lead in international relations.
- In both countries this power is limited by the legislatures:
  - Senate has a strong role, holding power to reject treaties negotiated by the president
  - Unwritten constitution in the UK makes this relationship unclear; parliament holds power to reject any treaties with financial implications and prime ministers often want to consult parliament on all treaties, out of political necessity.

Commander in chief

- US Constitution gives this role to the president, allowing them a great deal of control over military matters.
- Through royal prerogative, the prime minister effectively has this role, and can order military action.
- Lack of absolute clarity in both countries over who has the final say – Congress and parliament can assert some control.

Chief legislator

- In both countries, the head of the executive branch has assumed a major role in the legislative process, arguably acting as the dominant force.
- In the UK this is based on the prime minister's position as the head of the party with a majority (usually absolute) of seats in parliament, and their ability to use patronage and a whip system to control that majority. In the Unites States, the president has been able to use their national mandate and superior resources to become known as the chief legislator.
- US presidents face considerably greater opposition to their political agenda from the legislature than prime ministers. Congress takes much greater control of the legislative agenda and also rejects executive proposals much more than their United Kingdom counterparts.

> **EXTENSION ACTIVITY**
>
> Using the internet, find policies to both support and oppose the idea that President Trump and Prime Minister May are conforming to the ideology of their party.

Powers of the president and prime minister

As the head of government and state for the world's most powerful country, the president is often considered to be the world's most powerful person. However, it is important to compare the power of the president and the prime minister within their countries, looking at each person's ability to achieve their policy goals.

The role of prime ministers and presidents can be used to compare their relative powers. In practice the two hold power and are limited for quite different reasons, based on the different constitutions.

A common argument is that the prime minister is more powerful than the president in determining policy priorities for their country. This is to be expected given the nature of the checks and balances that the Founding Fathers imposed on the United States.

The prime minister has two key advantages.

- It is easier to pass legislation through parliament. The prime minister's party usually holds a parliamentary majority and they can use the whip to control this majority. While MPs from the prime minister's party may be naturally loyal, the prime minister can use patronage to encourage backbenchers to stay loyal and vote for government bills. The president has no such ability, due to the separation of powers. This robs presidents of patronage power and makes members of Congress more sensitive to public opinion than to presidential wishes.

- Prime ministers have arguably become even more powerful in recent years. The government dominates parliament, so a prime minister will be very powerful if they can dominate the rest of the executive branch. Any brake on prime ministerial power typically comes from the other senior members of the executive branch. This brake has been weakened in recent years as prime ministers have been able to adopt a presidential style, taking control over the rest of the executive branch.

By claiming a personal national mandate at election time, and by making heavy use of patronage and the Cabinet committee system to control policy-making, a prime minister can dominate executive processes. If prime ministers can now also dominate the executive branch, this suggests that they have much more power than US presidents.

However, prime ministers are not necessarily more powerful than presidents.

- The imperial presidency theory suggests that presidents may have similar levels of power as prime ministers because presidents can bypass some of the checks intended by the Founding Fathers using executive orders, executive agreements and signing statements.

- Some prime ministers will find it difficult to dominate the rest of the executive, especially if there are significant party splits or the prime minister cannot claim a national mandate (for instance, Gordon Brown and Theresa May until after the 2017 election).

- Prime ministers may be heavily curtailed by parliament if they lack or have a small majority in parliament. In these situations, the prime minister has a similar experience to a president, having to use others in the executive branch to persuade parliament to accept their policy priorities.

- Presidents may be as successful as prime ministers if they are popular and have a majority in both chambers of Congress (as George W. Bush did for most of his presidency).

Impact of the president and prime minister on politics and government
Key similarities:

- Both are the dominant political figures in their respective countries.
- Both act as a driving force using their political leadership as head of government to set a policy agenda for the country.
- Both are subject to constraints by the legislature, which can reject executive proposals.
- Both are subject to limits from public opinion, given that the basis of their power is derived from elections.

Key differences:

- The prime minister is more able to have an impact on politics and government due to their power over the legislature. The president is more constrained and has a lower impact, especially at a time of divided government.

- The prime minister is more able to have an impact because of the power of the judiciary. In the United States the courts can use the sovereign Constitution to overturn presidential policy and action. Parliamentary sovereignty makes this far more difficult in the UK where courts cannot overturn acts of parliament, which typically reflect the prime minister's will.

- The president has greater control within the executive branch than the prime minister. The president is elected nationally, unlike the rest of their executive team, and has constitutional authority over this branch. The impact of the prime minister can be limited more easily by their executive team, for example when Cabinet members are in conflict with the prime minister.

Accountability to the legislatures

As with roles and powers, the extent to which presidents and prime ministers are accountable to legislatures depends largely on the differing constitutional arrangements.

Presidents are more accountable in that they find it harder to pass legislation through Congress than prime ministers do

Parliament has the advantage of being able to remove a government – and therefore a prime minister – through a vote of no confidence. The president faces no such threat

The US Constitution allows the legislature to maintain stronger scrutiny, such as the need for appointments to be ratified by the Senate

Both executives face scrutiny and oversight form the legislature. The prime minister has to face parliament directly through Prime Minister's Questions; the president does not.

The US separation of powers means that presidents are more accountable. Congress is usually far more determined to hold the executive to account than parliament is

The extent of accountability depends on the nature of party majorities in the legislature

Figure 4.1: Accountability to the legislatures: key points

Rational, cultural and structural approaches

The rational approach reveals how both presidents and prime ministers are highly motivated to pursue their own self-interest by attempting to achieve their policy goals and use their position to maximise their power. Given their high levels of power, both have a great deal of ability to act, but the removal of political opponents shows a clear difference between the two. The prime minister has greater patronage power and usually appoints and dismisses Cabinet members based in part on loyalty. Here they are acting rationally to improve their own position. Presidents have less influence because they do not have the ongoing promise of promotion to all members of their own party in Congress. Donald Trump acted in his own rational self-interest by bringing like-minded people into his Cabinet and removing Attorney General Sally Yates in January 2017 when she criticised his immigration ban.

So there is a trade-off between the rational and structural: the more a structure restricts politicians, the less scope there is for them to pursue their own self-interest.

Case study: Applying the cultural approach to Cameron, Clinton, May and Trump

The cultural approach is important in understanding the way in which prime ministers and presidents carry out their roles. Both operate as part of a team and a political party, and may feel the need to conform to some of the dominant value systems of their party. Conservative prime ministers have been curtailed by the varying extents of Euroscepticism in the party and, regardless of their own view, have had to acknowledge this.

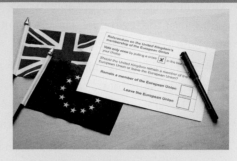

Referendums are rare in the UK, unlike in countries like Switzerland, where the electorate are directly consulted quite frequently. The 2016 EU referendum simply asked voters to indicate whether they wanted the UK to leave the EU or remain in it.

Arguably, this cultural approach helps to explain why David Cameron called an EU referendum even though he is a firm believer in the benefits of UK membership. He was responding to the dominant value system in his group. The extent to which leaders are guided by such cultural factors will always be difficult to measure. Theresa May, who campaigned to remain, has firmly accepted the dominant views of the country, opting for what many have described as a 'hard' Brexit. Hillary Clinton, as would-be president, adapted her language to the growing culture of progressive ideology in her party. This growth, alongside the relative success of Sanders, caused her to declare herself 'a progressive who gets things done'. US parties are more internally divided than those in the UK, so party leaders are less influenced by the values system of that party. Trump's rejection by many leaders in the Republican Party may mean that he is less influenced by any sense of the need to respect the shared value system of the Republican Party.

Questions

- What evidence is there that the cultural approach explains the behaviour of the prime minister and president?
- Does the case study suggest that cultural factors are greater in the UK or US?

Link

For more on structural explanations of the president and prime minister, see Section 6.2.

The structural approach is a powerful tool with which to assess similarities and differences here. Constitutional structures strongly influence the behaviour of the prime minister and president. It is clear that structures help to understand the power of the two. The prime minster has a higher level of power than the president. Much of this comes down to the basic principle of the separation versus the fusion of powers, which has a dramatic impact on political practice. This parliamentary system, coupled with the first-past-the-post voting system (which typically gives a single party an absolute majority of seats), is what makes the prime minister so powerful.

6.5 Judiciary and civil rights

Basis for and relative extent of powers

Judiciaries in both countries have the same role: to uphold the law and the constitution through its interpretation. The basis of their power is different, however. The Supreme Court in the US derives its power from the Constitution and has the role of upholding the sovereign Constitution. In the UK, courts derive their power from parliament through their ability to uphold acts of parliament. This leads to a central difference in the extent of their powers.

Scope

The US judiciary has greater scope than the UK judiciary to have major influence. In the US, justices uphold a codified sovereign Constitution, which allows the Court to overturn even the most powerful (and elected) bodies – including the president, the Congress and the states. In the UK, parliament is sovereign; the courts cannot overturn an act of parliament. UK judges are far more constrained than those in the US.

Having the final say

It is significantly easier to overturn decisions made by the UK judiciary than opinions delivered by the US Supreme Court. Overturning a decision made by a UK court involves passing a new act of parliament, which can be done relatively easily (for example, the government could use its parliamentary majority to have a new law made by parliament). Overturning a judicial ruling in the Unites States is technically possible, but hard to do. The vast majority of Supreme Court rulings remain intact because it is too difficult to achieve the supermajorities needed to amend the Constitution. US judges tend to have the final say; in the UK, government and parliament have ultimate power.

The attitude of judges

In both countries there may be a difference in how much power judges have and the extent to which they use it. The power of judges in each country is amplified by the vagueness of their constitutions. This gives individual judges latitude in achieving their policy preferences; the extent to which this is used depends on the judiciary themselves.

Arguably, this bias is far more apparent in the US because of the appointment process and because the Constitution is extremely vague. However, the extent to which this bias is used depends on individual judges and the judicial approach they apply.

Independence of the UK and US judiciaries

The independence of the courts

- Judges in both countries have high levels of independence through security of tenure. This allows them to exercise their power freely, without fear of political repercussions. In both countries judges can and do give rulings that undermine the executive in terms of their power or policy priorities.

- Arguably the appointment process in the US threatens the independence of the court, as Supreme Court justices are selected by the president and ratified by the Senate. UK judges are appointed by an independent body, the Judicial Appointments Committee. On the whole, this factor affects neutrality much more than it affects independence, as the president's pick for the top court introduces a bias. Once in office, a justice is not accountable to the president who picked them. US justices sometimes interpret the Constitution to restrict the power or policy of the president who appointed them.

- In both countries, the high-profile nature of constitutional cases means that there is often external pressure on justices. The US court faces much greater external pressure, in part because of the major constitutional issues it deals with, such as guns, abortion and gay rights – contested issues on which US society is deeply divided – and because court rulings may overturn acts of Congress. As a result, US justices face heavier informal restrictions – for example, through protests or presidential speeches – than in the UK.

Effectiveness of rights protection by the judiciary

In both countries the judiciary plays a central role in the protection of rights. They both uphold laws that safeguard civil liberties. In the US this is mainly through the bill of rights and key amendments, such as the 14th amendment providing equal protection. In the UK this protection comes mainly through rulings based on the Human Rights Act, where the courts are upholding an important piece of statute law.

Rights **are more** effectively protected in the US	Rights **are not more** effectively protected in the US
The sovereign Constitution allows US courts to overturn the actions of any institution, including Congress, if it restricts civil liberties. UK courts do not have the power to overturn acts of parliament even if they restrict human rights – they can issue a statement of incompatibility, which parliament can choose to reject.	The UK Human Rights Act provides extensive legal protection of civil liberties.
Because the US has an entrenched Constitution, court rulings cannot be easily overturned by other political bodies. This is particularly important in rights protection because it involves protecting individuals against powerful elected politicians. In the UK these politicians can overturn a ruling that protects civil rights by passing a new act of parliament.	Parliament is unlikely to reject decisions made by the court that have protected civil rights. The Human Rights Act can be described as quasi-entrenched. Despite the legal ability to remove the act, this would be politically very difficult without a reasonable degree of cross-party support. If the act is removed, it is likely to be replaced with a British bill of rights.
It depends The extent of protection depends not only on the ability to protect rights but also the willingness of judges to do so in their interpretations of the Constitution. Conservative justices may be more reluctant than liberal justices to find in favour of individuals. In the US there is a conservative majority on the Supreme Court, which may not favour civil rights protection (for instance, *Shelby County v Holder*). Even so, a significant number of cases in recent years have upheld minority rights (for example, *Obergefell v Hodges*).	

Table 5.1: Arguments for and against the effectiveness of rights protection

Link

For more on **interest groups** in the UK and US, see Section 1.3 of Democracy and Participation and Section 5.3 of US Democracy and Participation.

The effectiveness of interest groups in the protection of civil rights

The relative power of interest groups in protecting civil rights can be analysed by applying any of the points covered in the **interest groups** section of the Democracy and Participation chapters. The factors that allow US interest groups to hold so much power suggest that they have a greater impact than in the UK.

Arguments for UK groups being less effective

- **Weak parties:** The united nature of UK parties means that civil-rights-based interest groups (such as Liberty and Stonewall) may have less success in persuading legislative politicians than in the US. Given the higher tendency to vote in blocks and be subject to the whip system and patronage, the success of a group may depend more on their ability to persuade party leaders in the UK.

- **Access points:** This marks a central difference in explaining their relative success, with US civil rights groups enjoying a greater choice of powerful institutions to lobby and more opportunities to find a like-minded majority. In the US a civil rights group that is troubled by a Republican majority in Congress may find access with a Democratic president. In the UK a civil rights group that fails to convince the government is unlikely to achieve legislative success in parliament.

- **Rights protection:** With stronger levels of rights protection in the US, civil rights groups are likely to experience far higher levels of success than in the UK. This level of rights protection helps to account for much greater prominence of civil rights groups in the US, with groups such as the ACLU and NAACP being better known than groups such as Liberty in the UK. Interest groups in both countries have been active in taking cases to court.

Arguments for UK groups being more effective

The US political and constitutional system provides much greater opportunities for civil rights groups to be successful than in the UK. This does not mean that those rights are better protected in practice in the United States.

- The UK arguably has a stronger tradition of respecting civil rights than in the US. The level of constitutional protection does not necessarily explain the difference between the two countries. Given the maintenance of slavery and separate facilities in the United States long after they were banned in the UK, there are arguably greater concerns about racial rights in the US. In addition, concern over minority rights protection has grown in recent years, with the Shelby ruling, the growth of state-based measures that appear to discriminate, and the Trump approach to racial issues.

- There have been issues in both countries about the power of the state in matters of national security, a concern that has risen since 9/11 with increased police powers in both countries. Groups such as Liberty and the ACLU have been unsuccessful in fighting aspects of legislation such as the Patriot Act and Freedom Act in the US and the Prevention of Terrorism Act 2005 and Investigatory Powers Act 2016 in the UK. The Trump presidency has increased these concerns in the United States, and the Conservative plan to remove the Human Rights Act suggests a major failure of civil rights groups in the UK.

- **Which right?** There is debate in both countries about which rights should be respected. Liberals tend to push ideas of freedom from discrimination and freedom of expression, while conservatives might promote other types of rights, such as the right to bear arms.

Rational, cultural and structural approaches

The rational approach can be used to compare the two countries when judges appear to be able to act according to their own beliefs. In both countries judges have the scope to direct their own behaviour, operating as rational actors who can pursue their own ideological preferences. Despite the more apparent structures in the US, justices of the Supreme Court have much greater power as individuals to bring about change. The power given to the judiciary by the Constitution and the vagueness of the Constitution allow US judges great scope for interpretation, allowing them to have a major impact when delivering their rulings.

The cultural approach suggests that there is a more dominant rights-protection culture in the UK than in the US. It can be argued that UK citizens respect rights more than citizens in the US. In the US there are strong rival cultures based around competing parties and pressure groups that support or oppose civil rights. There are significant human rights concerns in the US despite apparently stronger structures to protect civil rights.

The structural approach is particularly useful in helping to understand similarities and differences in the power of judicial bodies of the two countries. The constitution strongly affects the extent to which judges have an impact on the political system as a whole. Similar arguments can be applied when examining the level of civil rights protection, as structures having a major impact on the extent to which rights can be upheld. This suggests that the US judiciary has a bigger impact on US politics and government by affecting:

- government policy (usually by overturning it)
- the power of political institutions (particularly regulating their use of power)
- the level of rights protection in the country.

6.6 Democracy and participation

Party systems

Regarding democracy and participation, there are similarities and differences between the party systems of the UK and US.

Similarities

In both the UK and US:

- There are two dominant parties, with only politicians from these two main parties heading the executive in recent years. The main two parties have also dominated the legislature.
- Third parties have some power at regional level.

Differences

- The UK has a stronger third-party presence than the US, and is arguably a multi-party system. The two main UK parties fall well below the near-100 per cent of seats held by Democrats and Republicans in the US.
- The two-party system in the UK is characterised by a pendulum effect, with power typically swinging between the two. At any one point, only one party usually holds significant power in Westminster. In the United States it is common for Democrats and Republicans to hold significant power at the same time. The separation of powers allows divided government, as in the last six years of the Obama presidency.
- There are strong regional variations in the UK. Third parties are the dominant force in some regions, such as the SNP in Scotland (Scotland has experienced Lab–Lib Dem coalitions as well as majority and minority SNP governments) and Plaid Cymru in Wales, which often has the second-highest number of seats in the Welsh Assembly.

Party unity

Party unity is significantly higher in the UK than the US.

In the US, structural factors prevent powerful party leaders and fragment parties. The separation of powers and federalism suggests that there is no one recognised party leader in the US and that the party is divided into executive, House, Senate, state and national committee parties. In the UK, parties are far more united mainly due to the parliamentary system, which gives party leaders great control over the parliamentary party through patronage and the whip system. It is less common for UK MPs to vote against their own party than it is for congressional politicians to do so. This makes the US much harder to govern.

The US party system is more factionalised than the UK's, including, for example, socially conservative, fiscally conservative and moderate factions. However, there are significant divisions within parties in both countries. In the UK, the Conservative Party has long been divided on the issue of Europe, while the Labour Party under Jeremy Corbyn has been divided between moderate New Labour forces and more traditional socialists. On the other hand, a recent growth in partisanship in the US has made parties more united, which suggests that the differences between the two countries are not as significant as they once were.

The party system and party unity have a major impact on the politics and government of the two countries.

- The two-party system suggests limited choice and restricts democracy.
- Party unity has an impact on the effectiveness of government.
- Factions and unity affect the power of party leaders, especially in the executive.

The policy profiles of the main parties

The easiest way to compare political parties across countries is to look at the policy direction they want to take their country in. In this sense the Democratic and Labour Parties have much in common, promoting policies that would typically move the country further to the left.

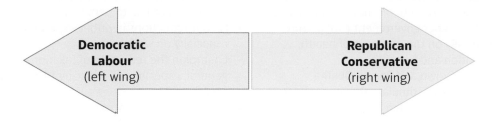

Figure 6.1: Ideological spectrum

Welfare and social justice

Similarities	
Labour and Democrats	**Conservatives and Republicans**
<ul><li>Typically champion the cause of social justice, viewing the state as having a positive role to play in society.</li><li>View the system as unfair, with inequalities caused by larger processes that individuals do not always have control over.</li><li>The provision of greater health care, access to education and benefits to help those who are most in need are central to the ideology of these two parties.</li><li>As the founder of the NHS, the Labour Party has a long history of putting in place measures to reduce socio-economic inequality.</li><li>Democrats supported the Affordable Care Act and food stamps (SNAP).</li></ul>	<ul><li>Tend to favour a reduction in the role of the state.</li><li>Critical of big government, attempting to reduce government expenditure as a percentage of GDP, leading to cuts to benefits when these parties have been in control.</li><li>Stress personal responsibility.</li><li>Conservatives introduced major welfare cuts since 2010, including the bedroom tax to reduce housing benefit.</li><li>Republicans opposed the Affordable Care Act and supported cuts to food stamps (SNAP).</li></ul>
But!	
Arguably the Conservative Party is much less right wing than the Republican Party in this area, reflecting the way in which the United States on the whole is more right wing in its policies than the UK. The Conservative Party has supported the concept of the NHS, which places it to the left of many Democrats who largely favour universal health insurance rather than health care that is free at the point of use.	

Table 6.1: Main party policies on welfare and social justice

Economic policy

Similarities	
Labour and Democrats	**Conservatives and Republicans**
• Favour an active role for government, using economic policy to promote social justice. • Favour higher government expenditure, especially on the provision of health, education and benefits. • Gordon Brown and Barack Obama attempted to stimulate the economy and protect jobs through a major increase of government expenditure.	• See government intervention in the economy as a risk to personal freedom. • Favour reductions in public expenditure, especially on welfare. • Champion the reduction of taxation in general, especially by reducing taxes on the wealthy. • Have resisted the introduction and increase in the national minimum wage.
But!	
There has been a debate in both countries about the extent to which the left-wing party is committed to centre-left policies. With the rise of both New Democrats and New Labour in the 1990s it is possible to see these two parties starting to have a lot more in common with the Republican and Conservative Parties, especially in terms of economic policy. In the UK the Labour Party dropped their previous commitment to nationalisation of key industries and did not increase the higher rate of income tax under the Blair-led government. In the United States, President Clinton signed a law to overturn the Glass-Steagall Act, which was created by Democrats in the 1930s to regulate the banking industry by splitting commercial and investment banking.	

Table 6.2: Main party policies on economic policy

Moral and social policy

Similarities	
Labour and Democrats	**Conservatives and Republicans**
• Adopt a liberal approach to civil rights. • Labour Party created the Human Rights Act of 1998, the landmark law that provides legal protection of civil liberties. • Democratic Party crafted both the Civil Rights Act and Voting Rights Act in the 1960s.	• Typically resisted or opposed extension and protection of civil rights. • The Conservative and Republican Parties opposed these acts in their respective countries.
But!	
In the UK it was Cameron's Conservative government that pushed legislation on gay marriage (with the support of most Labour and Liberal Democrat MPs), reflecting Cameron's one-nation conservative approach based on the desire for greater social harmony. Arguably US society is more divided over rights-based issues than the UK, with the result that there is greater agreement between the two main parties in the UK than there is in the US.	

Table 6.3: Main party policies on moral and social policy

EXTENSION ACTIVITY

Use the internet to find policies from the last election for the main opposing parties in the UK and the US. See if you can find similar policy debates in both the US and the UK. Where would you place each party's position on an ideological spectrum?

Campaign finance and party funding

The issue of campaign finance and party funding has been a highly controversial issue in both the UK and the US. In both countries legislation has been passed to regulate money and ensure greater fairness and transparency. The concerns in both countries centre around:

- the influence of donors
- the inequality of spending between parties
- transparency of donations, known as **hard money** in the US, and expenditure.

> **Key term**
>
> **Hard money**
> cash contributed directly to a political candidate, which may come only from an individual or a political action committee.

United Kingdom	United States
Major legal and constitutional developments	
The Political Parties, Elections and Referendums Act 2000 (PPERA) required all parties to register with the Electoral Commission and put controls on donations. **Transparency of Lobbying, Non-party Campaigning and Trade Union Administration Act 2014** regulated the expenditure of outside groups. Any pressure group spending £10,000+ during an election campaign (£20,000 in England) must register with the Electoral Commission.	**Federal Election Campaign Act 1974** introduced maximum donations, expenditure by presidential candidates and federal funding. **The Bipartisan Campaign Reform Act (BCRA) 2002** tried to close some of FECA's loopholes by limiting outside expenditure from interest groups during election campaigns. *Citizens United v FEC* **2010** undermined the BCRA, overturning regulations on outside spending and allowing for the creation of Super PACs.
Limits on campaign expenditure	
In 2015 parliamentary candidates could spend up to £30,000 in the long campaign (December to March) and £8,700 in the short campaign (March to May). Parties can spend up to £19.5 million if they field candidates in all 650 seats.	No real limit on campaign expenditure. The maximum limit only applies to presidential candidates who take federal funding, which is now rejected by candidates from both parties. The Clinton campaign spent $497 million; the Trump campaign spent $247 million.
The role of outside groups, such as business or pressure-group donations	
In 2015 no group could spend more than £9,750 per constituency in an election campaign. No limit on the amount an outside group can donate to a political party.	The creation of Super PACs means that donors can give unlimited money, even if this money cannot go directly to a candidate's official campaign. Donations to political parties (rather than candidates) are largely unregulated. Fahr LLC (owned by a billionaire hedge-fund manager) donated $67 million to candidates for different political offices, mainly to Democrats, in the two years up to the 2016 election. The second-highest spender was Renaissance Technologies, another hedge-fund company, which donated $57.7 million, splitting its money fairly evenly between the two parties.
Monitoring body for donations and expenditure	
The Electoral Commission	The Federal Election Commission

Table 6.4: Comparison of campaign finance and party funding in the UK and US

Similarities regarding campaign finance in both countries include:

- concerns about the involvement of money in US and UK elections
- legal regulations of campaign finance
- donors in both countries are not particularly limited, despite campaign finance laws.

Impact on politics and government

Influence of wealthy donors

Despite legislation there are still major concerns over the role of campaign finance in both countries. These have not been resolved by legislation, and donors can play a largely unlimited role, giving huge sums to help parties and candidates win elections. The concern is that excessive influence is held by wealthy donors, especially major corporations. This gives weight to the elitist theory, suggesting that politicians are responsive to the wishes of a small group of moneyed individuals.

Inequality and fairness of elections

There is clearly an inequality of expenditure between the main parties and candidates within each country. In the UK, the Conservative Party spent significantly more than Labour in 2015, while in the US Clinton outspent Trump in 2016. Both Clinton and the Conservative Party achieved significantly higher votes than their rivals.

Greater impact in the US?

It is often assumed that money plays a greater role in US elections than the UK, with far higher levels of expenditure and donations. UK political parties spent a total of £31.1 million at the 2010 general election. The Conservatives spent 53 per cent of this total, the Labour Party spent 25 per cent and the Liberal Democrats just 15 per cent. While total amounts donated and spent are higher, this does not mean that concerns about the role of money should be lower in the UK. Much depends on the extent to which money is giving excessive influence and helping one party or candidate to win over another.

Pressure groups

Methods that pressure groups use

UK and US pressure groups use similar methods, although the differences in the political and constitutional systems make some methods more common or successful than others. For example, in the US, legal methods are far more attractive than in the UK for pressure groups on the whole. Thanks to constitutional sovereignty, an interest group that succeeds in the Supreme Court achieves long-term gains, so legal methods are more intense in the US than the UK.

However, the choice of method depends on the interest group as much as the country they operate in. In both countries, groups that struggle to gain attention for their policies (usually because there is little ideological compatibility with any politicians) resort to demonstrations or direct action, rather than lobbying. Wealthy groups, such as corporations, will use political donations, whereas groups with fewer resources will rely on other methods.

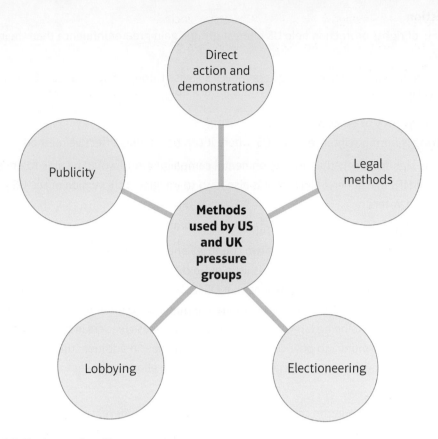

Figure 6.2: Tactics employed by pressure groups

The power and influence of pressure groups

A pressure group's power can be measured by the extent to which it achieves its policy goals. In general, it can be argued that US pressure groups are more powerful than those in the UK. In the UK the categorisation of 'insiders' and 'outsiders' suggests that some pressure group in the UK are significantly more powerful than others. In the US, arguably, insiders and outsiders do not exist, because most interest groups can gain influence. This difference is based on the specific political and constitutional differences between the UK and the US, which allow for different levels of influence.

This suggests that the US has a more pluralist system than the UK. Some pressure groups in the UK (insiders) have high levels of influence and many others (outsiders) do not, for several reasons.

Access points
- There are more access points in the US system because the separation of powers and federalism create a multitude of power centres.
- In the UK, because power is concentrated in the hands of the government, the only groups that gain power are those that can influence the government.

Weak parties
- The lack of powerful party leaders (caused largely by the separation of powers and primaries) allows US pressure groups to influence legislative politicians more than those in the UK.
- Stricter party discipline in the UK means that MPs are strongly accountable to political leaders.
- Interest groups know it will be difficult to persuade individual MPs to vote against the party line.

Rights protection

- Higher levels of rights protection help US interest groups gain greater influence than their UK counterparts.

- UK interest groups cannot achieve long-term policy success through Supreme Court rulings in the way that US groups can.

Number and frequency of elections

- Electioneering is far more intense in the US, where it can be a highly effective method.

- In the UK it is highly unlikely that an environmental campaign group would be able to unseat any of their target MPs in a general election. It is also hard to imagine a UK version of the US League of Conservation Voters.

Are US interest groups really more powerful?

Despite the constitutional differences in the two countries and the apparent supremacy of interest groups in the US, it can be argued that there is little or no difference in the power levels of UK and US groups. The elitist argument rejects the idea that US interest groups encourage power to be shared. In practice, in both countries only a small elite has significant influence, with the majority of groups and their interests being largely ignored. Wealthy business leaders in both countries can donate large amounts of money to politicians and political parties. In addition, they have a network of contacts, partly based on common social circles and funding, allowing power to be concentrated in the hands of the few.

Evidence for this can be seen in the change in income or wealth for different sections of society in the past 40 or 50 years. Wealth or income of the super wealthy and the wealthy has grown hugely, whereas for those on low income it has barely risen. The cake is bigger but the rich are taking an even bigger slice. Legislative outcomes created by parliament and Congress represent the influence of a very small number of interest groups in society.

Impact of interest groups on politics and government can be assessed in these key areas:

- on policy-making, which is arguably greater in the US than UK

- on the protection of civil rights

- on democracy, including representation and participation.

As well as examining the extent of impact it is also possible to discuss whether this impact is positive or negative.

Rational, cultural and structural approaches

EXTENSION ACTIVITY

Using the internet, find evidence for and against the elite theory view of US and UK interest groups. Which comparative theory (rational, cultural or structural) does the elite theory suggest is most useful in comparing US and UK groups?

The rational approach is particularly useful in comparing the two countries in relation to:

- individual voters

- the level of rights protection

- campaign finance

- individual politicians.

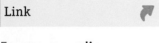

Link

For more on **policy networks** see Section 5.3 of US Democracy and Participation.

Arguably, in the US, individual members of the public have a greater ability to act rationally and pursue their own interests than in the UK. Greater number and frequency of elections as well as stronger rights protection both serve to empower individuals.

In both countries, self-interested actors donate money to gain political influence. Concerns over these donations have led to the imposition of structures in the form of campaign finance regulations. This creates a clash between the pursuit of rational self-interest and the structures that try to regulate it. The rational perspective is a useful theory here as the structures only provide basic restrictions. Politicians and donors are acting in a self-interested way, taking or giving funding because it helps them maintain their power without being restricted by structures or cultural expectations.

The rational approach can also be easily applied to individual politicians. Individuals may act according to their own views or interests regardless of the wishes of the party or party leaders. This is arguably true of the US with more fragmented parties. However, there is evidence for this in the UK. The Conservative Party has long been divided on the issue of Europe, which has limited the extent to which the structure of party leaders has been able to impose its view on the rational actors within the party, who have pursued their own ideological goals.

The cultural approach is useful in comparing groups such as voter groups, parties or factions. It is the common value system of a faction or caucus that influences the behaviour of politicians in Congress and parliament. In the UK, there is a more dominant culture of party unity. The concept of a rebellion is barely applied to politicians in the US, but in the UK it is seen as more serious. The collective culture of the Freedom Caucus in the US House of Representatives is a powerful force that unites those within it, often placing it in opposition to the party leadership.

The structural approach can be applied to all aspects of the comparison of democracy and participation. Structures such as the constitution determine the difference in the power of US and UK voters, interest groups and parties. The separation of powers, the number and frequency of elections, and the location of sovereignty all have an impact on their relative influence.

By having separate elections for the executive and legislature, the United States is arguably more democratic, giving more control to individual voters who can exercise greater choice over their elected politicians. In the UK, voters have only one choice, technically, for parliament, which then determines which party forms the government and who becomes prime minister – so the prime minister is not directly elected by the public. In the United States it is common for citizens to use their ability to vote for more than one institution to 'split their ticket', voting for different parties for different offices in the same election year.

Assessment support: 3.1.6 Comparative Approaches

Paper 3 Section A question

Question 1 on A-Level Paper 3 requires you to answer one question from a choice of two, worth 12 marks.

Examine the levels of independence of the Supreme Court in the US and the UK. [12 marks]

This type of question tests Assessment Objectives AO1 and AO2, with 6 marks available for each. This question asks you to examine: to explain direct comparisons between the US and the UK. You would typically explore three or four points of comparison, so you would write three or four paragraphs, comparing the US and UK in each one. This could involve similarities or differences or both depending on what the question is asking for.

Here is part of a student's answer.

The US Supreme Court has lower levels of independence than the UK Court. This is mainly because of the different appointment processes. In the UK justices are appointed by the judicial appointments committee, which is an independent body.

- The opening line shows a good approach to starting each paragraph of an answer.
- The student gives a direct answer to the question by comparing the two countries, followed by an explanation that relates to the question of independence.

Here is another part of a student's answer.

In the US, the president makes appointments, leading to accusations that justices will be reluctant to provide checks on the president who appointed them. Senate Democrats have expressed concerns that Trump's appointee, Justice Gorsuch, will act as a rubber stamp for some of the president's controversial policies that may break the Constitution. In the UK Supreme Court justices such as President of the Court Lord Neuberger had no problem defying the government over Brexit.

- The student does well by using contemporary examples from both the UK and the US.
- Ideally you should use examples from both countries in each paragraph, and explain what the examples tell us about the question.

Paper 3 Section B question

Question 2 on A-Level Paper 3 is a compulsory question – there is no choice. The question is worth 12 marks.

Analyse the difference between the power of the prime minister and the president. [12 marks]

In your answer you must consider the relevance of at least one comparative theory.

This type of question tests Assessment Objectives AO1 and AO2, with 6 marks available for each. These questions require you to compare the UK and US political systems. The question will ask you to analyse, which you need to do by applying at least one of the three comparative theories – rational, cultural and structural. AO2 marks are awarded for the application of the comparative theories.

You would typically explore three or four points of comparison, so you would write three or four paragraphs, comparing the US and UK in each one. This could involve similarities or differences or both depending on what the question is asking for.

Here is part of a student's answer.

The president is significantly less powerful than the prime minster because of the different levels of separation of powers and checks and balances. The structural theory shows how the president is more limited by the Constitution because he finds it difficult to pass legislation through a separately elected Congress. He has little patronage and may not even have a majority. Prime ministers, on the other hand, have fewer structural limits from the legislature. They can use their majority and patronage power to achieve their policy goals.

- The student follows the command to analyse by applying a comparative theory to the question, using the structural theory to explain differences between the two countries.

Here is another part of a student's answer.

The prime minister has greater freedom to act than the president. This suggests that the rational theory is more easily applied to the UK prime minister. The PM finds it easier to act in a self-interested manner to achieve their own policy goals. The president has less opportunity to act in a rational self-interested way, often compromising heavily on key policy goals or even giving up on them.

- Here the student analyses by showing how a comparative theory (rational) is more applicable to one country than another. It is important to apply these theories in each paragraph of your answer. You only have to use one theory, but you can use more – for example, using different theories in different paragraphs.

The State and Globalisation

States and **globalisation** are two of the key concepts in global politics. Importantly, states are said to have **sovereignty** – absolute and ultimate authority over their citizens and subjects. Globalisation is the idea that the world is becoming a more interconnected and interdependent place, where events and ideas from one part of the world have an impact far beyond their borders.

Key terms

Globalisation
emergence of a complex web of interconnectedness in many forms.

Sovereignty
absolute and unlimited power and authority.

Nation state
autonomous political community held together by citizenship and nationality.

The two concepts go hand in hand. States and state sovereignty are hugely affected by globalisation. In many ways, they work against each other. States are meant to be in control as sovereign entities, but globalisation can make states seem redundant, or even impotent. Arguably the more the world becomes globalised, the less sovereignty a state can have and the less significant states are. The more a state is affected by actions in another part of the world, the less it can realistically claim to have absolute and ultimate authority.

Furthermore, sovereignty and globalisation are similar in that they both appear to be simple and understandable concepts that are at the heart of the study of global politics. However, in reality, they are both extremely contested concepts whose meaning is debated. Both concepts are widely used by the public, and both stir up passions, but they can end up meaning what an individual wants them to mean.

1.1 The state: nation states and national sovereignty

Characteristics of a nation state

A common definition of a **nation state** is 'a political community bound together by citizenship and nationality'. You may feel that you know what a nation is, and have a good idea of what a state is, but looking more closely at the concepts behind these terms can help draw out the key aspects and issues involved.

Nation	State
Self-identifying community that does not necessarily have sovereignty.	Political entity with sovereignty.
Not necessarily recognised by the international community.	Recognised by the international community.
Not necessarily possessing a state, for example the Kurds.	Could contain more than one nation or community, such as the United Kingdom.
Defined territory not needed.	Defined territory needed.
Nations can live in more than one state.	States cannot cross the boundaries into other states.

Table 1.1: Key differences between nationhood and statehood

What is a nation?

A nation is a group of people who self-identify as belonging to the same group or community, with a strong sense of unity. The individuals may have certain characteristics in common – such as territory, language, ethnicity, history, traditions or religion – but none of these (apart from attachment to a territory) is absolutely essential. For a group to be a nation, they only need share some of these characteristics. For example, members of a nation may not share the same religion or even the same language but they still might see themselves as belonging to the same nation.

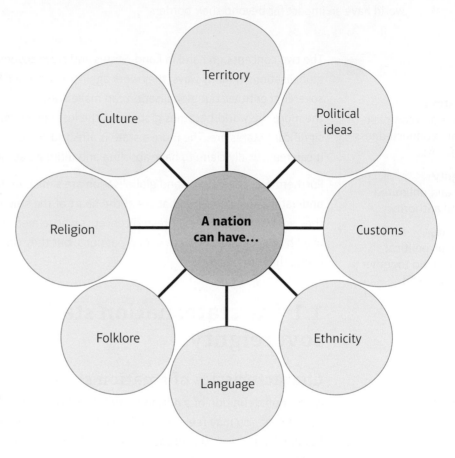

Figure 1.1: Characteristics that may be shared by members of a nation

In some respects, nations are easy to identify. You might think of the French, the Germans or the Italians as single nations. They meet some of the criteria: they all identify with a certain territory, have a common language, share a history, have the same traditions, and so on. However, there are Bretons in France, Bavarians in Germany, and South Tyroleans in Italy who all believe that they are a nation in their own right and could convincingly make a claim using the same criteria.

The concept of the nation is a fairly recent one. For many centuries people's loyalties were local – to their city, their church or a local prince – rather than any larger community. However, for the last two centuries, the idea of loyalty to and identification with the nation gained ground, and by the 20th century its real power was being felt.

Nationhood is important as it is the idea behind one of the most powerful forces in global politics: nationalism. Nationalism – the strong belief in one's own country – has been the force behind some of the greatest changes and conflicts in recent world history. Nationalism can be a force for good, uniting people and leading them to freedom from the tyranny of others, or a force for bad, leading countries and peoples to war and conflict.

What is a state?

A state is a specific form of political entity that meets four criteria, as shown in Figure 1.2.

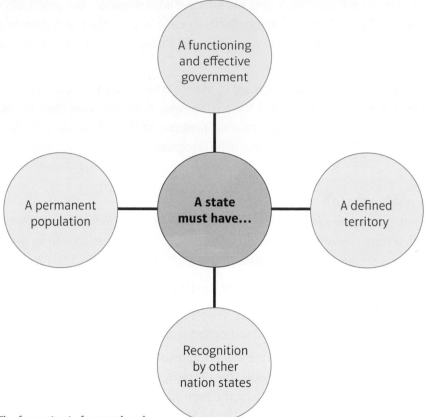

Figure 1.2: The four criteria for statehood

A defined territory

A state can only have sovereignty or absolute and unlimited power over somewhere. Much of the political conflict in the world is based on disagreements between states as to who owns which territory. Examples of conflict based on competing claims to territory include:

- the Falkland Islands/Malvinas conflict between the UK and Argentina
- Kashmir dispute between India and Pakistan
- disputes between the People's Republic of China and its neighbours over islands and sea rights in the South China Sea.

This criterion raises interesting questions over the future of low-lying Pacific island states, such as Vanuatu, if they succumb to rising sea-levels, and about the need for actual territory in cyberspace. But as it stands, physical land is essential for statehood.

A permanent population

For a state to exist it must have people permanently living in that territory. If there are no people, there is no state. For example, Antarctica does not have a permanent population so it does not meet this criterion.

A functioning and effective government

Some territories that meet the other criteria for a state are not in a position to enforce the law, or exercise their sovereignty over the territory and its population. They are more accurately described as 'failed states'. One recent example is Syria, which is engulfed by civil war. President Bashar al-Assad's government lost control of much of Syria to what it considered rebels and to Daesh (ISIS). Where it does not control the territory, it is not an effective state.

Recognition by other nation states

This is perhaps the most significant criterion of a state. A state-like entity may have a territory, a permanent population and a functioning and effective administration, but unless it is seen by other states as also being a state, it cannot effectively enter into relations with them or exercise its sovereignty in the international system (for example, through UN membership or having an embassy).

Kosovo is a state-like entity that is recognised by many of the world's states, but is not sufficiently recognised to be a member of the United Nations. Likewise, Palestine is not formally recognised by the UN although there is growing international pressure for the Palestinian authority to be recognised as a state. The most recent state to be recognised as such is South Sudan, which joined the UN in 2011.

What is a nation state?

The nation state is the prime political entity of the modern era and in the Westphalian system (see the Extension feature opposite). At its most basic a nation state is a nation with its own state, but this can be further developed. A nation state is:

- a state that represents the political wishes of a nation, and thus gains authority and legitimacy
- a self-governing state
- a state that is based on the principle of self-determination.

Although there are problems with both the identification of nations and the recognition of states, the nation state is now the dominant model. The UN recognises 193 states in the world, which are best described as nation states. To an extent, the term 'nation state' is used to differentiate the states of the world from the 50 states of the United States of America.

> **Pause & reflect**
>
> Are you clear on the differences between nations, states and nation states? Make some notes on the characteristics of each.

Issues with nationhood and statehood in the modern world

Nations without a state

There are ongoing claims for nations that do not have their own state. Scotland held an independence referendum in September 2014, where the people of Scotland exercised their right to decide whether they wanted to secede from the United Kingdom and become an independent state in their own right. On that occasion they voted not to leave the UK, but what is clear is that the Scots have a right to determine their own future. Any vote by the Scottish people to leave the UK would be legitimate.

This issue is not so clear for the Basque people and the Catalonians of Spain. Whereas the UK government gave its blessing to a Scottish independence referendum, and therefore would have honoured the alternative outcome, the Spanish government has not recognised the right of the Basque or Catalonian people to determine their own future outside of Spain. The secessionist movements of these parts of Spain play on the nationalist sentiment of their people, drawing on the history, traditions, folklore, language, politics and economics of these areas to try to convince the people to push for an independent and sovereign nation of Catalonia and the Basque country. These kind of secessionist movements have at times turned to violence, notably with ETA in the Basque country of northern Spain 'fighting for their freedom' – a stance which many others might call terrorism.

Case study: The Kurds

The largest nation in the world that is acknowledged not to have its own state is the Kurdish people of Turkey, Syria and Iraq. The Kurds feel they are a persecuted minority and some Kurds are using violence against the Turkish state to push for Kurdish self-determination. In Syria, the Kurdish people have been fighting against Daesh (ISIS) and have achieved some sort of autonomy in the country. In Iraq, the Kurds have had autonomy for a number of years and have effectively or de facto had their own country or state. However, the Kurds face a big problem in trying to achieve an independent, sovereign Kurdistan because the territory they claim as their own already belongs to sovereign states that are loathe to give it up. Furthermore, other states are unwilling to allow a precedent whereby parts of countries can be broken away from sovereign states without the permission of the original states.

Questions

- Is the United Kingdom of Great Britain and Northern Ireland a nation state or a multinational state?

- How viable are small nation states today?

National claims that cross borders

A further difficulty is that the territorial claims of a nation do not always coincide with the borders of states. Many states are in dispute with their neighbours over the sovereignty or ownership of territory, and this is complicated by the competing historical and traditional claims of the people who live in that territory. One of the ideas behind a nation is attachment to a territory or land, but what happens when two nations claim the same land? These types of conflict are particularly intractable.

The United Kingdom has its own example of this problem in Northern Ireland. Two different communities or nations claim the territory of Northern Ireland as their own. Both have strong historical arguments, both can claim a certain legitimacy, and both, in their own eyes, are right.

It is not just the Nationalists and Unionists of Northern Ireland who have competing claims. This type of dispute can also be seen in the Middle East, with Israeli and Palestinian claims to the same territory resulting in decades of conflict. The recent conflict in eastern Ukraine is founded on the same problem. Ethnic Russians who identify with the Russian nation and state are living in the internationally recognised state of Ukraine. The Russians want closer ties with Russia; the Ukrainians believe their state should be sovereign and independent of Russia.

States not recognised by other states

There are several examples of state-like entities that are not recognised by other states, so find it difficult to operate in the international system. Micro-nations are tiny parcels of land that claim they are independent and sovereign states, but are not recognised as such – so, for example, their issuing of passports and currency has no legal or practical value. One such micro-nation is Sealand, off the coast of Essex in England. They claim they are a state, but to all practical purposes, they do not exist. More pressing examples of states not recognised by other states are Kosovo, South Ossetia, Abkhazia and Transnistria.

Case study: The Turkish Republic of Northern Cyprus (TRNC)

Turkey invaded and occupied the northern half of the island of Cyprus in 1974, with the authorities there declaring it to be the Turkish Republic of Northern Cyprus. The TRNC exists insomuch as you can live and go on holiday there. However, in the international system the TRNC does not exist. The only country in the world to recognise the TRNC as an independent sovereign state is Turkey. The fact that other states do not recognise it has all sorts of ramifications. No country will allow travel into its territory on a TRNC passport. No country will recognise the government of TRNC. The TRNC is not a member of the United Nations or any other international body. There are no international flights to the TRNC. You cannot make international telephone calls to the TRNC (except via Turkey). The TRNC does not have internet domain letters, like .UK or .de. The TRNC cannot participate in the Olympics or the FIFA World Cup.

Questions

- What other state-like entities are not recognised by other states?

- Which countries have lost parts of their territory in this way?

Characteristics of national sovereignty

The state's absolute power over citizens and subjects

Sovereignty means absolute power. Within a state, the state has absolute power over its citizens and everyone who resides within its jurisdiction. The law applies to everyone, and there is no opting out. Should anyone break the law of the state, they can be arrested, put on trial in a court, sentenced to a prison sentence and, in some states, ultimately executed. Max Weber defined the state as having a monopoly on the legitimate use of force within a given territory. The state will seek to legitimise this monopoly.

On the face of it, sovereignty could not have a simpler definition: absolute and ultimate authority. But what does that actually mean – absolute and ultimate authority in theory, or in practice? If you give away the smallest amount of sovereignty, does that mean a state no longer has absolute and ultimate authority?

Sovereignty has become a widely debated concept and its use has come more into question due to globalisation. As each state is affected by the actions of other states and events in the world around them, do states lose the capacity in practice to control events in their own country? Is it sensible to talk about sovereignty as a concept if a state is left with no realistic choices?

At a basic level, sovereignty within a state or internal sovereignty is quite straightforward. It is easy to identify the location of sovereignty in the UK constitution. Parliament is the sovereign body of the UK – there is no higher body than parliament, there is no law that parliament cannot pass and only parliament can overturn an act passed by parliament. This is the most fundamental principle in the UK constitution. However, as a democracy it can also be argued that the people are sovereign; that there is 'popular sovereignty'.

In the USA, there are also complications. The preamble to the US Constitution declares 'We the people…' indicating that there is popular sovereignty and that this is upheld by the Constitution. However, the USA is also a federal country, meaning that there are two or more autonomous sovereign bodies in the USA. In fact, 50 individual states share sovereignty with the federal government. Furthermore, within the branches of government there is a system of checks and balances meaning that no one institution of government is sovereign (unlike in the UK, where parliament is sovereign).

EXTENSION ACTIVITY

Before the Treaty of Westphalia in 1648, states did not have sovereignty or absolute and unlimited power. Do some research to find out how the Treaty came about and what its impact was on notions of statehood and sovereignty. Consider the challenges to state sovereignty from **political globalisation, economic globalisation** and **cultural globalisation**.

1.2 Globalisation

Globalisation is a widely used term that has a simple enough idea at its heart: that the world is becoming more closely entwined and more of a complex web. However, there are many questions surrounding globalisation. Is it a phenomenon, a process or a policy? Is it Westernisation? Is it Americanisation? Is it a new thing? Can it be stopped? Can it be reversed? Can it be controlled? Is it economic, political, cultural, technological?

Different people have different views, but what is clear is that globalisation is having a profound effect on states and on people's lives. Globalisation can be seen to be having a significant effect on states' sovereignty, on democracy, on people's identities, jobs and communities. Some people feel left behind by what they term globalisation, by the changes it is making to their lives and their understanding of the world. Globalisation in its most broad terms has led to the closing of traditional industries, a loss of jobs, the lowering of wages and living standards, an increase in immigration, a loss of identity, the lowering of prices of goods and services, the ease and cost of international travel and – perhaps as significantly as anything else – the improvement of communication technology, not least the internet, which has shrunk the world. Time and place have become almost irrelevant.

The process of globalisation

Interconnectedness – the factors driving globalisation

People

People appreciate the benefits of this improved communication, the ease of conducting business and shopping transactions. They think nothing of going online and purchasing an item that is produced and dispatched from China, but they also have concerns about the loss of employment opportunities in their locality. People travel more freely, easily and cheaply than ever before. They travel to once-exotic destinations for short breaks, experiencing things and meeting people that in previous ages would have been only available to the very rich. As people travel and meet other people, they form relationships (often through social media), they fall in love and want to spend their lives together. This inevitably leads to immigration as couples choose one country to live in. Children born of these relationships have dual identities, and often dual nationalities.

Link

For more on the US system, see the US Constitution and Federalism chapter.

Key terms

Political globalisation
the growing importance of international organisations.

Economic globalisation
the increasing integration of national economies to create a single global economy of cross-border movement and trade in goods, services, capital and technology.

Cultural globalisation
the increasing transmission of ideas, meanings and values around the world.

Countries

State sovereignty implies ultimate and absolute authority within a territory and independence from interference from other states. However, the reality has always been that states are affected by the decisions of their neighbours. Whether they share rivers, coastlines, seas, oceans or the air above them, countries are linked. One state's decision can have an impact on another.

People, commodities, cultures and ideas have always been on the move. In an increasingly interconnected world the impact of the movement of all these things is more intense and significant than ever before. This is particularly the case if states are willingly agreeing to and enhancing this globalisation process.

Institutions

As the world becomes a more interconnected and interdependent place where there are global and regional problems, it is entirely logical that states and **non-state actors** will co-operate and create institutions to solve these shared problems. It is worth noting the proliferation of **intergovernmental** (IGOs) and **non-governmental organisations** (NGOs) in the world. The scale of IGOs has increased a great deal in the last 150 years or so, but particularly since the end of the Second World War. There are regional and global IGOs that serve many different functions, and some serve more than one function. For example, there is the United Nations and its associated agencies, including the World Meteorological Organization, the World Health Organization and the World Trade Organization. Other groupings of states dealing with shared issues include the Organization of American States, the European Union, the North Atlantic Treaty Organization, the Arab League, the International Whaling Commission and the Arctic Council. These are all forums and talking shops where states can engage with each other and try to solve shared problems at different scales, from regional to global.

The number of international NGOs is estimated to have risen from around 130 at the start of the 20th century to more than 6000 at the start of the 21st century. NGOs are extremely wide-ranging, campaigning for debt relief, for an end to poverty, for human rights, or against the destruction of the rainforests, against the death penalty and against the hunting of whales, elephants and rhinoceroses. NGOs familiar to the UK public include the International Committee of the Red Cross, Amnesty International, Save the Children, World Wide Fund for Nature (WWF) and Oxfam.

Culture

Cultural globalisation is the 'flattening out' of differences in culture between countries. Cultural diversity is replaced by cultural homogeneity. The world is increasingly a place where the same cultural commodities are consumed regardless of national borders. People listen to the same music, using the same technology, on the same devices. One in seven people on the planet is thought to have watched some of the 2014 Fifa World Cup final – a truly global event. The same brands can be bought throughout the world: McDonald's, Coca-Cola, Apple iPhones, Nike sportswear and more. Their trademarks are instantly recognisable to a large proportion of the world's population. The dynamic behind this process may be transnational corporations (TNCs) using their global economic power to further their reach and sell more products the world over by exploiting the benefits of economic development.

Allied to the role of TNCs in cultural globalisation is the transformation of technology in bridging barriers of time and space. Advances in information technology have revolutionised the speed and ability to transfer information around the globe and improvements in transportation and its cost have made the movement of goods and people vastly quicker and cheaper.

Key term

Non-state actors participants in international relations with significant power and influence that are not states.

Link

For more on **intergovernmental and non-governmental organisations**, see Global Governance: Political and Economic and Global Governance: Human Rights and Environmental chapters.

This process has been criticised by some as:

- Americanisation – due to the preponderance of US TNCs
- Westernisation – due to the role of Western companies and culture in this process
- imperialism – due to the supposed exploitative and coercive nature of the process.

Linked to the cultural **homogenisation (monoculture)** brought about through economic globalisation, and the spread of consumerism and capitalism, is the spread of Western ideas such as democracy, respect for human rights and individualism. This transmission of values, ideas and meanings may be having an immense impact on global politics. Some see a certain inevitability about the spread of liberalism and its associated ideas around the world. For some this spread of ideas is a good thing, emphasising freedom, but for others cultural globalisation, consumerism and individualism are bad news for the environment, for local communities and traditions, and for individuals who are manipulated by the lure of consumer products. For these critics, the only winners in globalisation are the USA, the West and the TNCs that lead the cultural globalisation march.

Economics

There has always been international trade but what is arguably unique about economic globalisation is the degree of **interconnectedness** and interdependence, and the fact that the global economy can be seen as a single entity.

A number of interrelated factors have led to economic globalisation. The starting point can be seen as the Bretton Woods economic system, introduced towards the end of the Second World War in an attempt to prevent the circumstances that led to pre-war economic catastrophe – and, indeed, to the Second World War itself. Politicians and economists at the Bretton Woods conference were aiming to learn the lessons of economic nationalism and beggar-thy-neighbour policies. The Bretton Woods system was a system of fixed exchange rates and regulations to encourage trade and stability in the international system. This global system, along with the post-war reconstruction of Europe through the Marshall Plan and Keynesian economic policies, led to a growth in production, trade and prosperity in the developed world until the early 1970s. This long boom led to high economic growth and full employment throughout the Western world, leading to significant social, cultural and political change.

The 1973 oil crisis and the collapse of the fixed exchange rates introduced by the Bretton Wood system led to the next stage in the process of economic globalisation. Floating exchange rates led to greater competition for national economies and a growth in transnational corporations investing globally. The collapse of communism opened up new markets and opportunities for investment, and the opening up of the Chinese economy was a further dimension in economic globalisation.

Economic globalisation is closely linked to the astounding strides in technology in the last 100 or so years (see below). It has taken little more than a century to move from the first powered flight to the transporting of fresh flowers by international air freight at an incredibly low cost. A major contribution to economic globalisation is the speed of development of information and communications-technology. Telegraphs, fixed-line telephones, the wireless, the television, personal computers, mobile phones and the internet have all played their part in making the world smaller, changing world economics along the way.

The ideologies and policies of states have played a role too. The decision by states to follow paths of co-operation and free trade in the post-war era have also been deliberate attempts to prevent

Key term

Homogenisation (monoculture)
the coming together of global cultures and development of a single, homogeneous culture without diversity or dissension.

Key term

Interconnectedness
mutual reliance of two or more groups.

war, increase stability, increase prosperity and perhaps spread democracy. This focus on the benefits of free trade is based in part on neo-liberal thinking, which sees the benefits of a laissez-faire approach bringing the most economic gains.

All of this has arguably led to the creation of a global economic system with interlocking and interconnected markets, and huge transnational flows of capital and money. Over $5 trillion is traded each day on global foreign exchange markets.

Technology

The process of globalisation has been underway for many years, but has quickened its pace in recent years not least due to the advances in technology. Part of the intensifying of globalisation and the reduction in the importance of time and space is due to modern communication methods. The speed, ease and low cost of conveying information, goods and people around the globe have massively changed the world. What used to take days or weeks can now be done almost instantaneously. There are now more mobile phones on the planet than people and it is estimated that 40 per cent of the global population use the internet.

News and information from around the world can be relayed virtually instantaneously to every smartphone or tablet computer. Social media has had major roles in the uprisings of the Arab Spring where atrocities committed were videoed and shared globally. Daesh (ISIS) uses the internet and social media to transmit its brutal propaganda. In July 2016, President Erdogan of Turkey was able to mobilise opposition to a military coup through the use of a smartphone broadcast.

Politics

Political globalisation is the growing significance of international organisations, by which states are making more and more decisions together – a form of **global governance**. States are turning to organisations like the UN, NATO, the EU, the IMF, the G20 and WTO in order to address the common challenges or dilemmas that states face together. These global and regional challenges, including economic globalisation (see above), are the main drivers behind this political globalisation.

One view of this process is to see states as reacting to challenges by working together to solve them, as with the environment and economic globalisation. Therefore, this process can be seen to further enhance globalisation.

Intergovernmental organisations can be seen as part of the problem of globalisation; states are encouraging globalisation by giving away or pooling their sovereignty with other states. On the other hand, political globalisation and the organisations that go with it can be seen as a safeguard or bulwark against globalisation. According to this view, states have been hollowed out and become less able to exert their sovereignty in the face of global challenges, not least from the power of transnational corporations. States can pool their sovereignty in response to these threats and come out more powerful and better able to control events. It can be argued that without political globalisation, states are unable to fight back against TNCs or have no chance of affecting climate change, for example. However, when states make decisions as part of an organisation, they have more power. In this way, states can control their own destiny more effectively as part of a group, club or gang than they can as individual states.

It seems counter-intuitive to give sovereignty away in order to have more, but this is the way the EU works. TNCs look for ways to incur the lowest costs for doing business, pay the least taxes and face the most lax regulations, and so will invest where they can make the biggest profits. To this end, they play states off against each other – but if states work together to maintain minimum standards in workers' rights, environmental standards or corporation tax, then TNCs cannot shop

Key term

Global governance
a broad and complex process of decision-making at a global level.

around for the best deal – they will receive the same deal everywhere. This is what the EU hopes to achieve in the single market, the WTO strives for through state subsidy rules and the G20 targets through co-operation on tax avoidance and evasion.

The impact of globalisation on the state system

The key relationship between globalisation and sovereignty is the extent to which independent sovereign states are able to control the forces of globalisation. Are states able to take effective action against internet fraudsters operating from other countries? Can states insulate themselves from economic and financial shocks in the international system?

There is a growing realisation among states that they need to work together to achieve common goals, that common problems need common solutions. Thus there has been an effort among states to pursue common approaches to global and regional problems through global and regional governance institutions such as the UN, the IPCC, the EU and ASEAN. All these institutions can be seen as an acknowledgement that states are no longer as sovereign as they once were.

Widening and deepening interconnectedness and interdependence

- **Cost of communication:** One of the key factors behind globalisation is the rising speed and frequency of communication. Technology has had a huge impact and brought huge changes over the millennia – from the development of writing to the invention of the printing press, from the telegram to the telephone to the digital technology of today. Mass communication that is virtually instantaneous is now available to billions of people, who can use the internet on tablets and mobile phones, and access the latest news 24 hours a day. The cost of communication has fallen just as rapidly. Today, sending an email or using social media to share information is virtually free.

- **Cost of transport:** Like communication, the speed and cost of transport have been hugely changed over the years. In 1800 it would take two months for a ship to cross the Atlantic Ocean with its cargo. Today, a ship can make the same journey in less than a week or a plane can cross the Atlantic in about 5 hours. As a result, the costs of transportation are reduced as well. Transportation costs are no longer prohibitive when it comes to moving goods around the world. This makes global-supply changes possible, it makes the production of goods in other parts of the world possible and it means fresh produce can be shipped from a field in one continent to a supermarket in another in a matter of days.

- **Human links:** The history of humankind is the movement of people, but what is perhaps different about modern migration patterns is the low cost of staying in contact and the relative low cost of travel to different countries or regions. Globalisation and economic growth have encouraged workers to move to countries with higher economic development in search of a better life. Gulf states like Kuwait and the United Arab Emirates are very wealthy due to oil production, and this has encouraged economic migrants to move to those countries to work. Well over 50 per cent of the population of these states is now made up of immigrants. Both Australia and Switzerland have migrant populations approaching 30 per cent of the total. Increasing wealth and leisure time have also led to a huge change in holiday patterns, with the growth of international tourism and, particularly today, long-haul travel. As people travel, they meet, experience different cultures and stay in touch.

Case study: Interconnected trade – imports to the UK

The UK imports almost half of its food. As well as food that needs to be grown in a warmer climate, such as bananas and oranges, there is also year-round demand for fruit and vegetables that would be off-season in the UK.

The UK is not self-sufficient in food despite having a significant farming industry that exports a considerable amount of its produce. Between 40 and 50 per cent of food consumed in the UK is imported from overseas, including about 25 per cent from EU countries. Examples of staple foods imported to the UK include tea, coffee, cocoa, bananas, oranges, rice and peanuts. The largest food-and-drink export from the UK is whisky, worth £5 billion pounds a year.

Both international trade and the country's food security are reliant on factors outside the control of the United Kingdom itself. Things like environmental disasters, poor harvests, animal epidemics and fluctuating currencies can all have an impact on the price and availability of food in the UK. This reliance on imported food is only likely to increase.

In addition, the UK imports vast numbers of cars and other vehicles, the oil and electricity to power these vehicles, pharmaceuticals, gems and precious metals, and clothing. Figures suggest that 90 per cent of clothes worn in the UK are imported from overseas. Of course, the UK is also reliant on exports of many products, including cars and food. This two-way trade is necessary for the prosperity of the UK, including securing employment and low-cost goods for consumers. The UK is part of an interdependent and interconnected world.

Questions

- What global factors affect the price of the petrol and diesel that fuels our cars?

- What, if anything, can the UK do to end its reliance on imports? Would that even be desirable?

Challenge to state control over citizens in areas such as law

In recent years, the emphasis on states as the key actors in the international system has been harder to sustain. It has become apparent that there is a host of actors in the international system, from terrorist organisations to transnational corporations, from global pressure groups to religious leaders, from NGOs to global movements. All these groups can be increasingly seen to have some influence in global politics. In addition, it can be argued that states are less likely to be able to exercise their sovereignty in the face of global challenges. Liberals argue that these non-state actors can be significant in influencing the world today.

Impact on the development of international law

Some would argue that there can be no such thing as international law. Laws are sets of rules that can be enforced, but one of the key aspects of the international system is the sovereign state – where there is no higher authority than the state. In the international system there are no global police that come and arrest a country and take them to a global court and perhaps throw them in a global prison. This is exactly what can happen within a country, where people are bound by the laws of the land and can be punished by the state as the law is superior to the individual. There is no compulsion in the international system, so no laws are enforceable internationally.

For others, international law means a set of international norms or standards of international behaviour. This is the behaviour that the community of states has approved of, involving rules over which there is a strong consensus.

Even though international law cannot be enforced in the way that national law can, there are a number of reasons why states would obey it.

- It is in their interests to do so. If they do not stay within international laws, nobody else will; obeying the rules makes life more predictable and ordered for everybody.
- International law can carry a certain legitimacy, and obeying it gives a country **soft power** or 'kudos' in the world.
- It is the morally right thing to do. States that believe in the rule of law should practise what they preach.
- Not obeying international law can lead to a state being isolated or, in some circumstances, punished. This does mean that international law can exist and there can be punishment of individuals who are personally responsible for crimes. There have been special tribunals dealing with crimes and there is now an international criminal court.

Humanitarian and forcible intervention

One of the key tensions in the international system is between the principle of non-intervention in the affairs of other states and the moral case for intervention when a humanitarian catastrophe is unfolding in another state. Should the world stand by when innocent men, women and children are facing genocide, crimes against humanity and war crimes? There is no easy answer to this question, but there have been numerous cases where the international community stood by and did nothing as human rights were routinely ignored.

It can be argued that in the period since the Holocaust, there has been greater support for the idea that the international community should act if crimes against humanity are taking place in another country. Using force in such situations raises considerable moral and legal questions. Forcible **humanitarian intervention** assumes there are universal moral absolutes that unite the world, but are these instead Western inventions and a form of cultural imperialism? Perhaps Western powers use intervention on humanitarian grounds as an excuse to increase their power and further their own national interests, or even as a pretext for the annexation of another state.

Humanitarian intervention is not guaranteed to make the situation better on the ground. Indeed, the use of force to prevent humanitarian catastrophes may lead to the loss of more lives, as war escalates. Humanitarian intervention can be seen to go against 'just-war' theory: it is not a last resort and could lead to disproportionate responses and the loss of more lives.

Of course, forcible humanitarian intervention goes against the principles of state sovereignty by interfering in the internal affairs of another state. If humanitarian intervention is increasingly permitted by the international community, this is clearly a challenge to state sovereignty.

> **Key term**
>
> **Soft power**
> the ability to attract and co-opt and to shape the preferences of others through appeal and attraction.

> **Key term**
>
> **Humanitarian intervention**
> military intervention carried out in pursuit of humanitarian rather than other objectives.

One attempt to square this circle of state sovereignty and humanitarian intervention has been the doctrine of responsibility to protect (R2P). This doctrine, in place since 2005, places the focus on the idea that state sovereignty comes with responsibilities. Part of a state's sovereignty is the responsibility to protect its own citizens. If a state fails to uphold this responsibility, the responsibility to protect falls on the international community, allowing – eventually – for humanitarian intervention through force.

Allied to the challenge of sovereignty from humanitarian intervention is the role of the International Criminal Court (ICC), which is based in The Hague, the Netherlands. While some significant global actors have not signed up to it – including the USA, China and Russia – the ICC is the first permanent international criminal court in the world. This has advanced considerably the concept of a higher international law. The fact that a large number of states have agreed definitions of genocide, war crimes and crimes against humanity, and have accepted that these crimes can be tried at an international level, suggests that there is a little less anarchy in the international system and that states are not as sovereign as they once were.

Pause & reflect

Look into recent cases of international humanitarian intervention. What sorts of events triggered a response from the international community?

EXTENSION ACTIVITY

Do some research to find out more about 'just-war' theory. You may want to look at the works of Thomas Aquinas and of Hugo Grotius on this subject.

- What are the principles behind the just-war theory?
- Is it significant that this theory is based on Christian ideas?
- Does the just-war theory still apply to modern conflicts?

Viewpoint	Explanation	Critique
Hyperglobalisers	Hyperglobalisers see the inevitability of globalisation as a consequence of advances in technology, and feel that humankind is entering a new age. There is no going back from growing globalisation; the world can only become more interconnected and interdependent. The borderless world will become a reality as states become irrelevant. Theorists differ on whether hyperglobalisation will be a good or a bad thing.	Are national governments now impotent and incapable of determining economic and other policies? Governments still play a large role in attracting inward investment and improving education. They have also pooled their sovereignty to work together to temper the effects of globalisation and related problems, like international crime and terrorism.
Sceptics	Sceptics see much of globalisation as a myth and argue that the so-called integrated global economy does not exist. In reality, regional, national and local economies are more significant. Sceptics also argue that international trade and capital flows are not new phenomena.	There has been a real change in technology that has made the world a smaller place. Economies are integrated into the global system, countries are working more co-operatively and there is a global flow of values, ideas and information.

Viewpoint	Explanation	Critique
Transformation-alists	Transformationalists tread a middle path between hyperglobalisers and sceptics. Yes, significant changes have occurred due to globalisation but they have not fundamentally changed the basic international system. National governments are changing, perhaps becoming less important. Interconnectedness has increased in terms of breadth, intensity and speed.	This approach waters down some of the exaggerations of the previous perspectives and perhaps is more balanced, focusing on the strengths of both previous views.
Realist	Realists are essentially sceptics. They believe that the state is still the main actor in the global system, and that globalisation has been made by states for states. Globalisation can make the world a more unstable place due to increasing competition and conflict.	Similar point of view to the sceptics. Globalisation is not new, states are still the most important actors, and states have promoted globalisation in their own interests.
Liberal	Liberals have a positive view of globalisation and its ability to bring trade, prosperity, peace, democracy, political freedoms and human rights. It is a win-win. Liberals are also glad to see a decline in nation states and an increase in international co-operation.	Globalisation is new and intensifying, states are in decline, and globalisation is a win-win for all economically and in preventing conflict.

Table 2.1: The debate between hyperglobalisers, globalisation sceptics and transformationalists, including the realist and liberal views

1.3 Debates about the impact of globalisation including its advantages and disadvantages

Hyperglobalisers and liberals argue that globalisation is a win-win in the world. Global markets bring trade, prosperity, lower prices for consumers, peace, democracy and human rights. What is not to like?

However, critics believe that globalisation favours the rich, the West, the USA and transnational corporations at the expense of the poor, working people, developing countries, the environment, democracy and national identity and culture.

The impact of globalisation, and its implications for the nation state and national sovereignty

The state has been central to the international system for many years. However, there are those who argue that the state can no longer be realistically considered sovereign. While the state still has de jure (legal) and theoretical sovereignty, the realities of the 21st century suggest that states are impotent or powerless in the face of the global and regional challenges they face.

Increasingly, states are considered by some to be post-sovereign – that is, states no longer have the ability to actually exercise their sovereignty. They may wish to exercise absolute and unlimited power within their territory or externally, but in reality they cannot achieve their goals. Liberals argue that the state is not sovereign; realists, by contrast, believe that the decline of the state is exaggerated and that states are still the major actors in the global system.

The argument is that, due to the creation of a single global economy, states are no longer the sovereign bodies they used to be. States are buffeted by global economic winds and no state can isolate itself from global economic challenges.

There is an increasing trend for decisions affecting states to be taken at global or regional levels, such as in the United Nations, the International Monetary Fund and the European Union. Decisions about economics, trade, and the environment are taken at these institutions, rendering the nation state a less significant actor, and reducing its sovereignty. Decisions taken by the European Court of Human Rights and the World Trade Organization can also impact on the sovereignty of the state.

Case study: the 2007–08 global economic crisis

This crisis started out in the US, where mortgage lenders faced difficulties in the sub-prime mortgage market because these riskier loans were not paid back. These bad debts were packaged and sold on in complex financial products to banks around the world, which had then taken on these risks. The ensuing uncertainty in the global banking system led to a credit crunch, where banks refused to do business with each other. What started out as homeowners in the USA unable to meet their mortgage payments almost led to a global financial collapse.

Questions

- Should there be more global rules governing banks?

- How could that be achieved?

1.4 Globalisation and contemporary issues

Globalisation is about a shrinking, more interconnected and interdependent world. The issues of poverty, conflict, human rights and the environment are increasingly shared issues. In this world, poverty in sub-Saharan Africa leads to the movement of peoples to Europe, where inequality and resentment can inspire terrorism, and conflict in one country or region can easily spill over into neighbouring countries, sucking in competing states.

Poverty

Some argue that globalisation has caused poverty. With the transfer of jobs to lower-cost countries – for example, outsourcing call centres to India or the production of clothing to the Far East, away from Europe and the USA – unemployment can be a consequence in countries that lose these industries. Likewise, the opening up of developing markets to Western competition can kill off local companies and the theory of comparative advantage can condemn developing nations to remain focused on the primary sector, such as crop production. However, there is considerable evidence that globalisation is lifting countries and people out of poverty. Those countries that have opened themselves up to trade in recent decades have seen economic growth and the improvement of living standards. Not all citizens are helped equally, but there have been positives.

Conflict

Poverty, inequality and fear can also lead to conflict. While Western states do not want to lose the considerable advantages they already have, developing nations do not want to be deprived of the gains of globalisation and growth they think they have earned and are entitled to. Around the world, nationalism has been rising, which has a tendency to blame others for a nation's misfortunes. Nationalism is a well-known threat to peace, and conflicts have a habit of spreading. This has been the case in Syria, where the civil war has led to increased regional tensions involving Russia, Turkey, Saudi Arabia and Iran, and also millions of refugees forced from their homes, heading to Europe or living precarious lives in neighbouring countries.

Human rights

The humanitarian plight of the Syrian refugees and the human rights abuses that they have suffered in the civil war – and are still vulnerable to – have pricked the conscience of many. However, the inability to protect these people has also damaged the reputation of the international community and its organisations.

The environment

Cimate change is a significant challenge for humankind – one which no state individually can solve. As people in developing nations start to consume at the levels of Western citizens, this will place a tremendous strain on the world's resources. Food and meat production, fish for human consumption, oil, coal and gas extraction, CO_2 emissions into the environment, other air, land and sea pollution are just some of the challenges facing the environment.

Assessment support: 3.2.1 The State and Globalisation

Question 3 on A-Level Paper 3 gives you a choice of answering two out of three essay questions. Each one is worth 30 marks and you should allow about 45 minutes to complete each answer.

Evaluate the extent to which the impact of globalisation on the state system has been exaggerated. [30 marks]

You must consider this view and the alternative to this view in a balanced way.

Your two chosen questions will require an essay-style answer in which you consider both sides of the argument ('evaluate the extent'). They test all three Assessment Objectives, with marks divided equally between them. Your essay structure should clearly reflect the question, with balanced arguments that relate logically to each other. You need to explain what the state system and globalisation are.

You should consider globalisation in terms of economic, political and cultural globalisation, explaining each term. You could use these three forms to structure your essay, evaluating the impact of each type of globalisation on the state system. Better answers are likely to draw on further references to globalisation from other chapters.

- Use your introduction to set up the debate. Establish the key different opinions – hyperglobalisers and liberals versus sceptics and realists. What do they differ about?

- Start with the view that the impact of globalisation on the state system has been exaggerated. Then challenge each point in a logical way, using linking words like 'however' or 'conversely'.

  ○ Sceptics/realists say states are the principal actors in the international system, that most economic activity takes place within states' borders and international organisations are still vehicles for state-interests, and are thus state-centric.

  ○ Hyperglobalisers/liberals argue that state sovereignty has been significantly impacted by globalisation in all its forms. Globalisation has seen a growth in non-state actors including TNCs, NGOs and criminal and terrorist groups. This decline in sovereignty has led states to co-operation.

Here is part of a student's answer – the introduction.

Globalisation is not denied by either sceptics (realists) or hyperglobalisers (liberals), but the extent to which it has impacted the globe and international relations is a point of contention. Hyperglobalisers would disagree with the statement as they believe we are living in a globalised world due to economic interdependence, political co-operation and the flattening out of cultures to form a global monoculture. On the other hand, sceptics would argue that globalisation has been exaggerated, particularly due to the fact that most economic activity takes place within nation states and the ineffectiveness of political co-operation.

- The student brings in the main protagonists (sceptics/realists and hyperglobalisers/liberals), acknowledges that globalisation is significant and addresses the question by using the word 'impacted'.

- The student does well to refer to the three types of globalisation (economic, political and cultural) but a short definition of globalisation would benefit this introduction greatly.

- The sceptic/realist position is also outlined briefly, giving a clue to the type of arguments that will be used in the body of the essay.

CHAPTER

2

Global Governance: Political and Economic

A system of global and regional institutions and organisations has developed to enable states to come together to agree on shared solutions to shared problems. States can engage in bilateral or country-to-country approaches, but many of the world's problems cannot be solved by such a piecemeal approach. Global environmental, economic and security challenges need a more concerted effort.

Co-operation on a global scale is epitomised by **the United Nations** (UN), but also includes the **North Atlantic Treaty Organization (NATO)**, the Intergovernmental Panel on Climate Change (IPCC), the International Monetary Fund (IMF) and the International Court of Justice (ICJ). All these organisations are set up jointly by states to serve a function or to solve a particular problem.

In this chapter you will look at:

- international organisations with a political focus
- international organisations focusing on economic issues
- the ways and extent to which these institutions address global issues.

Key terms

The United Nations
created in 1945 following the Second World War to promote international co-operation and to prevent another such conflict.

North Atlantic Treaty Organization (NATO)
military alliance based on the North Atlantic Treaty, signed in 1949.

World government
the idea of a common political authority with legislative and executive power over states.

Link

For more on **democracy**, see Democracy and Participation chapter.

2.1 Political

The Westphalian or International system is based on the sovereign independent state, implying that no government higher than the state can compel states to act – so no global government.

Global or **world government** implies compulsion. Some people are fearful of a world government as it goes against the principle of self-determination and the right of a nation to govern itself. Global government is also an anathema to democracy, as it takes away accountability and the decision-making capabilities of the people – two key features of **democracy**.

The United Nations (UN)

The UN is the only intergovernmental organisation where all the world's states can be members. It is the global forum, where all states – irrespective of their system of government or regime type – can meet and engage in dialogue over the challenges facing humanity in the 21st century. These include climate change, international terrorism, food production, human rights, poverty and humanitarian and health interventions.

Origins and development of the UN, including its 1945 charter

The United Nations

- Came into existence on 24th October 1945 based on proposals by China, the Soviet Union, the UK and the USA.
- Headquarters in New York City with main offices in Geneva, Nairobi and Vienna.
- Funded through contributions of the member states.
- Currently 193 member states.

The United Nations (UN) came into being after the horrors of the Second World War and the earlier failure of the League of Nations. From an initial 51 states, membership has now grown to 193.

Each member state agrees to uphold the terms of the 1945 UN Charter. The preamble talks of the UN's determination to rid the world of the scourge of war, reaffirm human rights and equality, establish the respect of the rule of law and international treaties and promote social progress and better living standards. The UN hopes to achieve this through states practising tolerance and behaving in a neighbourly way, working together to maintain international peace and security, avoiding the use of armed forces except in the common interest and to use international means for economic and social advancement.

Article 1 of the UN Charter

The Purposes of the United Nations are:

1. To maintain international peace and security, and to that end – to take effective collective measures for the prevention and removal of threats to peace, and for the suppression of acts of aggression or other breaches of the peace, and to bring about by peaceful means, and in conformity with the principles of justice and international law, adjustment or settlement of international disputes or situations that might lead to a breach of the peace;

2. To develop friendly relations among nations based on respect for the principle of equal rights and self-determination of peoples, and to take other appropriate measures to strengthen universal peace;

3. To achieve international co-operation in solving international problems of an economic, social, cultural, or humanitarian character, and in promoting and encouraging respect for human rights and for fundamental freedoms for all without distinction as to race, sex, language, or religion; and

4. To be a centre for harmonizing the actions of nations in the attainment of these common ends.

The UN's programmes, specialised agencies and other related institutions have grown over the years. For example, the Intergovernmental Panel on Climate Change (IPCC) was set up by the UN's World Meteorological Organisation in 1988. The International Atomic Energy Agency (IAEA) was set up in 1957 as a 'forum for scientific and technical co-operation in the nuclear field'.

Key term

Security Council (UNSC) the United Nations' most powerful body, with primary responsibility for the maintenance of international peace and security.

Role and significance of the UN's main organs

The UN has six main organs, which were all set up in 1945. They are the General Assembly, the **Security Council**, the Economic and Social Council, the International Court of Justice, the UN Secretariat and the Trusteeship Council.

The General Assembly is the main body for all 193 UN members, where they are all represented and meet annually for the General Assembly session. The General Assembly is the talking-shop of the world where each state has an equal say and all voices can be heard. The significance of the assembly is that it is the main representative, deliberative and policy-making body of the UN. All peace and security and budgetary questions require a two-thirds majority, as does any decision to admit a new member, which effectively recognises a state in the international community. Other decisions require a simple majority. The nature of the General Assembly has changed over time. With the process of decolonisation and the admission of new countries to the UN, the General Assembly is now more diverse with a greater range of interests than ever before.

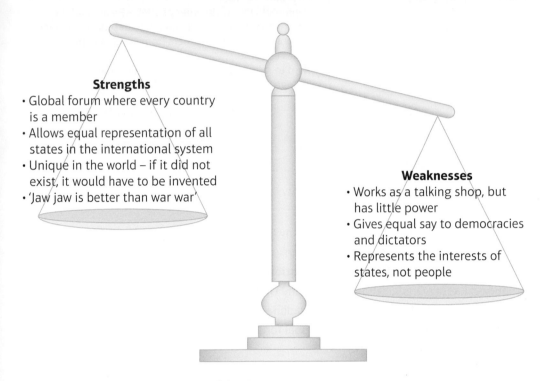

Strengths
- Global forum where every country is a member
- Allows equal representation of all states in the international system
- Unique in the world – if it did not exist, it would have to be invented
- 'Jaw jaw is better than war war'

Weaknesses
- Works as a talking shop, but has little power
- Gives equal say to democracies and dictators
- Represents the interests of states, not people

Figure 1.1: Strengths and weaknesses of the UN

The Security Council is the most important UN organ for maintaining peace and security in the world, and is probably the most important of all international organisations. The UNSC can authorise military action to enforce its resolutions and has done so – for example, against Iraq in 1990–91. The Council has 15 members, five of whom are permanent members and ten are non-permanent members elected by the General Assembly for a two-year period. Each member has one vote, but permanent members have a veto. The five permanent members are the great power victors of the Second World War: China, France, the UK, the USA and the Soviet Union (replaced by Russia). Decisions made by the Council are binding on all UN member states.

The fact that the permanent members of the UN Security Council have vetoes does have an impact on its effectiveness. When the interests of the big three permanent members (USA, China and Russia) are threatened, these powers will use their veto, preventing Security Council action.

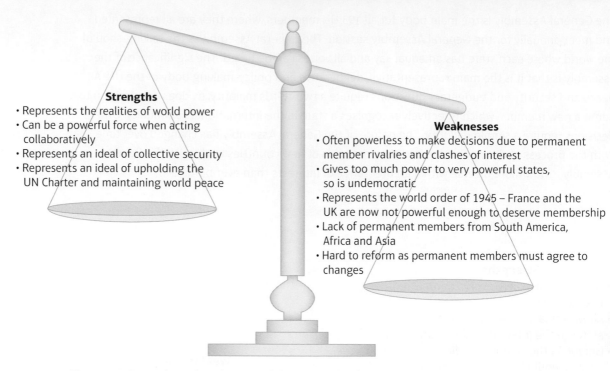

Figure 1.2: Strengths and weaknesses of the UN Security Council

The Economic and Social Council oversees the many UN agencies and their work on economic, social and economic issues. Its 54 elected members co-ordinate the International Monetary Fund, the **World Bank**, the **World Trade Organization**, the World Health Organization (WHO), the International Labour Organization (ILO) and the United Nations Educational, Scientific and Cultural Organization (UNESCO). While not as headline-grabbing as the Security Council, the Economic and Social Council is an important global forum for looking at some of humanity's most significant challenges.

Key terms

World Bank
international organisation that offers concessional loans and grants to the world's poorest developing countries in order to reduce poverty.

World Trade Organization (WTO)
organisation that regulates international trade.

Case study: The World Health Organization

The World Health Organization (WHO) is a specialist agency of the United Nations. It aims to increase international co-operation in the field of public health, working towards 'the attainment by all peoples of the highest possible level of health'. The WHO is particularly focused on fighting diseases, controlling epidemics and improving all-round health care. Historically, the WHO has worked on malaria, tuberculosis and AIDS. In recent years the WHO has been concerned with antibiotic-resistant 'superbugs', bird-flu outbreaks and fighting the ebola virus in West Africa in 2013–15. Successes have included the eradication of smallpox in the 1970s, and the removal of the scourge of polio from all but two countries. Child and maternal mortality have also been significantly reduced. However, the WHO has been criticised for its inadequate response to the ebola epidemic.

Questions

- What are the challenges the WHO may face in achieving its aims?

- What measures are used to assess the 'health' of a country?

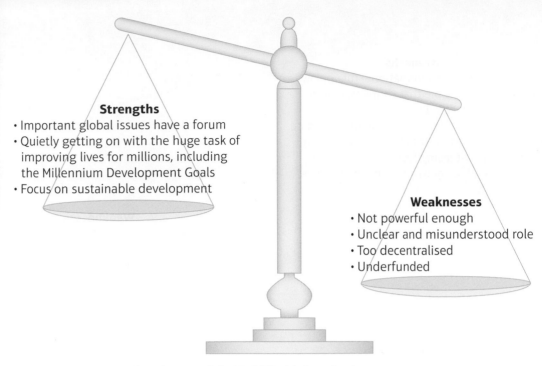

Figure 1.3: Strengths and weaknesses of the World Health Organization

The International Court of Justice (ICJ) is the principal judicial organ of the UN, and resolves disputes between member states. Based in The Hague, the Netherlands, it has 15 judges elected by the General Assembly for nine-year terms. The ICJ deals with sovereignty and border issues (at land or sea). One example was the dispute between Cambodia and Thailand over the sovereignty of the Temple of Preah Vihear, which was awarded to Cambodia.

Case study: The Temple of Preah Vihear

The Temple of Preah Vihear is a 900-year-old Hindu temple on the border between Cambodia and Thailand. In 1962 an ICJ ruling awarded sovereignty to Cambodia, but this has long been disputed. Fighting erupted between the two countries, first in 2009 and then more seriously in 2011. The fighting and mistrust between the two countries is fuelled by nationalism. The ICJ reaffirmed in 2013 that the temple belongs to Cambodia.

Questions

- Why do you think the temple was so important? Do some research to find out (for example, see www.bbc.co.uk/news/world-asia-pacific-12378001).

- How do 'borders' work at sea?

The Temple of Preah Vihear: the International Court of Justice ruled that the temple resided in territory that came under the sovereignty of Cambodia.

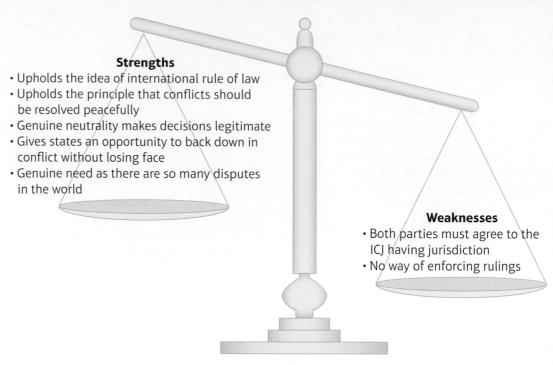

Strengths
• Upholds the idea of international rule of law
• Upholds the principle that conflicts should
  be resolved peacefully
• Genuine neutrality makes decisions legitimate
• Gives states an opportunity to back down in
  conflict without losing face
• Genuine need as there are so many disputes
  in the world

Weaknesses
• Both parties must agree to the
  ICJ having jurisdiction
• No way of enforcing rulings

Figure 1.4: Strengths and weaknesses of the International Court of Justice

The **Secretariat** comprises the secretary-general of the UN and the staff members who carry out the day-to-day work of the UN. The secretary-general of the UN, appointed by the General Assembly on the recommendation of the Security Council for a five-year term, is the head of the secretariat and therefore the chief administrator. The role is flexible and different secretaries-general interpret it differently, but they are seen as the world's number one diplomat. Their allegiance is to the UN and its values, not to their nation of origin, though they do have to maintain the support of member states with whom they work.

The **Trusteeship Council** suspended operations in 1994 when the last territory it was overseeing, Palau, gained independence. It had been set up to oversee the administration of 'trust territories', mostly former League of Nations mandated territories or territories of defeated powers, so that they were run with the best interests of their inhabitants and international peace and security in mind. All 11 trust territories are now independent, self-governing or have joined with neighbouring countries.

Strengths and weaknesses of the UN as a whole

The UN is a unique global organisation, as every state in the world is a member. This means that the UN and its associated agencies are the forum where the world as a whole can co-operate to find solutions to global problems, such as eliminating poverty and diseases. It also allows states to have worldwide communication networks, develop common frameworks for dealing with the sea, regulating space and space travel, protecting Antarctica and discussing climate change. The UN is often reduced in the public mind to the Security Council, but this ignores the many elements that enable states, corporations and people to interact on a daily basis. The existence of the UN shows the interconnectedness and interdependencies of the modern world.

One great strength of the UN is that it represents the states of the world as equals, irrespective of their power, size, wealth, dominant religion, culture or system of government.

Of course the UN has its problems. 193 sovereign states with competing national interests and outlooks will sometimes disagree. The UN does not take sovereignty away from states, so there is no compulsion. Critics highlight a range of weaknesses: it is too weak or too strong; it does not do enough or it does too much; it is undemocratic or it gives unsavoury governments an equal platform with the most liberal; it gives small countries too much say or it is dominated by powerful countries. The UN is also notoriously difficult to reform, and has been slow to react to humanitarian disasters.

North Atlantic Treaty Organization (NATO)

> **The North Atlantic Treaty Organization (NATO)**
>
> - Formed in 1949 by the signing of the Washington Treaty.
> - Originally had 12 members: the USA and Canada, plus ten states from western Europe.
> - Currently has 28 members.

The North Atlantic Treaty Organisation (NATO) was formed to provide collective security against the threat of military action in Europe from the Soviet bloc, and to promote deeper political integration and stability in Europe. Perhaps the most important article of the Treaty is Article 5, in which the signatories agree that an attack on one of them would be considered an attack on all of them, and that they should consider armed force in response.

Early role

At the end of the Second World War Europe was devastated: millions had been killed; millions more were displaced; and entire countries and economies were not working. It was feared that political instability would lead to communist parties winning elections. The Cold War was beginning.

The USA had signalled its intentions with the Marshall Plan, designed to kick-start the economies of Europe and restore economic and political stability. Attempts to restore military security to western Europe began with the Western Union in 1948, but it was felt that a truly North Atlantic approach – including the Americans – was needed. The Korean War and the Soviet Union's detonation of an atomic weapon in 1949 triggered deeper military integration. Lord Ismay, NATO's first secretary-general, supposedly said that NATO's purpose was 'to keep the Russians out, the Americans in and the Germans down'.

The Warsaw Pact

The Warsaw Pact (or Treaty of Friendship, Co-operation and Mutual Assistance) was formed in 1955 as a collective security organisation on the other side of the ideological divide from NATO in the Cold War. It was signed by seven countries under Soviet influence – Albania, Czechoslovakia, Poland, Hungary, Romania, Bulgaria and East Germany – as well as the Soviet Union itself.

NATO and Warsaw Pact countries never engaged in military conflict with each other, but the balance of power relations between these two blocs was the backdrop to much of the Cold War. Relations were often tense in a divided Europe – symbolised by the Berlin Wall, which was constructed in 1961 – but during the 1960s there was a movement towards *détente* (easing previously strained relationships).

After the 1979 Soviet invasion of Afghanistan, tensions between NATO and the Warsaw Pact increased with a new arms race for ballistic missiles, which created division in western Europe. From 1985 the rise of Mikhail Gorbachev, who was happier to negotiate with the USA and its NATO allies, meant that the Cold War was coming to an end.

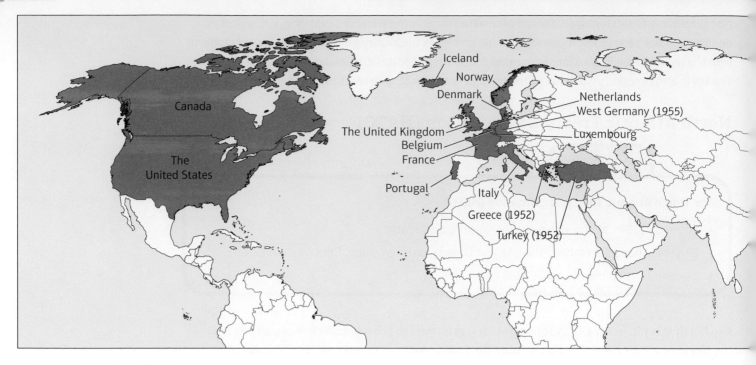

Figure 1.5: Early members of NATO

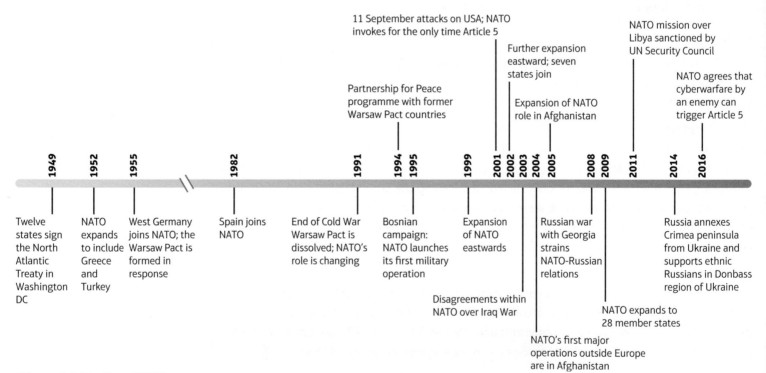

Figure 1.6: Timeline of NATO

Changing role

The end of the Cold War brought about an existential question for NATO, because the threat that NATO had been set up to counter had vanished. NATO was still committed to fighting militant nationalism in Europe, as well as promoting democracy and political integration. The ex-communist states of central and eastern Europe soon made it clear that they saw membership of NATO and the EU as key to embedding democracy and stability in their countries.

Involvement beyond Europe

NATO's primary role was collective security in Europe, and with the decline of the Soviet Union, people started to question its role. However, NATO's member states started to face different threats in the 21st century. On September 11th 2001, terrorists flew passenger airlines into the World Trade Towers in New York and into the Pentagon in Washington D.C. This triggered the first and only time that Article 5 of the NATO charter was invoked – this attack on one member state was an attack on all.

These terrorist attacks provoked a huge reaction from America and its allies. In Operation Enduring Freedom, America led the invasion of Afghanistan in October 2001 to take control from the Taliban regime, which had allowed Al-Qaeda to use the country as a base. NATO was called on to take command of the International Security Assistance Force (ISAF), aiming to provide security and stability so that peace and democracy could flourish. NATO maintained a presence in the country from 2003 to 2014.

NATO's role in Afghanistan was controversial on a number of fronts.

- Military personnel from NATO countries suffered considerable casualties. More than 2000 US and 400 UK personnel were killed. These losses were politically damaging. It was hard to make the case that NATO, perceived to be a defence organisation for Europe, was acting defensively in Afghanistan. People questioned how NATO troops serving and dying in Afghanistan helped the national interests of the member states.

- There were a number of 'friendly-fire' incidents in Afghanistan.

- Civilians were killed, particularly in airstrikes by NATO aircraft, such as the bombing of a wedding party by a US air raid in 2008. On top of the suffering, these casualties caused tensions between the Afghan government and foreign forces, and controversy among other NATO nations.

Growth and expansion into Eastern Europe and implications for peace and stability

The first expansion of NATO into former Warsaw Pact countries followed the reunification of Germany. As the Cold War came to an end, former Eastern bloc countries had ambitions to join both NATO and the EU. From 1990, 12 states from central and eastern Europe joined NATO; ten were former Warsaw Pact members and two were former republics of Yugoslavia.

Crucially, many states saw the Cold War as a period of oppression by the Russians in the guise of the Soviet Union. These new democracies were determined to entrench their freedom from Russia as well as their political and economic freedoms. Democracy, peace and stability would be ensured by a collective security arrangement with other European states and the sole superpower, the USA.

All 12 states that have joined NATO since the Cold War also wanted to join the European Union, and all but Albania have done so. Membership of NATO would guarantee security, while membership of the EU would embed democracy, human rights and market economies in those countries.

For Russia, this expansion of NATO into its former sphere of influence was not only a threat but also a betrayal. The Russians believed that the deal to bring about German reunification prohibited the expansion of NATO into central and eastern Europe. This expansion is seen by Moscow as part of the West's policy to 'encircle' and isolate Russia.

Relationship with Russia and the wider world

NATO's relationship with Russia and its predecessor the USSR has always been strained. In recent years, concerns about Russia's objectives in its 'near abroad' have raised tensions in the region to what some have described as a new Cold War.

After the collapse of the Soviet Union, Russia was not in a position to confront the power of the USA – economically, militarily or politically – so NATO did not feel under threat. As NATO took in more European countries and many joined the EU, Europe seemed like a haven of peace and stability. However, recently there have been several crises and tensions between Russia and NATO as Vladimir Putin has tried to regain Russia's position as a global power. Enlargement of NATO has caused disquiet and anger in Moscow, but there have been other issues where NATO and Russia have different interests, such as the USA's placement of an anti-ballistic missile system in former Soviet-bloc countries near Russia. The US maintains that the system is designed to protect against missiles from Iran and North Korea, but the Russians have their suspicions. The 2008 military conflagration between Russia and Georgia raised tensions, and Russia has sided with Serbia, its historic ally, over Kosovo's secession and pursuit of independence.

More recently, Russian actions in Ukraine – not a NATO member – caused alarm in the West. In March 2014, Russia annexed the Crimean peninsula, which belongs to Ukraine. Russian support for pro-Russian rebels and its actions in the Donbass region of eastern Ukraine are also a sign of the dangers that Russia poses. Russia is rearming and has used its military to support President Assad in the Syrian Civil War. NATO allies, particularly those with bitter memories of Soviet domination, are concerned that President Putin's tactics against Ukraine could be used against them too. Poland and the Baltic states are concerned about Russia's tactics, including using hybrid warfare – a mixture of conventional warfare, subversive and destabilising activities, and cyber-warfare – that could test the collective security commitments of the 28 member states of NATO. They fear that the Russians could manufacture a crisis involving ethnic Russian minorities in the Baltic states to muddy the waters, allowing Russia to intervene with troops who are not attributable to Russia (as occurred in Ukraine). In such a circumstance, Russia could plausibly deny responsibility, thus forcing NATO countries to decide whether to retaliate with limited evidence of the Russian state's involvement. Any differing views within NATO would massively weaken the alliance and give strength to the Russians. The stakes are high and both Russia and NATO have sought to bolster their borders by bringing in troops and military equipment to deter what each side sees as an aggressive neighbour. These movements suggest a re-play of the Cold War and a classic security dilemma and arms race.

Link

For more on **Cyprus and Turkey membership**, see Section 1.1 of The State and Globalisation.

Other countries in the neighbourhood of NATO and further afield have partnerships and dialogues with the bloc. Some of these are prospective members like Georgia; others are members of the EU but not members of NATO, like Sweden, Finland and Austria. **Cyprus** is a unique case because it is a member of the EU but is unlikely to join NATO in the near future, as **Turkey would veto its membership**.

NATO has quite close relationships with the EU as they share many member states, values and interests. Close co-operation between NATO and the EU can make the best use of the two organisations' specialisms. NATO can do much of the military work that the EU cannot do, while the EU has civilian expertise and soft power. One example of close co-operation was the two organisations deploying naval forces side-by-side in anti-piracy operations off the coast of Somalia.

Strengths and weaknesses

As with all intergovernmental organisations (IGOs), there are many criticisms that can be levelled at NATO, some fair and others not. Some of these criticisms will be contradictory and some are inevitable – member states will always have national interests that differ.

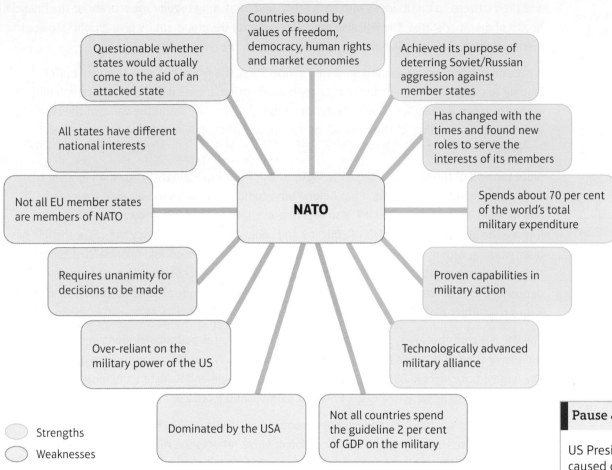

Figure 1.7: Nato strengths and weaknesses

NATO

Strengths

Weaknesses

Countries bound by values of freedom, democracy, human rights and market economies

Questionable whether states would actually come to the aid of an attacked state

Achieved its purpose of deterring Soviet/Russian aggression against member states

All states have different national interests

Has changed with the times and found new roles to serve the interests of its members

Not all EU member states are members of NATO

Spends about 70 per cent of the world's total military expenditure

Requires unanimity for decisions to be made

Proven capabilities in military action

Over-reliant on the military power of the US

Technologically advanced military alliance

Dominated by the USA

Not all countries spend the guideline 2 per cent of GDP on the military

2.2 Economic

International Monetary Fund (IMF)

International Monetary Fund

- Began in 1945.
- Based in Washington D.C. – a legacy of America's leading role in the Bretton Woods System.
- A specialised agency within the UN family, the IMF is independent from, but has a close working relationship with, the UN.
- Currently 189 members, from across the globe.
- Managed by Executive Board of 24 directors; run by 2700 staff drawn from 148 countries.
- Led by a managing director, appointed for a five-year renewable term.

The **International Monetary Fund** has three main tasks: surveillance (its primary purpose), capacity development and lending. The IMF maintains the stability of the international financial system, monitoring the system of exchange rates and international payments that allows countries

Pause & reflect

US President Donald Trump caused consternation among NATO members when, during the presidential election campaign, he declared that he thought NATO was obsolete. In April 2017 he changed his mind and declared that NATO was 'not obsolete'. What do you think? Is NATO an outdated relic from the Cold War? Is it a necessary bulwark against Russian expansion?

Key term

International Monetary Fund (IMF) works to foster global monetary co-operation, secure financial stability, facilitate international trade, promote high employment and sustainable economic growth, and reduce poverty around the world.

Country	% vote share
Australia	1.34
Belgium	1.30
Brazil	2.22
Canada	2.22
China	6.09
France	4.04
Germany	5.32
India	2.64
Italy	3.02
Japan	6.16
Korea	1.74
Mexico	1.80
Netherlands	1.77
Russia	2.59
Saudi Arabia	2.02
Spain	1.92
Switzerland	1.18
Turkey	0.96
UK	4.04
USA	16.53

Table 2.1: Voting shares of 20 IMF member countries

The IMF's current managing director, the former French finance minister Christine Lagarde follows in a long line of European, and mainly French, managing directors.

and their citizens to do business with each other, and producing regular reports about the financial health of member states. The IMF also promotes capacity development by giving policy advice to member states on financial matters.

While the Bretton Woods System remained in operation, the IMF acted as a 'currency buffer', lending to countries experiencing temporary balance-of-payments deficits to reduce volatility in exchange rates. Balance-of-payments deficits undermine confidence in the value of the currency, which can lead to selling of the currency by speculators and a fall in its value against other currencies.

Since the end of the system in the early 1970s, the IMF has increasingly focused on lending to the developing world. For example, it has helped post-communist states to liberalise their markets and develop economically. The IMF also acts to prevent financial crises. However, it did not foresee the global financial crisis of 2007–09 and could not prevent it. Since the crisis, the IMF has been working with member states and the European Union to encourage financial institutions to increase their capital reserves so that they can withstand a mass withdrawal of funds by depositors. In 2012, the mandate of the IMF was updated to include all macroeconomic and finance issues that affect global economic stability.

The IMF is a contributory system, meaning that member states pay subscriptions in relation to the size of their economies (quota) – and the size of loans available to states varies accordingly. The largest borrowers in 2016 were Portugal, Greece, Ukraine and Pakistan; the most expensive precautionary loans were to Mexico, Poland, Colombia and Morocco.

Policy decisions are made by the member countries. However, unlike the UN General Assembly where states are treated equally, the allocation of votes reflects the relative positions of the member states' economies in the world. Richer countries have more votes than poorer countries, and the USA – the richest country in the world – has the most votes of any single member.

Strengths and weaknesses

One of the IMF's strengths is that it seems to be effective. It was created to promote global economic stability, and was arguably successful in doing so, especially over the immediate post-war period. In the 1950s and 1960s the world experienced its longest period of sustained economic growth, and OECD countries – members of the Organisation for Economic Co-operation and Development, an international organisation founded in 1960 to stimulate economic progress and world trade – were enjoying growth rates of 4–5 per cent a year. However, this growth may have been the product of other causes, such as the application of Keynesian demand-management policies by domestic governments, or the stimulus effect of the US economy, which led to the globalisation of production, boosting economic growth beyond America's borders.

Another strength of the IMF is that it will lend to countries that can find no other source of finance. As such it acts as a bulwark against economic disasters that may spill over and affect other economies in the world. The IMF has taken the lead in bailing out a number of countries suffering debt crises as a result of the 2007–09 global financial crisis – including Cyprus, Greece, Ireland, Portugal and Spain – which prevented the further spread of the crisis. It has also acted as a source of expertise and information for member states to draw on to stabilise their economies.

A final strength of the IMF is that it has adapted to the changing international context. When the US suspended the dollar's convertibility to gold, bringing an end to the regime of fixed exchange rates, the IMF refocused its activities onto debt reduction and development (for example, helping eastern European states transition from communist to capitalist economies). More recently, the IMF has responded to criticisms about the under-representation of developing countries in decision-making by increasing the quotas for Brazil, India, China and Russia – now among the ten largest members of the IMF alongside France, Germany, Italy, Japan, the UK and USA. Following the widely unforeseen global financial crisis, the IMF refocused on surveillance, warning members when their debt burdens or economic policies are jeopardising economic growth.

However, the IMF has a number of weaknesses. One is that the IMF is dominated by the US – the country that was the organisation's leading architect and heavily influenced decisions about its role and functions. The US capital is home to the IMF's headquarters, facilitating US government influence, and because the US is the largest economy, it contributes the largest quota and enjoys the largest proportion of votes. As decisions require majorities of 85 per cent of votes and the US has nearly 17 per cent, it effectively exercises veto power.

The World Bank

The World Bank

- Partner organisation to the IMF.
- Based in Washington D.C.
- 189 member countries.
- Employs 10,000 people in 120 countries.
- Led by a president, appointed for a five-year renewable term.

The World Bank has close links with the IMF: they share the same building, make decisions in a similar way and are both guided by free-market economic principles.

The World Bank's purpose is essentially redistributive: to reduce global poverty. In 2016, it provided over $63 billion in low-interest loans, zero- to low-interest credits and grants to 275 projects in developing, post-conflict, fragile and middle-income states. In developing countries it has funded improvements to agriculture, roads and transport links. The aim of these projects is to reduce the proportion of the income that citizens spend on food so that they have more disposable income to spend in the domestic economy, stimulating economic development. Some of its loans are spent on what are known as global public goods (see Figure 2.1). The World Bank is also a source of expertise on economic and social development.

Some World Bank projects are jointly financed with governments, other multilateral institutions, commercial banks, export credit agencies and private-sector investors.

The World Bank also works in collaboration with other international organisations. With the Arab League it has been working to reduce unemployment and increase the economic participation of women in the Arab world, as this is a major cause of poverty. With the UN, it committed to achieving the UN Millennium Development Goals by 2015, such as reducing the number of people in the world earning less than $1.25 a day.

Strengths and weaknesses

One of the strengths of the World Bank is its redistributive role. It worked closely with the UN to halve extreme poverty in the world by 2015. It has two further targets to be achieved by 2030: to reduce the percentage of the world's population living on less than $1.90 a day to 3 per cent, and to boost the income growth of every country in the bottom 40 per cent.

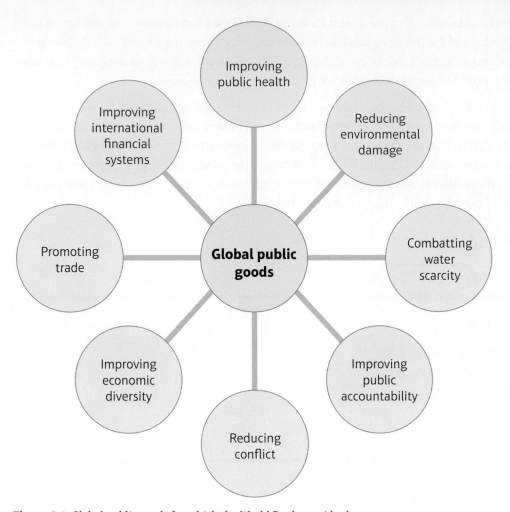

Figure 2.1: Global public goods for which the World Bank provides loans

Another strength is its willingness to adapt. It has evolved from being an organisation funding big infrastructure projects to one that focuses on promoting development and poverty reduction. It has also adapted its approach to its loans from dealing out high-handed technical remedies to involving local people and organisations in how loans are spent and giving greater consideration to their structural, social, human and environmental impact. The World Bank is also a key disseminator of information about development through its regular reports.

One weakness is that it often claimed the US has too much influence over the Bank and its policies. This has led to the World Bank being overly keen on deregulation, privatisation and the promotion of free trade – the economic orthodoxy practised by the US – while since the end of the Cold War, the rest of the developed world has subscribed to neo-liberal economic policy.

There may be some justification in the criticism of America's role in the appointment of the World Bank's president. An open system of appointment would be fairer and more transparent and it would be more appropriate to have a head from the developing world who was familiar with the challenges facing these countries. However, in 2012 the Obama administration did appoint Dr Kim as president, who is someone with expertise in global development.

The World Bank has also been criticised for other weaknesses.

- **It encourages poor countries to produce cash crops like cocoa and coffee:** This leaves developing economies dependent on developed-world markets and vulnerable to the transnational corporations that control processing and distribution. Cash-crop production also reduces the amount of land under cultivation to meet domestic food needs, which can lead to a continuing cycle of famine and poverty.

- **It has not made good governance a requirement of its loans:** Many of the World Bank's loans have gone to corrupt regimes, which squander the money or use it to line their supporters' pockets.

- **It encourages unsustainable development:** Marshland has been drained, hillsides terraced and trees felled to grow crops for export, lowering biodiversity and increasing the risk of landslides and flooding.

- **It spends too little on development:** The USA spent $600 billion on its military in 2016, while the World Bank spent just $63 billion on global economic development.

The World Trade Organization (WTO) and G7/G8 and G20

The World Trade Organization (WTO)

- Began in 1995.
- Based in Geneva, Switzerland.
- 164 member states, including Russia (joined in 2012).
- Currently 634 staff (lawyers, economists, statisticians and communications experts) led by Director-General Roberto Azevêdo.
- Budget of 197 million Swiss Francs (2015).

The World Trade Organization replaced the General Agreement on Tariffs and Trade (GATT), which was a series of meetings between member states' finance ministers. GATT reduced tariff barriers and made sure that any preferential trading agreements had to be extended to other member states. Also members could not impose asymmetrical tariffs – higher trading costs on one state than another.

The WTO was created as a permanent organisation with a wider focus. It settles trade disputes between member states and enforces international trade rules, making it the primary instrument of international trade law. The WTO also oversees the trade in services (via GATS, the General Agreement on Trade in Services), protection of intellectual property (via TRIPS, the Trade-Related Aspects of Intellectual Property Rights) and non-tariff barriers (which states put in place to protect domestically produced products).

Decision-making in the WTO prioritises speed over democracy. Whole packages of reform, known as a Single Undertaking, are presented at Ministerial Conference meetings to be accepted or rejected in full by members. Single Undertakings are negotiated before Ministerial Meetings, typically by members of the Quad, informal alliances of groups of four states that share the same interests on key trade issues. Historically, the US, the EU, Japan and Canada have formed the dominant Quad in the WTO. The US and EU represent the main trading nations, while Japan represents Asian countries and Canada the interests of NAFTA and states that want liberalisation of the trade in agricultural products. More recently, a competing Quad has emerged consisting of the US, EU, Brazil and India, which better represents the developing world.

EXTENSION ACTIVITY

Read about increasing electricity access in Tanzania to reduce poverty. What problems does Tanzania face? What help has the World Bank given it? In what ways does Tanzania illustrate the strengths and weaknesses of the World Bank?

Strengths and weaknesses

One strength of the WTO is that it is considered to be a more democratic institution than its fellow Bretton-Woods institutions. Decisions are made by simple majorities and two-thirds of members are developing states. The rules were written by its member states, many of which are democracies, and the member states elect its leadership. As a result, developing states are much more influential in the WTO than in the IMF and World Bank.

GATT and the WTO have been very successful in reducing tariff barriers. In 1947, average tariffs on imported manufactured goods were 40 per cent of the value of these goods; by 2000, this figure had fallen to 3 per cent. This has made it cheaper for states to trade, which has benefited ordinary citizens. In effect, the prices of manufactured goods have fallen, which makes them more affordable for consumers and allows disposable income to be spent on more goods, stimulating economic growth and leading to better job prospects. By promoting free trade the WTO has helped to raise living standards around the world.

However, one weakness is that, according to many commentators, the WTO is too powerful. It can compel sovereign states to change laws and regulations by declaring them to be in violation of free-trade rules. Decision-making in the WTO is dominated by the US and the EU. Through their membership of the Quad, they set the agenda on Single Undertakings, which have to be accepted or rejected in full. This has meant that the problems of developing countries have not been given significant weight.

In spite of the WTO, more-developed countries have not fully opened their markets to products from less-developed countries. For example, the US and the EU have been unwilling to abandon protection of their agricultural and textile industries, which has disadvantaged countries like China and India (who produce large quantities of these goods at a lower price than US and EU producers).

It is also claimed the WTO is indifferent to the impact of free trade on workers' rights, child labour, the environment and health. As a result many of its meetings have been the target of violent anti-capitalist protests, such as those in Seattle in 1999 and Cancun in 2003.

Although the organisation is internally democratic it lacks external accountability. Its hearings on trade disputes are closed to the public and the media. This leads to suspicions that judgements are not based on an impartial interpretation of the rules, but on the basis of quid pro quos and compromises.

Case study: The banana wars

The EU and USA had a long-running dispute over the EU's banana imports. As part of its international aid programme, the EU offered tenders on a first-come-first-served basis for bananas from countries in Africa, the Caribbean and the Pacific. The US argued that this favoured local producers in former colonies of EU member states over US-owned corporations in Latin America. The Clinton administration responded by imposing heavy tariffs on luxury goods produced in the EU, such as cashmere from Scotland. The Clinton administration took the banana wars to the WTO in 1999, after Chiquita (a major US-owned banana producer) made a $500,000 donation to the Democratic Party. The two sides reached an agreement in 2001, with the EU agreeing to gradually reduce its tariffs on Latin American bananas.

Case study: Boeing and Airbus subsidies

Boeing and Airbus dominate the aircraft manufacturing market for commercial planes.

Since 2005, there have been complaints to the WTO that Boeing has been receiving state subsidies from the US government – and Airbus from European states – in contravention of WTO rules. Airbus and Boeing have enjoyed a duopoly of commercial-aircraft market share since the 1990s, so the pressure to resolve this issue was intense. In 2012, the WTO finally ruled that Boeing had received illegal subsidies, but that Airbus had not. However, the dispute continues. The US has claimed that the EU has not fully complied with the terms of the 2012 ruling, so it will continue to subsidise Boeing as long as Airbus enjoys state support.

Questions

- What do these case studies show about:
  - the strengths and weaknesses of the WTO?
  - the role of the US and EU in the WTO?
  - the role of the WTO in dispute-resolution?
- Whose interests are best served by the WTO? Developed or less developed states? Transnational corporations (TNCs) or consumers?

Group of Seven/Eight (G7/G8)

The **G7** is an informal bloc of industrialised democracies – the United States, Canada, France, Germany, Italy, Japan, and the United Kingdom – that meets annually to discuss issues such as global economic governance, international security, and energy policy. The European Union also attends meetings. The organisation represents many of the advanced economies as reported by the International Monetary Fund, making it an important group; the G7 countries represent nearly 50 per cent of net global wealth. A very high net-national-wealth and a very high Human Development Index are the main requirements to be a member of this group.

The G7/G8 started off as the Group of Six, which was formed in 1975 as a forum for discussion of the global economy in the wake of the turbulence created by the Oil Crisis of 1973 and the end of fixed exchange rates. The initiative came from the French president, Valéry Giscard d'Estaing, and

> **Key term**
>
> **G7(8)**
> the Group of Seven (Group of Eight from 1998 to 2014) is an informal forum consisting of representatives from seven developed economies.

German chancellor, Helmut Schmidt. Its original membership was France, Germany, Italy, Japan, the UK and the USA. Canada joined shortly afterwards in 1976 – making it the Group of Seven – and Russia in 1998, to become the Group of Eight. However, the annexation of Crimea by Russia in 2014 led to Russia's suspension, and the group reverted to being the G7.

The G7 is not a permanent organisation and there are no formal criteria for membership. There are annual rounds of meetings under a rotating presidency. Member states take it in turns to preside over and host each annual round of meetings, and it is the responsibility of the presidency to set the agenda.

The focus of G7 meetings is primarily economic but, since the 1980s, it has expanded its remit to include foreign and security issues and energy policy.

> ### Pause & reflect
>
> Are global governance organisations necessary? If they did not exist, would you have to invent them?

G7 started off as G6, before Canada and Russia joined to make it the G8. However, Russia was suspended in 2014 bringing the number to the current number of members – seven.

Strengths and weaknesses of the G7

One of the strengths of the G7 is that it provides a forum where states can discuss common concerns openly and honestly in a way they could not do in other forums, such as the United Nations. The group is small enough for intimate discussions between leaders and finance ministers, which makes it easier to reach agreement. The G7 represents states with similar political and economic systems – liberal democratic capitalist economies – which facilitates consensus.

Another strength is that the G7 has made a number of important interventions in global politics. In 1999, it cancelled $100 billion of bilateral and multilateral debt. It went several steps further by doubling its aid to Africa and cancelling all debts of 19 countries owed to the IMF and the World Bank in 2005 at the Gleaneagles Summit in Scotland. In 2008, the member states met to co-ordinate their responses to the global financial crisis. Since 2014, the G7 has placed pressure on Russia to withdraw from Crimea and stop supporting Russian separatist rebels in eastern Ukraine.

However, the G7 has several weaknesses. What started as a rich countries' club to promote neo-liberal economic policy (to the detriment of developing economies, according to some critics) has become less relevant. It was formed in the 1970s by what were then the richest countries in the world. China and India have since broken into the top ten of the most economically developed countries in the world. At its peak in the late 1980s, G7 members produced nearly 70 per cent of the world's GDP, but that has declined to under 50 per cent. China and India are members of the Group of 20 (G20 – see below), a rival economic organisation that has become the key focus for dealing with the global financial crises.

Anti-globalisation protesters also criticise the G7 for its apparent inability or unwillingness to deal effectively with poverty, inequality and climate change. It has cancelled much of the debt of developing countries, but the gap continues to widen between them and developed countries. Despite sanctions and public condemnation, Russia continues to undermine the sovereignty of Ukraine and seems unconcerned about its exclusion from the G7, probably because it continues to enjoy membership of the G20, now generally thought to be a more important international forum.

Group of 20 (G20)

The **G20** was established in 1999 but its first summit was not until 2008. The purpose of the organisation is to promote international financial stability and replace the G7 as the main economic forum of wealthy nations.

The G20 is more diverse than the G7, with a membership including Argentina, Brazil, Canada, Mexico and the USA from the American continent, China, India, Indonesia, Japan, and South Korea from Asia, Saudi Arabia from the Middle East, South Africa and Australia – the sole representatives from Africa and Oceania – and France, Germany, Italy, Russia, Turkey, and the UK from Europe. The G20 works closely with a number of international organisations including the UN, IMF, World Bank, OECD, ILO and WTO. The twentieth member is the EU. The G20 represents two-thirds of the world's population, 85 per cent of global GDP and 75 per cent of world trade.

The G20 has no formal organisation or membership criteria. Instead, the main work of the organisation is conducted through a series of meetings. However, the G20 has created the Financial Stability Board to co-ordinate the activities of national financial regulatory bodies with international bodies to improve financial regulation. There is a rotating presidency, held for a year. The member state holding the presidency co-ordinates the year's activities in conjunction with its immediate predecessor and successor. The main annual meeting is hosted by the member state holding the presidency. All member states have equal representation, whatever their wealth or size.

> **Key term**
>
> **G20**
> the Group of 20 is similar to the G7, but is composed of the G7 nations plus 12 emerging economies and a representative from the EU.

G20 represents two-thirds of the world's population, but has no formal membership criteria.

Strengths and weaknesses

One of the G20's strengths is that, since 2009, it has become a more significant body than the G7. The G7/8 states were hit particularly hard by the global financial crisis, and realised they needed the help of developing states to weather the storm.

At the Washington (November 2008) and London (April 2009) summits – the G20's first meetings – a package of measures to aid economic recovery was agreed, with a fund of $500 billion to stimulate economic growth. Agreement was reached over the expansion of the IMF's borrowing programme, and voting shares in the IMF and World Bank were adjusted in favour of the developing countries. At the Pittsburgh summit in September 2009, members agreed that the G20 would replace the G7/8 as the main forum for economic co-operation.

However, the G20 has weaknesses. As with the G7/8, not all of its members are the richest countries in the world. Argentina, Indonesia and Mexico rank outside of the top 20. The G20 is also criticised for its lack of transparency and accountability. There is no formal charter and the most important meetings are held behind closed doors, and at remote locations, to deter protesters.

Significance of how global economic governance deals with the issue of poverty

The North-South divide and other measurements

North and South have replaced terms such as 'the West' and 'the third world' as descriptions of the variation of economic development in the world. The more economically developed and powerful states tend to be in the Northern Hemisphere and poorer and less politically influential states in the Southern Hemisphere. The largest percentage of the population living under $2 a day is in the global South. The term gained currency as a result of the 1980 Brandt Report into international development issues. However, it has not met with universal acceptance. Some question its relevance given the miraculous growth of the Chinese economy, the emergence of Brazil and India and the growing influence of these countries in international organisations, such as the G20.

EXTENSION ACTIVITY

List the criticisms of the IMF, World Bank, WTO, G7 and G20. How valid is each of these? What criticisms do these organisations have in common, and why might this be?

Key term

North-South divide
global socio-economic and political divide.

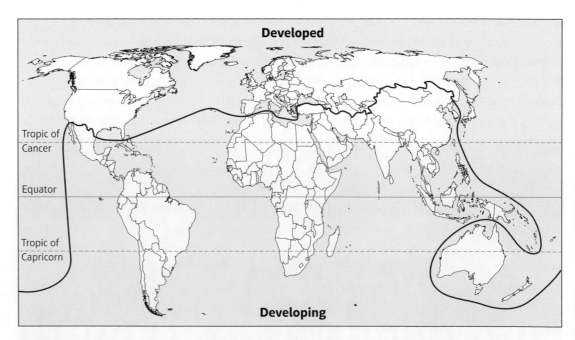

Figure 2.2: The Brandt Line showing the border between the global North and South

Theories of global inequality

Despite world economic growth there is an increasing gap between the richest and poorest countries. Between the early 1960s and the early 2000s, the richest 20 states got 300 per cent richer while the poorest 20 only grew by 20 per cent. Two theories of global inequality have been influential in understanding why unequal economic development continues: world-systems theory and **dependency theory**.

World-systems theory was developed by sociologist Immanuel Wallerstein. It is an approach to world history and social change that suggests there is a world economic system that has developed as a result of the expansion of capitalism since the 17th century, in which some countries benefit while others are exploited. As such it is a neo-Marxist theory. Wallerstein rejects the notion of a 'third world', claiming that there is only one world that is connected by economic relations. He argues that this system inherently leads to a division of the world into core, semi-peripheral and peripheral areas. Core areas are those that are economically advanced and dominate over peripheral areas. Peripheral areas are those parts of the world where wages are low, technology is basic and the economy is dependent on agriculture or the primary sector (low-tech industries, such as coal and steel). The semi-periphery areas have some of the features of core areas and some of those of peripheral areas. They act as a buffer area ensuring that the core areas do not face unified opposition from the rest of the world.

Dependency theory emphasises the structural imbalances within capitalism that impose dependency on poorer states. These structural imbalances were created by 19th-century imperialism. Western European countries exploited the natural resources and cheap labour provided by their colonies in Africa, South America and in the Middle and Far East. With decolonisation, former colonies became independent states politically but remained economically dependent on their former colonial masters for trade. This essentially neo-Marxist theory has much in common with world systems theory. It refers to core and periphery countries. Dependency theory starts from the notion that resources flow from the 'periphery' of poor and underdeveloped states to a 'core' of wealthy countries, which leads to the accumulation of wealth by the rich states at the expense of the poor states. When underdeveloped countries try to remove the Core's influence, the developed countries block their attempts to assume control. This means that poverty of developing nations is not the result of the disintegration of these countries in the world system, but because of the way in which they are integrated into this system. The poverty of the periphery countries is perpetuated by their structural dependence on the core countries. Hence, dependency theorists argue that underdeveloped countries remain economically vulnerable unless they reduce their connections to the world market.

Measurement of poverty

Poverty is a disputed term. Measures of absolute poverty include the level of deprivation of the necessities of life, such as food, fuel, shelter and clothing, or the measure used by the World Bank of earning less than $1.25 a day. However, absolute poverty does not capture the relative nature of poverty. The Organisation for Economic Co-operation and Development (OECD) and the European Union define poverty as income that is 50 per cent less than the average household. Moreover, the orthodox measure of poverty is the inability to meet material needs, but some commentators, such as Amartya Sen, Harvard Professor of Economics and Philosophy, argue that poverty is not just about income. He advocates an alternative measurement of poverty: the inability to meet non-material needs. Poverty restricts opportunities, such as access to education and equal treatment under the law or the protection of rights, which can be just as debilitating as lack of wealth.

> ### Key term
>
> **Dependency theory** emphasises structural imbalances within capitalism that impose dependency on poorer states.

Development theories

As there are competing views of poverty, so too are there different theories about how best to achieve economic development. They have come in and out of fashion over the post-war period. Their significance is that they have informed IMF and World Bank strategies for helping developing countries.

Classical economic development theory is inspired by the 18th- and 19th-century economic liberalism of Adam Smith and David Ricardo. It is closely linked to liberal international-relations theory. It claims that poverty is a lack of income or resources, which can be measured by comparing countries' GDP per capita (wealth per head). Economic development can be stimulated by Adam Smith's 'invisible hand' of the market, ensuring that all will ultimately benefit. Countries should free markets, privatise state-owned industries and focus their economies on producing products in which they have a comparative advantage.

Structural theory is an approach to development that originated in South America. It argues that poverty is the product of global inequality perpetuated by transnational corporations (TNCs) and the conditions attached to development aid by donor countries and organisations. In order to end structural inequality in the international system poorer states should intervene substantially in the domestic economy to promote industrialisation and reduce the reliance on the export of primary goods, such as agricultural and mining products. Developing states also should impose restrictive trade policies to protect domestic industries from external competition and promote trade with other developing countries. The logic of these strategies rests on the 'infant industry' argument, which states that young industries initially do not have the economies of scale and experience to be able to compete with foreign competitors, and thus need to be protected until they are able to compete in the free market.

Neo-classical development theory became influential towards the end of the 1970s, inspired by the economic policies of Margaret Thatcher in the UK and Ronald Reagan in the USA. At the same time, the World Bank shifted from its Basic Needs approach to a neo-liberal approach in 1980. Neo-classical development theory essentially is classical economic development theory. This approach inspired the Structural Adjustment Programmes imposed on recipients of loans in the 1980s.

2.3 Addressing and resolving contemporary global issues

> **Pause & reflect**
>
> Before reading on, remind yourself about the membership and structure of the UN Security Council detailed in Section 2.1.

States join these organisations voluntarily, as the most effective means of solving global problems, so members tend to support their agendas and decisions – but states will not always agree.

Powerful organisations like the UN and NATO receive a lot of criticism, for being both too powerful and too weak. On the one hand global governance organisations are accused of being a form of world government that imposes decisions on states, removing sovereignty and democracy. On the other hand, they are accused of being ineffectual and inefficient talking shops where nothing gets done because unanimity is required.

Intergovernmental decision-making

Intergovernmental decision-making is a form of decision-making in international organisations where all states have an equal say in the outcome. The decision requires consensus and unanimity, with each state having a veto (blocking vote).

Advantages

- Maintains state sovereignty, as no state is forced to accept decisions it does not want.
- States are in control of their own destiny.
- Gives smaller states a clearer, louder voice as they can stymie decisions.

Disadvantages

- Inefficient way to make decisions.
- Consensus is hard to achieve as each state can block the outcome.
- Outcome is usually the lowest common denominator.
- Everyone must compromise to achieve consensus.

Supranational decision-making

This form of decision-making is mostly associated with the European Union. Literally meaning 'above the nation', supranationalism is a form of decision-making that does not require unanimity or agreement of all parties. Each individual state can have its interests ignored but still be required to adopt or accept decisions.

Advantages

- Decisions are more likely to be made, as no one state can block them.
- More efficient and speedier way to make decisions.
- It is to the advantage of individual states to negotiate and compromise, knowing they cannot ultimately stop the decision.

Disadvantages

- State sovereignty potentially lost as states have to abide by decisions they may not have supported.
- Smaller countries may lose out to the bigger states.
- Bigger states may lose out to coalitions of smaller states.

The use of the veto in the UN Security Council

The five permanent members (the P-5) of the Security Council have a veto over decisions in the Council. In some respects, the veto represents the realities of power politics in the world. The USA, China and Russia are the three most powerful countries and any attempt to bypass their support to gain international legitimacy would be difficult, if not impossible. Sometimes the veto is not necessary, as a decision needs nine votes in total from the permanent five and the non-permanent ten. An abstention is not counted as a veto or a vote in favour.

During the Cold War, the UNSC and the UN as a whole were not particularly effective because both the USA and the Soviet Union would veto decisions where their interests were at stake, especially on the admission of new states to the UN.

This behaviour is quite commonplace again. In the last ten years, the USA has used its veto three times in the defence of Israel from criticisms of its actions over Palestine and the Occupied Territories. The UK and France have not used their veto since 1989. The USA last vetoed a resolution of the Security Council in 2011. More recently, Russia has been condemned for its use of the veto in its defence of President Assad and the Syrian regime. In February 2017, China and Russia vetoed the imposition of sanctions against Syria for their alleged use of chemical weapons. This was the seventh time Russia had used the veto to defend the Syrian government. China has done so six times. China has defended their use of the veto in the past by arguing that states should not intervene in the affairs of other states. Russia argued that sanctions would undermine the peace process, though they have interests in maintaining the current Syrian regime.

The use of the veto raises difficult questions about the P-5 or anyone having a veto, especially when it comes to humanitarian intervention and civilians suffering. As has been seen in Syria, and on other occasions such as in 1994 over the war in Bosnia and in 2015 over the situation in Ukraine, Russia has vetoed international condemnation and intervention. This may have exacerbated or prolonged conflict, though the Russians would deny this.

Table 3.1: Vetoes by UN Security Council members since 1993 and the issues they vetoed

Country	Issue	Times vetoed
China	Central America	1
	FYROM (Macedonia)	1
	Myanmar	1
	Zimbabwe	1
	Middle East – Syria	6
Russian Federation	Cyprus	2
	Bosnia and Herzegovina	2
	Myanmar	1
	Zimbabwe	1
	Georgia	1
	Middle East – Syria	7
	Ukraine	2
USA	Israel, Palestine, Occupied Territories, Middle East	13
	Bosnia and Herzegovina	1
France	n/a	
UK	n/a	

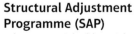
Pressure for reform of the IMF and World Bank
Structural Adjustment Programmes

The global economic system has its strengths and weaknesses, but two issues have emerged – whether it is fit for purpose and whether it perpetuates global structural inequality. The use of **Structural Adjustment Programmes** by the IMF and the World Bank has been criticised for attaching conditions to loans to poorer countries – such as privatising state-owned industries, cutting public spending, encouraging foreign investment and the production of goods for export – which leaves these countries vulnerable to the dictates of transnational corporations (TNCs) and reduces the living standards of citizens. The 2007–09 global financial crisis exposed the weakness of international financial regulation and cast doubt on the role of the IMF as a global financial regulator and a bastion of international economic stability.

The IMF and the World Bank began to adopt SAPs in the late 1970s. This was seen as a radical approach to promoting economic development, adopted because of the growing debt crisis and an ideological shift in global economic policy. Developing countries had been borrowing heavily from the West to finance economic development, but the 1973 oil crisis led to a world recession. For many countries their debts became unsustainable; their economic surpluses were lower than the interest payments on their loans. The debt repayments of these Heavily Indebted Poor Countries (HIPCs) were so big that there was a high risk that they would never be able to repay them. The stagflation of the 1970s gave rise to a new economic orthodoxy: monetarism, which focused on supply-side factors – instruments and policies that create the right environment for economic growth. When applied to developing economies, it was suggested that structural adjustment was needed to remedy the inefficiencies of developing economies and misguided government policies.

From the start, SAPs were controversial. Not all economists agreed that western neo-liberal economic policy was appropriate to the developing world. There was no empirical evidence that such an approach would work. Economic development in many western states had been fostered by state intervention and protectionism. Integrating weaker, less developed economies into the international economic system risked exposing these countries to the full brunt of competition.

By the 1990s, it became apparent that SAPs were making HIPCs' problems worse. Exposure to foreign competition drove down wages, led to worsening working conditions and increased unemployment. Many countries sold off state-owned utilities quickly to meet the conditions of loans, often cheaply to attract buyers, but this reduced the revenue available to repay loans, as well as depriving the government of revenue from potentially profitable businesses. Also TNCs demand incentives or sweeteners in the form of low corporation tax or fewer protections for workers.

Another effect of SAPs was to encourage HIPC economies to refocus their economies on production of goods for export – which for these less-industrialised countries usually means cash crops such as timber, coffee, tea, sugar, bananas and cocoa. This damaged the environment and the food supply, putting developing countries at a further disadvantage compared with the developed world. Many countries are suffering from the effects of deforestation because of logging. This leads to flooding and landslides, as well as raising carbon dioxide levels globally. Producing cash crops reduces the amount of land under cultivation to produce food for the local population, which increases food prices and can lead to famine. TNCs control the trade in products such as coffee, meaning that they dictate the price farmers receive for their crops, which is usually far lower than the price the product sells for in the West. This perpetuates global inequality.

SAPs required reduced public spending, which decreased the public services that would alleviate the effects of low wages and poor working conditions. Reduced spending on health and education programmes also meant poor health and low levels of education reducing the economic potential of citizens, most of all women and girls.

Above all, the record of SAPs is poor. Countries that have experienced the highest levels of growth have either refused loans, such as Malaysia, or employed their own national strategies, such as India and China.

The global financial crisis

In the early 2000s, the world was experiencing a prolonged economic boom. With low inflation and steady economic growth, interest rates were at historically low levels. Cheap loans encouraged consumer debt, in particular mortgage debt. The deregulation of financial services allowed more lenders into the marketplace, which encouraged competition and the development of increasingly creative financial products to entice customers. Continued economic growth led to rising real incomes and greater demand for mortgages. The boom also led to house-

Problems with sub-prime mortgages in the USA triggered a financial crisis that soon impacted on other economies. Exacerbated by risky banking practices in the UK, Britain's economy slipped into recession in 2009.

price inflation, which meant higher levels of borrowing to finance mortgages.

In the USA, sub-prime mortgages – loans to people with poor credit histories – became increasingly common, often with no proof of earnings required. In 2006, the US suffered a nationwide house-price slump. Large numbers of American mortgagees were unable to make the payments on their loans, but when their houses were sold, the sums recovered were not enough to repay the debt. Banks found that they were owed more than the sums in customers' savings. Northern Rock, a UK mortgage lender, had to be rescued in the autumn of 2007. Lehman Brothers, a major US bank, and AIG, an American insurance giant, collapsed in September 2008.

The crisis might have been contained. However, many European banks had stakes in US banks or had taken on some of their debt in the form of securities. The contagion spread, resulting in state governments bailing out financial institutions, which led to high levels of annual budget deficits and structural debt across Europe. The global financial crisis was the worst since the Great Depression of the 1930s.

Case study: The IMF and the global financial crisis

Some argue that the IMF should take some of the blame for the crisis. It encouraged the deregulation of international finance by promoting neo-liberal orthodoxy through the conditions on its loans and through its technical advice and annual reports on the financial health of member states. It did not anticipate that, in a deregulated environment, financial markets would engage in 'casino capitalism' – risky practices, such as parcelling debt out to other financial institutions under the guise of high-yielding securities. It was slow to recognise the signs of the global financial crisis and to take evasive action.

Before the global financial crisis the IMF was in danger of becoming irrelevant. Its currency-exchange role had lapsed after the end of Bretton Woods, its lending capacity was declining, its staff was shrinking and few countries paid attention to its surveillance reports. However, the IMF has played a prominent role in economic recovery, brokering rescue packages for Pakistan, Iceland, Hungary and Ukraine and providing $700 billion of crisis lending to member states. It has taken the leading role in developing and helping to finance a Europe-wide bailout fund, providing $430 billion in extra lending capacity for a $1 trillion European rescue fund. It has urged greater fiscal integration between Eurozone members to help stabilise the southern European economies. It has been outspoken in suggesting direct lending to European banks rather than state governments and in calls for the major recapitalisation of banks so that they have large enough deposits to withstand mass defaults on loans. The IMF has also strengthened its surveillance and risk analysis so that it can give early warnings of trends that might lead to financial difficulties.

Questions

- How did the IMF contribute to the global financial crisis?

- What has the IMF been doing to promote recovery from the crisis and help prevent future crises?

Pause & reflect

Think about the effectiveness of global institutions in promoting peace and security, economic stability and economic development. What successes and failures have they had? Why?

The role and significance of the global civil society and non-state actors

A variety of **non-governmental organisations** (NGOs), such as Greenpeace and Oxfam, and social movements – such as the women's movement, green movement, anti-capitalism and anti-globalisation movements – have drawn attention to the damaging effects of SAP conditions. In the light of criticisms and pressure from these organisations, the IMF and World Bank have replaced SAPs with Poverty Reduction Strategy Papers (PRSPs). They are more flexible, allow for more input from the recipient countries, place more emphasis on poverty reduction and allow longer loans of up to seven years. There has also been a shift from economic growth to sustainable development, which takes account of the impact on the environment and the lives of ordinary people, particularly women (what the World Bank and IMF call 'participation' and 'empowerment'). More attention is paid to promoting and rewarding good governance and democratisation. The World Bank, in particular, has devised guidelines that address the treatment of indigenous people, resettlement, the environmental impact of its projects, gender and the disclosure of information. It also develops social safety nets and provides microcredit (small-scale funds) to empower women. With the IMF, the World Bank has created a Heavily Indebted Poor Country Initiative. However, there has been no fundamental change in the belief in free-market solutions to promote economic development.

Key term

Non-governmental organisations (NGOs) any non-profit, voluntary citizens' group organised on a local, national or international level – e.g. Christian Aid. NGOs perform a variety of service and humanitarian functions, bring citizens' concerns to governments, advocate and monitor policies and encourage political participation through provision of information.

Assessment support: 3.2.2 Global Governance: Political and Economic

Question 1 on A-Level Paper 3 is worth 12 marks and you should allow about 15 minutes to write the answer. There is a choice of two questions.

Examine the criticisms that have been made of both the World Trade Organization and the G7/8. [12 marks]

This question requires a short answer – about one page of writing. These questions test Assessment Objectives AO1 and AO2, with the marks divided equally between the two. You are asked to show knowledge and understanding of the role of the World Trade Organization and the G7/8 as international institutions. You must also identify the main criticisms that have been made of them and analyse their validity. In a question of this length, analysis of three criticisms would be reasonable.

- Provide relevant facts about the WTO and G7/8: for example, their location, membership, functions and details about their organisation.

- Criticisms of these organisations might include: US dominance; they promote the interests of the developed countries at the expense of the developing world; they have done too little to promote sustainable development.

- Analyse the criticisms by questioning their validity. For example, US dominance is justified because it was the architect of these institutions and remains the most powerful state in the world; they are trying to address the problems of the developing world, such as cancelling poor countries' debts; and the environment has become a more important concern.

Here is part of a student's answer – analysis of a criticism of the WTO/G7/8.

One criticism that can be made of both the WTO and the G7/8 is that they are organisations created by rich countries to promote their own interests. Much of WTO time is taken up by agricultural disputes between the USA, EU and Japan. Foremost among these are disputes over Europe's Common Agricultural Policy (CAP) as nations subsidise their farming industry and give preferential treatment to banana producers in former colonies of European states. The G7/8 is made up entirely of rich countries. One way the organisation promotes its interests is by encouraging developing countries to adopt neo-liberal economic policies and free trade. This opens up developing countries to transnational corporations, which out-compete domestic industries. However, the WTO has reduced tariffs on imported manufactured goods from 40 per cent of the cost of a product to just 3 per cent. Cheaper exports help developing countries to compete and reduce prices for consumers. In 1999, the G7/8 cancelled the debt of 19 developing countries worth $100 billion dollars. The wiping out these countries' debts meant their government spending could be used for economic development, rather than servicing debt repayments.

- The opening phrase ('one criticism') indicates clearly to the examiner that the student is addressing the question.

- A major criticism is clearly explained with supporting evidence. Equal attention is devoted to the WTO and G7/8. This meets the requirements of AO1.

- The criticism is analysed by addressing the ways in which the two organisations have helped developing countries, rather than promoting their own interests. This meets the requirements of AO2.

CHAPTER

3

Global Governance: Human Rights and Environmental

As was discussed in the last chapter, states will often co-operate in order to meet their mutual interests. Whether those interests are collective security, economic stability or free trade, states will work together through intergovernmental organisations (IGOs).

This chapter looks at:

- the way IGOs have grown to deal with the issues of human rights protection and the increasing problem of environmental damage
- the way in which global problems need global solutions.

3.1 Human rights

Key terms

Human rights
rights that people are entitled to by virtue of being human.

Universal human rights
rights that apply to people of all societies regardless of cultural or other differences.

Human rights are entitlements that are inherent to all human beings irrespective of their sex, age, religion, nationality, sexuality, place of residence, language, colour of skin or any other characteristic.

Human rights are **universal** (applicable to all human beings) and inalienable (they should not be taken away except in specific circumstances after due process; for example, liberty may be curtailed if an individual has been found guilty of a crime).

The events of the Second World War led to the prioritising of human rights and the Universal Declaration of Human Rights (UDHR) in 1948 – the basis for the European Convention on Human Rights of 1950. The UDHR is widely acknowledged to be the foundation of international human-rights law.

It is important to understand the tension between the concept of universal and inalienable rights on the one hand, and the sovereignty of the state on the other.

> **Pause & reflect**
>
> Do some research on the UDHR and the covenants that make up the International Bill of Human Rights. Is there anything you are surprised to find there? Is there anything you think is missing?

EXTENSION ACTIVITY

Is it realistic to uphold these rights? Should the international community be doing more to defend these rights for all?

Origins and development of international law and institutions

Law is a requirement of an ordered society. There must be rules to regulate the behaviour of individuals. Normally, enforcement of those rules is required.

International law is essentially the rules governing relationships between states. There is considerable debate about the concept of international law, as law implies some sort of compulsion and higher authority, but in the international system there is no compulsion, because states are sovereign.

International law is not codified – written out in one place – but there are a number of sources, including:

- treaties and conventions between states
- international custom – such as diplomatic immunity
- the general principles of law recognised by civilised nations – things that are illegal in national law are probably illegal in international law
- judicial decisions
- legal writings.

Of particular significance in the development of international law on human rights are the Nuremberg and Tokyo tribunals after the Second World War.

International Court of Justice

The International Court of Justice was founded in 1945 as the main arbitration organ of the United Nations. Based in The Hague in the Netherlands, the court adjudicates on disputes between member states of the United Nations and to make judgements on issues brought to it by UN organisations and specialist agencies.

International Criminal Court

Also based in The Hague, the **International Criminal Court** is a separate court to the ICJ and is not a part of the UN family of organisations. The ICC is responsible for investigating and putting on trial individuals who have been accused of some of the most horrific and heinous crimes in the world – genocide, war crimes and crimes against humanity. In the future, the crime of aggression will also come under the remit of this court.

The ICC is a permanent court that replaces the ad hoc tribunals that have often been used to bring prosecutions against suspected war criminals and despots, for example after the wars in the former Yugoslavia and the genocide of Rwanda. The standing nature of the ICC is meant to ensure that all tyrants who may have considered committing crimes will be deterred from doing so.

The ICC was set up by the 1998 Rome Statute and came into force in 2002. The aim of the court is to work in addition to national courts, not to replace them. The ICC only tries a case where a national court system has not been willing or able to bring an individual to justice; the ICC is a court of last resort. 124 states have signed up to the Rome Statute but some countries are not bound by the full requirements of the court, including the USA, China, India and Israel. In October 2016, in a blow to the ICC, South Africa, Burundi and the Gambia announced that they were going to withdraw from the Rome Statute; other African countries may follow. This is because there is a perception among African countries that the ICC is biased against Africans. Most of the ICC's investigations and trials have been of Africans, and arrest warrants have only ever been issued against Africans. According to some African governments, this makes the ICC look like a colonial organisation. Russia also looks likely to remove its signature from the Rome Statute, perhaps predictably as it may face punishment over the annexation of Crimea and its actions in the Syrian Civil War.

Key terms

International law
laws that govern states and other international actors.

International Court of Justice (ICJ)
the principal judicial organ of the United Nations.

International Criminal Court (ICC)
organisation that prosecutes individuals for the international crimes of genocide, crimes against humanity and war crimes.

Special UN tribunals

There have been two notable UN **international tribunals** that were the forerunners to the International Criminal Court. Following atrocities and war crimes in the former Yugoslavia and the African state of Rwanda, the UN set up criminal tribunals or courts to punish the perpetrators. The International Criminal Tribunal for the former Yugoslavia was set up in 1993 to bring to justice those responsible for genocide, war crimes and crimes against humanity in the Balkans in the 1990s, including the genocide committed at Srebrenica. Likewise, the International Criminal Tribunal for Rwanda was set up as a response to the genocide and mass killings of 1994. The tribunal indicted 93 individuals, of whom 61 were sentenced for crimes.

> **Key term**
>
> **International tribunals** organisations set up to prosecute individuals in specific states for the crimes of genocide, crimes against humanity, and war crimes.

European Court of Human Rights (ECHR)

The Council of Europe (not to be confused with the Council of the European Union or the European Council) was set up in 1949 in response to the human-rights abuses of the Holocaust. The ECHR aims to promote human rights, democracy and the rule of law in Europe. It currently has 47 member states (the only European country not a member is Belarus). All member states are signatories to the European Convention on Human Rights (drafted in 1950), which is upheld by the European Court of Human Rights (ECHR) based in Strasbourg, France. The Council of Europe is not related to the European Union and nor is the ECHR (not to be confused with the Court of Justice of the European Union (ECJ). The Court, which came into being in 1959, is a court of last resort: individuals or groups who feel that their rights have been breached by a signatory state may appeal to the court to have their case heard if all other legal avenues have been exhausted. While the Court's rulings are not directly enforceable, all signatory states have agreed under international treaty to uphold the ruling of the Court.

Sources of authority, including the 1948 Universal Declaration of Human Rights

In the immediate aftermath of the Second World War there were two international tribunals to deal with those responsible for genocide, war crimes and crimes against humanity in Europe by the Nazis and in the Far East by the Japanese.

More commonly known as the Nuremberg Trials and the Tokyo Trials, these tribunals set the precedent for future war-crimes tribunals – and for the International Criminal Court. Such were the atrocities carried out by both regimes, it was felt that the perpetrators must be brought to justice. These trials were unprecedented because they were genuine international trials, not trials in one state under the legal system of one state. They can be considered controversial because they prosecuted individuals for crimes that were not a crime at the time they were committed. Nonetheless, the view that some crimes are so abhorrent and heinous that they must be punished has been the thinking behind the International Criminal Tribunal for the former Yugoslavia (ICTY), the International Criminal Tribunal for Rwanda (ICTR) and the ICC.

The 1948 Universal Declaration of Human Rights (UDHR) set out for the first time a set of rights that are applicable to all human beings. The UDHR is a remarkable achievement in that it was the first time that statesmen and women from different political, legal and cultural backgrounds agreed on a common set of fundamental rights that apply to all human beings.

Although not legally binding, the declaration has been a significant document in developing human rights around the world. It led to a collection of covenants that seek to underpin human rights in the world. The UDHR has also been followed by further covenants, such as the International Covenant on Civil and Political Rights and the International Covenant on Economic, Social and Cultural Rights, both adopted in 1966.

Not all states signed up to the UDHR in 1948. Most notably, Saudi Arabia refused to sign on the grounds that the UDHR was incompatible with Islamic law. Saudi Arabia does not allow citizens to renounce their religion which would be considered a breach of their human rights as guaranteed by the UDHR. The Cairo Declaration on Human Rights in Islam, signed in 1990, was an attempt by Islamic countries to give their view on human rights from an Islamic perspective. Freedom of religion is a key tension between the Cairo Declaration and the UDHR.

Case study: The Yugoslav Wars and International Criminal Tribunal for the former Yugoslavia

Slobodan Milosovic – Former Yugoslav president was put on trial at the International Criminal Tribunal for the former Yugoslavia.

In the 1990s the Federal Republic of Yugoslavia started to break up into its ethnic territories. Nationalism was the driving force. In 1992, Slovenia and Croatia broke away to form independent states after short wars. In 1993, further conflict erupted in Bosnia, with Bosnian-Serb nationalists determined to remain part of a Yugoslavia dominated by a greater Serbia. Muslim Bosniaks were forced from their homes in a process euphemistically called 'ethnic cleansing'. Over a million Bosniaks and Croatians were forced out. The Bosniak government was also besieged and the capital, Sarajevo, was shelled, with an estimated 10,000 people killed over 44 months. UN and international attempts to end the conflict failed. The war eventually ended after NATO bombed the Bosnian Serbs. A US-led peace deal was signed in 1995 creating a state of a Bosniak-Croatian federation and a Serb republic. More than 100,000 people had died.

The International Criminal Tribunal for the former Yugoslavia was established by UN Security Council Resolution 827 in 1993 to bring to justice political and military leaders accused of war crimes in the Yugoslav Wars. The ICTY was the first international tribunal since the Nuremberg and Tokyo trials, and the first to indict a sitting head of state – Slobodan Milosovic. In 1999, Milosovic was accused of genocide and war crimes, but he died before his trial ended. Radislav Krstić, a Bosnian-Serb army officer was the first person at the tribunal to be found guilty of genocide, at the 1995 Srebrenica massacre of 7500 Muslim men and boys. Radovan Karadzic, the Bosnian-Serb political leader, was found guilty of genocide and war crimes in 2016 and sentenced to 40 years in prison. Ratko Mladic, the Bosnian-Serb military commander is currently on trial in The Hague, charged with two counts of genocide and nine of war crimes and crimes against humanity.

The key issues of these institutions in dealing with human rights

One of the key tensions in the international system concerns intervention at times of humanitarian disaster. On the one hand, sovereign states have rights, including the principle that other states should not intervene in their affairs; on the other hand, many states feel a moral obligation to intervene if a catastrophe is taking place in another state. Should the world stand by when innocent men, women and children are facing genocide, crimes against humanity and war crimes? There is no easy answer to this question, but there have been many cases where the international community stood by and did nothing as human rights were ignored.

Auschwitz concentration camp: the largest Nazi concentration camp where more than a million people were murdered.

Since the Holocaust ended, there has been a growing view that the international community should act if crimes against humanity are taking place in another country. Using force in such situations raises both moral and legal questions.

- Forcible humanitarian intervention assumes that there are universal moral absolutes that unite the world, yet Western inventions could equally be seen as a form of cultural imperialism.
- States that intervene can be seen as using humanitarian grounds as an excuse to increase their power and further their own interests, or even as a pretext for the control or annexation of another state.

- Humanitarian intervention is not guaranteed to make the situation better on the ground. The use of force may lead to the loss of more life as war escalates.

- Of course, forcible humanitarian intervention goes against the principles of state sovereignty by interfering in the internal affairs of another state. If the international community increasingly allows humanitarian intervention, this is clearly a challenge to state sovereignty.

- Humanitarian intervention can be seen as contravening 'just-war' theory, as it is not a last resort. It could even be another way of starting a war.

One particularly problematic intervention was Western intervention in the Libyan civil conflict in 2011. This was ostensibly made on humanitarian grounds, to stop the bombing of innocent people, but this was soon claimed to be a cover for the overthrow of the Gaddafi regime. Gaddafi's overthrow also led to more chaos and killing in Libya.

'Just-war' theory

When should wars be fought? On what grounds should they be started? How should they be fought? 'Just-war' theory is an attempt by philosophers and thinkers to determine whether war is justifiable and permissible. There are two main focuses of just-war theory:

- *jus ad bellum*, dealing with when it is right to go to war

- *jus in bello*, dealing with the conduct of war.

A new focus has emerged on *jus post bellum*, concentrating on the situation after war has ended. In what circumstances is war permitted? How should wars be conducted?

Pause & reflect

Do some research into just-war theory. Look at the work of St Thomas Aquinas, Hugo Grotius and others. Do you agree with their criteria for war?

Impact on state sovereignty

The right of a state to determine its own policies is at the heart of what it is to be a state, as well as at the heart of sovereignty. Nothing is more controversial in a state – especially in a democratic state – than foreign interference in the affairs of another state. There is often a strong feeling that countries should 'keep their noses' out of others' affairs, whether they are foreign politicians, judges or the media. It is therefore remarkable that states that sign up to global governance organisations do achieve what can be best described as a greater good. However, there are always pressures on states to resist rulings from courts like the European Court of Human Rights – perhaps the most successful example of an international court – that some see as removing state sovereignty.

Rise of humanitarian interventions and growth in 1990s

The end of the Second World War saw the most immediate catalyst for human-rights protection, but the end of the Cold War in the early 1990s made practical help possible. The demise of the Soviet Union and the decline of Russia as a global power meant that the UN Security Council, in particular, was able to sanction humanitarian intervention missions. Also, the end of the Cold War seemed to issue a new era of liberal thinking that justified such protection of human rights.

Failures of UN interventions include Srebrenica in 1995 (see Yugoslavia case study in this section), Rwanda in 1994 and Somalia in 1995. However, intervention in Sierra Leone between 1999 and 2005 – where a peace-deal was successfully implemented to end a civil war and tens of thousands of fighters were disarmed – was widely deemed to have been successful.

Reasons for selective interventionism, development of responsibility to protect and conflict with state sovereignty

The world is, unsurprisingly, a very complex place. Clearly, the world is not always as we would like it to be. There are inequalities, injustices and innocents who suffer all around the world at any one time.

While the West may see itself as upholding liberal, humanitarian values, it may be the case that it cannot intervene to help people as much as it would like. There are sometimes practical difficulties with launching humanitarian interventions against states. The Syrian Civil War (beginning in 2011) is perhaps an example, as it would have been very difficult for Western military forces to be directly involved in a region such as the Middle East. There will often be domestic political pressures resisting intervention; why should troops from one nation fight and die for people in a country its citizens might not care about? This was often the argument against NATO involvement in Afghanistan in recent years. Is interventionism just another form of neo-colonialism, of Western states imposing their values on others? Is humanitarian interventionism a façade behind which Western states invade and exploit other countries? Some felt the 2003 invasion of Iraq was carried out just so the USA could gain access to Iraqi oil; claims that the Iraqi regime possessed weapons of mass destruction (WMDs) formed the legal basis, but overthrowing Saddam Hussein because he was a bad man and had violated the human rights of citizens was also a factor. Of course, the danger of humanitarian intervention is that the human-rights abuses are not stopped. Indeed, the situation may be further destabilised, as occurred following the overthrow of President Muammar Gaddafi of Libya in 2011 by NATO-backed forces.

One attempt to square the circle of state sovereignty and humanitarian intervention has been the doctrine of Responsibility to Protect (R2P). The doctrine has only been in place since 2005. The idea behind R2P is that part of a state's sovereignty is the responsibility to protect its own citizens. If a state fails to uphold this responsibility, then the responsibility to protect falls on the international community allowing, eventually, for humanitarian intervention through force. R2P places the focus on state sovereignty coming with responsibilities.

> ## Pause & reflect
>
> 'Never again' was the call after the liberation of Auschwitz and the realities of the Holocaust. Has the world learned the lessons? George Santayana's words that 'Those who cannot remember the past are condemned to repeat it' are often quoted but has the world done enough to prevent genocides since 1945 including Cambodia, Rwanda, Srebrenica and Darfur?

Alleged Western double standards

During the Cold War, the USA was heavily criticised in some quarters for preaching democracy and human rights on the one hand but overthrowing democratically elected governments and supporting military regimes that used torture on the other. The USA was particularly fearful of communist expansion in its 'backyard' – Central and South America. The USA saw this area as its sphere of influence and was not willing to tolerate any attempts by communists to get a foothold there. The USA was willing to tolerate and support military dictatorships that were also anti-communist in nature. The USA supported the Somoza family dynasty in Nicaragua, and attempted to overthrow Fidel Castro numerous times in Cuba. The USA justified this approach by arguing that the USSR was a greater threat to the USA, and Soviet expansionism needed to be stopped.

Today, there are still claims that the USA and the West operate double standards. There are numerous criticisms that could be levelled at the USA, including the use of the Guantanamo Bay

EXTENSION ACTIVITY

Do some research on the military coup in Chile in 1973. How might people claim that alleged Western double standards are illustrated by this event?

Naval Base as a detention camp for 'unlawful combatants' in the war against terror and the use of 'enhanced interrogation techniques', including waterboarding, which are widely viewed to be examples of torture. The Abu Ghraib prison in Iraq was also a scandal that seemed to show the hypocrisy of the USA when detainees were abused and maltreated in 2003. The US authorities were accused of inflicting 'grave breaches of humanitarian law'. British troops were implicated in the death of Baha Mousa in Basra, Iraq in 2003. The British were accused of using banned interrogation methods and 'gratuitous violence'. One soldier admitted a charge of inhumane treatment, becoming the first member of the British armed forces convicted of a war crime. In 2013 a British marine was found guilty at a court martial of executing an injured Afghan insurgent in 2011.

The USA has also been accused of breaching core liberal values in the war against terror through the use of 'covert rendition'. The US government is alleged to have unlawfully transported terrorist suspects to other countries to by-pass normal legal and human right protections. Detainees were often tortured, denied legal advice and fair trials. For a country that prides itself on upholding the rule of law, such acts can be seen as utterly hypocritical.

The West is meant to symbolise liberal values of democracy, respecting human rights and upholding the rule of law. However, it is often alleged that Western countries ignore these values when dealing with other countries if it suits the national interest of the Western country, or if it means making money.

Case study: UK hypocrisy or serving the national interest or both?

There are numerous examples of occasions when Western and UK governments have been accused of hypocrisy or double standards. The issue of the arms trade is one such example. Should the UK follow an 'ethical' foreign policy and prevent sales to questionable governments, even if it means UK workers will lose their jobs? Does it make sense in the national interest to protect British jobs? After all, if UK companies do not sell arms to these regimes, someone else will. Furthermore, there may be unintended consequences if one side in a conflict is able to obtain arms but the other is not, as was witnessed in the Bosnian War of 1992–95 when the Bosniak-Croats were not able to obtain arms to fight the well-armed Serbs.

The UK government claims to operate stringent rules on the misuse of UK-supplied arms. Arms should not be sold abroad if there is 'clear risk' that they may be used in a breach of international humanitarian law.

Examples

- The UK selling armaments to Saudi Arabia that have been used against civilians in Yemen. Saudi Arabia started a military campaign in 2015 against Iranian backed-rebels in Yemen. Alleged indiscriminate bombing has led to the killing of thousands of civilians and led to a humanitarian catastrophe in one of the world's poorest countries. Since 2015, the UK government has approved arms exports worth over £3.3 billion.

- The UK selling of armaments to Bahrain, which has a poor human rights record. Bahrain is the host of a new UK naval base. Since 2011, the Bahrain government has been accused of human-rights abuses in its attempts to put down pro-democracy protests. Bahrain is also a large buyer of UK arms.

- Alleged Western and UK silence or inaction over human-rights abuses in China, due to the economic power of China. The UK government believes that it can make more progress in persuading China to respect human rights by engaging in quiet diplomacy and encouraging trade rather than taking a harder line with the potential superpower.

These examples arguably demonstrate that the West does not practise what it preaches, and that liberal democratic states should have more ethical policies. Or is this more a question of dealing with a world as it is rather than a world as you would like it to be? What is your view?

Question

- Should the UK adopt an entirely ethical foreign policy even it damaged the economy and led to job losses? If so, why?

Allied to the challenge of sovereignty from humanitarian intervention is the role of the International Criminal Court, which is based in The Hague, the Netherlands. Though some significant global actors have not signed up to the court, such as the USA, China and Russia, the court is the first permanent international criminal court in the world. This has advanced the concept of an international higher law considerably. The fact that a large number of states have agreed the definitions of genocide, war crimes and crimes against humanity and have accepted that these crimes can be tried at an international court suggests that there is a little less anarchy in the international system, and that states are not as sovereign as they once were.

3.2 Environmental

The role and significance of the United Nations Framework Convention on Climate Change

The **United Nations Framework Convention on Climate Change (UNFCCC)** was created as a mechanism for developing global environmental policy. The UNFCCC was established at the Rio 'Earth Summit' – the UN Conference on Environment and Development – in 1992. The treaty came into force in 1994, and by 2012 it had been ratified by 194 states and organisations. Signatory parties have met every year since 1995 to assess progress in dealing with climate change.

Parties to the treaty have to make national inventories of their sources of CO_2 emissions and possible sinks (ways CO_2 emissions could be absorbed). At the 1997 Kyoto Summit, the 181 signatory states were required to freeze CO_2 emissions at 1990 levels from 2000 onwards. This paved the way for the introduction of legally binding emission targets.

Requirements on states were determined on the basis of equity and in accordance with states' 'common but differentiated responsibilities and respective capabilities'. States that had contributed most to global warming, had industrialised earlier or were more developed were expected to accept greater reductions in their emissions, while developing states were not expected to reduce theirs.

One criticism of the UNFCCC is that it did not take account of the fact that emissions by developing states would increase rapidly as their economic growth accelerated. Furthermore, the UNFCCC is merely a set of recommendations for further action – its rulings and requirements are not legally binding.

The creation of the Intergovernmental Panel on Climate Change (IPCC) and its role and significance

The **Intergovernmental Panel on Climate Change (IPCC)** was set up four years before the UNFCCC. It was created jointly by a United Nations agency, the World Meteorological Organization (WMO) and the United Nations Environment Programme (UNEP). Currently, it has 195 members.

The purpose of the IPCC is to provide impartial information and advice about climate change to decision-makers and interested organisations and groups. The panel consists of leading climate-change scientists, who volunteer to review the latest research on climate change. Three working groups look at:

- the physical science basis of climate change
- climate-change impacts, adaptation and vulnerability
- mitigation of climate change.

There is also a taskforce on national greenhouse gas inventories.

Key term

United Nations Framework Convention on Climate Change (UNFCCC) an international environmental treaty negotiated at the Earth Summit in Rio de Janeiro in 1992.

Key term

Intergovernmental Panel on Climate Change (IPCC) UN body set up in 1988 as an internationally accepted authority on climate change.

The Intergovernmental Panel on Climate Change seeks to improve understanding of climate change, through its reports, and to influence policy at state level.

The panel makes regular reports, the most important being *Assessment Reports*, which assess the risks of climate change, its current and its projected impact, and comment on the options for adaptation (coping with climate change) and mitigation (how to reduce emissions). There have been five assessment reports so far (1990, 1995, 2001, 2007, 2014). A sixth report is due in 2022.

Through its reports, the IPCC influences understanding of, and state policy-making on, climate change. It has established a consensus that climate change exists by providing evidence that the Earth's temperature is rising as a result of human activity – through the production of greenhouse gases, such as carbon dioxide, methane and nitrous oxide, from the burning of fossil fuels. The 2007 Assessment Report projected that, if nothing was done to curb greenhouse gas emissions, the world's mean temperature would rise by 2.4–6.4°C by 2099. The IPCC has made it increasingly difficult for states to ignore the issue. It was awarded the Nobel Peace Prize in 2007 for its efforts in raising awareness of climate change.

However, the IPCC can be criticised on a number of counts.

- Its reliance on already published research, which undergoes long, exacting reviews means that its reports may be years out of date, which could lead to an underestimation of the extent of climate change.

- Some people question the validity of some scientific assumptions on which the Assessment Reports' judgements are based – for example, assumptions about the oceans' capacity to absorb carbon dioxide, which are much disputed by the scientific community.

- The IPCC has been accused of scaremongering, making predictions that do not stand up to scrutiny. For example, the 2014 Assessment Report claimed that there is a 'risk of death, injury, and disrupted livelihoods in low-lying coastal zones and small-island developing states, due to sea-level rise, coastal flooding and storm surges.' Critics argue that the frequency and severity of flooding in many areas were higher during the Little Ice Age (1300–1870) and other cool eras than during the 20th century.

3.3 Addressing and resolving contemporary global issues

As we have seen, there have been numerous attempts to co-operate globally to deal with breaches of human rights, end conflicts and reduce poverty. It may be in the general interests of states to reduce global problems, but co-operation and consensus still remain disappointingly elusive due to the reasons outlined in this chapter.

Challenges to effective global environmental governance

The establishment of global environmental governance in the form of the Framework Convention on Climate Change and the Intergovernmental Panel on Climate Change has promoted a consensus on the existence of global warming and, to some extent, the scale of it. However, it has been difficult to reach agreement on how to mitigate it. There are a number of reasons for this. One is disagreement over whether to pursue gradual policies to discourage environmentally damaging behaviour or whether to take a more radical approach, which would risk lower levels of economic growth.

Shallow green ecologists support **sustainability**, believing that **sustainable development** is possible and that economic growth is compatible with environmental protection. Deep green ecologists, however, reject anthropocentrism (the prioritisation of human interests) in favour of an approach where nature takes priority. Another problem is the 'tragedy of the commons' – the idea that where resources are shared they will be misused or exhausted. If the **tragedy of the commons** is right it will be impossible to get states to agree to self-restraint in the exploitation of the Earth's resources. What further compounds the tragedy of the commons is the competing interests of states, especially between the developed and developing worlds. Why should any state accept limitations on its emissions that effectively limit its sovereignty, especially when the burden is shared unequally or there is a perception that others should take greater responsibility for the problem. Moreover, how should the share of responsibility be apportioned – according to current development or consumption, or based on historical levels? The various international conferences and the agreements reached at them highlight the obstacles in taking concerted action on climate change.

Competing views about how to tackle environmental issues
Shallow green ecology versus deep green ecology

Shallow green (reformist) and deep green (radical) ecology refer to two competing traditions in ecologism. Ecologism is a political ideology that argues that nature is an interconnected whole, where humans, animals and plants share a self-regulating and mutually sustaining ecosystem.

- **Shallow greens:** At one end of the spectrum, shallow green ecologists aim to reconcile the interests of humans with animals and plants, while still allowing for economic growth – within certain limits. Shallow greens recognise that environmental damage will inevitably affect human prosperity, whether through the depletion of fossil-fuel reserves or through the effects of climate change, such as more frequent flooding or more severe storms. To mitigate these potentially damaging effects of over-consumption, humans can curtail activities that

Key terms

Sustainability
the capacity to endure.

Sustainable development
development that meets the needs of the present, without compromising the ability of future generations to meet their own needs.

Link

For more on the **tragedy of the commons**, see Section 3.3 of Global Governance: Human Rights and Environmental

are damaging to the environment. This may involve some decline in living standards, or at least lower rates of economic growth, but shallow greens believe that a balance can be struck between economic growth and environmental concerns – what is called sustainable development.

Shallow green ecologists identify various ways in which sustainable development can be achieved. One way is for environmental costs to be factored in to economic decisions, so that it is more costly and less profitable to engage in activities or practices that are damaging to the environment. Examples are taxes on polluting practices or subsidies for the production of green energy. Shallow greens also look to human ingenuity and innovation to provide solutions to green problems, such as carbon capture and the development of drought-resistant crops. A third way is the development of international regimes, such as the UNFCCC, and international regulatory bodies, such as the IPCC, to ensure all states play their part in protecting the environment.

- **Deep greens:** Deep green ecology takes a more radical approach to the environment. Deep green ecologists reject the reformist shallow green position of sustainable development, because they argue that economic growth has caused environmental damage. The capitalist desire for profit has not only led to the exploitation of workers, but also to the plundering of the environment.

  Deep greens also disagree with the shallow greens' anthropocentric approach, which puts human interests above animals and plants. They argue instead that nature is equal if not superior to human interests – an ecocentric approach. Their solutions to climate change and degradation involve a paradigm shift away from a capitalist economic system to a more sustainable, less materialistic economic system. They advocate human population control as a way to minimise the human impact on the environment, and promote wilderness and biodiversity.

Sustainable development

The idea of sustainable development gained currency through the Brundtland Commission Report of 1987, *Our Common Future*. The report aimed to show how economic growth and poverty reduction should be linked to environmental protection. The report defined sustainable development as 'development that meets the needs of the present without compromising the ability of future generations to meet their own needs'.

Within this statement there is an implicit recognition that current economic growth should be limited to ensure that resources would be available to future generations – a concept of fairness between generations – as well as equity between the developed and developing world, ensuring that richer states would not plunder resources at the expense of poorer countries. Sustainable development as defined by the report has exerted considerable influence on development theory and has been adopted by shallow green ecologists to justify their reformist approach. The report, and the idea of sustainable development, paved the way for the Rio Earth Summit in 1992.

Today, the **tragedy of the commons** theory would apply to the seas and oceans, Antarctica, the atmosphere, the Moon and outer space – all of which do not fall under the sovereign jurisdiction of any state or authority, so are in danger. The seas and oceans are warming and are being over-fished; the polar and glacial ice is melting; greenhouse gas levels have risen by almost 50 per cent on pre-industrial levels; increasing amounts of satellite debris are orbiting the Earth.

The tragedy of the commons poses a potentially insurmountable problem for policy-makers and environmentalists. There seems to be no incentive for individuals and states to modify their

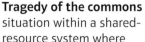

Key term

Tragedy of the commons situation within a shared-resource system where individual users acting independently and rationally according to their own self-interest behave contrary to the common good of all users by depleting that resource.

behaviour or accept restrictions on their freedom of action if they can gain all the benefits while others bear the cost. The world's common resources – like its seas and atmosphere – cannot be privatised.

Key concept: The tragedy of the commons

The tragedy of the commons is an economic theory about systems where resources are shared. The theory says that each individual will try to reap the greatest benefit from a given resource. As demand for the resource overwhelms supply, every individual who consumes another unit will directly harm others, who can no longer enjoy the same benefits.

The theory originated in the 1830s, when Victorian economist William Forster Lloyd looked at the example of common land, which tended to be overgrazed. Individual herders wanted to increase the number of their livestock grazing on the land, even though that led to the number of livestock exceeding the carrying capacity of the land, and ultimately to the loss of pasture – a tragedy for everyone. This tendency was driven by the fact that the positive benefit that each herder gained by adding one more animal (in meat, wool, leather or sale at market) always exceeded the negative impact on the quality of the pasture, which was small and shared by all herders.

The concept of the tragedy of the commons only became well known through an essay of the same name, published by Garrett Hardin in 1968. Hardin likened the environment to a **global commons** – areas and resources that are shared but are not regulated. He argued that the Earth has a limited carrying capacity for the size of the population. He believed the optimum carrying capacity had been reached by the last quarter of the 20th century, and any further increases in world population would bring about deterioration in the quality of the environment and of human life. As the number of people increased, there would be increased pollution, degeneration of the quality of agricultural land, deforestation and a lowering of air and water quality. To prevent this, Hardin believed that there should be limitations on world population growth.

Key term

Global commons
areas and resources that are un-owned and consequently beyond national jurisdiction.

However, international regimes have had some success in forcing states to comply with environmental regulations. The 1959 Antarctic Treaty ensures that the Antarctic remains the last great wilderness. It prevents the continent being used for military purposes, the detonation of nuclear devices or the storage of radioactive waste, and only allows access for scientific research. Another example is the Montreal Protocol of 1987. It banned the production of CFCs (chlorofluorocarbons), which were depleting the ozone layer – the part of the atmosphere that protects against the harmful effects of ultraviolet radiation. A fund was established in 1990 to help the developing world find alternatives to CFCs, and by 1996 the developed countries had stopped producing these gases.

Critics argue that the tragedy of the commons has been exaggerated. There are numerous examples of indigenous peoples, such as the Amazonian and North American Indians, the Bedouin and Mongolian Yak herders, who sustainably manage collective goods.

	Rio 1992	Kyoto 1997	Copenhagen 2009	Paris 2015
Description	• UN Conference on Environment and Development • Also known as the 'Earth Summit' • 3–14 June 1992 • 172 countries represented • 108 countries sent heads of government/heads of state • 2400 representatives of NGOs attended • Largest ever environmental conference held up to this point	• UN Climate Change Conference • December 1997 • 192 parties signed up to the Kyoto Protocol • 83 countries ratified it in their own nation • The Protocol ran until 2012 • In 2012 at the Doha Conference the binding targets of the Protocol were extended beyond 2012 for 37 countries	• UN Climate Change Conference • 7–18 December 2009 • 163 countries participated • 101 countries sent heads of government/heads of state, including President Obama and Premier Wen Jiabao of China • Resulted in the Copenhagen Accord, drafted by USA, China, India, Brazil and South Africa	• UN Climate Change Conference • Also known as Conference of Parties 21 (COP21) • The 21st conference since Rio in 1992 • 30 November–12 December 2015 • 195 countries represented • By April 2016, 174 countries had signed the Paris Agreement
Main decisions	• The Convention on Biological Diversity • The Framework Convention on Climate Change (FCCC) • The Principles for the Sustainable Management of Forests • The Rio Declaration on Environment and Development • Agenda 21 (UN programme of action from Rio)	• The Kyoto Protocol, under which developed countries agreed to cut emissions by at least 5.2 per cent on 1990 levels between 2008–12 • EU given a target of 8 per cent and the USA 7 per cent • Australia was allowed to exceed its 1990 level • Flexibility mechanisms allowed states to engage in carbon trading to meet their targets	• To keep the rise in global temperature below 2°C above pre-industrial levels • Developed countries to provide $30 billion (2010–12) in development aid to help poorer countries cut emissions and adapt to climate change • By 2020, developing countries to receive $100 billion a year in aid from richer countries, half from private sources • Developed countries to submit plans for cutting emissions to the UN for inspection and monitoring • Developed and emerging economies to submit to the UN reports on emissions for measurement and verification	• Long-term goal of keeping the increase in global average temperature to **well below 2°C** above pre-industrial levels • Aim to limit the increase to **1.5°C to** significantly reduce risks and the impacts of climate change • **Global emissions to peak as soon as possible**, recognising that this will take longer for developing countries • Undertake **rapid reductions thereafter** in accordance with the best available science • Every country to submit five-year plans on how to cut greenhouse gas emissions • The Agreement will not come into force until signed by at least 55 countries producing 55 per cent of global greenhouse gas emissions

	Rio 1992	Kyoto 1997	Copenhagen 2009	Paris 2015
Strengths	• An important step in the development of global environmental policy • Paved the way for the adoption of legally binding targets at Kyoto • Focus on sustainable development has led to an holistic approach to human rights, population control, poverty, gender inequality and the environment • Allowed NGOs to be represented and influence the agenda on environmental protection	• Introduced the first legally binding targets for reducing greenhouse gas emissions • Flexible targets and carbon trading made it easier for states to agree to binding targets • Carbon trading promotes investment by richer countries in poorer ones	• Copenhagen prepared the way for emission cuts • President Obama proposed to cut US emissions by 4 per cent by 2020 on 1990 levels • China and other emerging economies committed themselves to cutting emissions	• First ever universal, legally binding climate-change deal • The participation of the USA and China in the conference helped states to reach an ambitious target
Weaknesses	• The agreements reached at Rio lacked ambition and were not legally binding • Too many different positions made agreement difficult to reach • Developed and developing states disagreed over the responsibility for tackling climate change	• Carbon trading is open to abuse and allows richer states to avoid reducing their emissions • The Protocol did not come into force until 2005 – when Russia ratified the treaty – because it required signatories to be responsible for at least 55 per cent of 1990 emissions • Cutting emissions by on average 5 per cent is not enough to stop global warming • USA, the largest producer of greenhouse gases at the time, withdrew from the Protocol in 2001 • India and China did not sign the agreement, but are significant producers of greenhouse gases • Excluding developing countries, which have become significant polluters, from binding targets has compromised the effectiveness of Kyoto • Carbon dioxide levels are four times higher than they were in the 1990s	• Participants only required to take note of the Accord – no binding action to reduce emissions required • No date set for agreeing binding targets • The Accord is vague about where the developed countries will get the money for development aid and how it will be used • No detail provided about the measurement and verification process for checking emissions	• Doubts over whether the USA will ratify the Agreement – President Trump indicated he would not • States can set their own targets for cutting emissions, which are likely to be lower than needed for keeping the rise in global temperatures to just 1.5°C • No enforcement mechanisms or penalties if states fail to take action

Table 3.1: Strengths and weaknesses of international agreements

Obstacles to international co-operation and agreement

The tragedy of the commons explains in part why international co-operation and agreement on the environment is difficult to achieve. However, there are other obstacles, including:

- sovereignty
- divisions between developed and developing states
- disagreements about how far nations are responsible or should take action
- how pollution is measured – for example, whether current or cumulative levels should count.
- climate change denial

On most issues, such as health care, education, law and order and immigration, states enjoy sovereignty – they have the ultimate authority to decide policy in these areas. However, the environment is not confined within state borders. Pollution, rising sea levels and greenhouse-gas emissions cannot be solved by unilateral action; they require the collective action of many states, if not all. Collective action requires collective decision-making and collective implementation, which in turn lead to the creation of international organisations and regimes. Inevitably, this leads to a loss of sovereignty as decisions are made more easily by a majority rather than on the basis of unanimity. There will be times when individual states lose out in the interests of everyone.

Case study: The EU and greenhouse gas emissions

State co-operation on the environment has been possible within the EU. More than 80 per cent of environment regulations that are followed in EU member states have been devised and agreed at the EU level. The EU Commission was allowed to take a leading role in environmental policy formulation because a series of environmental agreements in the 1970s were threatening to frustrate movement towards the development of the common market. It was felt that co-ordination of environmental as well as economic policy was needed. The high level of integration in this area of policy led to an effective

The EU Commission has taken a leading role in formulating environmental policy at EU level.

burden-sharing agreement among member states on the Kyoto emissions-target reductions. The more-developed Northern European states agreed to reduce their emissions by up to a quarter, while allowing the less-developed Southern European states to increase their emissions by similar amounts. The ability to reach a consensus between member states and share the burden equitably has enabled the EU to set the most ambitious targets in the world in cutting greenhouse gas emissions.

Questions

- What led to the development of a common EU policy on the environment?
- How has the EU ensured that the burden of reducing greenhouse gas emissions has fallen fairly on more- and less-developed states?

Disputes over responsibility for climate change provide another significant obstacle to international co-operation and agreement on the environment. The scientific evidence suggests that global warming is caused by greenhouse gases, which are the by-products of burning fossil fuels. The consumption of fossil fuels began in earnest in the late-18th century with the Industrial Revolution. Countries industrialised at different rates and some countries in the developing world are still industrialising. The developed states were the earliest to industrialise, and they produce a greater share of greenhouse gases. In the 1990s, the USA produced about 25 per cent of the world's total carbon-dioxide emissions compared to China's 14 per cent, despite the fact that the American population accounted for less than 5 per cent of the total world population, while China's accounted for 20 per cent. Developed states are also responsible for much of the emissions in the developing world. Due to globalisation, around one-third of carbon dioxide emissions in the developing world come from the manufacture of goods that are consumed in the developed world. It would seem right that developed states should bear greater responsibility for the reduction in carbon dioxide, methane and nitrous oxide levels, especially when they have had longer to enjoy the benefits of industrialisation. Moreover, any requirement for developing states to reduce emissions would jeopardise their much-needed economic growth. In recognition of such concerns about equity and fairness, the principle of 'common but differentiated responsibilities' was enshrined in the 1992 Framework Convention on Climate Change. This places the onus on developed states to commit to greater reductions in greenhouse-gas emissions and to provide financial support to developing states to help them achieve reductions.

Adherence to the principle of common but differentiated responsibilities is highly contentious. Developed states argue that they cannot be held responsible for pollution produced in the past, when no one knew this would cause global warming. These countries argue that reduction targets should be set according to current rather than historical levels of emissions. They also take issue with the linking of emissions to a state's share of the global population. America may produce four times more greenhouse gas emissions per capita than China, but overall China is now producing the highest levels of emissions: 29 per cent to America's 16 per cent. Successive US administrations have disputed the fairness of targets based on per-capita measures, claiming that targeting the highest polluters would do more to combat climate change.

A further complication in agreeing binding targets is that climate change does not affect all parts of the world equally. Generally, the northern hemisphere has been only mildly affected by more extreme weather events, such as flooding and storms, thought to be caused by warming temperatures. The ice is retreating quickly in the Arctic, increasing the challenges for polar bears in hunting for food, but as a sparsely populated area this has little impact on human societies. Equatorial regions and the southern hemisphere, on the other hand, are more populated and seem to be bearing the brunt of climate change. The increasing incidence of drought in East Africa, the expansion of the Sahara and Namibian deserts, and the threat of rising sea levels to low-lying islands in the Pacific and river deltas in places such as Bangladesh may make such places uninhabitable in the future. For islands such as the Maldives, Nauru, Tuvalu and Vanuatu, urgent action on climate change is a matter of national survival. The Alliance of Small Island States (AOSIS) is lobbying for the more ambitious target of limiting the rise in global mean temperatures to just 1.5°C, rather than the 2°C accepted by most other states.

A significant obstacle to effective action on global warming is the reluctance of the most polluting countries – the USA and China – to sign up to binding emissions targets. The situation has developed into a quid pro quo or game of tit for tat. In the 1990s, China argued that it should not accept emissions targets because, as a developing country, it was not responsible for the damage done by other countries industrialising earlier. The US initially agreed to binding targets at Kyoto in

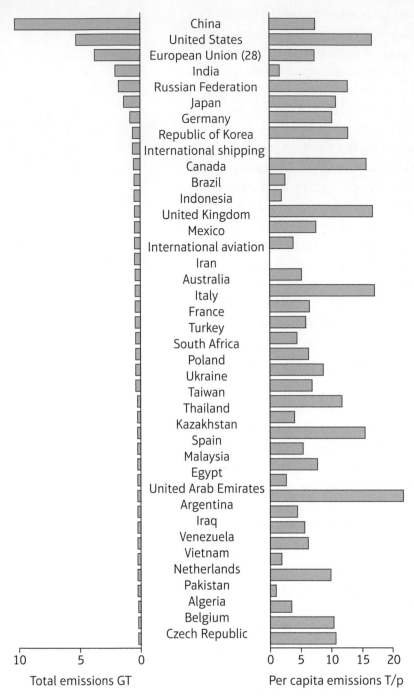

Figure 3.1: Total and per-capita CO$_2$ emissions by country with international shipping and aviation shown for comparison (EU Emissions Database for Global Atmospheric Research)

1997, but revoked its signature under George W. Bush in 2001, arguing that China had become the greatest net emissions producer, so it was unfair to expect the USA to make reductions when other countries were causing more damage to the environment. More recently, the USA and China have undergone a conversion to the climate-change cause. President Obama pledged to sign up to the Paris Agreement, although his successor Donald Trump has indicated that he will scrap the deal. China, in an attempt to combat the problem of smog in its major cities, has pledged to become the world's leader in renewable energy production.

A less tangible obstacle to agreement on tackling climate change, but, nonetheless, one that adds to the reluctance of states to take effective action is climate change denial. There is a significant lobby, especially in the USA, that challenges the science of climate change. The fossil fuel industry and right-wing libertarian think tanks sponsor scientists who question the role of human beings in global warming, the quality of the science and the seriousness of the threat. For example, they claim that current rising temperatures are due to natural variation, or that water vapour is a more important cause of global warming which is not accounted for in many models of climate change. It is hard to say whether such groups have reduced governments' ability to agree on what to do, but they may have influenced public opinion. In the UK, less than 1 per cent of voters consider the environment among the most important issues facing the country. If voters do not prioritise global warming there is less impetus for governments to act. Also, action on the environment might mean higher taxes or more restrictions on citizens, which would reduce their standard of living and their freedom of action.

Pause & reflect ✔

Create a timeline of the main developments in global environmental policy since 1990. Provide dates, achievements and consider how they improve on what has gone before.

EXTENSION ACTIVITY

Consider how the agreements reached at these climate-change conferences provide evidence of:

- the tragedy of the commons
- divisions in green thought
- differences between the developed and developing worlds.

The role of non-state actors in addressing and resolving environmental issues

Non-governmental organisations (NGOs) are non-state actors that seek to influence governments on wider social issues. NGOs – such as Greenpeace, Friends of the Earth and the World Wide Fund for Nature – have been active in pushing for more radical reductions in greenhouse-gas emissions. They are a familiar presence at the annual UN climate change conferences and actively lobby state governments and international organisations on environmental issues. In particular, NGOs have played a significant role in promoting the environment as a global issue.

Case study: Friends of the Earth

Friends of the Earth is an international network of environmental organisations. The first branch was created in the UK in 1969, by a group of anti-nuclear activists. The international network was created in 1971 by branches in the UK, Sweden, USA and France. There are now branches in 75 countries, with over 2 million members worldwide. Friends of the Earth aims to promote environmental protection and sustainable development. One of its greatest achievements was getting recognition of the 1.5°C threshold in the Paris Climate Agreement. Signatories to the agreement are committed to keeping the increase in the global mean temperature to below 2.0°C, but 1.5°C is the desired goal.

Question

- As a result of campaigning by Friends of the Earth, what did the Paris Climate Agreement recognise?

Case study: The green movement

The green movement emerged in the 1970s as an international movement, in response to concerns about the effects of testing nuclear weapons and emerging evidence of the damaging effects of human activities on the environment. It represents a range of organisations, from national to grassroots, private citizens, professionals, politicians, scientists and non-profit groups. The movement includes other movements with a more specific focus, such as the climate movement. It has no formal membership, but millions of people are members of environmental pressure groups and political parties. Followers of the green movement advocate sustainable management of the environment through changes in public policy and individual behaviour. The impact of the green movement has been to raise awareness of the damaging effects of humans on the environment and to increase the importance of the environment as a national and international political issue.

Question

- What has been the main achievement of the green movement?

EXTENSION ACTIVITY

Find out more about Greenpeace, Friends of the Earth and the World Wide Fund for Nature. Create an advertisement or a PowerPoint presentation on these NGOs, addressing the following questions and points.

- How and when were these organisations founded?
- What are their aims?
- How many members do they have and how many people do they employ?
- In what countries are they based?

Find examples of the influence of these organisations on the main climate-change conferences, on global environmental policies and on raising awareness of climate change.

Assessment support: 3.2.3 Global Governance: Human Rights and Environmental

Question 1 on A-Level Paper 3 is worth 12 marks and you should allow about 15 minutes to write the answer. There is a choice of two questions.

Examine the criticisms of the International Criminal Court (ICC). [12 marks]

This question requires a short answer – about one page of writing. These questions test Assessment Objectives AO1 and AO2, with the marks divided equally between the two. You are asked to show knowledge and understanding of the International Criminal Court, and identify the main criticisms made of the court. In a question of this length, you should aim to examine three criticisms in some depth.

- You need to start off by showing your knowledge of the ICC and its role in the field of international criminal law. Some context and examples would be useful, as would knowledge of the crimes that can be prosecuted.

- There are many criticisms of the ICC including:
  ○ the implications for sovereignty
  ○ Western cultural bias within the court
  ○ bias against African states
  ○ the slow process of cases, which delays justice
  ○ the double standards of Western states that criticise others but appear to act with impunity
  ○ the lack of arrest powers of the court allowing fugitives to avoid justice.

Choose three criticisms from this list that you can talk about in most depth, with a range that covers a clear variety of subjects.

Here is part of a student's answer – a brief criticism of the ICC.

A criticism of the ICC is that it can be seen to infringe on state sovereignty. Some countries, like China, have not signed up to the ICC because they believe that sovereignty is a fundamental right of states and they should be able to decide for themselves what happens in their country. The principle of non-intervention is at the heart of the Westphalian system and is enshrined in Article 2 of the UN Charter. They argue that states have the right to conduct affairs in their own territory without unwanted interference from states who have their own interests to pursue. These states may be politically motivated.

- The answer shows sound knowledge of the Westphalian system and its focus on state sovereignty. There can be tension within the international system between global co-operation and state sovereignty.

- The answer develops knowledge of the principle of non-intervention and the UN Charter Article 2.

- A correct criticism has been identified, but the answer would be stronger if it included specific examples of the ICC infringing state sovereignty or a politically motivated case.

CHAPTER
4

Power and Developments

Power can be exercised in different ways. There is hard power, which includes the use of military or economic rewards and punishments. There is soft power , which can be exerted through diplomatic relations and the sharing of cultural values. More recently, there has been the emergence of smart power – a combination of hard and soft power. In this section, you will consider these various ways and their effectiveness.

This chapter will discuss:

- the various types of power
- the hierarchy of state power in the international system and whether one, two or more states dominate
- alternative forms of government practised by states around the world
- the development and spread of liberal economies, the rule of law and democracy.

4.1 Different types of power

Power is the ability to exert influence over others to do something they would not otherwise do. It has nothing to do with legality or authority gained from elections; it is about having the resources, military might, persuasiveness or integrity to make others do what you want.

Power is an important aspect of international relations, but it is elusive. You will have an instinctive understanding of what power is, and will be easily able to identify the most powerful states in the world. However, it is harder to explain what makes states powerful or to measure their power.

This chapter will discuss the various types of power, explore how we might measure state power and debate the hierarchy of state power in the international system – whether one, two or more states dominate. You will also consider the alternative forms of government practised by states around the world.

> **Key term**
>
> **Hard power**
> the use of military and economic means to influence the behaviour or interests of other political bodies.

The use and effectiveness of types of power

Hard power: military and economic

Military power is the ultimate form of coercion.

Hard power is command or coercive power: the ability to make others do what you want, or to use some form of incentive to get what you want. Hard power encompasses military and economic 'carrots' and 'sticks'. Realists tend to conceive of power in these terms.

Military power is the capacity of a state to commit an aggressive act against another state, up to and including full-scale conflict. Recent examples of expansion in or demonstrations of military power include the following.

- As China's economic power has grown (it is now the second-richest state in the world) it has been building up its military capability. In 2009, military spend was about $70 billion; by 2016, it was $150 billion.

- Russia used its six-day invasion of Georgia in 2008 to retaliate against Georgia's suppression of Russian nationalist separatists in South Ossetia.
- The Iraq War of 2003 was fought to achieve a number of foreign-policy objectives for the USA, but principally its intention was to subdue America's enemies in the Middle East and in other parts of the world.

Economic power, on the other hand, involves inducements or incentives to a state to act according to the wishes of another state. For example, economic sanctions are commercial and financial penalties applied by one or more countries against a targeted country, including trade barriers, tariffs and restrictions on financial transactions. Trade agreements, which give countries privileged access to each other's markets, can also be used. Recent examples of the exercising of economic power illustrate the varied nature of this means of hard power.

- There were long-running sanctions against South Africa (1986–94) by the USA, Japan and the European Economic Community (EEC) in an attempt to end the racist apartheid regime. This prevented trade in certain commodities and financial services.
- Since 2014, the EU has imposed sanctions against Russia over its military support for Russian nationalist separatists in Ukraine. This includes the freezing of assets held in the EU by individuals and entities associated with Putin and his government, and a ban on certain exports to Russia.
- The USA and the EU were the first to insert clauses into their trade agreements protecting human rights and workers' conditions. More and more countries are using trade agreements to further their political objectives.

There are many facets to hard power, but its effectiveness can be questioned. China may have increased its military capability, but it has not been able to assert its legal claims over the South China Sea or establish military superiority in the region. US bases in Japan, South Korea, Guam, Philippines, Australia and the Malacca Straits effectively encircle China. Russia's intervention over South Ossetia has left the area in limbo, but Georgia has not been able to suppress the Russian nationalist movement there.

Sanctions have been unsuccessful in bringing about a withdrawal of Russian support for the separatists in eastern Ukraine. The consensus over the impact of the Iraq War for the USA is that it reduced its power in the Middle East and has even given rise to more terrorism and instability in the region. Sanctions against the apartheid regime in South Africa may have contributed to the emergence of black majority rule in the country, but the sanctions were not enforced by many important trading countries, such as the UK, and domestic factors were probably more important.

Whether the 'carrot' of trade agreements really works in promoting human rights is debatable, for two reasons.

- Countries seeking to make trade agreements are usually already on a path to democratisation, the adoption of rule of law and the protection of rights.
- Western states promote human rights but turn a blind eye when important trading partners have lower standards than they would like.

China is a good example of such double standards. Every Western leader who meets Chinese representatives lectures them about China's human-rights record, but concrete action is lacking even when the treatment of political prisoners and critics of the regime does not improve.

Military power is declining as a method of pursuing a state's interests. Inter-state conflict is decreasing and **economic interdependence** is on the rise. States are more likely to resort to

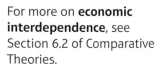

Link

For more on **economic interdependence**, see Section 6.2 of Comparative Theories.

economic sanctions or trade agreements to extend their influence. In Ukraine in 2016, although NATO increased its presence in Eastern European states bordering Russia, European states chose to use economic sanctions as their main tool in persuading Russia to withdraw its support for the Russian separatists. There was no immediate prospect of military intervention on behalf of Ukraine against its hostile neighbour.

Soft power: diplomatic and cultural

While hard power involves threats, punishments or incentives and rewards, soft power is based on attraction and identification, sharing common values and ideas – or 'cultural power'. The UK and the EU are widely recognised as leading 'soft powers' in the international system.

Soft power is about making friends and allies. Here, US President Barack Obama shakes hands with Chinese President Xi Jinping.

Rank	Country
1	United Kingdom
2	Germany
3	United States of America
4	France
5	Canada
6	Australia
7	Switzerland
8	Japan
9	Sweden
10	Netherlands

Table 1.1: Top ten soft powers in the world (Portland 2015)

Case study: The UK

The UK has topped recent league tables of soft-power states. One reason is that English is the most common second-language in the world, spoken by an estimated 1 billion people – about a seventh of the world's population. This is a product of both British imperialism in the 19th century and the global influence of the US in the 20th and 21st centuries. Familiarity with, and admiration for, British culture wins it friends across the world. Britain has also taken a leading role in the formation of international organisations. Britain helped to establish the Council of Europe in 1948, which produced the European Convention on Human Rights and the European Court of Human Rights, and is a member of the UN Security Council. Britain is also a leading member of the International Olympic Committee, with London the only city to have hosted the Olympic Games three times.

Questions

- Look at Great Britain's Olympic medal tally in 2016. How does it compare with China's?

- How might achievement at the Olympics give a state soft power?

Case study: The EU

The EU has emerged in the 21st century as a significant soft power, despite not being a state. Its strength lies in its economic power. The creation of the single market – the removal of all non-tariff barriers to trade in goods and most restrictions on trade in services, free movement of labour and capital, along with 19 of the 28 member states sharing the same currency – makes the EU an attractive marketplace. The EU expanded considerably in 2004 as newly democratised Eastern European countries sought to take advantage of the economic opportunities it offered. It has become a significant force in international relations. The creation of the role of High Representative, a 'foreign minister' for the EU, enables it to speak with one voice and send one representative to meetings of international organisations, such as the International Monetary Fund, G20 and G7.

The EU has been involved in 30 missions and operations since 2003 to help states with security, police training, customs, piracy and border management, as well as providing support in delivering humanitarian aid. The EU began negotiations with Iran in 2013 for the International Atomic Energy Agency's inspectors to have access to its nuclear-weapons programme, culminating in the 2015 Joint Comprehensive Plan of Action, signed by the five permanent members of the UN Security Council plus Germany, the EU and Iran – something the USA had failed to achieve alone through sanctions and breaking off diplomatic relations.

Liberals would argue that the EU's success over Iran's nuclear-weapons programme is testament to the superiority of soft power over hard power. Diplomacy can take a long time – over 12 years in the case of Iran – but in the long run it can achieve better outcomes. Liberals would also argue that the increase in the number of international organisations and the growth in world trade mean that soft power has the potential to be a more effective way for states to promote their interests than military force or economic penalties.

Question

• Why might a growth in world trade lead to greater co-operation between states?

Aesop's fable: The Wind and the Sun

One day, as the Wind and the Sun were debating which of them was the stronger, a man came along wearing a coat. The Sun said: 'See that man? I know a way we can decide which of us is the stronger. Whichever of us can remove his coat is the stronger.' The Wind agreed and the Sun allowed the Wind to have the first go. The Wind began to blow. The man clasped his coat tight. The Wind blew harder, but the man just clasped his coat even tighter. Then it was the Sun's turn. The Sun came out and shone brightly. Soon the man became too hot to wear the coat and took it off.

The Wind and the Sun illustrates two different approaches to influencing behaviour in order to get a desired outcome.

• What kind of power is represented by the Sun and the Wind?

• What kind of power would a realist or a liberal prefer and why?

Pause & reflect ✔

Compare hard and soft power. Think of other contemporary examples of the use of hard and soft power. Use the table below to help you.

Type of power	Definition	Methods	Examples	Effectiveness
Hard power				
Soft power				

Smart power

Smart power is a combination of hard and soft power. Liberal international-relations theorist Joseph Nye coined the term in his 2004 book *Soft Power: The Means to Success in World Politics*. Drawing on his experience as assistant secretary of defense during Bill Clinton's presidency, Nye argues that the most effective foreign policy employs a combination of hard- and soft-power strategies. Relying on hard or soft power alone in a given situation will usually prove inadequate.

Nye uses the example of the Taliban government in Afghanistan, which aided and supported the terrorist group Al-Qaeda that perpetrated the 9/11 attacks. Simply employing soft-power resources to change the hearts and minds of members of the regime would have been ineffective. Force was required to remove the regime and isolate Al-Qaeda. However, in developing relationships with the mainstream Muslim world, such as Saudi Arabia and Libya, the use of hard power would alienate them. In these cases, soft power would be a more fruitful strategy.

EXTENSION ACTIVITY

Find some relevant examples of smart power and assess their effectiveness. For example, consider the foreign policy of Barack Obama.

4.2 Differing significance of states in global affairs and how – and why – state power is classified

State power classifications

Different factors enable states to influence the behaviour of other states and gain power. A state can derive power through:

- **Capabilities:** Resources that it can draw on, such as population, wealth, military capability or geography. A poor country with a small population can never become a military power and will never be able to exercise hard power in any meaningful sense.
- **Relationships:** What is known as relational power. Making the right strategic alliances or joining certain international institutions can confer power on a state far beyond the extent of its resources.
- **Structures:** A state's establishment or control of knowledge, financial, security and production networks. The USA has significant structural power because it is the architect and leading power in a number of political and economic international organisations.

Link

For more on **structural power**, see Regionalism and the EU chapter.

Determining the origins of a state's power is not straightforward; it is debatable which, if any, of these are the most important. Power is as much about perception as about tangible qualities. It is mutable and dynamic, varying according to the issue – whether economic, social, political or military.

Great powers

The term '**great power**' originates from the early 19th century, when it was used to describe the combatants of the Napoleonic Wars – Austria, France, Great Britain, Prussia and Russia. There is no single agreed definition. Some thinkers have defined it in terms of military power or capability. Others, such as Kenneth Waltz – the founder of neo-realism – use these criteria.

- Population and territory.
- Resources.
- Economic development.
- Political stability.
- Competence and military strength.

A further relevant criterion is the ability to project power beyond the state's geographical region.

Of the five countries represented at the Congress of Vienna in 1814–15, which agreed a peace settlement to end the Napoleonic Wars, Great Britain came closest to satisfying all the criteria for great power status. In 1922, the British Empire covered nearly a quarter of the globe and ruled about one-fifth of the world's population. It was the foremost naval power and the richest and most developed economy in the world.

By the start of the 20th century, Germany was challenging Britain militarily and its rapid industrialisation at the end of the 19th century made it a rival economically too. The United States was also beginning to emerge, predominantly as a developing economy. The Monroe Doctrine – the guiding principle of US foreign policy since 1823 – prohibited the country from interference in European affairs, which stopped it becoming a military power until the Second World War.

Superpowers, including the USA

The term '**superpower**' emerged in the aftermath of the Second World War to describe the two main protagonists of the Cold War: the USA and the Soviet Union. These countries dominated the international order in ways in which Great Britain, as a great power in the 19th century, had not. What distinguished the USA and the Soviet Union was their mobility of power. Both countries had formed blocs (spheres of influence) in which they dominated. The North Atlantic Treaty Organization (NATO), led by the US, included much of Western Europe. The alliance was mainly a mutual defence arrangement: if one state was attacked, presumably by the Soviet Union or one of its allies, the other members would come to its aid. Likewise, the Warsaw Pact was formed by the Soviet Union to protect itself and Eastern European countries against possible attack from a NATO country.

These strategic military alliances were supplemented by political and economic associations beyond Europe.

The USA:

- allied with Japan and became involved in the Korean (1950–53) and Vietnamese (1955–74) conflicts to prevent communist regimes seizing power

- took an active interest in preventing the spread of communism in Central and South America, sponsoring right-wing opponents of Salvador Allende in Chile (1963–73) and providing arms to the right-wing Contra rebels in Nicaragua in the 1980s
- has long supported Israel to act as a counterweight to Soviet-backed regimes in Egypt, Syria and Afghanistan.

The Soviet Union:

- provided military and economic support to the communist insurgents in Korea and Vietnam
- supported communist Cuba – the stationing of Russian nuclear missiles there led to the 1962 Cuban Missile Crisis.

During the Cold War, every part of the globe acted as an arena for US–Soviet rivalry. They enjoyed global reach, which only Britain had come near to resembling at the height of the British Empire. The development of the nuclear bomb transformed these countries into superpowers. As the first countries to develop these weapons, they controlled their proliferation and use and, as a result, became the dominant military powers of the post-war era.

Emerging powers, including BRICS

There is no single agreed definition of '**emerging power**', in part because the term has only recently come into common use. However, it is generally agreed that a key characteristic of an emerging power is a growing economy, which gives a state the potential to be an important global actor.

There might be no emerging powers without globalisation. The growing volume of international trade requires the management of trading relations through international organisations, which brings states into closer contact with each other, providing opportunities to exert influence economically and politically.

A number of states are recognised as emerging powers. As well as the BRICS (Brazil, Russia, India, China and South Africa), there are Argentina, Australia, Indonesia, Iran, Mexico, Nigeria, Poland, Saudi Arabia, South Korea and Turkey. The **Group of 20**, seen by many as the forum through which these countries can exert influence, is arguably more important than the **Group of 7**.

4.3 Polarity

Polarity, or world order, is a description of the distribution of power and authority among states and others in the international system. There are three main ways in which power is distributed: **unipolarity**, **bipolarity** and **multipolarity**. These categories provide rival conceptions of where power lies, and suggest what implications these may have for global peace and security. Realists and liberals disagree about which of these systems is more likely to prevent conflict.

The implications of different polar structures

Unipolarity/hegemony

Unipolarity is where there is a lack of constraints or potential rivals to the one pre-eminent power, state or 'pole' in the world. When a single power is overwhelmingly dominant, this is known as hegemony. There can be predatory hegemony, where the dominant power acts aggressively, and benign hegemony, where the dominant power acts with good intentions.

Realists, in particular neo-realists, see unipolarity and the pursuit of hegemony as the natural consequence of states seeking power and security in an anarchic system. The surest way to protect the state from threats is to become the dominant power or hegemon. Unipolarity also

Link

For more on the **Group of 20** and the **Group of 7**, see Section 2.2 of Global Governance: Political and Economic.

Key terms

Emerging power
a state that is considered to be rising, primarily in economic power and influence.

Polarity
the nature of the international system at any given time in terms of how power is distributed.

Unipolarity
international system in which there is one dominant pole.

Bipolarity
international system revolving around two poles.

Multipolarity
international system revolving around three or more poles.

can have benefits for the wider international system. The dominant power can act as the 'world's police officer', intervening in conflicts between other states that threaten peace and security, or preventing human-rights abuses in civil conflicts. The hegemon can be the guarantor of economic and financial stability by setting and maintaining the ground rules for economic behaviour. The terms *Pax Britannicus* and *Pax Americana* refer to the roles played by Britain and the United States, at different points in their histories, in acting as guardians of the world order.

Liberals, by contrast, argue that unipolarity does not lead to the emergence of a benign force that promotes global peace and prosperity. Rather, they fear the emergence of a predatory hegemon that desires power at all costs. Other powers come to fear the megalomania of the dominant power, leading to a security dilemma. The very process of achieving dominance creates insecurity and hostility, which inevitably leads to conflict.

Bipolarity

Bipolarity is an international system that revolves around two poles or major power blocs: two states predominate, rather than one. For a system to be genuinely bipolar, there must be near-equality, or balance of power, between the two.

For realists, bipolarity is a natural tendency in the world order. States seek to establish such a balance to curb the hegemonic ambitions of all states. By establishing a balance of power, states are less likely to seek hegemony because they anticipate being countered by other states. Equilibrium is achieved, leading to peace and stability. For liberals, bipolarity does not curb the ambitions of states. Although the hegemonic ambitions of both are being curbed in the short term, there may come a point when circumstances allow one to emerge as the dominant power. In anticipation of this, the two power blocs vie with each other, often through an arms race, leading to tension and insecurity.

Case study: US and Soviet bipolarity

The US and the Soviet Union were the leaders of NATO and the Warsaw Pact respectively.

Between 1945 and 1989, two roughly equal blocs – NATO and the Warsaw Pact – dominated world politics. They were matched militarily, with armed forces of similar strength and roughly the same number of nuclear warheads, such that if they were to launch these warheads at each other there would be mutually assured destruction (MAD). NATO and the Warsaw Pact were led by superpowers – the US and the Soviet Union – that competed militarily but also politically and economically. They embraced the opposing ideologies of liberal democracy and capitalism in the West (the US-led bloc) and communism in the East (the Soviet-led bloc). The Berlin Wall – built in 1961 to separate the eastern zone of the city controlled by the Russians from the western zones controlled by the Americans, British, and French – epitomised the divisions between these blocs.

While the post-war world seemed to have the main characteristics of bipolarity, it can be argued this was an illusion. The Soviet Union matched American military might, almost tank for tank, nuclear warhead for warhead, and soldier for soldier, but it was never able to achieve economic parity. Resources were diverted to the arms and space races so that the production of consumer goods declined as a relative share of the Soviet economy, and the potential for economic development was squandered. When the superpowers' rivalry intensified in the 'Second Cold War', the Soviet Union could not match increases in US military spending. The glasnost (openness) and perestroika (economic reform) of the Gorbachev era (1985–91) were an acceptance of the Soviet Union's economic weakness, which was undermining its status as a military superpower. In 1989, the Berlin Wall fell as East Germany was permitted to open its border with West Germany, and the Soviet Union gave up its military and political domination of Eastern Europe – recognitions that the Soviet bloc was no match for the USA.

Questions

- In what ways was the power of the USA and the Soviet Union matched?

- Why did the era of bipolarity end?

Multipolarity

Multipolarity is an international system in which there are three or more power centres.

Neo-realists argue that multipolarity is inherently unstable. As the number of actors increases, so does the number of possible conflicts. When there are multiple power centres (anarchical polarity), even a small increase in power has the potential to make states a great power. This creates higher levels of uncertainty, intensifying the security dilemma.

Liberals are more optimistic about a multipolar world. They argue that such a world order promotes multilateralism, with greater co-operation and integration – what is known as interdependent polarity. States realise the futility of competition and conflict because the potential gains are relatively small, whereas co-operation produces benefits for all.

Consideration of changing nature of world order since 2000

At the start of the millennium, there was optimism that a 'new world order' would emerge to replace the tension and suspicion of the Cold War era. Two major obstacles remain to promoting peace and co-operation, which suggest this optimism was misplaced.

How the UN should be strengthened

Any strengthening of the UN's remit or powers threatens state sovereignty. The behaviour of the permanent members of the UN Security Council, particularly the USA and Russia's use of the veto, demonstrates how it is often difficult to reach agreement because states seek to protect their national interests. Peacekeeping has a mixed record and is often hampered by disagreements between the permanent members and the need to gain permission of sovereign states before peacekeeping missions can be deployed to them. **Reform of the UN**, in particular the much-criticised Security Council, has proved impossible.

How to promote partnership between USA and Russia

At first, the prospects seemed good. Russia transformed into a capitalist economy, but this was not followed by what the West would recognise as liberal democracy. There are elections in which a range of parties and candidates may stand, but there is the taint of ballot rigging in presidential

Link

For more on **reforming the UN**, see Section 2.3 of Global Governance: Political and Economic.

elections. The ideological conflict of the Cold War has disappeared, but closer co-operation has not materialised. Putin did declare support for the 'war on terror' in 2001 but relations with the USA deteriorated as NATO expanded to incorporate the former Warsaw Pact countries. Russia has been further offended by Western intervention in Kosovo on behalf of the ethnic Albanians against the Serbian government, traditional allies of Russia, and the willingness to support recognition of Kosovo as a sovereign independent state. During this time, Russian nationalism has been growing as a force in Russian politics. United Russia, a right-of-centre party that supports Vladimir Putin and encourages pride in the motherland and her achievements, dominates electoral politics. The party won nearly half of all votes in the 2011 Duma elections; the next nearest rivals, the Communist Party, gained only 20 per cent. Under Putin, there has been resurgence of Russian power and influence in the world, driven, in part, by rising economic prosperity. Russia is now an energy superpower, supplying the highest proportion of oil and gas of any country. However, Putin has become more assertive in pressing Russia's interests, such as over Ukraine and in defying American attempts to gain a UN resolution to intervene in the civil war between President Assad and the rebels in the Syrian conflict.

Hopes for a more peaceful world post-2000 have been dashed. The communist systems in states such as Yugoslavia and Chechnya had suppressed national and ethnic differences for many years. The fall of communism led to a power vacuum, which allowed minority groups to call for independence, creating potential flashpoints. The majority groups in these states desperately tried to cling on to power, resorting to ethnic cleansing, war crimes and genocide to maintain their dominance. The USA, by its 'war on terror' and its promotion of Western democracy, also unleashed destabilising forces. The Arab Spring started in Tunisia in 2010 and spread across North Africa and the Middle East, culminating in revolutions in Syria, Libya, and Yemen, civil uprisings in Egypt and Bahrain, and pro-democracy demonstrations in Algeria, Iraq, Jordan, Kuwait, Morocco, Oman, and even Saudi Arabia. The Syrian conflict has raged since 2011, with no immediate hope of a peaceful resolution. Arguably, the world is in a state of disorder, much like the pre-war era, making the Cold War appear to be an exceptional period of peace and stability.

Clearly, much has changed since 2000. The bipolarity of 1945–90 has not survived. The question is, what has replaced it.

A unipolar world order?

The obvious candidate for the pre-eminent power, pole or state in the world is the USA. Commentators have used various labels to describe its position in the international system: an empire, a global hegemon and even a hyperpower (a state that dominates all other states in every sphere).

To be a global hegemon, America would have to be vastly stronger than its rivals, economically, politically and culturally.

Case study: USA

The US does have the world's largest economy. In 2015, its gross domestic product (GDP) was just over $18 trillion. It is the world's strongest military power. In 2012, it spent more than 4 per cent of its GDP – more than half of global military spending – on its armed forces. It has a large population (over 320 million) that is highly educated with more than 80 per cent living in urban areas – all indicators of a highly developed economy. Politically, America can exert power as the chief architect of international political and economic institutions, such as the United Nations and the IMF. English is the most widely spoken second language in the world, driven by US economic development and the desirability of its products and its entertainment industry.

Coca-Cola is recognised in almost every country in the world. Apple has become a byword for technological chic. Hollywood is the highest grossing film industry in the world. American music and television programmes can be accessed across the globe. The USA is the 'Leader of the Free World'. American values, such as democracy and human rights, are embraced across the globe.

However, the USA is not vastly more powerful than other states. China's economy is catching up, and the combined GDP of EU states is not far short of the US at $16 trillion. The US has fewer nuclear warheads than Russia (6970 versus 7300), and has suffered some humiliating military defeats. It could not prevent the takeover of Vietnam by the communist Viet Cong. It failed to rescue American embassy officials taken hostage in Tehran in 1979. In 2001, the US suffered the 9/11 attacks, the worst terrorist atrocity in its history. In retaliation the US launched its 'War on Terror'. This led to the removal of the Taliban regime in Afghanistan and the Iraq War, but the Taliban have not been eradicated from Afghanistan and Iraq is not yet stable. It took ten years to track down Osama bin Laden, the mastermind of the 9/11 attacks. The USA has been powerless in resolving the Syrian crisis. It has taken Russian airstrikes and support for the Syrian Assad regime to bring IS to heel. Furthermore, it is debatable whether the US defeated communism in the Cold War. Communism was an unsustainable political and economic system that was bound to collapse. The Cold War may have prolonged it, as fear of an American attack caused Russians to be less critical of the system. To call the USA an empire is to overstate its influence. The USA is not a traditional imperial power. The US has no colonies and there has been no mass migration of American citizens to such colonies. There is resistance to American political and cultural leadership in the world. The emergence of groups such as Al-Qaeda and Islamic State, promoting a fundamentalist view of the Islamic religion and authoritarian political systems, can be seen as a rejection of American culture.

Questions

- In what ways is the USA powerful?
- What are the weaknesses of US power?
- Is the USA a global hegemon?

A multipolar world order?

In the 1970s, Japan and Germany emerged as leading economies. A decade later, the European Economic Community (now the EU) began to be recognised as a force in international relations. More recently, Brazil, Russia, India, China and South Africa (BRICS) have broken into the list of the top 20 most developed countries in the world. Altogether, these countries account for more than 50 per cent of the world's population, about 75 per cent of global GDP and 80 per cent of global defence spending.

Case study: China

The most obvious candidate to challenge American pre-eminence is China. While the 20th century is claimed to have been the 'American Century', many predict that the 21st century will be the 'Chinese century'.

One reason is China's rapid economic progress since the market reforms of Deng Xiaoping, beginning in 1978. Annual growth rates have been 8–10 per cent a year for almost 30 years, twice the levels of western economies. In 2009, China became the world's largest exporter. In 2010, it overtook Japan as the second-largest economy. It easily weathered the global financial crisis of 2008, being one of the few countries in the world to be running a surplus (spending less than it earns in tax revenue). It has the world's largest population at 1.3 billion (over one-sixth of the world's population), giving it a sizeable domestic market. If the rate of economic growth continues at this pace – in 2010 the Chinese economy was 90 times bigger than it had been in 1978 – China will soon have the most developed economy in the world.

Another reason is the growth in China's military capability. It has been a nuclear power since 1964, and has the second-largest military behind the US. It has been increasing its military presence in the South China Sea to reinforce its claims to Taiwan and to fishing rights and control of strategic shipping lanes.

China is also becoming a growing influence on global issues, such as climate change, through its memberships of the WTO and G20. Chinese membership of the G20 has led to this organisation being seen as more important than the G7. China has been strengthening its political and economic links with countries such as Australia and those in central Africa, parts of the Middle East and Latin America to gain access to natural resources. In return, Chinese companies provide financial investment for local infrastructure – roads, schools and hospitals. Many of these countries welcome Chinese investment not just for the material benefits of such a relationship but also because they have a shared dislike of Western imperialism. China's Asian neighbours share Confucian values, which provide a cultural basis for co-operation.

It is clear that China has the potential economically, militarily and politically to challenge American hegemony, but this depends on continued economic growth – something it may not achieve. Japan, Germany, Italy and France all experienced spectacular levels of growth in the 1960s and 1970s, but this has not been sustained in the 21st century. Japan, a near neighbour of China's with many cultural similarities, saw its economy stall in the 1990s. In 2016, the Japanese Central Bank adopted a negative interest rate of –0.1 per cent – charging people for saving money – in a desperate bid to stimulate economic growth. Also, the Chinese economy depends on cheap labour. This creates the risk of another country with even lower labour rates undercutting Chinese products.

China is yet to make the transition to a high-tech economy. An increasingly large and affluent middle class is demanding high-end products, such as Mercedes cars, but these are being supplied from abroad. There is evidence of Chinese economic growth beginning to falter. In 2015, the growth rate was 6.9 per cent. The one-child policy, established to control population size, has been so effective that China has a low birth rate and the most rapidly aging population in the world. Without young people to replace older generations, economic growth will be limited.

Some political commentators believe that China will prove to be a strong challenger to US pre-eminence as the 21st century progresses.

For other reasons, the Chinese century may not come to fruition. The liberalisation of China's economy has not been matched by political reform. Political opposition is banned and critics of the regime are suppressed. No figures have been released of the number of people killed or imprisoned in the Tiananmen Square protest of 1989, and it is still taboo to acknowledge the event. Tensions between the free-market economic system and the Stalinist-Communist political system may erupt into widespread social protest or even Arab Spring-style insurgency. Any political upheaval would adversely affect China's economic development. While China remains a communist system, its potential to become a world power is limited. Most states embrace liberal democracy and capitalism, which are at odds with communism. This may explain why China has been reluctant to take a leading world role, as was evident during the global financial crisis. Although China is emerging as a military power, it spends half of what the US does on its military as a percentage of GDP (2 per cent versus 4 per cent), and it does not have global reach.

Question

- What communist states are there currently in the world?

EXTENSION ACTIVITY

Do some research into China's claims in the South China Sea. You may want to look at the 2016 UN Permanent Court of Arbitration ruling.

Case study: Other contenders

Brazil has become the leading power in South America. It has the ninth-largest economy in the world. It is rich in natural resources, such as iron and timber, with a large agricultural sector producing foodstuffs that are in high demand internationally, such as coffee and cocoa. Brazil has a large population of over 200 million, giving it a large domestic marketplace. However, there is wide social inequality and below-average literacy rates, which will limit its economic potential.

India has become the seventh most developed economy thanks to its limited dependence on exports, high savings rates (and very low budget deficit), fast-growing population of mainly young people and rising middle class. It has also become a world leader in computer software and biotechnology. As a result, India recently overtook China as the fastest-growing large economy in the world. India's film industry, Bollywood, has become a global entertainment phenomenon. It is also a nuclear power. Nonetheless, India suffers from the same problems as Brazil that may hamper further economic development – wide social inequality and poor literacy rates, especially among women.

Russia has re-emerged as a power in recent years. An economic boom has been driven by the substantial expansion of oil and gas production. Russia has extensive natural resources, but these remained largely untapped during the communist era. With the advent of a capitalist economy there is both the incentive to exploit these resources more fully and access to foreign investment to do so. Russia's position as an energy superpower gives it great influence, as many countries have increasing energy needs that cannot be met at home. In particular, Russia retains strong influence over eastern Europe by supplying its energy needs. Economic growth and growing nationalism at home have made Russia increasingly assertive abroad, as demonstrated by the 2008 war with Georgia and by its resistance to Western military intervention to remove the Assad regime in Syria. It has been particularly active in exercising its veto in the UN Security Council. Russian net military spending lags far behind the US and NATO, although as a percentage of the country's GDP it is one of the highest in the world. Its support for the Russian separatists in eastern Ukraine has damaged its standing with the international community. It was excluded from the G8 in 2014 and EU sanctions led to a run on the rouble, causing it to fall in value by around 65 per cent.

Questions

- Which state is the best contender to rival US power and why?

- Evaluate the pros and cons of the case for multipolarity.

Country and ranking	GDP (trillion $)	GDP per capita ($)
1 USA	18.5	57,294
2 China	11.3	15,423
3 Japan	4.73	38,893
4 Germany	3.49	48,189
5 United Kingdom	2.65	42,513
6 France	2.48	42,384
7 India	2.25	6,658
8 Italy	1.8	36,313
9 Brazil	1.77	15,211
10 Canada	1.53	46,239

*Russia fell from 9th to 12th place 2015–16

Table 3.1: Top ten economies in the world (2016)

Ranking	Country	Spending (billion $)	Spending (% GDP)
1	USA	596	3.3
2	China	215	1.9
3	Saudi Arabia	87	13.7
4	Russia	66	5.4
5	United Kingdom	55	2.0
6	India	51	2.3
7	France	51	2.1
8	Japan	41	1.0
9	Germany	39	1.2
10	South Korea	36	2.6

Table 3.2: Top ten countries by military expenditure in the world (Stockholm International Peace Research Institute 2015)

Pause & reflect

Identify the key arguments for world order being unipolar and multipolar. Think of what evidence could be used to support these arguments. You might find it helpful to organise them according to three main categories – economic, military and political.

Types of argument	Unipolarity		Multipolarity		
	Argument	Evidence	Argument	Evidence	
Economic					
Military					
Political					

4.4 Different systems of government

In this section of the chapter, you will be introduced to different types of state. The main characteristics of these states are explained, along with descriptions of examples and evaluation of their consequences for global order.

Democratic states

Many states claim to be democracies but only about half of the world's countries satisfy all the necessary requirements. A true democracy is one where the government is elected by the citizens in elections that:

- are free and fair
- are free from intimidation (a secret ballot)
- count each person's vote the same
- have a choice of candidates/parties representing the ranges of interests and ideas in society.

This enables people to hold their representatives and the government to account by allowing them to be replaced by alternatives when they become dissatisfied with them.

Democratic states abide by the rule of law and citizens have various rights and freedoms, which can be exercised without interference from the state. For example, citizens enjoy freedom of speech, which allows them to criticise their representatives and ensure that representatives are responsive to them. There will be a range of pressure groups, allowing people to promote their interests on single issues – another way of holding those in power to account. Citizens should enjoy protection of their human and civil rights through an independent judiciary.

> ### Example: The UK
>
> The most familiar example of a democratic system is the UK – the first modern democracy. The UK evolved gradually from a monarchical system of government. Representation, an important element of any democracy, emerged in the 13th century with the creation of the English parliament. However, it was not until the 19th century that parliament represented a significant proportion of the people and it took until 1928 for there to be universal suffrage – somewhat later than many other democracies, such as the USA.
>
> The signing of Magna Carta in 1215 marked the beginning of the recognition of rights and government respect of the rule of law, and elections featured a choice of candidates from the 14th century. Political parties emerged in the late 18th century with the Whigs and the Tories, which became the modern-day Liberal Democrats and Conservatives. They were joined in 1900 by the Labour Party and throughout the 20th century a number of other political parties developed, including the Scottish National Party (1934), Plaid Cymru (1925), Green Party (1985) and UK Independence Party (1993). These parties represent a range of social groups (traditionally, Labour stood for the working class, while the Conservatives stood for the middle class) and ideas (nationalism, environmentalism and anti-Europeanism).
>
> British citizens enjoy protection of their rights through the Supreme Court and the European Convention on Human Rights. Elections are competitive and there is regular alternation of parties in government. There are thousands of pressure groups representing many different interests and viewpoints, and governments frequently change their policies under pressure from these groups.

Semi-democratic states

Some states can be considered to be **semi-democratic states** as have many of the characteristics associated with democracy, such as elections and representation, but elections may not be free

> ### Key terms
>
> **Democratic state**
> a state with a system of government in which all the people are involved in making decisions about its affairs.
>
> **Semi-democratic state**
> a stable state that combines democratic and authoritarian elements.

and fair, and representation may be skewed to allow one party to dominate the representative assembly. There will be a constitution and rule of law, but the judiciary may not be independent and the constitution may be subverted in whole or in part. In theory there may be freedom of speech and pressure groups may be allowed, along with a range of political parties, but the main media outlets may be state-controlled and political protest may be suppressed.

Example: The Russian Federation

For most of its history, Russia has had authoritarian systems of government: first tsarism and then communism. It became a democracy in 1991 with the fall of the Berlin Wall and the break-up of the Soviet Union. It adopted a semi-presidential system of government, with executive power shared between a prime minister, who leads the Council of Ministers, and a directly elected president. There is a representative legislature comprising two chambers: a lower chamber called the State Duma, with 450 elected representatives, and an upper chamber called the Federal Council with two representatives from each of the 89 federal units. There are regular elections of the Duma (parliament) and the presidency.

However, these elections have been subject to allegations of ballot rigging and intimidation. In 2012, many were surprised when Vladimir Putin was elected as president, as the opinion polls suggested that most Russians had voted for his opponents. Moreover, Putin had already served two terms as president between 2000 and 2008, and the constitution stipulates a two-term limit for the presidency. Putin circumvented the rules by serving as prime minister to his protégé Medvedev and then sought election as president in 2012.

The Putin presidencies have been dogged by accusations of press censorship, brutal repression of protest and claims that orders for the assassinations of political opponents came from the highest levels of government. There is a range of political parties but Putin's United Russia Party dominates the Duma. In 2016, it won 343 seats (76 per cent of the available seats).

> **Key term**
>
> **Non-democratic state**
> a state that lacks the central characteristics of a democratic state.

Non-democratic states

The distinguishing features of **non-democratic states** are an absence of the most important characteristics of democracy: free and fair elections and the choice of alternative candidates and political parties.

It is hard to find states that have no democratic qualities. The spread of liberal democracy and the promotion of democratic ideals by international organisations and social movements and pressure groups has meant the vast majority of states pay lip service to the idea of democracy, even if they do not practise it in full.

Example: China

China claims to be a democracy. There are elections to the 3000-member National People's Congress and there is some choice of candidates between independents, Communists and representatives of one of the eight communist-sanctioned parties created before 1950. However, rival political parties and pressure groups are banned. Turnout in these elections is exceptionally high (usually more than 90 per cent), but this is because failure to vote is seen as unpatriotic and criminal.

Congress debates issues put before it by the State Council (the executive) but rarely attempts to amend or delay legislation. Nor does it scrutinise the activities of the State Council. Rather, its purpose is to provide approval for government initiatives. Members of the State Council are elected by the Congress, but these are not open and transparent elections. Election depends on patronage, political favours and position in the administrative apparatus.

There is no freedom of speech in China. The media is state-owned and internet providers are

---

censored. Criticism of the regime is suppressed; it is taboo to discuss or attempt to commemorate the Tiananmen Square protest of 1989 and no figures have been released of the number of people who were killed or imprisoned. World-renowned artist, Ai Weiwei, has been censored and detained in what is thought to be punishment for his investigation of the deaths of students in the Sichuan earthquake in 2008, which he blames on poorly constructed student accommodation, and his support for democracy and human rights.

Autocratic states

Autocracy means rule by a single person or body. This form of government was the norm in the past, when it took the form of hereditary monarchy. There are few monarchies left, with some notable exceptions, such as Saudi Arabia. Autocrats in the 20th and 21st centuries have been leaders of political movements that either came to power through democratic elections, such as Mussolini in Italy and Hitler in Germany in the 1920s and 1930s, or by violent revolutions, for example Saddam Hussein in Iraq and Bashar al-Assad in Syria. Some autocracies are led by military leaders, such as Colonel Gaddafi of Libya.

Autocratic states ban opposition parties and brutally suppress protest. There may be a political party associated with the single leader, but it does not operate in the same way as a democratic political party. Membership of the political party may be necessary for holding government office and certain occupations. Advancement in the political party will depend on the patronage of the leader. The leader is not subject to any form of accountability and enjoys cult status. This status is claimed on the basis of superhuman qualities or divine appointment.

> **Key term**
>
> **Autocratic state**
> a state that is ruled by a single person with unlimited power.

> **Example: Syria**
>
> Syria was part of the Ottoman Empire, before being granted independence from the French mandate in 1945. The Syrian Arab Republic (Syria) suffered a number of military coups. There was a brief union with Egypt in the late 1950s, ending in 1961. The Ba'ath Party came to power in 1963, led by Captain Hafez al-Assad. He seized control of the party and became leader of Syria in 1971. On his death in 2000 he was replaced by his son, Bashar al-Assad.
>
> Syria maintains the appearance of democratic institutions and representation. There were elections to the People's Council of Syria in 2016 in the midst of the civil war, but votes were only held for the 250 seats in government-controlled areas. However, power rests with Assad, his family and members of the Alawite Shia minority that dominate the Ba'ath Party.
>
> Human Rights Watch, an international pressure group, declared in 2010 that Syria had one of the worst human-rights records in the world. There is strict censorship of the media and education by the Ba'ath Party.

Failed states

The Fund for Peace, a Washington-based non-governmental organisation that works to prevent violent conflict and promote sustainable security, uses four criteria to identify a **failed state**.

- The loss of control of a state's territory, or loss of the monopoly on the legitimate use of physical force within its borders.
- A government has lost legitimacy and lacks the authority to make collective decisions.
- The inability to provide basic services to citizens, such as health care and education, and to guarantee the supply of basic amenities, such as electricity and clean drinking water. Such a state may rely on substantial external support, such as development aid and non-governmental organisations to provide some basic services.

> **Key term**
>
> **Failed state**
> a state that is unable to operate as a viable political unit.

- The inability to interact with other states as a full member of the international community.

Many states have been identified as failed states. Most are in sub-Saharan Africa (for example, the Democratic Republic of the Congo, Eritrea, Liberia, Rwanda, Sierra Leone, Somalia, South Sudan and Sudan) but state failure has also affected Cambodia, Haiti, Syria and Yemen.

Example: Somalia

Since 2008, Somalia has topped the Fund for Peace index as the most fragile state. The government does not enjoy a monopoly over the use of force within the country or widespread legitimacy. Following the collapse of the military regime of Siad Barre in 1991, a ten-year civil war broke out between rival ethnic groups. During this conflict, warlords seized control of different parts of the country. More recently, the country has become a base for Al-Shabab, an Islamic fundamentalist group that is linked to Al-Qaeda. This group has launched attacks on neighbouring countries such as Kenya.

The provision of basic public services is limited. Children receive on average three years' worth of education, compared with an average of 14 years in the developed world. Infant and maternal mortality is high, and average life expectancy is 55 years – almost 30 years less than in the West – all signs of poor health care provision. There is extensive foreign intervention in the country. An internationally backed government has been in place since 2012. Non-governmental organisations such as Oxfam have provided food aid in recent famines. The African Union has been providing peacekeepers since 2007, while the European Union provides naval patrols off Somalia's coast to combat piracy off the Horn of Africa, which has disrupted trade and led to protracted hostage situations.

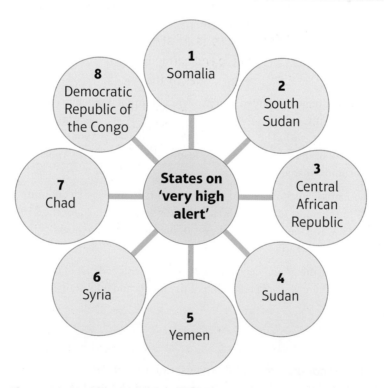

Figure 4.1: Fund for Peace Fragile States Index, 2016

Rogue states

A **rogue state** is a state that is considered a pariah by the rest of the international community. Such states flout international agreements and shun membership of international organisations, or are excluded because of their unco-operative behaviour.

President George W. Bush considered Iran, Iraq and North Korea to be rogue states when he declared them to be 'an axis of evil'. Iran has been brought back into the international fold with its

---

Key term 💬

Rogue state
a state that has a foreign policy that poses a threat to other states.

agreement to be subjected to inspections of its nuclear programme by the International Atomic Energy Agency. Saddam Hussein was removed from power in Iraq in 2003 and Iraq is now part of the international community. The Democratic People's Republic of Korea, however, continues to be shunned by the world.

Example: North Korea

North Korea's autocratic Stalinist-Communist political system follows the *juche* principle of self-sufficiency. The country is led by Kim Jong-un, the grandson of Kim Il-sung, who was the communist leader who came to power in 1948 in the Russian-occupied north. North Korean society is tightly controlled by the Workers' Party and the Kims are venerated as gods. Movement in and out of the country is tightly controlled. The media is heavily censored and mobile phones are banned.

The North Korean leadership is paranoid about the country's security, which is a legacy of centuries of Chinese and Japanese imperialism and the unresolved Korean War. Hostilities ended in 1953 and a truce was signed, but there has been no permanent peace treaty. North Korea feels surrounded by enemies. Japan to the east and adjoining South Korea are close allies of capitalist America, which sided with South Korea in the Korean War. Its traditional allies, Russia and China, have embraced capitalism, and Russia has democratised. North Korea feels it is the only truly communist state in the world. North Korea, therefore, is left with the classic **security dilemma**. It has developed a nuclear weapons programme to deter South Korea and the USA, but its posturing has led the USA and South Korea to strengthen their own military capability in the area.

Link

For more on **the security dilemma**, see Section 6.1 of Comparative Theories.

Consequences for the global order of different types of states

The wide variety of states can provide opportunities for peace and harmony in the international system, as well as pose threats to neighbouring states and countries further afield.

From the perspective of democratic peace theory – inspired by the works of the Prussian philosopher, Immanuel Kant, and the English political thinker, Thomas Paine – the increasing number of democratic states is an opportunity for peace and co-operation. Both claimed that republics – what we would now call democracies – are less war-like. They argued that people do not like war and would not vote for representatives who supported conflict. The theory received a boost in the late 20th century with Fukuyama's *End of History*, which claimed that conflict in the world would decline as more and more states adopted liberal democracy and capitalism. Empirical evidence also demonstrated that wars between democracies were far less common than between other types of states. Indeed, there are areas of the world where democratic states are more numerous and long periods of peace have been enjoyed, such as North America and Europe.

The norms and values of democracy and its structures are also thought to promote 'zones of peace'. The sharing of democratic values creates a cultural bond between states, which makes them likely to see each other as friends rather than enemies. Democracy promotes institutional structures and mechanisms that ensure peaceful resolution of conflict. Legislatures act as a neutral forum where competing views can be heard and votes are taken to decide which view has won the argument. Elections allow competing candidates and parties to demonstrate their suitability for office. In both legislatures and elections, losers accept the result peacefully, knowing they have had a fair opportunity to present their case. By participating in the process they agree to be bound by the outcome. A great strength of democracy is that changes in government take place without violent revolution. Democracies learn how to resolve conflicts peacefully, which means they are willing to exhaust all other possibilities in their dealings with other states before resorting to conflict.

On the other hand, the existence of non-democratic states, autocratic states, failed states and rogue states makes the world a more dangerous place. The examples above illustrate the dangers such states pose to other states. Take North Korea, a rogue state. Its position as one the few remaining states in the world that has chosen to follow a variant of communism that promotes self-sufficiency and autarchy puts it at odds with the rest of the world. It does not share the same values or political ideas as its neighbours or countries further afield. This leads North Korea to view its neighbours as potential threats, which it seeks to minimise through self-imposed seclusion and the development of a nuclear deterrent. Its unique political system makes dialogue with other countries difficult, which fosters misunderstanding and mutual suspicion. States react by building up their arms and holding military exercises in the vicinity to deter a potential attack. However, North Korea sees this as a threat, and every so often launches missiles to demonstrate its ability to defend itself. So far, these activities have amounted to nothing more than posturing, but such actions can trigger a chain of events that leads to war. The assassination of Archduke Franz Ferdinand, the heir to the Austro-Hungarian Empire, led to the outbreak of the First World War, a war that redrew the map of Europe.

Undemocratic and autocratic states threaten global peace when democratic states become concerned about the treatment of citizens by the governments of these states. China and Syria have been much criticised by countries such as the USA and the UK for their treatment of political opponents. In the case of Syria, these critics have recognised and supported rebel groups in their bid to topple the Assad regime.

However, the international community does not necessarily agree on what action to take to protect human rights. This can lead to delays in humanitarian intervention, which can allow situations to fester and spill over into neighbouring states. The uprising in Syria, inspired by the Arab Spring uprising across the Arab world, received support from three of the permanent members of the Security Council – the USA, the UK and France – but resolutions calling for the intervention in favour of the uprising were blocked by China and Russia. This stalemate has resulted in a protracted civil war, in which millions of people have fled the country. Neighbouring countries – such as Jordan, Lebanon and Turkey – have had to accommodate millions of refugees. Over a million Syrians have made their way to Europe with the help of criminal gangs. This has caused a migrant crisis in Europe, putting pressure on the public services of Italy and Greece, in particular, as these are the countries many migrants travel to in their bids to cross the Mediterranean. Other European countries refuse to take their share of migrants, such as the UK and Hungary. This strains relations in the EU and leads to domestic discontent from citizens who resent the influx of migrants. The Syrian crisis has also spawned a fundamentalist Islamic movement, ISIS, which promotes jihad (a war against non-believers). ISIS has been the inspiration for terrorist attacks in Europe and the USA, and has taken control of large parts of Syria and Iraq, subjecting the populations to terror and repression. Some commentators have argued that the Syrian conflict has had such far-reaching effects that it should be classed as a global conflict.

> ### Pause & reflect
>
> More states are becoming democratic. Will all states do this eventually? If so, will they share the same interests, promoting peace and stability, as liberals predict? Or will states continue to pursue their selfish national interests, as realists predict? Does the type of regime really make a difference to state interests?

4.5 Development and spread of liberal economies, the rule of law and democracy

Any serious discussion of the development and spread of liberal economies, the rule of law and democracy would take more pages than we have space for here. The story of their development and spread encompasses modern political history, the history of the industrial revolution, liberal political theory and the development of modern legal systems. What follows is a brief introduction to the emergence and growth of what amounts to a political regime known as '**liberal democracy**'. Liberal democracy is where there is **rule of law**, a capitalist economic system and what are recognised as the essential features of democracy: free and fair elections, choice, participation, representation and accountability. 'Rule of law' means a system in which no person or institution is above the law. Rulers and others in positions of power and responsibility may not disregard civil liberties and individual rights or act in contravention of the rules of the political system. These are guaranteed by statute law and the constitution and are enforced by an independent and neutral judiciary. A liberal economy or capitalist system is one where wealth creation is largely driven by the private sector, with the government playing a minimal role in regulating the operation of the market. Wealth and ownership of property is protected by law.

The origins of liberal democracy are to be found in medieval England. The rebellion by English nobles against King John's arbitrary government resulted in the signing of Magna Carta in 1215. This established the principle of the rule of law, in particular that subjects could not be imprisoned at the whim of the king. A legal process had to be followed in which charges were brought and a trial would take place. The establishment of parliament soon followed, where representatives of the nobility, and later the gentry, would be consulted on taxation. Charles I's attempts to rule without parliament brought about the English Civil War of 1642–49. Parliament won the war and for a brief period parliament became the sovereign power (ultimate authority). However, the restoration of the monarchy in 1660 saw a return to monarchy. Charles II's careful stewardship saw a revival of royal authority only to be squandered by his brother James II, who – like his father – tried to exercise absolute authority and revived religious controversy by his conversion to Catholicism. The Glorious Revolution of 1688 sealed the ascendancy of parliament and the demise of monarchical government. Gradually, a modern system of government emerged and a truly representative legislative with the extension of the franchise in 1832, 1867, 1884, 1918 and 1928.

The English Civil War began a gradual process of democratisation in England, but it also served as an example to other countries. The American revolutionaries echoed the English Civil War in their War of Independence from the British with the cry, 'No taxation without representation'. The French Revolution similarly took inspiration from the British to bring down the Ancien Regime. Over the late 18th and early 19th centuries a limited form of democracy representing a privileged elite spread to Germany, Italy, and other parts of Western Europe. The creation of new states in central and Eastern Europe in the aftermath of the First World War provided opportunities for the spread of liberal democracy, but these democracies were fragile and soon fell prey to the expansionist ambitions of Nazi Germany, or, in the case of Italy, to collapse because of the failure of the liberal political system to respond effectively to the aftermath of war and economic crisis. Eastern European countries had to wait until the fall of the Berlin Wall before they could complete the transition to liberal democracy, which had begun in the early 20th century. The spread of liberal democracy elsewhere in the world was also dependent on the end of the Cold War. In different ways, the USA and the Soviet Union promoted or sustained authoritarian political systems among their allies. The Soviet Union actively promoted communism through organisations such as Cominform and subsidies to fellow communist systems. Soviet subsidies to Cuba somewhat compensated for the trade embargo imposed by the USA. The USA was more concerned to stop

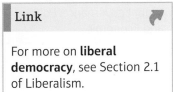

Link

For more on **liberal democracy**, see Section 2.1 of Liberalism.

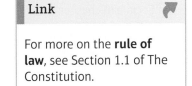

Link

For more on the **rule of law**, see Section 1.1 of The Constitution.

Link

For more on **the effects of globalisation on developed and developing states**, see Section 2.2 of Global governance: Political and Economic.

Link

For more on **communism**, see Socialism chapter.

For more on **capitalism**, see Conservatism and Liberalism chapters.

EXTENSION ACTIVITY

Choose a developed and developing country. Find out when these countries democratised and became modern industrial economies. Compare the circumstances in which these developments took place. Consider the ways in which their experiences are similar and different.

Link

For more on **conflict, poverty, human rights and the environment**, see Global Governance: Political and Economic and Global Governance: Human Rights and Environmental chapters.

the spread of communism rather than promote liberal democracy, which often meant support for right-wing dictatorships such as Pinochet in Chile. It was not until the beginning of the 21st century that most countries in the world became liberal democracies.

The spread of liberal economies through the industrial revolution seemed to go hand in hand with democratisation. As with democracy, England was the first to industrialise. It began in the late 18th century with a number of inventions that allowed for mass production of manufactured goods, such as iron and steel, and cotton and woollen cloth. Industrialisation then spread through western Europe and the United States of America in the 19th century. The acceleration of **globalisation** in the latter half of the 20th century due to the promotion of free trade and liberal economic policy by international institutions such as the IMF and the World Trade Organization has led to more states adopting the neo-liberal economic orthodoxy. However, the **developed states** have benefited most from the expansion of liberal democracy and continue to enjoy significant advantages over **developing states**.

By the end of the 20th century it seemed that liberal democracy had triumphed. Francis Fukuyama, first in his 1989 essay *The End of History and the Last Man* and then in a 1992 book of the same name, put forward the view that Marx's deterministic predictions of the end-point of human development being **communism** would not be realised. Instead, the intermediate stage of that development, which Marx had as **capitalism**, would in fact be the final stage of human development. Fukuyama was writing at the time of the fall of the Berlin Wall and the demise of the Soviet Union. Eastern European states were becoming democracies and even China was moderating its communism to allow for capitalist-style economic development. It seemed as if no other political idea could rival liberal democracy. In the 21st century, Fukuyama's predictions look less persuasive. The Arab Spring, which attempted to spread democracy to the Arab world, has faltered in Libya, Egypt, Syria and Yemen. A rival ideology has emerged in fundamentalist Islam, as promoted by Al-Qaeda and Islamic State, to challenge liberal democracy.

4.6 Impact of world order on conflict, poverty, human rights and the environment

The structure of power in the international system (world order) plays a key part in the extent of conflicts and poverty in the world. It can affect whether states protect the human rights of their citizens and whether states co-operate over environmental issues, such as climate change. The impact of different types of states on **conflict** and, to some extent, on human rights has been considered above. Throughout the other chapters on global politics, the role of states on poverty, human rights and the environment are discussed. What is appropriate to consider here is the impact of unipolarity and multipolarity. From the realist perspective, unipolarity could promote peace and the protection of **human rights** if the global hegemon acts as the world's police officer. States might be encouraged or forced by the dominant power into co-operation to reduce global poverty and to combat climate change. Liberals, however, see unipolarity as inherently unstable and more likely to lead to conflict and the abuse of human rights, especially if the hegemon is predatory. States may be less likely to co-operate on **poverty** and **the environment** if the dominant state does not set a good example. Realists and liberals also disagree about whether multipolarity is any more likely to have a beneficial effect on these issues. The impact of world order depends on what perspective one decides to take. There is evidence in the global politics chapters to support either. However, the most progress on climate change, poverty, human rights and conflict has been made since 2000, arguably an era of multipolarity.

Assessment support: 3.2.4 Power and Developments

Question 3 on A-Level Paper 3 gives you a choice of two out of three questions. Each one is worth 30 marks and you should allow about 45 minutes to complete each answer.

Evaluate the extent to which the rise of emerging powers has altered the nature of world order. [30 marks]

You must consider this view and the alternative to this view in a balanced way.

These questions require an essay-style answer in which you consider alternative views to that posed in the question ('evaluate the extent to which'). They test all three Assessment Objectives, with marks divided equally between them. Examiners are looking for comprehensive and precise knowledge and in-depth understanding of the topic, which are used to support the various arguments. You must consider alternative answers to the question: in this case, unipolarity, multipolarity and bipolarity. You should reach a clear judgement consistent with the balance of the argument in the main body of your essay. Remember that it is a strength when answers bring in relevant information from other sections of the specification.

- In your introduction, identify emerging powers (such as Brazil, Russia, India and China). Show that you understand that the question requires discussion of the different types of world order – unipolarity, bipolarity and multipolarity. A good way to do this is to divide your essay into three sections, each relating to a different type of polarity.

- Start with the argument suggested by the question, which is multipolarity. Identify a range of countries as rival powers to the US. Discuss evidence relating to their economic, military and political power. Then consider the case for unipolarity. Give facts and figures about the strength of the US economy, its military capability and its political influence. Finally, consider the evidence for either Russia or China as rivals to the US, economically, militarily and politically.

- In your conclusion, decide whether unipolarity, bipolarity or multipolarity is the more persuasive argument. Briefly restate the main arguments for that viewpoint.

Here is part of a student's answer – the introduction.

The extent to which the rise of emerging powers, such as Brazil, Russia, India and China (BRICs), has altered the nature of world order is debatable. Undoubtedly, the USA has been the dominant global hegemon post World War II. However, the emergence of the BRICs, due to globalisation, has arguably created a new world order, without the USA at its helm. The growth of supranational and intergovernmental institutions, such as the EU, also challenges US dominance of the world. However, the resurgence of Russia and the growing power of China as a counterweight to the USA suggest a return to Cold War bipolarity. Whether the world is unipolar, multipolar or bipolar is discussed below.

- This introduction uses words from the question ('rise of emerging powers') to show understanding and ensure relevance.

- There are clearly separated descriptions of unipolarity ('dominant global hegemon'), multipolarity ('emergence of India...') and bipolarity ('resurgence of Russia', 'growing power of China').

- The approach to the question and the main arguments are indicated by reference to 'economic, military and political power', 'globalisation' and 'supranational and intergovernmental organisations'.

Regionalism and the EU

In an increasingly globalised world, most states have seen it necessary to co-operate with their neighbours in formal regional organisations. These take different forms and do different things, but share the understanding – drawn from liberal theory – that common problems probably require common solutions, and that some form of co-operation is mutually beneficial. States realise that decisions taken by their neighbours can have an impact on themselves.

The most obvious example of this is making decisions about the environment. For example, a country polluting a river upstream from a neighbouring country has a significant impact on the river flowing through that country. This concern led to the formation of the world's first regional intergovernmental organisation, the Danube Commission, in 1856. The states that share the river Danube acknowledge that it is in all their interests to make sure the river stays navigable. No one country can protect the Danube; no one country can solve all the issues regarding the Danube on its own.

In this chapter you will look at:

- different forms of regionalism
- factors that have fostered integration
- the ways and extent to which regionalism addresses contemporary global issues.

5.1 Regionalism

In the modern technological world, interconnectedness and interdependence relate to economic and trade matters, as well as issues regarding health, science, communication technology, crime and security. With all these common problems facing states, there is an increasing move for states to form and join multilateral regional organisations rather than trying to deal with problems themselves or rely on bilateral (country-to-country) relationships.

Examples of **regionalism** and regional organisations are the **European Union (EU)**, the African Union (AU), the Arab League, the North American Free Trade Agreement (NAFTA) and the Association of South East Asian Nations (ASEAN).

Despite the dynamic of closer co-operation, regionalism faces challenges in the future. States do not like giving up **sovereignty**, and nations have a strong desire to govern themselves. This desire, driven by nationalism, can lead to a backlash against regional co-operation. In 2016 the British people voted to leave the EU, nationalistic parties gained support across Europe, and Donald Trump was elected president of the USA, promising to 'make America great again' and review trade deals such as NAFTA.

Different forms of regionalism

Attempts to differentiate types of regionalism fall into three categories: economic, security and political.

- Economic regionalism focuses on the financial and trade aspects of regional co-operation. These types of regional organisation are trade blocs of one type or another; the vast majority of countries now belong to a regional trade bloc.

Key terms

Regionalism
creation and implementation of institutions that express a particular identity and shape collective action within a geographical region.

European Union (EU)
political-economic union of 28 member states (2015) located in Europe.

Sovereignty
absolute and unlimited power and authority.

- Security regionalism involves regional organisations trying to achieve peace and security through one of two methods. Some aim to achieve stability within the group by enhancing interdependence and interconnectedness, making war impossible due to the closeness of interactions between member states. Others seek to achieve peace through binding the member states against a common enemy. ASEAN was originally viewed in this way, as the five original members had a shared fear of the growth of communism in South East Asia.

- Political regionalism is when states that share the same values seek to protect them, and to enhance their standing and voice in the world. Both the AU and the Arab League had their foundations in this type of regionalism.

One difficulty with this categorisation is that there is considerable overlap between the three types of regionalism, and they tend to feed each other. Security is achieved through economic co-operation; protection of values is achieved through security and economics. Regional organisations also develop over time and become more integrated. They may start out as one type of organisation, but adapt and become another type later.

Case study: Never again

The EU won the Nobel Peace Prize in 2012 for contributing to 'the advancement of peace, reconciliation, democracy and human rights in Europe'.

The first region to undergo the move to co-operation through a regional organisation was Europe after the Second World War. The horrors of the war and, in particular, the Holocaust led the leaders of Europe to resolve that Europe should never go to war again. The most war-torn continent on the planet should be peaceful.

In line with liberal theory, politicians in Europe hoped that they could design war out of the international system. The likes of Jean Monnet and Robert Schuman of France believed that the construction of a federal or United States of Europe would make war in Europe not just incredible, but impossible. After all, Germany had been to war with France three times in less than a century, including two world wars. These Euro-federalists believed that European institutions and integration, along with trade between European countries, would make war in Europe a thing of the past.

561

Key terms

European integration
the process of industrial, political, legal, economic, social and cultural integration of states in Europe.

Supranationalism
a large amount of power given to an authority, which, in theory, is placed higher than the state.

Intergovernmentalism
interaction among states based on sovereign independence.

Economics was to play a central role in this plan. An early attempt at **European integration** was the creation of the European Coal and Steel Community (ECSC) in 1951 by the Treaty of Paris. The aim of the ECSC was to make it impossible for the signatory states to go to war as their ability to produce coal and steel, necessary for rearming, was no longer in the hands of the states. A common market was created as well as **supranational** decision-making on coal and steel production.

Questions

- What were the aims of both the ECSC and the European Economic Community (EEC)?
- What are the similarities and differences between the ECSC and the EEC?

Debates about and the reasons and significance of regionalism

The relationship between regionalism and globalisation

Globalisation is the increasing interdependence and interconnectedness of states in the world. Economic, political and cultural globalisation are the main forms. Each can be seen to be heightened by regionalism, where states in a region co-operate on an economic, security or political level.

For example, attempts by the EU, NAFTA and ASEAN to increase trade between their member states – an increase in the flows of trade – is directly in line with economic globalisation. This can be seen as a positive or a negative. Many economists see more trade as a good thing for a state's economy, as it brings greater competition and economies of scale. However, there will always be individual losers who cannot effectively compete in larger and tougher markets. This can lead to scaling back of industries and job losses.

States join regional organisations because they enable the individual states to improve their leverage in the international system against global companies, and to develop their comparative advantage. Regional organisations also defend against globalisation by pooling their sovereignty. Similarly, political globalisation and regionalism are linked as they are effectively the same thing: the co-operation of states to aid governance and solve mutual problems.

Critics of globalisation criticise regionalism and regional organisations as enhancing and furthering globalisation. They see the impact on industries, on communities and on jobs brought about by the increasing ease of trade in regional economic bodies like the EU, NAFTA and ASEAN.

It is argued that democracy is undermined by supranational or **intergovernmental** bodies that make binding decisions beyond the reach of the people. These decisions lack accountability, and sovereignty and self-determination are undermined. The EU has been picked out for criticism over the freedom of movement it allows. EU citizens are free to live and work in other states, which has led to significant numbers of people emigrating around Europe. For example, about 750,000 Polish people have moved to the UK in recent years. However, the voting public has no ability to limit these numbers while their country is a member of the EU. This was undoubtedly one of the main reasons why UK citizens voted to leave the EU in June 2016.

Similarly, in the USA, NAFTA has been perceived as leading to the outsourcing of jobs to Mexico, resulting in industry closures and job losses in the US. In this atmosphere, immigrants can be blamed for taking what jobs there are or undercutting wages of 'local' people. People who have lost their jobs or feel alienated by the pace of change in a globalised era may blame regional organisations for exacerbating and deepening the process.

Regional organisations and globalisation are also seen to benefit 'big corporations' and transnational corporations (TNCs), such as Coca-Cola, GlaxoSmithKline and Unilever, rather than ordinary people. As trade increases and is seen to benefit TNCs over local or national producers, critics argue that consumers are all purchasing the same goods, services and culture. Big corporations with more competitive clout are pushing out smaller companies, leading to cultural **homogenisation**. States cannot protect their own industries or producers because the terms of economic regional organisations tend to limit this.

Some argue that this process benefits the USA most, as it controls much of the culture industry and many globally known products, such as Coca-Cola and McDonald's. A prime example is the Hollywood film industry, which can produce many popular, merchandisable films in English, which other countries cannot compete against.

Of course, this is a two-way street. Non-US producers also have access to the US market and can sell their goods and services to the Americans. For example, the German and Japanese car industries have been very successful at exporting and selling Mercedes, BMWs, Toyotas and Nissans, which has cost many jobs in the US car industry. Moreover, though there are losers in terms of jobs and industries, most people benefit from globalisation through more choice, cheaper prices and better-quality goods. Protecting industries usually leads to less choice and higher prices.

There is an alternative point of view. The EU, among others, would argue that these regional organisations are actually a way of controlling and limiting the impact of globalisation. Globalisation is a powerful force that can affect the sovereignty of countries, but co-operation and pooling sovereignty is an effective way for countries to fight back.

Consider the ability of states, big or small, to control or shape the world they exist in. Environmental issues do not respect borders: climate change affects every state, sea and river pollution affects all countries, and air pollution does not stop at boundaries. States have come together to try to halt the effects of climate change through the International Panel on Climate Change. States are co-operating to limit the impact of environmental change.

On a regional level, states have come together to limit the power of TNCs and their economic mobility. Some TNCs have more wealth than sovereign countries. For example, Apple has $200 billion in cash reserves – slightly less than the GDP of the entire Republic of Ireland, a country of about four and a half million people. In 2012, Samsung had $196 billion of revenue, more than the GDP of Morocco, with 32 million citizens. This makes TNCs potentially very powerful.

TNCs aim to lower their production costs and their tax liabilities. They will look to produce their goods in countries with low labour costs, lower tax obligations, less rigorous worker safety laws and more lenient environmental protection rules. In this situation, TNCs have huge power. Consider a company that can offer thousands of jobs. States will compete to attract – and keep – its investment. This can lead to a race to the bottom in tax rates, wage rates, health-and-safety laws and environmental and animal protection. It can also lead to huge amounts of state support to attract investment.

By adopting a regional and co-operative approach to these issues, as the EU and NAFTA do, regional organisations can ensure that states do not undercut each other, giving TNCs no benefit from shopping around for the best deal. By working together, states can fight back against globalisation.

So in Europe and North America, there are strong environmental protection laws that companies cannot avoid by looking at a neighbouring country; the protections are the same. The more a region adopts harmonised rules, the more level the playing field is in a region.

Key term

Homogenisation (or monoculture)
coming together of global cultures and development of a single, homogenous culture without diversity or dissent.

Pause & reflect

Think about how regional organisations can reduce the power of TNCs. Should they do more or less to restrict TNCs?

However, that is not to say that there will be competition *between* regional organisations. TNCs will seek to lower their costs and try and get regional organisations to lower regulations. States within the regional organisations may be able to stand firmer together under this pressure.

Currently, countries of the EU do not harmonise corporation tax at an EU level. There are significant differences in rates around the EU, ranging from over 33 per cent in Belgium and France to 10 per cent in Bulgaria. This means companies do look for the best deal. The Republic of Ireland has been successful in attracting companies like Apple to Ireland due its low corporation tax rates (12.5 per cent in 2016), even though the RoI has strict rules on environmental protection and workers' rights.

Regionalism can then control globalisation by pooling the power of states against TNCs. Small countries may not feel they can stand up effectively against powerful international firms, but together, standing united, they can win and limit the impact of globalisation.

Allied to the above argument is the supposed structural power that can be achieved through membership of regional organisations. Having pooled sovereignty, small states may be more able to stand up to other states or TNCs, and have a stronger voice within global governance organisations. For example, the EU played a significant role in global climate-change talks at COP 21, the climate change conference held in Paris in 2015.

This approach is also true with smaller states facing bigger states. Small states do not have much leverage in trade negotiations with big states: they do not have many consumers to sell to, and may not have much in the way of goods and services to sell. A small country like Malta with 430,000 inhabitants would be unlikely to negotiate a particularly equal trade deal with China and its 1.3 billion citizens. However, by negotiating as part of the EU, Malta can link itself to their 508 million consumers and their products and services, such as German cars and French cheese.

Regionalism can bring protections against the forces of globalisation, both in economic and cultural terms. For example, in 2016 the EU and the USA were negotiating the Transatlantic Trade and Investment Partnership (TTIP), designed to free up trade between them. There are differences of opinion on a number of issues, like the US allowing hormones in their meat and the EU not, and the French seeking protection for its French-language film industry from Hollywood. The EU wishes to maintain geographically protected names in the USA – for example, not allowing US companies to produce 'Champagne' or 'Parma' ham, which can only come from specific regions in the EU. The logic is that, by negotiating collectively, EU countries will be able to strike a more equal and fair deal. Individual deals can be struck, but the terms may not be as favourable as for a deal struck together.

This regional approach is controversial due to its impact on sovereignty and democracy. By co-operating or pooling sovereignty, states will not be able to control all aspects of the negotiations, and will have to make compromises. However, that is the nature of all negotiations.

Undoubtedly, adopting a regional approach to controlling globalisation has a profound and visible impact on states' sovereignty and the ability of the people to make their own democratic laws. For example, the Court of Justice of the European Union has made significant rulings on workers' rights. The Court has ruled that temporary and agency workers are entitled to the same holiday rights as full-time permanent workers. This applies to all workers in all countries of the EU. One of the arguments for the UK leaving the EU was that it would be free to set its own laws concerning workers and the environment. There is undoubtedly an argument that there is a 'democratic deficit' at the heart of the EU, and this is what concerns citizens who expect a democratic say in the way their country is governed.

EXTENSION ACTIVITY

The debate about sovereignty is a significant one. Is sovereignty zero-sum, or can it be increased through pooling? Does globalisation mean that states are losing sovereignty anyway, and regional organisations are the best way of controlling the process?

Prospects for political regionalism and regional governance

One of the key questions in international relations concerns the future of the nation state and its accompanying sovereignty. Global problems need global solutions; regional problems need regional solutions. How will these solutions be achieved? Through regional co-operation, or through formal regional organisations? These increasingly integrated organisations are facing difficulties regarding their legitimacy and effectiveness, particularly from a nationalistic and democratic perspective.

So what is the future for regionalism? Table 1.1 gives some arguments for more regionalism, and for less.

More regionalism	Less regionalism
Countries are queuing up to join the EU and most countries in the world are members of a regional trade bloc. There must be some reason for states to want to do this.	In 2016, the UK voted to leave the EU.
ASEAN is continuing to integrate not just economic areas, but also political-security and socio-cultural pillars.	ASEAN does not take bold steps and there are disagreements over democracy, human rights and good governance in the bloc.
The Arab League has been vociferous in the Syrian Civil War and has suspended Syria.	Beyond strong rhetoric, the Arab League has achieved very little in the Syrian Civil War. The countries are too disparate and self-interested.
Even with the UK voting to leave the EU, there will probably still be enhanced trade and co-operation between the EU and the UK.	There is significant opposition in the USA to NAFTA and other economic regionalism like TTP and TTIP, as shown through support for Donald Trump and Bernie Sanders in the 2016 election.
The problems that led to the formation of regional organisations have not gone away. Indeed, issues like climate change and immigration seem likely to get worse.	There is real democratic support for 'taking control' of decision-making in the UK, USA and much of Europe. The democratic nation state is still very popular.
There is a revival of traditional fears in Europe and elsewhere of the power and intentions of Russia, China and North Korea, among others. Security is still a key concern for states and people.	There is strong reaction to economic globalisation and the power of TNCs. Regionalism appears to many to benefit the big corporations at the expense of the 'ordinary person'.
What alternatives are there? Would people actually be better off if regionalism was reversed?	Co-operation is necessary, but it does not have to be achieved through such formal structures, which may seem illegitimate and ineffective.

Table 1.1: Some arguments for more regionalism, and for less

Considerations over regionalism highlight elements of the theoretical debate between **realism** and **liberalism**.

The impact on state sovereignty

Sovereignty is the key concept in international relations. Your view or interpretation of it will colour your ideas about the impact of regional organisations on state sovereignty. If you see globalisation as a negative, you are perhaps more likely to see regional organisations as a means by which globalisation is being furthered and enhanced. Alternatively, regional organisations can be seen as a way of states 'standing up' to TNCs and globalisation.

Link

For more on **realism and liberalism**, see Comparative Theories chapter.

Link

For more on **sovereignty**, see Section 1.1 of The State and Globalisation.

Type of sovereignty	Assessment of regional organisations' impact
Legal/ De jure	States can leave organisations, as the UK is due to leave the EU. There is no compulsion in the international system, so states are free to follow their own interests.
Political/ De facto	States need to co-operate through regional organisations and therefore may be seen to have surrendered sovereignty. Some states may feel they increase their sovereignty by pooling it with other states.
External/ State/ National	Sovereignty could be seen as reduced as states need to compromise and give up some controls to achieve common goals. Some states may feel they have more sovereignty through pooling it.
Internal	States are legally sovereign within their own territory but by co-operating through regional organisations they may lose control of their own law-making powers. For example, EU law is higher than national law for EU member states. National legislation may be overruled. EU states cannot control immigration from other EU states.
Zero-sum	Here it is clear cut that states have less sovereignty. The more sovereignty you give away to an organisation or supranational authority, the less you have.
Pooled	By pooling sovereignty, states can increase their power, influence and therefore sovereignty in the world.

Table 1.2: The impact of regional organisations on different types of sovereignty

5.2 Development of regional organisations, excluding the EU

Name	Original members	Role and objectives	Development
NAFTA Founded 1992, effective 1994	USA Canada Mexico	**Role** Free-trade agreement eliminating tariff and non-tariff barriers to trade and investment on goods and services. **Objective** To improve trade and prosperity for the three signatory states.	Donald Trump has pledged to re-write the agreement. He believes NAFTA was the 'worst trade deal ever' because Americans lost jobs.
AU Founded 1999, effective 2002	54	**Role** 'Accelerating the process of integration in the continent to enable it to play its rightful role in the global economy while addressing multifaceted social, economic and political problems, compounded as they are by certain negative aspects of globalisation' www.au.int/web/en/au-nutshell **Objectives** To rid the continent of the remaining vestiges of colonisation and apartheid. To promote unity and solidarity among African states. To co-ordinate and intensify co-operation for development. To safeguard the sovereignty and territorial integrity of member states. To promote international co-operation within the framework of the United Nations.	Replaced Organisation of African Unity (OAU).

Name	Original members	Role and objectives	Development
Arab League Founded 1945	Egypt Jordan Iraq Yemen Lebanon Saudi Arabia Syria	**Objectives** To encourage co-operation and the pursuit of common interests among Arab-speaking states in Africa and the Middle East.	Now has 22 member states, including Palestine, but the organisation is divided, not least on the issue of the Syrian Civil War.
ASEAN Founded 1967	Indonesia Malaysia Philippines Singapore Thailand	**Objectives** To encourage economic, social, cultural, technological and educational development. To promote peace and stability in the region. To ensure adherence to the principles of the UN charter and the rule of law. http://asean.org/asean/about-asean/history/	Grown from 5 to 10 members

Table 2.1: Development of regional organisations in Africa, Asia and the Americas

5.3 Factors that have fostered European integration and the major developments through which this has occurred

Formation, role, objectives and development of the European Union (EU)

How the European Union formed

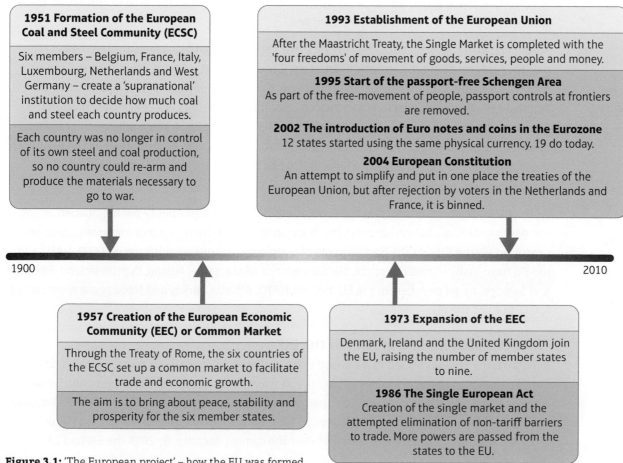

1951 Formation of the European Coal and Steel Community (ECSC)

Six members – Belgium, France, Italy, Luxembourg, Netherlands and West Germany – create a 'supranational' institution to decide how much coal and steel each country produces.

Each country was no longer in control of its own steel and coal production, so no country could re-arm and produce the materials necessary to go to war.

1993 Establishment of the European Union

After the Maastricht Treaty, the Single Market is completed with the 'four freedoms' of movement of goods, services, people and money.

1995 Start of the passport-free Schengen Area
As part of the free-movement of people, passport controls at frontiers are removed.

2002 The introduction of Euro notes and coins in the Eurozone
12 states started using the same physical currency. 19 do today.

2004 European Constitution
An attempt to simplify and put in one place the treaties of the European Union, but after rejection by voters in the Netherlands and France, it is binned.

1900   2010

1957 Creation of the European Economic Community (EEC) or Common Market

Through the Treaty of Rome, the six countries of the ECSC set up a common market to facilitate trade and economic growth.

The aim is to bring about peace, stability and prosperity for the six member states.

1973 Expansion of the EEC

Denmark, Ireland and the United Kingdom join the EU, raising the number of member states to nine.

1986 The Single European Act
Creation of the single market and the attempted elimination of non-tariff barriers to trade. More powers are passed from the states to the EU.

Figure 3.1: 'The European project' – how the EU was formed

The European Union's objective and role

After the Second World War, Europe was in a unique position. Leaders had personally experienced the horrors and destruction of war, and were determined not to repeat the mistakes of history; 'never again' was the call. These leaders also understood that it would take more than wishful thinking to prevent conflict. The Second World War came just 21 years after the end of the First World War, supposedly 'the war to end all wars'. The intervening 21 years saw the rise of nationalism in Germany and a global economic crisis that had devastating effects.

The forefathers of European integration had seen the dangers of cultural and economic nationalism. Nations have a strong drive to 'look after their own'. When jobs are being lost, governments are under pressure to help save them through public money and placing restrictions on foreign imports – but the countries affected by these import restrictions retaliate. Rather than saving jobs and improving domestic economies, this approach had made things worse. The same conclusions were drawn by the international leaders who met at the Bretton Woods Conference in the USA in 1944. They believed that the way to prevent the growth of nationalism and avoid damaging economic policies was to ensure global financial stability and to encourage as much global trade as possible.

This liberal view was that one of the ways to ensure peace in the world was to encourage interdependence and prosperity through trade. By trading, states co-operate to their mutual benefit, so it is not in anyone's interest to go to war. Trade also fosters better communication and greater understanding. This was the thinking behind the European project and also the US Marshall Plan after the Second World War. The Marshall Plan benefited American industry by giving European states money to spend, kick-starting the economies of post-war Europe and ensuring growing prosperity in Europe. This probably helped maintain peace and stability in the region and ensured that these countries remained part of the capitalist, democratic, 'free world', rather than succumbing to communism during the Cold War.

Part of the **EU**'s role is security. The very fact that the states are so closely entwined means that they rely on each other in security matters. Close co-operation takes place in terms of anti-terrorism, organised crime and people-trafficking. Europol enhances police co-operation in the EU, and there is also now formal foreign policy co-operation when there is a consensus through the European External Action Service (EEAS). States maintain their own foreign policies to serve their own national interest, but they also understand that their voice can be stronger if all the members speak together. This is not easy to achieve but, when it does happen, the foreign policy interests of the EU can carry more weight.

> **Link**
>
> For more on the **EU**, see Section 4.3 of Relations Between Institutions.

While the EU hopes to ensure that the conditions for peace and prosperity are maintained, it has not developed into a full-on security or military organisation. There is police and intelligence co-operation via the EU, but the best example of a regional security organisation is **NATO**. NATO and the EU have many shared members, but they are not all the same. Austria, Cyprus, Ireland, Finland and Sweden are all members of the EU, but not NATO; Albania, Turkey and Norway are members of NATO, but not the EU.

> **Link**
>
> For more on **NATO**, see Section 2.1 of Global Governance: Political and Economic.

The development and growth of the EU

In Europe, the EEC quickly led to increased trade and prosperity in the six member states. States outside the EEC, like the UK, looked on in envy at the economic growth that these countries were achieving. Despite attempts to emulate their success through the European Free Trade Association (EFTA), by the early 1960s, the UK had applied for membership of the EEC. The EEC and later the EU attracted more and more countries over the coming decades. By 2015 the EU had 28 member states.

It was not just economic concerns that encouraged newer members to join; both political and security concerns meant that states were eager to do so. Many states in Europe had been through turbulent times in the latter half of the 20th century. Some had been under right-wing dictatorships like Greece, Spain and Portugal; others, including Poland, Bulgaria and Estonia, were part of the Soviet bloc or even part of the Soviet Union itself. Defence against communism was also a factor in bringing states together in the early days of the EEC. For these countries, membership of the EU was a sign of their political maturity. From their perspective, joining the EU meant joining the club of the most respectable democracies in Europe, alongside the likes of Germany, France, the Netherlands and the UK. With human rights respected and democracy embedded, they could leave the past behind them.

Not all states or politicians believe that there should be a federal United States of Europe. Another theory that explains European integration is functionalism. The EU serves a function, as do its institutions and laws. Some politicians, while not being ideologically driven towards **federalism**, have taken a rational approach to EU membership, weighing up the costs and benefits and deciding that membership is in the nation's best interest.

One final explanation for the growth of the EU is neo-functionalism. Neo-functionalists say that greater European integration is inevitable because each stage of co-operation opens up the possibility and need for further co-operation and integration. Once you have a single market for goods and services aiming to increase trade between participating states, it is logical that there should be a single currency to trade in. Once states have agreed that a passport-free area in the single market will facilitate trade, but will also be open to abuse by criminals, it is logical that there should be greater police and border-control co-operation.

> **Key term**
>
> **Federalism**
> legal and political structures where power is distributed between two distinct levels of government on the basis that neither is subordinate to the other.

Establishment and powers of key EU institutions and the process of enlargement

Institution	Membership	Role	Represents
European Commission	28 European commissioners, one from each country but giving up their national loyalties. Each has a specific role as head of a Directorate-General	• Proposes laws and the EU budget • Oversees EU law implementation • Guardian of the Treaties	Europe and the common European interest
European Council	Heads of government of the member states	• Makes key political decisions • Sets political agenda	Member states
Council of the European Union	Ministers from the governments of the member states	• Passes, amends and rejects legislation	Member states
European parliament	751 directly elected MEPs from the 28 member states	• Passes, amends and rejects legislation • Approves the Commission	People of the European Union
Court of Justice of the European Union	1 judge from each member state	• Interprets EU law	Justice

Table 3.1: Organisation and role of key EU institutions

EU enlargement

Year	Country/Countries	Reason/dynamic	Membership
1958	• Belgium • France • Italy • Luxembourg • Netherlands • West Germany	Original and founder countries of the European Coal and Steel Community (ECSC) and the European Economic Community (EEC).	6
1973	• Denmark • Republic of Ireland • United Kingdom	UK felt they had missed the boat as EEC countries were growing economically faster.	9
1981	• Greece	Entrenching democracy after military dictatorship.	10
1986	• Portugal • Spain	Entrenching democracy after fascist dictatorships.	12
1995	• Austria • Finland • Sweden	Western democracies were neutral during the Cold War, which had now ended, enabling membership.	15
2004	• Cyprus • The Czech Republic • Estonia • Hungary • Latvia • Lithuania • Malta • Poland • Slovakia • Slovenia	Eight former Soviet or Soviet bloc countries entrenching democracy and capitalism joined Malta and Cyprus, which also met the accession criteria by 2004.	25
2007	• Bulgaria • Romania	Former Soviet bloc countries entrenching democracy and capitalism.	27
2013	• Croatia	Former Yugoslav country entrenching democracy and capitalism.	28
Candidate countries (as of 2017): Turkey, Macedonia (FYROM), Montenegro, Albania and Serbia. Bosnia Herzegovina and Kosovo are also potential candidates.			

Table 3.2: Historical timeline of EU enlargement

Key treaties and agreements

Treaty	Main features	EU development
Rome 1957	Set up the EEC, including the institutional framework.	EEC formed.
Single European Act 1986	Made provision for the single market.	Biggest transfer of sovereignty to the EU from states in order to make the single market work.
Treaty on the European Union (Maastricht) 1992	• Made the change from the EEC to the EU including further integration and co-operation. • Greater powers for European parliament. • More use of qualified majority voting (QMV) in the Council of Ministers. • Made provision for the single currency and the Social Chapter.	European project is now not just focused on economics, but also the pillars of Justice, Home Affairs and also Foreign Policy.
Amsterdam 1997	• Strengthened foreign policy co-operation. • Greater powers for European parliament. • More use of QMV in the Council of Ministers. • Some preparation for eastward enlargement.	**Widening and deepening** of the EU.
Nice 2000	• Further preparations for eastward enlargement. • Greater use of QMV in the Council of Ministers.	Widening and deepening of the EU.
The European Constitution 2004 (withdrawn)	• Intended to replace all previous treaties into one document. • More powers for the Commission and parliament. • Exit clause suggested.	Further integration. To many, the EU looks increasingly like a state itself.
Lisbon 2007	More powers for the Commission and parliament; European External Action Service; High Representative of the Union for Foreign Affairs and Security Policy/Vice president of the European Commission; President of the Council; and president of the Commission.	Further integration.

Table 3.3: Key EU treaties and agreements

> **Key term**
>
> **Widening and deepening** process by which the EU has attempted to expand membership while furthering integration.

Economic and monetary union

The introduction of the single European currency, the euro, is seen by some as the most significant act of integration of European countries since the European project began. It is clearly a major step on the road to binding the countries of Europe together in an economic, trade and political bloc, making war not only incredible but impossible. It may also be seen as a major advance towards political integration and even a United States of Europe.

For others, the euro is a symptom of the madness that is the European project. They see it as a triumph of ideology and dogma over reality and common sense, and an attempt to bind different countries together culturally, politically and economically with a one-size-fits-all approach. Critics see the economic project as damaging to states, companies and individuals, and even as the source of recent low growth and high unemployment in Greece, Italy, Spain and Portugal.

A closer look at Greece

Greece has been in deep recession. The state is having to make savings and increase taxation to help bring down the huge debt it owes to international bodies, states and private lenders. This debt was estimated by the BBC in 2015 as standing at 177 per cent of Greece's GDP – so Greeks owe more than one-and-a-half times the entire annual income of the country. As a result of this debt, the state has had to make major cuts to public services, youth unemployment is very high and the economy is being squeezed. Paying off the debt is an enormous challenge.

Both the causes and solutions to the Greek debt crisis are mired in the politics and economics of the EU and the euro. Greece's problems started before it joined the euro. Public spending was already too high and the 2004 Athens Olympics had to be paid for. Greece did not meet the strict economic criteria to join the euro in 2002, but it was felt that Greece should join the single currency for political reasons of solidarity. The introduction of the euro meant that Greece could borrow at cheaper interest rates than before, as stronger economies like Germany and the Netherlands were in the euro. However, with the international financial crash of 2008, recession hit and the cost of borrowing went up for Greece. Their debt became unsustainable and the country was at risk of defaulting, so they had to rely on loans from the European Union (and its member states), the International Monetary Fund and private lenders.

For critics of the euro, the Greek situation was brought on and exacerbated by the currency. This deepening of the EU has made the financial situation for ordinary Greek people close to catastrophic. Youth unemployment hit 60 per cent during the crisis, with young Greeks leaving the country for jobs abroad. Whole families were living off the dwindling income from grandparents' pensions. The economy had been squeezed so much it is struggling to get any growth at all. The euro is blamed because it relies on a single interest rate for the entire euro area, which includes strong manufacturing and exporting economies like Germany and the Netherlands, known for their prudence, but also weaker southern European economies like Greece and Spain. Cheap interest rates encouraged Greece to borrow too much. It is also argued that the Germans have been the biggest beneficiaries of the euro as German exporters have benefited from a weaker (compared to the German mark) euro and debt-laden countries like the Greeks purchasing the German exports. Furthermore, the traditional and orthodox way of getting out of a debt crisis such as the Greeks are in would be to devalue their currency to kickstart their economy, making exports cheaper. This is not an option as Greece is a member of the euro, making such a drastic move impossible. Greece has fewer options available to them because they are in the euro – they are in an economic straightjacket.

One option would be for the countries that have lent money to Greece to write off the debt, meaning that the Germans and others should say that the Greeks do not have to pay back the money they have been lent. There are a number of problems with this. Firstly, it is politically very difficult to achieve in the EU as it is currently set up. The German government is accountable to the German people through elections, and so any decision by the German government to effectively give the Greek people free money from the hard-working German taxpayers is politically impossible. Secondly, a writing off of the Greek debt would make it appear that the Greeks were getting away with being profligate and adopting spendthrift behaviour, and then not having to pay back their debts – a case of moral hazard. This would seem very unfair to taxpayers in other countries that have not overspent, who are having to give money to the Greeks, who have. All this seems to make a mockery of the idea of European solidarity and the European project.

So for critics, this economic and political deepening has made the Greece crisis. For them, the euro was ill-conceived, an accident waiting to happen, and will inevitably fail. You just cannot have one currency that works for 19 or more economies which are so different and so out of sync with each other. The euro is an integration too far.

On the other hand, there are arguments that the euro is an example of the lack of deepening within the European project. When the euro was introduced there was not enough integration; the solution to the Greek debt crisis is not less Europe, but more Europe. When the euro was constructed, the leaders of the member states did not pool the fiscal policies of the Eurozone countries, despite pooling the monetary policies. The EU leaders created a monetary union where the Euro countries shared a currency but left the collecting and spending of money in the hands of individual countries. So, despite sharing the currency, each country was left to its own devices when it came to public spending, tax rates and collection, and borrowing. Fiscal policy, as the Greek debt crisis has shown, can lead to shocks on the whole Eurozone economy.

One lesson learned from the debt crisis is that perhaps there should be a more supranational or pooled approach to fiscal policy. Arguably, Greece brought their troubles on themselves by borrowing too much, hiding their debts and expecting others to bail them out. In the meantime, the Greek debt crisis has stifled growth across the Eurozone. If all the countries could inspect each other's budgets, they would not be able to spend or borrow too much, reducing the likelihood of economic shocks to their Eurozone colleagues. This would impact sovereignty and the democratic deficit, but it would protect the euro and provide more economic stability.

This is also true for a banking union in the Eurozone. Currently each country is responsible for the regulation and solvency of its own banks. However, some countries' banks (like Ireland's) are so large compared to the size of their economy that failing banks can cause a shock to the whole economy and the finances of the state, with a knock-on effect for the whole Euro area. A banking union would create a level playing field for the banking industry, with all banks subject to the same rules and regulations wherever they were based, rather than encouraging banks to shop around for states with lax regulations to attract banks to their country.

Debates about supranational versus intergovernmental approaches

There is considerable debate over the advantages and disadvantages of supranational decision-making.

Intergovernmental decision-making is still used in the EU in some areas, although it has declined over the years. Intergovernmental decision-making requires unanimity, so all states have a veto or blocking vote. EU foreign policy still requires unanimity, with the obvious effect that it is harder to make decisions that are agreeable to all members. Likewise, there must be unanimity between all current members for new states to be admitted or treaties to be adopted or amended. The difficulty of achieving unanimity and the ability of one state to veto decisions makes the leaders of EU states reluctant to change treaties without pressing need. In late 2016, the regional parliament of Wallonia in Belgium threatened to veto the EU-Canadian free-trade deal known as CETA. This parliament threatened to derail the whole process. Wallonia's objections were eventually overcome and the treaty went ahead.

Supranational institutions make decisions that are binding on nations. The EU is the only truly supranational organisation in the world, with supranational bodies like the European Commission (EC) and the Court of Justice of the European Union (ECJ) and forms of supranational decision-making in the Council of the European Union (see below). The supranational nature of the EC and ECJ is like the neutral referee in a football match. If teams or players demanded the right to award their own fouls and penalties, the match would not be fair, effective or enjoyable.

A key requirement of membership of the EU is the acknowledgement that decisions of the EC and ECJ are binding. The EU would not work effectively if the states held on to their sovereignty.

The single market only works because the EC and the ECJ are independent of the states and their decisions are binding.

Particularly with the introduction of the single market it was felt that states could not be relied on to refrain from pursuing their own national interests. The single market requires states to allow the sale of products in their domestic market from other EU states, provided they are safe and not detrimental to public health.

Case study: Cassis de Dijon

The Cassis de Dijon case: an important case in EU law regarding the free movement of goods that provides for the mutual recognition of standards in EU member states.

The German authorities introduced a rule insisting that fruit liqueurs must be a certain alcoholic strength, which Cassis de Dijon was not. As a result, the liqueur was banned from sale in Germany. This ban was deemed unlawful by the ECJ as it was considered a protectionist move by Germany to help preserve the market for its own fruit liqueurs and Schnapps. Cassis de Dijon was not dangerous to public health and, as long as the product was properly labelled, no German consumer could be confused or misled about the product.

The EU single market requires the free movement of goods. Cassis de Dijon is a perfectly legal product made in France, and should not be banned in another EU member state.

Questions

- What impact did this case have on sovereignty?

- What would happen to the single market without this supranational approach?

Qualified majority voting (QMV)

The Council of the European Union is a legislative body of the EU on which each state's government is represented. The Council uses qualified majority voting – a special type of majority vote – in 80 per cent of legislation put before it.

The purpose of QMV is to make decision-making in the Council as fair as possible. The 'qualified majority' required is that:

- 55 per cent of member states (16 out of 28) must agree to the decision and
- the measure is supported by at least 65 per cent of the population of the EU.

This is known as the 'double majority' rule. QMV means that in theory no country has a veto, although blocs of countries can block the decision.

QMV is also designed to balance the interests of big and small states. Among the 28 current members of the EU, 20 have populations of less than 2.5 per cent of the EU's 508 million people, while Belgium, with its 11 million citizens is the 9th biggest population. The total population of the 20 smallest countries is less than that of Germany and the UK combined, while the largest four countries (Germany, France, the UK and Italy) have a combined population of around 273 million. QMV balances the right of the small member states not to be railroaded by the demands of the bigger states, and of the bigger states not to be thwarted by the smaller states. A double-majority vote requires a combination of both big and small states; neither big nor small states can gang up on the others.

QMV is rarely used to force countries to accept measures they do not want. Rather, it encourages those who might use their veto to negotiate as good a deal as they can get. Imagine you and your 27 classmates wanted to go to the cinema together. It would be difficult to get all 28 classmates to agree on which film to see, especially if each classmate had a veto. QMV makes each classmate realise that, if they are in a minority, they might have to accept the decision of the majority – and be in danger of watching a film they do not want to watch. To avoid this, they should start negotiating with their classmates to get the best deal they can.

5.4 Significance of the EU as an international body/global actor, including the constraints and obstacles

The EU's political, economic, structural and military influence in global politics

EU influence in the world	Strengths	Weaknesses
Political influence in global politics	• Most successful body of its kind • Through enlargement, the EU can get countries to change their ways to get in, e.g. Croatia, Serbia • Can mould global opinions on environmental issues. Influential at Paris and Kyoto conferences	• 28 member states – different national interests

EU influence in the world	Strengths	Weaknesses
Economic influence in global politics	• 508 million citizens • Largest single market in the world • TTIP • EU states represented at WTO by the Commission, giving leverage and clout	• Eurozone crisis • Brexit
Structural influence in global politics	• Different national interests within institutions • Agreement and habit of working together • UK and France both permanent members of the UN Security Council • EU represented at G20 in its own right • IMF has Europe office primarily to deal with the EU	• Different histories, traditions, cultures • Different geo-political priorities
Military influence in global politics	• NATO • EEAS Battlegroups • Berlin Group • Rapid Reaction Force • Example of Mali	• Separate national militaries • Not all EU members in NATO • Different defence priorities (Russia)

Table 4.1: Strengths and weaknesses of EU influences in the world

5.5 The ways and extent to which regionalism addresses and resolves contemporary global issues

As with global governance, regionalism is a recognition of the shared interests of states, such as reducing conflict and poverty or the protection of human rights and the environment. If global problems require global solutions, regional problems need regional solutions.

At the heart of the global order after the Second World War (certainly as far as Western liberal-democratic states were concerned) was the view that you cannot isolate yourself from the world's problems. A neighbour's problem would soon become your problem. President Roosevelt acknowledged this at the 1944 Bretton Woods Conference: 'The economic health of every country is a proper matter of concern to all its neighbours, near and distant.' Economic instability in one country will spread to other countries, a path that helped lead to the Second World War.

The European Union is a prime example of the linking of these two points; ASEAN is another. A peaceful and stable region can lead to trade – and trade leads to a peaceful and stable region.

Regional organisations are set up to avoid conflict, to improve relations between neighbours, and to facilitate trade, which should be a win-win for both or all parties. Growth of trade should reduce poverty, so trade should of course be encouraged.

Regionalism is a system set up in the anarchy of the Westphalian system. There is no compulsion in the international system, but regionalism imposes the rule of law on countries. States have to play by the rules; otherwise no one would play by the rules. Human rights can be protected by states agreeing to uphold and protect human rights. A perfect example of this is the European Convention on Human Rights and the European Court of Human Rights.

Most environmental problems need multilateral approaches. Regional blocs that have agreed on approaches or solutions can drive forward complex and difficult environmental negotiations. Regions can set an example for ambitious targets. If the argument is that states cannot put aside their economic interests to save the planet, then regions that do exactly that are powerful examples to the rest of the world.

Assessment support: 3.2.5 Regionalism and the EU

Question 3 on A-Level Paper 3 gives you a choice of answering two out of three questions. Each one is worth 30 marks and you should allow about 45 minutes to complete each answer.

Evaluate the extent to which the European Union is a unique example of regional integration. [30 marks]

You must consider this view and the alternative to this view in a balanced way.

These questions require an essay-style answer in which you consider both sides of the argument ('evaluate the extent'). They test all three Assessment Objectives, with marks divided equally between them. You should adopt a balanced approach before coming to a logical conclusion. Make sure you refer to the question and use words from it throughout your essay. You need to explain what the European Union is, and what a regional organisation is.

- The core of this essay is analysis of how the EU is special compared to other regional organisations, so you need to present a well-structured debate on the EU's unique features. Ideally, a small number of features or approaches would make the essay stronger.

- Examples may include examining EU and other regional organisations in terms of their history, their economic integration (including the single-market and monetary union of the EU) and their political integration (including the supranational role of the European Commission and the Court of Justice of the European Union, and decision-making in the European Council based on qualified majority voting).

Here is a short introduction from a student's answer:

The European Union is an organisation of 28 member states that have come together to reap the benefits of pooling sovereignty and trade using a single market. Starting with the economic coal and steel community in 1952 before becoming the European Economic Community with six members in 1957, the EEC has transformed over the years into a huge, powerful organisation. There are other regional organisations such as the Association of South East Asian Nations (ASEAN), the North American Free Trade Agreement (NAFTA) and the Arab League. The European Union differs in many ways but there are also significant similarities with these organisations. The extent to which the EU is a unique example of regional organisations will be discussed.

- This is one way to start the essay, with a significant amount on the EU and its history. Another way would be to explain what a regional organisation is then bring in examples of other organisations.

- The student addresses the question by suggesting there are similarities and differences, before using the phrasing from the question – a good way to keep the question in mind and make sure you answer it.

CHAPTER
6 Comparative Theories

Since the time of Thucydides, the ancient Athenian historian, and Sun Tzu, the Chinese general – both writing in the 5th century BCE – people have been writing about international relations.

There are many theories of global politics but their roots lie in one of two traditions – **realism** and **liberalism**. Realism is the older of the two theories and was the dominant theory until the early 20th century, when liberalism emerged to challenge realism's pessimistic conclusions about the inevitability of war. Drawing on different assumptions about human nature, the nature of power, and the motivations of states, liberals argued that states would co-operate to achieve peace and security.

This chapter looks at:

- the main assumptions of realism and liberalism and the main divisions between them
- ideas of the anarchical society and the theory of the society of states.

Key terms

Realism
wide school of thought in international relations theory that believes that world politics will remain a field of conflict among actors pursuing power.

Liberalism
wide school of thought in international relations theory that rejects power politics as the sole outcome of international relations and emphasises mutual benefits and co-operation.

Link

For more detail on **states**, see Section 1.1 of The State and Globalisation.

Pause & reflect

Before reading on, think about why theories of politics are necessary. How do theories help you in your study of global politics? What do they add to your understanding of how states behave towards each other? How can you use theories to explain war, trade and the creation of international organisation?

6.1 Main ideas of realism

Realism refers to being realistic, implying that realist theory will take a practical, down-to-earth, matter-of-fact approach to the study of international relations – one in which there is no room for sentiment or idealism.

States as key actors in global politics and the balance of power (state sovereignty)

According to realists, **states** are the most important actors in the global system. Certain characteristics of states lead to conflict.

Selfish human nature leads to selfish states

Realists differ as to what is the root cause of conflict between states. For classical realists, it is selfish human nature. Realist thinkers from Thucydides to Morgenthau have argued that human beings are fundamentally self-centred. People will pursue their own interests above and beyond those of others. States, which are ruled by people, also seek to promote their national interest at the expense of other states. It makes perfect sense for states to act selfishly in a world where there is uncertainty about the intentions of other states. As in the Prisoners' Dilemma (see page 579), states cannot trust other states to act in everyone's interests. The safest strategy is to expect betrayal and, therefore, pre-empt such an eventuality by being the first to betray. Today's friend could be tomorrow's enemy. So while it may seem that co-operating is optimal, states, like prisoners, do not know each others' intentions and have no means of guaranteeing co-operation. Not working together becomes the best strategy, even if it remains sub-optimal overall because there are losers as well as winners. Competition rather than co-operation between states inevitably leads to a clash of interests and this, in turn, leads to war.

Prisoners' Dilemma

In 1950, mathematicians Merrill Flood and Melvin Dresher posed a problem that came to be known as the Prisoners' Dilemma. The application of the problem can be found in economics, biology, politics and ethics.

Imagine a scenario in which two members of a criminal gang, A and B, are arrested. Each prisoner is held and questioned separately, with no way to communicate with each other. The police are forced to admit that they do not have enough evidence to convict either criminal on the original charge without one or both of the prisoners betraying each other. To maximise their chances of gaining successful convictions the police offer the criminals a Faustian bargain:

- If A and B both betray each other, they each serve five years in jail.
- If A denies the crime but B betrays A, B gets away scot-free while A has to serve 20 years in prison (and vice versa)
- If A and B both deny the crime, they each serve three months in jail on a lesser charge.

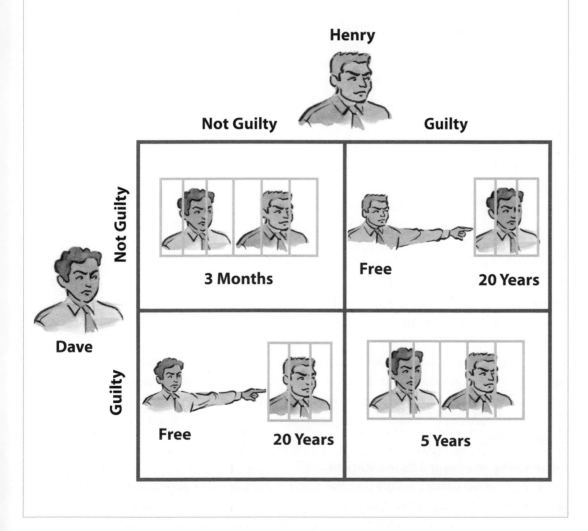

States are rational

States engage in dispassionate calculations of their interests, in the same way that individuals are assumed to act according to rational choice theory. Relations with other states, whether to go to war or make a trade deal, for example, are determined by the relative value of the costs versus the benefits of such an action. If the benefits are higher than the perceived costs then states pursue a policy or course of action. Vice versa and the policy or course of action is not adopted.

States are unitary actors

There is no division of opinion within the state as to what constitutes its interests. Some realists concede that the culture and the nature of the regime of a state may affect its interests, but others see interests as fixed, as it is always in states' interests to increase their power and, as a consequence, their security.

States are amoral

States do not act according to concepts of justice, rights or religious morality. States only act according to what is in their interests. Similarly, relations between states are not guided by universal principles. As Machiavelli advocated in *The Prince*, rulers of states should be ruthless in pursuing their interests and what matters is the achievement of these interests, not how they are achieved. Some realists have even gone so far as to say that 'a just war is one in the national interest' (Randall Schweller). That there can be anything noble in the pursuit of selfishness refutes the existence of a moral code underpinning state behaviour.

States seek power

States are motivated by the pursuit of the national interest; but what constitutes the national interest? Realists argue that it is power. Classical realists believe that power is a good in itself, while neo-realists see power as a means to security. The more powerful a state is the better able it is to protect itself against other states. It is not known how much power guarantees security, so neo-realists argue that the safest course is for a state to become the hegemon (the dominant power in the world). However, power is a finite resource. States must compete with each other for military and economic power and in doing so affect the balance of power between states. As one state gains power, other states inevitably lose power (known as a 'zero-sum game'). States' comparative economic and military power determines their security. States are reluctant to attack their more powerful neighbours, while attacking less powerful states is seen as less risky. Weaker states, aware of their vulnerability, try to increase their power, usually by increasing the size of their military or by acquiring more powerful weapons, such as a nuclear deterrent, and this then leads to a **security dilemma**. While an imbalance of power creates the potential for conflict, a balance of power, on the other hand, can create harmony. States naturally seek a balance of power to curb the hegemonic ambitions of more powerful states and so avoid the conflict that arises when great powers strive for dominance.

International anarchy and its implications

According to realists, states are the principal actors in international systems. As such, there is no higher authority than the state. States cannot be held to account for their actions or punished if they infringe the rights and interests of other states. Therefore, it is nonsensical to use the language of rights and justice in relation to state relations, as no actor has the authority to bring states to heel. The international system is therefore like Hobbes' state of nature where states can act with impunity. There is, hence, what is known as **international anarchy**. While some realists claim that selfish human nature causes states to act selfishly, which leads to conflict, others believe that the anarchy of the international system, allowing states to get away with acting selfishly, is the real cause of conflict.

Key terms

Security dilemma theory that any actions by a state intended to increase its security – such as increasing its military strength – can lead to other states responding with similar measures, producing increased tensions that create conflict.

International anarchy concept that the world system is leaderless: there is no universal sovereign or worldwide government.

> ### The state of nature
>
> The state of nature is a device used in political philosophy to imagine what life might have been like for people before the establishment of society and government. The 17th-century English philosopher Thomas Hobbes describes in *Leviathan* the state of nature as 'during the time men live without a common power to keep them all in awe, they are in that condition which is called war; and such a war as is of every man against every man'. In the absence of recognised authority, individuals are self-governing autonomous actors. There are no rules in the state of nature and nobody in a position to enforce them. Individuals are free to do as they will. Hobbes goes on to say that life is 'nasty, brutish and short'. Without government and the rule of law, people are free to give vent to their base instincts. They can rape, murder and pillage without restraint. States in the world are like individuals in the state of nature. They too are not subject to any higher authority and as they are ruled by human beings, they also act selfishly. Hobbes might have easily gone on to claim that the international system is like the state of nature (*Leviathan*, Chapters XIII–XIV).

Inevitability of war

The overwhelming logic of realism is that war is inevitable. It is not only the security dilemma that poses a threat to world peace but selfish human nature, states' desire for power and realist assumptions about the zero-sum nature of power (if one state gains power another state must have lost power).

Here are some of the reasons realists put forward for the inevitability of war.

- In a world where people are selfish and states act accordingly, there is bound to be disagreement and competition for resources.
- The lack of adherence to any moral principles coupled with the pursuit of power is bound to lead to misunderstandings and disharmony between states.
- Furthermore, the limited amount of power in the world means all states pose a threat, whether intentional or not. Even if there is not war, there is 'always the danger of war lurking in the background' (Randall Schweller).

Security dilemma

A security dilemma is where the actions that one state takes to increase its security cause other states to follow suit, which increases the likelihood of conflict even if states do not desire it.

A balance of power between states is rarely achieved. One exception was the Cold War (1945–91), when the United States of America and the Soviet Union dominated international relations. Mostly states find themselves in a competitive struggle for power, whether economically, politically, militarily or culturally. As all states possess some military offensive capability, the temptation is to increase that capability so as to increase their power and security. However, this is self-defeating because other states increase their military capability correspondingly, creating an arms race that increases the insecurity of all. The First World War is seen as a classic example of what can happen when there is a security dilemma.

The recognition of the security dilemma led to a refinement of realist theory. Kenneth Waltz argued that states become obsessed with security because of the anarchy in the international system. However, a state's action to increase its own security decreases other states' security. The result is 'bandwagoning' – an arms race. The consequence of more states with larger armies, more tanks and more nuclear warheads is to make the world a more dangerous place. States, being rational actors, reach the conclusion that gaining more power to increase security is counterproductive. They realise that, to avoid such a self-defeating situation, they must co-operate. The international system, therefore, is characterised by peace and stability, as it was during the Cold War.

Co-operating to escape the security dilemma

Reconnaissance photograph of Soviet missiles in Cuba.

The Cuban Missile Crisis of 1962 brought the USA and the Soviet Union to the brink of war. Reconnaissance photographs taken by an American U2 spy plane flying over Cuba showed that the Soviets had been deploying nuclear missiles in Cuba, despite public and private assurances to the contrary. The US president, John F. Kennedy, imposed a naval blockade of the island to prevent a deployment of further missiles. After 13 days of stalemate, the Russians backed down. In return for assurances that the US would not invade Cuba and would reduce the number of nuclear missiles stationed in Italy and Turkey, Russia agreed to withdraw the missiles. Hawks in the US military and Fidel Castro, the Cuban leader, had urged a tough stance but Kennedy and Khrushchev, the Soviet premier, realised that nuclear war would lead to their states' mutual destruction. They agreed to co-operate to avoid disaster. As a consequence, a hotline was established to create a direct line of communication between the White House and the Kremlin. In 1963, the Partial Test Ban Treaty was agreed, which banned testing of nuclear weapons in the atmosphere. Later on, in the 1970s, the Cold War superpowers signed two Strategic Arms Limitations Treaties (SALT I and II). Since then the US and Russia have continued to co-operate over the size of their nuclear arsenals in the Strategic Arms Reduction Treaties (START) of 1991 and 2010. The result has been an 80 per cent reduction in the number of nuclear warheads.

Some realists accept that the security dilemma can lead to instances of co-operation between states, but are pessimistic about institutionalised and permanent forms of co-operation – such as the United Nations or the European Union. Ultimately, selfish interests and the desire for power will lead to conflict, as states will always use international organisations to further their national interests. These interests inevitably clash with other states' interests and make effective co-operation difficult, if not impossible. Realists would point to the many examples of failures in UN peacekeeping as evidence. Whenever international organisations are able to promote effective co-operation, there is a usually a dominant power that can force this co-operation. Arguably, NATO has been a successful mutual defence body because it is dominated by the USA, and the EU has managed to develop a high level of integration because of the leadership of Germany and France. Even so, realists would argue that all alliances and institutions are doomed to fail because allies cannot be trusted, such as Hitler breaking the Nazi–Soviet non-aggression pact of 1939 by invading Russia in 1941.

Realists, such as Mearsheimer, see no escape from the security dilemma. Since no state knows how much power it needs to gain security, the most rational policy is to dominate – to become the global hegemon. This is regardless of what other states do because no state knows how much power is required to protect against threats. The struggle for hegemony is inescapable and war, therefore, becomes inevitable.

There are many illustrations of states behaving in a realist way. Here are two examples – the Melian Dialogue and the Iraq War.

Case study: The Melian Dialogue

The Melian Dialogue is a passage found in Book V (85-113) of the *History of the Peloponnesian War* by the ancient Greek historian, Thucydides. It describes a meeting in 416 BCE between the representatives of Athens and Melos, an island state in the Aegean Sea. The Melians were on friendly terms with Sparta, enemies of the Athenian Empire in the Peloponnesian War, but had remained neutral in the war. Athens wanted Melos to become part of the Athenian Empire on the grounds that:

- 'it is a necessary law of nature to rule wherever one can'
- Melos posed a threat to Athenian sea routes that had to be removed
- Allowing Melos to remain neutral would make Athens look weak and encourage members of the empire to rebel
- it would be in everyone's interest for Melos to comply and avoid bloodshed
- Sparta would not come to the aid of Melos
- if Melos did not comply, it would be destroyed.

The Melians, however, stubbornly resisted Athens' demands because:

- Athens was behaving aggressively and unfairly
- Athens may be the stronger power but this did not necessarily mean that Melos would be defeated
- Melos was standing up for what was right against what was wrong. The Gods would protect them
- if Athens defeated Melos, other states in Athens' Empire would rise up against it
- Sparta would come to the aid of Melos.

Athens immediately attacked Melos. It put up fierce resistance but there was treachery from within. Sparta, as Athens had predicted, did not come to the aid of Melos. Every man was put to death and the women and children were forced into slavery. Athens took control of the island and colonised it.

What the Melian Dialogue shows is that states are motivated by the selfish pursuit of power. Athens did not care about the rights and wrongs of its actions. Its only concern was to remove Melos as a threat to its shipping lanes and secure its power in the region in relation to its great rival, Sparta. It was willing to use any means at its disposal to achieve its ends.

Questions

- In what ways were the Athenians behaving like realists?

- How did the Melians justify their resistance to Athens?

Case study: The Iraq War

The Iraq War was a conflict between the USA and its allies against Iraq in March 2003. The USA accused Iraq of possessing weapons of mass destructions (WMDs) – chemical, biological and nuclear weapons – that it might use against the West. It was also accused of helping Islamic terrorist groups such as Al-Qaeda, which had carried out the 9/11 attacks against the USA in 2001. The USA and its allies invaded Iraq and removed Saddam Hussein's government. Realists would say that the real reasons for the war were:

The UK's role in the Iraq War sparked widespread controversy at home and saw the resignation of government ministers who did not support the invasion.

- **unfinished business from the first Bush administration of 1988–92:** Many of President George W. Bush's foreign policy and defence adviser had served under his father during the First Gulf War. Iraq had invaded the small oil-producing state of Kuwait in 1991. The USA led an international mission to remove the Iraqi army from the country but was unable to get UN support for an invasion of Iraq and the removal of the Saddam Hussein regime. The Iraq War provided the opportunity to achieve a policy that had proved impossible in 1991.

- **power and security:** The 9/11 attacks had shaken the American public badly. The Iraq War was intended to send a clear message to America's enemies in the world, such as North Korea, and in particular in the Middle East, that the USA would not tolerate states giving aid or support to terrorist groups seeking to attack the USA.

- **American national interest:** In the attempts to get a UN resolution to give legitimacy to the Iraqi invasion, the Bush administration claimed that there was evidence that Iraq had WMDs that could be launched at the West within 45 minutes. These claims were later found to be based on unreliable intelligence, suggesting that the US was prepared to go to any lengths to promote its national interest.

Questions

- What were the reasons for the Iraq War?

- In what ways are the reasons for the war realist?

EXTENSION ACTIVITY

The table below lists some of the key realist thinkers. Do some research to find out more about them, and use what you find to complete the table. 'Background' refers to when and where they lived, their occupation, and so on.

Name	Background	Main works	Main ideas	Type of realist
Thucydides				
Niccolo Machiavelli				
Carl von Clausewitz				
Hans Morgenthau				
Kenneth Waltz				
John Mearsheimer				

Pause & reflect ✔

Check your understanding of realist theory. Can you explain the realist view of states, power and international anarchy? Why do realists think that states act selfishly? What is the security dilemma and why do realists think that war is inevitable?

6.2 Main ideas of liberalism

You may remember that liberal theory developed much later than realist theory. Liberal theory is in part a reaction to the theoretical deficiencies of realism, but also a response to a number of developments in the latter half of the 20th century that could not be explained by realism.

- **The decline in conflict:** The number of deaths in battle had fallen to less than 10,000 in 2006 compared with 600,000 in 1951. The nature of conflict also had changed, from predominantly inter-state conflict (war between states) to intra-state conflict, or civil war.

- **The rise in democracy:** By 2006, over half of all countries had become democracies – a significant development as democracies tend to be less aggressive than authoritarian regimes. According to democratic peace theory, no two democracies have ever been to war with each other.

- **The growth in world trade:** Worldwide exports were worth $629 million in 1960. By 2010, they were worth $30 trillion. This suggests that states are becoming increasingly interdependent, which is thought to reduce the potential for conflict between them. States will not risk conflict if it jeopardises the sale of exports and the supply of imported goods.

- **The growth in the number of intergovernmental organisations:** The post-war era has witnessed a burgeoning of international organisations – the United Nations, the European Union, NATO, the IMF, the International Criminal Court and more. This demonstrates a desire on the part of states to co-operate rather than to go to war with each other.

A meeting of the League of Nations, 1936.

Liberalism may appear a less highly developed theory than realism. There are good reasons for this. One is that liberalism developed in reaction to realist theory, so there is less need for *a priori* reasoning (theoretical deduction). The other is that much of liberal theory develops from observable facts about the world. It is a fact that states want to co-operate – they do so through alliances, trade agreements and international organisations.

The significance of morality and optimism on human nature

Liberalism takes the polar opposite view of human nature to realism. According to realists individuals are selfish and put their interests before all others, but liberals argue that individuals are altruistic and capable of a selfless concern for others. This is demonstrated theoretically and practically. Rousseau uses the Stag Hunt Scenario to illustrate how humans are naturally altruistic.

The Stag Hunt Scenario

Two hunters have tracked a large stag and found that it follows a certain path. If they work together, they can kill the stag and will both enjoy a hearty meal. If they are discovered, or do not co-operate, the stag will flee, and both will go hungry. The hunters hide and wait along a path. An hour goes by, with no sign of the stag. Two, three, four hours pass, with no trace. A day passes. The stag may not pass every day, but the hunters are reasonably certain that it will come.

Meanwhile, a hare appears on the path. If one hunter leaps out and kills the hare, he will eat. However, this will scare off the stag and the other hunter will starve. Yet, there is no certainty that the stag will arrive, whilst availability of the hare is guaranteed.

Here is the dilemma. If one hunter waits, he risks his fellow hunter killing the hare for himself, ruining the prospects of the stag being caught. There is also the risk that the stag will never come.

Rousseau claims that the hunters will wait for the stag, because:

- there is no communication between the two hunters (as in the Prisoners' Dilemma)
- the stag yields more food than the hare
- in any given scenario at least one hunter is guaranteed food
- both hunters are rational and equally informed
- The benefits to each hunter in waiting for the stag far outweigh the benefit to any individual hunter in catching the hare.

The Scottish philosopher, David Hume, presents two further scenarios where selflessness is more beneficial for everyone. One scenario concerns rowing a boat. Two people are needed to row the boat. If both choose to row they can successfully move the boat. However, if one does not row, the other wastes his effort and no progress is made. The other scenario is draining a meadow. Two neighbours want to drain a meadow. If they both work together they will be successful, but if either fails to do his part the meadow will not be drained.

Practically, the benefits of selflessness can be seen in the animal world. Killer whales 'carousel feed': they work together in groups to corral large schools of fish to the surface and stun them by hitting them with their tails; each then takes its share of the kill. Similarly, wolves hunt in packs and lions in prides. Ant nests and beehives are highly sophisticated units, with each individual ant and bee performing a necessary role for the greater good of the whole community.

Possibility of harmony and balance

- If altruism is possible in human nature, states – groups of people – can also act selflessly; they are not necessarily the self-interested actors described by realism. Furthermore, liberals reject the realist assumption that states are unitary actors. Rather, liberals claim that states' interests reflect the plurality of interests in a state. This allows for the possibility that states' interests change according to which political groups control the executive and legislature, or even according to public opinion and pressure-group activity.

Case study: Public pressure over the Vietnam War

As more young men were drafted (conscripted) to fight in Vietnam and the number of American casualties increased from the mid-1960s onwards, more Americans protested against the war. Protest reached its height in 1970 when the fatal shooting of four students at an anti-war protest at Kent State University led to nationwide student protests. In the same year, opinion polls showed that only a third of Americans supported the war. Shortly after this, the US government began to drastically reduce troop numbers in Vietnam. On 30 April 1975, the last US personnel were evacuated from the Vietnamese capital, Saigon, as the Viet Cong entered the city.

Protest against the Vietnam War.

Questions

- What led to a decline in public support for the Vietnam War?
- Can you think of other examples where public opinion has led to a change in foreign policy?

Liberals also argue that the constitutional and political organisation of a state affects its behaviour towards other states. In this, liberals have something in common with classical realists.

- By constitutional organisation liberals are referring to mechanisms that protect human rights or provide for judicial review of the executive. Such states tend to be less aggressive but they also tend to intervene in the affairs of other sovereign states when they feel that human rights are being threatened.

- By political organisation liberals mean whether a state is a democracy or a dictatorship. Democracies, which value the rule of law and where government change takes place through elections in which the losing parties and candidates accept the result, are better placed to resolve differences with other states. This is because they are used to settling internal political disputes peacefully. Dictatorships, used to using terror and oppression against political opponents, resort to the same tactics against other states.

As liberals make rather different assumptions from realists about the nature of states and their motivations, they draw the conclusion that the international system is characterised by co-operation. As J.D. Bowen of St Louis University puts it, the world is like a high school or college campus. States, like students, can choose to make what they will of their environment. They can choose to be the high school bully or join the football team or cheerleading squad. Similarly, states can choose to be aggressive or work with other states. Crucially, states have a choice. Conflict is not inevitable. Harmony and balance in the international system, therefore, are possible.

Evidence suggests that the international system is characterised by co-operation. Many **international institutions** emerged in the post-war era with the express purpose of preventing a third world war. It seems that states have consciously chosen to make the best of the world they find themselves in, just like the college- or high-school student. This is a significant advantage of liberalism over realism. Realism is in a conflict straitjacket. According to it, given its assumptions about human nature and the motivations of states, the only response states can make is to engage in military conflict. States are predestined to act aggressively. What is attractive about liberalism is that it is not necessarily pessimistic about the state of international relations.

Link

For more on **international institutions**, see Global Governance: Political and Economic and Global Governance: Human Rights and Environmental chapters.

Key term

Complex interdependence where states and their fortunes are inextricably tied together economically, politically, militarily and culturally.

Complex interdependence

Complex interdependence is a term coined by Robert Keohane and Joseph Nye in the 1970s to describe how states and their fortunes are inextricably tied together. They noted that various and complex connections and interdependencies were taking place between states and that these relationships were increasing, while the use of military force was decreasing, although still important.

Keohane and Nye's ideas draw on liberal theories of how trade promotes interdependence between states. Classical liberal economists, such as David Ricardo and the 'Manchester' liberals Richard Cobden and John Bright, argued that free trade promotes economic interdependence – states rely on each other for goods and trade promotes the exchange of values and ideas. A 'cobweb of interdependence' develops that makes conflict unthinkable, in contrast to the 'billiard ball model' associated with realist theory, which views states as autonomous and self-contained units.

Complex interdependence is characterised by three characteristics.

- The development of multiple channels of action between societies in interstate, transgovernmental and transnational relations, meaning that states are no longer autonomous international actors.

- The growing prominence of economic and other issues ('low politics') in world politics over defence and foreign policy ('high politics').
- States increasingly prioritising trade over war, leading to a decline in the use of military force and coercive power.

In 1795, Immanuel Kant published an essay entitled *Perpetual Peace: A Philosophical Sketch* in which he put forward a recipe for international peace that advocated the kind of complex interdependence between states that Keohane and Nye identified in the 1970s. Kant suggested that 'three definitive articles' would be required.

- The civil constitution of every state should be republican.
- The law of nations shall be founded on a federation of free states.
- The law of world citizenship shall be limited to conditions of universal hospitality.

The Kantian Triangle, as it became known, has been adapted to meet the conditions of the modern world and the state of liberal thinking. Kant originally referred to 'republican government', by which he meant a separation between the legislature and the executive. He was not thinking of democracy in the modern sense where there is universal suffrage. However, as this is now the most prevalent form of representative government, democracy is used in the triangle instead of republican government. A federation of free states is now interpreted as international institutions, while the second pillar of Kant's *Perpetual Peace*, universal hospitality, now refers to free trade.

Figure 2.1: The Kantian Triangle

Case study: The European Union

The European Union is a federation of free states, meaning that members give up some of their sovereignty (self-determination) while remaining independent states. All members are democracies – a precondition of membership and a guarantee against dictatorships emerging in member states. The union has the highest level of economic interdependence of any regional or international organisation. It is a completely tariff-free zone: there are no import or export duties on all goods and many services traded across the union. There is a single currency, called the euro, for 19 of the 28 member states. Above all, there is free movement of people and capital. EU citizens have the right to live and work in any member state, whether they are a citizen of that country or not. It is inconceivable that EU member states would go to war with each other. Politically, economically and culturally the member states and their citizens are mutually dependent and interconnected.

Questions

- In what respects are the countries of the EU interdependent?
- Identify the ways in which the EU promotes democracy and economic interdependence, and has established international organisations.

Key term

Global governance
a movement towards the political integration of states in order to address problems that face more than one state or region.

Link

For more on **climate change**, see Section 3.2 of Global Governance: Human Rights and Environmental.

Link

For more on **business**, see The State and Globalisation chapter.

Likelihood of global governance

The willingness of states to act co-operatively allows for the development of **global governance** and the creation of international institutions. However, liberals also argue that co-operation is driven by other developments. States are not necessarily the principal actors in the international system. A number of non-state actors, including religious groups, social movements and businesses are highly influential in international relations.

- **Religious groups:** The Catholic Church was an influential force in politics in the Middle Ages. It was so powerful that some European rulers broke with the Church to gain greater control over domestic politics. In recent years, the spread of so-called Islamic State in Iraq and Syria (ISIS) has led to American, French, British and Russian air strikes to eradicate it from the region.

- **Social movements:** The women's movement and the green movement have led to reforms of national laws and policies. Many countries have laws against sex discrimination and states are attempting to agree **climate-change** targets to limit global warming.

- **Business:** Business is a powerful lobbying group at the national and international level. The promotion of its interests are behind many of the regulations initiated by Brussels. States struggle to raise corporation tax from transnational corporations (TNCs), which can use legal loopholes to claim that profits are being earned in lower tax jurisdictions. However, the influence of TNCs is not necessarily a modern phenomenon. The British East India Company, formed in 1600 to exploit trade with India, had such a profound effect on international relations that it led to the development of the British Empire.

Impact and growth of international organisations

Some liberals go as far as to claim that the state is in decline as an actor in the international system. They point to the growth in the number of intergovernmental (IGOs) and non-governmental organisations (NGOs), as well as transnational corporations (TNCs), as evidence of this declining importance.

Certainly, intergovernmental and non-governmental organisations are becoming more numerous. Most of them have been created since the Second World War, although it is difficult to put precise figures on this growth. Undoubtedly, their influence is increasing. Intergovernmental organisations, such as the United Nations, are taking a leading role in combating climate change. Oxfam, the international charity, is both a significant provider of disaster relief – much of which is funded by national governments – and an influential voice in the formulation of state international-development aid policy. The number of transnational organisations has grown considerably: in 1970, there were 7000 TNCs; by 2013, their number had grown to 63,000. They account for over 50 per cent of production and over 70 per cent of world trade. A major factor in the escalation of these non-state actors is globalisation. To argue, as realists do, that states are the principal actors in the international system ignores the evidence and renders an increasingly important part of international relations inexplicable.

While realists are pessimistic about the prospects for international co-operation via international organisations, liberals are optimistic. They see more to be gained from working together. This stems from a recognition that many problems and challenges in the world do not respect state borders and that power is not a zero-sum game. Norway cannot take effective action to prevent acid rain without the co-operation of its more industrialised neighbours in curbing their nitrogen and sulphur oxide emissions. Like Hume's scenario of draining a meadow, all states need to reduce their emissions of these gases for action to be effective. Although there are costs associated with reducing emissions – such as more expensive energy – states also benefit by having cleaner air,

410

61616161

which reduces incidences of conditions that are costly to health care systems, such as asthma, lung disease and heart attacks caused by poor air quality.

Liberals put great faith in international organisations to promote co-operation in the international system. Woodrow Wilson, a leading liberal thinker of the early 20th century and American president (1913–1921), proposed a 'League of Nations' to guarantee the political and territorial independence of states. Unfortunately, it failed – but its successor, the United Nations, has had more success, including ensuring that the Cold War did not turn into a 'hot' war. However, realists would argue that the development of nuclear weapons did more to promote peace by making the prospect of war too awful to contemplate.

Pause & reflect ✔

How does the liberal view of human nature lead to state co-operation? How do liberals explain the growth of international organisations?

The best examples of liberal theory in action are the various current **regional and international institutions**. Here is an explanation of how liberal theory can be used to understand the United Nations.

EXTENSION ACTIVITY

The table below lists some of the key liberal thinkers. Do some research to find out more about them, and use what you find to complete the table. 'Background' refers to when and where they lived, their occupation, and so on.

Name	Background	Main works	Main ideas	Type of liberal
Immanuel Kant				
Woodrow Wilson				
Robert Keohane				
Joseph Nye				

Sidebar:

EXTENSION ACTIVITY

Watch the liberal clip – from a series called *Theories in Action* – in which J.D. Bowen of St. Louis University describes liberal theory www.youtube.com/watch?v=tZbDMUaqwE8. What does Bowen say about morality and optimism about human nature, the possibility of harmony and balance, global governance and the impact of international organisations?

Link

For more on **regional and international institutions**, see Global Governance: Political and Economic; Global Governance: Human Rights and Environmental; Regionalism and the EU chapters.

Case study: The United Nations

The United Nations General Assembly Hall in New York.

The United Nations is the embodiment of liberal ideas. It succeeded the League of Nations, which was inspired by Woodrow Wilson's 'Fourteen Points', which promoted many liberal ideas such as the self-determination of states, free trade, disarmament and co-operation between states. The UN continues to promote these liberal ideas through its charter. The aims, as set out by the charter, are to promote peace and security, to protect human rights, to uphold respect for international law and advance social progress and better standards of living. Co-operation between states is encouraged by the principle of sovereign equality, which is upheld in the General Assembly by each state having only one vote each in the General Assembly, regardless of size or power. The UN protects the idea of self-determination by requiring the express consent of host member states before the deployment of peacekeeping missions to protect human rights. It upholds respect of international law through the International Court of Justice that arbitrates in disputes between member states, helping to resolve them peacefully rather than states resorting to conflict. The UN oversees many agencies and programmes that promote social progress and better standards of living across the world, such as the World Food Programme and UNICEF. In recent years, the UN has set targets to reduce extreme poverty and the spread of diseases such as HIV/AIDs and malaria through its Millennium Development Goals. This concern with the social and economic welfare of the world's population shows that states do not necessarily act in their own national interest, but are capable of altruism.

Questions

- How does the UN promote liberal ideas of international relations?

- How would a realist explain the existence of the UN?

6.3 Divisions between realism and liberalism

Realism and liberalism take different views of a number of issues in international relations. Table 3.1 identifies the key areas of difference and directly compares them.

Main features	Realism	Liberalism
Human nature	Human nature is selfish.	Human nature is altruistic.
Power	There is a finite amount of power in the world. States compete for power in a zero-sum game.	Power is unlimited and all states can gain power. The pursuit of power is not a game of winners and losers.
Order and security	The anarchic nature of the international system means that states act with impunity. The lack of trust between states leads to a security dilemma. Peace can only be maintained by the emergence of a global hegemon or a balance of power.	The international system is characterised by co-operation and complex interdependence.
Likelihood of conflict	For offensive neo-realists, the security dilemma means that conflict is inevitable.	It is in states' interests to co-operate so conflict can be avoided.
International organisations	International organisations are doomed to fail or, at best, be ineffective. The lack of trust between states and the pursuit of national interests will render co-operation difficult. There is a danger of domination by great powers or a global hegemon.	International institutions are growing in number and influence.
Significance of states	States are the principal actors in the international system. They reflect selfish human nature by pursuing their national interest. States are unitary and rational and they are not guided by any sense of morality or justice.	States are not the only important actors in the international system and they are declining in importance. States are not necessarily self-interested. States can be guided by moral principles.

Table 3.1: Key differences between realism and liberalism

6.4 Main ideas of the anarchical society and society of states theory

Hedley Bull, Montague Burton professor of International Relations at Oxford University, wrote *The Anarchical Society*, published in 1977. Bull's text is seen as the founding text of the English School of International Relations. In it, he accepts the neo-realist premise that there is anarchy in the international system, but says that among the chaos a society of states has emerged.

Acceptance that there is anarchy in the global system

Bull's core idea is that of society being anarchical. States do not accept any higher authority, and therefore exist in a condition of international anarchy. However, this does not lead inevitably to a struggle for power that can only be avoided by a balance of power, as claimed by realists. Conflict can be avoided by the existence of a **society of states**, which is distinct from the realist system of states. In this way, Bull squares the circle between the anarchy of realism and the interdependence of liberal theory. Therefore the **anarchical society** can be seen as a form of liberal realism.

> **Key term**
>
> **Anarchical society and society of states**
> theory that the states of the world can be members of a society, despite the anarchical nature of the international system.

States have an informal understanding that ensures a degree of co-operation

According to Bull, states become aware that they share a set of interests and values and so develop institutions and a set of rules, norms and values by which they agree to be bound. This idea of a 'society of states' allows Bull to analyse and assess the possibilities of order in world politics. He explores the meaning of order in social life and the roles that balance of power, international law, diplomacy, war and the great powers play in creating a society of states. He concludes that alternative forms of organisation exist, such as regional and international organisations (the 'new medievalism'), but state co-operation provides the best chance of achieving order in world politics. The society of states falls short of the idea of global governance or supranationalism. States co-operate as sovereign entities; they do not give up power to a higher authority. The United Nations would be a more appropriate example of the society of states than the European Union. Indeed, the concept of the society of states can be criticised because it does not explain or account for the development of supranational bodies, such as the World Trade Organization or the International Criminal Court.

Case study: The United Nations

Looking at the UN from the perspective of the anarchical society and the society of states casts a different light on the organisation than looking at it from the liberal perspective. An important insight that the English School of International Relations can provide is that states co-operate to advance their national interests, but are not capable of acting selflessly as a liberal would claim.

The use of the veto by the permanent members of the Security Council of the UN shows how states co-operate, but only as far as it is in their national interests. Between 2007 and 2017, Russia used its veto ten times – mostly over its intervention in Ukraine and to protect the Assad regime in Syria. Over the same period, the USA used its veto three times – to protect Israel from censure over settlements in the occupied West Bank. In terms of the UN developing a set of rules, norms and values reflecting the shared values and interests of states, in the preamble to the UN Charter there is a commitment to the protection of human rights. The UN went further in 2005 with the adoption of the principle of 'the responsibility to protect', which requires states to protect their citizens from genocide, war crimes, ethnic cleansing and crimes against humanity. It also requires the international community, through the UN, to use appropriate diplomatic, humanitarian and other peaceful means to protect human rights. This agreement goes back to the origins of the UN, which was created at the end of the Second World War when states agreed to not let another Holocaust happen again.

Questions

- How does the UN illustrate the claim of anarchical society that states co-operate but only as long as it is in their national interest?

- How does the UN promote a society of states – a set of rules, norms and values reflecting the shared values and interests of states?

Pause & reflect

Think about what you have learned so far in this chapter. What ideas do the anarchy of states and the society of states share with realism and liberalism? How do they modify realist and liberal assumptions?

6.5 The extent to which realism and liberalism explain recent developments in global politics

State and globalisation, global governance in all its forms (international institutions), power and regionalism can all be understood from a realist or liberal perspective. Table 5.1 offers guidance about how realist and liberal theories can help us to understand developments in international relations.

Topics	Realist perspective	Liberal perspective
State and globalisation	Realists are sceptical about the novelty and extent of globalisation. They argue that globalisation is nothing new and that its impact has been exaggerated. They point to the East India Company and the Silk Route as historical examples of trade and cultural influence. The state continues to be the most important actor internationally. States, not ordinary citizens, are represented in international organisations such as the UN. States have promoted globalisation in their own interests, especially the West and the USA. The USA created the Bretton Woods system of fixed exchange rates pegged against the dollar to promote financial stability to ensure markets for US goods. Greater interdependence will lead to 'mutual vulnerability'. Arguably, Brexit came about because the UK voters felt British interests were being undermined by EU membership.	Liberals argue that globalisation is novel and intensifying. Trade and the number of TNCs grew exponentially in the latter half of the 20th century. Globalisation is leading to the declining importance of the state as an international actor and the rise of organisations such as the EU – now the largest aid donor in the world, and a leader in addressing climate change. Everyone is a winner from globalisation. The integration of national economies allows for 'comparative advantage' – the production of goods at the lowest price and to the best quality. China has become the workshop of the world because its goods are cheap but well made. Economic interdependence spreads ideas and values, such as democracy and human rights. The Arab Spring of 2011 can be seen as a product of globalisation. Globalisation promotes economic, political and cultural interdependence, which leads to peace and co-operation. The UN has prevented a third world war.

Topics	Realist perspective	Liberal perspective
Global governance (including political, economic, human rights, environmental and regionalism and the EU)	Realists are sceptical about the ability of international organisations to deliver systems of global governance, seeing them as weak and ineffective. States will not co-operate because they are competing for power. This is why, for example, there have been so many failures in UN peacekeeping. The growth of international organisations is undesirable as they undermine state sovereignty. This explains Euroscepticism across EU member states. International organisations can be useful. Powerful states can use them to promote their national interests, for instance US domination of NATO, IMF and The World Bank.	Liberals advocate global governance through international organisations as a way to promote peace and co-operation in the world. The UN, through the General Assembly and the UN Charter, provides a forum and a set of rules to promote peaceful co-operation. States co-operate because it is in their interests to do so, which is why there has been a growth in the number of international organisations and in the level of integration, as in the EU. International organisations promote complex interdependence by enforcing a set of rules that prevents states from 'free-riding' or defecting, as the EU does with its regulation of the single market.
Power	Realists argue that in a unipolar system the dominant power can act as the 'world's police officer' (for example, *Pax Britannicus* and *Pax Americana*) and guarantee economic and financial stability by setting and maintaining ground rules for economic behaviour. The USA was the guardian of peace and security at the end of the 20th century. Realists favour a system of bipolarity between states because it is stable and relatively peaceful. In their view, bipolar systems tend to produce a balance of power – a natural tendency in the world order. States seek to establish a balance to prevent the emergence of a hegemon. The Cold War produced a bipolar system that was stable and relatively peaceful. Neo-realists claim that multipolarity leads to fluidity and uncertainty, which can only lead to instability and an increased likelihood of war (anarchical polarity). Arguably, the world has become a more uncertain and dangerous place with the rise of China and the re-emergence of Russia.	Liberals claim that bipolarity causes tension and insecurity, resulting from its tendency to breed hegemonic ambition and prioritise military power. Bipolarity led to an arms race that came near to producing a nuclear conflict in the Cuban Missile Crisis. Liberals argue that unipolarity promotes megalomania on the part of the dominant power, and fear, resentment and hostility towards the dominant power among other powers. The USA's invasion of Iraq was an act of megalomania that increased hostility to it in the Middle East and spawned new enemies, such as Islamic State. Liberals argue that multipolar systems are characterised by a tendency towards multilateralism – greater co-operation and integration. The agreement at the Paris Climate Change conference to keep global warming below 2°C above pre-industrial levels shows how co-operation can increase in a multipolar world.

Table 5.1: Differing realist and liberal perspectives on recent global developments

Assessment support: 3.2.6 Comparative Theories

Question 2 on A-Level Paper 3 is worth 12 marks. You should allow about 15 minutes to write your answer. There is one compulsory question.

Analyse the divisions regarding the inevitability of war that exist between realists and liberals. [12 marks]

In your answer you must discuss any relevant core political ideas.

This question requires a short answer – about one page of writing. These questions test assessment objectives AO1 and AO2, with the marks divided equally between the two. You are asked to show knowledge and understanding of realist and liberal views of the inevitability of war. You must identify the main differences in their views and explain why the theories lead to different conclusions about the inevitability of war.

- Realists think that conflict cannot be avoided, while liberals see war as a last resort, only to be considered after all other possibilities have been exhausted.

- There are three main reasons why there are divisions between realists and liberals over the inevitability of conflict: their view of human nature; differences over the possibility of international co-operation; and the importance of states.

- You will need to explain these elements of realist and liberal theory and explain how they lead to different conclusions.

Here is part of a student answer – an explanation of the differences between realist/liberal views of human nature and what they tell us about the likelihood of conflict.

Realists and liberals differ in their portrayals of human nature. From the realist view, as Machiavelli asserted, humans are 'malignant, iniquitous, violent and savage'. In this view, all humans are self-seeking and primarily motivated by a quest for power, reflected in the principle of egoism. Individual egoism gives way to state egoism, meaning international relations is characterised by selfish interests. To this end, humans and states alike exist in a Hobbesian 'state of nature' in which life is 'nasty, brutish and short'. In contrast, liberals argue that individuals and states are capable of a selfless concern for others, as illustrated by many states providing 0.7 per cent of their GDP as international development aid. Even when humans do act in their self-interest this is best achieved by co-operation, as illustrated by Rousseau's 'Stag Hunt' or Kant's 'Perpetual Peace'. Realist and liberal views of human nature lead to different conclusions about the inevitability of conflict. According to the realist view, states are bound to come into conflict because their selfish interests will clash. Liberals believe that conflict can be avoided if states choose to work together to promote their mutual interests.

- This answer clearly states the realist and liberal view of human nature and compares them by using the phrase 'in contrast'.

- It uses evidence in the form of quotes and references to realist and liberal thinkers.

- The last part of the excerpt shows how realists and liberals reach different conclusions about the likelihood of conflict.

Glossary

Additional member system (AMS) A hybrid electoral system with two elements. The voter makes two choices. Firstly, the voter selects a representative on a simple plurality (first-past-the-post) system, then a second vote is apportioned to a party list for a second or 'additional' representative.

Affirmative action A policy of favouring historically disadvantaged members of a community.

Altruism Concern for the interest and welfare of others based on a belief that humans are social beings with a capacity for social solidarity.

Anarchical society and society of states Theory that the states of the world can be members of a society, despite the anarchical nature of the international system.

Anthropocentric Humans are separate from and superior to nature. Humans have intrinsic value while the rest of nature is just a resource that may be exploited to benefit humanity.

Anti-permissiveness A rejection of permissiveness, which is the belief that people should make their own moral choices.

Apathy Lack of interest, enthusiasm, or concern; for example, not caring about political activity, as manifested in low turnout at elections and poor awareness of contemporary events.

Assimilation The processes affecting change and the relationship between social groups are one-way, with minorities adopting the values, customs and beliefs of the majority.

Atomism The idea that society is made up of self-interested and self-sufficient individuals (also known as egoistical individualism). Can also describe increasing social breakdown and isolation.

Authoritative works Works written by experts describing how a political system is run, which are not legally binding but are taken as significant guides.

Authority For conservatives, the idea that people in higher positions in society are best able to make decisions on behalf of other people or society as a whole; authority comes naturally from above and rests on an accepted obligation from below to obey.

Autocratic state A state that is ruled by a single person with unlimited power.

Autonomy A form of self-government involving a combination of freedom and responsibility, in which the individual is not subject to the will of the state or any other person.

Backbenchers The rank and file MPs who do not have a ministerial or shadow-ministerial position. They occupy the benches in the debating chamber behind their leaders. Their main role is to represent their constituencies. They are also expected to support the leaders of their respective parties.

Biodiversity The diversity of species within a biotic community, which brings the benefits of health and stability to the community.

Biocentric equality The radical idea that all beings within the biotic community have equal intrinsic value.

Bipolarity International system revolving around two poles.

Bipartisanship Attempts within the structure of the US Congress to try to ensure that the two main parties must work together in order to fulfill congressional functions.

Black nationalism A reaction to white oppression originating in the mid-20th century.

Buddhist economics The idea that economics should be built on the principles of 'right livelihood' rather than on an obsession with economic growth.

Cabinet The group of senior ministers, chaired by the prime minister, which is the main collective decision-making body in the government.

Campaign finance Any money raised or spent in order to influence election campaigns.

Capitalism Financial system in which wealth is privately owned and goods and services are produced for profit, as determined by market forces. The capitalist system has developed over the last five centuries to become the economic driving force of the modern global economy.

Change to conserve The idea that society should adapt to changing circumstances by introducing moderate reforms, rather than reject change outright and risk rebellion or revolution.

Chauvinistic nationalism A form of nationalism that believes one nation is superior to others, regarding them as a threat to survival.

Checks and balances The division of power between the three branches of government, where each branch has a direct ability to prevent action from another branch.

Civic nationalism A form of nationalism based on a shared vision and on an individual's duty to observe given laws and, in turn, receive legal privileges, such as in the USA. This type of nationalism requires simply a commitment to these values in order to become part of the nation.

Class consciousness The self-understanding of social class that is a historical phenomenon, created out of collective struggle.

Class dealignment The process where individuals no longer identify themselves as belonging to a certain class and – in political terms – fail to make a class connection with their voting choice.

Classical liberals Early liberals who believed that individual freedom would best be achieved with the state playing a minimal role.

Coalition government A government formed of more than one political party, normally accompanied by an agreement over policy options and offices of state (e.g. the Conservative–Liberal Democrat coalition of 2010–15).

Codification Writing a constitution down in one document.

Codified A constitution in which laws and practices are set out in a single document.

Collective responsibility Principle by which ministers must support Cabinet decisions or leave the executive.

Collectivisation The abolition of private property and its replacement by a system of common ownership.

Colonialism Also known as imperialism, the extension of control by one country over another by settlement or economic domination.

Common law Laws made by judges where the law does not cover the issue or is unclear.

Common ownership The common ownership of the means of production so that all are able to participate in its running and to benefit from the wealth of society.

Communism An economic and political system advocated by Karl Marx in which private ownership of the means of production is abolished in favour of common ownership, a classless society is established, production is based on human need, and the state withers away. Marxists argue that it is only under such a system that humans can realise their full potential.

Complex interdependence Where states and their fortunes are inextricably tied together economically, politically, militarily and culturally.

Confidence and supply A type of informal coalition agreement sometimes used in the event of a hung parliament where the minority partner agrees to vote with the government on key issues, usually in exchange for policy concessions. The minority partner also agrees to support the government in the event of a no-confidence vote.

Congressional caucuses Groups of US legislators who share special interests and meet to pursue common legislative objectives, such as black caucus, women's caucus, Hispanic caucus.

Conservative justice A US justice who interprets the Constitution and produces conservative outcomes. This might mean favouring the authority of the government over civil rights, overturning liberal policies of law-makers or upholding conservative ones, or protecting freedoms championed by conservatives, such as the right to bear arms or the right to life.

Constitution A set of laws and guidelines setting out how a political system works, and where power is located within the system. It defines the powers and functions of government and the rights of ordinary citizens in relation to the government.

Constitutional rights The rights specifically outlined for citizens within the US Constitution, Bill of Rights and subsequent amendments.

Consumerism A psychological and cultural view that focuses on consuming goods and services as a means to feel good about oneself and drive economic growth.

Conventions Traditions not contained in law but influential in the operation of a political system.

Co-operation Working collectively to achieve mutual benefits.

Cosmopolitan integration Integration that entails the maximum freedom for minority, as well as majority, individuals, to mix with, borrow and learn from all cultures.

Cultural feminism A form of difference feminism that seeks to challenge the dominance of male culture in society by promoting 'women's values'.

Cultural globalisation The increasing transmission of ideas, meanings and values around the world.

Culture Values, customs and beliefs that are passed on down the generations through learning.

Decentralisation Basing society around communes, villages or bioregions that can achieve sustainability through a high level of self-sufficiency, making them dependent on their natural environment.

Democratic deficit A perceived deficiency in the way a particular democratic body works, especially in terms of accountability and control over policy-making.

Democratic state A state with a system of government in which all the people are involved in making decisions about its affairs.

Dependency theory Emphasis of structural imbalances within capitalism that impose dependency on poorer states.

Developmental individualism The idea that individual freedom is linked to human flourishing.

Devolution The dispersal of power, but not sovereignty, within a political system.

Dialectic A process of development that occurs through the conflict between two opposing forces. In Marxism, class conflict creates internal contradictions within society, which drives historical change.

Difference feminism Feminism that argues that men and women are fundamentally different from one another.

Direct action A range of political actions, both non-violent and violent, that are taken outside the legal and constitutional framework.

Direct democracy A form of popular self-government in which citizens make law and policy decisions in person, rather than through elected representatives.

Discrimination Less favourable treatment of one group of people compared to other groups.

Disillusion Disappointment from discovering something is not as good as one believed it to be; for example, having no confidence in politics and politicians as being able to solve issues and make a difference.

Diversity The view that different races and cultures co-existing happily within a state is possible, positive and should be celebrated, although the extent to which diversity should extend is contentious.

Divided government When the US House of Representatives, Senate and presidency are not all controlled by one party.

Domestic politics Issues within the USA that directly concern citizens, such as health care, gun control and race issues.

Ecocentric A nature-centred rather than human-centred system of values that gives priority to ecological balance.

Economic globalisation The increasing integration of national economies to create a single global economy of cross-border movement and trade in goods, services, capital and technology.

Egoistical individualism The idea that individual freedom is associated with self-interest and self-reliance.

Elective dictatorship A government that dominates parliament, usually due to a large majority, and therefore has few limits on its power.

Electoral mandate The permission granted to a political leader or winning party to govern and act on their behalf, usually via the results of an election. The mandate is more or less in effect for as long as the government is in power.

Emerging power A state that is considered to be rising, primarily in economic power and influence.

Empiricism The idea that knowledge comes from real experience and not from abstract theories.

Enabling state A larger state that helps individuals to achieve their potential and be free.

Entrenched A constitution protected by a higher court, requiring special procedures to amend it.

Entrenchment A system by which a constitution is protected from change by law.

Enumerated powers Powers explicitly stated – such as article I, section 8 in the US Constitution, which provides a list of congressional powers.

Equality feminism Feminism that seeks equality for men and women in society whose advocates believe that the biological differences between men and women are inconsequential.

Equality of opportunity The idea that all individuals should have equal chances in life to rise and fall.

Essentialism In difference feminism this is the belief that biological factors are significant in the different behaviour of men and women.

Ethnicity The sense of belonging to a social group that shares a common and distinctive culture, religion, language and history.

European integration The process of industrial, political, legal, economic, social and cultural integration of states in Europe.

European Union (EU) An association of 28 states (including, at present, the UK), originally founded as the European Economic Community (EEC) in 1957, which has evolved into a political and economic union.

Evolutionary socialism A form of socialism advocating a parliamentary route to deliver a long-term, radical transformation in a gradual, piecemeal way through legal and peaceful means.

Exclusive nationalism A form of nationalism that holds that it takes time to be a part of the nation, as membership is based on shared history and/or language.

Executive The decision-making branch of government, centred on the prime minister and the Cabinet and its committees.

Executive branch One of the three branches of government, alongside the legislative branch and the judiciary.

Executive order A direction to the US federal bureaucracy on how the president would like a piece of legislation to be implemented.

Factions Subgroups – ideological wings, particular age and occupation groups, and citizens concerned about particular issues – that make up political parties.

Failed state A state that is unable to operate as a viable political unit.

Federalism System in which sovereignty is shared between a central government (federal government) and individual states, with each having their own specific rights.

Federalism Legal and political structures where power is distributed between two distinct levels of government on the basis that neither is subordinate to the other.

Filibuster A process in which a politician gives a prolonged speech to obstruct legislative progress of a bill.

First past the post (FPTP) An electoral system, sometimes known as a plurality system, where the candidate with the largest number of votes is elected. Victory is achieved by having at least one more vote than other contenders.

Formal equality The idea that all individuals have the same legal and political rights in society, based on Aristotle's idea that things that are alike should be treated alike.

Foundational equality Rights that all humans have by virtue of being born, which cannot be taken away.

Four freedoms The principle of free movement of goods, services, people and capital within the EU's single market.

Franchise/suffrage The ability, or right, to vote in public elections.

Fraternity Literally a 'brotherhood' – humans bound together by comradeship and a common outlook, because they share the same basic nature and interests, while differences due to class, religion, nationality and ethnic background are far less significant.

G7 (8) The Group of Seven (Group of Eight from 1998–2014) is an informal forum consisting of representatives from seven developed economies.

G20 The Group of 20 is similar to the G7, but is composed of the G7 nations plus 12 emerging economies and a representative from the EU.

Gender equality The belief that men and women are of equal value in society and should be treated the same.

Gender stereotypes The dominant and usually negative views in society on the different ways men and women should behave.

Global commons Areas and resources that are un-owned and consequently beyond national jurisdiction.

Global governance A movement towards the political integration of states in order to address problems that face more than one state or region.

Globalisation Emergence of a complex web of interconnectedness in many forms.

Governing competency The perceived ability of the governing party in office to manage the affairs of state effectively. It also applies to how voters regard the potential competency of an opposition party, if it were to win office.

Government A system of rule, from monarchism to dictatorship to liberal democracy, where a group of representatives run a country on behalf of its citizens.

Government department A part of the executive, usually with specific responsibility over a policy area such as education, health or defence.

Great power A state that is recognised as having the ability and expertise to exert its influence on a global scale.

Green capitalism The idea that the market will deliver environmental solutions, based on a faith in technology solutions and capitalism's response to ecologically aware consumers.

Gridlock A situation in US politics where the president and Congress are equally powerful and constantly prevent each other from acting, resulting in difficulty passing legislation.

Group-differentiated rights Rights – including self-government rights, polyethnic rights and representation rights – that belong to a group, in contrast to a right held by individuals.

Hard money Cash contributed directly to a political candidate, which may come only from an individual or a political action committee.

Harm principle The idea that individuals should be free to do anything except harm other individuals.

Hard power The use of military and economic means to influence the behaviour or interests of other political bodies.

Hierarchy The conservative belief that society is naturally organised in fixed and unequal tiers, where one's social position or status is not based on individual ability.

Historic materialism Marxist theory, which holds that the economic base (the economic system) forms the superstructure (culture, politics, law, ideology, religion, art and social consciousness).

Homogenisation (or monoculture) Coming together of global cultures and development of a single, homogenous culture without diversity or dissent.

House of Commons The primary chamber of the UK legislature, directly elected by voters.

House of Lords The second chamber of the UK legislature, not directly elected by voters.

Human imperfection The traditional conservative belief that humans are flawed in a number of ways, which makes them incapable of making good decisions for themselves.

Humanitarian intervention Military intervention carried out in pursuit of humanitarian rather than other objectives.

Human rights Rights that people are entitled to by virtue of being human.

Identity The sense that someone has of who they are and what is most important about them.

Imperial judiciary An all-powerful judiciary on whom checks and balances are weak and ineffective.

Imperial presidency A dominant presidency with ineffective checks and balances from the other branches.

Imperilled presidency A presidency where the president does not have enough power to be effective particularly because of complexity or direct resistance in the executive branch – the opposite to an imperial presidency.

Inclusive nationalism A form of nationalism that holds that joining a nation is straightforward and quick as it is not based on shared previous experiences.

Incumbent The current holder of a political office.

Individualist integration Institutional adjustments for migrants or minorities as individual claimants and bearers of rights as equal citizens. Everyone is treated as an individual and not on the basis of difference.

Individual responsibility The principle by which ministers are responsible for their personal conduct and for their departments.

Industrialism Based on large-scale production, a faith in science and technology, and limitless growth to satisfy material needs.

Informal powers Powers of the US president not listed in the Constitution but exercised anyway.

Intergovernmentalism Interaction among states based on sovereign independence.

Intergovernmental Panel on Climate Change (IPCC) UN body set up in 1988 as an internationally accepted authority on climate change.

International anarchy Concept that the world system is leaderless: there is no universal sovereign or worldwide government.

International Court of Justice The principal judicial organ of the United Nations.

International Criminal Court Organisation that prosecutes individuals for the international crimes of genocide, crimes against humanity and war crimes.

International law Laws that govern states and other international actors.

International Monetary Fund (IMF) Works to foster global monetary co-operation, secure financial stability, facilitate international trade, promote high employment and sustainable economic growth, and reduce poverty around the world.

International tribunals Organisations set up to prosecute individuals in specific states for the crimes of genocide, crimes against humanity and war crimes.

Insurrection Violent uprising against those in power.

Integral nationalism An intense, hysterical form of patriotism in which the individual is absorbed into the nation.

Interconnectedness Mutual reliance of two or more groups.

Intersectionality An idea that challenged the notion that 'gender' was the singular factor in determining a woman's fate, arguing that black and working-class women's experiences of patriarchy are different from that of white, middle-class women.

Invisible primary The period before the primaries take place, in which candidates attempt to establish their ability to be successful in the primaries. It is also sometimes called the 'money primary' as candidates spend most of their time raising money in an effort to show their political strength.

Judicial activism An approach to judicial decision-making that holds that a justice should use their position to promote desirable social ends by overturning political institutions or court precedent.

Judicial independence The principle that judges should not be influenced by other branches of government, particularly the executive.

Judicial neutrality The principle that judges should not be influenced by their personal political opinions and should remain outside of party politics.

Judicial restraint An approach to judicial decision-making that holds that a justice should defer to the executive and legislative branches, which are politically accountable to the people, and should put great stress on the principle established in previous court decisions.

Judicial review The power of the judiciary to review, and sometimes reverse, actions by other branches of government that breach the law, or that are incompatible with the Human Rights Act.

Judicial review The ability of the court to review the actions or laws of any other body (including president, Congress and state) and overturn those actions if they break the constitution.

Keynesian economics The economic theory developed by British economist John Maynard Keynes that requires government involvement to stimulate the economy to achieve full employment and price stability.

Laissez-faire Minimal intervention in business and the state by the government.

Laissez-faire capitalism An economic system organised by the market, where goods are produced for exchange and profit, and wealth is privately owned.

Left wing Individuals or parties desiring change, reform and alteration to the way that society operates, including socialists, who are critical of the capitalist or free-market economy.

Legal equality No one is above the law and the law applies equally to all.

Legal sovereignty The right to ultimate legal authority in a political system; in the UK, this belongs to parliament.

Legislative bills Proposed laws passing through parliament.

Legitimacy The legal right to exercise power (for example, a government's right to rule following an election).

Liberal internationalism The idea that sovereign nations should co-operate and create a level of interdependency to avoid international conflict.

Liberalism A range of political beliefs with a strong focus on individual liberty and equality.

Liberal justice A US justice who interprets the Constitution more broadly in order to give the people more freedom and bring about social change.

Limited government The role of government is limited by checks and balances, and a separation of powers, as a bulwark against corruption.

Limits to growth The finite Earth, with the scarcity it implies, places limits on industrial growth.

Living Constitution The idea that the US Constitution is an evolutionary document that can change over time through re-interpretation by the Supreme Court (linked to **loose constructionism**).

Lobbyist Someone who is paid by clients to seek to influence government or parliament on their behalf, particularly when legislation is being considered.

Loose constructionism A legal philosophy that favours a broad interpretation of a document's language.

Mandate The authority to govern, which a government derives from an election victory. This means that it has the right to introduce its policies as stated in its manifesto. It also allows the government to take decisions on other issues as they arise during its term of office, which could not have been foreseen when the manifesto was produced.

Manifesto The document in which a political party details what actions and programmes it intends to introduce if it is successful in an election – a set of promises for future action.

Marginal seats Those won by a small margin of votes, where a small swing to an opposition candidate can cause the seat to change hands. There is no precise percentage or winning margin to which this aligns, but a 10 per cent margin would need only a 5 per cent swing to the rival party to take it. Although marginal seats comprise only a minority of seats at Westminster, they are where general elections are commonly determined. Parties focus their resources heavily on these seats, spending large amounts of money on campaigning and enlisting the support of high-profile figures to lend support to their candidates.

Marxism An ideological system, within socialism, that drew on the writings of Marx and Engels and has at its core a philosophy of history that explains why it is inevitable that capitalism will be replaced by communism.

Mechanistic theory The theory that people created the state to serve them and act in their interests.

Mechanistic world view The post-Enlightenment view in science that nature is a machine where the parts can be understood, fixed or replaced in isolation.

Meritocracy A society organised on the basis that success is based on ability and hard work.

Mid-term elections Congressional and state-based elections held mid-way through a president's four-year term.

Minimal state The idea that the role of the state must be restricted in order to preserve individual liberty.

Minister A member of either the House of Commons or the House of Lords who serves in government, usually exercising specific responsibilities in a department.

Minority government A government that takes office but does not have a majority of seats in the legislature (parliament). This makes passing legislation very difficult. After an indecisive general election, Labour leader Harold Wilson took office in March 1974 as leader of a minority government, although he was able to win a small majority in a further election in October.

Modern liberals Liberals who believe that, under free-market capitalism, many individuals were not truly free, and that the state must help them in a more active way.

Mutual aid The idea that the most successful species are those that employ solidarity and co-operation rather than individualistic competition.

Multicultural integration Integration in different ways for different groups and individuals, to create a new national identity where all citizens have not just rights, but a sense of belonging to the whole, as well as to their own group.

Multipolarity International system revolving around three or more poles.

Mutualism A system of equitable exchange between self-governing producers – organised individually or in association – and small-scale private property based on use or possession.

Nation state Autonomous political community held together by citizenship and nationality.

Negative freedom Freedom from interference by other people.

New Labour (Third Way) A revision of traditional 'Old Labour' values and ideas, involving a shift in emphasis from a heavy focus on the working class to a wider class base, and a less robust alliance with the trade unions.

New Right An approach that combined the thinking of neo-conservatives, who wanted the state to take a more authoritarian approach to morality and law and order, and the thinking of neo-liberals who endorsed the free-market and the rolling back of the state in people's lives and businesses.

Noblesse oblige A French phrase that encapsulates the idea that nobility and privilege bring with them social responsibilities, notably the duty and obligation to care for those less fortunate.

Non-democratic state A state that lacks the central characteristics of a democratic state.

Non-governmental organisations (NGOs) Any non-profit, voluntary citizens' group organised on a local, national or international level – e.g. Christian Aid. NGOs perform a variety of services and humanitarian functions, bring citizens' concerns to governments, advocate and monitor policies, and encourage political participation through provision of information.

Non-state actors Participants in international relations with significant power and influence that are not states.

North Atlantic Treaty Organization (NATO) Military alliance based on the North Atlantic Treaty, signed in 1949.

North-South divide Global socio-economic and political divide.

Old Labour (social democracy) Key Labour principles embodying nationalisation, redistribution of wealth from rich to poor and the provision of continually improving welfare and state services – an approach which largely rejected the more free-market approach associated with Thatcherism or New Labour.

One nation A paternalistic approach adopted by Conservatives under the leadership of Benjamin Disraeli in the 19th century – and continued by David Cameron and Theresa May in the 21st century – revolving around the idea that the rich have an obligation to help the poor.

Opposition The official opposition is usually the party with the second-largest number of seats in the Commons. Its role is to criticise the government and to oppose many of its legislative proposals. It also seeks to present itself as an alternative government.

Originalism The idea that the meaning of the US Constitution is fixed and should not be subject to interpretation.

Otherness The idea that women were considered to be fundamentally different from men, who were seen as the 'norm'; women were deviants from this norm.

Oversight The ability of one branch of government to supervise the work of another.

Parliament The British legislature (law-making body), made up of the House of Commons, House of Lords and monarch.

Parliamentary privilege The right of MPs or Lords to make certain statements within parliament without being subject to outside influence, including law.

Parliamentary sovereignty The principle that parliament can make, amend or unmake any law, and cannot bind its successors or be bound by its predecessors.

Participation crisis A lack of engagement with the political system, for example where a large number of people choose not to vote, join a political party or stand for office.

Partisan dealignment The process where individuals no longer identify themselves on a long-term basis by being associated with a certain political party.

Partisanship Extreme loyalty to a political party.

Party systems The way in which the political parties in a political system are grouped and structured. Possible variants that could apply to the UK include one-party dominant, two-party, two-and-a-half party and multi-party systems.

Pluralist democracy A type of democracy in which a government makes decisions as a result of the interplay of various ideas and contrasting arguments from competing groups and organisations.

Polarity The nature of the international system at any given time in terms of how power is distributed.

Policy group In US politics, a group that attempts to influence a whole policy area.

Political Action Committee (PAC) In US politics, a body that raises and spends money in order to elect or defeat electoral candidates, with a donation limit of $5,000 per candidate, per election.

Political equality Equal right to vote and protest.

Political globalisation The growing importance of international organisations.

Political sovereignty The ultimate political power; in the UK's democracy, the electorate holds this power, which it delegates to parliament.

Positive discrimination Preferential treatment for groups within society to correct structural inequality or to compensate for historical wrongs.

Positive freedom Having the capacity to act on one's free will.

Power The means or instruments – such as the law, the police and the use of ideology – by which the state and other social institutions secure their authority.

Powers of persuasion The informal power of the US president to use the prestige of their job and other bargaining methods to get people to do as they wish.

Presidential government An executive dominated by one individual. This may be a president but can also describe a strong, dominant prime minister.

Principle A fundamental and organising idea that runs throughout something.

Private sphere The area in society where relationships are seen as private, specifically home and domestic life.

Professional group A group that represents the economic interests of its members.

Progressive Ideas, movements or groups that move towards improving society.

Public bill committees Committees responsible for looking at bills in detail.

Public policy In US politics, legislation and judicial decisions made on any policy that affect the population.

Public sphere The area in society where relationships are public, specifically life outside the home, particularly society and work.

Racial equality An equal regard to all races. It can refer to a belief in biological equality of all human races, and also to social equality for people of different races.

Radical A term used to describe beliefs, ideas or attitudes that favour drastic political, economic and social change.

Rational Using or being able to use reason or logic in making decisions.

Realism Wide school of thought in international relations theory that holds that world politics will remain a field of conflict among actors pursuing power.

Reformist Seeking to change society gradually and peacefully.

Regionalism Creation and implementation of institutions that express a particular identity and shape collective action within a geographical region.

Regressive Seeking to revert society to a former or less advanced state.

Religious right In the US, an ultraconservative religious response to the sexual revolution, promoting family values, opposing abortion and the 1973 *Roe v Wade* judgment, same-sex marriage, civil partnerships and non-discrimination laws.

Representative democracy A form of democracy in which an individual selects a person (or political party) to act on their behalf to exercise political choice.

Reserve army of labour The idea that women constitute a spare workforce that can be called upon as and when needed.

Revisionism A revised political theory that modifies the established or traditional view.

Right wing Supporting the status quo – for little or no change. Supporters of right-wing parties (often known as conservatives) stress the importance of order, stability, hierarchy and private property.

Rogue state A state that has a foreign policy that poses a threat to other states.

Royal prerogative A set of powers and privileges belonging to the monarch but normally exercised by the prime minister or Cabinet, such as the granting of honours or of legal pardons.

Safe seats Constituencies in which the sitting MP has a secure majority over the nearest rival, and is largely immune from swings in voting choice. The same political party holds these seats in every election. In the run-up to the 2015 general election the Electoral Reform Society estimated that 364 seats – 56 per cent of the total – were safe seats. An example is Theresa May's Maidenhead constituency in Berkshire, which she held with a majority of 29,059 in 2015, and which has been Conservative since 1885.

Salisbury convention The convention whereby the House of Lords does not delay or block legislation that was included in a government's manifesto.

Secondary legislation Powers given to the executive by parliament to make changes to the law, within certain specific rules.

Security Council (UNSC) The United Nations' most powerful body, with primary responsibility for the maintenance of international peace and security.

Security dilemma Theory that any actions by a state intended to increase its security – such as increasing its military strength – can lead to other states responding with similar measures, producing increased tensions that create conflict.

Semi-democratic state A stable state that combines democratic and authoritarian elements.

Separation of powers Where the three key bodies of government – legislature, executive and judiciary – each have their own powers, personnel and buildings. The principle behind the separation of powers ensures that a system of checks and balances prevents too much power residing with any one body.

Segregation Multiculturalism has led to ethnic and religious groups becoming increasingly separated, inward looking and protective of their own cultures.

Select committees Consisting of backbench MPs, the composition of Commons select committees reflects the make-up of the Commons. Select committees in the Commons investigate and report on the activities of government departments. Their counterparts in the Lords (such as the Constitution Committee and the Science and Technology Committee) carry out topic-based inquiries.

Single-interest group A group that advocates policy surrounding a limited, specific issue.

Single transferable vote (STV) An electoral system that allows voters to rank their preferences in numerical order. In order to win a seat, a candidate must obtain a quota. After the votes are cast, those candidates with the least votes are eliminated and their votes are transferred. Those candidates with excess votes above the quota also have their votes transferred.

Social contract An unofficial agreement shared by everyone in a society in which they give up some freedom in return for security.

Socialist internationalism The idea that class solidarity is more powerful and politically significant than national identity.

Social justice A commitment to greater equality and a more just distribution of wealth in order to achieve a more equitable distribution of life chances within society.

Soft money Cash contributed to a political party with no limits attached to the amount that can be received.

Soft power The ability to attract and co-opt and to shape the preferences of others through appeal and attraction.

Solidarity A relationship of sympathy, co-operation and harmony between people that means that they have no need to be regulated by the state (any regulation makes solidarity impossible).

Sovereignty Absolute and unlimited power and authority.

Stare decisis Doctrine built on the idea of standing by decided cases, upholding precedents and maintaining former adjudications – it tends to favour the status quo.

State A sovereign body that exerts total authority over all individuals and groups living within its defined geographical limits.

Statute law Laws passed by parliament.

Strict construction A philosophy that favours looking solely at the written text of the law.

Structural Adjustment Programme (SAP) A loan provided by either the IMF or the World Bank to a country experiencing economic crisis, which requires the recipient state to meet certain conditions.

Super PACs In US politics, Super Political Action Committees raise and spend unlimited amounts of money to support or oppose political candidates, but without directly donating or co-ordinating with these candidates.

Superpower A state with a dominant position in international relations, pre-eminent among great powers, and characterised by its unparalleled ability to exert influence or project power on a global scale.

Supplementary vote (SV) A majoritarian electoral system that gives the voter two choices. If one candidate obtains more than 50 per cent on the first vote, then he or she is elected. If no candidate attains this level, all but the top two candidates remain. Then the supplementary choices are redistributed to produce a single winner.

Supranationalism A large amount of power given to an authority, which, in theory, is placed higher than the state.

Supreme Court The highest court in the UK.

Sustainability The capacity of the ecological system to maintain its health over time – one of the most contested ideas in ecologism.

Sustainable development Development that meets the needs of the present, without compromising the ability of future generations to meet their own needs.

Swing justice In the US judiciary, an informal name for the justice on the Supreme Court who falls ideologically in the centre of the nine current justices and sometimes swings towards a liberal interpretation and at other times acts more conservatively.

Syndicalism Revolutionary trade-unionism that uses direct action and the mass strike as an expression of working-class power to inspire popular revolt.

The rule of law The principle that all people and bodies, including government, must follow the law and can be held to account if they do not.

The United Nations International body created in 1945 following the Second World War to promote international co-operation and to prevent another such conflict.

Think tank A body of experts brought together to investigate and offer solutions to economic, social or political issues.

Tolerance A willingness to accept values, customs and beliefs with which one disagrees.

Tragedy of the commons A situation within a shared-resource system where individual users acting independently and rationally according to their own self-interest behave contrary to the common good of all users by depleting that resource.

Treaties Formal agreements with other countries, usually ratified by parliament.

Ultra vires Literally 'beyond the powers' in Latin. An action that is taken without legal authority.

Unanimous consent In US politics, a Senator or Congressperson may request unanimous consent on the floor to set aside a specified rule of procedure so as to expedite proceedings.

Unipolarity International system in which there is one dominant pole.

Unified government A situation in US politics where both Houses of Congress and the presidency are controlled by people from the same political party.

Unitary A political system where all legal sovereignty is contained in a single place.

United Nations Framework Convention on Climate Change (UNFCCC) An international environmental treaty negotiated at the Earth Summit in Rio de Janeiro in 1992.

Universal human rights Rights that apply to people of all societies regardless of cultural or other differences.

Universalism The belief that certain values are applicable to all individuals and all societies, regardless of culture, history, geography or any other differences.

Value pluralism The idea that there is no one absolute conception of the 'good life', but rather multiple competing and equally legitimate conceptions.

Volksgeist The 'spirit' of a nation; the unique identity of a people based on their culture.

Widening and deepening Process by which the EU has attempted to expand membership while furthering integration.

World Bank International organisation that offers concessional loans and grants to the world's poorest developing countries in order to reduce poverty.

World government The idea of a common political authority with legislative and executive power over states.

World Trade Organization (WTO) Organisation that regulates international trade.

Index